Our Reviewers Agree: **Macroeconomics *is*...**

A highly readable and relevant text:

"The text is easy to read and understand. The chapters are technical in nature, but the language is quite lucid...this book is better than my current textbooks."

"The writing style of the chapters is simple and very approachable."

"It is written in a lucid manner and is useful for teaching. The chapters contain some standard material and also cover some specific approaches by specific authors."

"The language is lucid, the examples make the message clearer, and the emphasis on Indian examples makes it easier to relate to our own surroundings and apply the knowledge readily."

Uniquely detailed and provides in-depth explanation of topics:

"The text narrows down the explanation from a larger unit to individual units. This approach is not followed in other texts and that makes this book unique and special. One really comes to know the basics."

"This book is much more detailed than most books I've read so far! After reading through all the 'extra' portions (detailed reasons for a phenomenon, for instance, while most other books would just define the phenomenon and mention a few reasons), students can understand the topic much better than they would have from other books."

"Another thing that impresses me is the importance given to details and explanation. The book scores a point with its detailed structure and ability to strengthen the basics of a student."

Replete with a host of innovative and value-adding features:

"The marginalia and macrofocus boxes are illuminating and make the reading quite interesting. The online application problems are quite innovative."

"The definitions and the extra information are highly value-adding to the readers. The end-of-chapter readings and appendices are useful to the students who would want to learn more than what is discussed in the chapter."

"Where this book really shines is in the clarity and presentation of the mathematical relationships, and its analytical content, which is clearly ahead of others. This book is far superior to any other macroeconomics textbook written in India."

Praise for **Macroeconomics**

"This is macroeconomics at its best—both old and new at the same time."
—Romar Correa, *University of Mumbai*

"Written in a lucid manner ..."
—Sanjaya Baru, *Media Adviser to the Prime Minister of India and former editor-in-chief of* The Financial Express

"It is a comprehensive and complete book with excellent features."
—Suma Damodaran, *XLRI, Jamshedpur*

"The book will be considered as the bible for students of economics."
—Mihir Mahapatra, *Goa Institute of Management*

"The novelty of the book is its excellent balance between theory and practice and the numerous examples and data."
—Sunil Mani, *Centre for Development Studies, Thiruvananthapuram*

"Owning this book would be tantamount to holding a lifelong treasure."
—K. S. S. Uduman Mohideen, *University of Madras*

"A well-written book."
—A. G. Moss, *OU College for Women, Hyderabad*

"*Macroeconomics* by Errol D'Souza is probably the first book written by an Indian author that caters significantly to the needs of the management students."
—Jaydeep Mukherjee, *Xavier Institute of Management, Bhubaneswar*

"The book is sure to get the attention of students for its lucidity."
—Paramita Mukherjee, *The ICFAI Business School, Kolkata*

"The pedagogical features like macrofocus boxes, summary, test yourself, and online-application questions are really interesting."
—K. C. Padhy, *Institute of Management and Information Sciences, Bhubaneswar*

"Concepts are explained using Indian data, which is really good."
—C. Bhujanga Rao, *Madras School of Economics*

"The book will provide a knowledge base to the students, researchers, and teachers in the area of macroeconomics."
—S. N. Sahdeo, *Birla Institute of Technology, Ranchi*

"The depth and 'correctness' of theory coupled with a very clear focus on learning from the Indian economy make it a much-needed book on macroeconomics."
—Runa Sarkar, *Indian Institute of Technology Kanpur*

"The organization of the book is worth mentioning ... [The book] seeks to present the chapters in such a manner as to facilitate comprehension of the subject on a graduated and staggered basis."
—Prabal Kr. Sen, *XLRI, Jamshedpur*

"The USP of the book is the analysis of the variables in relation to real world, that is, the practical aspect of macroeconomic variables."
—Kumudani Sinha, *Patna University*

"Errol D'Souza has written a text on macroeconomics in a way that allows students to understand the basic macroeconomic issues."
—T. H. Thangiah, *International School of Business and Media, Pune*

"The book covers a wide range of macroeconomic issues and theories."
—I. Thiagarajan, Loyola Institute of Business Administration, Chennai

Macroeconomics

Errol D'Souza
INDIAN INSTITUTE OF MANAGEMENT AHMEDABAD

Pearson

Associate Editor – Acquisitions: Neeraj Bhalla
Assistant Editor – Development: Bimbabati Sen
Associate Editor – Production: Vipin Kumar

ISBN: 978-81-317-6101-4

First Impression 2012
Fifteenth Impression 2023
Sixteenth Impression

Published by Pearson India Education Services Pvt Ltd, CIN: U72200TN2005PTC057128.

Head Office: 1st Floor, Berger Tower, Plot No. C-001A/2, Sector 16B, Noida – 201 301, Uttar Pradesh, India.

Registered Office: Featherlite, 'The Address' 5th Floor, Survey No 203/10B, 200 Ft MMRD Road, Zamin Pallavaram, Chennai - 600044
Website: in.pearson.com, Email: companysecretary.india@pearson.com

Compositor: Bookcraft Publishing Services (I) Pvt Ltd.

Printed in India by: Rakmo Press Pvt. Ltd., New Delhi

For
Saachi and Hriya

About the Author

Errol D'Souza studied economics and statistics at the University of Mumbai, where he was awarded the Kashinath Trimbak Telang gold medal for obtaining the first rank in his MA degree. He went on to obtain his Ph.D. as a University Grants Commission National Research Fellow from Jawaharlal Nehru University, New Delhi, with a study of the fiscal limitations on state intervention in post-Independence India. He then joined Goa University as an assistant professor in the Department of Economics and, for some time, was a consultant to the Finance Department, Government of Goa, on fiscal issues. In 1994, he moved to the University of Mumbai as an associate professor in industrial economics and public finance. In 1995, he was awarded a Ford Foundation fellowship and was a visiting scholar at Columbia University, New York, where he did theoretical work on the effectiveness of fiscal policy and tax evasion. Subsequently, in January 1999, he was appointed the Industrial Finance Corporation of India Chair Professor at the Department of Economics, University of Mumbai.

Currently, Professor D'Souza teaches economics at the Indian Institute of Management Ahmedabad. He is also the current chairperson of the doctoral programme—the Fellow Programme in Management (FPM)—at IIM Ahmedabad. He has been the India Chair Professor at SciencesPo., Paris; a visiting professor at the Indian Institute of Advanced Study, Shimla; an honorary senior fellow of the Institute of South Asian Studies at National University of Singapore; and a visiting professor at the Turin School of Development—a joint venture between the International Training Centre of the International Labour Organization, the University of Turin, related United Nations agencies, and the Ministry of Foreign Affairs, Italy. He is a consultant to the banking and industrial sectors in India, the United Nations Development Programme, the International Labour Organization, as well as the central and various state governments. He has worked as a member of the academic committees of the University Grants Commission and the Indian Council of Social Science Research. Apart from these, he has been associated with the Reserve Bank of India and the Planning Commission of the Government of India in various capacities. He is on the academic councils of the Tata Institute of Social Sciences as well as the Indira Gandhi Institute of Development Research, Mumbai. Currently, he is a member of the Technical Advisory Committee on Monetary Policy, Reserve Bank of India.

Professor D'Souza's main areas of interest include macroeconomics, public policy, and labour issues.

Brief Contents

Contents

MacroFocus Boxes: Tying Theory to the Real World

Preface

What is New about the Second Edition?

Based on the feedback and review concepts received for the first edition of the book, the second edition of *Macroeconomics* has undergone significant changes in order to make it more comprehensive. The primary goal while developing this edition was to make sure that the concepts explained in the book are streamlined and are easily grasped by the students. The second edition also reflects the latest developments in macroeconomics, including the emergence of the recent global financial crisis.

Certain advanced concepts (e.g., the dynamic Phillips Curve) that were part of the main book in the first edition have been either included as downloadable material for interested students or have been rewritten or dropped to make the book more lucid and accessible to students.

A new chapter (Chapter 15) has been added to the second edition. This chapter provides a framework for understanding issues such as the economic implications of public investment that is financed by deficits and the emergence of the recent financial crisis.

What is *Macroeconomics*?

It would be naïve to assume that most students taking a course in economics want to go on to specialize in the discipline. Instead, *Macroeconomics* understands that what they will definitely do is participate in the economy and want to understand how policy influences their economic lives.

Thus, the focus of this textbook rests, first and foremost, on the analysis of macroeconomic thought in terms of the intuition and underlying logic that forms its basis.

This book has been designed to help students think independently about real-world situations by helping them master the basic technical tools that enable them to do this. Therefore, macroeconomics is discussed in the form in which researchers, policy watchers, and policymakers think about the economy.

Introducing Students to Foundational Issues

Most macroeconomics texts are based on the presumption that students will feel intimidated if they are required to grasp the methodologies essential for developing an understanding of the basic concepts. *Macroeconomics*, on the other hand, bases itself on the belief that students who are first introduced to the economic intuition behind a fundamental concept are motivated to think more deeply about the rigour that underlies the intuition.

Providing Insight into a Real-world Economy

The techniques and tools employed in this book are not discussed as ends in themselves. Books that have the sole aim of being "accessible" are forced to be merely descriptive, and gloss over many real-world complications. This book, on the other hand, understands that students are prepared to "dirty their hands" with technique, provided it is not overwhelming. This, ultimately, helps them relate to the practical world.

Focusing on Current Issues

Over the years, macroeconomics has progressed from one controversy and school of thought to another, and attached itself to school after school of thought. Over time, however, some consensus has begun to emerge about the methods of the discipline. This emphasizes thinking about macroeconomics as involving the interactions between aggregate markets. These are where choices are made in the knowledge that they result in current as well as future consequences—what economists refer to as intertemporal models. *Macroeconomics* maintains focus on the most current and relevant issues, while also understanding the fluidity of the subject.

Organization

The unique strengths of *Macroeconomics* are highlighted through a conceptual framework, which organizes the chapters into five major modules. The following flowchart

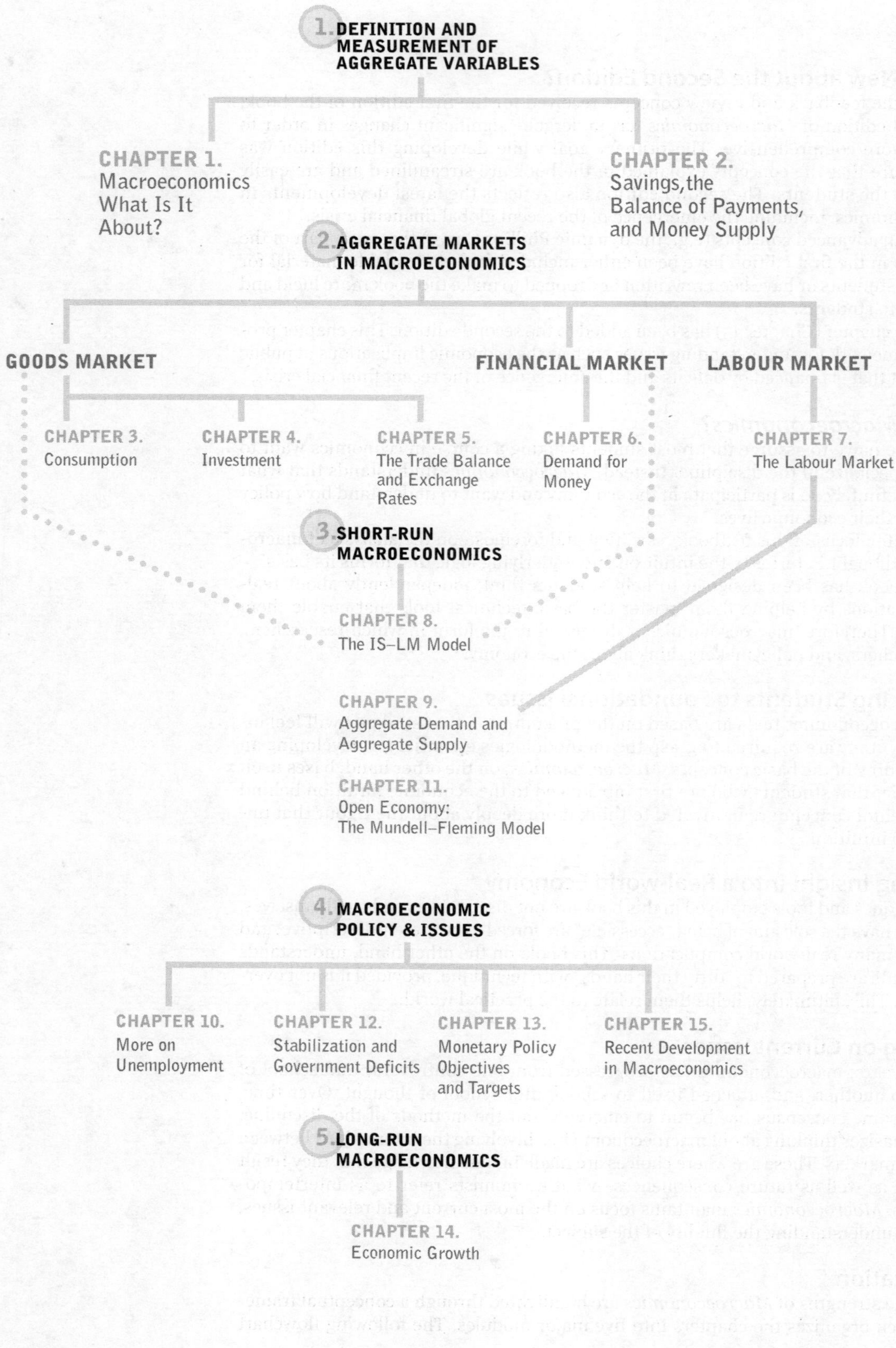
1. DEFINITION AND MEASUREMENT OF AGGREGATE VARIABLES
CHAPTER 1. Macroeconomics What Is It About?
CHAPTER 2. Savings, the Balance of Payments, and Money Supply
2. AGGREGATE MARKETS IN MACROECONOMICS
GOODS MARKET
FINANCIAL MARKET
LABOUR MARKET
CHAPTER 3. Consumption
CHAPTER 4. Investment
CHAPTER 5. The Trade Balance and Exchange Rates
CHAPTER 6. Demand for Money
CHAPTER 7. The Labour Market
3. SHORT-RUN MACROECONOMICS
CHAPTER 8. The IS–LM Model
CHAPTER 9. Aggregate Demand and Aggregate Supply
CHAPTER 11. Open Economy: The Mundell–Fleming Model
4. MACROECONOMIC POLICY & ISSUES
CHAPTER 10. More on Unemployment
CHAPTER 12. Stabilization and Government Deficits
CHAPTER 13. Monetary Policy Objectives and Targets
CHAPTER 15. Recent Development in Macroeconomics
5. LONG-RUN MACROECONOMICS
CHAPTER 14. Economic Growth

presents an outline of the topics within the structure of the book. The topics addressed in each of the chapters are as follows:

Part I: Definition and Measurement of Aggregate Variables

Macroeconomics studies a broad aggregation of markets in an attempt to explain what happens in the economy as a whole, rather than what goes on in an individual market. The first building block in macroeconomics, thus, involves the definition and measurement of aggregate variables.

Chapters 1 and 2 define and measure aggregate measures of income, output, inflation, savings, the balance of payments, and money supply in the economy. These chapters also examine what the data reveal about these variables and familiarize readers with the substance that macroeconomics deals in.

Macroeconomics, at its core, is concerned with the interaction between choices made in four aggregate markets—the market for goods or the demand for output; the money market; the bonds market; and the market for labour services, which enables the production of the output. Insights into these foundations of macroeconomics are presented in a staggered manner in Parts II and III.

Part II: Aggregate Markets in Macroeconomics

Part II examines how choices are made, given the opportunities available in each of the aggregate markets. Having introduced readers to some of the major terms in macroeconomics in Part I, Part II develops a conceptual framework that provides them with insights into the determinants of the aggregate measures central to macroeconomics. Chapters 3 to 7 deal with the foundations of macroeconomics, and are, thus, the building blocks of the subject.

In macroeconomics, the expenditure on goods is partitioned into expenditure by individuals on consumption and expenditure by businesses on investment. (There is also public expenditure by a government which macroeconomists, in a first cut, take as given or exogenous.) Chapters 3 and 4 focus on the determinants of consumption and investment expenditure. Some expenditure is incurred by domestic residents on goods produced abroad (imports). Also, some goods produced domestically are sold abroad (exports). Chapter 5 examines the determinants of these expenditures. Subsequently, Chapter 6 discusses the financial market—the markets for money and bonds—and Chapter 7 deals with the market for labour.

Part III: Short-run Macroeconomics

Part III discusses how the interactions of the markets discussed in Part II result in aggregate outcomes. It combines the goods and financial markets to generate a framework for considering how the demand for output and the interest rate are determined in the short run—a period within which the economy's capacity is underutilized and where the price level does not vary. This is the famous workhorse *IS–LM* model of macroeconomics, which is introduced in Chapter 8. The immediate short-run impacts of macroeconomic policy, such as fiscal and monetary policy, are analysed in this chapter.

The *IS–LM* model ignores the supply of output. Therefore, we need to integrate the aggregate supply relationship with the aggregate demand relationship implicit in the *IS–LM* model. This is the basic aggregate demand–aggregate supply model or *AD–AS* model, which determines the price level and aggregate output in the economy and, by implication, the level of employment, interest rate, and (for some versions of macroeconomics) the nominal wage rate as well. This *AD–AS* model, discussed in Chapter 9, is very useful when confronted with a macroeconomic question.

Given that economies are increasingly integrating themselves with the global economy, Chapter 11 extends the basic approach of Chapter 8 to an open economy. The openness of an economy is not just a matter of trading in goods and services—the extent to which an economy that is closed to capital flows affects macroeconomic outcomes is discussed in Chapter 11. Moreover, the way different exchange rate regimes—fixed versus flexible—mediate policy changes in terms of macro outcomes is also shown to be an important insight that the closed-economy approach does not offer. Therefore, a basic macroeconomic course would require a student to master Chapters 1 to 9 and Chapter 11.

Part IV: Macroeconomic Policy and Issues

Part IV deals with additional issues that fall within the realm of macroeconomic policy. Chapters 10, 12, 13, and 15, deal with contemporary macroeconomic-policy issues. These involve questions such as: should governments be put on a leash as far as deficits and the incurring of debt go? Is unemployment the result of employer policy, or can workers collude to exclude others from the labour market? What should the operating instruments and targets of monetary policy be? How do people form expectations about the evolution of economic variables? Do fiscal deficits, that are associated with public investment expenditures, have beneficial effects on the economy? How did the global financial crisis of 2007 occur and what can policymakers do to offset the impact of the crisis?

Part V: Long-run Macroeconomics

One of the central issues in macroeconomics concerns how policy can impact the cyclical fluctuations of the economy that result in variations in output, employment, and prices. Another central issue is concerned with the questions of why some economies, over long periods, grow faster than others. This is the subject matter of economic growth, dealt with in Chapter 14.

Features

Each chapter includes some key features aimed at helping readers gain an in-depth understanding of the concepts discussed in the chapter.

CRITICAL QUESTIONS

- » *What is macroeconomics and what are its distinguishing features?*
- » *What is gross domestic product (GDP) and how is it measured?*
- » *How is the aggregate output related to the aggregate income and expenditure?*
- » *How do international transactions affect the measurement of the GDP?*
- » *What is the difference between the nominal GDP and real GDP?*
- » *What is the difference between price indices such as the producer price index, consumer price index, and the GDP deflator?*

Learning Goals: The learning goals of each chapter are stated upfront in terms of Critical Questions.

› **Figure 1.2**
Components of GDP at Market Prices. The aggregate domestic income earned from the production of output within the nation is the major component of measured GDP. This figure is based on Table 1.1.

Source: Central Statistical Organisation, Government of India, National Accounts Statistics, 2011.

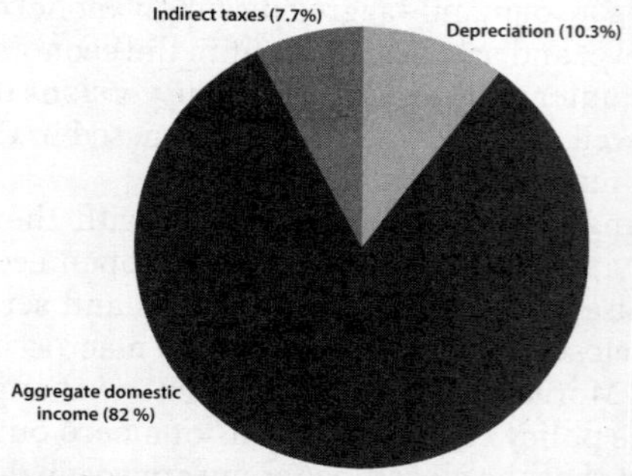

Real-world Validation: Each chapter highlights the salience of the results of the conceptual framework developed in terms of whether the economy's behaviour matches the way theory depicts it. This makes macroeconomics about theory in the real world. Graphs and tables are used throughout the book to explain each concept and its application as well.

› **Table 1.2**
GDP (Factor Cost) by Industry (INR billion)

Source: Central Statistical Organisation, Government of India.

	1999–2000	2000–2001	2005–2006	2006–2007	2007–2008	2008–2009	2009–2010
Agriculture and allied activities	4,465.15	4,497.46	6,377.72	7,229.84	8,365.18	9,289.43	10,892.97
Industry	3,502.33	3,921.38	6,852.38	8,177.68	9,413.62	10,390.3	11,521.64
Mining and quarrying	415.94	457.06	944.62	1,067.87	1,248.12	1,386.49	1,542.69
Manufacturing	2,641.13	3,003.92	5,216.69	6,348.28	7,327.20	8,162.17	9,052.24
Electricity, gas, and water supply	445.26	460.40	691.07	761.53	838.30	841.64	926.71
Services	9,897.78	10,835.31	20,666.11	24,114.89	28,035.42	33,141.03	38,917.69
Construction	1,020.07	1,119.99	2,686.34	3,224.29	3,889.14	4,514.14	5,017.06
Trade, hotels, transport, and communications	3,875.14	4,288.55	8,457.24	9,973.44	11,493.74	13,086.40	14,774.56
Financing, insurance, real estate, and business services	2,335.50	2,547.72	4,931.02	5,865.95	6,914.64	8,491.83	10,271.58
Community, social, and personal services	2,667.07	2,879.05	4,591.51	5,051.21	5,737.90	7,048.66	8,854.49
GDP_{FC}	17,865.25	19,254.15	33,896.21	39,522.41	45,814.22	52,820.86	61,332.30

Notes: (1) For 2008–2009, quick estimates and for 2009–2010, revised advance estimate.
(2) Agriculture and Allied Activities + Industry + Services = GDP_{FC}
(3) GDP_{FC} + Indirect Taxes less Subsidies = GDP_{MP}

Recent Research and Data: Data from government organizations like the Central Statistical Organisation of India and the Reserve Bank of India are used to illustrate and clarify concepts.

what follows, the emphasis will be on INTERTEMPORAL CHOICES—choices that have consequences across more than one time period. This stress on intertemporal choices is because major decisions, such as decisions about how much to work, save, and consume, are heavily influenced by our mental images of the future. The choice to work less or consume more today necessarily involves a choice to work more or consume less in the future. The choice about how much to work or consume as a result of a decision of today has both present and future consequences. As a result, today's decisions will be made with an eye to the future.

Choices in an intertemporal setting are, of course, from an economic point of view, made in the context of markets. In MACROECONOMICS, we are concerned with the choices related to four markets.

The first market is the goods or output market—the market for goods available for immediate use, or current goods. There are, of course, separate markets for textbooks, iron and steel, shoes, cars, and clothes. The interactions between

› **Intertemporal choices** are choices that take into consideration the consequences for the current and future periods.

› **Macroeconomics** is concerned with choices in an intertemporal setting within four markets—the markets for goods, bonds, labour, and money.

Margin Notes: The marginalia, or margin notes, along the text recreate some of the student–teacher interactions that take place in the classroom and provide material that is complementary to the matter contained in the text. These notes are also used to summarize crucial points and highlight definitions.

Summary: Each chapter ends with a summary of the main topics covered in the chapter.

SUMMARY

- Choices made in markets result in macroeconomic outcomes like aggregate income. Macroeconomics concerns itself with the market for goods, the market for bonds, the market for labour, and the market for money.
- Macroeconomists' interest in aggregate income stems from its being an approximate measure of welfare.
- Measures of aggregate income are incomplete due to underreported income and participation in underground and nonmarket activities.
- GDP is a measure of aggregate income and output in an economy. It is the total value of the current production of final goods and services within the national territory during a given period of time.
- In macroeconomics, aggregate output equals aggregate income, which, in turn, equals aggregate expenditure.
- As some citizens work for foreign-owned business organizations and some foreigners work for domestically-owned organizations, gross national product (GNP) measures aggregate output by citizens regardless of where in the world they work.
- National income is the sum of aggregate domestic income and net factor incomes from abroad.
- Aggregate expenditure (Y) is the sum of domestic expenditure plus net exports (or exports less imports).
- Aggregate domestic expenditure equals aggregate expenditure on consumption (C) by households, on investment (I) by business units, and aggregate expenditure by government (G).

$$Y = C + I + G + X - M$$

- In order to understand whether income increases represent an increase in command over goods and services, we differentiate between real income (income measured in constant prices) and nominal income.
- The rate of change in prices or inflation in the price of goods and services is measured by a producer price index, such as the wholesale price index (WPI), a consumer price index (CPI), or the GDP deflator.

MACROFOCUS 1.1

The Underground Economy: Beneficial or Subversive?

The underground economy constitutes economic activities that are not recorded in government statistics. These activities have also been referred to as the shadow economy, unofficial economy, black economy, and parallel economy. Scholars who have attempted to indirectly estimate the share of the underground economy in GDP have found that this activity is of a significant size. Schneider and Enste* found the underground economy in Nigeria, Egypt, and Thailand to be nearly three-quarters of the officially recorded GDP as averaged over 1990–1993. The OECD countries' underground economies ranged from 8 per cent to 30 per cent of their GDP. In India, the estimates vary from 22 to 50 per cent; in Taiwan, from 25 to 45 per cent; and in Pakistan, from 20 to 50 per cent. In Brazil, the estimates started at 7 per cent in the early 1980s and shot up to more than 100 per cent by the early 1990s. In the 1980s, Mexico's underground economy is reported to have trebled while the legal economy registered virtually no growth.

While there is a natural tendency to think of the underground economy as undesirable, this is a contentious issue. One of the reasons for the existence of the underground economy, for instance, is that it is a refuge for entrepreneurs from a government that resorts to excessive taxes, regulation, and even graft. In response to a demand by corrupt government officials (say, for a license), an entrepreneur can make one of three decisions—(1) to pay the bribe and enter the business, (2) to stay out of business, or (3) to produce without the required license in the underground economy. The last saves the cost of bribes but bears the cost of possible detection and subsequent punishment and evasion of law-enforcement costs. In such a situation where entrepreneurs take the outside option and move to the underground sector, corrupt officials are constrained in their ability to demand graft. As a result, there is a lower handover required to be paid to corrupt officials from business than would be the case if this outside option of migrating to the underground sector did not exist. This lowers the cost of doing business in the official sector and induces more entrepreneurs to enter, which, in turn, results in additional economic activity. The official economy, then, is complementary to the underground economy, which is beneficial to its growth. The underground economy in such a situation improves social welfare and efforts to eradicate it are not socially valuable unless corruption is curtailed in the first place.

*F. Schneider and D. H. Enste, "Shadow Economies: Size, Causes, and Consequences," *Journal of Economic Literature*, no. 38 (2000): 77–114.

MacroFocus Boxes: Each chapter has at least a couple of boxed items that discuss applications, present curious and interesting macroeconomic details, or indicate the areas of current research in the discipline.

Test-Yourself Questions: Test-yourself questions at the end of each chapter are designed to help students gauge their understanding of the concepts discussed in the chapter.

TEST YOURSELF

1. Economics is the study of choices. In macroeconomics, choices are studied in relation to which markets?
2. Why does GDP, as reported in the national accounts, not correctly measure total output?
3. Explain how cutting down trees to make furniture may increase a country's GDP but causes economic welfare to decline at the same time.
4. GDP only counts the production of goods in their final form during a given period of time. What are the various components of the final demand for goods?
5. What is the difference between GDP and GNP?
6. Is the balance of merchandise trade a good indicator of a nation's trade position, if the nation has a comparatively large service sector?
7. Why is the output of the private sector measured in market prices and that of the government measured at cost?
8. Why may the GDP deflator overstate the average annual inflation rate for the economy?
9. When the prices of different goods change at different rates, how can we measure inflation?
10. Why is the wholesale price index more widely used as a measure of inflation than the consumer price index?

Online Application Questions: Students are exposed to the available databases on the economy and online applications of the tools and techniques are indicated.

ONLINE APPLICATION

1. (a) Go to the home page of the Reserve Bank of India URL: www.rbi.org.in/home.aspx.
   (b) Click on the "DataBase" icon.
   (c) Then under the classification of annual data, click on "Handbook of Statistics on Indian Economy."
   (d) Click on "Table 1: Macro-economic aggregates (at current prices)" and create a spreadsheet of data on GDP for the 20 data points corresponding to the period 1990–1991 to 2009–2010.
2. (a) Then click on "Table 2: Macro-economic aggregates (at constant prices)" and access data for GDP at constant prices for the same time period.
   (b) Calculate the GDP deflator for this time period using the formula from the text.
3. Inflation is the percentage change in the price index. Calculate the inflation based on the GDP deflator by taking the percentage change in the GDP deflator price that you have calculated.
4. (a) Next click on "Table 39: Wholesale price index—annual average". Access the data on this price index for the period 1990–1991 to 2009–2010. The data are provided for 3 different base periods—1981–1982, 1993–1994, and 2004–2005. Using the overlapping years amongst these base periods construct a data series that is consistent for the time period selected.
   (b) Again click on "Table 40: Consumer price index—annual average". Access the data on this price index for the period 1990–1991 to 2009–2010 for the consumer price index for industrial workers. The data are provided for 2 different base periods—1982 and 2001. Using the overlapping years amongst these base periods, construct a data series that is consistent for the time period selected.
5. Calculate the inflation rate based on the wholesale price index and the consumer price index for industrial workers.
6. Plot the three series of inflation rates over time. Which price index results in higher average inflation rates over time? Why do you think this is so? (Hint: You should obtain the plot given in Figure 1.6).
7. Plot the data on GDP at constant prices and GDP at current prices over time. Observe whether these curves cross one another. Why do you think that occurs? What do you observe in the graph you have plotted about the relationship between real GDP and nominal GDP?

Appendix 1.1 The GDP Deflator

If there were two goods, 1 and 2, and p stands for price, and q for output, then, the prices of the two goods in the base year and current year (Year 1) could be as depicted in the following Table 1.13.

Let i stand for a good (i = 1, 2) and j depicts the years where j takes the value 0 if it is the base year and any positive number for a year that comes later.

Define C_{jx} as the expenditure in year j in the prices of year x. Then, the figure for nominal income in Year 1 is given by

$$C_{11} = q_{11}p_{11} + q_{21}p_{21} = (4 \times 3) + (12 \times 2) = 36$$

The real income in Year 1 is given by

$$C_{10} = q_{11}p_{10} + q_{21}p_{20} = (4 \times 1) + (12 \times 1) = 16$$

Note that the common weights of the prices p_{i1} and p_{io} in the above are the current year's expenditures on the commodities, q_{ij}. When prices are weighted by current year quantities, the price index generated is said to be a *Paasche Index*.

The inflation rate of the economy is found by deriving the implicit GDP deflator which is the current price estimate divided by the constant price estimate. Thus,

$$\text{GDP Deflator} = \left(\frac{C_{11}}{C_{10}}\right)100 = \left(\frac{\text{Nominal GDP}}{\text{Real GDP}}\right)100$$

Appendices: Mathematical derivations for each chapter are provided in the appendices at the end of the chapter so that the student can become well-versed in the theory behind the concepts.

The Teaching and Learning Package

The companion Web site of this book contains a full range of resources that support teaching and learning. These include:

- Resources for instructors, which include introduction to the major concept of each chapter, definitions and background for each concept, application of data, analytical problems to be offered to students, and related issues that can be discussed in the class.
- Resources for students, which include an extensive question bank and animations to explain key concepts.
- A detailed image bank that makes all the images readily accessible.
- PowerPoint lecture slides that provide a set of outlines, summaries, graphs, and equations for each chapter.
- Certain difficult concepts that were part of the main book in the first edition have been included as downloadable material for interested students in the second edition.

A Note on the Language and Terms Used in the Book

- We have used the ISO 4217 code for the Indian currency—*INR*—instead of *Rs* throughout the book.
- The terms *million* and *billion* have been used to represent large numbers, and the use of *lakh* and *crore*, although common in Indian English, have been avoided wherever possible.

The Development of This Book

Macroeconomics has benefited from an extensive development process. Over 150 faculty reviewers, students, and industry professionals provided feedback about the accuracy and relevance of the content as well as suggestions for its improvements. While we could not incorporate every suggestion from everyone, we do acknowledge that their feedback was invaluable in our attempt at creating the best possible macroeconomics textbook.

Consultant Board

The consultant board provided us with a detailed and critical analysis of each chapter and worked with us throughout the development of the book. We would like to thank the following for their time and commitment:

Sujoy Chakravarty
Indian Institute of Technology Delhi

M. Sundara Rao
Andhra University

Ajitava Raychaudhuri
Jadavpur University, Kolkata

V. K. Seth
Faculty of Management Studies, Delhi

S. N. V. Sivakumar
K. J. Somaiya Institute of Management Studies and Research, Mumbai

Romar Correa
University of Mumbai

Supplement Authors

T. J. Joseph of the ICFAI Institute of Management Teachers and C. S. Shylajan of the ICFAI Business School prepared the Instructor's Manual for *Macroeconomics*. This supplement includes introduction to the major concepts of each chapter, definitions and background for each concept, application of data, and analytical problems that can be discussed in the class.

Student Reviewers

We took the help of many students who class-tested the manuscript, evaluated it for clarity, and assessed each feature. Their comments helped us expand the book's content, improved the pedagogical features, and strengthened the assessment features. We are thankful to the following:

Sandip Agarwal
University of Delhi

Richa Bhardwaj
University of Delhi

Yajnaseni Das
Jadavpur University

Yasodhara Das
University of Calcutta

Kunal Singh Dhaliwal
Rabindra Bharati University

Chinmayee Gopal
Delhi School of Economics

Sheikh Azeem Hussain
Jadavpur University

Ishita Mohanty
London School of Economics

Amiya Sharma
Delhi School of Economics

Ashish Tyagi
Jawaharlal Nehru University

Reviewers

The guidance and thoughtful recommendations of many helped us improve this book. We are grateful for the comments and helpful suggestions received from the following reviewers:

Debashis Acharya
Indian Institute of Technology Chennai

Sunil Ashra
Management Development Institute, Gurgaon

Benni B. S.
Sinhgad Institute of Management, Pune

Sanjaya Baru
Prime Minister's Office, New Delhi

Bimal Beri
Narsee Monjee Institute of Management Studies, Mumbai

Laveesh Bhandari
Indicus Analytics

Manisha Chakrabarty
Indian Institute of Management Calcutta

Harnita Choudhary
Symbiosis Institute of Management Studies, Pune

Suma Damodaran
XLRI, Jamshedpur

Mrutyunjay Dash
Asian School of Business Management, Bhubaneswar

V. Renuka Devi
Ethiraj College for Women, Chennai

A. C. Fernando
Loyola Institute of Business Administration, Chennai

Mridula Goel
Jaipuria Institute of Management, Lucknow

C. Kanagaraj
Happy Valley Business School, Coimbatore

Raj Kumar
Maharaja Agrasen Institute of Management and Technology, Jagadhri

Mihir Mahapatra
Goa Institute of Management

Sunil Mani
Centre for Development Studies, Thiruvananthapuram

B. Deevena Margaret
Yogi Vemana University, Kadapa

Meeta K. Mehra
Jawaharlal Nehru University, New Delhi

K. S. S. Uduman Mohideen
University of Madras

A. G. Moss
OU College for Women, Hyderabad

Jaydeep Mukherjee
Xavier Institute of Management, Bhubaneswar

Paramita Mukherjee
The ICFAI Business School, Kolkata

Ram Ji Narayan
PGDAV College, New Delhi

Amar Nath
National Institute of Public Finance and Policy, New Delhi

P. C. Padhan
XLRI, Jamshedpur

K. C. Padhy
Institute of Management and Information Sciences, Bhubaneswar

Pranab. K. Pani
Indian Institute of Management Indore

G. A. Prabhakar
GVP College for PG Studies, Visakhapatnam

C. Bhujanga Rao
Madras School of Economics

D. Tripati Rao
Indian Institute of Management Lucknow

S. N. Sahdeo
Birla Institute of Technology, Ranchi

Runa Sarkar
Indian Institute of Technology Kanpur

Prabal Kr. Sen
XLRI, Jamshedpur

Rudra Sensharma
Indian Institute of Management Lucknow

Anup K. Sinha
Indian Institute of Management Calcutta

Kumudani Sinha
Patna University

T. H. Thangiah
International School of Business and Media, Pune

I. Thiagarajan
Loyola Institute of Business Administration, Chennai

N. S. Viswanath
Bharatiya Vidya Bhavan, Bangalore

A Word of Thanks

This book began as lectures delivered at the University of Mumbai and the Indian Institute of Management Ahmedabad. I have always maintained that the quality of the output of institutions of higher learning is directly attributable to the quality of the students (that determines the extent and the depth of the disciplinary ground that can be covered), the knowledge embodied in the teacher (that accumulates as the teacher engages in research and not just teaching), and the time and effort devoted to teach-ing by the teacher. Over the years, many students have made critical observations whenever they spotted an error, an inconsistency, or an ambiguity in my presentation of the subject matter. I have been fortunate to have this intervention from their side. In particular, I would like to thank my doctoral students Vanditaa Dar, Anjani Sarma, and Vineet Virmani.

Over the years, I have also had the good fortune to obtain the support of the following academic associates in my teaching—Indrani Manna, Swapan Chakraborty, Poonam Arora, Dipti Lalit, Suparna Banerjee, Vivek Pandey, and Renu Pothen.

The writing of this book was made easier by the able secretarial assistance and word-processing prowess of Reena Narendran and Sarala Nair. I am grateful to the Research and Publications Committee at the Indian Institute of Management Ahmedabad for providing me with a grant. The credit for the author photo goes to Madhuri Pandey.

The editorial and development support that I received from Amarjyoti Dutta and Jonaki Ray at Pearson Education made the task of completing this manuscript a pleasurable one.

A part of this book was completed in the summer of 2007, which I spent at the Institute of South Asian Studies, National University of Singapore. The hospitality of the Institute faculty and staff, the Director, Tan Tai Yong, and the Head of Research, S. Narayan, provided a conducive environment in which I could work on parts of this book.

Over the years, I have benefited from seminars on macroeconomics and discus-sions with numerous colleagues, which have influenced my thinking on the discipline. I must state the disclaimer that some of them may not recognize and may indeed dis-agree with some of the writing they see in this text. I would like to acknowledge my debt to Amit Bhaduri, the late Krishna Bhardwaj, Shubham Chaudhuri, Vikas Chitre, Romar Correa, Devesh Kapur, Satish Jain, Shubhashis Gangopadhyay, Subir Gokarn, Arun Kumar, Sugata Marjit, Anjan Mukherji, Dilip Nachane, Avadhoot Nadkarni, R. Nagaraj, Mihir Rakshit, M. Ramachandran, Ajit Ranade, the late M. J. Manohar Rao, Abhijit Sen, Pushpa Trivedi, and John Williamson. I am especially grateful to Partha Sen for his remarks on the exposition in parts of the book.

I am grateful to a number of people for their help in bringing out the second edition of *Macroeconomics*. Numerous people from different parts of the world have sent me e-mails over the past few years, encouraging me to revise the book and bring out a new edition. Their feedback has resulted in many changes that have occurred in the second edition of the book. Some chapters have been deleted, large parts of many chapters have been rewritten and simplified, and some of the most difficult parts, like the section on the dynamic Phillips Curve of Chapter 7, are now part of the companion Web site of the book. Instructors and students who are interested in these more advanced materials can download these chapters from the companion Web site. A new chapter has been added at the end of the book to enable the reader to understand some recent developments in the macroeconomic environment. This last chapter provides a framework for understanding issues such as the economic implications of public investment that is financed by deficits as well as the emergence of financial crises and policy responses to them.

The opportunity to revise the book was partly made possible by academic associates like Aswini Mishra, Preeti Mishra, Bhuwan Chandra Bhatt, Amey Sapre, Sonal Katyal, and Sunny Kumar Singh, who provided able assistance in teaching courses on macroeconomics since the time the first edition was made available. Several members of various faculties also helped by discussing the problems they faced when they taught courses from the first edition of the book. The comments of Snehal Herwadkar, Avadhoot Nadkarni, and Vineet Virmani were particularly useful in suggesting the changes that have been made in the second edition. The editorial support provided by Bimbabati Sen and Shabnam Dohutia of Pearson Education was quite helpful in bringing out this edition.

Errol D'Souza

1

Macroeconomics—What is it About?

CRITICAL QUESTIONS

» *What is macroeconomics and what are its distinguishing features?*

» *What is gross domestic product (GDP) and how is it measured?*

» *How is the aggregate output related to the aggregate income and expenditure?*

» *How do international transactions affect the measurement of the GDP?*

» *What is the difference between the nominal GDP and real GDP?*

» *What is the difference between price indices such as the producer price index, consumer price index, and the GDP deflator?*

1.1 Aggregate Income and Its Dimensions

Why do some countries have higher incomes than others? Why are the incomes of some countries growing faster than others? How is income related to employment, wages, prices, and interest rates? How do government policies affect incomes? Are higher incomes sure to make us better off?

These are the questions that macroeconomists try to answer, and one of the ways they do it is by studying income. The income that macroeconomists focus on is aggregate income—the income of an entire country. Macroeconomists study aggregate income using the same methods by which economists study everything else—through examinations of how people make choices. In what follows, the emphasis will be on INTERTEMPORAL CHOICES—choices that have consequences across more than one time period. This stress on intertemporal choices is because major decisions—such as decisions about how much to work, save, and consume—are heavily influenced by our mental images of the future. The choice to work less or consume more today necessarily involves a choice to work more or consume less in the future. The choice about how much to work or consume as a result of a decision made today has both present and future consequences. As a result, today's decisions will be made with an eye to the future.

› **Intertemporal choices** are choices that take into consideration the consequences for the current and future periods.

Choices in an intertemporal setting are, of course, from an economic point of view, made in the context of markets. In MACROECONOMICS, we are concerned with the choices related to four markets.

› **Macroeconomics** is concerned with choices in an intertemporal setting within four markets—the markets for goods, bonds, labour, and money.

The first market is the goods or output market—the market for goods available for immediate use, or current goods. There are, of course, separate markets for things like textbooks, iron and steel, shoes, cars, and clothes. The interactions between these separate markets are the subject matter of microeconomics. Macroeconomics, on the other hand, aggregates all these markets into a single market for goods and uses a single unit in which all of these goods can be measured.

The second market studied by macroeconomics is the market for future goods, or equivalently, the market for bonds. A bond is a promise to deliver commodities at some specified time in the future. The bond market allows goods that will be produced in the future to be traded for goods currently produced. If we purchase a bond for one Indian rupee, or INR 1, and get paid back a sum of INR 1.17 (inclusive of interest) when we redeem the bond after a year, then the interest on the bond is 17 per cent per annum. At the same time, if the price of a good like an apple changed from INR 1 to INR 1.05 between the time of the bond's purchase and its redemption, then the bond can equivalently be thought of as exchanging an apple today for 1.17/1.05 or 1.11 apples tomorrow.

For goods to be exchanged, they must be produced, and that requires factors of production. Macroeconomics, therefore, denotes the third market to be the market for a factor of production—the labour market. In this market, the availability of goods changes as the amount of labour utilized in production varies.

Finally, in order to exchange goods, individuals need an asset that can be used to purchase and sell things—money. In economics, assets that are actually used to purchase goods are referred to as money. Such assets include coins or pieces of paper that bear pictures of national leaders.[1] The final market that macroeconomics deals with is, accordingly, the market for money, or the market for the holding and provision of money balances.

Macroeconomics, thus, attempts to understand the markets for goods, bonds, labour, and money, and the way in which they influence each other. Agents making intertemporal choices in these four interconnected markets then become the natural subject domain of macroeconomics.

Before examining these four markets, we need to get familiar with some of the jargon used by macroeconomists. Let's begin with income.

In a sense, all of us know what income is. Individuals work or own small or big businesses that fetch them an earning, which is deployed for expenses on food, shelter, clothing, and education, as well as other items of expenditure. Included in their income would also be the earning on interest or dividends, or rents from savings, or holdings of equity stock, or housing stock. Thus, there are various sources of income—wages and salaries, rental income, interest income, and profits from business activity. The AGGREGATE INCOME of a country is the sum of all the incomes that accrue to all its citizens within a given period of time—a year or a quarter. The sum total of all incomes or aggregate income divided by the population of the country is the PER CAPITA INCOME.

› The **aggregate income** is the sum of all incomes accruing to the citizens of a country within a given period of time—a year or quarter.

› The **per capita income** is the aggregate income divided by the population of the country.

1.1.1 Income and Welfare

Another reason economists are interested in income is because it is an indicator of the welfare of the citizens of a country. The notion is that, with greater incomes people are better off as they can live more comfortably and afford more goods. They also feel more secure as they can save more for the future. Economists are actually more interested in welfare—or rather, happiness as measured in terms of welfare—and would like to increase it. Unfortunately, it is not easy to measure and most economists measure income as a rough approximation of welfare. But is income really a true measure of welfare?

While Robert Redford seemed to think so in the film *Indecent Proposal*, the fact is that money can't buy love, as declared by the Beatles. Still, greater income can get people a better education and memberships to clubs, as well as access to many other things. Many economists also argue that improvements in the quality of life—lower crime rates, cleaner air, less congestion, more parks, less violence against women—matter more than incomes. Macroeconomists would only point out that higher aggregate incomes are surely of some relevance when we tackle each of these issues.

However, the correlation between income and happiness is not certain. As economists like Lane[2] have shown recently, giving money to people below the poverty line makes them happy. However, above the poverty line, this relationship between the level of income and subjective well-being is weak or non-existent. The rich are no more satisfied with their lives than the merely comfortable. They, in turn, are only slightly, if at all, more satisfied with their lives than the lower middle classes. Lane found that it is people, (family solidarity, social inclusion, and warm friendships) and not money that makes people happy.

It is also important to recognize that an increase in aggregate income is not the only way to solve all social and economic problems. It is not true that all increases in income make individuals better off because there is no perfect correspondence between income and welfare. For instance, the government could cause aggregate income to increase by mandating that everyone work harder and for longer hours. The retirement age could also be relaxed and the increased work life may contribute to increased incomes while not making people better off.

Again, aggregate income is a deceptive measure of welfare when inappropriate goods are produced. The Soviet Union in the 1980s, for instance, had a measured income that was relatively high because of the production of all kinds of machinery and military equipment that were of not much good for average citizens. For the average citizen, another warplane or machine was not of much value when the only way to buy bread was by lining up at the bakery every morning. Similarly, greater income was meaningless when married couples and their children lived with their grandparents in two-room apartments and were not allowed to move elsewhere.

Finally, macroeconomists do not pass judgments on important ethical problems involving aggregate income. For example, opinion regarding whether a country where everyone has exactly the same income is better off than a country where some people have extremely high incomes and everyone else has an extremely meagre income is outside the purview of macroeconomist.

These omissions, however, do not imply that there is no merit in studying the determinants of aggregate income. A caricature of macroeconomists is that they believe that the worth of a person is revealed when he dies and goes to heaven, where Saint Peter stops him at the gates and asks what his contribution to aggregate income has been so that he may decide whether to let him in. Of course, income is not identical to welfare. However, it is well worth studying because it is a gauge, however imperfect, by which macroeconomists can evaluate whether the welfare or well-being of citizens has been enhanced.

1.1.2 Omissions in the Measurement of Aggregate Income

A country can find out the aggregate income of its citizens by requiring them to fill out forms detailing their income. Since this is time consuming and people would surely vote out a government that required them to spend valuable time reporting their income to a bureaucrat each day, most countries measure income on an annual basis. However, when individuals report their income to the tax authorities, the resulting aggregate misses significant sources of a country's income.

An important omission in measures of aggregate income includes underreported income. Business people often overstate their expenses and understate reported incomes; teachers often do not report earnings from tuition classes; and secretaries often take in an extra income by taking up typing jobs on the side. All these individuals understate their incomes so as not to pay taxes. They also work with an accounting system that leaves no paper trail so that the government finds it difficult to track their true incomes.

In addition, people engaged in underground activities like drug dealing and gambling do not report their incomes. Telgi allegedly selling fake stamp paper, Dawood reportedly indulging in extortion from celebrities and film stars, or arms dealers paying off politicians are instances of people who do not report their incomes to the government. As these activities are illegal, it may be just as well that these incomes are not included in aggregate incomes. However, when an illegal activity promotes personal welfare without harming others, it might merit being included in a measure of aggregate income. An example of such an activity would be betting on cricket matches of one's own free will without directly decreasing someone else's welfare, as would be the case with extortion.

Finally, there are many activities performed that are not marketed through formal markets. These non-market activities do not get included in aggregate income. In India, many farmers live in subsistence and produce their own food—a form of income that many farmers do not reckon as income and which may not show up in official statistics as the goods (food) produced are not traded in markets. In developing countries, many households do much of their own production that do not get traded in the markets. This makes comparisons of per capita incomes between countries problematic.

Another problem arises when, say, instead of washing your own dishes, cooking your own meals, and scrubbing your own floors, you contracted out these activities for a market wage. Just as much work gets done, and you probably have as well-run a house, but the measured income has grown since other people are getting paid. So why do goods and services that we provide ourselves instead of contracting out not enter into official statistics? They do not because we do not pay ourselves for such activities and so do not report such income. Ignoring these activities in measures of aggregate income distorts the correspondence between income and welfare. For example, if more women start going to work and start paying for services like housekeeping and child care (as happened in the 1990s), measured income can go up. However, since women themselves used to provide these services earlier without payment, to what extent such a rise of measured income rises welfare, is a subject of many unending household debates.

As long as the level of non-market activities and underreported incomes stays constant, we can still compare incomes from one year to another and make inferences about changes in welfare that correspond to the change in income. A change in the level of these activities should, however, induce cautions in data handling. For instance, tax rates were cut in the mid-1990s, which reduced the disincentive to report income. This resulted in a situation where the reported income might have increased while the actual income did not change at all. It is a problem worthy of consideration as to how much of the increase in the reported aggregate income of India in the 1990s is due to increased compliance with the tax system.

MACROFOCUS 1.1

The Underground Economy: Beneficial or Subversive?

The underground economy constitutes economic activities that are not recorded in government statistics. These activities have also been referred to as the shadow economy, unofficial economy, black economy, and parallel economy. Scholars who have attempted to indirectly estimate the share of the underground economy in GDP have found that this activity is of a significant size. Schneider and Enste* found the underground economy in Nigeria, Egypt, and Thailand to be nearly three-quarters of the officially recorded GDP as averaged over 1990–1993. The OECD countries' underground economies ranged from 8 per cent to 30 per cent of their GDP. In India, the estimates vary from 22 to 50 per cent; in Taiwan, from 25 to 45 per cent; and in Pakistan, from 20 to 50 per cent. In Brazil, the estimates started at 7 per cent in the early 1980s and shot up to more than 100 per cent by the early 1990s. In the 1980s, Mexico's underground economy is reported to have trebled while the legal economy registered virtually no growth.

While there is a natural tendency to think of the underground economy as undesirable, this is a contentious issue. One of the reasons for the existence of the underground economy, for instance, is that it is a refuge for entrepreneurs from a government that resorts to excessive taxes, regulation, and even graft. In response to a demand by corrupt government officials (say, for a license), an entrepreneur can make one of three decisions—(1) to pay the bribe and enter the business, (2) to stay out of business, or (3) to produce without the required license in the underground economy. The last saves the cost of bribes but bears the cost of possible detection and subsequent punishment and evasion of law-enforcement costs. In such a situation where entrepreneurs take the outside option and move to the underground sector, corrupt officials are constrained in their ability to demand graft. As a result, there is a lower handover required to be paid to corrupt officials from business than would be the case if this outside option of migrating to the underground sector did not exist. This lowers the cost of doing business in the official sector and induces more entrepreneurs to enter, which, in turn, results in additional economic activity. The official economy, then, is complementary to the underground economy, which is beneficial to its growth. The underground economy in such a situation improves social welfare and efforts to eradicate it are not socially valuable unless corruption is curtailed in the first place.

*F. Schneider and D. H. Enste, "Shadow Economies: Size, Causes, and Consequences," *Journal of Economic Literature*, no. 38 (2000): 77–114.

1.2 Measuring Output

Before measuring income, we must consider how we are earning income. When an income gets earned, an economic unit must produce something like shoes, haircuts, and entertainment. Goods and services that are produced are called production or output. The addition of the values of all the goods produced in a particular period in a country is that country's aggregate production of goods.

Let us for a moment suppose that there are only two goods in an economy—*lungis* and shoes. If, in a year, 20 *lungis* were produced and sold for INR 12 each, and 8 pairs of shoes were produced and were sold for INR 32.50 each, then the aggregate production of the economy in that year is (INR 12 × 20) + (INR 32.5 × 8) = INR 500.

GDP of a country is the total value of the current production of final goods and services within the national territory during a given period of time—a quarter or a year. This definition implies that measuring output is an exercise fraught with difficulties. For instance, the fact that GDP includes only current production implies that we do not count the resale of items. Similarly, since only final goods are included, it means that we do not count raw materials and the intermediate goods used as inputs. Let us illustrate this through an example.

› **GDP** is the market value of the final goods and services produced in a country during a given time period.

Let a farmer produce INR 50 worth of wheat, which is then sold to a baker. The baker, in turn, puts in effort worth INR 50 to produce bread from the wheat, which is then sold for INR 100 (see Figure 1.1). If we ask the farmer and the baker to report their output and simply add them, we would falsely conclude that INR 150 of output has been produced in the economy. What has caused the error in this operation of counting is that we have counted the wheat, which is not a final, but an intermediate good. Wheat disappears once it is converted into bread.

We could define an INTERMEDIATE GOOD (or service) as one that is used up in the production of other goods (and services) during the same period in which it was produced. Intermediate goods like wheat, oil, and advertising should not be double-counted when output is computed.

› An **intermediate good** is used up in the production of other goods during the same period in which it was produced. Such goods are not counted as part of the GDP.

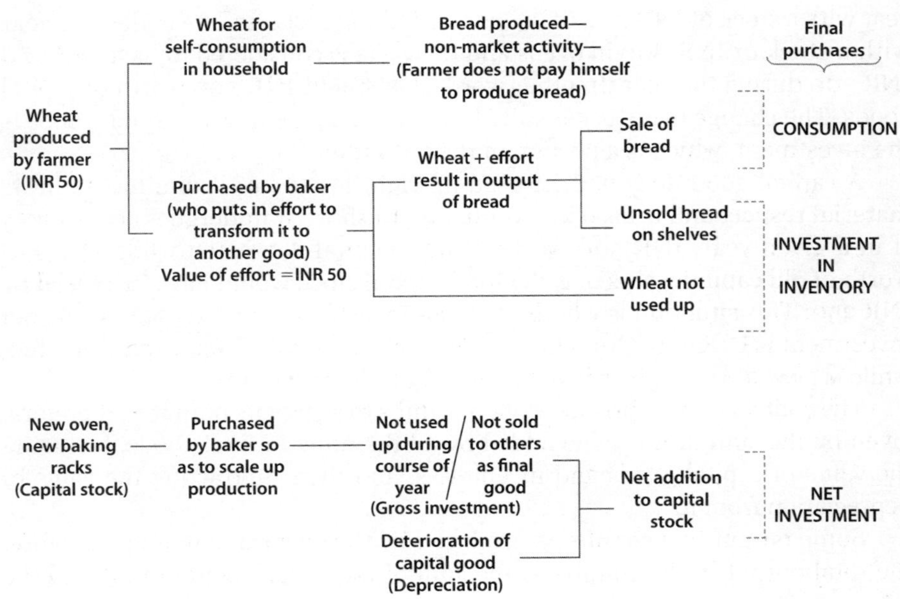

› **Figure 1.1**
Production Processes and the National Income. The production of goods includes intermediate goods and goods for self-consumption, that are not counted as final goods. Final goods include purchases for consumption, additions to inventory or investment in inventory, and net additions to the capital stock or net investment.

To avoid errors due to inclusion of intermediate goods, economic agents would be asked either to report their sales of final goods to consumers (the baker reports INR 100 and the farmer INR 0), or to report the contribution each makes to the total output (the baker reports INR 50 of effort and the farmer, INR 50 worth of wheat, which totals to an aggregate output of INR 100). An economic agent's contribution to output is called his VALUE ADDED. In the baker's case, the value added is calculated by subtracting costs (INR 50 of wheat) from his revenue (INR 100). The baker's value added is INR 50. The farmer's value added is INR 50 as in the example we did not allow him to pay for any costs. Adding the value added by all the economic entities gives us a measure of GDP.

› The **value added** is the market value of the product or service of an agent, minus the cost of intermediate inputs purchased from other agents or firms.

We now need to think about the estimation of aggregate output when the baker does not sell all the bread during the accounting period, or he does not use up all the wheat purchased from the farmer in that period. The unused wheat and unsold bread is not used up, and so cannot be deemed to be intermediate goods. Rather, they are both deemed to be inventories that are classified as final goods and counted as part of output (see Figure 1.1). The accounting is done by classifying the change in the value of an economic unit's inventory from one year to the next as a final good called the INVENTORY INVESTMENT. If the baker had an inventory worth INR 200 at the end of one year and INR 300 at the end of the next year, the baker is considered to have undertaken INR 100 worth of inventory investment during that year. This INR 100 is reported as output in the form of inventory.

› A firm's unused raw materials or unsold output is its inventory. The change in the stock of inventory in an accounting year is treated as **inventory investment** and is classified as a final good.

Now, suppose the baker wants to scale up his business and buys new baking racks and a new oven. These objects are not used up during the accounting period, and so, cannot be intermediate goods. The baker also does not sell them as final goods. Rather, these objects are called capital goods and the economic entity (here the baker) who purchases them is considered to be the final user of the CAPITAL GOOD (see Figure 1.1). As the capital good is not used up during the period in which it was bought, it is thought of as a final good. A capital good is a long-lived good that is itself produced and is used to produce other goods. It is similar to an intermediate good in that it is used to produce other goods. However, unlike an intermediate good, it is not used up right away. The total quantity of a country's capital good is called its capital stock. The change in the country's capital stock from the beginning to the end of the year is denoted as the country's INVESTMENT for that year. If the baker began the year with a stock of INR 500 of ovens and baking racks and he ended the year with a stock of INR 800 in ovens and racks, he is considered to have invested INR 300 during the year. In other words, he bought INR 300 worth of capital goods. The change in a stock is called a FLOW. Thus, the flow of capital goods is the investment, which is a portion of the output for the year.

› A **capital good** is a long-lived good that is used in the production of other goods and services.

› The expenditure resulting in the increase in the stock of capital goods is **investment** expenditure.

› A measure that is defined at a point in time is a stock. A measure that is defined per unit of time is a **flow**.

A capital good does not get used up right away, but it diminishes in its material respect and is used up eventually. In short, it undergoes DEPRECIATION. If in a given year, INR 500 worth of new capital is created while INR 150 worth of old capital wears out, the total capital stock would have increased by INR 350. This situation is where the gross investment is INR 500 and the net investment is INR 350. Gross investment is the amount of new capital created, while NET INVESTMENT is gross investment minus depreciation.

› The decrease in the value of a capital good as it is used or becomes old or obsolete is **depreciation**.

› **Net investment** is gross investment less depreciation.

The contribution of private economic units to aggregate output is, therefore, given by the sum of the value added by all the units to final goods, including the value of capital goods and inventories, and then subtracting the value of depreciation from it.

Some output in a country is produced by the government, and therefore, the total output in the country is the sum of the government output and the private sector output. Measuring the contribution of government to the output, however, is not an easy task. Many things that the government produces, such as defence and police services, are not income generators. Also, the vehicle taxes and tolls the government charges for roads are never enough to cover the costs incurred in constructing and maintaining the roads. In practice, therefore, the output of the government is measured by its costs which, in turn, are the expenses it incurs on its employees and what it pays for goods and services. The valuation of the output of the government by members of society could be more or less than what it costs to produce that output. However, due to the lack of a proper metric, valuing government output at cost is the best that we can do.

The aggregate output of a nation is, thus, computed by its GDP and is the sum of the private-sector output and the government costs.

1.2.1 Connecting Output with Income

GDP is a measure of the aggregate output of the economy, and this output must be either sold or added to stocks. It is important to remember that in macroeconomics, aggregate output or the GDP refers to the production associated with final goods and services. The proceeds from the sales of goods produced must cover the costs of production and allow for profits, which could be negative. Hence, the total value of the production must equal the total value of incomes generated from that production.

The equivalence of output and income may be seen by recollecting that production is (a) either sold, or (b) not sold, or (c) the firm may not have used up all its intermediate goods. The change in the stock of unsold finished goods or the intermediate goods not used up in production constitute a change in stocks or investment in inventory.

Production = Output Sold + Change in Stocks (Inventory Investment)

The output sold, in turn, comprises the following elements:

Output Sold = Final Purchases by Consumers (Consumer Goods)
+ Final Purchases by Producers (Capital Goods)
+ Intermediate Input Purchases by Producers (Interfirm Purchases)

The change in stocks is an inventory investment and considered to be a FINAL PURCHASE by producers. Accordingly, we may write,

› The **final purchase** or demand is the goods and services consumed by the ultimate user who is what the end product of the production process serves. This equals final purchases by consumers and producers, which includes the changes in stocks or inventory investment.

Production = Final Purchases by Consumers and Producers
+ Interfirm Purchases

A firm produces goods so as to generate revenues for the business. A firm has two initial claims on its revenues. It must pay for intermediate goods it has purchased from suppliers and it must pay compensation to the employees it has hired.[3] After these claims on its revenues have been discharged, the residual amount left is the net operating surplus of the firm. Thus,

Revenues = Payments to Inputs from Other Firms (Suppliers)
+ Compensation of Employees + Net Operating Surplus

The net operating surplus is deployed by the firm in two ways. A part is distributed as interest payments to the owners of debt capital from whom the firm borrowed. The remainder constitutes the gross profits[4] of the firm.

Net Operating Surplus = Interest Payments + Gross Profits

Interest payments (return to debt capital) and gross profits (return to equity capital) may be considered as returns to capital assets delegated to the management of the firm by their original owners, or, capital incomes. Another way to categorize the net operating surplus, then, is that it is equivalent to capital incomes. Also, the payments to inputs from suppliers is none other than intermediate input interfirm purchases. Then,

$$\text{Revenues} = \text{Interfirm Purchases} + \text{Compensation of Employees} + \text{Capital Incomes}$$

With revenues equal to the value of production,

$$\text{Interfirm Purchases} + \text{Compensation of Employees} + \text{Capital Incomes} = \text{Final Purchases by Consumers and Producers} + \text{Interfirm Purchases}$$

Cancelling out Interfirm Purchases from both sides,

$$\text{Compensation of Employees} + \text{Capital Incomes} = \text{Final Purchases}$$

Recall that value added is the revenue received from the product, minus the cost of intermediate inputs purchased from other firms. Thus,

$$\text{Value Added} = \text{Revenues} - \text{Interfirm Purchases} = \text{Compensation of Employees} + \text{Capital Incomes}$$

Thus, we may write,

$$\text{Compensation of Employees} + \text{Capital Incomes} = \text{Final Purchases}$$

as,

$$\underset{\text{(Income)}}{\text{Value Added}} = \underset{\text{(Output)}}{\text{Final Demand}}$$

However, when we get down to the actual measurement, we must take care to relate measured output to income. A part of the revenues received by the firm is in the form of indirect taxes levied by the government, over which the firm has no claims. Then again, a part of the revenues must be set aside to replace the equipment worn out during the production process—a process called depreciation. The revenues a firm has after selling its output constitutes its net output. Ideally, data on both the output and income side of the national accounts should be net of depreciation. This is because the physical plant and machinery "used up" in production is in one way like an intermediate good like cloth used up in the making of garments. A firm must then make allowances for the maintenance of its physical capital in calculating the funds it can allocate to those who provided it with capital. Say, while producing an output of INR 10 million, if the equipment and plant depreciated by INR 1 million, then even though the gross output of the firm is INR 10 million, its net output is INR 9 million. It is the revenue from the net output that covers the claims on the firms by its suppliers, its employees, and those who have delegated their funds to the firm.

First, then, a part of current output must be reinvested in any given period simply to make up for depreciation. The value of the output of the firms left after replacing the depreciated capital is called the NET DOMESTIC PRODUCT or NDP. Thus

› **Net domestic product** at market prices is GDP less depreciation.

$$\text{GDP} - \text{Depreciation} = \text{NDP}$$

It is the NDP that constitutes the output sold to generate revenues, which the business then uses to pay out to suppliers, employees, and owners of capital or assets. Second, before that income is paid out, firms have to pay indirect taxes. Sales taxes are imposed on the sales of goods to final consumers so that the sum of the consumer's final expenditures on output will exceed the proceeds of sales by the amount of tax imposed. Only after paying out that indirect tax to the government, will firms be able to pay out to suppliers, employees, and asset owners. Thus,

NDP − Indirect Taxes = Aggregate Domestic Income

Combining the two previous equations gives us the following:

GDP = Aggregate Domestic Income + Indirect Taxes + Depreciation

Or, Output = Income

Thus, macroeconomists measure income as the sum of aggregate domestic income, indirect taxes, and depreciation. And income, as measured this way, always equals output.

For macroeconomists, GDP is a measure of both output and income as the two are identical. Aggregate domestic income is *not* the measure a macroeconomist would use to measure the aggregate income or output of a country.

1.2.2 Aggregate Income Categories

When aggregate output is measured at the prices at which it is actually sold, it is referred to as GDP at market prices. When the net output—GDP less depreciation—is measured at market prices, it is referred to as NDP at market prices. Subtracting indirect taxes less subsidies paid by the businesses to the government from the net output sold to final consumers gives NDP AT FACTOR COST. NDP at factor cost is the aggregate of domestic incomes earned from the output produced within the national territory.

› **Net Domestic Product at factor cost** is GDP at market prices less depreciation less indirect taxes (net of subsidies). This is identical to aggregate domestic income.

Table 1.1 provides data on the Indian economy for the last few years for which we have firm data available on GDP, depreciation, indirect taxes less subsidies, and aggregate domestic income. As Table 1.1 shows, depreciation over the last few years was 10.3 per cent of the aggregate output on average, and indirect taxes was 7.7 per cent of the GDP. Aggregate domestic income, thus, constitutes 82 per cent of GDP in India (see Figure 1.2).

Before we continue, it is appropriate to consider how macroeconomic data is made available in India. In January of every year, quick estimates of the national accounts are released by the Central Statistical Organisation for the financial year ending in March of the preceding year. This means a lag of ten months. At that time, the estimates for earlier financial years are revised and advance estimates for the current financial year are also released about two months before the close of the year. Thus, in January 2012, quick estimates of

› **Table 1.1**
GDP and its Components (INR billion)
Source: Central Statistical Organisation, Government of India, National Accounts Statistics, 2011.

	1999–2000	2000–2001	2005–2006	2006–2007	2007–2008	2008–2009	2009–2010
GDP (market prices)	19,520.35	21,023.75	36,924.85	42,936.72	49,864.26	55,826.23	65,502.71
Depreciation	1,855.93	2,062.95	3,637.13	4,186.11	4,845.58	5,632.90	6,556.73
NDP (market prices)	17,664.42	18,960.80	33,287.72	38,750.61	45,018.68	50,193.33	58,945.98
Indirect taxes less subsidies	1,655.10	1,769.60	3,028.64	3,414.31	4,050.04	3,005.37	4170.41
NDP (Factor Cost) = Aggregate Domestic Income	16,009.32	17,191.20	30,259.08	35,336.30	40,968.64	47,187.96	54,775.57
Net factor incomes from abroad	−154.31	−227.33	−261.16	−332.34	−205.12	−329.23	−380.00
NNP (Factor Cost) = National Income	15,855.01	16,963.87	29,997.92	35,003.96	40,763.52	46,858.73	54,395.57

Note: All figures are in INR billion at current prices.

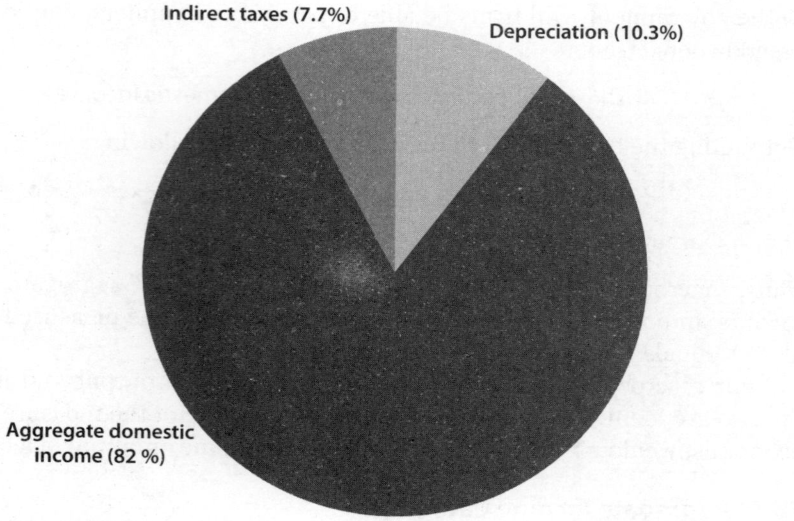

› **Figure 1.2**
Components of GDP at Market Prices. The aggregate domestic income earned from the production of output within the nation is the major component of measured GDP. This figure is based on Table 1.1.

Source: Central Statistical Organisation, Government of India, National Accounts Statistics, 2011.

2010–2011 are released along with advanced estimates for 2011–2012. The advanced estimates are then updated and published as revised estimates in June 2012. The tables of this chapter do not report the more current advanced estimates as they are subsequently revised.

Finally, GDP is decomposed in another way on the basis of citizenship. Some Indian citizens work for foreign-owned companies and some people who work for Indian-owned companies are foreign citizens. This means that the revenues from the sales of output of Indian firms do not automatically become incomes in the hands of Indian citizens. Some of it becomes incomes earned by foreign citizens. So, if we take the output of Indian firms to measure Indian aggregate income, we commit an error by including incomes paid to foreign workers. We also mistakenly exclude the incomes earned by Indian citizens working for foreign-owned firms.

› **Net factor incomes from abroad** is the income paid to domestic factors of production by the rest of the world less the income paid to foreign factors of production by the domestic economy.

To take care of this, we consider the net factor incomes from abroad (NFI). NET FACTOR INCOMES FROM ABROAD refer to the income paid to the domestic factors of production by the rest of the world minus the income paid to the foreign factors of production by the domestic economy. When the NFI are added to the total value of output in India, we get the gross national product or GNP. Thus,

› **GNP** equals GDP plus net factor incomes from abroad.

$$\text{GNP} = \text{GDP} + \text{NFI}$$

The difference between the two measures is that GDP is the output produced within a country's borders, regardless of whether or not it is produced by the country's citizens. GNP is the output produced by a country's citizens regardless of where in the world they work. The difference between GDP and GNP essentially boils down to how many of a country's citizens and their assets work abroad. Payments to domestic factors of production by the rest of the world amounted to INR 620.22 billion in 2009–2010. 7 per cent of this amount was in the form of compensation to Indian employees and 93 per cent comprised payments in the form of property and entrepreneurial incomes to Indians from the rest of the world. In the same year, payments made out to factors of production from the rest of the world by India amounted to INR 1,000.22 billion, of which 8.1 per cent was in the form of compensation to foreign employees. The NFI in 2009–2010 was accordingly in deficit by INR 380.00 billion (Table 1.1).

For countries such as Egypt and Turkey that have many citizens working abroad, the distinction between the two measures is significant because incomes earned by citizens abroad are part of a country's GNP and not GDP. For India, net factor payments abroad are a small percentage of GNP in the last few years—0.60 per cent on average (see Table 1.1). GDP and GNP are, therefore, roughly equal for India. Even though GNP is a better measure of the welfare of citizens, most countries are interested in how policies and programmes translate into effects within national borders. So, GDP is the measure of output that is generally used.

Not surprisingly the NATIONAL INCOME of a country comprises two components. One is the net output produced within a country's borders valued at production prices, which is the national domestic product at factor cost, NDP_{FC}, or the domestic income. The other component is the NFI. The national income is also known as NNP_{FC} and can be written as:

› The **national income** is the sum of the Net Domestic Product valued at factor cost plus the Net Factor Incomes from abroad.

$$\underset{\text{(National Income)}}{NNP_{FC}} = \underset{\text{(Aggregate Domestic Income)}}{NDP_{FC}} + NFI$$

As net factor incomes from abroad are a very small proportion of national income (see Table 1.1), there is not much harm in interpreting the net domestic product at factor cost (NDP_{FC}) as the measure of the national output and income in the country. GDP is thus treated as the aggregate measure of output in macroeconomics. Of course, given that output equals income, GDP is also the measure of income.

Output is often referred to in terms of production from a sector—agriculture and allied activities—such as forestry and fishing, industry, and services. The data of output by sector of production for the Indian economy is given in Table 1.2. As Figure 1.3 depicts, services is the largest production sector in the Indian economy—close to 62 per cent of GDP. Till recently, agriculture was the second-largest production sector and industry was a close third. Most economies develop from being primarily agricultural to industrial and eventually to service economies. The Indian economy has only just begun to have agricultural output of a smaller denomination than industrial output.

The incomes earned as a result of the output produced are usually attributed to the factor that is the source of earnings—wages to labour, rent to land, buildings and equipment, interest on loans, and profit to entrepreneurs.

› Table 1.2
GDP (Factor Cost) by Industry (INR billion)
Source: Central Statistical Organisation, Government of India.

	1999–2000	2000–2001	2005–2006	2006–2007	2007–2008	2008–2009	2009–2010
Agriculture and allied activities	4,465.15	4,497.46	6,377.72	7,229.84	8,365.18	9,289.43	10,892.97
Industry	3,502.33	3,921.38	6,852.38	8,177.68	9,413.62	10,390.3	11,521.64
Mining and quarrying	415.94	457.06	944.62	1,067.87	1,248.12	1,386.49	1,542.69
Manufacturing	2,641.13	3,003.92	5,216.69	6,348.28	7,327.20	8,162.17	9,052.24
Electricity, gas, and water supply	445.26	460.40	691.07	761.53	838.30	841.64	926.71
Services	9,897.78	10,835.31	20,666.11	24,114.89	28,035.42	33,141.03	38,917.69
Construction	1,020.07	1,119.99	2,686.34	3,224.29	3,889.14	4,514.14	5,017.06
Trade, hotels, transport, and communications	3,875.14	4,288.55	8,457.24	9,973.44	11,493.74	13,086.40	14,774.56
Financing, insurance, real estate, and business services	2,335.50	2,547.72	4,931.02	5,865.95	6,914.64	8,491.83	10,271.58
Community, social, and personal services	2,667.07	2,879.05	4,591.51	5,051.21	5,737.90	7,048.66	8,854.49
GDP_{FC}	17,865.25	19,254.15	33,896.21	39,522.41	45,814.22	52,820.86	61,332.30

Notes: (1) For 2008–2009, quick estimates and for 2009–2010, revised advance estimate.
(2) Agriculture and Allied Activities + Industry + Services = GDP_{FC}
(3) GDP_{FC} + Indirect Taxes less Subsidies = GDP_{MP}

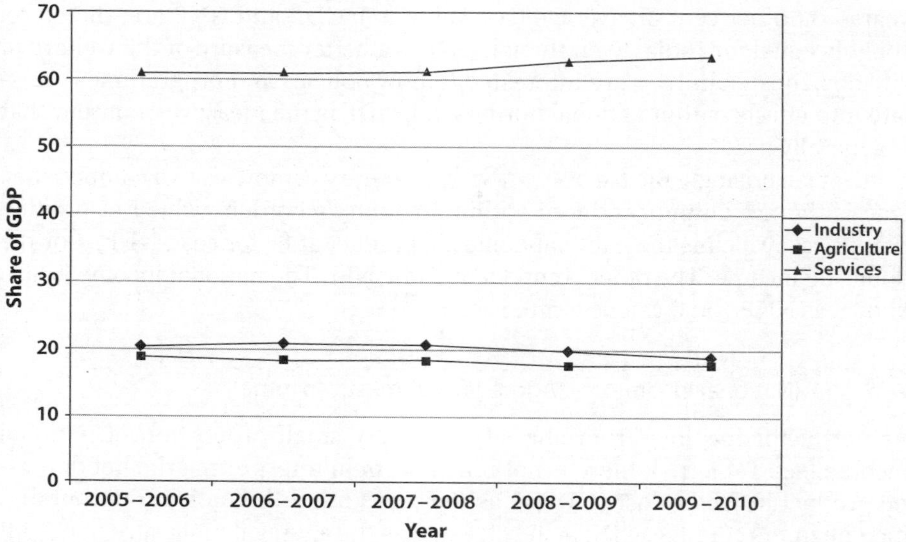

› Figure 1.3 Components of GDP (Factor Cost). In terms of sectoral contribution to output, services comprise the major share of output (62.1 per cent) with agriculture and industry contributing 18 and 19.9 per cent respectively. This figure is based on Table 1.2.

Source: Central Statistical Organisation, Government of India.

In India, a predominant number of people are self-employed. In 2009–2010, 50.7 per cent of workers were self-employed, 16.4 per cent had regular salaried employment, and 32.9 per cent had casual employment (Government of India 2011). Self-employed individuals do not attribute their incomes under pure categories like entrepreneurship or labour. Their incomes are, therefore, classified as mixed income. The national income in India is thus classified under two account heads—compensation of employees and mixed income (see Table 1.3). In 2009–2010 the compensation of employees was 34 per cent of the aggregate domestic income. In countries like the United States, the compensation of employees is around 70 per cent of the national income. A major reason for the lower share of labour in India is because a large part of the returns to labour gets counted in as the mixed income of the self-employed.

1.2.3 Components of Aggregate Expenditure

Now that we have looked at income, let us look at the way it is spent. Just as output is produced by the private sector and by the government, expenditure in an economy is subdivided into expenditure by the private sector and expenditure by the public sector, or government. The public sector constitutes approximately 20.7 per cent of GDP in the last few years (see Table 1.4).

Expenditures by the government are of three types—consumption, investment, and transfers.

Consumption expenditure includes, amongst other items of expenditure, wages paid for labour, expenditure on trash collection, general administration, public order and safety, and relief expenditure on calamities.

Investment expenditure by the government includes actions like the building of roads, the purchase of aircraft expenditure on railways, and on community and social services.

Transfer payments are direct payments that agents in the economy receive without having to sell anything in return to the government. These are mainly

› Table 1.3
NDP_{FC} by Factor Incomes (INR billion)

Source: Central Statistical Organisation, Government of India.

	1999–2000	2000–2001	2004–2005	2009–2010
Compensation of employees	5,929.93	6,516.66	9,125.34	18,671.88
Mixed income	10,126.50	10,757.86	17,390.40	36,103.67

Note: Compensation of Employees + Mixed Income = NDP_{FC}

	1999–2000	2000–2001	2005–2006	2006–2007	2007–2008	2008–2009	2009–2010
GDP_{FC}	17,865.25	19,254.15	33,896.21	39,522.41	45,814.22	52,820.86	61,332.30
GDP (public sector) (per cent share)	4,570.06 (25.6)	4,818.61 (25.0)	7,290.42 (21.51)	8,188.89 (20.72)	9,138.21 (19.95)	10,736.23 (20.33)	12,978.17 (21.16)

› Table 1.4
GDP of Public Sector (INR billion)
Source: Central Statistical Organisation, Government of India.

welfare payments such as subsidies on food and fertilizers as well as interest payments on previous borrowings that the government made from citizens. Transfers are simple redistributions of income—the government taxes from some people and distributes to others. They are not counted as part of a country's expenditures as they do not represent any additional economic production. By counting those, the incomes earned that were taxed and then redistributed back amongst citizens would have been counted twice.

Government expenditures include spending on consumption and investment and transfers. However, only the spending on consumption and investment is included in expenditure by the public sector. Table 1.5 shows that for central government expenditures, on average, transfers constituted 60.6 per cent of it in the last few years.

The expenditure by the private sector, in turn, is subdivided into expenditure by households and businesses. Most household expenditure is on consumption, whether of non-durable goods such as food, or durable goods like refrigerators and television sets. Even though expenditure on college education or health is fundamentally an investment, the national accountants count it as consumption expenditure. Similarly, most investment expenditure (such as the purchase of machinery and factory space and additions to inventory) is usually deemed to be done in most countries by businesses or firms rather than individuals or households. In India, however, given the high extent of self-employment, investment expenditure or capital formation in the private sector is by firms and households, with households having the largest share in capital formation till recently (see Figure 1.4).

Before looking at the data on expenditure, we have to account for the fact that most countries have open economies—citizens sell and buy goods from foreigners. If an Indian citizen buys goods worth INR 100 from another Indian citizen, the value of Indian income is INR 100—the same as expenditure. However, if the Indian citizen spends INR 75 on Indian goods and imports or spends INR 25 on foreign goods, then the Indian expenditure is INR 100, but the Indian income is INR 75. To maintain equality between expenditure and income, the total expenditure by Indian citizens should be reduced by the value of imports. Similarly, some goods produced by Indian business are sold to foreigners or exported. If a foreigner buys INR 15 worth of Indian goods then the Indian income is INR 15 but the Indian domestic expenditure for those goods is INR 0. Again, to maintain the equality between expenditure and income, we must add the value of exports to expenditure.

› Table 1.5
Economic Classification of Central Government Expenditures (INR billion)
Source: Economic & Functional Classification of Central Government Budgets, or, Economic Survey 2010–2011, Table 3.8.

	1999–2000	2000–2001	2005–2006	2006–2007	2007–2008	2008–2009	2009–2010
Consumption expenditures	688.31	719.77	1,163.05	1,216.09	1,313.96	1,743.45	2,269.87
Transfers*	1,615.49 (52.5%)	1,836.96 (56.0%)	2,972.67 (59.3%)	3,565.60 (62.5%)	4,086.76 (59.3%)	5,433.47 (62.8%)	5,949.89 (59.2%)
Capital formation	77,129 (25.1%)	72,592 (22.1%)	875.11 (17.5%)	920.16 (16.1%)	1,488.36 (21.6%)	1,468.38 (17.0%)	1,833.21 (18.2%)

Notes: *Transfers = Subsidies + Interest Payments + Grants
Figures in brackets are percentages to total central government expenditures

› Figure 1.4
Shares in Capital Formation. The private corporate sector contributes towards 39 per cent of capital formation, followed by the household sector (33%), and the public sector (25%). The figure is based on Table 1.6.
Source: Central Statistical Organisation, Government of India.

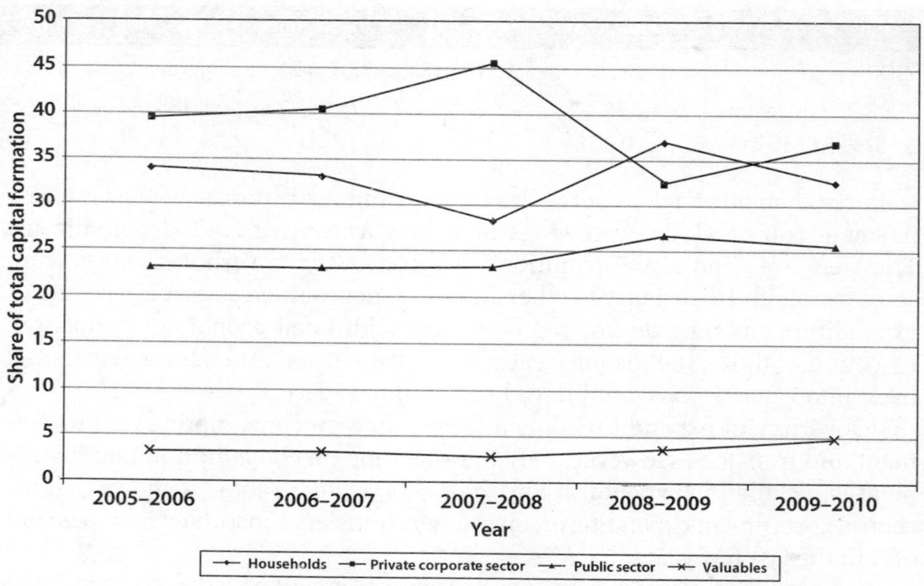

For any country, then, we must add the value of exports and subtract the value of its imports—exports-less imports is called net exports—from the domestic expenditure to obtain the equality:

$$\text{Output} = \text{Income} = \text{Domestic Expenditure} + \underbrace{\text{Exports} - \text{Imports}}_{\text{Net Exports}}$$

However, domestic expenditure is the expenditure by households, business, and the government, not inclusive of transfers. Given that household and business expenditures are mainly on consumption and on investment goods, we may write:

$$\text{Income} = \text{Consumption} + \text{Investment} + \text{Government Expenditure} + \text{Export} - \text{Imports}$$

where we keep in mind that government expenditure also has two components—consumption expenditure and investment expenditure on capital formation. In symbols this may be written as:

$$Y = C + I + G + X - M$$

Where, Y is the country's output, income, or GDP;
C is private consumption expenditure;
I is private investment expenditure;
G is government expenditure on consumption and capital formation;
X is exports; and
M is imports.
G could further be written as

$$G = G_c + G_I,$$

where, G_c is the government's consumption expenditure; and
G_I is the government investment expenditure.

However, conventionally, these two components are clubbed together into a single value for government expenditure, G.

For the year 2009–2010, the numbers for this equation for the Indian economy are as follows:

$$\underset{(65{,}502.71)}{Y} = \underset{(37{,}820.13)}{C} + \underset{(17{,}425.61)}{I} + \underset{(13{,}870.61)}{G} + \left(\underset{(-5{,}182.0)}{X - M}\right)$$

where the numbers are in billions of Indian rupees.

	1999–2000	2000–2001	2005–2006	2006–2007	2007–2008	2008–2009	2009–2010
Private final consumption expenditure	12,536.43	13,401.09	21,525.99	24,763.89	28,404.21	32,578.00	37,820.13
Government final consumption expenditure	2,527.44	2,654.01	4,016.19	4,434.77	5,130.21	6,164.30	7,854.43
Gross capital formation	5,095.18	5,061.81	12,662.45	15,407.49	18,965.63	19,735.35	23,441.79
a. Households	2,059.14	2,269.17	4,308.45	5,103.28	5,378.94	7,308.92	7,645.44
b. Private corporate sector	1,434.75	1,199.01	5,006.58	6,241.56	8,631.54	6,411.99	8,646.43
c. Public sector	1,446.10	1,446.39	2,933.50	3,565.56	4,419.23	5,292.31	6,016.18
d. Valuables	155.19	147.24	413.92	497.09	535.92	722.13	1,133.74
Exports	2,276.97	2,781.26	7,120.87	9,048.72	10,189.07	13,287.65	12,983.71
Imports	2,657.02	2,975.23	8,134.66	10,405.35	12,191.09	16,140.40	16,398.72
Discrepancies	−258.65	100.81	−265.99	−312.80	−633.77	201.33	−198.63
GDP (market prices)	19,520.35	21,023.75	36,924.85	42,936.72	49,864.26	55,826.23	65,502.71

Note: Valuables excludes works of art and antiques.
Gross Capital Formation = Gross Fixed Capital Formation + Change in Stocks
Gross Domestic Capital Formation = Gross Capital Formation + Errors and Omissions

› Table 1.6
Components of Aggregate Expenditure
Source: Central Statistical Organisation, Government of India.

The data for the Indian economy showing the various components of final expenditures by domestic citizens and the government on consumption, capital formation and imports, and foreign nationals on exports is given in Table 1.6.

Figure 1.5 reveals the salience of these components for the period 2005–2006 to 2009–2010 through a pie diagram. Private consumption expenditure on average is 57.8 per cent of GDP, followed by private investment expenditure, which is 27.1 per cent of the GDP. Government consumption expenditure is 11 per cent of the GDP and its investment expenditure is 8.9 per cent of the GDP. Indians spent 25.1 per cent of GDP on foreign goods via imports. Foreigners spent 20.9 per cent of GDP on Indian goods, which comprise Indian exports.

A country's record of trade in goods and services and other current transactions is recorded in the current account. There are four sub-accounts

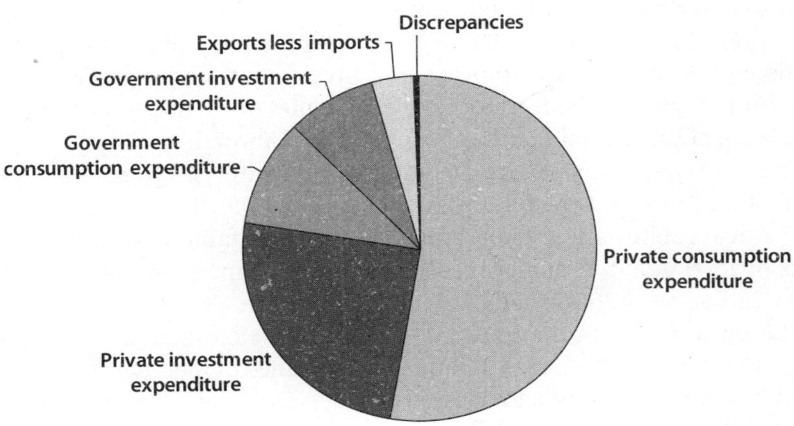

› Figure 1.5
Components of Aggregate Expenditure. Private consumption is the dominant component of expenditure (57.8%). This is followed by private investment (27.1%), government consumption (11%), and government investment (8.9%) expenditure. Net exports are –4.2% of GDP. This figure is based on Table 1.6.
Source: Central Statistical Organisation, Government of India.

MACROFOCUS 1.2

Chinese and Indian GDP: Re-emerging Economies?

Definitions of emerging economies vary. The United Nations counts Hong Kong, Singapore, South Korea, and Taiwan as emerging economies. The International Monetary Fund, however, counts all four as "developing economies" in its *International Financial Statistics*, but as "advanced economies" in its *World Economic Outlook*. In policy discussions, these are labelled as emerging economies. By 2005, the emerging economies accounted for about 30 per cent of the world GDP and they have new begun to dominate the global economy in terms of exports, energy consumption, and foreign-exchange reserve holdings. Currently, two fast-growing emerging market economies are China and India, which together contributed to about 25 per cent of the increase in emerging market economies' GDP in 2005.

In a study of the world economy, the economic historian, Angus Maddison* found that until the late 19th century, China and India were the world's two biggest economies. These two economies dominated the world output before the steam engine and the industrial revolution placed Britain at the top. Maddison estimates that in the eighteen centuries up to 1820, the current emerging market economies produced, on average, a staggering 80 per cent of the world GDP. After a gap of about 180 years, they are now back amongst the fastest growth rates of GDP currently.

Given this perspective, it may be more appropriate to label these economies as re-emerging economies. Two important features of economies of countries such as China, Hong Kong, Indonesia, Malaysia, Oman, Malta, Singapore, and Thailand that have seen sustained high increases in the GDP in the past couple of decades have been: (1) the high levels of investment—attempting high growth without investment in infrastructure and skills increase inflation and (2)the large fraction of GDP associated with exports and imports—an indicator of a country's ability to leverage the demand and resources of the global economy. For instance, in 2004, China's total investment expenditure was 43.2 per cent of its GDP, compared to India's 27.2 per cent. Similarly, international trade (exports plus imports) as a percentage of GDP was 58.2 per cent in China, whereas it was 27.4 per cent in India.

*Angus Maddison, *The World Economy: A Millennial Perspective*, OECD, 2001.

associated with the current account of a nation. These are the balance of merchandise trade, net receipts from non-factor service incomes, net factor incomes from abroad, and transfers.

› The **balance of (merchandise) trade**, otherwise known as net exports, is the value of exports less the value of imports of goods.

The BALANCE OF (MERCHANDISE) TRADE is the value of exported goods minus the value of imported goods. This records exports and imports of all movable goods that are sold or transferred between domestic and foreign parties involved in the transaction. This balance, however, does not include services of any kind.

The measure of the trade in services is the net receipts from non-factor service incomes, which includes trade in banking services, travel, transportation, tourism, and business and professional services. Transportation services including freight and insurance charges for the international movement of goods and expenditures on international travel are included in this sub account. Business and professional services, such as software that are commonly referred to as international outsourcing transactions, are also recorded in this sub account. These include software exports as well as the services of engineering firms and management consultants.

The third sub-account, net factor incomes from abroad, has already been introduced earlier. These include net payments for the services of factors of production that work abroad. These payments for factors of production abroad include compensation of employees and investment, or property and entrepreneurial income in the form of interest payments, or dividends—payments for services of the capital that has been deployed abroad.

The final component of the current account comprises transfers[5]—private transfers and official transfers between governments. These consist, respectively, private remittances from emigrants to their families and government grants or foreign aid. Transfer receipts in India comprise mainly remittances sent by Indian workers abroad.

› The term $X - M$ in the **equation for aggregate income** equals expenditure is the sum of the balance of merchandise trade (or trade in goods), and the net receipts from non-factor service incomes (or trade in services).

The term $X - M$ in the EQUATION FOR AGGREGATE INCOME equals expenditure, or, $Y = C + I + G + X - M$ is the sum of the balance of merchandise trade and the net receipts from non-factor service incomes. Only these two sub-accounts of the current account are included in the measure of the aggregate expenditure of the economy. $X - M$ is referred to as the balance of trade in goods or services or the net exports of an economy.

The balance of trade and the CURRENT ACCOUNT BALANCE for India are given in Table 1.7. In addition to depicting some of the major items of exports and imports, Table 1.7 also reveals how private transfers have, in the recent past, turned a large negative balance of trade into a smaller current account deficit balance.

› The **current account balance** is the statement of a country's payments to and from the rest of the world for goods and non-factor services transacted in, for factor incomes from abroad, and for transfers.

The current account balance is a broad measure. However, it is not exhaustive and many major services are not included in it. For instance, Indian students going to the United States for education are not included as an import of a service, and meals purchased by foreign travellers at a *dhaba* in Rajasthan is not reported as an export of cuisine.

› **Table 1.7**
India's Foreign Trade (INR billion)

Source: Reserve Bank of India, *Handbook of Statistics on Indian Economy*.

	2000–2001	2005–2006	2006–2007	2007–2008	2008–2009	2009–2010
Merchandise exports	**2,078.52**	**4,657.48**	**5,828.71**	**6,680.08**	**8,579.60**	**8,623.33**
Agriculture	272.88	452.20	573.92	742.09	806.49	841.36
Gems and jewellery	337.33	687.52	722.95	792.27	1,285.75	1,375.68
Chemicals and related products	268.89	653.90	784.42	853.28	1,044.42	1,086.87
Engineering goods	311.50	961.57	1,337.90	1,504.35	2,174.82	1,815.72
Textiles	515.55	726.18	786.13	782.09	920.62	941.89
Petroleum products	85.42	515.33	845.20	1,141.92	1,233.98	1,328.99
Merchandise imports	**2,645.89**	**6,954.12**	**8,628.33**	**10,356.72**	**14,054.12**	**14,230.79**
Petrol oil and lubricants	714.97	1,946.40	2,585.72	3,206.55	4,199.68	4,116.49
Capital goods	408.47	1,667.62	2,129.86	2,822.69	3,303.84	3,124.85
Gold and silver	211.89	501.08	662.72	719.34	1,047.86	1,404.40
Chemicals—organic and inorganic	111.65	309.21	354.33	398.45	561.25	564.73
Pearls, precious and semi-precious stones	219.64	404.41	338.81	320.94	762.63	766.78
Balance of merchandise trade	**−567.37**	**−2,296.64**	**−2,799.62**	**−3,676.64**	**−5,474.52**	**−5,607.46**
Net non-factor services incomes, of which:	**79.05**	**1,026.11**	**1,330.64**	**1,562.44**	**2,484.06**	**1,698.43**
Foreign travel	33.23	54.39	108.78	83.35	68.90	118.05
Transport	−68.08	−89.05	−4.55	−60.79	−64.58	−34.96
Insurance	2.30	−2.71	25	23.93	13.01	14.96
Software exports (net)	263.08	1,008.03	1,311.44	1,485.26	2,006.34	2,281.69
Exports less imports	**−488.32**	**−1,270.53**	**−1,468.98**	**−2,114.2**	**−2,990.46**	**−3,909.03**
Net factor incomes from abroad	−227.33	−261.66	−332.34	−205.11	−329.23	−380.00
Transfers (net)	599.67	1,094.32	1,357.49	1,684.52	2,043.38	2,482.77
Invisibles (net)	**451.39**	**1,859.27**	**2,355.79**	**3,041.85**	**4,198.21**	**3,801.20**
Current account balance	**−115.98**	**−437.37**	**−443.83**	**−634.79**	**−1,276.31**	**−1,806.26**

Notes: (1) Only major components of exports, imports, and invisibles have been depicted. The list is not exhaustive.
(2) Chemicals as well as pearls, precious, and semi-precious stones are mainly for further processing and re-export.
(3) "Exports less imports" is the sum of "balance of merchandise trade" and "net non-factor services incomes".
(4) "Invisibles" or trade not involving movable goods is the sum of "net non-factor services incomes" and "net factor incomes from abroad" and "transfers (net)".
(5) "Current account balance" is the sum of "balance of merchandise trade" and "net non-factor services incomes" and "net factor incomes from abroad" and "transfers (net)".

1.3 Real and Nominal Incomes

› The **growth rate** of GDP is the percentage change in aggregate income or output over a unit of time, usually a year.

The percentage change in a country's output or income from one year to the next is the GROWTH RATE of the country's economy. Table 1.8 shows per capita income for the past few decades. This table reveals that an average person's income increased by 3.2 times in the decade beginning in 2000—from INR 20,651 to INR 66,425. In the previous decade of the 1990s, income increased by 3 times. Most people comparing this with their own family income history would find these statistics unbelievable. Did anybody's income increase 9.8 times between 1990–1991 and 2010–2011? Maybe some business houses like the Ambani family reported such a growth in income, However, on average, incomes surely did not increase by that amount. The reason the data of Table 1.8 is misleading is that the rupees we earn as income are only as valuable as the goods we can purchase with them. If our rupee incomes rise and the prices of the things we buy also rise, then our REAL INCOME may not be increasing as fast as our rupee incomes or NOMINAL INCOMES.

› **Real incomes** are incomes measured in physical terms, i.e., in terms of the quantities of goods and services.

› **Nominal incomes** are incomes measured in terms of current rupee values.

To understand this, suppose that there is only one good in the economy, which happens to be pizza. Table 1.9 gives the nominal income and real income in Year 0 (the base year) and Year *j* (the current year). The table shows that despite your rupee income increasing by 12.5 per cent, your real income declined by 10 per cent. Even though the nominal income increased, you could buy less pizza with it.

1.3.1 Comparing Income Across Time

If there were more than one good (we cannot live only on pizzas) in the economy, we proceed as follows to calculate the real income:

1. Pretend that prices in the current year are the same as in the base year
2. Calculate the value that the output would have in the current year at these constant prices of the base year

To see how such a comparison is done across time we will calculate the price index for a student who spends the annual pocket money of INR 5,000 on two goods—pizzas and books. The student's expenditure is on 30 pizzas a year for INR 3,000 (each pizza costs INR 100), and on four books a year for INR 2,000 (each book costs INR 500).

In a subsequent year, the competition increases and the price of pizzas decline to INR 85 per pizza. However, there is no new entrant in the booksellers market and the price of books goes up to INR 615 per book because of the increase in the cost of paper. The student's income and expenditure go up to INR 5,625 in the subsequent year and he purchases the same quantity of pizzas and one additional book this year—the additional book being purchased with the intention to study more and do better in the examinations. This situation is depicted in Table 1.11.

› **Table 1.8**
Per Capita GDP (Rupees)

Year	Per Capita Income	Percentage Increase (Per Decade)
1960–1961	395.6	42.9
1970–1971	844.3	113.4
1980–1981	2,117.3	150.8
1990–1991	6,778.0	220.1
2000–2001	20,650.6	204.7
2010–2011	66,424.5	221.7

› **Table 1.9**
Real Incomes with One Good

	Year 0	Year j
Nominal income	INR 5,000	INR 5,625
Price (of pizza)	INR 100	INR 125
Real income	50 pizzas per year	45 pizzas per year

› **Nominal GDP** or aggregate income is the sum of the quantities of goods produced times their current price.

NOMINAL GDP OR EXPENDITURE is the expenditure in a year in the prices of that year. The nominal expenditure in Year 1 valued in the prices prevailing in that year, denoted by C_{11}, will then be,

$$C_{11} = (30 \times 85) + (5 \times 615) = 5{,}625$$

› **Real GDP** or aggregate income is the aggregate income measured in the prices of a base year. It measures aggregate income in constant rupees or adjusted for inflation.

REAL GDP OR EXPENDITURE is the expenditure in a year in the prices of the base year. The real expenditure or income in Year 1 valued in the prices of the base year 0, denoted by C_{10}, will then be,

$$C_{10} = (30 \times 100) + (5 \times 500) = 5{,}500$$

› The **GDP deflator** is Nominal GDP divided by real GDP.

The inflation rate of the economy is found by deriving the implicit GDP DEFLATOR, which is the current price estimate divided by the constant price estimate. Thus,

$$\text{GDP Deflator} = \left(\frac{C_{11}}{C_{10}}\right)100 = \left(\frac{\text{Nominal GDP}}{\text{Real GDP}}\right)100$$

For our example with just two goods—pizzas and books—the deflator is given by:

$$\left(\frac{C_{11}}{C_{10}}\right)100 = \left(\frac{5{,}625}{5{,}500}\right)100 = 102.27$$

The obtained deflator indicates that inflation was 2.27 per cent in the economy with two goods. This summary indicator makes sense if we note that the proportion of expenditure devoted to pizzas in real terms is the share of real expenditure on pizzas, denoted by w_1, where,

$$w_1 = \frac{30 \times 100}{(30 \times 100 + 5 \times 500)} = \frac{3{,}000}{5{,}500} = 0.545455$$

The proportion of expenditure devoted to books in real terms is the share of real expenditure on books, denoted by w_2, where,

$$w_2 = \frac{5 \times 500}{(30 \times 100 + 5 \times 500)} = \frac{2{,}500}{5{,}500} = 0.454545$$

The price of pizzas declined to 85 per cent of its original price—from INR 100 to INR 85. The price of books increased by 23 per cent from—INR 500 to INR 615. The weighted average of price increase in the overall economy is then given by:

$$\begin{aligned}\left[0.545455(0.85) + 0.454545(1.23)\right]100 &= (0.463636 + 0.559091)100\\ &= (1.022727)100 = 102.27\end{aligned}$$

This is exactly what the summary indicator calculated. (See the Appendix 1.1 for a derivation of the formula for the GDP deflator for the case of n goods.)

1.3.2 Measures of Inflation

The GDP Deflator is the only measure of inflation that takes into account the inflation in all the goods and services produced in the economy. Other measures of inflation are the wholesale price index (WPI) and the consumer price index (CPI). These are calculated by selecting a fixed set of goods, rather than all goods available in an economy, and then tracking the prices of these specific goods and services from one time period to another. The bundle of goods used in calculating the WPI is different from that incorporated into the calculation of the CPI.

› The **consumer price index (CPI)** is the cost of a standard basket of goods and services consumed by a typical domestic consumer.

The CPI is a weighted sum of prices of the set of goods and services that the statistical agency of the government determines through surveys of the typical domestic consumer purchases each year. The government conducts a survey to determine the importance of different expenditures by the average household. Weights are assigned to the different expenditure categories to reflect the importance of each in the household spending. For example, expenditure on fuel and light by industrial workers receives a weight of 6.43 out of 100, and clothing, bedding, and footwear receive a weight of 6.58 (see Table 1.11). In addition to a CPI for industrial workers, the government also calculates alternative consumer price indices for agricultural workers and urban non-manual employees.

› The **wholesale price index (WPI)** is a price index of goods that are domestically produced.

The WHOLESALE PRICE INDEX measures the average level of prices of goods sold by producers. Unlike the CPI, the WPI measures price changes from the perspective of the seller (Table 1.11 indicates the weighting pattern for this index). The WPI is useful because it indicates what is likely to happen to consumer prices in the proximate future. If producers are receiving higher prices from their sales to wholesalers, we might expect that sooner or later retailers will have to charge higher prices. This will then get reflected in a higher CPI. Both the WPI and the CPI are measured using base year quantities as weights. Price indices that do this are called LASPEYRE INDICES. The expenditure proportions in a LASPEYRE INDEX are those prevailing in the base year. Both the WPI and the CPI represent only a subset of all the goods and services produced by the entire economy and so may not reflect all changes in price levels.

› A **Laspeyre price index** is calculated from a basket of fixed quantities of a given list of goods. We first calculate the total price of the basket of goods in the base period. Let the price index in the base period be 100. Then we calculate the total price of exactly the same basket of goods in a subsequent year *j*. Next we compute the ratio of the total price of the basket of goods in period *j* divided by the total price of the basket in the base period. The price index in year *j* then is this ratio multiplied by 100. It tells us the expenditure that must be incurred in year *j* as a fraction of the expenditure in the base year in order that we may obtain the same bundle of goods as that in the base year.

In price indices such as the CPI, we are interested in finding out how much it costs in the subsequent year to purchase the same basket of goods that was purchased in the base year. If the student whose expenditure pattern is represented in Table 1.10 were to purchase the same basket of goods the subsequent year, he would have to pay INR 2,550 for pizzas (30 pizzas at INR 85 per pizza) and INR 2,460 for book (4 books at INR 615 per book). The expenditure on the same basket of goods in the subsequent year is then equal to INR 5,010. In the subsequent year then the student's cost of living has increased. Setting the value of the index equal to 100 in the base year, the price index in the subsequent year is calculated as $100 \times (5{,}010/5{,}000) = 100.2$. The inflation rate is the percentage change in the price index. The price index rose from 100 in the base year to 100.2 in the subsequent year—an increase of 0.2 per cent. Inflation as measured by the price index with base year quantities as weights is 0.2 per cent in the subsequent year.

The advantage of an index is that once calculated for a base year we can compare it with any other year. For instance, if the index were to rise to 103.04 in a later year, then, between the subsequent year and the next year

› **Table 1.10**
Real Incomes with Two Goods (1 and 2)

	Pizzas		Books	
	Quantity	Price	Quantity	Price
Year 0	30	100	4	500
Year 1	30	85	5	615

the index rose by 103.04 − 100.2 = 2.84. Hence, the inflation for this time period is the percentage change in the index or 100 × (2.84/100.2) ≐ 2.83 per cent.

Before looking at the weighting pattern of WPI and CPI, it is worth pointing out that all price indices could overstate the true inflation due to two factors:

1. Price indices cannot account for price changes in newly-invented goods, as the indices are calculated on a bundle of fixed goods and undergo revision with a lag. For example, the prices of new computers tend to start high and come down rapidly as output expands, and so the price index in the initial years would overstate inflation.
2. Existing goods change in quality over time. For example, attributes of automobiles over time have improved significantly. Apart from improved engine performance, there have been a number of innovations in luxury, comfort, and safety features. As time goes by, a given brand and vehicle of a given engine size (small, mid-size, or luxury segment) may be available with

› **Table 1.11**
WPI and CPI—A Comparison

WPI		CPI	
Movement in wholesale prices of 676 commodities in all trade and transactions		CPI for industrial workers measures retail prices of goods and services for 260 items	
Index released on a provisional monthly basis on the 14th of each month. WPI of articles in the primary and fuel group is released weekly on a Thursday. Provisional data is finalized in a period of two months		Index constructed on a monthly basis	
Widely used in business and industry and by government as indicator of inflation			
Base year is 2004–2005		Base year is 2001	
Weighting diagram of WPI and CPI (industrial workers)			
Primary products	**20.12**	Food	46.19
Food articles	14.34	Pan, supari, tobacco and intoxicants	2.27
Non-food articles	4.26		
Minerals	1.52		
Fuel group	**14.91**	Fuel and light	6.43
Coal mining	2.09		
Electricity	3.45		
Mineral oils	9.37		
Manufactured products	**64.97**	Housing	15.27
Of which		Clothing, bedding and footwear	6.58
Food products	9.97	Miscellaneous	23.26
Textiles	7.33		
Chemicals	12.02		
Basic metals	10.75		
Machinery and machine tools	8.93		
Transport equipment and parts	5.21		
Differences between WPI and CPI			
Fuel group gets a much higher weight		Food gets maximum weightage	
Services not included		Miscellaneous group includes services such as transport, education, and health	

› Table 1.12
Inflation Rates Based on GDP Deflator, WPI, and CPI (Industrial Workers)
Source: Central Statistical Organisation.

Year	GDP Deflator	WPI	CPI (IW)
1990–1991	10.68	10.26	11.56
1991–1992	13.73	13.74	13.47
1992–1993	8.97	10.06	9.59
1993–1994	9.81	8.35	7.50
1994–1995	10.00	12.60	10.08
1995–1996	9.08	7.99	10.21
1996–1997	7.55	4.61	9.27
1997–1998	6.46	4.40	7.02
1998–1999	7.98	5.95	13.11
1999–2000	3.80	3.27	3.38
2000–2001	3.53	7.16	3.74
2001–2002	3.03	3.60	4.28
2002–2003	3.80	3.41	4.10
2003–2004	3.56	5.46	3.73
2004–2005	5.57	6.48	4.00
2005–2006	4.18	4.50	4.23
2006–2007	6.41	6.60	6.83
2007–2008	5.75	4.67	6.40
2008–2009	6.69	8.06	9.02
2009–2010	7.54	3.81	12.41
Average (1990/1991–2009/2010)	6.91	6.75	7.70
Standard deviation	2.88	3.04	3.42
Trend growth rate	–4.20	–4.25	–3.24

additional features such as colour-coded bumper, disc brakes, driver airbags, and a digital odometer. The price index overstates the inflation in the price of the commodity because it records a higher price which is the sum of the old, unimproved good plus the premium for higher improved quality.

To account for differences in consumption patterns across households, the CPI is compiled for industrial workers, urban non-manual employees, and agricultural labourers. In Table 1.11 we list some properties of the CPI for industrial workers, which are published by the Labour Bureau of the Ministry of Labour, Government of India. The table also includes the WPI, which covers the prices of goods purchased and transacted in, mainly by producers of goods. The WPI, however, excludes the prices of all services.

Table 1.12 gives statistics for the inflation rate calculated using the three indicators of inflation—GDP deflator, WPI, and CPI (industrial workers). As Figure 1.6, which is drawn on the basis of the data in Table 1.12, depicts, inflation in India has been on the decline since 1994–1995. The WPI shows the steepest decline in inflation compared to the other two indicators of inflation.

Index numbers help us to understand whether we are better off in terms of real incomes today. They are computed by fixing a base year in which the cost of a fixed bundle of goods and services is determined and the cost of this bundle over time is then tracked. However we also have to account for the changes in the available goods and services.

One reason why life is better today than it was, say, 25 years ago is not just that average real incomes have risen, but that there are many more goods

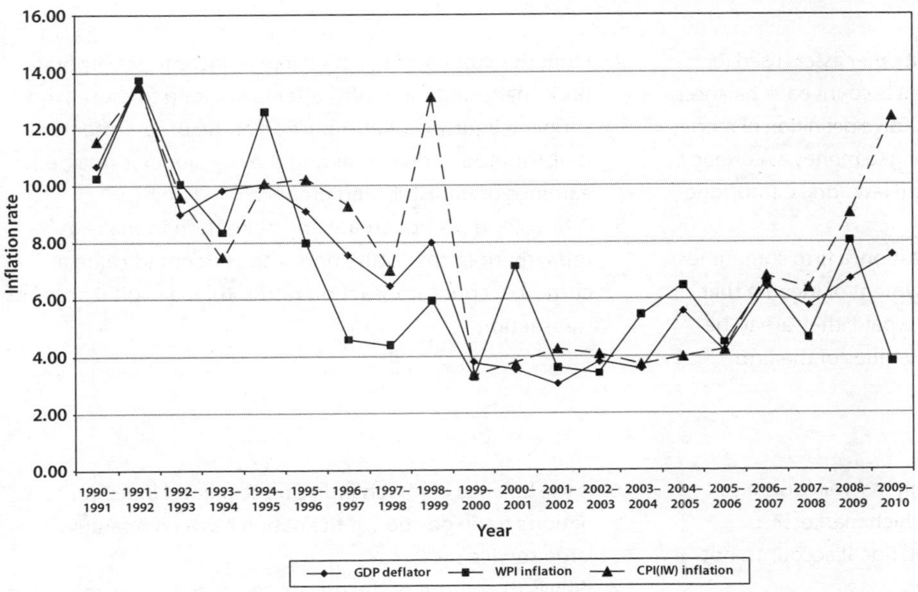

› **Figure 1.6**
Inflation Rates. Inflation has been declining over the past two decades with the steepest decline measured by the WPI.

available. In 1980 people were still using typewriters instead of computers, they were lucky if they got to watch just one channel on a black-and-white television set, and they could not speak with their families and loved ones while driving back from work. There are a greater variety of ways to spend incomes today, and measuring one's income by correcting for inflation is not going to capture that very important transformation in our lives. Even if someone today has a real income that is lower than that of a person who was in a comparable position 50 years ago, the person has a larger range of products to spend his income on. As was emphasized in the beginning of this chapter, the way in which we measure income is not a perfect manifestation of the welfare we experience.

SUMMARY

» Choices made in markets result in macroeconomic outcomes like aggregate income. Macroeconomics concerns itself with the market for goods, the market for bonds, the market for labour, and the market for money.

» Macroeconomists' interest in aggregate income stems from its being an approximate measure of welfare.

» Measures of aggregate income are incomplete due to under-reported income and participation in underground and non-market activities.

» GDP is a measure of aggregate income and output in an economy. It is the total value of the current production of final goods and services within the national territory during a given period of time.

» In macroeconomics, aggregate output equals aggregate income, which, in turn, equals aggregate expenditure.

» As some citizens work for foreign-owned business organizations and some foreigners work for domestically-owned organizations, gross national product (GNP) measures aggregate output by citizens regardless of where in the world they work.

» National income is the sum of aggregate domestic income and net factor incomes from abroad.

» Aggregate expenditure (Y) is the sum of domestic expenditure plus net exports (or exports less imports).

» Aggregate domestic expenditure equals aggregate expenditure on consumption (C) by households, on investment (I) by business units, and aggregate expenditure by government (G).

$$Y = C + I + G + X - M$$

» In order to understand whether income increases represent an increase in command over goods and services, we differentiate between real income (income measured in constant prices) and nominal income.

» The rate of change in prices or inflation in the price of goods and services is measured by a producer price index, such as the wholesale price index (WPI), a consumer price index (CPI), or the GDP deflator.

NOTES

1. Money includes not just currency but other assets used for purchases such as savings and current account bank balances. In Chapter 2, we adopt this more inclusive definition of money, but here, for simplicity, we are referring to money as currency.
2. Robert Lane, *The Market Experience* (New York: Cambridge University Press, 1991).
3. In addition to employees compensation, a firm sometimes also pays proprietors' income, a payment of income that we are ignoring. If such incomes are paid, they are to be treated as an initial claim on the revenues of the firm.
4. From the gross profits, a payment of income or corporate tax is made and the profits after tax belong to those who supplied equity capital. A portion of the profits after tax is distributed as dividends and the remainder is retained earnings or undistributed profits.
5. A transfer does not create any obligation to make a repayment in the future and is thus deemed to be a current account transaction rather than a capital account transaction.

TEST YOURSELF

1. Economics is the study of choices. In macroeconomics, choices are studied in relation to which markets?
2. Why does GDP, as reported in the national accounts, not correctly measure total output?
3. Explain how cutting down trees to make furniture may increase a country's GDP but causes economic welfare to decline at the same time.
4. GDP only counts the production of goods in their final form during a given period of time. What are the various components of the final demand for goods?
5. What is the difference between GDP and GNP?
6. Is the balance of merchandise trade a good indicator of a nation's trade position, if the nation has a comparatively large service sector?
7. Why is the output of the private sector measured in market prices and that of the government measured at cost?
8. Why may the GDP deflator overstate the average annual inflation rate for the economy?
9. When the prices of different goods change at different rates, how can we measure inflation?
10. Why is the wholesale price index more widely used as a measure of inflation than the consumer price index?

ONLINE APPLICATION

1. (a) Go to the home page of the Reserve Bank of India URL: www.rbi.org.in/home.aspx.
   (b) Click on the "DataBase" icon.
   (c) Then under the classification of annual data, click on "Handbook of Statistics on Indian Economy."
   (d) Click on "Table 1: Macro-economic aggregates (at current prices)" and create a spreadsheet of data on GDP for the 20 data points corresponding to the period 1990–1991 to 2009–2010.
2. (a) Then click on "Table 2: Macro-economic aggregates (at constant prices)" and access data for GDP at constant prices for the same time period.
   (b) Calculate the GDP deflator for this time period using the formula from the text.
3. Inflation is the percentage change in the price index. Calculate the inflation based on the GDP deflator by taking the percentage change in the GDP deflator price that you have calculated.
4. (a) Next click on "Table 39: Wholesale price index—annual average". Access the data on this price index for the period 1990–1991 to 2009–2010. The data are provided for 3 different base periods—1981–1982, 1993–1994, and 2004–2005. Using the overlapping years amongst these base periods construct a data series that is consistent for the time period selected.
   (b) Again click on "Table 40: Consumer price index—annual average". Access the data on this price index for the period 1990–1991 to 2009–2010 for the consumer price index for industrial workers. The data are provided for 2 different base periods—1982 and 2001. Using the overlapping years amongst these base periods, construct a data series that is consistent for the time period selected.
5. Calculate the inflation rate based on the wholesale price index and the consumer price index for industrial workers.
6. Plot the three series of inflation rates over time. Which price index results in higher average inflation rates over time? Why do you think this is so? (Hint: You should obtain the plot given in Figure 1.6).
7. Plot the data on GDP at constant prices and GDP at current prices over time. Observe whether these curves cross one another. Why do you think that occurs? What do you observe in the graph you have plotted about the relationship between real GDP and nominal GDP?

Appendix 1.1 The GDP Deflator

If there were two goods, 1 and 2, and p stands for price, and q for output, then, the prices of the two goods in the base year and current year (Year 1) could be as depicted in the following Table A1.1.1.

Let i stand for a good ($i = 1, 2$) and j depicts the years where j takes the value 0 if it is the base year and any positive number for a year that comes later.

Define C_{jx} as the expenditure in year j in the prices of year x. Then, the figure for nominal income in Year 1 is given by

$$C_{11} = q_{11}p_{11} + q_{21}p_{21} = (4 \times 3) + (12 \times 2) = 36$$

The real income in Year 1 is given by

$$C_{10} = q_{11}p_{10} + q_{21}p_{20} = (4 \times 1) + (12 \times 1) = 16$$

Note that the common weights of the prices p_{i1} and p_{io} in the above are the current year's expenditures on the commodities, q_{ij}. When prices are weighted by current year quantities, the price index generated is said to be a *Paasche Index*.

The inflation rate of the economy is found by deriving the implicit GDP deflator which is the current price estimate divided by the constant price estimate. Thus,

$$\text{GDP Deflator} = \left(\frac{C_{11}}{C_{10}}\right)100 = \left(\frac{\text{Nominal GDP}}{\text{Real GDP}}\right)100$$

Now, $$C_{11} = q_{11}p_{11} + q_{21}p_{21}$$

Adding and subtracting p_{10} in the first part of the right-hand side of the expression for C_{11} and p_{20} in the second part of the expression,

$$C_{11} = q_{11}(p_{10} + p_{11} - p_{10}) + q_{21}(p_{20} + p_{21} - p_{20})$$

This may be rewritten as

$$C_{11} = q_{11}p_{10}\left(1 + \frac{p_{11}}{p_{10}} - 1\right) + q_{21}p_{20}\left(1 + \frac{p_{21}}{p_{20}} - 1\right)$$

Inflation in the price of commodity i measured in year j (π_{ij}) is defined as the percentage change in prices. We can define this as:

$$\pi_{ij} = \frac{\text{Change in Price}}{\text{Original Price}} = \frac{p_{ij} - p_{io}}{p_{io}}$$

Then, $$\pi_{11} = \frac{p_{11}}{p_{10}} - 1 \quad \text{and} \quad \pi_{21} = \frac{p_{21}}{p_{20}} - 1$$

We can then write

$$C_{11} = q_{11}p_{10}(1 + \pi_{11}) + q_{21}p_{20}(1 + \pi_{21})$$

	q_1	p_1	q_2	p_2
Year 0	$q_{10} = 2$	$p_{10} = 1$	$q_{20} = 4$	$p_{20} = 1$
Year 1	$q_{11} = 4$	$p_{11} = 3$	$q_{21} = 12$	$p_{21} = 2$

› **Table A1.1.1**
Real Incomes with Two Goods (1 and 2)

Dividing throughout by the expression for C_{10},

$$\frac{C_{11}}{C_{10}} = \frac{q_{11}p_{10}}{q_{11}p_{10} + q_{21}p_{20}}(1+\pi_{11}) + \frac{q_{21}p_{20}}{q_{11}p_{10} + q_{21}p_{20}}(1+\pi_{21})$$

$$= w_1(1+\pi_{11}) + w_2(1+\pi_{21})$$

where, $w_i = q_{i1}p_{io}/(q_{11}p_{10} + q_{21}p_{20})$ is the proportion of commodity i's contribution to GDP in the base year, or the weight that commodity i has in the overall output produced. (Note that the sum of the weights equals unity.)

Generally, the GDP deflator involving the expression C_{jj}/C_{jo} in year j is defined as:

$$\text{GDP Deflator} = \left[w_1(1+\pi_{1j}) + w_2(1+\pi_{2j}) + \cdots + w_n(1+\pi_{nj})\right]100$$

where, $w_i = q_{ij}p_{io}/(q_{1j}p_{10} + q_{2j}p_{20} + q_{nj}p_{no})$.

For the example above:

$$w_1 = \frac{4\times 1}{(4\times 1)+(12\times 1)} = \frac{4}{16} = \frac{1}{4}$$

$$w_2 = \frac{12\times 1}{(4\times 1)+(12\times 1)} = \frac{12}{16} = \frac{3}{4}$$

Also, $\pi_{11} = \frac{p_{11}}{p_{10}} - 1 = \frac{3}{1} - 1 = 2$ and $\pi_{21} = \frac{p_{21}}{p_{20}} - 1 = \frac{2}{1} - 1 = 1$

Plugging these values into the expression for C_{11}/C_{10},

$$\left(\frac{C_{11}}{C_{10}}\right)100 = \left[\frac{1}{4}(1+2) + \frac{3}{4}(1+1)\right]100$$

$$= \left(\frac{3}{4} + \frac{6}{4}\right)100$$

$$= \left(\frac{9}{4}\right)100$$

$$= 225$$

Note that the price of good 1 increased by [(3 − 1)/1], or 200 per cent. The price of good 2 increased by [(2 − 1)/1], or 100 per cent. The weighted average of price increase in the economy is:

$$\frac{1}{4}(100+200) + \frac{3}{4}(100+100) = \frac{300+600}{4} = \frac{900}{4} = 225 \text{ per cent}$$

2

Savings, the Balance of Payments, and Money Supply

CRITICAL QUESTIONS

- *How is the aggregate savings of an economy used?*
- *What is the balance of international payments and what are its components?*
- *How is the exchange rate determined and what is its relationship with the financing of the balance of payments?*
- *What is the difference between the monetary base, or reserve money, and the money stock?*
- *How does the interaction between the public, the commercial banks, and the central bank determine the money supply?*
- *What is money multiplier?*
- *What is an open market operation and how does it affect the money supply?*

2.1 The Sources and Use of Savings

In Chapter 1, we derived the fundamental macroeconomic identity that output equals income equals expenditure (domestic expenditure plus net exports). This is a truism from the perspective of an aggregate economy. You might, for an instant, think that at an individual level income is not equal to expenditure because some of it gets taxed and it is only after some of it gets saved that we get to spend on goods like ice creams and computers. Yet, what is true at an individual level is not true in the aggregate. This is an insight that macroeconomics provides.

From your income, a certain amount leaks out as taxes, but that is what the government spends. What happens when you save and put your money into a bank account? The bank then lends your money to firms who plan to spend on setting up new factories, or to the government which plans to spend on, say, the salaries of professors at the Indian Institutes of Technology and Indian Institutes of Management. So, in the final analysis, even if we do not spend all our income, it turns out that all of our income does get spent. From the perspective of an aggregate economy, therefore, all income is spent.

To probe this perspective further, we begin with the identity that income in the aggregate equals expenditure, which we explained in Chapter 1 as:

$$Y = C + I + G + X - M$$

The term $X - M$ here denotes the balance of merchandize trade plus net receipts from non-factor service incomes such as software exports and foreign travel. As our interest is currently on savings which is due to current income (from all sources) being set aside rather than being spent, we expand the identity above to include NFI and transfers (mainly remittances) from abroad. Adding NFI and transfers from abroad to both sides of the above identity,

$$Y + \text{NFI} + \text{Transfers from Abroad} = C + I + G + X - M + \text{NFI} + \text{Transfers from Abroad}$$

Taking the terms in consumption and government expenditure on the left hand side,

$$Y + \text{NFI} + \text{Transfers from Abroad} - C - G = I + (X - M + \text{NFI} + \text{Transfers from Abroad})$$

However,

$$(X - M + \text{NFI} + \text{Transfers from Abroad}) = \text{CA}$$

where the left-hand side is the net exports of goods and services (or non-factor incomes) plus the net factor incomes and transfers from abroad, and this is the definition (see Chapter 1) of the term on the right-hand side, the current account surplus (CA). We may then write,

$$Y + \text{NFI} + \text{Transfers from Abroad} - C - G = I + \text{CA}$$

To connect the savings in the economy with the above identity, we need to define private and public savings.

PRIVATE SAVINGS is that income which is left over after the private sector spends whatever income is available for spending. The private disposable income is the amount of income the private sector has available to spend. This equals income

› **Private saving** is the value of the private sector's disposable income minus its consumption.

received from private sector activities plus payments received from government less tax paid to government.

$$\begin{aligned}\text{Private Disposable Income} = \text{GDP} &+ \text{Net Factor Incomes Abroad}\\ &+ \text{Transfers from Abroad}\\ &+ \text{Transfers Received from Government}\\ &- \text{Taxes}\end{aligned}$$

Recollect that NFI is income paid to domestic factors of production by the international economy less income paid to foreign factors of production by the domestic economy. Transfers from abroad are mainly remittances by Indians working abroad. Transfers from government include subsidies and interest payments on the public debt.

As consumption is spending by the private sector to meet current needs, savings of the private sector is defined as private disposable income minus consumption.[1]

$$\text{Private Savings} = S_{pvt} = \text{Private Disposable Income} - \text{Consumption}$$

Similarly, the income of the government is the taxes paid by the private sector to the government. The net government income is the tax revenues of government less the TRANSFERS it makes.

› **Transfers** by government include subsidies and interest payments on government borrowing from the private sector.

$$\text{Net Public Sector (Government) Income} = \text{Taxes} - \text{Transfers (to Private Sector) by Government}$$

› **Government saving** is equal to net government revenues less government spending.

GOVERNMENT SAVINGS then is the net government income less government purchases of goods and services for the current needs (government consumption expenditure).

In most macroeconomic models, the government purchases are the sum of government consumption and investment expenditure and are treated as though they are entirely expenditures on current needs. In that case, we need not differentiate between the kinds of government expenditure that we take to be current government outlays.

$$\begin{aligned}\text{Government Saving} = S_{govt} &= \text{Net Government Income} - \text{Government Expenditure}\\ &= \text{Taxes} - \text{Transfers by Government}\\ &\quad - \text{Government Expenditure}\end{aligned}$$

A commonly used term for government savings is the government fiscal surplus.[2]

› The sum of private and public saving is **national saving**.

NATIONAL SAVING, or the saving of the economy is equal to private saving plus government saving.

$$\begin{aligned}\text{Saving} &= S_{pvt} + S_{govt}\\ &= (\text{GDP} + \text{Net Factor Incomes Abroad}\\ &\quad + \text{Transfers from Abroad} + \text{Transfers from Government}\\ &\quad - \text{Taxes} - \text{Consumption})\\ &\quad + (\text{Taxes} - \text{Transfers by Government}\\ &\quad - \text{Government Expenditure})\\ &= Y + \text{NFI} + \text{Transfers from Government} - C - G\end{aligned}$$

Since we had written the "aggregate income equals expenditure" identity as $Y + \text{NFI} + \text{Transfers from Abroad} - C - G = I + \text{CA}$, we can substitute this into the above expression for national savings,

$$\text{Saving} = I + \text{CA}$$

or,

$$S_{pvt} + S_{govt} = I + \text{CA}$$

or,

$$S_{pvt} + S_{govt} - \text{CA} = I$$

The previous identity or AGGREGATE INVESTMENT EXPENDITURE states that the investment expenditure in the economy is financed through three sources:

1. Private savings
2. Government savings
3. Foreign savings

› The **aggregate investment expenditure** of an economy is financed from three sources—(1) private savings, (2) government savings, and (3) foreign savings (current account deficit).

A negative current account surplus, or a current account deficit ($M > X +$ NFI + Transfers from Abroad) implies that what foreigners receive from us (as monetary payment when we import goods and services from them) is more than the amount that we receive as payments on the Indian goods and services they demand (Indian exports). The money coming into the Indian financial system from abroad as payment for exports, and returns to factors of production (NFI) as well as remittances is insufficient to pay for the import demand of residents. The country then must raise the money required to finance the excess imports from abroad. It does this by borrowing from abroad. A CURRENT ACCOUNT DEFICIT, thus, requires borrowing from abroad, which means that domestic residents are utilizing the savings of foreigners to finance expenditures. A current account deficit is thus financed by an increased indebtedness abroad and it represents the savings of foreigners.

› A **current account deficit** implies that a country's payments to the rest of the world exceeds the payments received from the rest of the world. This deficit in payments to be made to the rest of the world increases the country's indebtedness abroad and is plugged via a use of the savings of foreigners to finance the gap in payments.

Aggregate investment in the economy is, therefore, equal to aggregate savings. Aggregate savings, in turn, is the sum of national savings—private savings (S_{pvt}) plus government savings (S_{govt})—and foreign savings (−CA).

The aforementioned identity, that investment is financed through three sources of savings, is always true by definition. Being an identity, a reduction in any component of the identity must result in an increase in another component or a combination of components so that the identity continues to hold true. Hence if the government decides to splurge and reduces its savings—the government deficit increases—at least one of three things or a combination of them must occur: private saving rises, investment decreases, and/or the current account balance deteriorates.

Figure 2.1 graphs data on the sources of savings and aggregate investment in the Indian economy from 2004–2005 to 2009–2010. The upper portion of the graph shows that aggregate investment has consistently been higher than private savings. On average, during this period, aggregate investment has been 35.5 per cent of GDP and private savings has been 31.5 per cent of GDP. This leaves a gap of 4 per cent of GDP that indicates the extent to which that private savings has been unable to finance investment expenditures. The gap has been filled to some extent by government savings, which, in the lower portion of the

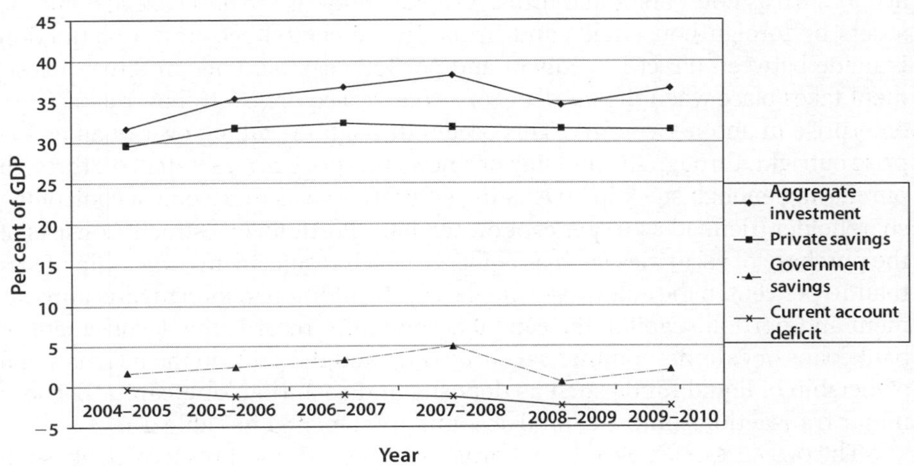

› **Figure 2.1**
Sources of Savings and Investment. Aggregate investment is financed by private savings, government savings, and the current account deficit (foreign savings). Aggregate investment which has averaged 35.5 per cent of GDP in the recent period has been financed by private savings (31.5 per cent of GDP), government savings (2.5 per cent of GDP), and foreign savings (1.5 per cent of GDP).

graph, has been, on average, 2.5 per cent of GDP. The residual in the gap has been financed by a current account deficit that on average has been 1.5 per cent of GDP. This means that Indians have been borrowing an amount equivalent to 1.5 per cent of GDP from foreigners to finance capital formation in the economy.

A change in the current account of an economy is associated with a change in the capacity to hold the assets of the residents of a country, as compared to the residents of other nations. With each flow of goods, services, and income[3] that comprises the transactions reflected in the current account, there will be an associated outflow of domestic assets abroad as well as inflow of foreign assets into the domestic economy. For instance, the export of software services by India will result in an inflow of foreign exchange as payment received for such exports.

These flows of financial assets are recorded separately in an account that depicts the income and asset transactions between domestic residents and residents of other nations and is called the balance of payments accounts of a country. The increase in the stock of foreign exchange by the economy will also get reflected in the asset and liabilities position of the banking system since that is where these assets will be held. That, in turn, will affect the money supply in the economy. We thus turn to a study of the balance of payments and the money supply of an economy.

2.2 The Balance of Payments

› The **balance of payments** summarizes a country's transactions—monetary payments for goods and services, and acquisition of financial assets—with the rest of the world.

The BALANCE OF PAYMENTS account is a summary of the nation's financial relationship with the rest of the world. It records the market value of goods, services, and financial assets that domestic residents exchange with foreigners from other nations during an accounting period. There are three balance of payments concepts—the balance on current account, the balance on capital account, and the overall balance.

› The **current account** is the summary of the country's payments to and from the rest of the world.

The CURRENT ACCOUNT measures the flow of goods, services, and income across national borders. The income recorded in this account is the compensation of employees working outside the geographical borders, investment income of the interest, and dividend payments received by residents from the holding of financial assets abroad less similar payments made to foreign residents (NFI). International transfers comprising government grants and private remittances are also a part of this account.

› The **capital account** is a summary of the country's financial asset transactions with the rest of the world.

The CAPITAL ACCOUNT measures the capital outflow and the capital inflow into the economy. A capital outflow is the purchase of foreign assets by domestic agents such as households and firms. A capital inflow is the purchase of domestic assets by foreign households and firms. In the capital account, a distinction is made between direct investment and portfolio capital. Foreign direct investment takes place when the residents of a country acquire control over a business enterprise in another country. This occurs through the taking over of an enterprise outright, through the building of a new enterprise from scratch, or, through purchasing enough stock in an existing enterprise so as to become a controlling shareholder (defined as 10 per cent ownership). Portfolio investment consists of the purchase of securities such as equities (which results in an ownership of less than 10 per cent in the enterprise) and bonds. In addition to foreign direct investment and portfolio capital, the capital account also records the devolvement of bank loans or external commercial borrowings and the shifts in the international ownership of liquid funds such as deposits and cash (banking capital). These major transactions on the capital account are depicted in Table 2.1.

› The **overall balance** records the changes in a country's stock of international reserves during the year. International reserves are the foreign currency and other assets held by the government for the purpose of purchasing the domestic currency in the foreign-exchange market.

The OVERALL BALANCE account records the transactions of reserve assets such as gold and foreign currencies by official government agencies.

	1999–2000	2006–2007	2007–2008	2008–2009	2009–2010
Current account balance	−203.31	−443.83	−634.79	−1,316.14	−1,807.57
Capital account					
Foreign investment (net)	225.01	667.91	1,743.95	1,178.60	2,482.25
a. FDI	93.96	349.10	637.76	768.31	942.58
b. Portfolio investment	131.05	318.81	1,106.19	−650.45	1,539.67
Commercial borrowings and external assistance	69.51	1,104.34	1,634.91	3,638.8	566.36
Banking capital (including NRI deposits)	92.17	84.77	471.55	−192.05	98.44
Total capital account balance*	481.01	2,080.17	4,331.67	344.99	2,449.94
Overall balance#	277.70	1,636.34	3,696.88	−971.15	642.37
Monetary movements	−277.70	−1,636.34	−3,696.88	971.15	−642.37
a. IMF, Net	−11.22	0	0	0	0
b. Foreign-exchange reserves (increase −, decrease +)	−266.48	−1,636.34	−3,696.88	971.15	−642.37

Notes: * Inclusive of errors and omissions.
Overall Balance = Current A/c Balance + Capital A/c Balance
Figures for 2008–2009 are partially revised, and figures for 2009–2010 are preliminary.

› **Table 2.1**
India's Overall Balance of Payments (INR billion)
Source: Reserve Bank of India, Annual Reports.

The balance of payments is a bookkeeping system which records both sides of any transaction involving a domestic resident and a resident abroad. A DEBIT ENTRY is made if a transaction results in a domestic resident making a payment abroad. Another way of stating this is that a debit entry is made whenever a good, service, or financial asset enters the country. A credit entry is made if a transaction results in a domestic resident receiving a payment from abroad. Alternatively, whenever a good, service, or financial asset leaves the country, a credit entry is made.

› In the balance of payments, a **debit entry** is made whenever a domestic resident makes a payment abroad, or when a good, service, or financial asset enters the country. A credit entry is made whenever a good, service, or financial asset leaves the country, or a domestic resident receives a payment from abroad.

If the total of debit entries or imports recorded in the current account exceeds (is less than) the sum of the credit entries or exports as well as net factor incomes and transfers from abroad, then there is a deficit (surplus) in the current account.

Similarly, the purchase of domestic financial assets (bonds, stocks) by foreign residents is a capital inflow which is a credit entry. The rule for recording a transaction as a credit entry is that the asset, or the claim to the asset and the returns associated with it, leaves the country. Thus, capital inflows get recorded as a credit entry. A purchase of foreign financial assets by domestic residents is a capital outflow (the asset enters the country) and is a debit entry. When the debit entries exceed (are less than) the credit entries—capital outflows are greater (lesser) than capital inflows—there is a net capital outflow (inflow) or a deficit (surplus) in the capital account.

The sum of the current account balance and capital account balance is the OVERALL BALANCE that states a net debit or credit. If it is a net credit, as has been the case in India in the recent past, then domestic residents are receiving more payments from abroad than they are making payments abroad. This surplus in the overall balance requires the central bank to accumulate the excess foreign assets, and add to its holding of foreign currencies as foreign-exchange reserves.

› The **overall balance** is the sum of the current account balance and the capital account balance. A surplus overall balance is a net increase in the country's stock of international reserves over the year. A deficit overall balance is a net decline in the country's stock of international reserves over the year.

The accounting of the balance of payments thus is:

$$\text{Current Account Balance} = CA$$
$$\text{Capital Account Balance} = KA$$
$$\text{Overall Balance} = (CA + KA)$$
$$\text{Official Reserves, } R = -(CA + KA)$$

The overall balance is achieved through official financing—the authorities absorb the finance required for overall balance by accumulating forex reserves, or by making a deposit with monetary authorities overseas such as the International Monetary Fund when there is an overall surplus. This accumulation of reserves is shown as a negative value of the sum of the capital and current accounts. A negative value to the reserves thus represents an increase in the official reserves held. On the other hand, positive value is a decrease in the holding of official reserves by the central bank.

To understand this role of the government, whereby it absorbs or releases foreign exchange in the foreign-exchange market, we employ the diagram illustrated in Figure 2.2. A foreign-exchange market is where commercial banks, foreign-exchange dealers, and the central bank buy and sell the currency of other nations. The exchange rate is the market price at which foreign exchange is bought and sold. The EXCHANGE RATE expresses the value of a currency relative to another. In Figure 2.2, the vertical axis depicts the exchange rate measured as the number of units of domestic currency (rupees) per US dollar, $E_{INR/USD}$. The exchange rate thus expresses how many domestic currency units (Indian rupees) it takes to purchase one dollar, or, rupees per US dollar. The exchange rate we are concerned with here is the SPOT MARKET EXCHANGE RATE—the rate for immediate purchase and delivery of the foreign currency.

› The **exchange rate** is the value of a currency relative to another.

› A **spot exchange rate** is the market price for immediate purchase and delivery of foreign exchange. The forward exchange rate and real exchange rate are studied in Chapter 5.

When the number of rupees required to purchase one US dollar increases, we say that the rupee price of the dollar rose, or, the rupee DEPRECIATED relative to the US dollar. When the number of rupees required to purchase a dollar decreases, we say that the rupee price of the dollar has fallen, or the rupee has APPRECIATED relative to the US dollar.

› A **depreciation** occurs when the price of the foreign currency in terms of the domestic currency rises—an increase in the exchange rate.
› An **appreciation** occurs when the price of the foreign currency in terms of the domestic currency decreases—a decrease in the exchange rate.

In Figure 2.2, higher values of E represent a depreciation of the currency and lower values represent an appreciation. On the horizontal axis, we measure the flow of dollars per period (a year).

Now, take the case of an economic agent who imports goods and services and is thus required to pay the foreign supplier in dollars. The importer goes

› **Figure 2.2**
Exchange Rate and Balance of Payments. The demand for foreign exchange from importers and due to capital outflows and the supply of foreign exchange by exporters and due to capital inflows determines the exchange rate and the balance of payments.

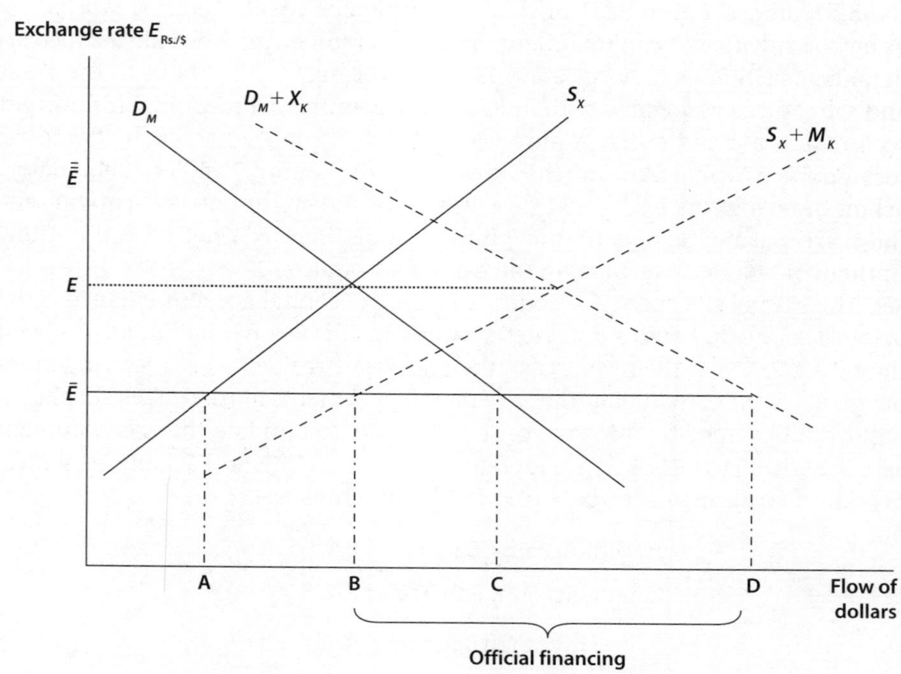

to the foreign-exchange market with his rupees that he wants converted into dollars—he has a demand for dollars in the foreign-exchange market. A depreciation of the currency requires the importer to give up more rupees for the dollars that are required to pay for the imports of goods and services. We should then expect that depreciation by raising the foreign-exchange cost of imports would reduce the demand for imports. An appreciation would have the opposite effect. The demand for dollars as a result of the demand for imports of goods and services is, therefore, downward sloping and depicted as D_M. Similarly, exporters supply dollars that they receive from customers abroad in exchange for rupees in the foreign-exchange market. As the rupee depreciates, foreigners will find Indian goods cheaper, exports will increase in volume and value, and the supply of dollars by exporters will be an upward sloping line as depicted by S_X. If the exchange rate is fixed by the government at $\overline{E}$, then, the current account balance is the distance *AC* and is in deficit as drawn.

We now take into consideration the capital account. If an economic agent wishes to export capital, say, to buy shares on the New York Stock Exchange, he supplies rupees to be converted to dollars. From the viewpoint of the impact on currency demand, this is like an import of goods and services as there is a demand for dollars. We thus add the capital export X_K to the D_M schedule and denote the total demand for dollars as $D_M + X_K$. Conversely, we may have agents overseas who want to buy stock on the National Stock Exchange in India. These agents supply dollars in exchange for the rupees that will allow them to buy the shares. The impact on foreign currency supply is like that of an export of goods and services. We add the capital import, M_K, to the S_X schedule and denote the total supply of dollars as $S_X + M_K$. The amount of capital export at exchange rate $\overline{E}$ is *CD,* and the distance *AB* measures the capital import. The capital account deficit is, therefore, $CD - AB$.

Combining the deficit on current account (*AC*) and capital account ($CD - AB$), we obtain an overall deficit of $AC + (CD - AB)$, or *BD*. This is the amount that the government acting through its central banker—the Reserve Bank of India (RBI) in the case of India—is required to finance from reserves or by borrowing from overseas monetary authorities. In the figure, the excess demand for foreign exchange, *BD*, arising from transactions on the current and capital account, is what the RBI would be required to finance. It does so by selling rupees in exchange for dollars, by decreasing its holdings of foreign-exchange reserves, or by incurring a debt to the Federal Reserve by asking a foreign monetary authority such as the Federal Reserve Board in the US to buy rupees on its behalf. If the exchange rate were at $\overline{\overline{E}}$ instead of $\overline{E}$, then the overall balance *BD* would be in surplus, and the RBI could just accumulate the excess supply of foreign exchange as reserves. The reader is encouraged to draw a diagram similar to Figure 2.2 depicting this situation of a surplus overall balance. The alternative to decreasing the holding of foreign-exchange reserves or running up a debt to a foreign monetary authority when the exchange rate is $\overline{E}$ is to stop controlling the exchange rate and to let it float. The exchange rate would depreciate to *E* where the overall balance would be zero. Most economies, however, do not "free float", but pursue a MANAGED OR DIRTY FLOAT in which official financing of the overall balance goes on.

› A **managed** or **dirty float** is a system of flexible exchange rates but with periodic intervention in the foreign-exchange market by official agencies.

Table 2.1 depicts India's balance of payments in the last few years. Some items in the capital account, such as rupee debt servicing, have not been reported here. The current account has been in a deficit in the recent past.

MACROFOCUS 2.1

Forex Reserves: Index of Economic Strength?

Japan, during the last months of 2005, was the largest foreign-exchange reserve holder in the world, valued at USD 843.5 billion. China was in second place. However, China's ratio of foreign-exchange reserves to GDP is 37 per cent, whereas that of Japan is 18 per cent. India holds the fifth largest stock of reserves among emerging market economies. It is often claimed that a greater stock of foreign-exchange reserves reflects a country's economic strength and an enhancement of its international status. Is such thinking justified?

In order to determine a rational amount of foreign-exchange reserves, a policy maker must take into account the extent of foreign trade, the utilization of foreign investment and the capacity to finance internationally, the level of opening up of economy, the associated efficiency of adjustment and regulation, etc. A developed economy may exhibit a lower demand for foreign-exchange reserves because its currency is convertible and can be used for international payments. In contrast, an emerging economy's currency is not generally acceptable for international use because of doubts about the efficacy of their macroeconomic regulatory framework. Thus, such countries usually have a stronger demand for foreign-exchange reserves. Besides, an emerging economy needs reserves to handle contingencies such as financial risks due to insufficient liquidity with financial institutions. It also needs foreign-exchange reserves due to its high requirement of oil that is subject to price fluctuations in the international market.

Foreign-exchange reserves are accumulated by continual surpluses in the current and capital accounts of the balance of payments. Reserves emanating from a surplus in the current account are mainly due to the capacity of domestic firms to export products in international markets and compete with other countries. This reflects economic supremacy only to the extent that exports do not comprise resource-based primary products that give a quantity-based advantage, include more products that are of high quality, and have high value added. To some extent, reserves are accumulated to keep the exchange rate stable and protect the export competitiveness of domestic firms, as has happened in China. In such cases, expectations are generated towards revaluation of the currency, and that results in an influx of "hot money" from speculators betting on the revaluation. Foreign-exchange reserves, then, are the result of a policy objective of weakening exchange rates so as to steer the economy's external demand. To the extent that it results in speculative flows, it increases the likelihood of financial crisis and increases the riskiness of the economy, rather than strengthening it.

To sum up, reserves that come from the capital account surplus are largely debt based (FDI) or equity based (FII flows), and result in an increased indebtedness to the rest of the world. They are an indicator of economic power only to the extent that they finance investments which raise the productivity and efficiency of the economy sufficiently so that the returns after compensating these capital inflows increase the incomes received by domestic citizens.

MACROFOCUS 2.2

Does Money Have a Future?

The central bank has a monopoly in the supply of bank reserves. In order to transact, individuals require money, and banks can only cater to this if they hold reserves in parallel to their outstanding deposits. For many goods and services today, neither cash in one's wallet nor an adequate balance in the bank account is necessary at the time of purchase. Credit cards and other electronic cash have contributed to this trend. In Hong Kong, you can buy fast food with an Octopus stored-value card, and in Finland you can pay for a car wash by using your mobile. Even if you do not have the cash up front when undertaking a transaction, you need it for the final settlement of the transaction. For example, if you have used a credit card, you must make a payment by transferring money out of your bank account. You still have a need for money balances. The central bank influencing the money supply through the control of reserves is still relevant.

What if a telephone service provider (TSP) sells you an advance payment smart card? You would still pay for it using cash or a bank cheque. Now suppose the TSP convinces merchants to accept its smart cards in payment for purchases, which is a growing possibility according to Friedman (1999). You could then walk into a store and pay for merchandize using the telephone service's smart card. If the TSP settled with merchants by transferring balances with banks, then they would be providing a service akin to that of a credit-card provider. However, if it could convince merchants that its smart card is widely used, then the merchants would be willing to accept balances on the books of the TSP as payments for transactions undertaken with the smart card. The merchant runs up a credit with the TSP and uses this credit to square off debits it incurs elsewhere. As the acceptance of the smart card issued by the TSP becomes widespread, the merchant's balances on the TSP's books are accepted in payment for transactions. The TSP, in effect, swaps balances on its books as settlement of transactions and does not have to maintain bank balances to meet its payment liabilities. Transactions can then be settled independent of any bank money. The monopoly of the central bank loses relevance and it is unable to affect interest rates and economic activity through the control of bank reserves.

This is an emerging reality. For those bidding on eBay, the biggest Internet-auction site, PayPal is the most popular method of payment. It can be used for payment at over a million other business Web sites as well as for person-to-person payments. PayPal has even encouraged buyers away from using credit cards by paying interest on deposits in a PayPal account that can be used for payments to other PayPal accounts. Banks are losing their hold over the start and finish of each payment transaction.

Direct-investment flows and portfolio flows provide support to the balance of payment with foreign-exchange reserves rising sharply in the last few years. Foreign-exchange reserves declined in the year 2008–2009 during the global financial crisis. India has one of the highest net capital flows among the emerging economies of Asia. India's foreign-exchange reserves are the seventh largest in the world, after countries like China, Japan, Russia, and Brazil.

The purchase and sale of foreign exchange is often mediated through the banking system and affects the asset and liability position of commercial banks and the central bank. We thus turn next to the balance sheet of the banking system and the determination of money supply.

2.3 The Money Supply

We normally think of money as coins or notes. These are financial instruments that we use to make payments in exchange for goods and services. Economists agree that coins and notes are money, but suggest that other financial instruments such as a cheque drawn on a savings deposit in a bank are also acceptable in exchange for goods and services. Economists say that these are to be included in the definition of money. Money is best understood by the three roles it plays in an economy:

1. *Medium of Exchange*—This function of money results from people accepting money in return for the sale of a good or service, and buyers parting with money when they purchase a good or service. Without money people would have to exchange goods and services directly. This is a barter system that is inefficient because it would involve trading a tangible good or service in return for a good or service. This could be quite costly or inconvenient as it requires individuals to search for others who are willing to exchange the goods each other currently possess. Consider, for instance, that you are a young IT professional who can offer software services and you wish to purchase pizzas. You would need to track down a pizza vendor who is at that moment in need of the software services you can deliver. It could take a long time before you and the pizza vendor come across each other, and by that time you could be very hungry indeed. If you could be freed from what is called the double coincidence of wants—your willingness to supply a service (software) so as to satisfy your demand for a good (pizza), i.e., matching the supply of the pizza and demand for software by different agents in the economy—your life would be considerably improved. Money does just that by providing the medium of exchange so that you can sell your service to whoever wants it (not just pizza vendors) and use the money you get from this transaction to purchase the pizza you want. Money's *fundamental role* is as a MEDIUM OF EXCHANGE.

› A **medium of exchange** is something that is used to pay for goods and services.

2. *Store of Value*—This property of money means it can be put aside until a time arrives when you are required to make a transaction. An asset such as money must be something we can draw upon for future purchases, as otherwise pizza vendors will not be willing to accept your money in exchange for selling you pizza. The vendor accepts your money because he can use it a week later to make payments to his suppliers. Many assets can be used as STORES OF VALUE. For instance, you may hold shares in a firm, or gold jewellery that can be sold to acquire the money required to make payments that are due to an exchange transaction you have entered into. Unlike shares and jewellery, however, money as a store of value is the most liquid asset as it is immediately usable in making an exchange for a good or service.

› A **store of value** is the property of an asset whereby it has purchasing power over time.

3. *Unit of Account*—Here money plays the role of measuring the value of goods, services, and assets in an economy. A UNIT OF ACCOUNT provides a yardstick for easy comparisons of the value of economic goods, services, and assets. For instance, grain is measured in bushels and petrol in litres, and in order

› A **unit of account** is anything that is used to measure value in an economy.

to judge whether a bushel of grain is more or less valuable than a litre of oil, their value has to be expressed in money terms. In this way, the use of money as a unit of account is related closely to its use as a medium of exchange—as money is used to buy and sell things, it is sensible to have the prices of all economic things expressed in money terms.

It is also important to distinguish money from income. When laypersons say that someone makes a lot of money, economists interpret that, as a statement, a person has a high income. Income is a flow variable—a measure defined per unit of time. Money, on the other hand, is a stock variable—a measure defined at a point in time. The distinction between the two is clear if we consider a person earning a high income over a year. Such a person may not hold a large stock of money if he is a spendthrift and spends his income on goods and services. Thus he has a high income over the unit of time defined as a year but he has little money as measured at a point in time. Money then is the stock of a type of asset which is the primary medium of exchange and distinct from the flow of income over a period of time. It is true that if you are employed as a manager, your salary is paid at the end of the month (more often than not) in the form of money. But this is because money is the unit of account and the medium of exchange for the managerial services you render to the firm over the month. As the transaction cost of accounting for and paying for each minute of services rendered is high, the convention is to pay at the end of a larger time interval, such as a month. During that time interval, your rendering of services to the firm is compensated for in the form of income, and accounted for in the unit of account or money. You receive an income equal to your contribution to the output of the firm, as income equals output. Both income and output are measured in units of money.

One component of money we use as a medium of exchange is the currency that is issued by central banks. Cheques drawn on our accounts held with commercial banks also serve as a medium of exchange. It is natural then that money supply is the result of the interactions between central banks, commercial banks, and the public. In India, the central bank is the Reserve Bank of India, which determines how much currency should be in circulation. A central bank of a country has two main responsibilities. First, it sets a target for the overnight loan rate (or call money rate) for RESERVES—the rate at which commercial banks borrow from each other in the interbank market. In this market, banks that have excess reserves lend to other banks that are short of reserves. The central bank influences the overnight call money rate by announcing a target rate called the repo rate, which it supports through the use of three instruments—(i) by the purchase and sale of GOVERNMENT SECURITIES in the financial market, (ii) through changes in RESERVE REQUIREMENTS, and (iii) by allowing banks to borrow from the central bank. We shall soon see how the use of these instruments of monetary policy influences the supply of money in the economy. Second, central banks are also responsible for the regulation of financial markets and have a large role to play during periods of financial crisis.

› **Reserves** are the holdings of deposits of commercial banks in accounts with the central bank, plus currency held by banks. At this point, think of reserves as liquidity that enable banks to honour payments to creditors.

› A **government security** or bond is a financial instrument issued by the government to raise funds necessary to pay for its expenses.

› A **central bank** can influence the money supply by requiring banks to hold a percentage of their deposits in a reserve account with it so that banks cannot loan out this amount. In India, it is called the cash reserve ratio.

To understand the money supply process, it pays to begin by looking at the balance sheets of the central bank and commercial banks—their holdings of assets and liabilities. A bank's balance sheet is the list of its sources of bank funds (its liabilities) and the uses to which the funds are put (its assets). This list of sources and uses of funds must balance so that total assets are equal to total liabilities.

The main sources of funds, or the liabilities of a central bank are currency in circulation and deposits held by commercial banks with the RBI (Table 2.2). The main uses of funds or the assets are in the form of credits advanced to the government, the commercial banks, and the private sector.

› **Table 2.2**
Central Bank Balance Sheet

Assets	Liabilities
Credit to Government = Holdings of Government Debt (Including Loans to Government) − Government Deposits	Currency in Circulation = Currency with Public (C^P) + Currency with Banks } RESERVES
Credit to commercial banks	Deposits held by commercial banks (a) Required reserves (b) Working fund reserves } RESERVES
Advances (credits) to commercial private sector	Net non-monetary liabilities of central bank

The currency in circulation and deposits held by commercial banks comprise what is known as the monetary liabilities of the RBI because changes in these liabilities lead to changes in the money supply. The monetary liabilities of the central bank are also referred to as base money, high powered money, or reserve money (Table 2.2). As the non-monetary liabilities and assets of the RBI do not impact the money supply, they are entered on the balance sheet as the difference between non-monetary liabilities and assets/net non-monetary liabilities (NML).

2.3.1 Liabilities of a Central Bank

The liabilities of the central bank are sub-divided into two categories—currency in circulation in the hands of the public (C^P), and reserves (R). All liabilities of the central bank that are corresponding assets of commercial banks are for analytical puposes treated as RESERVES. The currency in the hands of the public, in contrast, is a liability of the central bank and a corresponding asset held by the non-bank public and will not be treated as a reserve. There is an important distinction between the analytical definition of reserves being used here and the accounting definition used by the RBI that considers only deposit balances of the commercial banks held with the RBI as reserves. Though currency with banks is a liability of the RBI that is held by banks, it is not counted as a part of reserves in the accounting definition of reserves by the RBI. The mechanism by which the money supply of an economy is arrived at is best described with the assistance of the analytical definition of reserves.

› **Reserves** are the liabilities of the central bank that are the corresponding assets of commercial banks. They include currency with banks and deposits held by commercial banks at the central bank (required reserves and working fund reserves.)

Currencies issued by the central bank are an IOU from it. The term IOU is a contraction of "I owe you" and refers to a written evidence of a debt signed by the debtor. In the case of a currency note, it is a promise to pay back the holder of the note the amount of currency denoted on the note. For instance, if you hold a 100 rupee note, you will see a signed statement by the Governor of the RBI on it stating, "I promise to pay the bearer the sum of one hundred rupees". The central bank of a country is a special type of IOU debtor in that an IOU is paid back with other IOUs. So if you submit a 100 rupee note to the RBI and demand payment you will receive two 50 rupee notes or ten 10 rupee notes or some combination of notes that amount to a 100 rupees.

Money is willingly held by the public because of the expectation that it will be acceptable in exchange. The currency and coins we hold are also called fiat money. The world fiat comes from the Latin "let it be done", and a legal authority does something by fiat when it declares something to be so. Thus, a currency note is money because the central bank declares it to be money. Your currency note, therefore, has the declaration printed on it that it is "Guaranteed by the Central Government."[4] This declaration works because people are in agreement that the currency note has value, and are, therefore, willing to accept it as a medium of exchange. If people stop agreeing that the currency note has value (as when they lose confidence in the value of their money which occurs during high inflations), then the medium of exchange function of the money issued by the central bank gets impaired.

The other components of monetary liabilities are reserves. Reserves consist of commercial bank deposits held with the central bank as well as the currency with the banks. Banks hold deposits at the central bank mainly for two reasons—for maintaining what is called the cash reserve ratio, and as working funds for meeting payment requirements. The cash reserve ratio is what is otherwise called REQUIRED RESERVES. A central bank requires that for every hundred rupees of deposits at a bank, a certain fraction called the required reserve ratio or cash reserve ratio must be held as reserve. Any additional reserves above this that banks hold, are working fund reserves. These working fund reserves are held at the central bank because the central bank operates as a banker's bank. An important daily operation of the central bank is the use of deposits made by commercial banks at the central bank to clear cheques drawn on one bank and deposited in another. When a cheque is drawn on a bank, it goes to a clearinghouse set up by the central bank. The commercial bank's account at the central bank is then debited by the amount of the cheque. The bank which deposited the cheque at the clearinghouse will have its account at the central bank credited with the funds. These deposits of a commercial bank can also be used to make payments to the central bank in exchange for currency, whenever a commercial bank is in need of currency or vault cash (so called because currency is stored by banks in bank vaults).

› **Required reserves** or the cash reserve ratio is the fraction of deposits that a central bank requires to be kept as funds in an account with the central bank.

The non-monetary liabilities of the central bank include a number of components such as its paid-up capital and other liabilities. The paid up capital is the amount the RBI received from the government. The paid up capital by the government in the RBI is INR 50 million. The RBI, strictly speaking, is not owned by the government, and is not a profit-making institution. It is an independent entity within the government. However, the government does receive all of the RBI's surplus after establishment, interest rent, printing and stationery, etc. have been paid for. This amounted to INR 150 billion in 2010–2011. The government does exercise some control on this independent entity by appointing its highest level employees such as the governor and deputy governors and setting their salaries. The other liabilities include items such as a contingency reserve the RBI maintains to enable it to absorb unexpected and unforeseen contingencies. A currency and gold revaluation account is also part of its other liabilities. In this account gains or losses on the valuation of foreign currency assets and gold, arising from movements in the exchange rate and price of gold are recorded. The increase in the value of foreign currency assets and gold with the RBI in 2010–2011 was INR 631.5 billion. From these non-monetary liabilities, if we net out the value of items such as fixed assets (the physical assets such as bank buildings, computers, and equipment owned by the bank), we obtain the NML of the bank. In 2010–2011, this was INR 3,682.7 billion. Monetary liabilities, on the other hand, were 3.7 times this at INR 13,768.8 billion.

2.3.2 Assets of the Central Bank

The two major monetary assets on the central bank's balance sheet are the credit it gives to the government and to commercial banks.

The central bank's credit to government is the difference between its investment in government securities and the deposits held by the government with the central bank. The government holds a deposits account at the RBI, which is actually a liability of the RBI. To keep the accounting simple, these liabilities are deducted from the asset of the RBI or its holdings of government debt (Table 2.2). An INCREASE IN GOVERNMENT DEPOSITS is thus shown as a reduction in the assets of the RBI rather than as an increase in its liabilities. In much the same way as individuals keep an account at a bank, the government also keeps a checking account with the RBI, through which incoming tax deposits and outgoing government payments are handled. Tax payments are collected in the government's accounts at a commercial bank. The government then draws out funds from these accounts in the commercial banking system and transfers them to its deposit account at the RBI. This replenishes the balance in its deposit account at the RBI and allows it to make payments. In the process, there is a decline in the government's deposit account at the RBI when it makes a payment, but a corresponding increase in the deposit of a commercial bank that receives the government's payment order in the form of a cheque. Conversely, when the tax receipt in the commercial bank account is transferred to the RBI, there is a reduction in the deposits of commercial banks but an increase in the government's deposit at the RBI.

› An **increase in the deposits** of government at its deposit account with the RBI is captured as a reduction in the net assets of the RBI.

Subtracting the value of the government's deposit at the RBI from the investment in government securities by the RBI, gives us the central bank or RBI's credit advanced to the government. The RBI can also make direct loans to the government—a rare phenomenon with modern day central banks—and when this happens credit to the government increases on the assets side of the RBI's balance sheet.

The main asset of the RBI in a closed economy is the credit given to government. This asset is created through OPEN MARKET operations. The purchase of existing government securities by the RBI is called an open market purchase and the sale of government securities by the RBI is called an open market sale. Generally, the RBI makes purchases of government securities from commercial banks. It pays for this purchase by crediting the bank's account (a corresponding increase in liability) by the amount of the purchase. It makes funds available to the commercial bank's account at the RBI by issuing a cheque and simply declaring that the credit in this account is now higher. How does it do this? Recall that currency in circulation was fiat money, the value of which depended on the government's declaration that this is money. In a similar way, the funds of a commercial bank that are deposited with the RBI are declared to be higher when the RBI pays for the government securities with a cheque. If we list only the changes that occur in the balance sheet of the banking system due to an open market purchase of government securities by the RBI it would look something like in Tables 2.3A and 2.3B.

› The buying and selling of government securities by a central bank in the **open market** in order to control the money supply is an open market operation.

In Table 2.3A, the RBI purchases INR x of government securities from a commercial bank and pays for it with a cheque that is deposited by the commercial bank with the RBI as the commercial bank wishes to increase the working funds at the RBI that can be used for payment purposes. The commercial

› Table 2.3A
RBI's Balance Sheet

Assets		Liabilities	
Purchase of government securities	+INR x	Deposits held by commercial bank	+INR x

› Table 2.3B
Commercial Bank's Balance Sheet

Assets		Liabilities	
Sale of government securities	−INR x		
Deposits held at central bank	+INR x		

bank then correspondingly sees a reduction in its holdings of government securities—Table 2.3B—and a corresponding increase on its assets side in the form of an increase in credit available in its deposit account with the RBI.

Another option commercial banks sometimes resort to is to cash in the cheque of the RBI for currency. The RBI will then withdraw currency from its vaults and hand it over to the commercial bank. The currency in the vault of the RBI is not currency in circulation, i.e., currency in the hands of the public or with banks. As it is not in the hands of the public or banks to be used as a medium of exchange, it is not a liability of the RBI or an asset of any agent in the economy. For this reason, such currency is not treated as part of the monetary liabilities of the RBI. The moment it comes into circulation, however, it becomes the liability of the RBI and the asset of the commercial bank. The changes in the balance sheet of the banking system would then be depicted as shown in Tables 2.4A and 2.4B.

The changes in balance sheets for an open market purchase of government securities by the central bank are similar (reads are encouraged to write out the balance sheet positions for such a transaction at this juncture so as to be absolutely familiar with open market transactions by the central bank). Apart from the outright sale and purchase of government securities, the central bank is also engaged in the purchase and sale of government securities through transactions that are self-reversing. Such temporary transactions are called reverse repo and repo agreements.

› A **reverse repo** is the purchase of a security by a buyer with an agreement to resell it at a higher price at a specific future date (overnight in India).

› A **repo** is a contract in which the seller of a security agrees to buy it back at a specified time (overnight) and price. It is also called a buyback.

Commercial banks that are temporarily short of liquidity approach the inter bank market with a demand for funds, while banks with surplus liquidity supply such funds. The RBI attempts to influence the call money or overnight interest rate in this market by undertaking temporary transactions called REVERSE REPURCHASE AGREEMENTS (REVERSE REPOS) and REPURCHASE AGREEMENTS (REPOS). In a reverse repo, the RBI sells government securities and the buyer agrees to sell them back, to the RBI in a short period of time. In India, this period is usually a day.[5] In a repo, the RBI purchases government securities with an agreement that the seller will repurchase them overnight. Such actions temporarily affect the availability of liquidity, and through that, influence the short-term inter-bank interest rate. A repo temporarily increases the reserves of a commercial bank, giving it liquidity, and correspondingly decreases its holding of government securities. It is a temporary open market purchase of government securities by the central bank, involving transactions identical to those associated with Table 2.3. The only difference is that this purchase will be reversed the next day and the balance sheet accounts will revert to the situation before such a temporary transaction was undertaken. In 2008–2009, for instance, the RBI used this mechanism to inject liquidity through repo operations on 158 days and used reverse repos to absorb liquidity on 169 days. At the end of the accounting year, the outstanding securities sold (reverse repos) are treated as a reduction in investment in government securities or a reduction in assets held by the

› **Table 2.4A**
RBI's Balance Sheet

Assets		Liabilities	
Purchase of government securities	+INR *x*	Currency with banks	+INR *x*

› **Table 2.4B**
Commercial Bank's Balance Sheet

Assets		Liabilities	
Sale of government securities	−INR *x*		
Currency with banks (vault cash)	+INR *x*		

RBI. In a similar vein, securities purchased (repos) are counted as an addition to the RBI's investment in government securities. The difference between the addition to the investment in government securities (repos) and the reduction in holding of government securities (reverse repos) is added to the value of the existing holding of government securities by the RBI. It is reported on the assets side of the balance sheet as investments in government securities.

A second asset on the balance sheet of the central bank is its credit to commercial banks. Here, commercial banks in sound financial condition are allowed to borrow from the central bank at very short maturities (usually overnight). Commercial banks are supposed to turn to this lending facility from the central bank only as a back up source when they face a shortage of funds in the interbank market. In India, this operates through the marginal standing facility whereby banks can borrow funds up to 1 per cent of their deposit liabilities with the RBI at a rate which is pegged at 1 per cent above the repo rate. The RBI has the discretion not to accept such a request from commercial banks that, therefore, only access the facility when they face considerable shortfalls of liquidity. The discount rate is also set above the usual level of short term overnight market interest rates so as to discourage commercial banks from requesting for funds through this route. This type of discount lending facility was created so that a central bank can be a LENDER OF LAST RESORT and prevent bank failures due to temporary shortages of liquidity from spinning out of control. By providing liquidity when it is unavailable elsewhere, the central bank can prevent banking and financial panics. The effect on the balance sheets of the central bank and commercial bank when a discount loan of INR x is made is depicted in Table 2.5.

› The **lender of last resort** is a function of a central bank in which it lends money to a bank which is facing unusually heavy withdrawals and a temporary liquidity shortage and no one else is willing to provide resources to it.

Finally, the central bank provides credit to the private sector as well. For instance, it makes loans to primary dealers in the government securities market. A primary dealer is a bank or a securities broker which is required to make bids or offers when the central bank conducts open market operations or auctions of government securities. Such bank primary dealers in India include Bank of Baroda, Citibank, Bank of America, and stand alone primary dealers include ICICI Securities Primary Dealership Ltd., SBI Discount and Finance House of India Ltd., Morgan Stanley India Primary Dealer Pvt. Ltd. The RBI also provides credit to institutions such as the National Bank for Agriculture and Rural Development (NABARD) which provides credit to agriculture and small scale industries in rural areas. Such loans show up on its balance sheet as a credit to the private commercial sector. Finally, the RBI has an investment in the bonds/shares of financial institutions, which is also considered to be a part of central bank credit to the private sector.

Reserve money or the monetary liabilities of the central bank may then be written as:

$$\text{Reserve Money} = \text{Currency in Circulation} + \text{Deposits Held by Commercial Banks at the Central Bank}$$

The recent trend in reserve money is shown in Table 2.6.

› **Table 2.5A**
RBI's Balance Sheet

Assets		Liabilities	
Credit to commercial banks (discount loans)	+INR x	Deposits held by commercial bank with RBI	+INR x

› **Table 2.5B**
Commercial Bank's Balance Sheet

Assets		Liabilities	
Deposits held at central bank	+INR x	Loan from central bank	+INR x

In terms of its sources (or assets side), we may write reserve money as:

Reserve Money = Credit to Government
+ Credit to Commercial Banks
+ Credit to Commercial Private Sector
− Net Non-monetary Liabilities

2.3.3 The Balance Sheet of Commercial Banks

In a similar way, we can write the balance sheet of a commercial bank in the manner as depicted in Table 2.7. Commercial banks issue deposits and borrow funds which are its sources of funds, or its liabilities. The funds obtained in this manner are used to acquire assets such as government securities (commercial bank credit to government) and loans to the private sector.

› A **demand deposit** allows the owner of the account to write cheques to third parties.

› A **time deposit** is a non-transaction deposit that cannot be used as a medium of exchange.

The deposits of commercial banks are broadly classified as demand deposits and time deposits. A DEMAND DEPOSIT is a bank account that allows the owner of the deposit to write cheques as means of final settlement of dues with respect to a transaction. Such checkable deposits are payable on demand and with the presentation of the cheque at the bank it must pay out the funds immediately. In contrast, TIME DEPOSITS such as fixed deposits (which are a major source of bank funds) are non-transaction deposits and cannot be used to settle dues. Such deposits have a maturity ranging from a few months to several years and can only be accessed by the depositor on payment of a substantial penalty, which involves the forfeiture of considerable interest for early withdrawal. Demand deposits were approximately 15 per cent of bank deposits and time deposits were 85 per cent of deposits in the end of March of 2009. The major source of funds in Indian banks is deposits, which account for over 75 per cent of their liabilities.

Banks also obtain non-deposit funds by borrowing from other banks and through borrowings in the capital market. If bank A borrows from another bank B, the liability of bank A is the asset of bank B. If we consolidate the balance sheets of all banks in the economy, then this form of inter-bank borrowing will cancel out and not appear on the consolidated balance sheet. Thus, only borrowings from the non-bank private sector would show up on the consolidated balance sheet of commercial banks. Borrowings are not yet an important source of bank funds in India, and amount to about 7 per cent of bank liabilities. In advanced market economies such borrowings can account for over 30 per cent

› **Table 2.6**
Components of Reserve Money (INR billion)
Source: Reserve Bank of India, Annual Reports.

	31 March 2007	31 March 2008	31 March 2009	31 March 2010	31 March 2011
Currency in circulation	5,040.99	5,908.01	6,911.53	7,995.49	9,496.59
Bankers' and other deposits with RBI	2,047.91	3,375.01	2,968.45	3,561.37	4,272.22
Reserve money (M_0)	7,088.90	9,283.02	9,879.98	11,556.86	13,768.81

Note: Other deposits are the deposits of foreign central banks, multilateral institutions, and financial institutions with the central bank.

› **Table 2.7**
Commercial Bank's Balance Sheet

Assets	Liabilities
Deposits with central bank (a) Required reserves (R^r) (b) Working fund reserves currency with banks (vault cash) } (R^0)	Deposits (D)
Commercial bank credit to government ($G_{b/B}$)	Loans from central bank
Advances (credits) to commercial private sector (A_B)	Net non-monetary liabilities of commercial banks (NML_{CB})

of bank liabilities. Since banks borrow from the private sector and also give out loans to the private sector, we net out the borrowings (a liability) from the advances (credits) to the private commercial sector on the asset side of the balance sheet. Thus, the advances to the private commercial sector are, in net terms, net of borrowings from the private sector.

In India, a fraction of credit advanced to the private sector by banks is mandated to be towards what is called the priority sector—agriculture, micro and small enterprises, micro credit, education, and housing.[6] The idea is to channelize credit to these vulnerable sectors of the economy, which may not be attractive for banks from the point of view of profitability, but are nevertheless important for economic development. Domestic banks and foreign banks have to extend 40 per cent and 32 per cent of their non-bank credit respectively to the priority sectors.[7] The treatment of advances to the private sector in net terms is equivalent to the accounting treatment for credit advanced to government, which, being the loans to government less the deposits of government with commercial banks is also in net terms.

Commercial banks in India are mandated to hold a certain fraction of their deposit liabilities in the form of government securities. This is called the statutory liquidity ratio, or SLR, which is set at 25 per cent of bank deposit (demand and time) liabilities. Banks almost always maintain a larger fraction of government securities, sometimes up to at least 2 per cent over the SLR requirement, as these securities can be used as collateral to borrow funds on the interbank market or from the central bank. In times of uncertainty, banks hold an even greater fraction of government securities as these are low risk financial instruments. Such securities are also very liquid because, if requires they can be traded and converted into cash at low transaction costs. In the end of March 2011, investments of commercial banks in such securities amounted to 28.4 per cent of deposit liabilities. Such investments are advances by commercial banks to government, and if we subtract from this the deposits of government in commercial banks, through which are managed the government tax receipts and payments, we obtain in net terms the commercial bank credit to government.

The other items on the balance sheet are by now familiar to the reader. The net non-monetary liability of commercial banks are the value of physical assets owned by the bank, such as bank buildings, furniture, and equipment subtracted from the capital of the bank or the bank's net worth (its liability in the form of the value of its paid up capital and retained earnings). As we saw earlier, the commercial banks keep deposits with the central bank in the form of mandated required reserves and working fund purposes to meet its obligations when a cheque is written on its account. Banks also keep a certain amount of currency in their vaults to honour withdrawals made by their depositors. Finally, commercial banks may also take out discount loans from the central bank when there are acute shortages of liquidity in the short-term money markets.

2.3.4 Consolidated Bank Balance Sheet

We now consolidate the balance sheets of the central bank and commercial banks to obtain the consolidated balance sheet of the banking system. Consolidation requires that all claims and liabilities between individual commercial banks and between commercial banks and the central bank are netted out. For instance, currency with banks that is a monetary liability of the central bank is at the same time an asset of the commercial banks (see Tables 2.8A and 2.8B). The consolidated balance sheet of the banking system (see Table 2.8C) will, therefore, not depict this item as the sources of funds because one entity has a counterpart in the uses of funds by another entity of the banking system. The assets of the balance sheet of the consolidated banking system then include two entries. One is bank credit to government (G_b), which is the sum of credit to government by the central bank ($G_{b/CB}$) and credit to government by commercial banks ($G_{b/B}$). The other is advances or credit given to the private sector (A), which is the sum of advances given by the central bank to the private sector (A_{CB}) and advances by commercial banks to the private sector (A_B). The liabilities of the banking system comprise three components. These are the currency in circulation with the public (C^P), deposits at commercial banks (D), and NML of the central bank and commercial banks.

So far we have been examining the balance sheet of the banking system on the presumption that the economy is closed to monetary transactions with agents abroad. We now relax this assumption and examine the change in the balance sheet when the economy is open to international transactions. In that case the central bank has an additional asset of foreign-exchange that include holdings of gold (FE_{CB}) as depicted in Table 2.9A. Gold coins and bullion are occasionally held by central banks outside the country.[8] It is only as a matter of accounting convenience that gold is counted as an asset along with foreign-exchange assets. For commercial banks, international transactions involve two assets and one liability (Table 2.9B). The assets are the net foreign-exchange assets of banks (FE_B) and the advances or credit given by commercial banks

› Table 2.8 A
Central Bank Balance Sheet

Assets	Liabilities
Credit to Government = Holdings of Government Debt (Including Loans to Government) − Government Deposits ($G_{b/CB}$)	Currency in Circulation = Currency with Public (C^P) +
~~Credit to commercial banks~~	~~Currency with Banks~~ ~~Deposits held by commercial banks~~ ~~(a) Required reserves~~ ~~(b) Working fund reserves~~ } ~~RESERVES~~
Advances (credits) to commercial private sector (A_{CB})	Net non-monetary liabilities of central bank (NML_{CB})

› Table 2.8B
Commercial Bank's Balance Sheet

Assets	Liabilities
~~Deposits with central bank~~ ~~(a) Required reserves (R^r)~~ ~~(b) Working fund reserves~~ ~~Currency with banks (vault cash)~~ } (R^0)	Deposits (D)
Commercial bank credit to government ($G_{b/B}$)	~~Loans from central bank~~
Advances (credits) to commercial private sector (A_B)	Net non-monetary liabilities of commercial banks (NML_{CB})

› Table 2.8C
Consolidated Balance Sheet of Banking System

Assets	Liabilities
Bank Credit to Government $G_b = (G_{b/CB} + G_{b/B})$	Currency in circulation currency with public (C^P)
Advances (Credits) to Commercial Private Sector $A = (A_{CB} + A_B)$	Deposits (D)
	Net Non-monetary Liabilities NLM = ($NML_{CB} + NML_{CB}$)

to non-residents (A_{FE}). The additional liabilities of commercial banks are the deposits of non-residents (D_{FE}).

The additional items on the consolidated balance sheet of the banking system (Table 2.9C) are the additional assets—the foreign-exchange assets (net) of the banking sector (FE). In this consolidated balance sheet, the holding of foreign currency deposits (D_{FE}) have been netted out from foreign currency advances (A_{FE}).

The net foreign-exchange assets of the banking system so defined is then added to the other assets of the consolidated banking system to obtain the consolidated balance sheet of the banking system in an open economy (Table 2.10).

In terms of an identity, the consolidated balance sheet of the banking system may be written as:

$$C^P + D = G_b + A + \text{FE} - \text{NML}$$

Not surprisingly, this is also the definition of the money supply (M^S). The money supply then is given by

$$M^S = C^P + D = G_b + A + \text{FE} - \text{NML}$$

The various components in terms of the sources of money supply in India are shown in Table 2.11. The definition of the money supply makes apparent the monetary impact of capital flows into an economy. When foreigners express a demand for holding the assets of an economy—either by purchasing shares of a company as in the case of foreign institutional (or portfolio) investors or by setting up a business unit as in the case of foreign direct investment—they first exchange foreign currency for domestic currency. The foreign-exchange assets of the banking system (FE) then increase and the direct impact of this, when

› **Table 2.9A**
Additional Items on Central Bank Balance Sheet in an Open Economy

Assets	Liabilities
Foreign-exchange assets (including gold holding) (FE_{CB})	

› **Table 2.9B**
Additional Items on Central Bank Balance Sheet in an Open Economy

Assets	Liabilities
Advances (credit) in foreign currency (A_{FE})	Deposits (claims on banks) in foreign currency (D_{FE})
Net foreign-currency assets of banks (FE_B)	

› **Table 2.9C**
Additional Items on Central Bank Balance Sheet in an Open Economy

Assets	Liabilities
Foreign-exchange assets (net) of banking sector (FE)	
$FE = FE_{CB} + FE_B + (A_{FE} - D_{FE})$	

› **Table 2.10**
Consolidated Balance Sheet of Banking System in an Open Economy

Assets	Liabilities
Bank Credit to Government $G_b = (G_{b/CB} + G_{b/B})$	Currency in circulation with public (C^P)
Advances (Credits) to Commercial Private Sector $A = (A_{CB} + A_B)$	Deposits (D)
Foreign-Exchange Assets (Net) of Banking Sector $FE = FE_{CB} + FE_B + (A_{FE} - D_{FE})$	Net Non-monetary Liabilities $NML = (NML_{CB} + NML_B)$

	31 March 2007	31 March 2008	31 March 2009	31 March 2010	31 March 2011
Net bank credit to government (G_b)	8,276.26 (25.0%)	8,995.18 (22.4%)	12,773.33 (26.7%)	16,691.86 (29.9%)	19,827.71 (30.6%)
Net bank credit to commercial sector (A')	21,288.62 (64.3%)	25,789.90 (64.2%)	30,148.93 (63.0%)	34,914.09 (62.4%)	42,354.06 (65.3%)
Net foreign-exchange assets (FE)	9,131.79 (27.6%)	12,951.31 (32.2%)	13,521.84 (28.3%)	12,814.69 (22.9%)	13,933.27 (21.5%)
Net non-monetary liabilities (NML)*	5,595.99	7,557.56	8,596.52	8,506.02	11,246.80
Money supply	33,100.68	40,178.83	47,847.58	55,914.62	64,868.24

Notes: *Government's currency liabilities to the public have been netted out of these figures.
Figures in parentheses are percentages to total money supply

› **Table 2.11**
Sources of Money Stock (INR billion)
Source: Reserve Bank of India, Annual Reports

other items on the balance sheet remain unchanged, is an equivalent increase in the money supply (M^S). If the central bank wants to negate the impact of capital flows on the money supply, say, because it finds the increased money supply to be inflationary, then it can undertake to offset this through a process known as sterilization. Sterilization involves a reduction in central bank credit to government ($G_{b/\text{CB}}$) in response to an increase in foreign-exchange assets. A complete offsetting of the increased capital inflow (written in symbols as ΔFE) by sterilization, so that there is no impact on the money supply, would require the reduction in central bank credit to government ($DG_{b/\text{CB}}$) to be of such a magnitude that $\Delta\text{FE} = -DG_{b/\text{CB}}$. The recent spurt of capital flows to India since 2003 required the Reserve Bank of India to sterilize the capital inflows to the economy to a considerable extent. In March 1991, for instance, central bank lending to government ($G_{b/\text{CB}}$) was 33.4 per cent of the money supply and the net foreign-exchange assets of the banking sector (FE) was 5 per cent of the money supply. By 2009, there was a drastic reversal. In 2009, the central bank lending to government was a much reduced 1.3 per cent of the money supply as the central bank sought to sterilize the impact of capital inflows which resulted in the net foreign-exchange assets of the banking sector to constitute 28.3 per cent of the money supply.

The money supply in India, as read out of the balance sheets of the banking system, is referred to as broad money or M_3. A narrower definition of money is M_1 or narrow money. This includes only the demand deposits of the banking system in the definition of money and leaves out time deposits. A demand deposit is more currency-like than a time deposit. Unlike a time deposit, a demand deposit can be transferred into currency at a very low transaction cost—indeed demand deposits are defined as those deposits that we make with banks that allow us to get our money back on demand. Broader definitions of money include components that are less perfect substitutes of currency in circulation. M_2, for instance, is M_1 plus time deposits with a maturity of less than a year—post office savings bank deposits. M_3 includes all time deposits, regardless of their maturity. And to complete the naming ceremony, M_0 is the symbolic name for high-powered money or the monetary base. To sum up:

Different Measures of Money

M_0 = Currency in Circulation + Deposits Held by Commercial Banks at the Central Bank

M_1 = Currency in Circulation with the Public + Demand Deposits

M_2 = M_1 + Time Deposits with Maturity of Less than a Year (Post Office Savings Bank Deposits)

M_3 = M_2 + Time Deposits with Maturity of 1 Year and More

	March 31, 2007	March 31, 2008	March 31, 2009	March 31, 2010	March 31, 2011	Average Share of M_3
Currency with the public (A)	4,828.54	5,684.10	6,654.50	7,674.93	9,141.97	14.03%
Demand deposits (B)	4,851.00	5,874.26	5,942.58	7,218.09	7,213.73	12.84%
Time deposits (C)	23,421.13	28,620.46	35,351.05	41,134.30	48,639.79	73.13%
Narrow money (M_1)	9,679.54	11,558.36	12,597.08	14,893.02	16,355.70	
Broad money (M_3)	33,100.67	40,178.82	47,948.13	56,027.32	64,995.49	

Note: Demand deposits is inclusive of other deposits at the RBI

M_1 = (A) + (B)

M_3 = (A) + (B) + (C)

› **Table 2.12**
Applications of Money Stock (INR billion)

Source: Reserve Bank of India, Annual Reports.

Broad money or M_3 is the monetary aggregate that is taken to be the reference for the money stock in India. The components of the money stock in terms of its uses (or liabilities) are given in Table 2.12.

2.3.5 The Banking System and the Creation of Money

The analysis of the central bank's balance sheet reveals that it can change the monetary base by operating with the monetary policy tools as follows:

1. *Reserve Requirements*—The central bank can change the mandated reserve requirements that all deposit-taking financial intermediaries need to hold as a percentage of their deposits in a reserve account with the central bank.
2. *Open Market Operations*—By selling or purchasing government securities the central bank changes its balance sheet. There is a change in the assets it holds in the form of a change in its holdings of government securities or its credit to government. There is also a change in its liabilities in the form of a change in the working fund reserves held by commercial banks at the central bank. We saw, for instance, how an open-market purchase of government securities by the central bank results in an increase in the central bank's assets in the form of government securities as well as an increase in its liabilities in the form of deposits held by commercial banks with the central bank. A change in the deposits held by commercial banks at the central bank amounts to a change in the monetary base or M_0.
3. *Discount Lending*—These are the borrowings by banks from the central bank whenever they find the market for short-term overnight funds to be expensive (as occurs when the interest rate here is higher than the discount rate). It also happens when they are constrained in their ability to borrow in this market. In this case, the central bank's assets in the form of credit to commercial banks change to the extent of the discount loan. As the proceeds of the discount loan are credited to the deposit account of the commercial bank at the central bank, the liabilities of the central bank change by the same amount as the change in its assets. The change in the monetary base equals the change in liabilities in the form of a change in deposits held by commercial banks with the central bank.[9]

Through these actions—a change in open-market operations, the required reserve ratio, or the discount rate—the central bank affects the supply of money in the economy. Recall that in the beginning of this section we emphasized that the money supply results from action taken by three players—central banks, commercial banks, and the non-bank public which operate a deposit account with banks. Let us examine the process of credit and deposit creation resulting from the use of one monetary tool by the central bank—the required reserve ratio. To focus on the essentials, let us rewrite the balance sheet of commercial banks in the following way. As a commercial bank's major liability is the deposits it issues, let us, in what follows, ignore the loans it takes from the central bank (discount loans) and its NML. Let the initial deposits be of a value of INR 100 (see Table 2.13). On the assets side of the balance sheet, let us club together the advances it makes in the form of credit to government and credit to the private commercial sector as credit advanced by the commercial bank, or advances. Let the advances by the commercial bank be INR 75. The commercial bank's balance sheet then may be written as shown in Table 2.13.

The commercial bank receives funds in the form of deposits at its branches. The bank knows that except in the case of a banking panic, all the depositors are not likely to show up at the same time, demanding their funds in cash. Some depositors will withdraw funds in the form of currency, for which the bank holds cash in the vaults. Some payments will have to be made to clear cheques that depositors make out to agents who hold accounts with other banks—to enable this, the commercial banks keep working funds on deposit at the central bank. From past experience, in our example in Table 2.13, the commercial bank finds that keeping 10 per cent of deposits as vault cash, or working funds at the central bank provides sufficient liquidity to take care of withdrawals and depositor payments to creditors through the writing of cheques. Apart from ensuring sufficient liquidity for withdrawal and depositor payments of funds, the bank also has a mandate to hold 15 per cent of its deposits as required reserves with the central bank. After ensuring it has funds for required reserves and for payments and withdrawals, the bank can use the remainder of the deposits it holds to obtain earnings. It does so by making out loans or advances—in this case, of INR 75.

Thus, for a hundred-rupee deposit, the bank keeps 15 per cent aside as required reserves and 10 per cent in liquid forms to manage deposit outflows in the form of withdrawals and demand deposit payments, and loans out 75 per cent to obtain profits. The fundamental tradeoff for a bank is to hold sufficient liquidity to honour deposit outflows, but the cost of that is forgone earnings on loans advanced. Banks will, therefore, not hold too much of extra liquidity beyond that required for depositor outflows, and will attempt to give out excess liquidity as loans.

Suppose now the central bank decided to reduce the required reserve ratio from 15 per cent to 10 per cent of deposits. This leaves the commercial bank with INR 5 of surplus liquidity in the form of vault cash and deposits at the

› **Table 2.13**
Commercial Bank's Balance Sheet

Assets		Liabilities	
Deposits with central bank			
(a) Required reserves	15		
(b) Working fund reserves currency with banks (vault cash)	10	Deposits	100
Advances	75		

› **Table 2.14**
Commercial Bank's Balance Sheet

Assets		Liabilities	
Deposits with central bank			
(a) Required reserves	(15 − 5) = 10		
(b) Working fund reserves currency with banks (vault cash)	(10 + 5) = 15	Deposits	100
Advances	75		

central bank. With this change in central bank policy, the balance sheet of the commercial banks will now be altered to Table 2.14.

Commercial banks now have surplus liquidity—they operate with a 10 per cent liquidity ratio that is sufficient to manage depositor outflows. The current liquidity ratio, however, is 15 per cent. The additional liquidity of 5 per cent is sitting on the books of the banks and the banks are forgoing earnings. The banks, therefore, lend this surplus liquidity to the private commercial sector. The commercial banks make out loans of INR 5 to customers.

Let us assume that there are only two banks in the financial system—Bank ABC and Bank HIJ. For simplicity, suppose that both banks are symmetric and each bank, therefore, finds that the reduction in the required reserves of INR 5 in the financial system results in additional liquidity of INR 2.5 in its working fund reserve account. Let us begin with Bank ABC, which, having this surplus liquidity, makes out a loan of INR 2.5 by opening a checking account for the borrower (if they do not already have one) and putting the sanctioned loan amount into this deposit account. Bank ABC increases its liabilities with INR 2.5 of deposits and its assets with INR 2.5 of advances or loans. The change in the balance sheet of Bank ABC will be as depicted in Table 2.15A.

The customer who obtains the loan from Bank ABC uses the amount to make payments for an income-generating project that was the basis for the sanctioning of the loan. When the receiver of the payment has an account with Bank HIJ, the cheque written out on Bank ABC will be deposited at Bank HIJ. Bank HIJ then presents the cheque for payment at the central bank. The central bank credits Bank HIJ's working fund reserves with an amount of INR 2.5 and debits the working fund reserves of Bank ABC by INR 2.5. With this transaction, the amount in the deposit account of INR 2.5 has been transferred to Bank HIJ, and Bank ABC's balance sheet is as in Table 2.15B.

Bank HIJ, which got paid INR 2.5 into its working funds reserve account, accordingly credits the deposit account of the customer who brought in the cheque from Bank ABC. The change in the balance sheet of Bank HIJ will be as in Table 2.15C.

We now consolidate the balance sheets of Bank ABC and Bank HIJ. This involves adding up the change in the balance sheets of Bank ABC and Bank HIJ as depicted in Tables 2.15B and 2.15C. While adding up we must keep in mind that the banks are symmetric and that the sequence of transactions that occurred on Bank ABC's balance sheet will also occur on Bank HIJ's balance sheet. Similarly, the change depicted in Bank HIJ's balance sheet (Table 2.15C) will also show up on Bank ABC's balance sheet. When consolidating, then, we

› Table 2.15A
Bank ABC's Balance Sheet

Assets		Liabilities	
Required reserves	−INR 2.5		
Working fund reserves	+INR 2.5		
Advances	+INR 2.5	Deposits	+INR 2.5

› Table 2.15B
Bank ABC's Balance Sheet

Assets		Liabilities	
Required reserves	−INR 2.5		
Advances	+INR 2.5		

› Table 2.15C
Bank HIJ's Balance Sheet

Assets		Liabilities	
Working fund reserves	+INR 2.5	Deposits	+INR 2.5

must take care to double the denominations of the transactions reported in Table 2.15B and Table 2.15C. The consolidated change in the balance sheet of commercial banks can then be written as in Table 2.15D.[10]

The balance sheets of commercial banks at this stage of the deposit creation process (after all these transactions have occurred in the banking system) is now as shown in Table 2.16.

Commercial banks now find that they have deposits of INR 105. Required reserves that the central bank mandates are 10 per cent of deposits. The banks must then hold 10 per cent of 105 or INR 10.5 as required reserves—an increase of INR 0.5. The banks also operate with a liquidity ratio of 10 per cent to manage deposit outflows. Working fund reserves at the central bank and vault cash must then also be INR 10.5 so as to attain the desired liquidity ratio. The balance sheet at this stage is given in Table 2.17.

Banks again find that they have excess reserves of INR 4 and would want to make loans of this amount. Again, the borrower deposits the loan amount in the bank, resulting in the balance sheet shown in Table 2.18.

Yet another round of balance-sheet adjustments is called for. For deposits amounting to INR 109, the required reserves at 10 per cent is an additional INR 0.4 to make it INR 10.9. Similarly, the liquidity ratio of 10 per cent requires extra

› **Table 2.15D**
Consolidated Bank Balance Sheet

Assets		Liabilities	
Required reserves	−INR 5		
Working fund reserves	+INR 5		
Advances	+INR 5	Deposits	+INR 5

› **Table 2.16**
Commercial Banks' Balance Sheets

Assets		Liabilities	
Deposits with central bank			
(a) Required reserves	15 − 5		
(b) Working fund reserves currency with banks (vault cash)	10 + 5	Deposits	100 + 5
Advances	75 + 5		

› **Table 2.17**
Commercial Banks' Balance Sheets

Assets		Liabilities	
Deposits with central bank			
(a) Required reserves	10.5		
(b) Working fund reserves currency with banks (vault cash)	10.5 + 4	Deposits	105
Advances	80		

› **Table 2.18**
Commercial Banks' Balance Sheets

Assets		Liabilities	
Deposits with central bank			
(a) Required reserves	10.5		
(b) Working fund reserves currency with banks (vault cash)	10.5 + 4	Deposits	105 + 4
Advances	84		

reserves to be kept at INR 10.9 as well. The balance sheet now reads as shown in Table 2.19.

Yet again there are excess reserves of INR 3.2. The commercial banks will again loan out this amount. Advances by commercial banks are now INR (84 + 3.2) or INR 87.2. There are new deposits of INR 3.2 as the loan amount is put into a deposit account (taking the deposits to INR 112.2). Excess reserves of INR 2.56 are again got that will again be loaned out. The process will continue until the balance sheet eventually reaches the position depicted in Table 2.20. Deposits that were initially INR 100 have now become INR 125, and loans advanced similarly have increased from an initial INR 75 to INR 100.

The process of increments to deposits, loans advanced, and reserves—required reserves plus other reserves in the form of working funds and vault cash—is depicted in Table 2.21.

› **Table 2.19**
Commercial Banks' Balance Sheets

Assets		Liabilities	
Deposits with central bank			
(a) Required reserves	(10.5 + 0.4) =10. 9		
(b) Working fund reserves currency with banks (vault cash)	10.9 + 3.2	Deposits	109
Advances	84		

› **Table 2.20**
Commercial Banks' Balance Sheet

Assets		Liabilities	
Deposits with central bank			
(a) Required reserves	12.5		
(b) Working fund reserves currency with banks (vault cash)	12.5		
Advances		Deposits	109
(a) Before policy change	75	(a) Before policy change	100
(b) Initial new advances after policy change	5	(b) Initial new deposits after policy change	5
(c) Subsequent new advances	20	(c) Subsequent new deposits	20
Total	125	Total	125

› **Table 2.21**
Process of Deposit Creation When Required Reserves are Decreased by 5 per cent

	Increase in Reserves Held	Increase in Loans	Increase in Deposits
Stage 1	.5 + .5 = 1	5	5
Stage 2	.4 + .4 = .8	4	4
Stage 3	.32 + .32 = .64	3.2	3.2
Stage 4	.256 + .256 = .512	2.56	2.56
Stage 5	.2048 +.2048 = .4096	2.048	2.048
	.	.	.
	.	.	.
	.	.	.
	.	.	.
Total	2.5 + 2.5 = 5	25	25

2.3.6 Multiple Deposit Creation Process

When banks lend out excess reserves, there are subsequent increments to deposits. Banks keep reserves on hand to fund deposit outflows. Excess reserves above this amount can be safely given out as a loan and increase the earnings of a bank. An increase in a unit of reserves due to a change in policy by the central bank (a reduction in required reserves in our example) results in an increase in loans and deposits by a multiple of this amount—a process referred to as multiple deposit creation.

We can generalize. The required reserves, R^r, are a fraction x_1 of deposits D (10 per cent in our example) that commercial banks must hold as a deposit with the central bank.

$$R^r = x_1 D$$

where x_1 is a policy tool set by the central bank. The liquidity ratio for maintaining other reserves R^o in the forms of working funds and vault cash is a fraction x_2 of deposits.

$$R^0 = x_2 D$$

Let ΔD_0 represent the initial increase in loans advanced and new deposits in commercial banks as a result of the policy change. In our example, the reduction in the required reserve ratio from 15 per cent to 10 per cent resulted in banks making an initial increase in loans advanced by INR 5. Then, in the example, $\Delta D_0 = 5$. Then, the process of deposit creation and loans advanced will continue until the change in total deposits in the banking system, ΔD, is given by:

$$\Delta D = \frac{\Delta D_0}{x_1 + x_2}$$

In our example, with $\Delta D_0 = 5, x_1 = 0.1, x_2 = 0.1$, the process of deposit creation by banks ends when deposits have increased by

$$\Delta D = \frac{5}{0.2} = 25$$

Indeed, the total change in deposits and loans advanced due to the policy change is shown as INR 25 in the final balance sheet position of the commercial banks.

The multiple creation of deposits is a direct implication of a fractional reserve banking system, where only a fraction of deposits need to be kept as reserves to manage deposit outflows. If all banks were required to keep the entire deposit as a reserve, then, $x_1 + x_2 = 1$. In that case, the banks would not be able to loan out any money as they would have to keep deposits as reserves till the depositor withdraws the money. In a 100 per cent reserve system, banks can never make loans and will never be able to earn profits either. With $x_1 + x_2 = 1$,

$$\Delta D = \frac{\Delta D_0}{1} = \Delta D_0$$

and the increase in deposits exactly equals the initial increase in deposits.

2.3.7 The Money Multiplier

There is an additional complication that we need to address. What if the person who receives a loan decides to withdraw some of the amount from his deposit account as currency in order to facilitate transactions? In this case, a fraction of the loan made leaves the commercial banking system through withdrawals of cash. This is a deposit outflow that reduces the level of excess reserves available with banks that may be advanced as loans. If, for instance, the initial INR 5 that was given out as a loan was taken out in the form of currency and not deposited, then there is no increase in deposits and the multiple deposit creation process ceases. It is only deposits that can be the source of multiple deposit creation and currency are incapable of multiple deposit expansion. The expansion of money (defined as currency with the public plus deposits) is diminished as there is an increase in the holding of currency. Again let us generalize. Suppose a fraction θ of money is held as currency with the public. Then, a fraction θ of an increase in money supply due to the advancing of a loan will be withdrawn. Then $(1 - \theta)$ of a new loan/deposit remains with the banks, which can then use this amount to make out another loan after keeping aside reserves for liquidity purposes up to the fraction $x_1 + x_2$. We can then show that the banks can create new advances and deposits to an extent, given by,

$$\Delta D = \frac{\Delta D_0}{(x_1 + x_2)(1 - \theta) + \theta}$$

or,

$$\frac{\Delta D}{\Delta D_0} = \frac{1}{(x_1 + x_2)(1 - \theta) + \theta}$$

$\Delta D/\Delta D_0$ is the ratio of the final increase in deposits to the initial increase in deposits, or the multiple increase in deposits as a fraction of the initial increase in deposits. $\Delta D/\Delta D_0$ must be greater than unity as the terms in the denominator of the right hand side are fractions and less than unity resulting in the right hand side being greater than unity.

Economists define the money multiplier, m, as the ratio of the money supply M_3 to the monetary base M_0.

$$m = \frac{M_3}{M_0} = \frac{\text{Money Supply}}{\text{Monetary Base}}$$

The initial increase in deposits in our example above occurred due to a change in the monetary base as the central bank reduced required reserves. The multiple increase in deposits was the resulting increase in the money supply. Hence,

$$m = \frac{1}{(x_1 + x_2)(1 - \theta) + \theta} = \frac{M_3}{M_0}$$

Another way of writing this is to cross multiply and write the above expression as follows:

$$\text{Money Supply} = \text{Money Multiplier} \times \text{Monetary Base}$$

or

$$M^s = m \times M_0$$

In the end of March 2009,

$$M_0 = \text{INR } 9{,}880.01 \text{ billion}$$
$$M^s = M_3 = \text{INR } 47{,}640.19 \text{ billion}$$

The money multiplier in end March 2009, then, was

$$m = \frac{47{,}640.19}{9{,}880.01} = 4.82$$

Alternatively, the Reserve Bank of India had set required reserves as,

$$x_1 = 0.05$$

Commercial banks operated with a liquidity ratio for maintaining reserves in the form of working funds and vault cash given by,

$$x_1 = 0.0285$$

The public held a fraction of the money as currency given by,

$$C^p/M^s = \theta = 0.1399$$

Then, the money multiplier in end March 2009 was,

$$m = \frac{1}{(x_1 + x_2)(1 - \theta) + \theta} = \frac{1}{(0.05 + 0.0285)(0.8601) + 0.1399} = 4.82$$

The money multiplier tells us by how much the money supply will change for a given change in the monetary base or high powered money. The central bank influences the monetary base mainly through changes in reserve requirements and open market operations. An open market purchase of government securities, for instance from commercial banks, results in an increase in the working fund reserves of commercial banks held at the central bank. The central bank pays for purchasing the securities by crediting this account of commercial banks. Commercial banks then find themselves holding excess reserves and advance these funds as loans. This results in the process of multiple deposit creation. A money multiplier of 4.82 means that the open market purchase of government securities results in a 4.82 times increase in loans and deposits in the financial system.

The money supply in the economy is influenced not only by policy changes undertaken by the central bank. Commercial banks and the public can also influence the money supply with a change in their financial behaviour. For instance, if commercial banks decide to increase the amount of excess reserves they hold rather than lend it out (as occurs during times of uncertainty), a speed breaker is created in the process of multiple deposit creation and the money supply reduces. You can check that an increase in the liquidity ratio with which commercial banks operate, x_2, indeed reduces the money multiplier. Finally, if the public decides to hold more currency, then again there is a deposit outflow that reduces the process of multiple deposit creation. Again, an increase in currency with the public—an increase in θ—reduces the value of the money multiplier. The money supply then is the result of decisions taken by the central bank, commercial banks, and depositors.

› A **bank run** or a bank failure occurs when a bank cannot meet its obligations to pay its depositors and creditors.

The central bank is the crucial agent, however, in the money supply process in a fractional reserve banking system. Without a central bank, the chance of a bank run increase. A BANK RUN occurs when depositors lose their confidence in the bank and attempt to withdraw their funds at the same time. As the bank has given out those funds as loans that are difficult to call in at a moment's notice, the bank is not in a position to pay all its depositors who want to withdraw. It is here that the central bank anchors the stability of the banking system by serving as a lender of last resort. As banks can turn to the central bank for funds when there is a wave of depositor withdrawals, it induces a certainty to depositors that the bank can meet its obligations, and makes them less liable to run and withdraw their deposits. By setting required reserves, the central bank also restricts commercial banks from being reckless and lending out all their deposits and not having funds on hand to honour deposit outflows. Besides, central banks also protect depositors' funds by insisting that banks maintain a certain fraction of deposits in the form of equity or NET WORTH—called capital requirements. The money put in by the owners of the firm in exchange for shares in the ownership of the firm determines the bank capital or initial net worth of the firm. The higher this capital put up by owners, the higher their stake in the bank and the more careful they will be with how they invest the funds of depositors as the owners are the ones bearing the first loss. Thus, apart from influencing the money supply, the central bank also ensures the safety and soundness of commercial banks.

› The **net worth** of a bank or its equity capital is the difference between its assets (what it is owed) and its liabilities (what it owes).

SUMMARY

- Private saving is private disposable income less consumption expenditure.
- Government saving is tax revenues less transfers and government consumption expenditure.
- Total national saving is the sum of private and government saving, or GNP (GDP plus NFI) plus transfers from abroad less private consumption expenditure and government expenditure.

$$\text{Saving} = Y + \text{NFI} + \text{Transfers from Abroad} - C - G$$

- The private-sector savings of an economy is used to finance investment expenditures by firms, or to finance a current account surplus (equivalent to a purchase of foreign financial assets), or to finance the government's budget deficit (equivalent to dissaving by the government).

$$S_{\text{pvt}} = I + CA - S_{\text{govt}}$$

- The sum of the current account balance and capital account balance gives the overall balance of payments which is financed mainly by the stock of foreign-exchange reserves held by the central bank.
- The demand for foreign exchange is by importers and by domestic resident decisions on capital outflows. The supply of foreign exchange is by exporters and capital inflows from abroad. The exchange rate regime in a free float is determined where the demand equals the supply of foreign-exchange.
- In a managed exchange-rate regime, foreign-exchange reserves are used to meet the excess demand for foreign exchange and reserves are accumulated when there is an excess supply of foreign exchange.
- The money supply in an economy is the outcome of the interplay between the central bank that influences the monetary base, the public's behaviour in holding currency relative to deposits, and the commercial banks demand for bank reserves.
- Reserve money or the monetary base (M_0) is the currency in circulation plus bank reserves.
- Money supply is the sum of bank credit to government (G_b) plus advances to the commercial sector (A_R) plus foreign-exchange assets of the banking sector (FE) less NML.

$$M^S = G_b + A_R + \text{FE} - \text{NML}$$

- The money multiplier is the ratio between the money supply stock and reserve money.
- The money supply increases with a decline in the mandated reserve ratio that commercial banks are required to hold against deposits and with an increase in the propensity to hold deposits relative to currency by the public.
- An open-market operation is the purchase or sale of government securities by the central bank. This could be an outright sale/purchase of a security or a repurchase agreement. Open market operations are used to influence the monetary base.

NOTES

1. Investment is a part of private sector expenditure, and is not deducted from private disposable income. This is because investment is expenditure on capital goods that are long lived or purchased to enhance future productive capacity rather than to satisfy current needs.
2. The fiscal surplus equals the government non-debt related receipts comprising taxes net of transfers minus government outlays. Since government outlays are devoted partly to meet current needs (government consumption) and partly on long-lived capital goods (government investment), the fiscal surplus equals government savings only when government purchases are made up entirely of government consumption, that is, government investment equals zero.
3. These are income flows due to the holding of financial assets. They include interest and dividend payments to foreigners who hold domestic financial assets and similar payments received by domestic residents who hold financial assets abroad. See the components of the Current Account in Chapter 1.
4. The Governor of the central bank makes the promise even though ultimately the currency is the liability of the government.
5. The period after which the security is sold back to the RBI could also be three days if a transaction is undertaken on a Friday and the earliest the reversal of the transaction can take place is on a Monday.
6. These are subject to certain caps on loan amounts in each sector. For example, housing loans up to INR 2.5 million only are treated as priority sector lending. Similarly, for education loans the cap is INR 1 million.
7. Actually, this is expressed as a per cent of adjusted net bank credit, or the credit equivalent amount of off balance sheet exposures of banks, whichever is higher.
8. In India, gold that was pledged outside the country and sent out in 1991 in exchange for foreign currency when a currency crisis occurred has not been brought back and yet is at present completely owned by the RBI.
9. Students are encouraged to write out the balance sheet of the central bank which reflects the change in monetary base if discount-lending is increased by INR 100.
10. As an exercise, write out the changes to the consolidated balance sheet: (a) when the two banks are not symmetric and (b) when there is a single bank. You will find that the outcome in both cases is as shown in Table 2.15D.

TEST YOURSELF

1. Why is it that despite an individual saving (spending less than his/her income), the aggregate income equals expenditure?
2. Explain how aggregate investment in the economy is supported from savings by (a) the private sector, (b) by the government, and (c) by foreigners.
3. Why should a nation's overall balance of payments always equal its foreign-exchange reserves?
4. Which actions by agents result in the demand and supply of foreign exchange in the economy? Explain how this influences the determination of exchange rates when they are freely floating.
5. What is the role of foreign-exchange reserves in the determination of the balance of payments?
6. What are the components of the monetary base of the central bank in terms of its sources and applications?
7. Write out the consolidated balance sheet of the banking system in an open economy and then define the money supply on the basis of this.
8. What is the money multiplier and what are the alternative currency holding behavioural ratios that are considered in explaining the magnitude of the multiplier?
9. What is sterilization and how does an act of sterilization by the central bank affect the supply of money in the economy ?
10. Describe how the balance sheets of the central bank and commercial banks change when there is an open market purchase of government securities by the central bank.

ONLINE APPLICATION

1. Go to the home page of the Reserve Bank of India URL: www.rbi.org.in/home.aspx.
2. Click on the "DataBase" icon.
3. Then under the classification of Annual data, click on "Handbook of Statistics on Indian Economy."
4. Click on "Table 43: Components of the Money Stock" and create a spreadsheet of data on Reserve Money for the period 1993–1994 to 2009–2010.
5. Then from the same Table 43, download data for the same time period for Broad Money.
6. Calculate the money multiplier for this time period and create a graph of the money multiplier for this time period. What does the slope of this graph indicate?
7. Now click of "Table 44: Sources of Money Stock" and download data on the Net foreign-exchange assets of the RBI. Calculate the fraction of the central bank's monetary base that is sourced from foreign-exchange assets over time. Create a graph of this ratio.
8. Create a graph of the Net Foreign-exchange assets of the RBI and of Broad Money over time. Which graph is rising at a faster rate? What does this indicate about how the central bank is offsetting expansions in the money supply?

3

Consumption

CRITICAL QUESTIONS

» *What are the marginal and average propensities to consume and how are they related?*

» *What is the savings rate and how is it related to changes in disposable income?*

» *How are rational decisions about consumption over time (intertemporal consumption) made?*

» *What is permanent income?*

» *What is the effect of a shock to the income on the consumption decision?*

» *What is the effect of a change in the interest rate on the current consumption?*

» *How is consumption affected by the age cohort that an individual belongs to?*

3.1 Keynes on Consumption

We began by stating that macroeconomics deals with the relation between choices in four markets—the markets for goods, money, bonds, and labour. In the goods market, in the aggregate, we demonstrated the truism that output is always equal to income which is always equal to expenditure. Aggregate expenditure comprises domestic expenditure and net exports. In symbols, we had written,

$$Y = C + I + G + X - M$$

In this chapter, we will focus on the determinants of aggregate private consumption expenditure, C.

Recall that consumption expenditure by households is a very significant 57.8 per cent of GDP, and so an examination of the determinants of this component of GDP is crucial to understanding aggregate expenditure.

The first formal attempt to understand consumption was that of J. M. Keynes, who related it to the current income by adopting a behavioural approach. According to Keynes,[1] "The fundamental psychological law, upon which we are entitled to depend with great confidence both *a priori* from our knowledge of human nature and from the detailed facts of experience, is that men are disposed, as a rule and on the average, to increase their consumption as their income increases, but not by as much as the increase in their income".

This was the basis of the model of consumption that linked current income and current consumption. That can be written algebraically as:

$$C = a + cY^d \tag{3.1}$$

where C is consumption, Y^d is personal disposable income, and a and c are constants. Recall that private disposable income[2] is GDP plus net factor incomes from abroad plus transfers from abroad, as well as government less direct taxes paid. For the Eq. (3.1) to be a representation of Keynes' psychological law, it would require that $0 < c < 1$. Here c is referred to as the MARGINAL PROPENSITY TO CONSUME (MPC), and MPC < 1 is another way of saying that for any increment to income, the incremental consumption resulting from this will be less than the incremental income. More formally, suppose there is an increment to personal disposable income that we write in symbols as ΔY^d. Then the increment to consumption (ΔC) that occurs in response to a marginal increment in personal disposable income which is written as $\Delta C/\Delta Y^d$, may be expressed from Eq. (3.1) as:

> › The **marginal propensity to consume (MPC)** is the amount by which consumption rises when disposable income rises by INR 1. It is assumed that the increase in consumption is less than the increase in disposable income, or, MPC < 1.

$$\frac{\Delta C}{\Delta Y^d} = c$$

If $c < 1$ then $\Delta C/\Delta Y^d < 1$, or $\Delta C < \Delta Y^d$, which inequality states that the increment to consumption is less than the marginal increment to personal disposable income. Summarizing the marginal propensity to consume is given by,

$$\text{MPC} = \frac{\Delta C}{\Delta Y^d} = c < 1 \tag{3.2}$$

The AVERAGE PROPENSITY TO CONSUME (APC) is defined as the average consumption per unit of disposable income. Dividing throughout Eq. (3.1) by Y^d,

> › The **average propensity to consume (APC)**, is the ratio of consumption to disposable income.

$$\text{APC} = \frac{C}{Y^d} = \frac{a}{Y^d} + c \tag{3.3}$$

The graphs of MPC and APC are given in Figure 3.1. As can be seen, an implication of Keynes' theory is that MPC < APC. Also, since disposable income is either consumed or saved, $Y^d = C + S$, private savings can be written as

› Figure 3.1
Average and Marginal Propensities to Consume.
The average propensity to consume declines with an increase in disposable income. The marginal propensity to consume is constant.

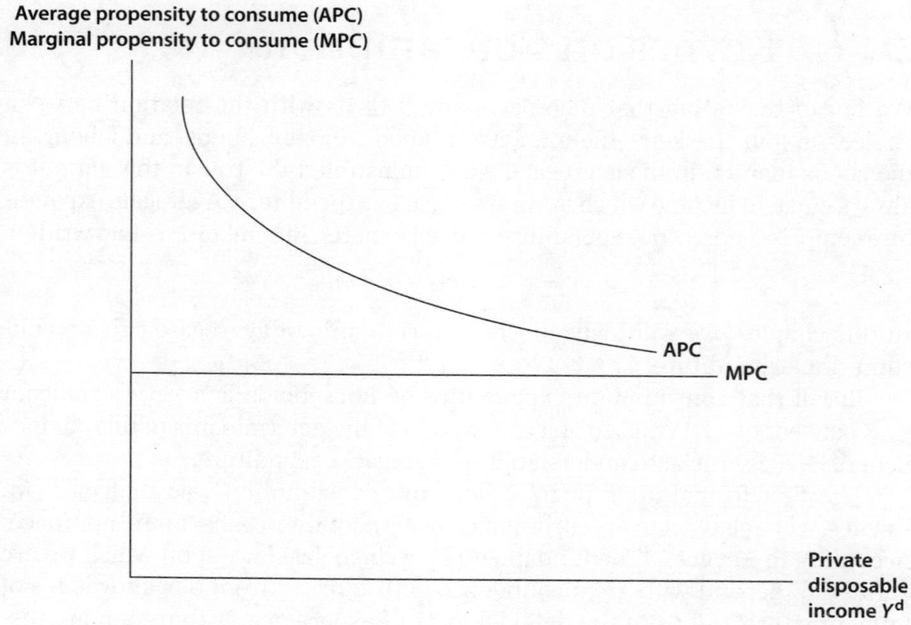

$$\begin{aligned} S &= Y^d - C \\ &= Y^d - \left(a + cY^d\right) \\ &= -a + (1 - c)Y^d \end{aligned} \tag{3.4}$$

› The **average propensity to save** or the savings rate is the ratio of savings to disposable income.

The AVERAGE PROPENSITY TO SAVE (APS) is given by Eq. (3.5) and is depicted in Figure 3.2:

$$\text{APS} = s = \frac{S}{Y^d} = -\frac{a}{Y^d} + (1 - c) \tag{3.5}$$

The average propensity to save is also known as the *savings rate.* Figure 3.2 implies that as disposable incomes rise, the savings rate rises or individuals in the aggregate save, increasing proportions of their incomes.

› Figure 3.2
Average Propensity to Save.
The average propensity to save or the savings rate increases with disposable income.

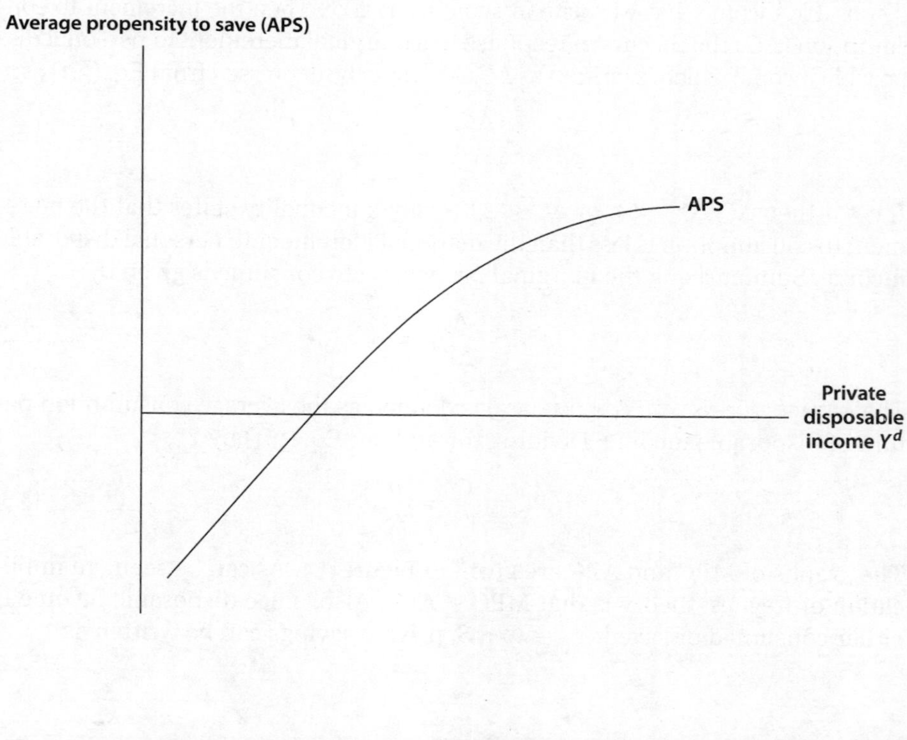

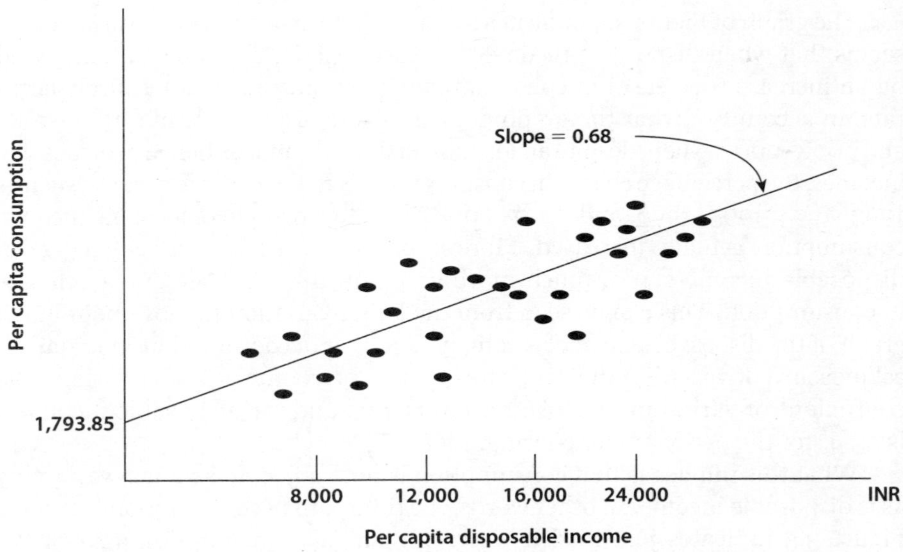

› Figure 3.3
Relationship between Consumption and Disposable Income. The relationship between per capita consumption and per capita disposable income is linear.

Source: Data taken from CSO, National Accounts Statistics.

Figure 3.3 depicts the measured consumption function for India from 1980–1981 to 2009–2010. The estimates[3] for the parameters of the consumption function are as follows:

$$C = 1793.85 + 0.68Y^d \quad (3.6)$$

where the variables in Eq. (3.6) have been stated in per capita terms. From this we can see that the measured value of the marginal propensity to consume is MPC $= c =$ 0.68. The average propensity to consume in this time period was 0.80. The average propensity to consume declined from an average of 0.87 during 1980–1981 to 1993–1994 to an average of 0.77 during 1994–1995 to 2009–2010.

The dotted points in Figure 3.3 are the actual values of consumption and disposable income, and Eq. (3.6) gives the best fit for a straight line through those points. Figure 3.3 would lead us to contend that changes in disposable incomes in a given period are closely associated with changes in consumption. To check out this contention, we can examine Figure 3.4 which graphs the changes in consumption and disposable income.[4]

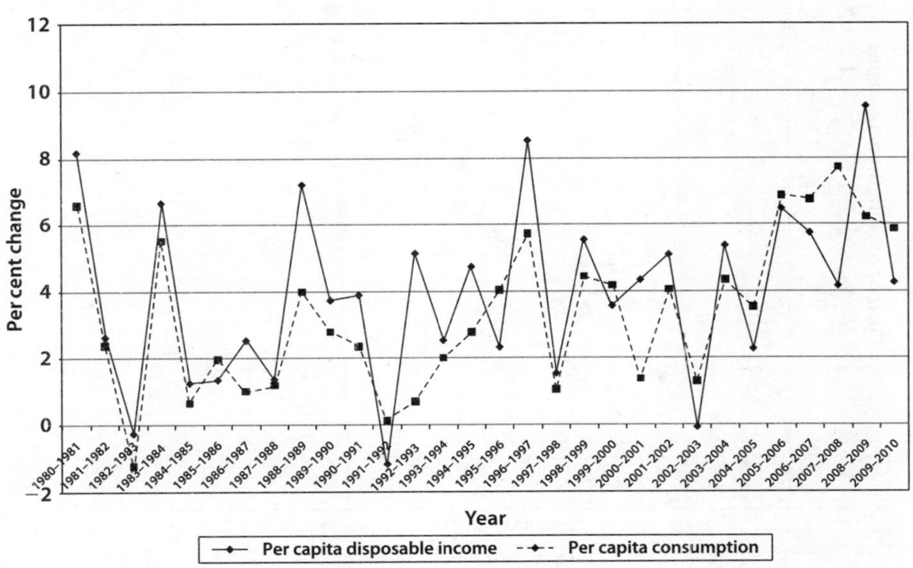

› Figure 3.4
Percentage Change in Real Per Capita Consumption and Disposable Income. The variability of disposable income is greater than the variability of consumption. Also, an increase in income does not automatically translate into an increase in consumption.

The graph of Figure 3.4 indicates a connection between the two variables—it seems that when disposable incomes increase (decrease), this is accompanied by an increase (decrease) in consumption. However, this is not entirely accurate an account of what the graph depicts. There are periods like 1986–1987 and 2008–2009, when, despite an increase in the percentage change in disposable incomes, the percentage charge in consumption declined. In some periods, such as 1993–1994, 1995–1996, and 2007–2008, despite a drop in disposable income, consumption actually increased. More importantly, the percentage change in disposable income shows much more variation than the percentage change in consumption. This can be seen from the larger variation in movement in the graph of the disposable income as compared to that of consumption. One statistical measure of variation that indicates this is the coefficient of variation. The coefficient of variation in consumption is 28.5 and for disposable income it is 33.4[5] for the period under consideration.

› The data on consumption reveals that it is not subject to as much variability as is income–consumption over time has a flat or **smooth** profile.

What this implies is that consumption is not subject to as much variability as is disposable income. In other words, the time path of consumption is SMOOTH. Figure 3.5 indicates just this. If we graph current consumption against the previous period's consumption, we get the graph indicated in Figure 3.5.

In fact, consumption in a given year is 1.041 times the consumption in the previous year as estimated by the straight line through the scatter of points in Figure 3.5.

$$C_t = 1.041\, C_{t-1} \tag{3.7}$$

In Eq. (3.7), C_t is consumption in some time period t and C_{t-1} is consumption in the period previous to this or period $t-1$. The Eq. (3.7) indicates that we seem to continue our consumption patterns inherited from the previous period with of course some growth in consumption overtime, which is implied by the growth factor that increases C_{t-1} to C_t next period.[6] Also, the scatter of points in Figure 3.5 is clustered closer to the straight line than the scatter in Figure 3.3, indicating a much better fit of the straight line to the raw data.

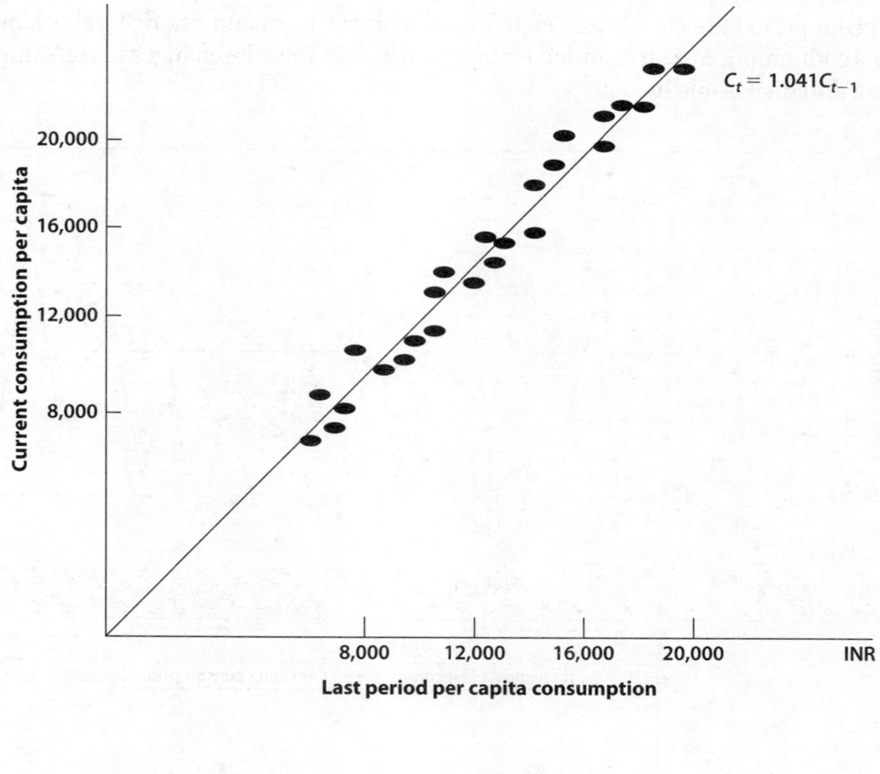

› Figure 3.5 Current and Lagged Consumption 1980–1981 to 2009–2010. The time path of consumption is smooth, with consumption today proportional to consumption yesterday.

That consumption demonstrates smoothness in its pattern calls for an explanation. Moreover, an implication of a Keynes type consumption function is that savings rates tend to rise over time, as shown in Figure 3.2. Simon Kuznets[7] tested the data to prove this, and instead found that in the US, for over the period of a century, the savings rate had not risen. This contradicted what the Keynesian consumption function was proclaiming. To explain the smoothness in consumption, the fact that savings rates can be pretty static became an important area for research in economics. Two economists who led the research in this area were Franco Modigliani of MIT and Milton Friedman of the University of Chicago. Their theories are the Life-Cycle theory and the Permanent Income theory of consumption respectively. With sincere apologies to the two Nobel laureates, we will treat the two theories as providing analogous explanations for the smoothness of consumption and identify their contribution as the consumption smoothing theory of consumption.

3.2 Consumption Smoothing

There are two hallmarks of the consumption smoothing approach. One is that unlike Keynes, who appealed to behavioural inference, the consumption smoothing approach uses the standard tool of economics, i.e., that agents optimize subject to constraints. Thus, in this theory, consumption is the consequence of rational agents seeking to maxi mize their preferences, subject to the opportunities that they face. The second differentiating factor in the CONSUMPTION SMOOTHING THEORY is that agents are not just reactive and tied in solely to the present—where current consumption moves in step with current income—but are also treated as forward looking-proactive agents. They have foresight about what is in store for them in the future and take decisions today keeping that in mind. The fact that the future casts its shadow on the present requires that a successful portrayal of economic behaviour involves taking into consideration at least two periods—a present and a future—in our analysis. This type of analysis is known as INTERTEMPORAL ANALYSIS. A lot of economics is concerned with tradeoffs between alternatives in the present—the choice between eating Thai food and an *idli-dosa* meal, or between buying the latest Harry Potter book and treating your girl or boy friend to a dinner and a movie. In intertemporal analysis, by contrast, the fundamental consideration is that alternatives chosen today affect the menu of alternatives available in the future.

› **Consumption smoothing theory** is not a behavioural but a preference maximization theory where individuals are forward looking.

› **Intertemporal analysis** is about the tradeoffs when present choices affect the alternatives available in the future.

3.2.1 Intertemporal Constraints and Preferences

For instance, when deciding what to do with their incomes, people may consume them all now or save a part for the future. So the question that the intertemporal approach will focus on is: How do rational consumers distribute their consumption over time? To keep the analysis manageable, and also to allow us to draw diagrams, we suppose that there are only two time periods, namely, current and future. So the alternatives facing the consumer are current consumption (C_1) versus future consumption (C_2). To derive the intertemporal budget constraint facing a consumer, we begin by noting that a consumer always has the choice of consuming his entire income in each period. So, with Y_1 and Y_2 denoting current and future income, the consumer sets $C_1 = Y_1$ and $C_2 = Y_2$. This is the point E in Figure 3.6.

Another option open to the consumer is to deposit all the income earned in period 1 in a bank and with the interest rate of r per cent he would be able to get $(1 + r)Y_1$ as the principal plus interest payment in the future. He would

› **Figure 3.6 Intertemporal Budget Constraint.** The intertemporal budget constraint depicts the current and future consumption possibilities from the stream of income available across time.

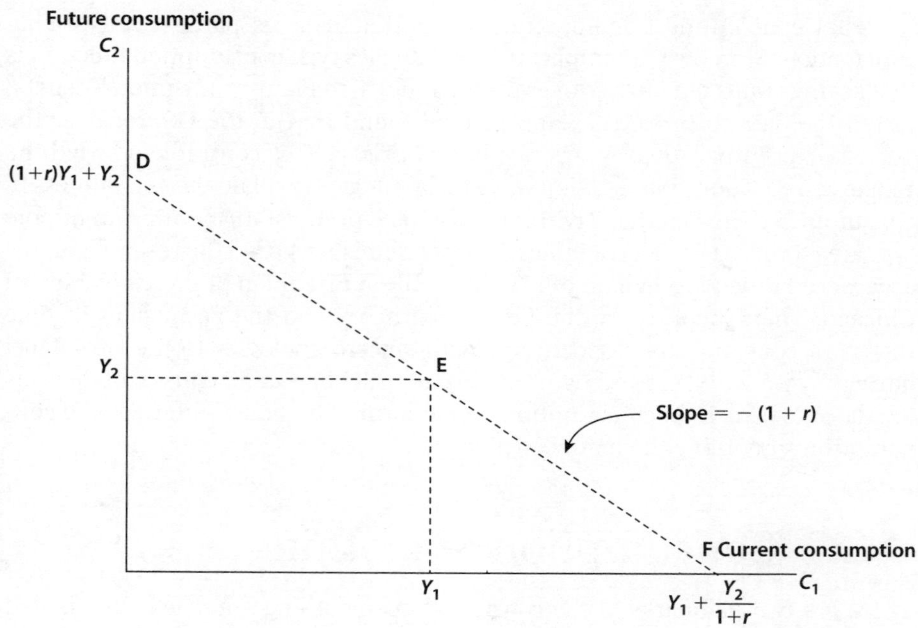

not consume any income in the present ($C_1 = 0$) and by saving it all derive an income from his savings of $(1 + r)Y_1$. Due to there being only two periods and no opportunities for leaving bequests to heirs, he must consume along with his second period income Y_2 so that $C_2 = Y_2 + (1 + r)Y_1$. This alternative of consuming only in the future is represented by point D in the diagram. Of course, we might presume that if there is no consumption today, the consumer might not live to see another day. So, point D does not seem like a practical alternative. Though extreme behaviour for a consumer, it is still a theoretical possibility, and as we want to be exhaustive about the possibilities open for consumption, we include that point in our analysis.

The other extreme behaviour is to forget that there is a future altogether, and to consume all the future and present income today. Consuming tomorrow's income requires borrowing that future amount today, and in present value terms, Y_2 of future income is equivalent to $Y_2/(1+r)$ income today. This follows from the observation that if we were to put $Y_2/(1 + r)$ in a deposit in a bank today, we would get back $[Y_2/(1 + r)](1 + r)] = Y_2$ in the next period as repayments on our deposit. So, consuming both tomorrow's and today's income today amounts to $C_2 = 0$ and $C_1 = Y_1 + Y_2/(1 + r)$ which is represented by point F. Obviously, it is not necessary to save or borrow the maximum amounts possible. If from current income Y_1, the individual consumes only a part of it such that $C_1 < Y_1$ and saves $(Y_1 - C_1)$, then the earnings on that savings in the next period amounts to $(1 + r)(Y_1 - C_1)$. This must be spent along with next period's income Y_2 on next period's consumption C_2 (given that there are only two periods). Thus,

$$(1 + r)(Y_1 - C_1) + Y_2 = C_2$$

Dividing throughout by $(1 + r)$ gives,

$$Y_1 - C_1 + \frac{Y_2}{(1+r)} = \frac{C_2}{1+r}$$

Rearranging this expression gives us,

$$C_1 + \frac{C_2}{1+r} = Y_1 + \frac{Y_2}{1+r} \quad (3.8)$$

This is the equation for the INTERTEMPORAL BUDGET CONSTRAINT drawn as the line DEF in Figure 3.6.

› The **intertemporal budget constraint** states the present value of consumption possibilities over time from the present value of the flow of income over that period.

Another way of interpreting Eq. (3.8) is that with only two periods and no heirs to worry about the present value of life-cycle, consumption $C_1 + C_2/(1+r)$ must equal the present value of life-cycle income $Y_1 + Y_2/(1 + r)$. As depicted, the slope of the intertemporal budget constraint is $(1 + r)$ as that is the opportunity cost of the interest foregone when money is spent rather than saved. If an individual reduces current consumption, C_1, by a rupee, and puts that amount into the bank, he gets back INR $(1 + r)$ in the future which is the amount of the increase in future consumption, C_2, that is enabled.

Which point will the consumer select on this intertemporal budget constraint? We need to know his preferences over current and future consumption to answer this and that is given by his preference function. The preferences are defined by a utility function as is done in the atemporal case in microeconomics texts, and can be written as

$$U = U(C_1, C_2) \tag{3.9}$$

This utility function can be represented by an indifference map as in Figure 3.7, where the consumer is indifferent between two consumption bundles that lie on the locus of any given indifference curve. For those readers who would like to do a quick revision, the concept of indifference curves is summarized in Appendix 3.1. The indifference curves that are more to the north-east represent more desirable consumption for the consumer and provide the consumer with greater satisfaction or utility. As the level of utility along an indifference curve is constant, the slope of an indifference curve gives us the rate at which we can substitute one dimension of consumption (or one good) for another without any change in the level of utility.

The slope of an intertemporal indifference curve in Figure 3.7 measures the marginal rate of substitution (MRS) between future and current consumption. It is the rate at which present consumption can be substituted for future

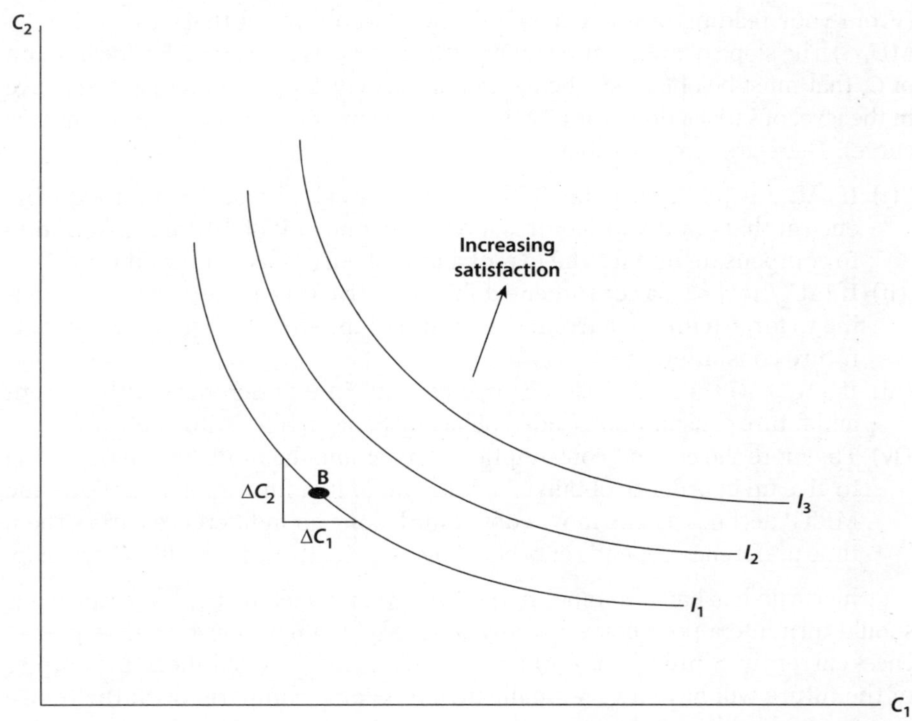

› **Figure 3.7**
Intertemporal Indifference Curves. The preferences of an individual for consumption today versus tomorrow are depicted by indifference curves. Along any indifference curve, the individual is indifferent between the consumption possibilities depicted by any two points on the curve.

consumption with no change in the utility obtained. A marginal change in consumption results in a change in utility as expressed by the marginal utility of consumption, or MU_C. If then, at point B in Figure 3.7, we reduce present consumption by an amount ΔC_1, then, the reduction in utility due to this reduction in consumption will be $MU_{C_1}(\Delta C_1)$. To compensate the individual for the loss in utility from the decline in present consumption, he would require future consumption to be augmented. If we raise future consumption by an amount ΔC_2, then, the increase in utility arising from the increase in consumption will be $MU_{C_2}(\Delta C_2)$.

An individual's time preference for consumption is usually such that the utility from consumption received in the future is valued less than the utility from consumption today. Let the subjective discount rate at which an individual values future consumption relative to current consumption be given by θ. We assume that $\theta > 0$. Accordingly, the value of the gain in utility from an increase in future consumption is given by,

$$\frac{MU_{C_2}(\Delta C_2)}{1+\theta}$$

For the individual to be on the same indifference curve, the value of the gain in utility from increased future consumption must exactly offset the loss in utility from a reduction in present consumption:

$$\frac{MU_{C_2}(\Delta C_2)}{1+\theta} = -MU_{C_1}(\Delta C_1)$$

or,

$$-\frac{\Delta C_2}{\Delta C_1} = (1+\theta)\frac{MU_{C_1}}{MU_{C_2}} \tag{3.10}$$

The slope of the intertemporal indifference curve is called the marginal rate of time preference (MRTP) to differentiate it from the slope of an atemporal indifference curve which is the marginal rate of substitution (MRS). The MRTP is,

$$MRTP = -\frac{\Delta C_2}{\Delta C_1} = (1+\theta)\frac{MU_{C_1}}{MU_{C_2}}$$

› The slope of an **intertemporal indifference curve** measures the rate of time preference for present consumption versus future consumption.

(From your reading of microeconomics, you would recall that $MRS = MU_{C_1}/MU_{C_2}$.) The slope of an INTERTEMPORAL INDIFFERENCE CURVE is a measure for the amount of C_2 that must be obtained when a unit of C_1 is given up and there is no change in the level of satisfaction or utility (i.e., the consumer is on the same indifference curve). There are three possible cases:

(i) If $|\Delta C_2/\Delta C_1| > 1$, at point B, the consumer exhibits positive time preference at that point and requires more than one unit of future consumption to compensate him for the loss of a unit of current consumption.
(ii) If $|\Delta C_2/\Delta C_1| < 1$, a consumer exhibits negative time preference and is willing to forgo a unit of current consumption in return for less than a unit of future consumption.
(iii) If $|\Delta C_2/\Delta C_1| = 1$, a consumer has neutral time preferences with present and future consumption traded off against one another with a ratio of 1:1.
(iv) The more the current consumption of a person, the more he will be willing to give up in order to obtain an additional unit of future consumption—the MRTP declines as one moves downward along an indifference curve. Then, time preference depends on where one is currently on the indifference map.

A farmer who has had a bumper harvest this year, which by the law of averages should turn into a poor harvest next year, is likely to have negative time preferences currently. Similarly, the son of a tycoon who is due to inherit the empire in the future will have a very small current income compared with the future income, and is likely to have positive time preference.

MACROFOCUS 3.1

Emotions and Intertemporal Decisions

Is decision making based solely on rationality? An emerging field in economics that goes by the name of neuroeconomics argues that decision making draws on emotions even when reason is clearly involved. As humans evolved, new capabilities such as the ability to deliberate about the broader consequences of our actions were gradually added to the basic pre-historic brain system. The neural anatomy essential for full rationality—the pre-frontal cortex—emerged only in the last 150,000 years of humanity's six million year existence.

Neuroeconomists conceive human behaviour as a struggle between affective and cognitive systems. Affective systems embody not only emotions such as anger and jealousy, but also drive states such as hunger and sexual desire, and motivational states such as anger and physical pain. These motivate us to be aggressive and take steps to ease the pain. Cognitive systems assess the options available to an individual with a broad, goal-based perspective, such as posited in the standard rational choice approach. The affective system has primary control over behaviour. However the deliberative system chooses which behaviour to implement by trading off its objectives against the cost of exerting cognitive effort or willpower so as to influence the affective system's choice.

With regard to intertemporal choice, people are often of two minds—they often find themselves encouraged to take myopic actions such as eating high-calorie foods or eschewing contraception, whilst concurrently realizing these activities are not in their self-interest. This is because even though the deliberative system recognizes the desirability of certain actions motivated from the affective system (that focuses on near-term environmental stimuli and payoffs), it also incorporates the willpower it must exert to control these affective motivations. The individual can then make myopic choices such as extravagant spending with credit cards, which defers the pain of paying to the future. However, the interaction between affect and cognition can help us understand not just impulsivity, but also the opposite problem of high self-control—people with dominant deliberative systems can exhibit miserliness and cannot get themselves to spend enough. Workaholics who cannot take a break are in the same category.

Source: C. Camerer, G. Loewenstein, and D. Prelec, "Neuroeconomics: How Neuroscience can Inform Economics," *Journal of Economic Literature*, no. 43 (March 2005): 9–64.

3.2.2 Time Preference and Permanent Income

Exactly as is the case in standard choice theory, the consumer's problem is to maximize his utility subject to the budget constraint,

$$\text{Max } U = U(C_1, C_2)$$

such that:

$$C_1 + \frac{C_2}{1+r} = Y_1 + \frac{Y_2}{1+r} = W \tag{3.11}$$

In Eq. (3.11), W is the present value of the two-period income. The problem stated here in Eq. (3.11) is akin to the consumer selecting the point along his budget constraint (as depicted in Figure 3.6) that corresponds to the highest attainable indifference curve (from those depicted in Figure 3.7). This implies (in the normal case without corner solutions) a tangency solution to the maximization problem stated in Eq. (3.11), where the slope of the indifference curve is equal to the slope of the budget line as depicted in Figure 3.8.

The consumer consumes $C_1^* < Y_1$ of his current income and saves $(Y - C_1^*)$ so as to consume tomorrow $C_2^* = Y_2 + (Y_1 - C_1^*)(1 + r)$.[8] Of course, different consumers will have different preferences and will allocate current and future consumption differently. In Figure 3.9A, for instance, we have a consumer whose preferences are heavily in favour of future consumption—we could consider this person to be patient as he is willing to postpone the bulk of his consumption to the future. Figure 3.9B depicts a consumer who cares much more about present consumption—he is much more impatient and prefers consuming more today, rather than tomorrow.

If the utility function is written in additively separable form,

$$U = U(C_1, C_2) = U(C_1) + \frac{U(C_2)}{1+\theta} \tag{3.12}$$

› θ is the subjective discount rate for valuing future consumption relative to current consumption. The **higher is** θ the more impatient is the individual for current consumption relative to future consumption.

where, $\theta > 0$, is the measure of impatience of a consumer. HIGHER VALUES OF θ imply higher impatience and a consumer preference for consumption today rather than tomorrow (see Figure 3.9B).

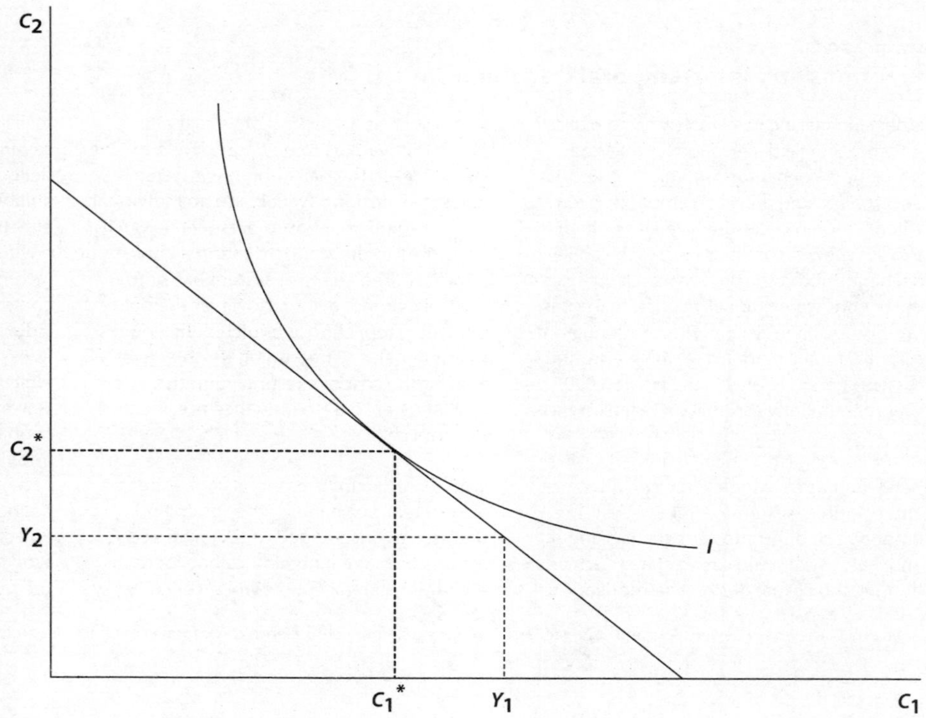

› **Figure 3.8**
Equilibrium of the Individual. Optimal consumption is where an indifference curve is tangential to the intertemporal budget line. In this case, the individual saves some of their current income with a view to increasing the consumption possibilities in the future.

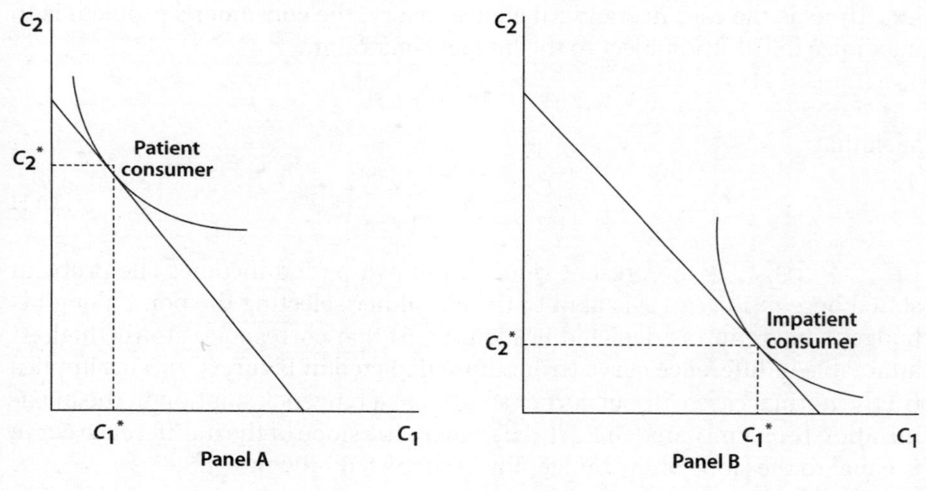

› **Figure 3.9**
Time Preference and the Individual. A patient individual has a high preference for consumption in the future. An impatient individual prefers consumption today at the expense of less consumption in the future.

In order to fix the idea of impatience further, let us give a form to the utility function. Suppose the utility of consumption is logarithmic in consumption, that is,

$$U = U(C_1, C_2) = U(C_1) + \frac{U(C_2)}{1+\theta} = \log C_1 + \frac{\log C_2}{1+\theta} \tag{3.13}$$

A logarithmic form to the utility function has been found in experimental work to adequately represent the preferences of individuals. The logarithmic form also has the standard properties that marginal utility is positive and that individuals eventually face diminishing marginal utility as they increase their consumption. Then, the slope of an indifference curve[9] is given by,

$$-\frac{\Delta C_2}{\Delta C_1} = (1+\theta)\,\frac{C_2}{C_1} \tag{3.14}$$

The highest utility that an individual can obtain is graphically depicted by the highest indifference curve that is attainable. This is the indifference curve that is tangent to the budget line. As maximizing preferences requires tangency—the slope of the indifference curve equals the slope of the budget line—we can write the condition for optimal consumption as,

$$\underbrace{(1+\theta)\frac{C_2}{C_1}}_{\text{Slope of Indifference Curve}} = \underbrace{1+r}_{\text{Slope of Budget Line}} \tag{3.15}$$

or

$$\frac{C_2^*}{C_1^*} = \frac{1+r}{1+\theta} \tag{3.16}$$

> If the utility function is separable in consumption across time periods, then consumption today is consumption yesterday times the ratio of one plus the market rate of interest to one plus the marginal rate of time preference, **Consumption smoothing** occurs when the rate of interest equals the rate of time preference, or , when, $C_2 = C_1$.

Equation (3.16) implies that $C_2^* = [1 + r/1 + \theta]C_1^*$. That individuals prefer to maintain a stable consumption pattern rather than allow consumption to rise or fall with variations in income is the essence of the theory of consumption in an intertemporal framework. If $\theta = r$, then, $C_2^* = C_1^*$, or, the consumer equates consumption in the two time periods. This is what is referred to as CONSUMPTION SMOOTHING. In Figure 3.10, consumption smoothing with $C_1^* = C_2^*$ occurs at the point where a 45-degree line from the origin intersects the point where the slope of the indifference curve equals the slope of the intertemporal budget constraint.

> **Consumption tilting** is because the consumer's impatience for present versus future consumption is not equal to the interest rate at which income is discounted.

CONSUMPTION TILTING, in contrast, is the case where the consumer is impatient and tilts his consumption towards the present $C_1^* > C_2^*$ and $\theta > r$ as depicted in Figure 3.11A, or the consumer is patient and tilts his consumption towards the future – $C_1^* < C_2^*$ and $\theta < r$ as depicted in Figure 3.11B. Empirically, we had found that $C_2 = 1.041C_1$ for India. This suggests that $\theta < r$ or those individuals are willing to be more patient than the rate at which the market discounts the future. When θ is less than r, individual's value future consumption more than current consumption and tend to postpone consumption to the future. However, given that the coefficient attached to last period's consumption is

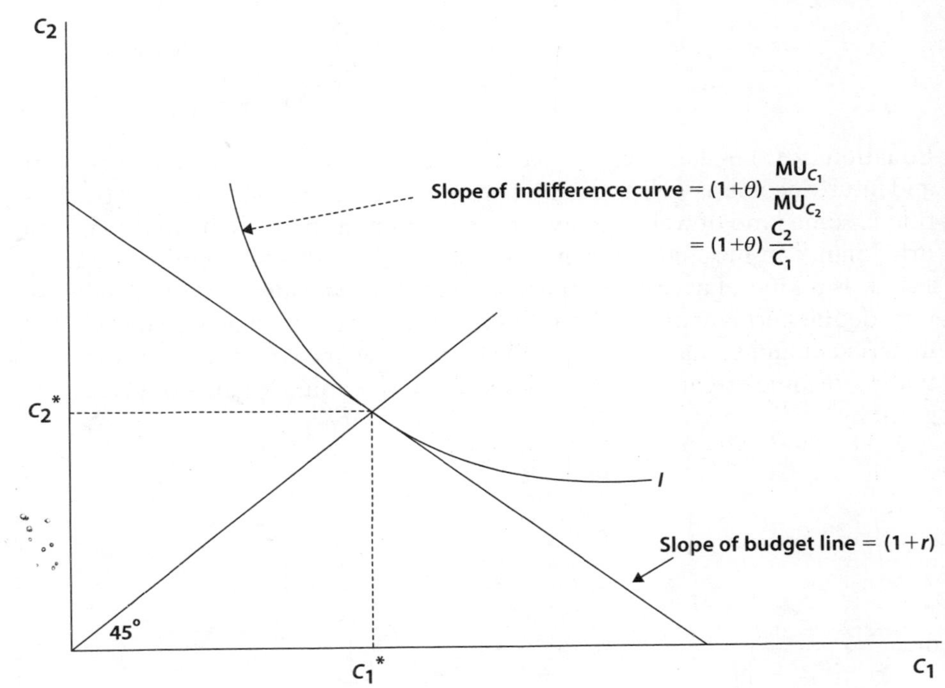

> **Figure 3.10**
Consumption Smoothing. Consumption smoothing, $C_1^* = C_2^*$, results when the marginal rate of time preference given by the slope of the indifference curve equals the slope of the intertemporal budge line and the subjective rate of time preference equals the market rate of interest, or $\theta = r$.

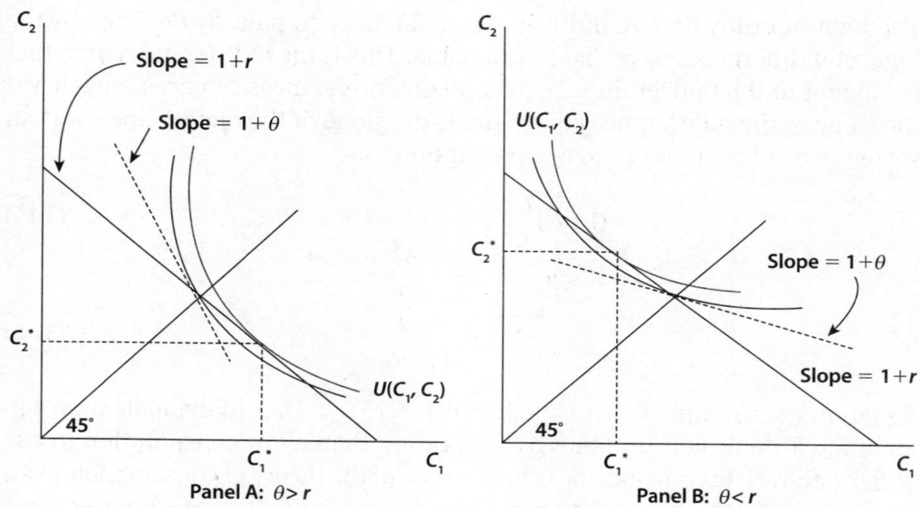

› Figure 3.11
Consumption Tilting.
Individuals who are impatient and prefer more consumption today (panel A) and those who are patient and prefer more consumption in the future (panel B) depict consumption tilting behaviour.

close to 1, it is difficult to reject the hypothesis that individuals do not pursue a strategy of smoothing consumption.

The essence of the approach of consumption smoothing is that current consumption depends not only on the current income but also on the future income. It is also dependent on the interest rate which determines the slope of the budget constraint, and on the preferences of individuals which determine the shape of the indifference curves. Suppose the individual's preferences are such that he smoothens his consumption over time, $C_1^* = C_2^*$. Substituting this allocation of lifetime consumption into the intertemporal budget constraint $C_1 + [C_2/(1+r)] = Y_1 + [Y_2/(1+r)] = W$, and solving for current consumption, we obtain,

$$C_1^* + \frac{C_1^*}{1+r} = W$$

or,

$$\frac{2+r}{1+r}C_1^* = W$$

or,

$$C_1^* = \frac{1+r}{2+r}W = \frac{1+r}{2+r}\left(Y_1 + \frac{Y_2}{1+r}\right) \tag{3.17}$$

Equation (3.17) makes it clear that current consumption depends on current and future income as well as the interest rate. It indicates that current consumption is some kind of weighted average of present and future incomes. Milton Friedman,[10] in his study on consumption, pursued this by defining PERMANENT INCOME as a kind of average of present and future income. More precisely, we may define permanent income (Y_p) as that constant-income stream (Y_p, Y_p) in periods 1 and 2, that gives the same lifetime income stream as does the fluctuating income stream (Y_1, Y_2). In short, Y_p, the annuity value of (Y_1, Y_2), is given by

› **Permanent income** is that constant stream of income that equals the present discounted value of the fluctuating stream of current and future incomes.

$$Y_p + \frac{Y_p}{1+r} = Y_1 + \frac{Y_2}{1+r}$$

or,

$$\frac{2+r}{1+r}Y_p = Y_1 + \frac{Y_2}{1+r}$$

or,

$$Y_p = \frac{1+r}{2+r}\left(Y_1 + \frac{Y_2}{1+r}\right) \tag{3.18}$$

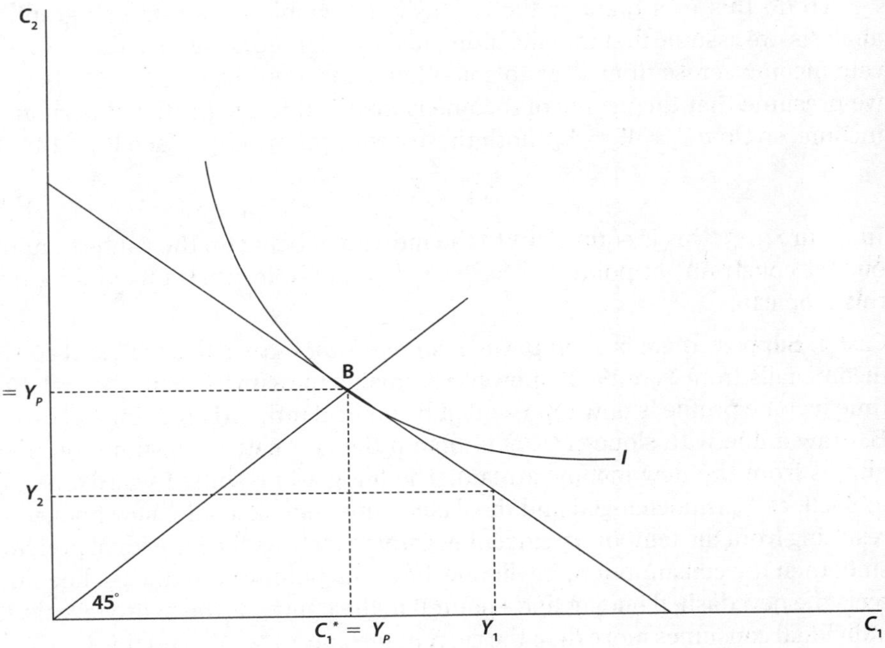

› **Figure 3.12**
Permanent Income and Consumption. Consumption smoothing is identical to the individual consuming permanent income and saving the difference between actual income and permanent income.

It turns out that permanent income Y_p in Eq. (3.18) is the same expression as the right hand side of Eq. (3.17), and noting this we can then write,

$$C_1^* = C_2^* = Y_P \tag{3.19}$$

Thus, when the individual possesses preferences which lead him to maintain a stable consumption path, consuming the same every period, we can say that CONSUMPTION is set equal to permanent income.

› Consumption smoothing is identical to **consumption,** each period being equal to **permanent income**.

In other words, the individual decides on his consumption levels on the basis of his PERMANENT INCOME, and not current income as in Keynes. In graphical terms, permanent income is a constant stream across periods, and so its value is represented by the point where a 45° line from the origin intersects the intertemporal budget constraint, point B in Figure 3.12.

Consumption smoothing is akin to the individual setting current consumption equal to permanent income. SAVING is thus the gap between current and permanent income, or,

› An individual who smoothens consumption across time periods, has **savings** given by the difference between permanent income and actual income.

$$S_1 = Y_1 - C_1 = Y_1 - Y_P \tag{3.20}$$

When individuals pursue consumption smoothing, it implies that the savings of individuals is the amount of the difference between current and permanent income.[11]

3.3 Temporary and Permanent Shocks

Up to now, we have treated future income as a known variable. In fact, Ando and Modigliani[12] demonstrated that, on the average, future income is proportional to current income, or $Y_2 = \beta Y_1$, where $\beta > 0$. However, there are always shocks to income and to expect it to grow smoothly by a proportional amount from one period to the next is not realistic. We need to accordingly discuss the effects on consumption and saving of SHOCKS to income.

› A **shock** is a disturbance that changes the value of a variable by a random amount.

To do this in a manner that is easily amenable to non-messy graphical analysis, we assume first that the individual's preferences are such that they allocate income across time so as to smoothen consumption, or $C_1^* = C_2^*$. Second, we presume that the profile of income is identical to the profile of permanent income, so that $Y_1 = Y_2 = Y_p$. Both these assumptions imply [see Eq. (3.19)]:

$$C_1^* = C_2^* = Y_1 = Y_2 = Y_p \tag{3.21}$$

In Figure 3.13, this is equivalent to the individual being on their intertemporal budget constraint at point A. There are five possible situations arising from this scenario:

Case 1: Suppose there is a *temporary current shock*, say a drought, and current income falls from Y_1 to Y_1'. Y_2, however, remains the same. The individual's lifetime income profile is now represented by point E rather than point A. Through E, draw a line with slope $(1 + r)$ to obtain the alternative consumption possibilities from the new income stream. The budget line shifts inwards, parallel to itself, as Y_2 is unchanged and the dashed line represents the new budget line resulting from the temporary current negative shock. As the individual prefers to smoothen the consumption, it will now be at the point where the 45° line intersects the new dashed budget line—point B in the figure. As the figure reveals, the individual consumes more than the current income, $C_1'^* > Y_1'$, and this is possible because the shock is temporary and the individual borrows part of future income to finance current consumption.

Savings were zero before the shock as $C_1^* = Y_1 = Y_p$, and after the shock $C_1'^* = Y_p' > Y_1'$ and there is dissaving. A temporary current shock that results in a decline in current income is thus accompanied by a decline in savings. This is because individuals prefer to smoothen out their consumption and absorb the decline in income by reducing consumption a bit but allowing the shock to hit their saving considerably more.

Case 2: In contrast, if the temporary shock to current income is a favourable positive shock (the individual wins a lottery, for instance) then, as Figure 3.14 depicts, lifetime income is now given by point E rather than point A. This results

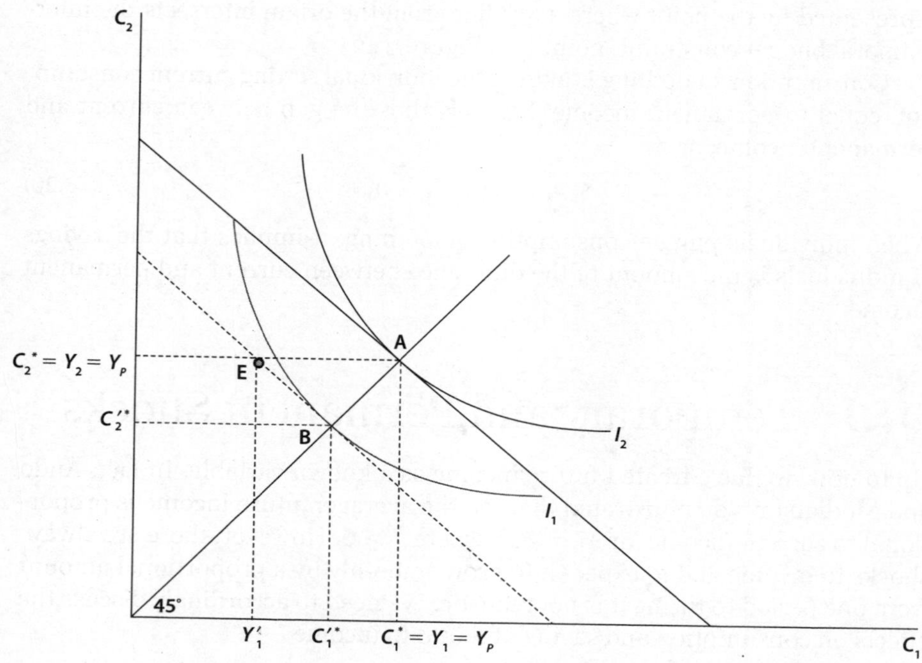

› **Figure 3.13 Temporary Current Negative Shock.** Individuals adjust to a temporary current negative shock that reduces income by dissaving and maintaining the smoothness of consumption.

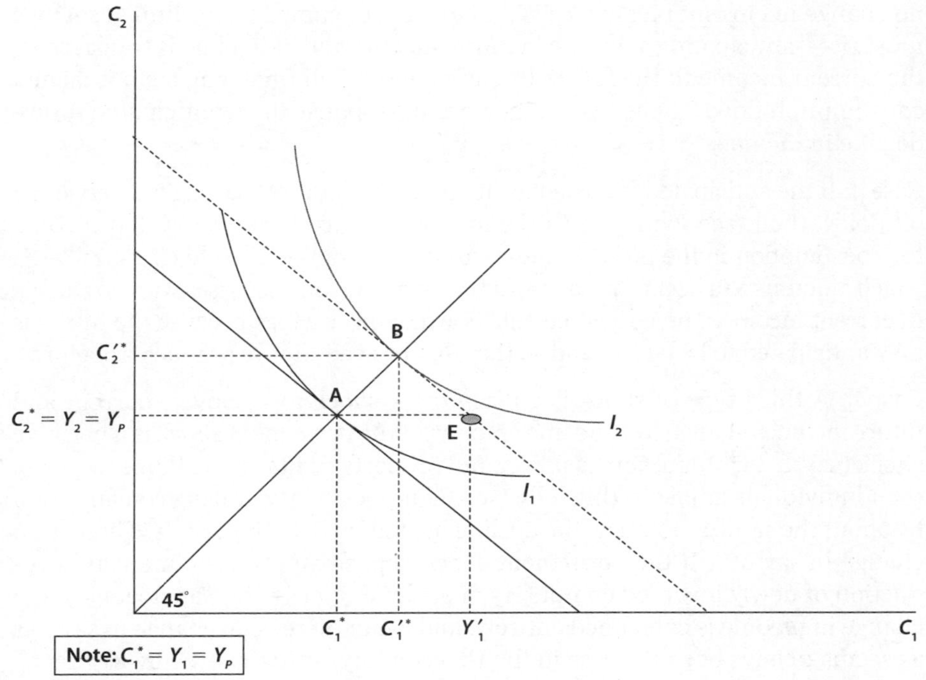

› **Figure 3.14**
A temporary current positive shock that increases income results in an individual increasing savings while smoothening consumption.

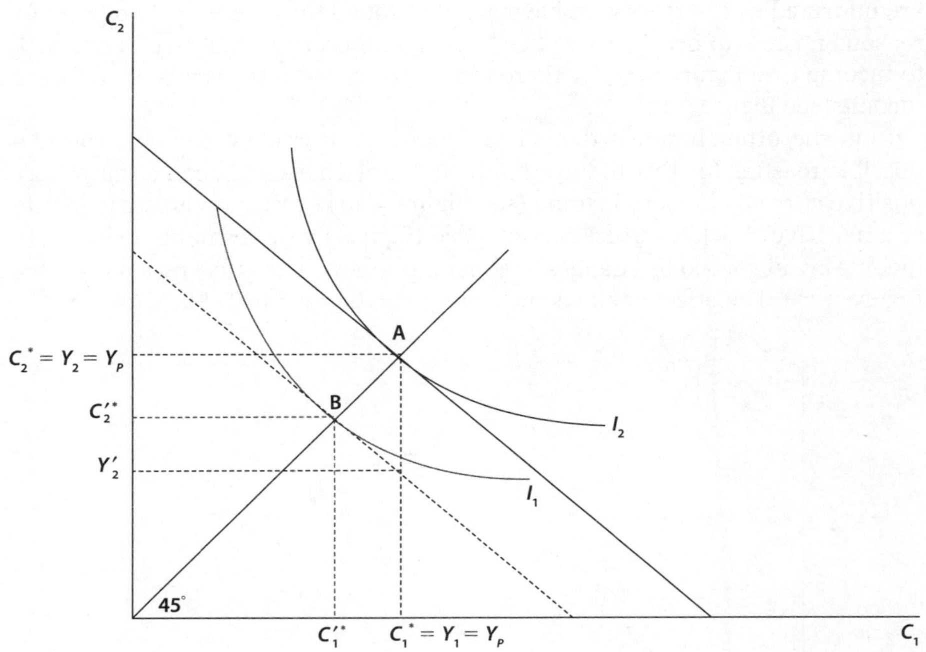

› **Figure 3.15**
Anticipated Future Negative Shock. Anticipating a decline in future income, an individual increases savings today to smoothen consumption.

in an increase in current savings to $Y_1' - C_1'^*$, and an increase in current consumption to $C_1'^*$. With temporary current shocks, therefore, increases in consumption and savings absorb the impact of the shock.

Case 3: A second type of shock is an *anticipated future shock*. In this case, current income is unchanged at Y_1, but there is an expectation of a future decline in incomes to Y_2', say, due to a war that could break out. Figure 3.15 depicts this situation with the dashed budget line indicating the post-shock situation.

The consumption path moves from point A to point B with the individual adopting consumption smoothing. Current consumption declines to $C_1'^*$ despite no change in current income Y_1. With current consumption declining, savings must rise—anticipating a decline in future income, the individual is transferring the current income to the future by saving more and financing a smoothened consumption flow. Savings, thus, increase in response to an anticipated future decline in income.

Case 4: If the anticipated future shock to income is positive (say, a discovery of an oil field), then (see Figure 3.16) the individual borrows some of that income for consumption in the present, and current consumption rises to $C_1'^* = Y_P' > Y_1$, which amounts to a decline in savings as current consumption rises with no change in current income. The individual cuts down on his savings because the future is now anticipated to be better, and so they do not need to save as much as before.

Case 5: A third type of shock is a *permanent shock* to incomes—current and future incomes change by the same amount. If the permanent shock is a negative shock (say, a dictator assumes power and property rights are no longer secure), then individuals adjust to this fully (see Figure 3.17) by reducing consumption by about the same amount as the decline in income in both periods. There is no change in savings. If the permanent shock is positive—the commercial introduction of newly invented computers or steam engines—then analogously, the change in income is consumed entirely, and again there is no change in savings as seems to have been the case in the US economy, as discovered by Kuznets.

To summarize the discussion, if we see a decline in current savings, we are informed by the theory we have just developed that there are two possible reasons for this to occur—there has been a temporary negative current shock to income (see Figure 3.13) or there is an anticipated positive shock to future income (see Figure 3.15).

On the other hand, if there is an increase in current savings, the two possible reasons for this to have happened are—there has been a temporary positive current shock to income (see Figure 3.14) or there is an anticipation of a negative shock to future income (see Figure 3.16). Permanent shocks to income are absorbed by changes in consumption with no effect on savings (see Figure 3.17). The effect of shock on savings can be seen in Table 3.1.

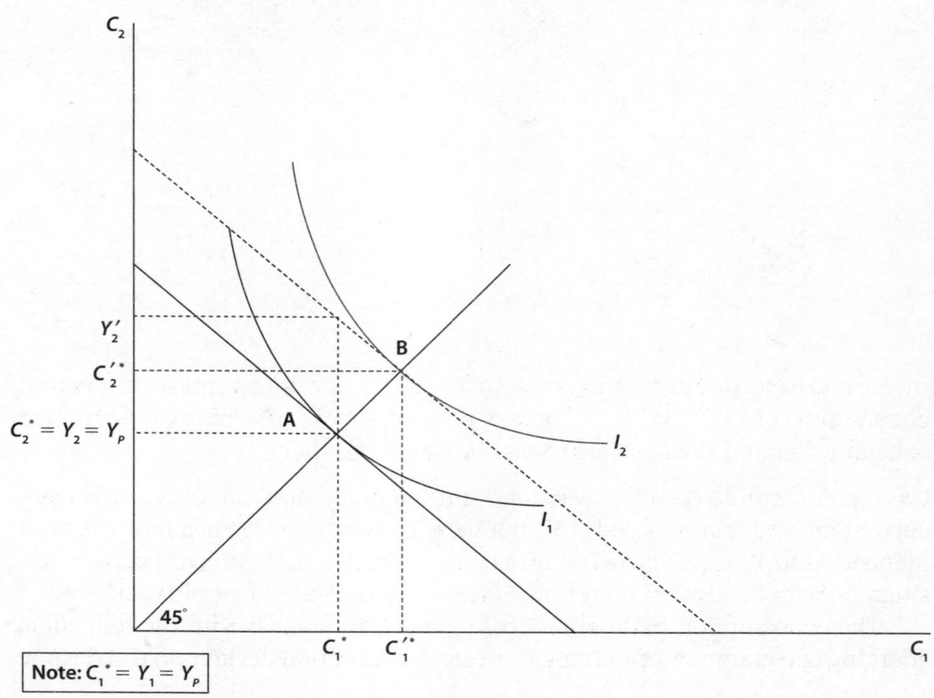

› **Figure 3.16**
Anticipated Future Positive Shock. Anticipating an increase in future income, the individual decreases savings today and increases present consumption as with an improved future income there is no need to save as much as before.

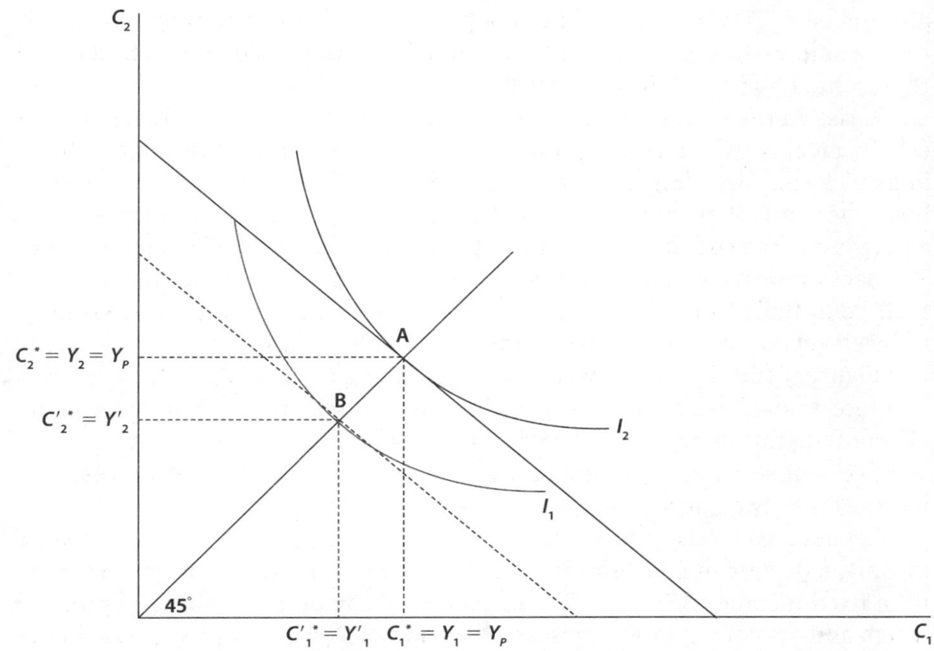

› Figure 3.17
Permanent Negative Stock. If the decline in income will persist in the future, then the individual adjusts by reducing consumption by the extent of the decline in income.

› Table 3.1
Effect of Shock on Savings

Outcome	Type of Shock to Income
Decline in savings	Temporary negative current shock
	Anticipated positive future shock
Increase in savings	Anticipated negative future shock
	Temporary positive current shock

MACROFOCUS 3.2

Joint Families and Borrowing Constraints

An implication of life-cycle theory is that saving is a vehicle for transferring income from high-income to low-income earning phases of the life cycle. In developing countries, however, households tend to be larger and there is also a tendency for quite a few generations to live together. Such households resort to internal transfers between workers and dependents, and in the process take care of expenditures that are related to health or maintenance during old age. This happens to the extent that individuals belonging to such households are ensured of such transfers, they would not require savings to compensate for shortfalls in income in any time period. Aggregate savings in societies, which are less individualistic, may be, therefore, lower.

The life-cycle model also assumes that individuals are free to borrow and lend at a given rate of interest. In developing economies, however, financial institutions are often unwilling to lend because individuals have little or no collateral, and even if they do, legal difficulties in securing the transfer rights of assets to creditors in case of defaulting makes them impose constraints on borrowing. Knowing that the possibility of borrowing is limited, individuals would forsake high consumption even when it is possible out of their current income, as a way of getting ready for periods of misfortune when incomes would be low. This is a *precautionary motive* for saving where individuals take precautions against bad times in which they know they will be unable to borrow.

This motive also provides us an insight expounded on by Deaton*, as to why many households save even when the return on their assets is negative. Poor households often save in the form of grain stocks or cash. The stocks of grain often have a real annual rate of return that is negative, as stocks depreciate due to pests and desiccation. Similarly, cash has negative return due to inflation. Yet, grain and cash are major vehicles for savings, especially by poor households as a precaution against dramatic drops in income due to bad harvests.

*A. Deaton, "Household Saving in LDCs: Credit Markets, Insurance and Welfare," *Scandinavian Journal of Economics* 94(2) (1992): 253–273.

3.4 Effect of Interest Rates

So far, we have examined how shocks to income affect consumption and savings. We now examine the effects of interest rate changes. It is often thought that as the interest rates rise, the rate of return to savings rises, and so savings would also increase. However, the relation between interest rates and savings is a bit more complex than that. Consider an individual with income stream (Y_1, Y_2) represented by point E in Figure 3.18.

A rise in the interest rate will make the slope of the budget line given by $(1 + r)$ steeper—the intertemporal budget constraint rotates through point E in a clockwise direction and is represented in the figure by the dashed budget line. The individual who was originally consuming at point P in Figure 3.18A as a result of the rise in interest rates, changes his allocation of consumption to P′ where present consumption has declined and future consumption has risen relative to their values at point P. That is because higher interest rates have reduced current consumption and raised current savings.

Figure 3.18B, however, portrays a contrasting picture. The very same rise in interest rates results in an increase in consumption and a fall in savings. The effect of the rise in the interest rates on saving is, therefore, ambiguous.

› A **substitution effect** indicates the change in consumption due solely to a change in the interest rate, and is measured along the initial indifference curve.

› An **income effect** is the change in consumption due to the change in purchasing power or income implicit in the change in the interest rate.

Economists explain the ambiguity by dividing the effect of the interest-rate increase into two parts—a SUBSTITUTION EFFECT and an INCOME EFFECT.

Let us consider the substitution effect. As consumption plus savings exhaust income, a decline in consumption must be matched by an equal rise in saving for a fixed income, $\Delta S_1 = -\Delta C_1$. The increased saving earns a rate of return r which adds to consumption in the next period, $\Delta C_2 = (1 + r)\Delta S_1$. A rise in the interest rate, thus, enables more future consumption and in effect has made future consumption cheaper relative to current consumption. Individuals thus substitute away from current consumption and increase future consumption. More technically, the substitution effect measures the change in the individual's desired allocation of present and future consumption when interest rates rise, assuming that individuals remain on the initial indifference curve. Along the original indifference curve, this implies a move from point P to Q where the slope of the indifference curve equals the new higher interest rate. As can be seen at point Q, the higher interest rate unambiguously leads to a reduction of C_1 and a rise in C_2, which means that savings rises. The effect of interest rate increase on savings is given in Table 3.2.

› The **substitution effect** of a rise in the interest rate causes current consumption to decline and savings to rise. The income effect is ambiguous. A net lender reduces savings and a net borrower increases savings.

The SUBSTITUTION EFFECT always tends to rise saving but the same is not true of the income effect. The impact of the income effect depends on whether the individual was a net lender or a net borrower. In panel A, the individual is a net borrower as consumption in the first period exceeds the individual's income, whereas in panel B, the individual is a net lender as consumption is

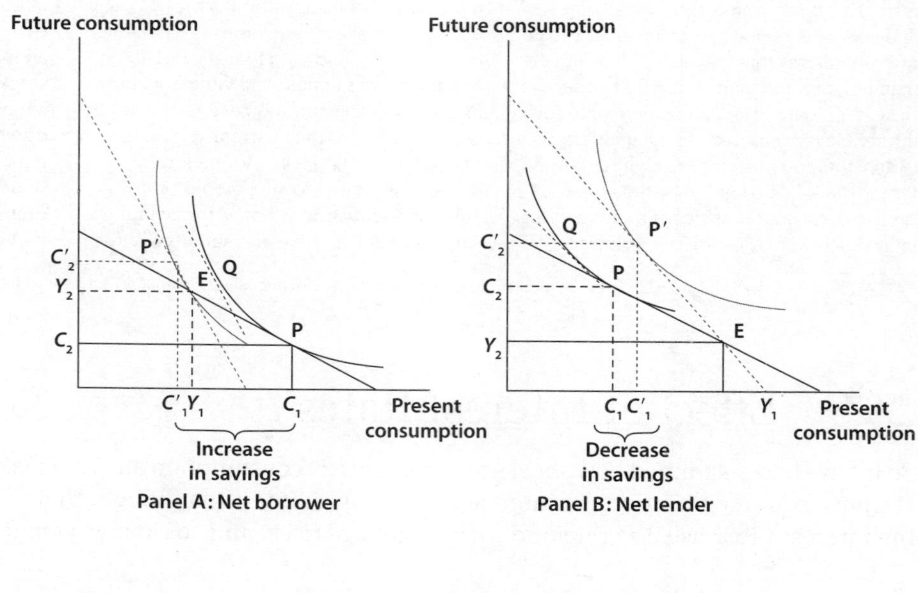

› **Figure 3.18**
Effect of Rise in Interest Rate. An increase in the interest rate increases savings only if the individual is a net borrower or if the substitution effect dominates the income effect.

	Net Lender	Net Borrower
Substitution effect	+	+
Income effect	–	+
Total effect	?	+

› **Table 3.2**
Effect of Interest Rate Increase on Savings

less than his first period income and lends that saving which contributes to the individual's future consumption. If the individual is initially a net lender (see Figure 3.18B), the rise in interest rates makes the individual richer. Note that in the situation when current consumption is unchanged, the individual can afford a higher level of future consumption due to the higher interest rate—the dashed new budget line around point P is above the solid budget line that indicates lifetime income prior to the change in the interest rate. The income effect of this increased allocation of future consumption, possible due to an expanded budget set, makes the individual richer, and the individual tends to raise the consumption levels of both C_2 and C_1. This is a positive income effect which is shown in Figure 3.18B as a shift from Q to P′, which raises current consumption C_1 and reduces savings.

If the individual is initially a net borrower (see Figure 3.18A), the rise in interest rates makes that individual poorer, as evidenced by the fact that with current consumption unchanged the individual can no longer afford the original level of C_1. This is because the new dashed budget line representing the rise in the interest rate is below the solid budget line prior to the change in interest rate. The income effect of this diminished allocation of current consumption, possible due to a contracted budget set, makes the individual poorer, and the individual tends to reduce the consumption levels of C_1. This is an income effect which is shown in Figure 3.18A as a shift from Q to P′, which reduces current consumption C_1 and raises savings.

The substitution effect, then, always causes individuals to transfer incomes to the future by increasing saving, as the rise in interest rate makes future consumption cheaper. The income effect reduces savings for net lenders and raises savings for net borrowers. The total effect of a rise in interest rates is to raise or lower savings for an individual who is a lender, depending on whether the substitution or income effect dominates. For an individual who is a borrower, the rise in interest rates unambiguously raises saving. The aggregate economy comprises a mix of borrowers and lenders. If the income effects of net borrowers and net lenders tend to cancel each other at the aggregate level, the substitution effect will dominate. It is this presumption about the offsetting income effects that generates the expectation that a rise in interest rates will reduce current consumption and raise aggregate saving. The empirical evidence backs up the validity of this presumption for developing countries.[13]

3.5 Aggregating Across Individuals

So far, we have looked at the decision to split the income between consumption and savings from the perspective of an individual's decision making. In the aggregate, individuals not only have different incomes but also belong to different age groups. When they are young, individuals have low incomes and tend to dissave (or incur debt) as they know they will be earning more later in their lives. During working years, incomes rise to reach a peak, at maybe just after middle age, and individuals repay their debts incurred earlier and save for their

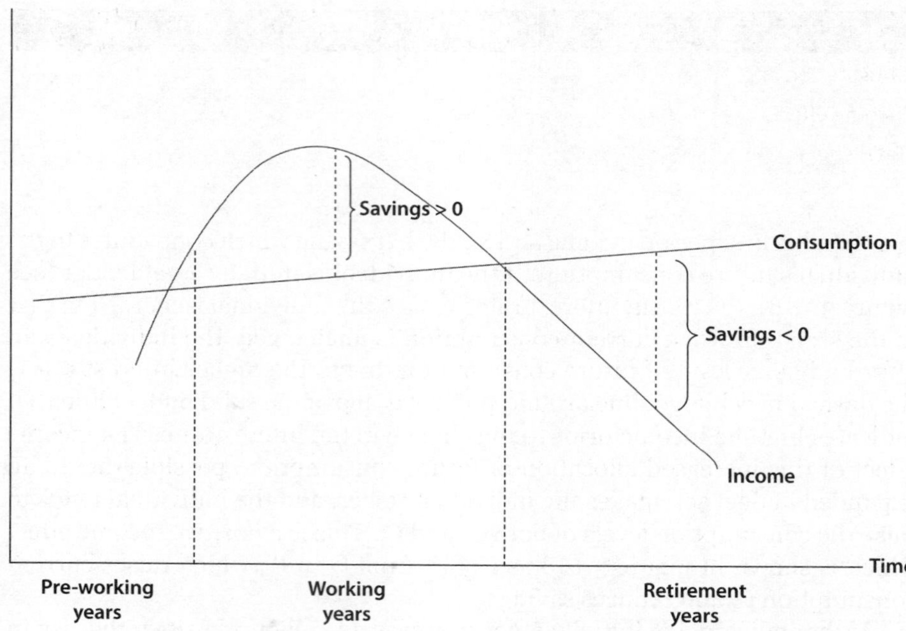

› **Figure 3.19** **Life-Cycle Income and Consumption.** Over the life cycle an individual tends to begin to be a net saver around the time of middle age. Dissaving is typical prior to joining the workforce and during retirement.

retirement years. When individuals finally reach the retirement phase of their lives (see Figure 3.19), their incomes due to them from past work (pensions) are much lower, and they top this up with incomes accruing from past savings to maintain a steady level of consumption. It was MODIGLIANI[14] who pointed out to this observation that there are two periods of dissaving in an individual's life—early years prior to working and retirement years—and that savings is, therefore, determined by one's stage in the life cycle.

› Franco **Modigliani** emphasized that the planning horizon of individuals is their lifetime, which in a two period set up includes a working period and a retirement period.

Figure 3.19 depicts the typical patterns of consumption, saving, and income across a person's life cycle. If we temporarily ignore the fact that an individual has a younger period of life (because we cannot use two dimensional graphs to depict three periods of life as shown in Figure 3.19), then, our two-period model with the current period as working years and the future period as retirement years can be used to understand the right hand two-thirds of Figure 3.19.

In Figure 3.20, higher incomes during working life relative to retirement life is depicted by the point E. Consumption smoothing makes individuals transfer income from working years (when incomes are larger) to provide for retirement (when incomes are smaller). The hump-shaped pattern of income over the life cycle as depicted in Figure 3.19 and represented by point E in Figure 3.20 generates a time path of consumption and savings that arises due to individuals pursuing consumption smoothing across time.

Aggregation across individuals is, therefore, complicated. Individuals differ in their preferences for consumption today versus consumption in the future, and they also differ in their stage in the life cycle. Young savers coexist with even younger and older dissavers. The aggregate saving in the economy is the outcome of the balance of saving and dissaving averaged over the entire population. In a static economy with no population growth as well as no growth in incomes per person, and with the young and old population evenly distributed, we could expect aggregate saving to be very low as the older generation would be dissaving at about the rate at which the young are saving for retirement.

In most economies, however, overall savings is positive—savings by the young exceeds dissaving by the old—due to population growth and a growth in output

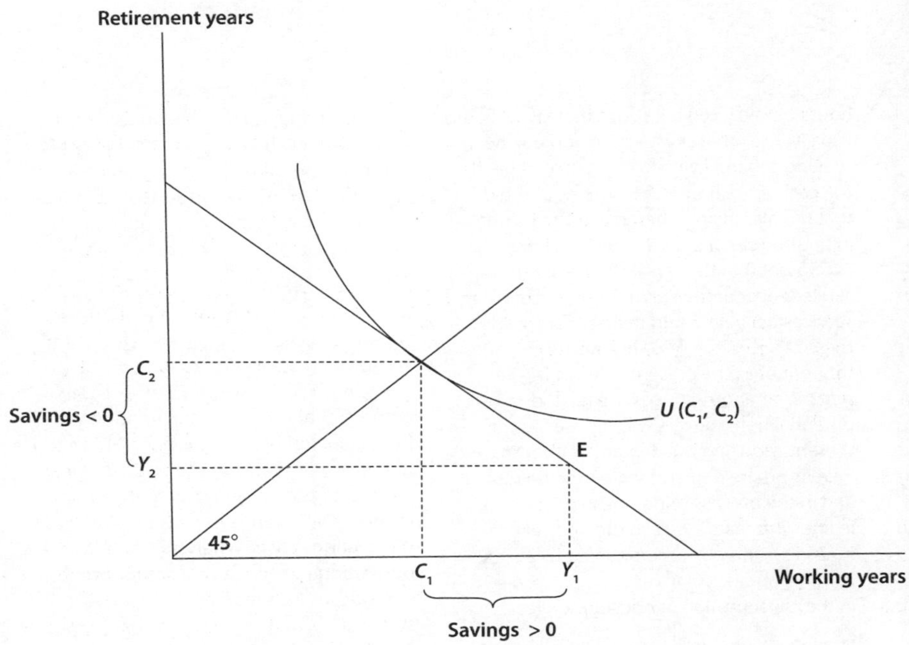

› **Figure 3.20**
Life-Cycle Income and Savings. Individuals save during working years so as to smooth consumption as income is low during retirement years.

per person, stemming from technological change that fosters improvements in productivity. So, demographic profile (as proxied by the DEPENDENCY RATE in a country—the proportion of the very young and the retired to the working population) and technical change are important determinants of aggregate savings. However, why some countries save at a very high rate while others save so little is still a topic that is being extensively researched. In 1987, for instance, aggregate savings to GDP was 34 per cent in Japan whilst it was just 14 per cent in the US, which prompted research into the causes for this.[15] Currently, the same question is being asked about the high saving rate in China, which is over 40 per cent of GDP. China's per capita income ranks below 100th in the world. Its savings rate, however, has been one of the highest worldwide in recent decades. Just before he passed away, Modigliani along with his co-author, Shi,[16] put together data to show (predictably) that income growth as it turned into a market-oriented economy has been the dominant factor behind the dramatic increase in China's saving rate, with demographic structure and inflation also having significant impacts.

› The **dependency rate** is the ratio of dependents (the young and the old population) to the working population.

We could summarize that in the aggregate, consumption is positively related to the aggregate level of disposable income as Keynes had indeed stated. However, as individuals are forward looking and the consumption decision is the outcome of rational decision making when individuals take into account the opportunities available both in the present and the future, consumption is related to permanent income which is a weighted average of the present value of current and future income. Aggregate consumption, then, also increases with an increase that is anticipated in future income. If future income is expected to decline, then current aggregate consumption also declines. An increase in the market rate of interest also causes current consumption to decline. Finally, life-cycle issues affect consumption and countries with a larger fraction of the population being young have lower aggregate consumption. Also, if a country experiences continuous productivity increases stemming from technological progress, then consumption increases along with the income that results from such productivity changes.

MACROFOCUS 3.3

House Prices and Consumption

Housing is a dominant component of wealth for many households, with more households owning homes than owning stocks. In many economies, house price rises have been accompanied by a consumption boom. For example, Barata and Pacheco* state that "the housing market appears to be more important than the stock market as a factor influencing consumption" and find that a 1 per cent increase in housing wealth leads to a 0.1 to 0.2 per cent increase in consumption for various European countries. In Taiwan, the savings rate reached a peak of 38.5 per cent of GDP in 1987, and subsequently dropped to a low of 24 per cent by 2001. The real average housing prices in Taiwan increased almost three times from 1987 to 1990 and then remained stable. Hseuh** found that the rise in house prices had a windfall effect on consumption in Taiwan.

An increase in house price may not impact positively on the consumption expenditure of all households through a wealth effect. (A wealth effect is the tendency of changes in asset prices to affect household wealth and their spending on consumption goods. As wealth is the value of assets minus liabilities such as outstanding debt, an increase in house prices being an increase in the value of real estate assets is an increase in wealth). A young household with limited savings is typically 'short' in housing services and must purchase these services in a spot market—it must rent in housing services—and/or it must save to make the initial down-payment on the house before it can take out a mortgage. Banks usually insist that prospective homeowners seeking a loan pay up front a percentage of the cost of the house. An older household that has already purchased a house is 'long' in housing services as a house is a long-lived asset that delivers a stream of housing services over time. With the value of housing services per year being the rent for leasing these services, the price of a house can be thought of as the present value of future rents. When house prices rise relative to rents, potential homebuyers will choose to rent, thereby reducing the demand for houses and increasing the demand for leasing on rent, and in the process bring house prices back in line with rents. A rise in the price of housing is thereby accompanied by a commensurate rise in rent or an increase in the consumption of housing services.

(1) For young homeowners who remain in their houses over the long term, the increase in house prices is roughly offset by the increase in the cost of housing services and there should be no impact on consumption. For older homeowners, the increase in their wealth is more than the cost of housing services over their remaining lives. If real estate can be used as collateral for borrowing, then an increase in the value of real estate will increase the value of collateral and with it the availability of funds for consumption. Consumption by older homeowners will increase. Campbell and Cocco† find that in the UK, there is a large positive effect of house prices on consumption for old households who are homeowners and a close to zero effect for young households. In the aggregate, then consumption may be responsive to house prices as older homeowners become an increasing fraction of the population.

(2) If homeowners cannot borrow by pledging their ownership of real estate as collateral (because banks are reluctant to accept such assets due to the difficulty of securing such assets in a weak legal enforcement regime), consumption will be unaffected by housing prices. Even those homeowners who want to trade down and consume less housing may find barriers in their way in terms of high moving and transactions costs. When transactions costs pertaining to service charges for brokers and document preparation by lawyers, stamp duty, and registration charges are significant (estimated as varying between 8 and 27 per cent of housing costs in India—NHB††), homeowners are unable to realize windfall capital gains and will not treat them as an increase in wealth or savings.

(3) In contrast, young households who intend purchasing a housing unit will have to save more to make a higher down payment for the house when house prices increase and their consumption declines.

(4) Those who view housing price increases to be so drastic that it makes it impossible for them to save enough money for the down-payment to buy a housing unit may respond by increasing their consumption.

*J. M. Barata and L. M. Pacheco, "Asset Prices and Monetary Policy: Wealth Effects on Consumption," *The Twentieth Symposium on Banking and Monetary Economics*, University of Birmingham, June 2003.

**L.M Hsueh, "The Relationship between Housing Price, Tenure Choice, and Saving Behaviour in Taiwan," *International Real Estate Review*, 3 (2001): 11–33.

†J. Y. Campbell, and J. F. Cocco, "How Do House Prices Affect Consumption? Evidence from Micro Data," *NBER Working Paper Series*, Report No. 11534 (August 2005).

††National Housing Bank, "Transaction Cost of Housing in India: An Analysis," Occasional Paper No. II (New Delhi: National Housing Bank, May 2007).

SUMMARY

- Keynes' fundamental psychological law of consumption states that an increase in disposable income is accompanied by an increase in consumption but of a smaller magnitude.
- The marginal propensity to consume is the incremental consumption arising from the increment to disposable income and is less than unity.
- The average propensity to consume is consumption per unit of disposable income. The marginal propensity to consume is less than the average propensity to consume.
- The average propensity to save or the savings rate rises with income.
- The variation in consumption is significantly less than the variation in disposable income.
- The consumption smoothing approach to consumption employs the decision framework that people choose rationally from amongst the opportunities available that one which best furthers their preferences for consumption today versus in the future and that people are forward looking.
- The intertemporal budget constraint represents the present discounted value of current and future income (life-cycle income).
- An individual exhibits positive (negative) time preference if they require more (less) than one unit of future consumption to compensate himself for the loss of a unit of current consumption. The rate of time preference declines as one moves downwards along an indifference curve.

- If the utility function is separable in consumption across time periods and if the marginal rate of time preference equals the interest rate, then consumption smoothing occurs.
- Consumption tilting is because the consumer's impatience for present versus future consumption is not equal to the interest rate at which income is discounted.
- Permanent income is that constant stream of income that gives the same lifetime income as the fluctuating income stream that occurs.
- Saving is the difference between current income and permanent income when consumption smoothing occurs.
- Savings declines when there is a temporary negative current shock or an anticipated positive future shock.
- Savings increases when there is an anticipated negative future shock or a temporary positive current shock.
- A rise in the interest rate increases savings for an individual who is a net borrower and has an ambiguous effect on an individual who is a net lender.
- Over the life cycle, there is a hump-shaped pattern of income causing individuals to transfer incomes via savings from working years to provide for retirement.

NOTES

1. John M. Keynes, "The General Theory of Employment, Interest and Money," *The Collected Writing of John Maynard Keynes* (London: Macmillan, 1992).
2. In the national accounts, there is a distinction between personal disposable income and private disposable income which we ignore here.
3. The data on consumption and disposable income contain a unit root but co-integration is rejected. Even when using instruments to correct for endogeneity, the GMM estimates are no different from the OLS estimates.
4. The national accounts in India do not report real personal disposable income. We have estimated this series using a comparison with real net national product at factor cost.
5. We should expect this because with a linear relation between C and Y^d, we should have Var $(C) = c^2$ Var (Y^d).
6. From Eq. (3.7), $C_t/C_{t-1} = 1.041$, or, $(C_t/C_{t-1}) - 1 = 0.041$. However, $(C_t/C_{t-1}) - 1 = (C_t - C_{t-1})/C_{t-1}$ which is the growth rate of consumption. This implies that consumption is growing at a steady rate of 4.1 per cent each period.
7. Simon Kuznets, "National Income, a Summary of Findings," (New York: National Bureau of Economic Research, 1946).
8. Note that as the slope of the budget line is $(1 + r)$, an indifference curve tangent at this slope implies a positive marginal rate of time preference.
9. From high school algebra, we know that when we have a function such as $y = \log x$, then the slope of this function or the amount by which there is a change in the variable y written as Δy, when there is a change in x (written as Δx, is given by $\Delta y/\Delta x = 1/x$.
10. Milton Friedman, *A Theory of the Consumption Function* (Princeton, NJ: Princeton University Press, 1957).
11. $C_t = 1.041C_{t-1}$ does not strictly indicate a marginal tilting of consumption and the patience of waiting for slightly more consumption in the future because of high dependency ratios (ratio of old to young and economically active population) and a higher share of a younger population in the demographic profile of the country. This is an issue that requires a more advanced treatment and we leave it as is.
12. A. Ando and F. Modigliani, "The 'Life Cycle' Hypothesis of Saving: Aggregate Implications and Tests," *American Economic Review*, no. 53(1) (March1963): 55–84).
13. A. Giovannini, "Savings and the Interest Rate in LDCs," *World Development*, (July 1983), 11(7), pp. 601–607.
14. F. Modigliani, "Life Cycle, Individual Thrift and the Wealth of Nations," Nobel Lecture, *American Economic Review*, (June 1986), 76(3), pp. 297–313.
15. F. Hayashi, "Why is Japan's Saving Rate So Apparently High?" In Stanley Fischer ed. *Macroeconomics Annual* (New York: National Bureau of Economic Research, 1986).
16. F. Modigliani, and L. C. Shi, "The Chinese Saving Puzzle and the Life-Cycle Hypothesis," *Journal of Economic Literature* 42(1) (March 2004): 145–170.

TEST YOURSELF

1. Suppose the consumption function (in INR billion) for a closed economy is $C = 20 + .8Y^d$. Suppose also that disposable income increases from INR 50 billion to INR 150 billion. By how much would the consumption rise? By how much would the savings rise? What has happened to the savings rate?
2. If current income is INR 100 billion and future income is INR 150 billion and the rate of interest is 20 per cent, draw the intertemporal budget constraint associated with this stream of income. What is the slope of this constraint? Indicate the point on this constraint that depicts the income stream.
3. When does an individual use consumption smoothing and when does his consumption tilt?
4. What is permanent income and how can we determine the savings behaviour on the basis of this?
5. Demonstrate how a temporary current positive shock to income and an anticipated negative future shock affect the consumption behaviour.

6. Show how a decline in the interest rate affects the savings behaviour of a net borrower and a net lender.
7. If the labour ministry decides to rise the age of retirement by a few years because of an increase in longevity, what would be the impact on the current savings in the economy?
8. What sort of marginal rate of time preference would you expect a cricketer like Sachin Tendulkar—who is towards the end of his career—to have and why?
9. Suppose there are two time periods— in Period 1, income is given by INR 200 thousand. In Period 2, it is INR 110 thousand. The rate of interest is 10 per cent. If consumption in Period 1 is INR 150 thousand, is the individual consumption smoothing or consumption tilting?
10. Two youngsters A and B have similar qualifications and earn the same income. However, A comes from a family with a longer history of coronary problems and expects to die at an earlier age. Who will have a higher present consumption and why?

ONLINE APPLICATION

1. Go to the web site of the Reserve Bank of India (URL: www.rbi.org.in/home.aspx). Click on the "Database" icon. Then, click on "Handbook of Statistics on Indian Economy".
2. Click on the Table 2, "Macroeconomic aggregates (at constant prices)". Download data on NDP at factor cost from 1980–1981 to 2009–2010. From Table 1, "Macroeconomic aggregates (at current prices)", download data on population for the same period. Data on population are in millions unlike the aggregate income data which are in rupees crore. Find NDP at factor cost per capita.
3. Click on Table 3a, "Components of Gross Domestic Product (at market prices)" and download data on Private Final Consumption Expenditure at constant prices for the period 1980–1981 to 2009–2010. Find Private Consumption Expenditure per capita.
4. In what way is NDP at factor cost different from Personal Disposable Income? See Statement 4 of the National Accounts Statistics which shows this accounting relationship on the web page of the Central Statistical Organisation. (URL: www.mospi.nic.in/mospi_cso_rept_pubn.htm) Unfortunately, personal disposable income data is only available in current prices and so cannot be used unless we deflate it appropriately. For our purposes, we will use NDP at factor cost as an indicator of private disposable income. This understates private disposable income by about 3.8 per cent.
5. Find out the average propensity to consume and draw a graph of this. Interpret this graph in terms of what it states about the behaviour of savings in India.
6. You have calculated the average propensity to consume on the assumption that direct taxes do not vary with income—as it is consumption out of income and not disposable income that you have calculated. To what extent would your calculation be incorrect if this assumption were not true?

Appendix 3.1 Indifference Curves

Consumer preferences are given by utility functions. Consider a world with only two goods, X and Y. The utility function *U*(X, Y) is a preference ordering for a consumer that ranks all possible combinations of the two goods in order of preference. When we say that a consumer is able to rank different combinations of the two goods, all that is being stated is that the consumer is able to make statements about their relative desirability. The consumer is not required to make a precise quantitative statement about how much more satisfaction one combination of the two goods (say, 3 units of X and 2 units of Y) gives over another combination of the two goods (say, 2 units of X and 3 units of Y). A preference ordering only ranks the combinations of goods.

Four properties that preference orderings are assumed to have are the following:

1. Completeness: A preference ordering is considered to be complete if the consumer can rank all possible combinations of goods. Suppose there are only two goods and there are two combinations of the two goods, A (consisting of 3 units of X and 2 units of Y) and B (consisting of 2 units of X and 3 units of Y). Then, the consumer should be in a position to make one of three possible statements about the two combinations of goods given by A and B: (i) A is preferred to B, (ii) B is preferred to A, or (iii) the consumer is indifferent between A and B as they are considered to be equally attractive combinations of the two goods X and Y. A person who can rank all combinations of goods is a person who knows their mind and so can make evaluations about the relative attractiveness of different combinations of goods.
2. Non-satiation: This property of a preference ordering states that, other things equal, an individual always prefers more of a good to less. Individuals are never satisfied and as long as there are no restrictions on individuals getting rid of any surplus goods they do not want, having more of a good will surely not make them worse off.
3. Transitivity: This property states that if there are three combinations of the two goods given by A, B, and C, and if the individual prefers A to B and prefers B to C, then it must be the case that the individual prefers A to C. Similarly, if it turns out that the individual is indifferent between A and B, and the individual is also indifferent between B and C, then, the individual is indifferent between A and C. This assumption is justified in that it negates the possibility of the chance that a person is made a sucker. For instance, consider a person with intransitive preferences. Suppose the person prefers *A* to B and B to C. The person also prefers C to A. Then, start with an initial position where the person currently has the combination of goods given by C. Since B is preferred to C, the person will be willing to pay a small amount to obtain B. Now with an endowment of B the person will also be willing to make a small payment to obtain A as A is preferred to B. Finally, since C is preferred to A, the person will be willing to pay a small amount to exchange the combination of goods given by A to obtain the combination C. The individual has made a series of three payments and ended up with exactly the same combination of goods they had initially. Surely an individual is better off retaining the combination of goods and not trading. It is to eliminate the possibility of such preferences that go against the self interest of the individual that transitivity is assumed.
4. Convexity: This assumption is made to rule out extreme preferences. Convexity requires that if you are indifferent between the combinations of

goods given by A and B, then, you will prefer a combination of goods that contains any fraction of A (say 1/3) and the residual fraction (2/3) of B to either combination A or combination B. This assumption captures the notion of the attribute of individuals of a sense of balance, where having both goods are preferred over extreme preferences that only want one good and there is never an inclination for the other good.

These properties of preference orderings are used to generate indifference curves that represent consumer preferences. In Figure A3.1.1, consider the combination of goods X and Y as depicted by point A in the diagram. The assumption of non-satiation implies that all combinations of goods to the north-east of point A and lying in the region to the right of the vertical line PA and above the horizontal line AQ which represent more of both goods will be preferred to point A. The same assumption of non-satiation implies that all combinations of goods inside the rectangle ORAS will be less preferred than the combination at A simply because point A gives more of both goods. We can then state that non-satiation implies that point E is preferred to point A and in turn point A is preferred to point D.

Draw a straight line joining points D and E. Consider the combinations of goods as we move along this straight line from point D towards point E. Point D is less preferred to point A, that is, less preferred to point E. As we move along the straight line till we approach the vertical line AS, it is the case that all points on the line DE will be less preferred to point A as they represent less of both goods than at point A. As the straight line leaves the intersection with the vertical line AS, the axiom of completeness will allow us to compare each point with point A. Either such points on the line DE will be less preferred to A, or they will be more preferred than A, or, it will be the case that the individual is indifferent between the point on the line and point A. Points on the line close to point E are preferred to point A and points close to point D are less preferred than point A. Then logically as we move along the line from point D towards point E we are slowly transiting from points that are less preferred than point A to points that are more preferred than point A. Somewhere along the line then there must be a point that separates points that are less preferred than A from points that are more preferred over the combination of goods at A. Such a point, which we label as point B, will be a point where the individual is indifferent between the combination of goods at B and the combination at A. Non-satiation implies that points to the right of B on the line DE will represent situations where more of both goods are available and so will be preferred over

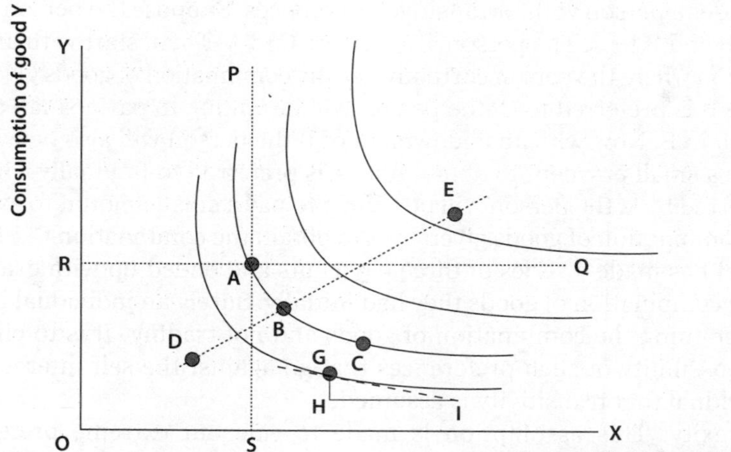

› Figure A3.1.1 Construction of Indifference Curves. Using the assumption of non-satiation, point A is preferred to point D and point E is preferred to point A. As we transit along the straight line from D to E, we move from points that are less preferred to A towards points that are more preferred to A. At some point in the transit then we will arrive at a point such as B where the individual is indifferent between the goods available at B and those available at A. We can find a point C in a similar manner. Then, the points A, B, and C lie on an indifference curve that represents the same level of utility or satisfaction obtained from the consumption of the combinations of goods that are available along the curve. Similar curves above the indifference curve ABC represent higher levels of utility and those curves below represent lower levels of utility.

point B. Similarly, points below and to the left of B will represent combinations of goods that are less preferred than the goods at point B.

Having found point B, which is indifferent to point A, we can, in a similar way, find another point C that the individual finds to be a point of indifference with or equally as attractive as point B. Now we can apply the assumption of transitivity. Since the individual is indifferent between points A and B and is also indifferent between points B and C, it must be the case that the individual is indifferent between points A and C. Continuing this process, we can find other such points like A, B, and C that represent combinations of goods which the individual finds equally attractive or is indifferent between. Joining all such points gives the INDIFFERENCE CURVE that depicts the various combinations of the two goods X and Y that the individual finds equally attractive or is indifferent between. Indifference curves are labelled with the help of utility functions. The utility function assigns an index or rank to a combination of goods. The various combinations of goods along an indifference curve being equally attractive have the same rank or index of valuation or utility.

› An **indifference curve** is a set of combinations of goods that the individual prefers equally. The utility associated with any point on an indifference curve is therefore constant.

Now take a combination of the two goods as represented by point G. The point G depicts less of both goods than available at point C. Point G will then be less preferred to point C and a point that is less preferred will be associated with lesser utility. We can find other points that represent combinations of the two goods which the individual prefers equally to point G (in a similar manner that we did for point A). Joining such points will give the indifference curve through point G. The indifference curve through G will be associated with a level of utility that is less than the utility associated with the indifference curve through point C. Generally, combinations of goods that lie below an indifference curve are less preferred and have lower utility whilst combinations of goods that lie above an indifference curve are more preferred and have higher utility.

The assumption of completeness implies that for each combination of the two goods that we may choose in the figure, there will be an indifference curve that will pass through it. We then can generate many indifference curves—called an indifference map—that represent the consumer's preferences. In Figure A3.1.1, we have depicted only four such indifference curves. As we move in the north eastern direction along an indifference map, we encounter indifference curves that represent combinations of goods with more of the goods in each combination and thereby associated with higher levels of utility or satisfaction. The indifference map is a complete description of the preferences of the consumer. If we want to know how the individual ranks any two combinations of goods, it is required that we compare the utility associated with the indifference curves associated with those combinations of goods. The combination of goods with higher utility or goods lying on a higher indifference curve will be ranked higher or preferred more by the individual.

The rate at which a consumer is willing to exchange or trade off one good for another is described by the slope of an indifference curve. Suppose the individual is at the point G. If we take away an amount of good X represented by the distance HI from the individual, then, how much of the other good Y would we have to give to the individual so as to make him exactly as well off as before? We would have to compensate the individual with GH units of good Y so that they are able to attain the same level of preferences or utility. The change in utility when we take away (or provide) one unit of a good is known as the MARGINAL UTILITY, written as MU. If HI units of the good X are taken away then the total change in utility is $-HI \times MU_X$. The minus sign depicts the loss of good X to the extent of HI units of X. With GH units of good Y provided to the

› The additional utility gained from consuming an additional unit of a good is known as the **marginal utility**.

individual to compensate for the loss of good X, the change in utility associated with this will be $GH \times MU_Y$. Since the loss of X is compensated for with a gain in Y in a manner such that there is no change in utility, it must be the case that:

$$GH \times MU_X = -HI \times MU_X$$

or

$$-\frac{GH}{HI} = \frac{MU_X}{MU_Y}$$

The ratio of *GH* to *HI* is the ratio of a vertical distance to a horizontal distance, which is the definition of the slope of a line. The slope of the line associated with these vertical and horizontal distances is the dashed line through point G, that is, a tangent to the indifference curve passing through G. Hence,

$$\text{Slope of Indifference Curve} = \frac{MU_X}{MU_Y}$$

› The **marginal rate of substitution** is the slope of an indifference curve and is the ratio of marginal utilities. It is the rate at which the individual is willing to substitute or trade off or exchange one good for another such that there is no change in the level of satisfaction or utility.

The absolute value of the slope of an indifference curve—MU_X/MU_Y—is the rate at which an individual is willing to exchange or trade off one good for another. In economics literature, this is referred to as the MARGINAL RATE OF SUBSTITUTION (MRS). The MRS is the rate at which an individual is willing to substitute one good for another without changing the total level of satisfaction or utility that is obtained from the consumption of the goods.

Appendix 3.2 Borrowing Constraints

In the lifecycle model of consumption, individuals synchronize their income and preferred consumption profiles by borrowing and lending at a single rate of interest, r. However, capital markets are not perfect and usually impose quantitative restrictions on borrowings, or charge higher interest rates on borrowings than the rate at which individuals lend to the capital markets when they place their savings in various financial instruments. For instance, if you place your savings in a bank deposit, the interest rate you will receive is much less than that you would pay if you were to borrow an identical sum of money from the bank. Borrowing constraints prohibit individuals from consuming today the income they would receive in the future.

To understand the role played by capital market imperfections assume that loans and savings instruments are available at constant, but unequal rates of interest. The interest rate at which the individual lends to the capital market when he puts his savings into financial instruments, r_L, or the interest rate received on lending, will be taken to be smaller than the interest rate at which he can take a loan or borrow from the capital market, r_B. When the individual is a net lender, then his consumption in Period 1 must be less than income, $C_1 \leq Y_1$, and $(Y_1 - C_1)$ is the amount loaned to the capital market at interest rate r_L. If the individual is a net borrower, he is consuming more than his current income, $C_1 > Y_1$, and $(C_1 - Y_1)$ is the amount of borrowing from the capital market at interest rate r_B. The interest rate faced by an individual can then be written as

$$r = \begin{cases} r_L & \text{if } C_1 \leq Y_1 \\ r_B > r_L & \text{if } C_1 > Y \end{cases}$$

This implies that the intertemporal budget constraint is truncated about the point (Y_1, Y_2)—the coordinates representing current and future income. All

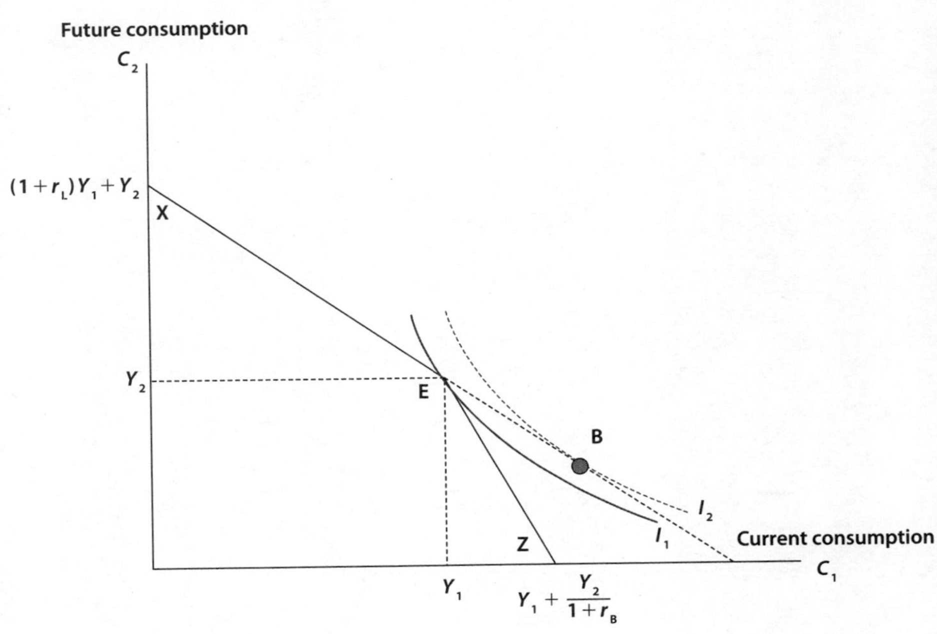

› **Figure A3.2.1 Borrowing Constraints and Consumption.** The presence of borrowing constraints with the interest rate on borrowing larger than the interest rate on lending results in the budget constraint XEZ. An individual who would have preferred to consume at point B, where he would have borrowed against future income is now forced to limit his consumption by the amount of current income and consume at point E.

points to the left of point E that depicts incomes (Y_1, Y_2) in Figure A3.2.1 are points where current consumption is given by $C_1 \leq Y_1$ and r_L is the operative interest rate.

All points to the right of point E depict current consumption, where $C_1 > Y_1$ and the operative interest rate is the borrowing rate $r_B > r_L$. The locus XEZ then depicts the budget constraint of the individual with the segment XE having a slope given by $1 + r_L$ and the slope of the segment EZ is $1 + r_B$.

Let the indifference curves of the individual be given by I_1 and I_2 in Figure A3.2.1. The individual's maximizing choice of consumption would be at point B where the slope of the indifference curve equals the slope of the dashed budget line that represents borrowing and lending at a uniform interest rate in perfect capital markets of $r = r_L$. When capital markets are imperfect, individuals are forced to operate along the locus XEZ and their preferences are maximized at a lower utility level at point E. The individual is then able to consume only up to his current income and cannot finance consumption beyond this by borrowing against the prospect of future income. Of course, if the indifference curves of the individual were tangential along the segment XE, then the presence of borrowing constraints does not affect the optimal consumption decision of the individual. The presence of borrowing constraints implies that consumption is driven by current income, and life-cycle income may have a marginal impact on consumption behaviour.

4

Investment

CRITICAL QUESTIONS

- » *What is the cost of employing the factor input of physical capital for a firm?*
- » *How does the firm select the optimal stock of capital?*
- » *What is Tobin's marginal Q?*
- » *What are the determinants of investment in housing and inventory?*
- » *How does the irreversibility of investment affect the decision to invest now rather than later?*
- » *What are the other circumstances applicable to developing countries that affect investment behaviour?*

4.1 Profit Maximization and the Optimal Capital Stock

When using the term "capital", people usually associate it with the finance that is required to run a business. Finance involves the use and acquisition of funds from bank loans, bond sales, and the sale of stock in equity markets for business projects. It enables a business to acquire and organize factors of production that produce the output, which is then sold in the market with the intention of generating a profit for the business. Financial capital is distinct from physical capital. Financial capital is essentially money, or some other form of paper asset or security (such as a bank loan, a bond, or a share) that functions as contracts for the exchange of commodities or money. Physical capital, on the other hand, is a piece of productive equipment that is long lived. An example of this is a lathe or Xerox machine which generates a flow of productive services over time. In this chapter, we will be directly concerned with real or physical capital—capital as a factor of production.

A firm or business requires capital inputs along with other inputs such as labour (N) so that it can produce an output that is sold on the market. Suppose the firm was to hire capital equipment and use it in the production process. For simplicity, let us assume that the firm operates in competitive markets where it can sell all its output at the going market price, p, and it can hire any amount of capital it wishes at a rental rate of k per year. To see how this rental rate could be determined, put yourself in the position of a business organization that rents out machines. Let us say that the purchase price of a particular machine is INR 100, and the interest rate at which money can be borrowed or loaned is 10 per cent per annum. In order to cover the OPPORTUNITY COST of the INR 100 tied up in the machine, you would have to charge INR 10 per year for it. There will be additional costs as well. A machine loses some of its value each year. This is partly because newer and more efficient machines are designed each year and existing machines lose economic value when this happens. This is a situation referred to as technological obsolescence. Also, as the machine is used, it undergoes wear and tear, and needs maintenance. Sometimes, parts could even require replacement. The effect of this physical wear and tear and technological obsolescence could result in the price of the machine to fall by, say, INR 20 per year. At the very minimum, then, you would be willing to supply the machine in the market for services of capital inputs at a cost of INR 30 per year—INR 10 in forgone interest and INR 20 in lost market value. Generalizing, let δ stand for physical and technological depreciation, expressed as a fraction of the price of the capital good, and r denote the market rate of the interest expressed in decimal form. Then, the annual rental rate on capital, K, will be given by,

> The **opportunity cost** of a factor is what it could have earned in an alternative use. Here it is the cost of services from the machine measured in terms of the forgone alternative earnings if instead the money was put into a bank that paid interest on it.

$$K = r + \delta$$

The unit cost to the firm of hiring capital equipment is then given by,

$$p^K K = p^K (r + \delta)$$

where p^K is the supply price at which the capital good may be purchased. $p^K (r + \delta)$ is the UNIT CAPITAL RENTAL or the user cost of capital.

> The **rental cost of capital** also referred to as the user cost of capital is the cost of using capital over a given period of time (a year) and is the sum of the real interest rate and depreciation rate into the unit price of the capital good.

The other FACTOR OF PRODUCTION that the firm hires is labour, (N man-days) which is paid compensation in the form of a wage rate of INR w per man-day. The total input costs incurred by the firm can then be written as,

$$\text{Total Cost} = wN + p^K (r + \delta)K \tag{4.1}$$

> We are considering only primary **factors of production,** or, inputs that facilitate production but neither become a part of the product or get significantly transformed in the process of production (as occurs with intermediate inputs). A primary factor that we also do not explicitly consider for simplicity is land.

The compensation to labour, wN, is referred to as a variable cost and the cost of capital, $p^K(r+\delta)K$, is the fixed cost of production. In what follows, we simplify the discussion by assuming that the firm has static expectations regarding all prices and the interest rate, and technology is constant.[1] Numerous alternative combinations of capital and labour can be hired by the firm towards the production of the output. The PRODUCTION FUNCTION specifies how much output Y we get when we employ specific quantities of K and N. This may be expressed as

› The **production function** describes how inputs like capital and labour are transformed into output.

$$Y = F(K, N) \tag{4.2}$$

A property of the production function is that it is subject to diminishing marginal productivity. As we add more of a factor of production, with the other inputs held fixed, the resulting increments to output will eventually diminish. This property of a production function can be stated in terms of the MARGINAL PRODUCT (MP) of a factor of production, defined as the resulting change in output when an additional unit of the input is hired (with no change in the amount of the other input used). For instance, the marginal product of capital, MP_K, is the increment to output when an additional unit of capital is hired. Diminishing marginal productivity of capital is, then, the diminishing tendency for the increment to output with the hiring of additional units of capital.

› The **marginal product** is the change in output that occurs in response to a unit change in the application of an input.

The firm selects that level of output which maximizes profits. Given the firms' objective is profit (Π) maximization, this requires,

$$\text{Max } \Pi = \text{Total Revenue} - \text{Total Cost}$$
$$= pY - \text{Total Cost}$$

Substituting the input cost function given by Eq. (4.1) into the profit function, we may write this as,

$$\text{Max } \Pi = pF(K, N) - wN - p^K(r+\delta)K$$

In this equation, for a given output price (p) and given input prices [w, $p^K(r+\delta)$], maximizing profits is akin to selecting the amount of employment and capital stock that produces the output, that, when sold, gives the firm maximum profits. In what follows, we focus on the capital stock decision that informs us as to what choice of stock of capital results in an output that maximizes profits to the firm.

An additional unit of capital will cost the firm $p^K(r+\delta)$, and it will produce an additional output given by the marginal product of capital, MP_K. This additional output generates revenue to the firm. This is given by the price times the additional output produced and sold, pMP_K. So long as the additional revenue pMP_K exceeds the additional cost $p^K(r+\delta)$, the input is adding more to the revenue than the cost of the input, and the firm will continue to hire additional units of the input. Thus, capital will be hired as long as the additional benefit from adding to the stock of capital exceeds the additional cost incurred to add to the stock of capital, or, as long as,

$$pMP_K > p^K(r+\delta)$$

or,

$$\frac{pMP_K}{p^K(r+\delta)} > 1 \tag{4.3}$$

The optimal stock of capital to deploy in production is then given by the condition[2] where the marginal benefit of doing so equals the marginal cost, or,

$$pMP_K = p^K(r+\delta) \tag{4.4}$$

Similarly, labour will be hired till the additional revenue it generates will equal the additional cost of the labour, or,

$$pMP_K = w \tag{4.5}$$

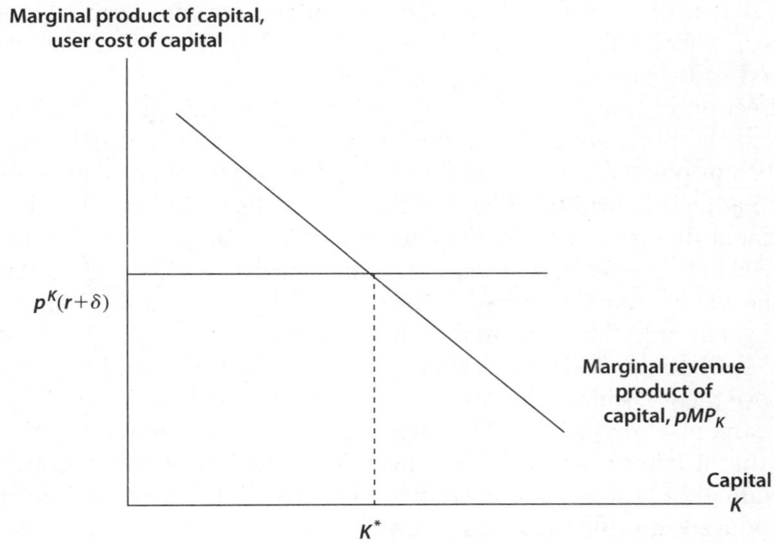

› **Figure 4.1**
Optimal Stock of Capital. The additional benefit from employing an additional unit of capital is the marginal revenue product of capital. The additional cost of employing an additional unit of capital is the user cost of capital. Profit is maximized by employing K^* units of capital, where the marginal revenue product equals the user cost.

Hence, profit maximization by the firm requires it to select that capital stock and employment levels where the additional revenue generated by these inputs equals the marginal cost of putting these inputs into producing an output.

The optimal stock of capital that a firm which maximizes profits should employ is depicted in Figure 4.1. As the marginal product of capital (MP_K) diminishes with additions to the stock of capital, and the output price is given to the firm, pMP_K, or the additional revenue generated from employing an additional unit of capital decreases as the stock of capital is increased. In Figure 4.1, this is depicted by the downward sloping curve, labeled as the marginal revenue product of capital curve and it is the diagrammatic counterpart of the left hand side of Eq. (4.4). The right hand side of Eq. (4.4) is the user cost of capital that is taken as given by the firm, and it is the horizontal line in Figure 4.1. The OPTIMAL stock of capital, K^*, then, is arrived at in the diagram as the solution to the profit maximizing condition stated in Eq. (4.4). The firm that is a profit maximizer, and which asks itself how much of the input capital to hire, would get the answer at K^* of capital.

› For the interested reader, the Appendix 4.1 derives the **optimal** stock of capital when the production function takes a particular form known as the Cobb–Douglas production function.

4.2 Adjustment Costs and Investment Decisions

Up to now we have proceeded by considering how much capital the firm should hire when it seeks to maximize profits. However, a distinguishing feature of capital is that whereas other inputs are normally hired on a period-by-period basis, capital equipment is usually owned outright by the firm. Rather than paying a rental of equal installments per period over the capital equipment's life, the firm purchases the capital equipment outright at a cost of p^K.[3]

The second thing to note about our discussion is that, so far, it was concerned solely with finding out the optimal capital stock that the firm should acquire in order to maximize profits. If the actual capital stock at any moment in time differs from the optimum capital stock, i.e., $K_t \neq K^*$, then at what speed should the firm go about acquiring new capital stock? Should it acquire capital slowly or should it adjust its capital stock to the optimal level immediately? Recall that investment is the change in capital stock, and so another way of stating this is that with a divergence between actual and optimum capital stock, we can have investment at any rate between zero and infinity. The theory we have followed so far advises us about the adjustment to the stock of capital and the direction of that adjustment. It does not, however, prescribe the speed at which the process should evolve. It is a STATIC THEORY that helps us locate equilibrium positions, and it is silent about movements between equilibria. How to adjust the capital stock is a topic that falls within the jurisdiction of investment theory, which, accordingly, must be dynamic. It informs us about the speed at which we should acquire capital when a new stock of capital other than the current one is required in the pursuit of profit maximization.

› **Capital theory** informs about the optimal stock of capital to be used as an input. It does not indicate the speed at which the stock of capital should be acquired, which is a dynamic problem that belongs to the realm of the theory of investment.

To get around the problem that firms should instantaneously adjust their capital stock to the desired level, a partial adjustment mechanism is added to the above theory, which talks about the choice of capital stock to yield a model of investment. Proponents of this approach, such as Eisner and Strotz (1963), argue that it takes time to put new machinery into place, to integrate it into the production process, and to train workers to use the new machinery. This is introduced into the theory as a convex COST OF ADJUSTMENT. For low levels of investment, these adjustment costs are low, but the costs rise more than proportionately with the level of investment. This implies a cost of adjustment, $\phi(I)$, which is given by the following equation that is graphed in Figure 4.2:

› **Adjustment costs** are the costs of integrating new capital goods into the production process. The larger the investment, the larger will be the cost of adjustment.

$$\phi(I) = \frac{b}{2} p^K I^2 \tag{4.6}$$

If investment is increased by the amount OA in Figure 4.2, the adjustment cost of doing this is given by AB. Doubling the investment to OC causes adjustment cost to increase to CD which is more than double the adjustment cost AB. It is the presence of steeply rising adjustment costs that inhibits undertaking investment activity in one go in order to attain the optimal stock of capital in a firm. The marginal cost of adjustment resulting from an increase in investment by the firm is given by Eq. (4.6) by $bp^K I$. This rises with the cost of investment, $p^K I$, as well as that of parameter b that indicates how steeply adjustment costs rise with the level of investment. An increase in b will cause

› **Figure 4.2**
Adjustment Costs of Investment. Adjustment costs rise more than proportionately with the level of investment.

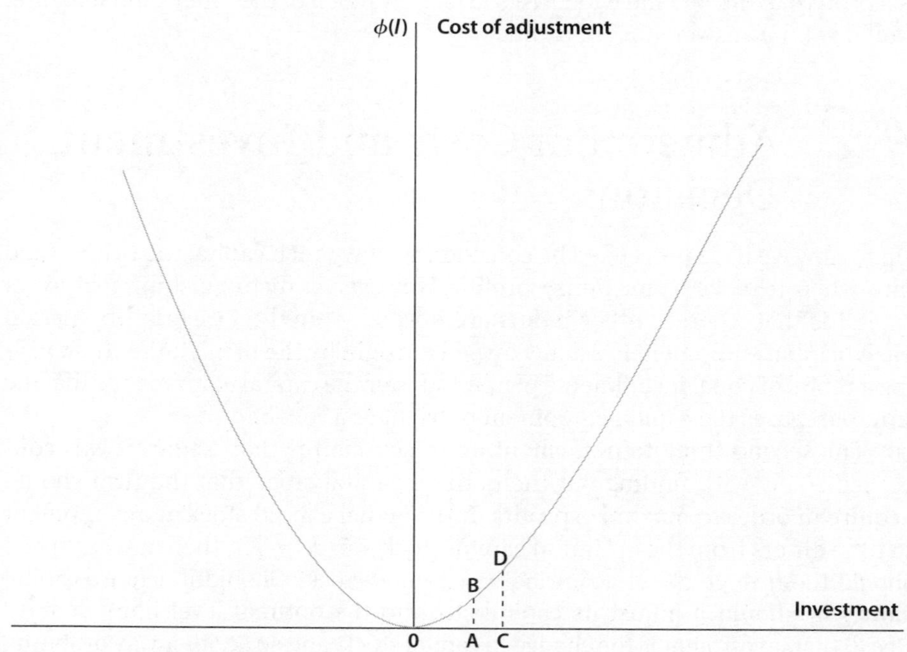

the adjustment cost curve in Figure 4.2 to be steeper, or adjustment costs will rise faster for any given level of investment that is undertaken.

The cost of current investment activities, thus, has two elements—current expenditure on purchasing capital goods, $p^K I_t$, and the adjustment costs, $\phi(I_t)$, incurred in absorbing increases in its productive capacity. Thus, the total cost to the firm of investment activities at time t is given by $p^K I_t + (b/2)p^K I_t^2$.

The motivation of the firm for increasing its capital stock is that the new capital will bolster the firm's rate of product not only in the current period, but also in the future. That extra output will enhance the firm's total revenue in the coming years. We ignore that there is a maintenance cost of the new capital, and that at the end of its economic life it will have a scrap value.

To keep things simple, we proceed by assuming that output is produced solely from the capital stock and that employment does not enter the picture. Fortunately, the result we are about to derive regarding the determinants of investment continue to hold even when we take into account the level of employment in the firm. To keep the exposition simple, then, we ignore the decision to hire the other primary input, labour. The output produced in that case is given by $Y = F(K)$. Our conclusion is also not affected if we allow the production function to be linear—output is a linear function of the capital stock. Therefore, for simplicity, we allow the production function to be linear:

$$Y = F(K) = AK \tag{4.7}$$

where, A is a constant. In this case, the marginal product of capital is given by,

$$MP_K = A \tag{4.8}$$

The marginal product results from noting that if we start out with no capital stock, $K = 0$, and no production, $Y = 0$, and then increase the capital stock by one unit, $K = 1$, the corresponding output is $Y = A$. Hence the increase in output as a result of an increase in the stock of capital by one unit or the marginal product of capital is A. We may alternatively write the production function as,

$$Y = AK = MP_K K$$

This states that the total output is the output produced by one unit of capital or MP_K times the number of units of capital K employed in production. The firm is the usual profit maximizer—it maximizes the present value of profits resulting from the sale of the output produced by the firm. The revenue that the firm earns when the price level is given by p is $pY = pMP_K K$. However, the capital stock depreciates at a constant rate of δ in each period, and for the period $t + 1$ the capital stock K_{t+1}, is the undepreciated capital stock plus gross investment, or,

$$K_{t+1} = (1 - \delta)K_t + I_t \tag{4.9}$$

The capital stock K_t depreciates at the rate δ so that the undepreciated capital stock at the end of period t is $(1 - \delta)K_t$. In addition, there is an addition to the stock of capital in period t given by the amount of investment undertaken, I_t. At the beginning of period $t + 1$, then, the stock of capital K_{t+1} is that given by Eq. (4.9).

We begin the analysis in time period 0 where new investment I_0 is undertaken at a cost of $p^K I_0 + (b/2)p^K I_0^2$, that contributes to the output of subsequent periods (see Table 4.1). This investment has a gestation of one time period and begins to produce an output from period $t = 1$. In order to focus on a single investment decision, we take it that the firm makes no subsequent investments in later time periods. At time $t = 1$, the capital stock produces an output that

Time Period	Capital Stock	Investment	Cost of Investment	Value of Output
$t = 0$	0	I_0	$p^k I_0 + \frac{b}{2} p^k I_0^2$	0
$t = 1$	$K_1 = I_0$	0	0	$pMP_K K_1$
$t = 2$	$K_2 = (1-\delta)K_1$	0	0	$pMP_K K_2 = pMP_K K_1 (1-\delta)$
$t = 3$	$K_3 = (1-\delta)K_2 = (1-\delta)^2 K_1$	0	0	$pMP_K K_3 = pMP_K K_1 (1-\delta)^2$
–	–	–	–	–

Note: $K_{t+1} = (1-\delta)K_t + I_t$

› **Table 4.1**
Investment, Capital Stock, and Output over Time

results in a revenue of $pY_1 = pMP_K K_1$ to the firm. As the investment decision is taken in $t = 0$, the present value of the discounted revenue to the firm, when discounted at the rate $(1 + r)$, yields $pMP_K K_1/(1 + r)$ of revenue in present value terms at time $t = 0$.

In the next time period, $t = 2$, the capital stock depreciates at the rate δ, so that output in that period is produced from an input of the period $t = 1$ capital stock that now equals $K_1(1 - \delta)$. At time $t = 2$, the total revenue earned from the output produced by the capital stock is $pMP_K K_1(1 - \delta)$ and we discount this at rate $(1 + r)^2$ to get the present discounted value of revenue earned in $t = 2$ of $pMP_K K_1(1 - \delta)/(1 + r)^2$.

In a similar way, at $t = 3$, the capital stock $K_1(1 - \delta)$ depreciates again by δ, so the output at that time is produced from a capital input given by $K_1(1 - \delta)^2$. The present discounted value of revenue earned at $t = 3$ is $pMP_K K_1(1 - \delta)^2/(1 + r)^3$. Hence, the discounted present value of total revenue as a result of the investment in time period 0 is,

$$\frac{pMP_K K_1}{(1+r)} + \frac{pMP_K K_1(1-\delta)}{(1+r)^2} + \frac{pMP_K K_1(1-\delta)^2}{(1+r)^3} + \ldots$$

We can write this[4] as,

$$\frac{pMP_K K_1}{(1+r)} + \frac{pMP_K K_1(1-\delta)}{(1+r)^2} + \frac{pMP_K K_1(1-\delta)^2}{(1+r)^3} + \ldots = \frac{pMP_K K_1}{r+\delta} \tag{4.10}$$

The total cost to the firm with only capital as an input in production is the cost of purchasing new capital goods $(p^K I_0)$ and the adjustment costs $[(b/2)p^K I_0^2]$, or,

$$\text{Total Cost} = p^K I_0 + \frac{b}{2} p^K I_0^2 \tag{4.11}$$

The firm chooses the level of investment to maximize the present value of its profit V_0. This is the present value of total revenue [Eq. (4.10)] less the cost of investment [Eq. (4.11)], or,

$$V_0 = \frac{pMP_K K_1}{r+\delta} - p^K I_0 - \frac{b}{2} p^K I_0^2$$

However, (note from Table 4.1) $K_1 = I_0$ as the analysis is from a period $t = 0$, in which $K_{-1} = 0$. Substituting this value of K_1 into the above equation for the present value of profit,

$$V_0 = \frac{pMP_K I_0}{r+\delta} - p^K I_0 - \frac{b}{2} p^K I_0^2$$

Maximizing this expression for the value of the firm, with respect to the level of investment $I = I_0$, we obtain,

$$\frac{pMP_K}{r+\delta} - p^K - bp^K I = 0$$

which, upon solving for I, gives us,

$$I = \frac{1}{b}\left[\frac{pMP_K}{p^K(r+\delta)} - 1\right] \tag{4.12}$$

$[pMP_K/p^K(r + \delta)]$ is known as TOBIN'S MARGINAL Q or Q^M. Q^M is the ratio of addition to the value of the firm or the marginal value of the firm, (pMP_K), to the user cost of capital $[p^K(r + \delta)]$. Recall that an addition to the stock of capital increased the output by MP_K, and the value of that increment to output, or the marginal value of output from the increment to the stock of capital, is pMP_K. Equation (4.12) reveals that investment is positive as long as $[pMP_K/p^K(r + \delta)] > 1$ or $Q^M > 1$. Earlier, we had obtained the result in Eq. (4.3) that additional capital should be acquired by the firm when an identical condition holds. The difference now is that the sensitivity of adjustment costs b appears on the right hand side of (4.12) and indicates that the higher the adjustment costs associated with an increase in the level of investment, the lower should be the investment undertaken by the firm. Tobin had defined Q as,

› **Tobin's marginal Q** is the ratio of the marginal value of the capital stock (computed by adding the market value of the additional equity and the debt raised by the firm to finance the addition to capital stock) to the rental cost of capital.

$$Q = \frac{\text{Market Value}}{\text{Replacement Cost}} = \frac{pF_K K}{[p^K(r+\delta)]K}$$

Our analysis implies that what is relevant for investment is marginal Q or Q^M—the ratio of the market value of a marginal unit of capital to its replacement cost [Hayashi (1982)].[5] The factors that have a bearing on investment according to Tobin's Q theory are:

1. *Value of marginal product of capital* (pF_K)—A higher price for the produced output increases the revenue and raises investment. Also, technological progress that alters the marginal product of capital favourably affects the investment by the firm.
2. *Price of capital goods* (p^K)—A change in the price of the capital good changes the relative price of capital (p^K/p) and induces a change in the stock of capital. For instance, a reduction in the relative price of capital causes the firm to increase the stock of capital.
3. *Interest rate* (r)—A reduction in the interest rate decreases the opportunity cost of the stock of capital that has been invested and causes investment to rise.
4. *Depreciation rate* (δ)—Even though we took this to be a constant, if there is technological progress, there would be a reduction in the profits from current investments when that occurs.
5. *Adjustment cost* (b)—The adjustment cost function depicts that adjustment costs increase more than proportionately with the amount of investment. A rise in the adjustment cost parameter will, thus, slow down the pace of investment towards the desired level of the capital stock.

Recall that MP_K is the marginal product of capital. For simplicity, we had taken this to be constant in the equation for output, Eq. (4.7). Generally, however, output produced is subject to diminishing marginal productivity, which gives us a downward sloping curve as the stock of capital increases. This implies that for a given price, pMP_K is downward sloping. The cost of capital, $p^K(r + \delta)$, at any moment of time, is a known constant. Hence, $[pMP_K/p^K(r + \delta)]$ is a downward sloping curve that we can interpret as the investment opportunities curve,

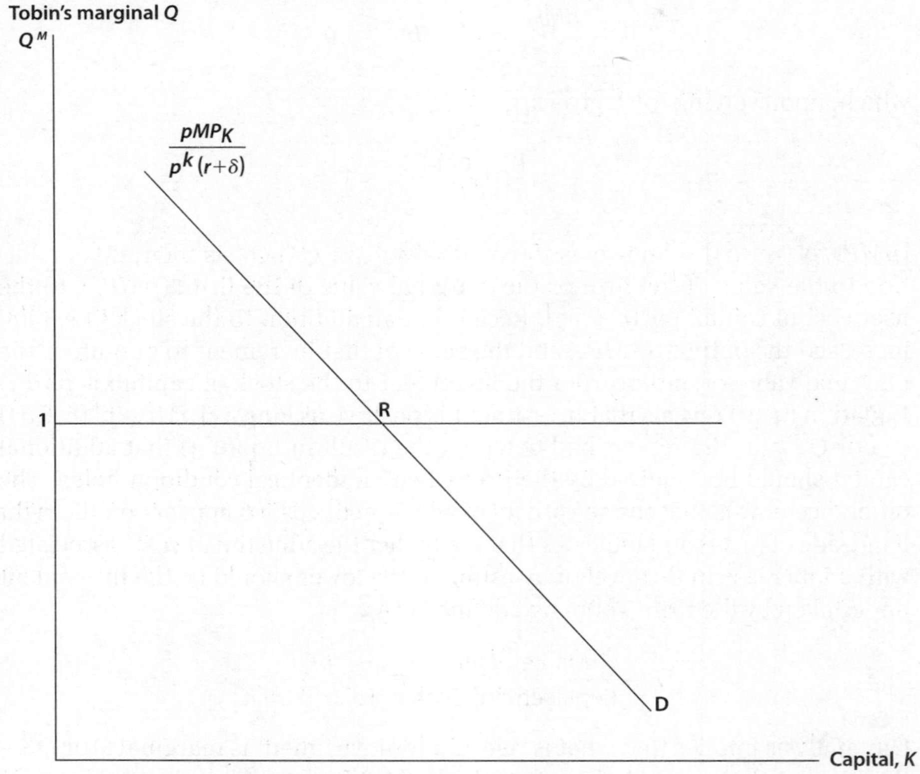

› **Figure 4.3 Investment Opportunities.** Tobin's marginal *Q* is positive when the revenue from a unit of output produced by hiring additional capital, pMP_K, is greater than the rental on capital. As the marginal product of capital decreases with an increase in the capital stock—diminishing marginal productivity—Q^M is a downward sloping line.

which we represent by D in Figure 4.3. To the left of the point R, investment is positive as the investment opportunities are greater than the ratio of marginal market value and replacement cost (which is unity). An improvement in investment opportunities shifts the D curve to the right, increasing the desired capital stock; a decline in investment opportunities shifts the D curve to the left, decreasing the desired capital stock.

Empirical applications require that we have a measure of Q^M. If financial markets are efficient, the value of an extra unit of capital would be given by the financial market value of that extra unit. Q^M is related to the change in market value. This would be the financial market's valuation of the profit stream from a small change in the firm's stock of capital. Though Q can be observed, Q^M cannot be directly observed (see Hayashi, 1982) and is much more difficult to measure. The market value of a firm is the stock market value of its shares (price of a share times the number of shares) plus its net debt or total value of bonds outstanding. Dividing this total market value by the value of the capital stock of the firm at replacement cost—the price firms have to pay to replace their current productive capacity of plant, machines, etc.—gives us a measure of Tobin's Q.[6] We also need an estimate of the adjustment cost parameter b in Eq. (4.7) to estimate the investment function. Summers, Bosworth, Tobin, and White (1981) found an estimated value of $b = 32$, but more sophisticated econometric analysis has shown that the cost of adjustment parameter is varying through time, whereas in the theory developed above it is time invariant.[7]

Given the problems of measurement in the real world, it is never an easy task to verify a theory. A way out that has been adopted in macroeconomics is to go with a reduced form version of the investment decision rule as given in Eq. (4.12). It can be shown (see Appendix 4.2) that TOBIN'S Q is equivalent to

› An equivalent expression for **Tobin's Q** is the ratio of the internal rate of return to the rate of interest.

the ratio of the internal rate of return (r_N) on a project involving an addition to capital stock divided by the rate of interest. That is to say,

$$Q = \frac{r_N}{r} \tag{4.13}$$

The internal rate of return is the break even discount rate that equates the present value of the revenues from a project—$\sum_{t=1}^{n} [pMP_K I_0(1-\delta)^{t-1}/(1+\text{internal rate of return})^t]$—to the cost of the project given by $p^K I_0 + (b/2)p^K I_0^2$. The internal rate of return is then given by (see Appendix 4.2),

$$r_N = \frac{pMP_K I_0}{p^K I_0 + (b/2)p^K I_0^2} - \delta \tag{4.14}$$

The internal rate of return captures all the other factors other than the interest rate that determine investment, as given in Eq. (4.12). Specifically, the internal rate of return increases with a rise in the value of the marginal product of capital, pMP_K, and decreases with an increase in the price of capital goods, the depreciation rate, and adjustment costs. As long as marginal Q, which is the ratio of the internal rate of return to the market rate of interest, is larger than unity, investment that maximizes the value of the firm is profitable. For a given value of the internal rate of return, investment is then inversely related to the interest rate. It is this investment function that we will employ later. To summarize this in a linear form, we will write investment as,

$$I = a - br \tag{4.15}$$

where a is a parameter representing the factors that determine the internal rate of return. The parameter a then is the value of the internal rate of return and it increases with an increase in the value of the marginal product of capital, while decreasing with an increase in the price of capital goods, the depreciation rate, and adjustment costs.

MACROFOCUS 4.1

Overconfidence and Investment

Are investment decisions solely due to the characteristics of the firm such as the market value of assets, or do the personal characteristics of decision-makers in firms affect such decisions? The literature on behavioural finance has increasingly documented evidence of biases in beliefs such as overconfidence in managerial decision making. A large body of experimental literature has recorded the tendency of individuals to consider themselves above average on positive characteristics. A substantial fraction of entrepreneurs have been found to rate their chances of success as above average and consider themselves unlikely to experience failure. Corporate executives and management students have been found to be especially prone to this self-serving bias (Larwood and Whittaker, 1977).

The tendency of certain individuals to expect their behaviour to produce success leads them to attribute a successful outcome to their actions. If they fail it is attributed to bad luck and is deemed to be disconnected to their endeavours. Such a self-serving attribution of outcomes reinforces overconfidence. The tendency of individuals to be optimistic about their own future prospects also makes them prone to overestimate outcomes to which they are highly committed.

Malmendier and Tate (2005) have constructed a measure of CEO overconfidence. Many CEOs receive extensive stock-based compensation. Since most of their income is in this form, one would expect them to diversify their portfolio by selling company stock beyond the vesting period, especially when it is profitable to exercise the stock option. Many CEOs, however, do exactly the opposite and hold options till their date of expiration, even when they would have been better off by exercising earlier. Such CEOs display overconfidence and bet their personal wealth on the company's performance in the future.

Overconfident CEOs, as identified by their option holding behaviour, are sensitive to cash flows. However, it is for a different reason than that provided by the asymmetric information literature where external finance is restricted to avoid diluting the undervalued shares of the company (because good types are taken for bad types). Overconfident CEOs overestimate the returns on investment and overinvest if they have sufficient internal funds. If internal funds are not sufficient, overconfident CEOs do not issue new equity because they perceive their company's stock to be undervalued. This is "perceived asymmetric information" by overconfident CEOs, who restrict their investment and use additional cash flows to invest closer to their, desired level. Overconfident CEOs display investment behaviour that is sensitive to cash flows, as is the case in the asymmetric information approach.

4.3 Residential and Inventory Investment

› The **total investment expenditure** in the economy comprises (1) business investment, (2) residential investment, and (3) inventory investment.

So far, we have discussed business investment. There are two other COMPONENTS OF INVESTMENT EXPENDITURE in macroeconomics that we now discuss. These are residential or housing investment and inventory investment.

Investment in housing and residential structures refers to expenditure on new housing units as well as on the maintenance and improvement of existing units. Residential investment spending constitutes a large fraction of total private investment spending in an economy. A dominant component of household savings is in the form of housing. Our understanding of the determinants of investment in housing is developed with reference to the market for rental apartments. The market for owner-occupied housing is similar in nature, because the owner of a house implicitly pays a rental price which has been paid up front at the time of the purchase.[8]

At any point of time, there is a fixed supply of housing units that results from the accumulated past investment that has occurred. The supply of housing at any moment is the stock of housing units in existence at that time. The flow of investment in housing by builders and developers (the suppliers of housing) adds to the stock of housing units and increases the supply of housing in a later time period. Let the initial total stock of housing units be denoted as K_h. Lags in housing construction result in an INELASTIC SUPPLY OF HOUSING units with respect to the rental rate—the supply of housing is fixed and can only increase after the interval of time it takes to construct new housing stock.

› The supply of housing units at any point in time is the result of accumulated past investment in housing and is a given **constant stock of housing**.

› The **demand for housing** decreases as the rental on housing increases.

The DEMAND FOR HOUSING is like the demand for any good. As the rental on housing (the price paid for purchasing housing services) increases, the demand for the stock of housing declines—a downward sloping demand curve. What is the rental price of housing? Consider a housing unit that can be purchased at time t at a price p_t^h. The rate of depreciation of the housing unit is δ, and there is a resale value to the house which fetches a price p_{t+1}^h, one period hence. If you purchase the house at time t, rent it for a unit time period at a rental rate R, and then sell the house in the next time period, your return would be the rental plus the value of the house next period. As the housing unit is subject to depreciation, a unit of housing next period is reduced to $(1 - \delta)$ of a unit of today's housing. Then, the value of the house next period is $p_{t+1}^h(1 - \delta)$. Your return next period is then given by $R + p_{t+1}^h(1 - \delta)$. The rate of return on purchasing a housing unit, earning a rent on that unit, and reselling it next period, is then given by,

$$\text{Rate of Return} = \frac{R + p_{t+1}^h(1 - \delta)}{p_t^h}$$

To purchase the housing unit in period t, your cost of funds would be the interest rate on the loan market. If the rate of return in the market for housing were higher than the interest rate on taking out a loan, you would see a profit opportunity and keep taking out loans and purchasing housing units. Of course, your ability to continue earning such a profit opportunity or free lunch cannot continue indefinitely due to ARBITRAGE, which will ensure that the rate of return in the market for housing must equal $(1 + r)$. Thus,

› **Arbitrage** is the proposition that the expected rates of returns on two assets must be equal.

$$1 + r = \frac{R + p_{t+1}^h(1 - \delta)}{p_t^h}$$

For the stationary simple case where price appreciation does not occur, $p^h_{t+1} = p^h_t$, the RENTAL RATE can be solved out as,

› The **rental** on housing is the price of a unit of housing times the rate of interest plus depreciation.

$$R = p^h(r + \delta)$$

This is the formula for the rental with reference to the housing capital stock. Compare this with the equation in Section 4.1 for the rental on capital equipment. If we took into account that there is appreciation in housing prices, or that the inflation in the price of housing is π^h, such that $p^h_{t+1} = (1 + \pi^h)p^h_t$, then it can be shown that the rental will be given by $R = p^h(1 + \pi^h)(r + \delta)$ instead of the value above.[9] Concentrating on the stationary case, the rental price is the interest rate (r) plus a rate of depreciation (δ) times the price of housing (p^h). With the demand for housing inversely related to the rental price, the desired demand for the stock of housing units, or the amount of housing agents in the economy would like to consume, is then given by K^*_h in Figure 4.4.

Now, suppose the stock of housing units in the market is $K_h = K^*_h$. As the supply of housing at any point in time is the result of accumulated past investment in housing, it is the vertical line through $K_h = K^*_h$ in Figure 4.5(a). The DEMAND FOR HOUSING STOCK equals the supply of housing stock, and the housing market is in equilibrium. A disturbance to this equilibrium position can arise due to, say, a shift in the demand for housing. An increase in incomes associated with an economic boom acts through an income effect to increase the demand for housing. Alternatively, a rise in the population also causes a rise in the demand for housing. Both these factors cause the demand for housing to shift to the right to D' in Figure 4.5(b).

› The **demand for housing** increases with an increase in income and population.

The current stock of housing is now less than the demand for housing, $K_{h,t} < K^{**}_{h,t+1}$. With excess demand the rental rate in the housing market will rise to R'. With no change in r and δ, the higher rental rate is capitalized into a higher selling price for housing units, and the price of housing increases to $p^{h\prime} > p^h$. As the price of existing homes has been driven up, the market valuation of the existing housing stock has increased. Builders and developers respond to this demand for housing by consumers by building new homes

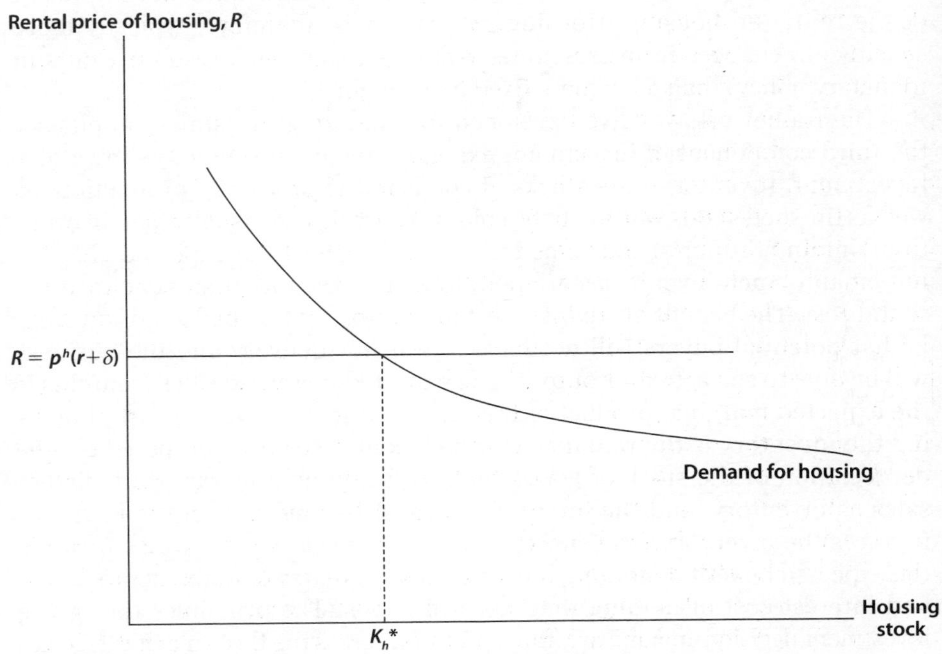

› **Figure 4.4**
Demand for Housing Services. The demand for housing is inversely related to the rental on housing.

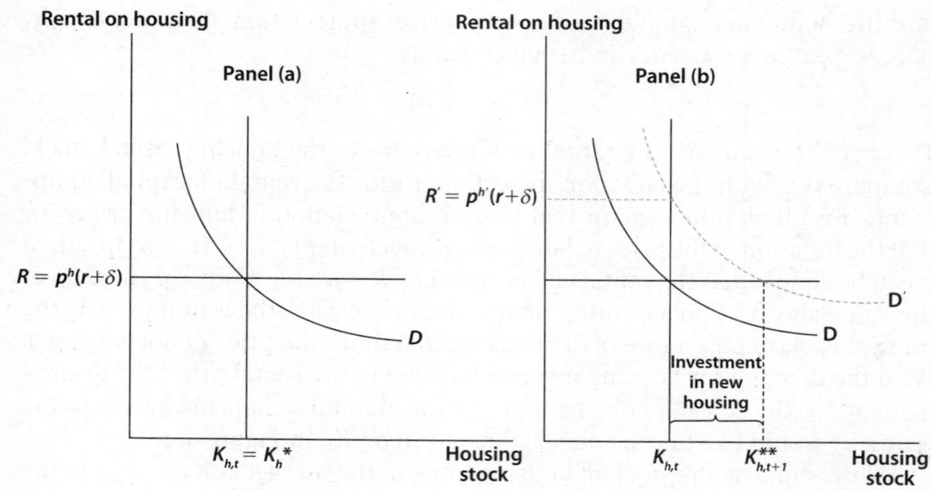

› Figure 4.5 Investment Expenditure on Housing. The demand for housing increases with an increase in income and population. This makes existing homes expensive as compared to the cost of building new homes, and induces an increase in investment in housing.

when the existing home prices are high as compared to the price of new homes. The amount of investment in building new homes, I_h, is,

$$I_h = K^{**}_{h,t+1} - K_{h,t}$$

› **Investment expenditure** in housing results when the price of existing homes is expensive as compared to the price of new homes. Alternatively, investment in housing occurs when the market valuation of housing stock exceeds the replacement cost, or Tobin's $Q > 1$.

This amount of investment expenditure is depicted in Figure 4.5(b). An alternative way of thinking about what drives the INVESTMENT EXPENDITURE is to ask what the replacement cost of the existing stock of housing assets is. How much would it cost to buy the existing housing stock again, off the production line? That would be the cost of new housing, which is p^h. As the current market valuation at $p^{h\prime}$ is larger than the replacement cost, Tobin's Q is greater than unity and investment takes place. So housing investment is the outcome of decision making akin to the decision behind a firm's investment in plant and machinery. The difference between housing investment and business investment is that housing depreciates at a low rate of around 2 per cent per year, compared to business depreciation rates in plant and machinery that is typically well over 6 per cent. Hence, the interest rate is the dominant component of the rental on housing. Housing investment is, therefore, typically more sensitive to changes in interest rates (which happens as a result of shifts in monetary policy) than a business fixed investment.

The framework we have developed for analyzing investment applies to the third component of investment expenditures in an economy—inventory investment. Inventories are stocks of goods in the process of production, as well as finished goods waiting to be sold. Inventories are usually held in order to maintain a buffer stock, so as to be able to cater to unexpected changes in demand. Such inventories are held to equate the marginal benefit to the rental cost. The benefit of having a certain number of finished goods on hand is that potential buyers will not have to wait for delivery and the business will be able to sell a greater output. The expected increased sales from this is the expected marginal product of the increased inventory. The cost of holding the inventory is the rental price which comprises two components—the depreciation of the stock of goods that are being held in excess of current sales as inventory, and the interest that must be paid out on the loan that finances the inventory. The business will make the INVENTORY INVESTMENT when the expected benefit of holding the inventory is greater than the depreciation and interest cost of holding that stock of goods. The principles that guide investment decision-making are, thus, common across the three major categories

› **Inventory investment** occurs when the marginal productivity of the inventory exceeds the rental on the inventory, or Tobin's $Q > 1$.

MACROFOCUS 4.2

India: An Inverted Pecking Order?

It is well known that managers of firms who have hands-on daily experience are better informed about the investment opportunities available to a firm than external suppliers of funds. Asymmetric information is then prevalent when investors in the firm are not as equally well-informed as managers about the prospective returns from new investment projects. External investors then typically tend to undervalue projects compared to managers. The costs of external capital are accordingly greater than those for the internal capital or cash flow of the firm due to asymmetric-information problems between managers and the external investors in the capital market, or because of the transactions costs of issuing bonds and equity. There is, therefore, a pecking order in financing investments—internal funds are cheaper and ought to be exhausted first before resorting to external funds obtained from bond and equity markets. One would presume that cash flow would be an even more important source of finance in developing countries such as India where the transactions costs are more prohibitive and asymmetric information is more severe. The finding of Singh and Hamid (1992) that firms in developing countries finance their growth from external capital sources more than firms in developed countries, is, therefore, surprising. Moreover, Indian firms rely much more heavily on external debt as a source of finance than firms in advanced countries like the United States.

Gugler, Mueller, and Yurtoglu (2003) find that Indian firms earn returns on their investments that are less than their cost of capital, implying that marginal Q is less than unity for Indian firms. They attribute this to the existence of weak corporate governance structures in India. The low efficacy of legal institutions in enforcing contracts as well as weak accounting standards prevent shareholders from protecting themselves against self-serving managers who feel secure that low returns investments will not cost them their jobs. Moreover, most debt financing of investment in the Indian context has been by public sector financial institutions which have implicit government guarantees that they cannot fail. This imparted a confidence to depositors and borrowers that banks are safe and served to weaken financial discipline by bankers who did not pursue efficient screening of projects and resorted to imprudent lending. With government shouldering the loss arising in the event of bank failure, and banks absorbing the full returns otherwise, banks in India had an incentive to overlend (D'Souza, 2000). Also, as interest rates in the financial system prior to liberalization were administered, banks competed through non-price competition by overlending so as to gain market share. Thus, the financial system in India for those medium and large firms that had access to bank finance was characterized more by a credit-liberal regime rather than a credit-constrained one. Managers making poor return investments were not constrained by their internal cash flows. With financial liberalization, however, as banks seek prudent balance-sheet positions, managers will find that credit constraints are akin to those in developed countries.

of investment expenditures—business fixed capital formation, investment in housing, and inventory investment. The general form of the investment function that the Q approach suggests [see Eq. (4.15)] is that it depends positively on a shift parameter that represents the value of the marginal product of capital, price of capital goods, depreciation, adjustment costs, and negatively on the interest rate.

4.4 Irreversibility and Investment

We now study a more recent approach to investment. Readers may skip this section in a first reading and move directly to the next section without any loss of continuity from the previous section. An alternative theory of investment that this section presents is the theory of irreversible investment. IRREVERSIBILITY refers to the fact that many firms may not be able to sell their capital stock. A firm faces total irreversibility when resale markets are absent, which is equivalent to the situation where the resale price of capital is zero. In such a case, once the firm invests, it cannot get rid of additional capital stock even if economic conditions warrant a lower desired capital stock. As it cannot access resale markets, it can only allow the excess capital stock to depreciate through time. The firm can always adjust its capital stock upward, but it cannot adjust it downward by disinvesting ($I_t \geq 0$). Irreversibility usually arises because capital is industry or FIRM-SPECIFIC. Industry level uncertainty tends to affect all firms simultaneously. As a result, if a firm wishes to sell excess capital in response to an adverse demand shock, it may not be able to find buyers willing to purchase it. For example, a steel plant is industry-specific in the sense that if the demand for steel falls, the market value of the plant will fall. Though the plant could be

› **Irreversibility** of investment occurs when the cost associated with the investment is not completely recoverable if the firm wants to sell the capital stock subsequently.

› **Firm-specific** capital enhances productivity only in the firm where it is acquired, and the value of the capital is lost if the capital is transferred out of the firm.

› A **sunk cost** is an investment in an asset with no alternative use—also referred to as a specific asset. A sunk cost is, therefore, an investment in an asset with no opportunity cost (the value of the next best alternative use of the asset).

› A **lemons problem** arises when the seller of a good has inside information about the quality and performance characteristics of the good, and will be unwilling to accept the terms that a less-informed buyer requests. This would usually result in a discount to the price that would prevail under full information. A sale of a used capital good is always suspected to involve the sale of a lemon that does not perform according to expectations, and so, sells at a discount.

sold to another steel company, there is little gain from doing so as all steel manufacturers will be facing adverse conditions during a drop in demand and will be willing to offer to pay a reduced price. The investment in the plant must be viewed as a SUNK COST.

Most investments in marketing and advertising are also firm-specific and, so, are sunk costs. Even less specific capital such as computers and office equipment and general-use machinery are partially irreversible due to LEMONS PROBLEM of adverse selection. Secondary markets for such capital are inefficient. Finally, irreversibility also arises due to government regulation or institutional impediments. For example, capital controls may make it impossible for foreign investors to sell assets and reallocate their funds.

Not only does traditional investment theory assume that invested capital is reversible, it also assumes that each investment opportunity facing the firm is a unique opportunity. If the firm declines the opportunity, it will never have the choice to reconsider. In such a case, the firm faces a "now or never" situation.

To get a flavour of what irreversibility and delay can result in, let us take a simple two-period example as expounded in Pindyck (1991). Assume investment is totally irreversible, i.e., the firm will not be able to recover any of the investment. The firm in question is a German firm contemplating investment in a new steel factory. For simplicity, let us assume that there is no gestation lag—efficient Germans can build the factory instantly at a cost of INR 800 (million). Let us also assume that the factory can produce a unit of steel forever, with zero operating costs. The current price of a unit of steel (100 tones) is INR 100 (million), but the price will change next year to either INR 150 (million) with probability one half or to INR 50 (million) with probability one half. The price will then remain at this new level, forever. The evolution of steel prices has been shown in Table 4.2.

The firm can discount future cash flows using the rate of return, which is the risk-free rate if the risk is fully diversifiable of, say, 10 per cent. Suppose the firm is deciding whether to invest now. Is this a good investment? One decision rule is that the net present value should be positive. Let us use this rule.

The expected future price of steel in any time period is,

$$\text{INR } 100 = (0.5)(150) + (0.5)(50)$$

Hence, the present value of the factory's revenue is $100 + \frac{100}{1.1} + \frac{100}{(1.1)^2} + \ldots$

The factory costs INR 800, and so the net present value is,

$$NPV_{\text{invest now}} = -800 + \sum_{t=0}^{\infty} \frac{100}{(1.1)^t} = -800 + 1100 = 300$$

The factory should be built on this decision criterion. We can also use the value of Tobin's Q to guide our decision. This can be calculated as:

$$Q = \frac{1100}{800} = 1.375, \text{ which is greater than 1.}$$

Hence, this criterion also supports the decision to invest.

› **Table 4.2**
Evolution of Steel Prices

Time: $t = 0$	$t = 1$	$t = 2$	$t = 3$	—	—
$q = \frac{1}{2}$	$P_1 = 150$	$P_2 = 150$	$P_3 = 150$	—	—
Price: $P_0 = 100$					
$(1 - q) = \frac{1}{2}$	$P_1 = 50$	$P_2 = 50$	$P_3 = 50$	—	—

Note: q = Probability of price change

These calculations, however, ignore a cost—the opportunity cost of investing now, rather than waiting, and thereby keeping open the possibility of not investing should the price fall. As an alternative, suppose the firm's managers wait a year and build the factory only if the price increases from INR 100 to INR 150.

In year zero, there is no expenditure and no revenue. In year 1, the cost of investment is incurred only if the price rises and the present value of that cost is 800/1.1. The present value of returns from investing when the price increases is $\sum_{t=1}^{a} \frac{150}{(1.1)^t}$.

Hence, if we wait a year and invest only if the price goes up, an event that occurs with a probability of half, the net present value is[10],

$$NPV_{delay} = 0.5\left[-\frac{800}{1.1} + \sum_{t=1}^{\infty} \frac{150}{(1.1)^t}\right] = \frac{425}{1.1} = 386$$

The NPV is higher if we plan to wait a year. So, clearly, waiting is better than investing now. Likewise, Tobin's Q in the "delay" case is given by,

$$Q_{delay} = \frac{\sum_{t=0}^{\infty} [(150)/(1.1)^t]}{800/1.1} = \frac{1650}{727} = 2.27$$

and $$Q_{delay} > Q_{invest\ now}$$

It is important to note that if our only choices were to invest today or never invest, we would invest today. In that case, there is no option to wait a year, and hence, no opportunity cost to killing such an option. The "real option"—the value of the call option of delay—is INR 386. The less completely irreversible the investment, the lower the VALUE OF WAITING. This description of changes in the value of the option to delay follows the connected effects on the value of financial call options.[11]

› The **value of waiting** is the expected present value of the irreversible mistake that would be revealed in the future should the returns fall short of the costs.

An irreversible investment opportunity is akin to a financial-call option. A call option gives the holder the right, for some specified amount of time, to pay an exercise price and, in return, receive an asset (for example, a share of stock that has some value). As with a financial-call option, the firm's option to invest is valuable in part because the future value of the asset that the firm gets by investing is uncertain. If the asset rises in value, the pay-off from investing rises. If it falls in value, the firm need not invest and will only lose what it spent to obtain the investment opportunity.

There are situations where a firm cannot wait, or wait very long, to invest. For instance, if the firm anticipates the entry of a competitor into a market that can sustain one large firm, waiting is costly. Also, if there is no patent or a mineral resource lease is about to expire, the wait will irreversibly affect the investment decision. The example above focused on uncertainty over future product prices. Investment, however, is sensitive to uncertainty in various forms: uncertainty over operating costs that determine cash flows; uncertainty over future interest rates; and uncertainty over the cost and timing of the investment itself.

This has strong policy implications. If a goal of macroeconomic policy is to stimulate investment, stability and CREDIBILITY may be much more important than tax incentives and a low-interest rate regime. Indeed, if uncertainty over the economic environment is high, tax and related incentives may have to be very large to have any significant impact on investment.

› **Credibility** refers to the degree to which individuals and markets believe that a policy announcement will be implemented, even when there are short term economic costs that may be imposed.

The implication of irreversibility is that the cost of investing includes the discounted marginal call option in addition to the market price for capital goods, p^K. By investing one additional unit at any point in time, the firm loses the opportunity to invest that unit in the future and incurs the loss of a call option. This additional cost tends to discourage investment. Greater uncertainty increases the value of the call option and reduces the incentive to invest. In an equilibrium situation, the sum of the costs must equal the marginal benefit of investing an additional unit of capital. This marginal benefit of investing an additional unit can be shown to be the sum of two terms. First is the discounted expected marginal value of capital if the firm never invests in the future and simply allows its capital stock to depreciate (Tobin's Q). The second component of marginal benefit is the expected value of the unused portion of the capital stock, assuming the firm does not invest in the next period (or there is increase in the expected marginal value of capital due to future marginal call options available to the firm).

The intuition that is prevalent here is that the value maximizing investment decision must consider the value of the option of delay when comparing the marginal benefit and cost of investing.

4.5 Investment in Developing Countries

There has been very little empirical work on the determinants of private investment in developing countries.[12] Investment theories formulated for industrial countries need to be changed to fit the circumstances in developing countries. For instance, given that financial variables influence investment behaviour, investment is sensitive to the institutional environment in the financial system. Equity markets are typically small and underdeveloped and the prevalence of FINANCIAL REPRESSION implies that Tobin's Q must be applied cautiously. The cost of funds in informal markets has been found to influence private investment when the firms are credit rationed in the formal financial sector. Then again, in many developing countries with fledgling capital-goods sectors that resort to imports of capital goods, foreign exchange rationing and the cost of foreign exchange in unofficial curb markets can be important determinants of private investment. Also, the existence of a debt overhang, which indicates the possibility of future taxation that will be used to finance future debt service, has been found to inhibit private investment.[13]

› **Financial repression** refers to the controls on financial intermediaries such as credit and operational controls as well as interest rate controls that restrict a banks' choices on the supply of loans and their demand for deposits.

Developing countries also tend to have large public sectors and there is accordingly a need to incorporate complementarity–substitutability relationships between public and private investment in empirical work on investment in these countries. The relation between public and private investment is *a priori* positive or negative. Public sector investment can crowd out private investment expenditure if it uses scarce physical and financial resources that would otherwise be available to the private sector. The financing of public investment through taxes, issuance of debt, or inflationary finance can reduce the resources available to the private sector and depress private investment. Alternatively, public investment that expands infrastructure and the provision of public goods can raise the productivity of private capital and is complementary to private investment. To sum up, public and private investment can be complementary or substitutes to one another.[14]

An important source of uncertainty for private investment decision has been macroeconomic instability associated with economic policy making. Some studies have found that political uncertainty—government instability, rapid government turnover, and social unrest—vary negatively with investment.[15]

Volatility of output growth is an indicator of the unpredictability of demand, and the volatility of inflation is an indicator of macroeconomic uncertainty. Both of these and other indicators of uncertainty have been found to adversely impact private investment.[16]

Finally, corruption has been found to have a significant adverse impact on investment. Corruption tends to increase the number of projects undertaken and expand their size. Thus, while increasing the share of public investment to GDP, corruption also lowers the quality of public investment put in place.[17]

Thus, when investigating the substitution-complementary effects of public investment, we need to capture the indirect effect of corruption via its impact on the quality of public investment. Empirical work usually includes an interaction term between the corruption index and the level of public investment to capture this effect. It has been found that higher corruption for a given level of public investment is associated with lower quality of public investment, which tends to lower private investment.[18] Clearly, the behaviour of aggregate investment is subject to many influences that empirical and theoretical work is slowly uncovering.

4.5.1 Investment in India

A recent attempt to understand the determinants of private corporate investment in India (Athukorala and Sen, 2002) gives us an indication of the importance of some of these variables. Drawing on the literature focusing on finance constraints on investment decisions, which argue that external finance may be more costly than internal finance because of transaction costs, contract enforcement problems, and asymmetric information, Athukorala and Sen include the availability of finance—measured in terms of real bank credit to the private sector, BC—as a determinant of investment. Similarly, public sector fixed capital formation I_{public}, as argued before, can affect investment from the supply side through infrastructure investments, or the demand side through competing for investible funds. Other variables that are included in investment functions are the cost of capital[19] (*CC*), GDP (*Y*), and the capital stock in the private sector (*K*). The GDP and the capital stock are included as explanatory variables as the marginal product of capital depends positively on output produced (see the definition for the Cobb–Douglas case in the Appendix 4.1) and negatively on *K* (a large capital stock base diminishes the marginal productivity of capital).

The equation was estimated for 1954–1996 and all variables were measured in natural logarithms, except, of course, the cost of capital which is measured in proportional form. In addition, because the credibility and sustainability of reforms could affect the perception of firms about investment opportunities, a post-reform intercept dummy (PRD), which takes the value one for the post-reform years and zero otherwise, is included in the estimation.

The estimated equation[20] for private corporate investment (*I*) is as follows:

$$\Delta I_t = -1.28 + 0.13\Delta BC_{t-1} + 2.98\Delta Y_t - 3.89\Delta CC_t + 0.68\Delta I_{\text{public}} + 1.06 I_{\text{public},t-1} - 0.50K_{t-1} - 0.45I_{t-1} + 0.75PRD$$

The equation clearly indicates that business investment in any given year accelerates with changes in GDP (ΔY) and there is a positive effect of bank credit (BC). Moreover, public investment has a strong complementary effect on business investment in India. As predicted by investment theories, the cost of capital (CC) and the initial capital stock K_{t-1} have negative effects on investment. The positive coefficient on PRD indicates that the reforms have had an investment enhancing impact over and above the impact from other explanatory variables. When incorporating the effects of future uncertainty on investment through measures such as moving averages of standard devitions of the change in output as well as the change in the cost of capital, it was found that they had insignificant effects on investment. Uncertainty in the Indian context, however, may be more associated with the variability of inflation, rather than the variability of output or the rental on capital. Despite this, that investment in India is responsive to bank credit and public investment indicates the importance of proper economic policy-making so that there may be salutary effects on private investment in the economy.

SUMMARY

- The rental on the stock of capital is the sum of the market rate of interest, r, and the constant rate of depreciation, δ, multiplied by the unit supply price of the capital good, p^K.
- The optimal capital stock is determined where the value of the marginal product of capital equals the user cost of capital.
- Convex adjustment costs that rise more than proportionately with the level of investment determine the speed at which the stock of capital adjusts to its optimal level.
- The investment undertaken by a firm is positive as long as Tobin's $Q^M > 1$.
- The supply of housing stock with respect to the rental rate on housing is inelastic and increases with the flow of investment in housing by builders and developers. The demand for housing is inversely related to the rental on housing.
- When the rental price of housing is higher than the rental cost of building new homes, the market value of housing exceeds the replacement cost and investment in housing increases.
- Inventory investment increases when the expected value of the increased sales from holding inventory exceeds the depreciation and interest cost of holding the increasing inventory.
- Irreversibility arises due to the investment being a sunk cost when it is industry or firm specific. This makes it very costly to redeploy the capital stock. With irreversibility it is sometimes worth waiting for future uncertainty to be resolved before investing.
- Investment in developing countries is influenced by institutional factors such as the existence of financial repression, foreign-exchange rationing, macroeconomic uncertainty, the complementarity between public and private investment, and the prevalence of corruption.

NOTES

1. δ is just the physical wear and tear of the machine expressed as a fraction of the price of the capital good
2. This profit maximizing condition is also obtained by maximizing the profit function with respect to the capital stock, K. This first order condition is the same as the one we have intuitively obtained.
3. The two acquisition schemes—renting and outright purchasing—will be equivalent for entrepreneurs when the cost of the two schemes are equal. Thus, when the present discounted value of rental payments is identical to the purchase price of the equipment, renting and purchasing are equivalent actions. Under perfect competition this would always be true.
4. In what follows we use the result that the sum of the infinite series $S_n = 1 + x + x^2 + \ldots = (1/1-x)$.
5. See Hayashi, F. (1982).
6. For the difficulties in measuring Tobin's Q in developing countries, see Athey and Reeser (2000).
7. See also Demers, F. S., M. Demers, and H. Schaller (1994).
8. A key difference between renting and owning that we are overlooking here is that homeowners get an offsetting benefit to owning in the form of tax deductibility of mortgage interest and property taxes. This means that from the interest and maintenance (depreciation) costs we must subtract out mortgage and property tax payments that are tax exempt. See Himmelberg, Mayer, and Sinai (2005).
9. In that case, the rate of interest on the left hand side of the arbitrage equation will be the nominal rate of interest and not the real rate of interest, r. In Chapter 6, we prove a result that the nominal interest rate i is given by $1 + i = (1 + r)(1 + \pi^h)$. The right hand side of the arbitrage equation with inflation will be $\{[R + p_t^h(1 + \pi^h)(1 - \delta)]/p_t^h\}$. Solving the revised arbitrage equation, then for R gives us $R = p_t^h(1 + \pi^h)(1 - \delta)$.
10. $S_n = X + \dfrac{X}{1+r} + \dfrac{X}{(1+r)^2} \ldots = \sum_{t=0}^{\infty} \dfrac{X}{(1+r)^t} = \dfrac{(1+r)X}{r}$

    and $S_n = \sum_{t=1}^{\infty} \dfrac{X}{(1+r)^t} = \dfrac{X}{r}$ for $n \to \infty$
11. See Brealey, R. A. and Myers, S. C. (1991).
12. See Serven, L. and Solimano, A. (1992).
13. See Sachs, J. A. (1989).
14. See Rama, M. (1993).

15. See Barro, R. (1996), "Democracy and Growth", Journal of Economic Growth, 1, January.
16. See Serven, L. (1998).
17. See Tanzi, V. and Davoodi, H. (1997). Tanzi and Davoodi measure corruption from the Political Risk Service's International Country Risk Guide which provides a measure of corruption based on whether government officials are likely to demand special illegal payments. Infrastructure quality is measured through proxies such as paved roads in good condition as a percentage of total roads, electric power system losses as a percentage of total power output, and telephone faults per 100 mainlines per years.
18. See Everhart, S. S. and Sumlinski, M. A. (2001).
19. The cost of capital that is estimated is $CC = [p^K(r + \delta)/p]$, that is, relative to output price.
20. To guard against simultaneity bias, the equation was estimated using two-stage least squares. We do not present the diagnostic tests here for simplicity. See Athukorala, P. C. and Sen, K. (2002).

TEST YOURSELF

1. Differentiate between savings, financial investment, and investment in physical capital. For a macroeconomist, is the purchase of shares in the stock market saving or investment?
2. Why is the investment-opportunities curve downward sloping? Explain the role of diminishing marginal productivity in determining the slope of the investment-opportunity schedule.
3. What factors govern a firm's decision to buy a given piece of capital equipment?
4. Explain the role of adjustment costs in the theory of investment.
5. Suppose the upfront cost of a two year MBA programme is INR 200,000. You estimate that your salary in the current year if you work would be INR 165,000 and a year from now it will be INR 275,000. The interest rate is 10 per cent per annum. How much income are you forgoing by joining the MBA programme? Explain why pursuing the MBA might be a good investment.
6. What are the various factors that affect Tobin's marginal Q and thereby the investment in the economy.
7. Suppose there exist rent controls or caps on what landlords can charge to rent out their premises. Analyze what will happen to the housing market when there is an increase in demand for housing due to an increase in income.
8. You live in an economy where the government subsidizes diesel but charges a market price for petrol. You are considering purchasing a car and weighing the options of a diesel versus a petrol vehicle when you hear that the policy may change and diesel may no longer be subsidized. How does this information affect your decision to invest in a diesel car?
9. What is the advantage of investing later rather than now? What does uncertainty require of macroeconomic policy?
10. In a developing economy what factors other than Tobin's marginal Q would you consider as important for the decision-making process?

ONLINE APPLICATION

1. Go to the home page of the Reserve Bank of India URL: www.rbi.org.in/home.aspx
2. Click on the "DataBase" icon
3. Under the classification of annual data, click on "Handbook of Statistics on Indian Economy"
4. Click on "Table 2: Macro-economic aggregates (at constant prices)". Download data for the last 15 years on Gross Domestic Capital Formation (GDCF) and GDP (at market prices).
5. Calculate the GDCF/GDP ratio and draw a graph of this ratio over time. If GDCF is increasing (or decreasing) as a proportion of GDP what does this indicate about other components of GDP?
6. Calculate the growth rate of GDP and the growth rate of GDCF. Graph the growth rates. Which variable, GDP or GDCF, depicts greater variability? What could be the reason for this?

Appendix 4.1 Optimal Capital Stock when Production Function is Cobb–Douglas

To find an explicit solution for the optimal capital stock allow the production function to be of the Cobb–Douglas type, or,

$$Y = AK^{a} N^{1-a} \qquad (0 < a < 1) \tag{A4.1.1}$$

where, A which represents technology is a constant.

Then, $$MP_N = \frac{\partial Y}{\partial N} = (1-a)AK^{a}N^{-a} = (1-a)\frac{Y}{N}$$

and $$MP_K = \frac{\partial Y}{\partial K} = aAK^{a-1}N^{1-a} = a\frac{Y}{K}$$

Substituting these values for MP_N and MP_K into Eqs (4.4) and (4.5) in the text gives us,

$$\frac{(1-a)\frac{Y}{N}}{a\frac{Y}{K}} = \frac{w}{p^{K}(r+\delta)}$$

or, $$\frac{1-a}{a}\frac{K}{N} = \frac{w}{p^{K}(r+\delta)}$$

or, $$K = \frac{a}{1-a}\frac{w}{p^{K}(r+\delta)}N \tag{A4.1.2}$$

From the production function given in Eq. (A4.1.1),

$$N^{1-a} = \frac{Y}{AK^{a}}$$

or, $$N = \left[\frac{Y}{AK^{a}}\right]^{\frac{1}{1-a}}$$

Substituting this into the expression (A4.1.2),

$$K = \frac{a}{1-a}\frac{w}{p^{K}(r+\delta)}\left[\frac{Y}{AK^{a}}\right]^{\frac{1}{1-a}}$$

$$= \frac{a}{1-a}\frac{w}{p^{K}(r+\delta)}\left(\frac{Y}{A}\right)^{\frac{1}{1-a}}K^{-\frac{a}{1-a}}$$

or, $$K^{1+\frac{a}{1-a}} = K^{\frac{1}{1-a}} = \frac{a}{1-a}\frac{w}{p^{K}(r+\delta)}\left(\frac{Y}{A}\right)^{\frac{1}{1-a}}$$

or, $$K^{*} = \left[\frac{a}{1-a}\frac{w}{p^{K}(r+\delta)}\right]^{1-a}\frac{Y}{A} \tag{A4.1.3}$$

Given that A and a are constants as they represent the current technology of production, if we take the cost of factor inputs to also be given, then the optimal capital stock depends only on output Y. This has led some economists to argue that as the demand for output increases, there is an increase in the stock of capital by the firm. As the change in capital stock is investment when we ignore depreciation ($I = \Delta K$)—investment is a function of the change in output from (A4.1.3)—a proposition referred to as the ACCELERATOR THEORY of investment. Whenever there is an acceleration in the growth of output, firms respond by increasing investment. When factor prices are not constant, however, the optimal capital stock to hire is increasing in output, Y, and decreasing in the rental to be paid per unit of capital, $k = p^K(r + \delta)$. We may then write generally, that

› The effect of a change in output (or an acceleration in output) on investment is called the **accelerator**.

$$K^* = K\left[Y, \frac{w}{p^K(r + \delta)}\right] \tag{A4.1.4}$$

Appendix 4.2 Tobin's Q and the Rate of Interest

Tobin's Q is given by the ratio of the market value of a business unit to the replacement cost of its assets. The market value is the present value of the future stream of revenues generated by the firm. We found that the present value of revenues that the firm earns is given by

$$\frac{pMP_K I_0}{(1+r)} + \frac{pMP_K I_0(1-\delta)}{(1+r)^2} + \frac{pMP_K I_0(1-\delta)^2}{(1+r)^3} + \ldots = \sum_{t=1}^{n} \frac{pMP_K I_0(1-\delta)^{t-1}}{(1+r)^t}$$

The market value of the firm is then given by the expression

$$\text{Market Value} = \sum_{t=1}^{n} \frac{pMP_K I_0(1-\delta)^{t-1}}{(1+r)^t}$$

The replacement cost of the assets of the firm (RC_0) is the initial expenditure on investment $p^K I_0 + (b/2)p^K I_0^2$ that yields a stream of future revenues to the firm. The present value of the future revenues to the firm (left hand side of the following equation) which exactly offsets the cost of the assets that generated these revenues (right hand side of the following equation) involves a discount rate for the future revenues that results in the outcome given by

$$\sum_{t=1}^{n} [pMP_K I_0(1-\delta)^{t-1}/(1+\text{Discount Rate})^t] = RC_0$$

This discount rate that gives the *net* present value of the earnings or revenues minus costs as equal to zero is known as the internal rate of return (r_N). The formula for the internal rate of return is then obtained by setting r_N equal to the discount rate in the above equation so that

$$-RC_0 + \sum_{t=1}^{n} \frac{pMP_K I_0(1-\delta)^{t-1}}{(1+r_N)^t} = 0$$

or,

$$-p^K I_0 - \frac{b}{2} p^K I_0^2 + \sum_{t=1}^{n} \frac{pMP_K I_0(1-\delta)^{t-1}}{(1+r_N)^t} = 0$$

or,

$$RC_0 = p^K I_0 + \frac{b}{2} p^K I_0^2 = \sum_{t=1}^{n} \frac{pMP_K I_0(1-\delta)^{t-1}}{(1+r_N)^t}$$

The internal rate of return is the rate of growth the investment project is expected to generate. Solving the above equation for r_N, we obtain

$$r_N = \frac{pMP_K I_0}{RC_0} - \delta$$

It turns out then that the internal rate of return is the gross rate of return on investment per period of time ($pMP_K I_0/RC_0$) minus the rate of depreciation, or r_N is the net rate of return per period when an investment costing $p^K I_0 + (b/2)p^K I_0^2$ is undertaken. We may write the Q relationship as

$$Q = \frac{\text{Market Value}}{\text{Replacement Cost}} = \frac{\sum_{t=1}^{n}[(pMP_K I_0[1-\delta]^{t-1})/(1+r)^t]}{\sum_{t=1}^{n}[(pMP_K I_0[1-\delta]^{t-1})/(1+r_N)^t]}$$

$$= \frac{\sum[1/(1+r)^t]}{\sum[1/(1+r_N)^t]}$$

Now, the geometric series $1/x + 1/x^2 + 1/x^3 + \ldots + 1/x^n$ sums to $1/x$ as $n \rightarrow \infty$.
We may then write Tobin's Q as

$$Q = \frac{1/r}{1/r_N} = \frac{r_N}{r}$$

This states that a project should be undertaken when $Q > 1$, or where the internal rate of return is greater than the rate of interest. Alternatively, investment is inversely related to the rate of interest. With $I_0 = 1$, the same holds true for marginal Q. As a result investment is taken to be impacted positively when the rate of interest declines.

5

The Trade Balance and Exchange Rates

CRITICAL QUESTIONS

- *What is a real exchange rate?*
- *How is a country's trade balance influenced by the competitiveness of its goods and services?*
- *How does a devaluation affect the short-run and long-run trade balance?*
- *What is uncovered and covered interest rate parity, and how is the exchange rate determined in asset markets?*
- *What is the Law of One Price? How does it determine purchasing power parity in the foreign-exchange market?*
- *What are the various types of exchange rate regimes in between fixed and floating exchange rate systems, and what effect do they have on macroeconomic management?*
- *What sort of exchange rate regime is implied by (a) a currency board, (b) dollarization, and (c) monetary union?*

5.1 The Real Exchange Rate

Up to now, we have been dealing with a closed economy. However, economies are open to trade as well as world capital markets, and are increasingly integrating into the global economy. In order to export or import goods, any agent must give up or obtain the foreign-exchange that is accepted in the market where the transaction is made. In what follows, we simplify by lumping the rest of the world into one category so that we can speak of "the" exchange rate.[1] In Chapter 2, we had defined the dimension of the exchange rate as the rupee price of the dollar,

$$\text{Dimension } [E] = \frac{\text{INR}}{\text{USD}}$$

As we had discussed earlier, there are two polar systems for setting exchange rates. Under fixed exchange rates, the central bank posts the price at which it is willing to buy or sell foreign currencies, and then tries to maintain those rates administratively. Under a flexible exchange-rate system, rates are established in the private markets for foreign currencies. These rates may be influenced by, but are not controlled by central bank actions. When the dimension of the exchange rate rises, the rupee is said to depreciate under a system of flexible exchange rates, or to be devalued under a system of fixed exchange rates. When the dimension of the exchange rate falls, the rupee appreciates under flexible rates, or is revalued under fixed rates.

The exchange rate is a nominal price for exchanging one currency for another. Adjusting for differences in the price levels in the two countries gives us the real exchange rate (RER), or,

$$\text{RER} = \frac{EP^*}{P} \tag{5.1}$$

where P^* is the average foreign price level (i.e., dollars per unit of US goods). The nominal exchange rate is the price of the domestic currency in terms of the foreign currency. The real exchange rate is the price of the average foreign good or service in terms of the average domestic good or service. When we inquire whether, on average, the goods and services produced by a particular country are expensive as compared to the goods and services produced by other countries, we are asking a question about the real exchange rate. A country's REAL EXCHANGE RATE is the price of the average foreign good or service as compared to the price of the average domestic good or service, when prices are expressed in terms of a common currency.

› A country's **real exchange rate** is the price of the average foreign good or service relative to the price of the average domestic good or service, when prices are expressed in terms of a common currency.

$$\text{RER} = \frac{EP^*}{P} = \frac{\text{INR}}{\text{USD}} \frac{\text{USD/US Goods}}{\text{INR/Domestic Goods}}$$

Cancelling the dollar terms which appear in the numerator and denominator of the above expression, we obtain,

$$\text{RER} = \frac{EP^*}{P} = \frac{\text{INR/US Goods}}{\text{INR/Domestic Goods}}$$

We cannot express the real exchange rate as the ratio P^*/P, as the two price levels are expressed in different currencies. When P^*/P, which is the price of the foreign goods relative to the price of domestic goods, is measured in a common currency, we have the real exchange rate. The real exchange rate incorporates nominal exchange rate, E, as well as relative prices of goods and services across countries.

As you would have noticed, economists focus on real variables. When we were examining how to measure income, for instance, we wanted a measure that corrects for changes in the general level of prices—real, rather than nominal incomes. In a similar vein, a distinction is made between the nominal exchange rate and the real exchange rate. It is the change in the real exchange rate, rather than the nominal exchange rate, that affects the exports and imports of a nation—a distinction that is often mistakenly overlooked.

Let us take an example. Suppose you are planning to purchase furniture for your home, and one option is to import it from Italy. The furniture you have chosen costs EUR 1,000 for being delivered at your home, according to the price list of the Italian furniture brand, Friuli. If you were to purchase an Indian brand such as Style Spa, it would cost you INR 60,000. At the time you are contemplating your purchase, the current exchange rate for the euro is INR 57 per euro. In order to purchase the Italian furniture for EUR 1,000, you would need to exchange INR 57,000. When you compare the price of the Italian furniture with the Indian furniture, you find that the latter is costlier by INR 3,000, or 5.3 per cent. To come to this conclusion, you required three pieces of information—the euro price of the Italian furniture, the rupee price of the Indian furniture, and the nominal exchange rate.

However, if prices rise by 3 per cent a year in Italy, and 5 per cent a year in India, then the price of Italian furniture would increase to EUR 1,030, whereas that of Indian furniture would rise to INR 63,000, in a year's time. If the nominal exchange rate does not change (INR 57 = EUR 1), then the rupee price of the Italian furniture would be INR 58,710. The Indian furniture is now costlier by INR 4,290, or 7.3 per cent. Even without a change in the nominal exchange rate, Indian furniture is relatively more expensive than Italian furniture and Indian purchasers of furniture would purchase more Italian furniture—a situation of more imports.

Suppose, on the other hand, the rupee depreciates against the euro so that INR 58.11 equals EUR 1. Then, the rupee price of Italian furniture would rise to INR 59,853.30 (1,030 × 58.11), which is INR 3,146.70 lower than the cost of Indian furniture (INR 63,000). Indian furniture would now cost 5.3 per cent more than Italian furniture, just like before the price change. Indian furniture being relatively less costly (5.3 per cent costlier, instead of 7.3 per cent), Indians would tend to purchase less abroad. Imports would be less than when the nominal exchange rate was constant.

This example illustrates that it is not only changes in the nominal exchange rate, but also changes in the price levels in two countries that affect imports and exports. That is why the real exchange rate, which considers the relative price of domestic and foreign goods rather than just the nominal exchange rate, affects the decision to export or import.

5.1.1 Real Exchange Rates and Net Exports

When the real exchange rate is high, foreign goods are, on an average, more expensive than domestic goods when they are priced in the same currency. A high value of the real exchange rate means that domestic producers will find it easy to export to other countries, while foreign goods will be expensive as compared to goods produced at home. Thus, an increase in the value of the real exchange rate will tend to increase exports and reduce imports. Exports and imports are affected by changes in the real exchange rate. The real exchange rate always floats, even for a country that may fix its nominal exchange rate. When the nominal exchange rate is fixed or pegged to the value of another country's currency, the price level at home will adjust vis-à-vis prices abroad, and the real exchange rate will fluctuate in response to mismatches between the demand and supply for goods traded between the countries. The real exchange rate of the Hong Kong dollar is, thus, a floating rate, even though the nominal rate is fixed by Hong Kong's currency board.

The graph of the real exchange rate[2] and the nominal exchange rate of the rupee vis-à-vis the US dollar is depicted in Figure 5.1. The real exchange rate for the Indian economy has mildly fluctuated around a constant trend from 1993 onwards. It depreciated till 2002 and appreciated since then till 2007. However, the nominal exchange rate has been depreciating faster from 1993 to 2002 at a trend growth rate of 3.6 per cent, from INR 31.4 per US dollar in 1993 to INR 48.2 per US dollar in 2002. It appears that as the inflation differential between the two economies widened, the RBI intervened in the foreign-exchange market by allowing the nominal exchange rate to depreciate up to 2002, and then appreciate subsequently till 2007, so as to stabilize the real exchange rate[3]. Since 2008, the nominal exchange rate has been depreciating and the real exchange rate has been appreciating. In this period, the central bank did not intervene in the foreign-exchange market, and the exchange rate was more market-determined.

The real exchange rate is also important for the definition of the trade balance, or the difference between exports (X) and imports (M). Exports and imports are incommensurable, as the former are domestic goods and the latter are foreign goods. To measure imports in the same units as exports, we need to multiply the volume of imports by the real exchange rate.

Let a country produce only one good which is used for both exports and domestic consumption. Let Q_M denote real imports. Then, P^*Q_M is the nominal value of imports in the foreign currency. The nominal value of imports in domestic currency terms will then be EP^*Q_M, where E is the nominal exchange rate. The trade balance or net exports—exports less imports—in nominal terms will then be given by,

$$\text{Nominal Net Exports} = PQ_x - EP^*Q_M$$

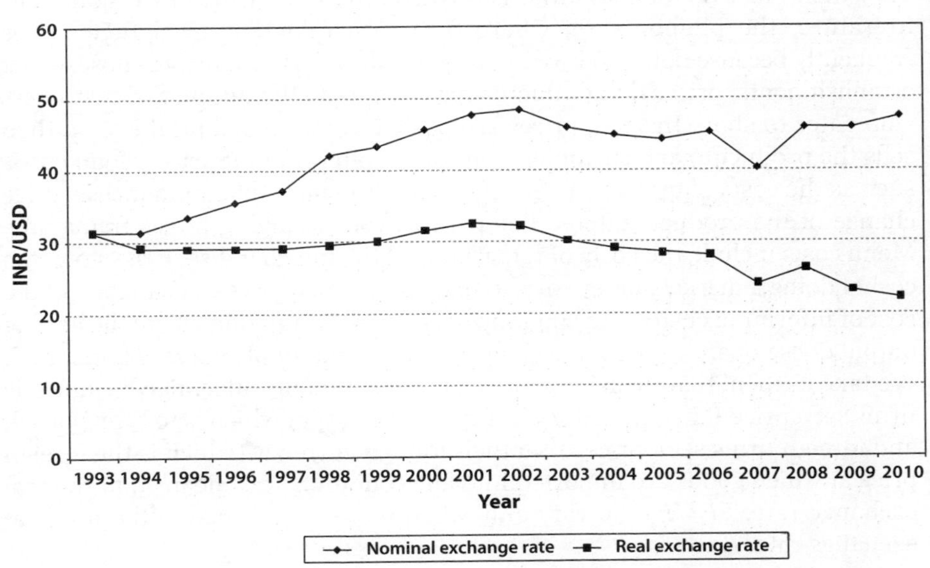

› **Figure 5.1**
Real and Nominal Exchange Rates. The nominal exchange rate of the Indian rupee per US dollar has been depreciating till 2002, and then has appreciated till 2007, after which it again began to depreciate. The real exchange rate has mildly depreciated till 2002 and has been appreciating since then.

In real terms—in terms of the price of domestic goods, net exports will be:

$$NX = Q_X - \frac{EP^*}{P} Q_M$$

$$= Q_X - qQ_M$$

where, $q = (EP^*)/P$ is the real exchange rate.

Hence, net exports (NX) as defined in the national income accounts is given by[4],

$$NX = Q_X - qQ_M$$

$$= X - M \quad (5.2)$$

5.1.2 The Marshall–Lerner Condition

How does a change in the real exchange rate affect the trade balance account of a country? The answer to this question is provided by the Marshall–Lerner condition, named after the two economists who discovered it—Alfred Marshall and Abba Lerner. At this stage, to determine the impact of a change in the real exchange rate on net exports, we ignore the influence of net factor incomes and transfers from abroad as well as capital flows on the exchange rate. Alternatively, international transactions involving payments for the services of labour and capital working abroad (net factor incomes from abroad) and transactions on the capital account can be considered to be constant for our current purposes. This is equivalent to stating that the balance of payments is simply the balance of trade plus a constant. Also, we begin the analysis at a point of time when the economy is experiencing balanced trade, or net exports is equal to zero. This starting point of the analysis implies that a change in the real exchange rate can have one of three impacts—net exports will stay unchanged at zero, net exports will improve and we will obtain a surplus trade balance, or net exports will worsen and we will obtain a deficit in the balance of trade. The Marshall–Lerner condition then informs us how starting from a position of balanced trade, a change in the real exchange rate affects the net exports of an economy.

To facilitate diagrammatic analysis, we will assume that the period of analysis is the short run where the level of output does not affect prices. In the short run, producers post a price for their product which is unchanged. They then meet the demand that is forthcoming at that price. In economics literature, the phenomenon where firms are reluctant to change prices frequently because doing so is costly is referred to as MENU COSTS. At most selling establishments, prices do not fluctuate according to the number of customers who enter to shop. Instead, prices are posted by the shop and the shop then sells the product to any customer who wants to buy at that price. Menu costs, such as the costs of printing a new menu or a brochure that announces a price change of the products offered deter firms from changing prices frequently. Menu costs include the costs of remarking all the merchandise in the store, the cost of doing a market survey so as to figure out which price to change, and the cost of informing customers about price changes. A situation where the level of output does not affect prices is a situation where the supply curve is horizontal. We take it, then, that firms set a price and this remains unchanged. Domestic firms set a price $\overline{P}$ in domestic currency for the output which is to be exported, and foreign firms set a price $\overline{P}^*$ in their foreign currency (which is the foreign price at which goods are imported into an economy). This means that the real exchange rate, $E\overline{P}^*/\overline{P}$, can vary only when there is a change in the nominal exchange rate, E.

› **Menu costs** are the costs to a supplier of changing listed prices.

A resident of a country that is importing a good will be concerned with what the price of that importable is in terms of domestic currency. Since the price has been set by producers abroad at $\overline{P}^*$, the price the domestic economy experiences when the good is imported is $E\overline{P}^*$. The supply of the imported good is then infinitely elastic at $E\overline{P}^*$ (see Figure 5.2). The demand for the import is a usual demand curve where the demand is decreasing in the price of the imported good expressed in domestic currency units. We can write the demand for imports, M, as inversely related to the real or (equivalently) the nominal exchange rate given that the foreign currency price of the good has been set by the producer—this is depicted in Figure 5.2. The demand curve reflects the situation where residents buy fewer products from abroad when the domestic currency price of those products increases.

In a symmetric way, the supply of exports is set by domestic producers at $\overline{P}$ and is an infinitely elastic supply curve (Figure 5.3). The demand for exports is by agents abroad, who like any agent on the demand side of a transaction, will demand less the higher the price. In this case, the price of the exportable good for a person abroad is in a foreign currency, P. Converting that price into the currency units of the person abroad makes the prices of the exportable good P/E. If, for instance, the price of an export item from India is $P =$ INR 100 and the exchange rate is $E =$ INR 40 per USD, then the export item in foreign currency units abroad costs USD $P/E =$ USD(100/40) $=$ USD 2.5. Finally, the customers abroad will compare the price of the average foreign good that is exported to them with the price of the average domestic good,

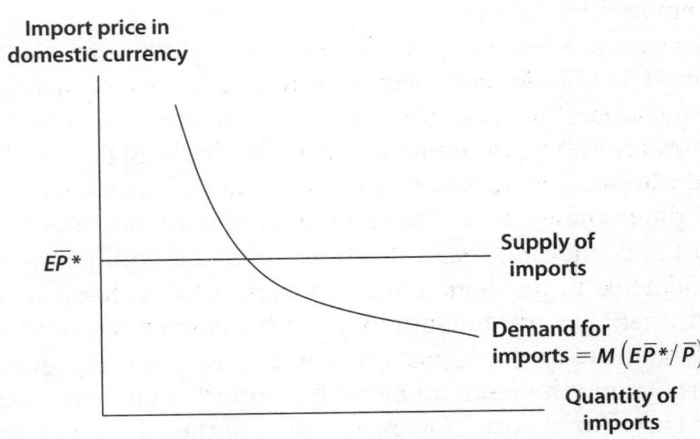

› **Figure 5.2**
The Imports Market. With supply prices fixed, suppliers are willing to supply any quantity of imports at $E\overline{P}^*$. The demand for imports is decreasing in the price of the imported good in comparison to domestic goods, $E\overline{P}^*/\overline{P}$.

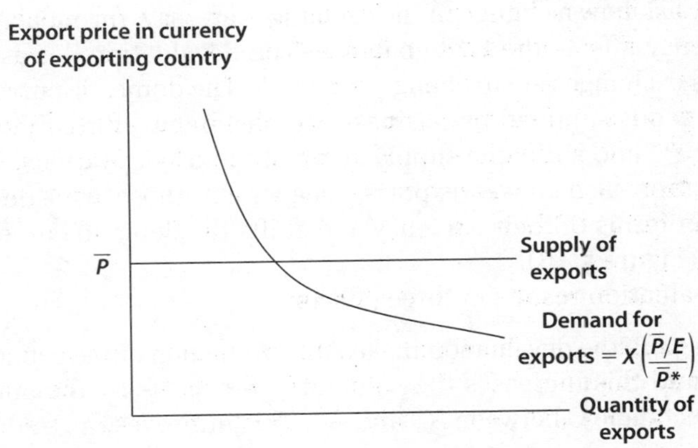

› **Figure 5.3**
The Exports Market. With supply prices fixed due to menu costs, producers are willing to supply any amount of exports at the price $\overline{P}$. The demand for exports is negatively related to the relative price of the foreign good to the domestic good, $(\overline{P}/E)/\overline{P}^*$.

with prices expressed in terms of a common currency. That is, as discussed earlier, the demand depends on the real exchange rate in this case, the real exchange rate for these abroad is the price of the foreign good in terms of the domestic good. The demand for exports is then a decreasing function of $(P/E)/P^*$, and we can write $X = X(\overline{P}/E)/\overline{P}^*$. The demand and supply of exports is depicted in Figure 5.3.

Notice that in Figure 5.3, the demand curve for exports is drawn for a given nominal exchange rate—the price on the vertical axis is in terms of the currency of those who export the good and not in terms of the currency of those who demand the good. A change in the nominal exchange rate, then, will result in a shift of the entire demand curve for exports. A demand curve is the relation between the quantities demanded at the different prices represented on the vertical axis, with all the other factors affecting demand held constant. As the price on the vertical axis, changes, there is a movement along the demand curve. If any of the other factors that affect demand changes, there will be a shift in the demand curve. To continue the earlier example, the rupee price of the export is $P =$ INR 100. However, let us assume that the nominal exchange rate has depreciated to $E^1 =$ INR 50 per USD instead of $E =$ INR 40 per USD. Prices abroad, P^* has not changed. Then, the export in foreign currency units is USD $P/E^1 =$ USD (100/50) = USD 2. The foreign price of the export has declined from USD 2.5 to USD 2. As the exports have become cheaper, the demand for exports will increase and the demand for exports curve will shift rightwards at every price to reflect the increased willingness to demand exportables abroad. If the nominal exchange rate appreciates, on the other hand, then exportables become more expensive in foreign currency units, and the demand for exports curve shifts leftwards.

In Figure 5.2, the demand curve for imports is with reference to the price of the imported good in domestic currency units, EP^*. A nominal depreciation of the currency raises the price of imports to domestic residents and this is a movement upwards along the demand curve. The demand function for imports is expressed after converting the foreign price into domestic currency that is inclusive of the exchange rate. The nominal exchange rate effect of the price of an importable, then is already factored into the willingness to demand imports as depicted in the demand curve for imports. A change in the NOMINAL EXCHANGE RATE, then, is a movement along the demand curve for imports and a shift of the demand curve for exports. A depreciation of the currency is a movement upwards along the demand curve for imports and a rightward shift of the demand curve for exports. An appreciation of the currency is a movement downwards along the demand curve for imports and a leftward shift of the demand curve for exports.

› A change in the **nominal exchange rate** causes a movement along the demand curve for imports and a shift of the demand curve for exports.

We now ask how a change in the exchange rate, say, through a devaluation of the currency affects the trade balance. The devaluation, let us say, causes the nominal exchange rate to change to $E^1 > E$. The domestic currency price of importable goods supplied by business establishments abroad now increases to $E^1\overline{P}^* > E\overline{P}^*$ and shifts the supply curve of imports upwards (Figure 5.4A). The devaluation also makes exports cheaper for those who demand these exportable in terms of their currency and shifts the demand curve for exports to the right (Figure 5.4B).

The devaluation results in three effects:

1. In Figure 5.4B, the devaluation makes the production of the country relatively cheaper and this increases the value of real exports by the amount of the shaded rectangle C between X^0 and X^1. This improves the trade balance.

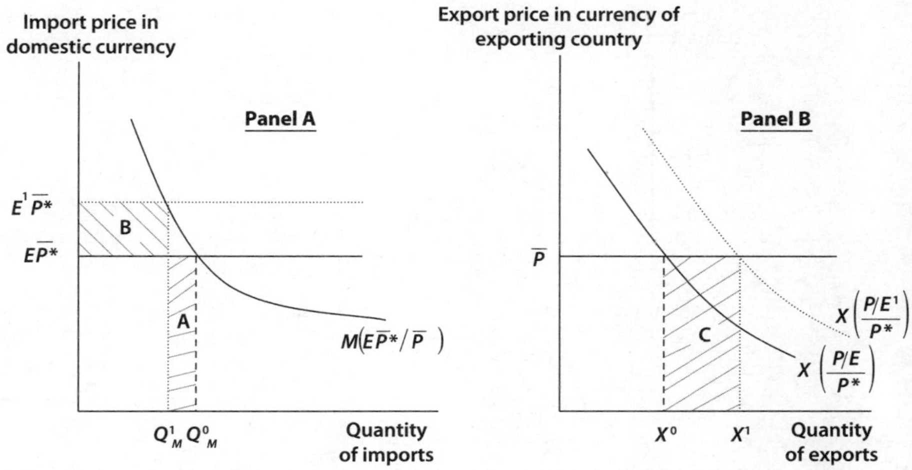

› **Figure 5.4**
Effect of a Devaluation.
A devaluation of the currency shifts up the supply curve of imports in panel A and shifts to the right the demand curve for exports in panel B. It (a) increases the volume of exports (area C), (b) reduces the volume of imports (area A), and (c) increases the price paid for imports or the value of imports (area B).

2. In Figure 5.4A, the devaluation reduces the real quantity of imports from Q_M^0 to Q_M^1. This reduction in imports improves the trade balance.
3. In Figure 5.4A, the devaluation raises the price that has to be paid for imports from $E\overline{P}^*$ to $E^1\overline{P}^*$. This increases the price of the foreign good as compared to the domestic good. This change in the valuation of imports worsens the trade balance as more domestic output is being exchanged per unit of foreign goods imported. Suppose the shaded rectangular area B representing this valuation change in imports is larger than shaded rectangular area A representing the reduction in the volume of imports at the original valuation E. Then, even though the volume of imports has declined, the country is paying out more in value terms on that reduced import volume. Think of imports as spending on foreign goods and paying for it in terms of domestic goods. When the price of a good increases, demand falls, and yet the increase in price could be large enough that the expenditure on the reduced demand is higher than earlier.* In a similar vein, the rise in the exchange rate can reduce the quantity of imports and yet the expenditure on imports in terms of the value of the domestic output equivalent of the volume of imports increases. Such is the case if rectangle B is larger than rectangle A.

The net outcome on the trade balance of a devaluation of the currency, then, is unclear. If the third effect is larger than the first two, the net outcome could be a worsening of the trade balance. The trade balance would improve if the third effect is small and the first two effects are large. The first effect is large if the volume of exports increases substantially when the exchange rate is devalued, if exports are elastic with respect to the exchange rate. The second effect dominates the third effect depending on the elasticity of import demand.

In Figure 5.5, we depict two import demand curves—the elastic curve M_{elastic} and the inelastic curve $M_{\text{inelastic}}$. At the domestic currency cost of imports $E\overline{P}^*$, the quantity of imports is initially the same, Q_M^0, on both these demand curves. After the devaluation which increases the domestic currency cost to $E^1\overline{P}^*$, the quantity of imports declines relatively more to $Q_{M_e}^1$ along

*This occurs when the price elasticity of demand is less than unity. For example, suppose at a price of INR 20, 6 units of a good are purchased. If the price doubles to INR 40, the demand reduces to 4 units. Expenditure on the good has increased though the demand for the good has declined.

› Figure 5.5
The Elasticity of Imports. When the import demand is elastic, devaluation reduces the volume of imports to a greater extent than when it is inelastic. However, when the import demand is inelastic, a devaluation increases the relative price of foreign to domestic goods or the value of imports more than when it is elastic.

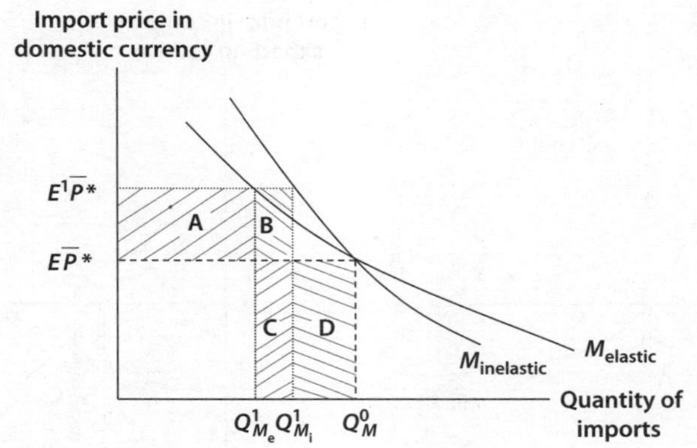

the elastic demand curve and the change in imports is smaller at $Q^1_{M_i}$ along the inelastic demand curve. In contrast, the devaluation increases the relative price to be paid for imports and raises the valuation of imports more for the inelastic demand curve (given by the sum of areas A and B), than for the elastic import demand curve (given by the area A). The sizes of the second and third effect arising from the devaluation of the currency are summarized in the Table 5.1.

It is clear that the third effect is larger and the second effect smaller when import demand is inelastic. The valuation effect, then, is larger when imports are inelastic with respect to the exchange rate.[5] The trade balance will then have a higher likelihood of worsening when the import demand curve is inelastic.

This implies that the more elastic are the import demand and the export demand curves, the more likely is it that the trade balance will improve. In fact, it can be proved (see the Appendix 5.1) that starting from a position of balanced trade, a devaluation will improve the trade balance if the sum of the elasticity of demand for exports (η_X) and the elasticity of demand for imports (η_M) exceeds unity. This is the MARSHALL–LERNER CONDITION and may be written as,

› The **Marshall–Lerner condition** states that the trade balance improves following a devaluation or real depreciation of the currency if the sum of the export and import elasticities is greater than unity.

$$\eta_X + \eta_M > 1 \tag{5.3}$$

The Marshall–Lerner condition holds if the elasticities of exports and imports were defined with respect to the real exchange rate instead of the nominal exchange rate. With the supply prices fixed by producers in the currency of their countries, the real exchange rate is $E\overline{P}^*/\overline{P}$. A change in the real exchange rate, then, is identical to a change in the nominal exchange rate as the producer prices do not change. It is the real exchange rate which influences the demand for importables and exportables. We should accordingly interpret the Marshall–Lerner conditions in terms of the elasticities with respect to the real exchange rate rather than the nominal exchange rate.

The Marshall–Lerner condition applies when the initial position is one of trade balance. If a country has a trade deficit and seeks to reduce the deficit, then, for the trade deficit to improve the elasticities must be larger

› Table 5.1
Impact of Devaluation on Imports

	Elastic Import Demand	Inelastic Import Demand
Second effect: Reduction in volume of imports valued at original exchange rate	Area C + D	Area D
Third effect: Valuation change effect of devaluation	Area A	Area A + B

than the value of unity as given by the Marshall–Lerner condition. This is because with real imports larger than exports as in a trade deficit situation,** the valuation effect of a change in the exchange rate is much larger as the value of imports initially were relatively large. The demand curves for imports and exports we have considered have been specified as functions of the relative price of foreign versus domestic goods. A more complete demand function would be in terms of the incomes in the country from which the demand originates as well. With exports and imports a function of the real exchange rate as well as income abroad and domestic income, a change in the real exchange rate changes the income of a country and has induced indirect effects on demand. For instance, an increase in the real exchange rate increases the exports and income of an economy. This increase in income will cause an increase in expenditure on goods—both domestic as well as imported goods—and result in an indirect increase in imports. These indirect effects have been suppressed in the Marshall–Lerner elasticity approach.

5.1.3 The J-Curve

Goldstein and Kahn (1985) found that the medium to long run elasticities (measuring the response of trade flows to real exchange rate changes over an adjustment period of greater than two years) are about twice as large as the short-run elasticities (measuring the response of trade flows in the first six months after the change in the real exchange rate). Furthermore, the short run elasticities almost always fail to sum to unity while the long run elasticities almost always sum to greater than unity. The possibility that in the short-run the Marshall–Lerner condition may not be fulfilled, although it generally holds in the longer run, is the J-CURVE effect. Following a real devaluation at time t_1 (Figure 5.6) the trade balance deteriorates and after some time (greater than two quarters of a year) it improves.

› The **J-Curve** is the phenomenon where a depreciation of the currency causes the trade balance to initially worsen before it eventually improves.

The J-curve depicting rising demand elasticities over time occurs due to a number of reasons. First, most orders for exports and imports are usually placed a few months in advance. The real depreciation or devaluation of a currency then raises the value of the quantity of imports that have been precontracted for. As exports are measured in domestic output, the level of

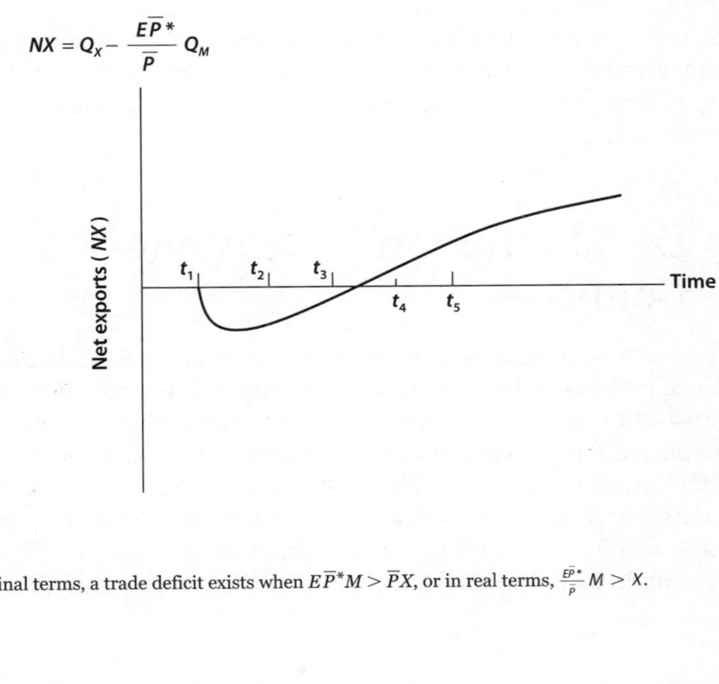

› **Figure 5.6**
The J-Curve. A real devaluation at time t_1 results initially in a deterioration of the trade balance. After some time t_3, the trade balance improves as exports and the demand for imported goods respond to the devaluation.

**In nominal terms, a trade deficit exists when $E\bar{P}^*M > \bar{P}X$, or in real terms, $\frac{E\bar{P}^*}{\bar{P}} M > X$.

MACROFOCUS 5.1

Does Devaluation Raise the Price of Imported Goods?

From 2002 to 2005, the dollar depreciated about 15 per cent against an import-weighted index of currencies. The decline of the dollar should have helped correct the US trade deficit by altering the relative price of US and foreign goods. As the cost of foreign goods rose, US demand for imports ought to have weakened. Similarly, US exports ought to have increased as those goods became less costly abroad. Yet, the US trade imbalance has not shrunk in response to the depreciation of the currency.

One explanation for this puzzle is that pass-through—the degree to which a change in the value of a country's currency induces a change in the price of the country's imports and exports—can vary across industries because foreign firms may have different levels of market power as compared to domestic firms (Froot and Klemperer, 1989). For instance, if a foreign firm exports goods in an industry in which domestic firms have considerable market power, it may be reluctant to raise prices when the domestic currency depreciates. The foreign firm will adjust its markup downward to maintain market share and exchange rate pass-through will be lower. If, on the other hand, a foreign firm exports goods in an industry in which domestic firms have less market power, it may have less incentive to keep prices low.

Many other countries also experienced episodes of large real exchange rate depreciations in the 1990s that did not result in significant increases in the prices of imported goods. Renowned examples of this include Sweden and the UK after 1992 and Brazil after 1999. Another reason advanced for this phenomenon is the increased emphasis by central banks on inflation stabilization (Gagnon and Ihrig, 2004). When a central bank acts aggressively to stabilize inflation, it tightens policy to offset any inflationary impetus from a rise in import prices. Agents anticipating the central bank's actions are less likely to pass through cost increases arising from exchange rate depreciations.

An important implication of import prices becoming less responsive to changes in currency values is that larger devaluations of the currency would be required to narrow trade imbalances. Also, a depreciation of the currency would not result in rising import prices, and to that extent, would not have an inflationary impact on the economy.

precontracted export does not change. However, imports are valued in domestic output and this measure of imports (the real exchange rate) rises following a real depreciation. Then, the trade balance initially declines because it is measured in domestic output.

Second, the pass-through effects of a change in the exchange rate may be partial. A pass-through effect occurs when a change in the exchange rate results in a change in domestic prices of imported goods. Often, however, retailers do not immediately pass exchange rate changes through to domestic currency prices. Instead, they absorb the increase in the cost of imports by reducing profit margins as would prefer to retain their market share (see Macrofocus 5.1).

Finally, the quantity response to a change in the real exchange rate occurs with a lag. Producers who are exporters require time to scale up output by increasing plant and machinery and hiring new workers. Importers, if they are importing intermediate goods, will also install production units that economize on the use of these intermediate inputs. As these quantity changes become larger, the trade balance improves and at some point the trade balance is more favourable than the pre real exchange rate depreciation level and the J-curve tapers off.

5.2 Devaluation in Developing Countries

› A devaluation can be contractionary in a **developing country** if it decreases the share of workers in national income or the increase in the import price of crucial inputs causes a contraction in supply.

Until the late 1970s, it was widely believed that devaluation would improve the trade balance and expand output and employment. An alternative approach that emerged at the end of the 1970s raised the possibility that devaluation would be contractionary, especially in DEVELOPING COUNTRIES. This approach is sometimes referred to as structuralist as it considers the economic problem of developing countries to be structural.[6] One of the channels identified by Krugman and Taylor (1978) through which devaluation might cause a reduction in national output is the income-distribution channel. This income distribution effect arises because there are two different classes of consumers in the society: wage earners and profit (including rent) earners. The marginal propensity to consume for wage earners is higher than that for profit earners, as the income level of workers is lower and saving possibilities are limited for them. A devaluation[7] increases the price of traded goods and real wages, (w/P), decline since nominal wages are the same but prices are now higher. While the workers' share in national income falls, profit earners' share increases. As the marginal propensity to consume for wage earners is higher than profit earners, there is an eventual decline in aggregate demand.

Yet another channel through which devaluation works is the imported input cost channel. In many developing countries, the production process is highly dependent on imported inputs in the form of raw materials, intermediate, or capital goods. Devaluation via imported inputs increases the cost of imports in particular, and the cost of domestic production in general. Decreasing imports results in insufficient inputs that are necessary for production. Eventually, due to the lack of inputs and increasing costs, production slows down leading to a contraction in total supply. This occurs especially in oil-importing developing countries. A rise in the price of oil increases the cost of production. As the cost of production increases relative to the price of the product, firms tend to produce less. This leads to a reduction in aggregate supply and an increase in unemployment. Devaluation creates negative effects similar to oil price shocks on output and employment through increased production costs in developing countries.

The evidence of devaluation is that the effect of exchange rate changes on the balance of trade in India does not yield a J-Curve (Singh, 2004). Singh used quarterly data from 1975 to 1996 for the exchange rate in terms of the trade weighted real effective exchange rate, and found that the first and sixth quarter lags of this variable affect the trade balance with a negative coefficient whilst the other lags (upto the eighth lag) are positive. However, only the coefficient of the first lag is statistically significant—suggesting no J-Curve effect. Whilst the real exchange rate and domestic income significantly explained the behavior of the balance of trade in India, Singh found that the world income had no effect on the trade balance. As the lack of a significant relation between the trade balance and the real exchange rate could be due to the use of aggregate trade data, it is advisable to study the short-run and long-run effects of real depreciation of the rupee on the Indian trade balance using bilateral trade and real exchange rate data. Arora, Bahmani-Oskooee and Goswami (2003) do such a study for the seven largest trading partners of India, who together counted for more than 50 per cent of Indian trade during the quarters of 1977 to 1998. Again, there is no J-Curve effect, but long-run real depreciation of the rupee against the currencies of Australia, Germany, Italy, and Japan has a positive impact on India's trade balance with each country. However, the UK, USA, and France do not show any significant impact of the bilateral real exchange rate on the bilateral trade balance.

5.3 Exchange Rates and Assets

As the nominal exchange rate is the price of one country's money in terms of another's, it is also an asset price. The exchange rate, therefore, affects not only the flow of goods and services on the trade account but also the purchase and sale of assets such as bonds, equities, and real estate on the capital account.

We should, thus, expect that the principles governing the behaviour of other asset prices also govern the behaviour of the exchange rate. If foreign-currency assets are taken to be a foreign bond or a foreign-currency deposit, what are the determinants of the demand for these assets? The demand for a foreign-currency deposit will be influenced by the same considerations that apply with regard to the demand for other assets. The expected returns on holding the asset influence the demand for an asset. This is associated with the asset's future value, which, in the case of a foreign-currency deposit, depends on two factors—the interest rate offered abroad and the expected change in the country's exchange rate against other currencies.

Of course, assets are valued by savers for attributes other than the expected rate of return. Savers care about the risk or the variability that the asset contributes to a savers' wealth and the liquidity, or the ease with which the asset can be sold. We will assume here that the foreign and domestic financial assets are perfect substitutes so that they have equivalent risk and liquidity attributes. Also, we assume that international capital markets are free from capital controls and there are no restrictions on the purchase and sale of foreign currency denominated assets. These assumptions allow us to unravel, with reference to asset demand, the determination of the exchange rate.

5.3.1 Uncovered and Covered Interest Parity

We now consider the demand for an asset in terms of the return on the asset vis-à-vis competing assets. Under these conditions, consider an agent who must choose between investing an amount INR X domestically or abroad. If she invests domestically, she will receive over a given period (such as a year) a rate of return on the domestic financial instrument E_D measured in the domestic currency, where,

$$E_D = (1 + i)X \tag{5.4}$$

and i is the domestic interest rate on domestic deposits.

› When two parties agree to an exchange of financial instruments and execute the deal immediately, then the exchange rates governing such "on-the-spot" trading are called **spot exchange rates**.

If, on the other hand, the money is invested abroad, the amount INR X must first be converted into foreign currency units at the SPOT EXCHANGE RATE, E. With INR E equal to USD 1, INR X will give USD X/E. The earnings in foreign currency on this amount will be USD $(1 + i^*)(X/E)$, where i^* is the interest rate on the foreign-currency deposit.

This earning must be converted back into domestic currency at the end of the investment period. However, when the investment decision is taken, it is not known what the exchange rate will be at the end of the investment period, and so an expectation is formed concerning the future exchange rate, E^e. The expected domestic currency return on the foreign financial instrument will then be,

$$E_F^e = (1 + i^*)\frac{X}{E}E^e \tag{5.5}$$

The domestic financial instrument will be preferred as long as the return obtained on it exceeds the return on the foreign financial instrument,

$$E_D > E_F^e$$

or,

$$(1 + i)X > (1 + i^*)\frac{X}{E}E^e$$

or,

$$\frac{1 + i}{1 + i^*} > \frac{E^e}{E}$$

or,
$$\frac{1+i}{1+i^*} - 1 > \frac{E^e}{E} - 1$$

or,
$$\frac{i-i^*}{1+i^*} > \frac{E^e - E}{E}$$

Multiplying throughout by (1+ i^*), we get,

$$i - i^* > \frac{E^e - E}{E} + i^*\left(\frac{E^e - E}{E}\right)$$

The product $i^*\,[(E^e - E)/E]$ is usually a small number and ignored. Hence, the savers will continue to prefer the domestic financial instrument as long as,

$$i - i^* > \frac{E^e - E}{E} \tag{5.6}$$

or, as long as the interest rate differential exceeds the depreciation expectation regarding the domestic currency. The inequality in Eq. (5.6) will eventually tend towards an equalization of the domestic and foreign rates of return, $E_D = E_F^e$, through the operation of three mechanisms:

1. A capital inflow as savers abroad seek higher returns domestically, which create an additional supply of capital and cause a fall in domestic interest rates.
2. A tightening of the supply of capital abroad due to the savers there preferring the higher return on financial instruments outside their country, which leads to a rise in foreign interest rates.
3. The capital inflow increasing the supply of foreign currency, which causes the spot exchange rate to appreciate (the $S_X + M_K$ curve in Figure 2.2 shifts to the right, causing the exchange rate to appreciate) and leads to an increase in the percentage by which the exchange rate is expected to depreciate, i.e., an increase in $(E^e - E)/E$.

Hence, equalization of the return on financial instruments domestically and abroad results in:

$$i = i^* + \frac{E^e - E}{E} \tag{5.7}$$

This is referred to as the UNCOVERED INTEREST PARITY condition; "uncovered" because the investment involves an exchange risk which could be eliminated by selling forward the foreign currency amount as soon as the funds are invested abroad. Knowing that an amount of dollars given by USD $(1 + i^*)(X/E)$ is due to them a year from now, an agent could currently enter into an agreement to sell this amount when it comes due and request a forward market trader to quote an exchange rate at which he would purchase the amount. A forward market trader would quote an exchange rate at which he would be willing to purchase USD $(1 + i^*)(X/E)$ a year from now and that quoted rate is the forward rate of Indian rupees per dollar of F. If agents hedged the exchange rate risk via a FORWARD TRANSACTION, they could earn a return E_F^f by selling forward the foreign currency amount as soon as the funds are invested abroad, where, $E_F^f = (1 + i^*)(X/E)F$.

Then, the equilibrium condition is,

$$i = i^* + \frac{F - E}{E} \tag{5.8}$$

› **Uncovered interest parity** relates interest differentials of two countries $i - i^*$ to the expected change in the spot exchange rate between those countries.

› The exchange rate quoted for a date on which the parties actually receive the funds they have purchased is a **forward exchange rate**. Forward exchange rates are typically for 30 days, 90 days, 180 days, and 365 days. The forward exchange rate F in the text is a one year forward rate.

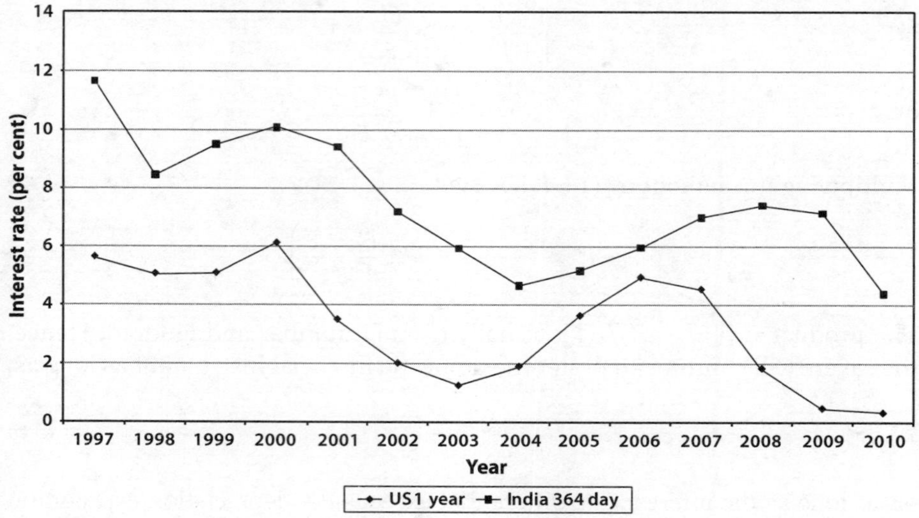

› **Figure 5.7**
Interest Rates on U.S. one Year Government Securities and Indian 364 Day Treasury Bills. That interest rates on one year US government securities and 364 day Indian Treasury bills show a similarity in the pattern of variation is an indication that the interest parity conditions hold.

› **Covered interest parity** relates the difference between the interest rate domestically and abroad to the forward premium or discount.

› The **Law of One Price** applied to assets states that if international arbitrage is unhindered (the market is efficient), then identical assets (with the same risk and liquidity characteristics) must earn the same rate of return.

which is referred to as the COVERED INTEREST PARITY condition. The interest parity conditions are an example of the LAW OF ONE PRICE for asset markets. The reason we expect the law to prevail is arbitrage—the process of buying or selling an asset in order to exploit a price differential and to make a riskless profit. The interest parity conditions define the foreign-exchange market to be in equilibrium when the deposits of all currencies offer the same expected rate of return (when measured in the same currency).

An implication of interest parity is that if there is a change, say, in the foreign interest rate, i^*, then in response to that change assets will be redeployed between the domestic and foreign country. If the foreign interest rate increases then the attractiveness of higher interest rate abroad causes asset holders to reduce their demand for assets domestically and increase their demand for assets abroad. The reduction in the demand for domestic assets reduces the supply of capital by savers and this in turn causes the domestic interest rate to rise. Hence, the interest parity condition implies that domestic and foreign interest rates should move in tandem. Figure 5.7 plots the interest rates on 1 year government securities in the US and 364 day Treasury bills in India. As can be seen from Figure 5.6, there is a similarity in the pattern of annual variation of interest rates indicating that interest parity applies.

5.3.2 Exchange Rate Determination

To understand how the foreign-exchange market finds its equilibrium, consider how the current exchange rate affects the expected return on a foreign-currency deposit. From Eq. (5.5), a depreciation of the country's currency today (an increase in E) reduces the expected domestic currency return on foreign currency deposits, E_F^e. Similarly, appreciation of the domestic currency today (a decrease in E), raises the domestic currency return expected of foreign currency deposits. For a fixed value of the expected future rupee/dollar exchange rate, E^e, and the foreign currency interest rate, i^*, the expected return on foreign-currency deposits is, therefore, a downward sloping schedule, as in Figure 5.8. The reason for this is that a current depreciation of the domestic currency that affects neither the exchange rate expectations (E^e), nor interest rates (i, i^*), leaves the expected future payoff of a foreign currency deposit in rupee terms the same, but raises the foreign currency deposit's current rupee cost.[8]

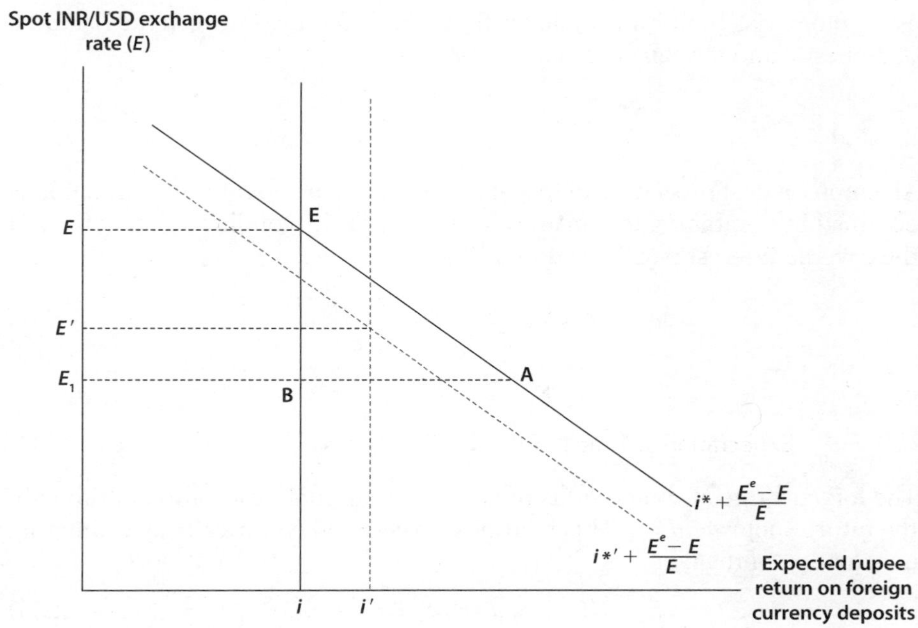

› **Figure 5.8 Equilibrium Exchange Rate.** The demand for foreign-currency deposits increases with an appreciation of the currency. With a domestic interest rate i, interest parity determines the exchange rate at E. If the exchange rate, instead, is E_1, individuals will purchase the higher return foreign-currency deposits. The increased supply of capital abroad decreases the foreign interest rate to $i^{*\prime}$ and the reduced holding of domestic deposits raises the domestic interest rate to i'. The exchange rate then settles at E'.

The vertical schedule in Figure 5.8 represents the given level of the return on domestic currency deposits, i. The intersection of the two schedules at point E gives the equilibrium exchange rate, E. Any exchange rate not equal to E will tend to gravitate towards E. To see why, consider an appreciated exchange rate E_1. At this exchange rate the rate of return on foreign-currency deposits (distance E_1A) is greater than the rate of return on domestic deposits (distance E_1B). Individuals would prefer selling their domestic deposits for the more lucrative foreign-currency deposits. As domestic residents purchase foreign exchange whilst seeking higher returns on deposits abroad, they bid up the exchange rate—the curve $D_M + X_K$ shifts to the right in Figure 2.2 of Chapter 2—till the return on domestic and foreign currency deposits are equal and there is no longer an incentive to get out of domestic deposits.

Of course, as discussed earlier, as savers withdraw their holdings of domestic deposits there is a tightening of the supply of capital. This raises the domestic interest rate—the point i shifts to i', where $i' > i$. Similarly, the capital inflow abroad creates an additional supply of capital that results in a decline in the foreign interest rate—i^* declines to $i^{*\prime} < i^*$. Hence, the final equilibrium exchange rate[9] will be at E' where the dashed lines intersect.

As long as domestic and foreign-currency assets are perfect substitutes, the foreign-exchange market is in equilibrium when the interest parity condition given by Eq. (5.7) holds. When imperfect asset substitutability exists, it is possible for the expected returns of the assets to differ in equilibrium. The main factors behind imperfect asset substitutability are risk (when the return on an asset fluctuates widely) and liquidity (the high cost and speed at which savers can dispose of an asset). If assets denominated in different currencies have different degrees of risk, investors who are risk averse may be willing to earn a lower expected return on assets that are less risky. This means that they will hold a risky asset only if the expected returns it offers is relatively high. Equilibrium in the foreign-exchange market now requires that the domestic interest rate equals the expected domestic currency returns on the foreign asset, plus a risk premium (ρ) that reflects the difference between the riskiness of domestic and foreign currency assets:

$$i = i^* + \frac{E^e - E}{E} + \rho \tag{5.9}$$

An empirical test procedure of this approach to exchange rate determination is obtained by combining the uncovered interest parity condition, Eq. (5.7), and the covered interest parity condition, Eq. (5.8). Then,

$$i^* + \frac{E^e - E}{E} = i^* + \frac{F - E}{E}$$

or,
$$E^e - E = F - E$$

or,
$$\text{Expectation at Time } t \text{ of } E_{t+1} = E^e = F_t \tag{5.10}$$

The forward rate at time t, F_t, is the market's rational expectation at time t of the future spot rate, E_{t+1}. This relationship is tested empirically by estimating an equation of the type:

$$E_{t+1} = \alpha + \beta F_t + \varepsilon_{t+1} \tag{5.11}$$

where ε_{t+1} is a random error term. If α is close to zero and β is close to 1, then, the interest parity approach to exchange rates is valid. The estimates for most currencies lead to results that tend to support this approach.[10] Bhoi and Dhall (1998) examine the data for India and find that covered interest parity holds for the Indian economy in the post-reform period.

5.4 Purchasing Power Parity

› **Purchasing power parity** states that if arbitrage across national borders is unhindered, the price of a good or service in one nation should be the same as the exchange rate adjusted price of the same good in another nation.

Interest rate parity is the application of the law of one price for assets. Applying this law to goods results in PURCHASING POWER PARITY (PPP). It is an old theory of exchange rate determination.[11] It is based on the Law of One Price, which states that apart from tariffs and transaction costs (inclusive of transportation costs), international commodity arbitrage will equalize the prices for tradable goods in all locations when quoted in the same currency. The principle here is that when trade is open and costless, identical goods should trade at the same relative prices regardless of where they are sold. If a good i sells in a market abroad at a foreign currency price of USD P_i^*, and the same good fetches a price of INR P_i in the domestic market (ignoring tariffs and transactions costs) the domestic price should be the foreign price times the exchange rate, or,

$$P_i = EP_i^* \tag{5.12}$$

If $P_i > EP_i^*$, then an arbitrageur would have an incentive to buy the good abroad where it is cheap and ship it into the domestic market where it is dear. In the process he will push up the price abroad and push down the domestic price until prices are equal in the two locations. If we assume that the domestic price index, $P = f(P_1..., P_i,..., P_n)$, and the foreign price index, $P^* = g(P_1^* ..., P_i^* ,..., P_n^*)$, are made up of the same goods with the same weights—the reference commodity baskets are identical in the two countries[11]—the Law of One Price applied to individual goods becomes a law of price levels, which is the ABSOLUTE VERSION OF THE PPP,

› **Absolute PPP** states that the domestic price level should equal the foreign price level times the spot exchange rate.

$$P = EP^* \tag{5.13}$$

The left-hand side is the rupee price of the reference commodity basket domestically, and the right hand side is the rupee price of the reference basket when purchased abroad. These two prices are the same when PPP holds. PPP is, thus, the proposition that the price levels of all countries are equal when measured in terms of the same currency. If purchasing power parity holds, then the exchange rate between countries can be obtained by rearranging Eq. (5.13) to obtain,

$$E^{PPP} = \frac{P}{P^*} = \frac{\text{Domestic Price of the Reference Basket of Goods}}{\text{Foreign Price of the Same Reference Basket}} \tag{5.14}$$

Though the Law of One Price applies to individual commodities, the PPP applies to the general price level, which is a composite of the prices of all commodities contained in the reference basket. The PPP holds as long as the reference basket used to calculate different countries' price levels are the same.[12] When goods become more expensive in one country than in others, the demand for its currency and products declines, and this depreciates its currency and pushes domestic price down in line with PPP.

Irving Kravis, a student of the father of national income accounting, Simon Kuznets, started the Penn World Tables or the International Comparisons Program along with Alan Heston and Robert Summers. This is where the data on prices across countries are collected for a common reference basket of goods and services. This enables them to calculate the international price of the reference basket, P^*. Dividing the domestic currency weighted average of prices of the reference basket of goods, P, by P^*, gives the purchasing power parity exchange rate for a domestic economy, $E^{PPP} = P/P^*$. Suppose the market exchange rate, as obtained in the foreign-exchange market for an economy, is greater than the PPP value of the exchange rate. Then,

$$E > E^{PPP} = \frac{P}{P^*}$$

Cross multiplying, we obtain,

$$EP^* > P$$

› The domestic currency is undervalued when the market exchange rate exceeds the purchasing power parity exchange rate. Products in a country with an **undervalued** exchange rate are cheaper than abroad when prices across countries are compared using the spot exchange rate.

or, the cost of goods abroad valued in terms of the spot exchange rate of the domestic currency is greater than the cost of goods in the domestic economy. As goods produced domestically cost less or are valued less than goods abroad, the domestic currency is considered to be UNDERVALUED. When a currency is undervalued, a person traveling to the country which uses that currency will find that many products there seem cheaper than in his own country after converting the prices there using the spot exchange rate. Similarly, a currency is considered to be OVERVALUED when the cost of goods from abroad valued in terms of the spot exchange rate of the domestic currency is less than the cost of goods domestically, i.e., goods are more expensive domestically than abroad, or, $EP^* < P$. A person traveling to a country where the currency is overvalued compared to his own country will find that products there are more expensive than in his home country after converting the prices there using the spot exchange rate. Figure 5.9 plots the market and PPP exchange rates for India from the Penn World Tables. The market exchange rate in India is greater than the PPP exchange rates. On average for the period 1994 to 2009, the market exchange rate in India was 3.4 times the PPP exchange rate. This qualifies the Indian exchange rate as being undervalued. China's market exchange rate for the same period was on average 2.7 times the Chinese PPP exchange rate. According to this measure, then, India is a cheaper economy than China.

› The domestic currency is **overvalued** when the market exchange rate is less than the purchasing power parity exchange rate.

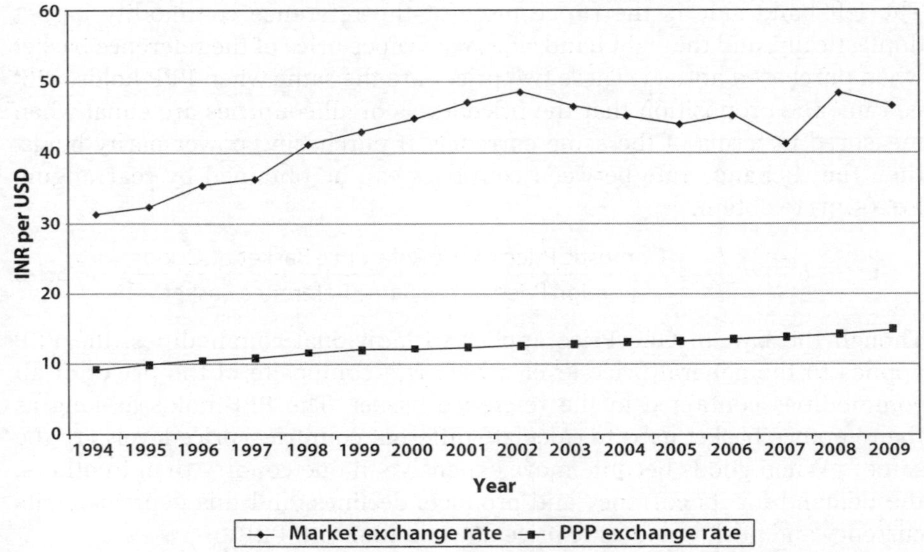

› **Figure 5.9 Market and PPP Exchange Rates.** Market exchange rates in India are higher than the PPP exchange rate, implying that the Indian currency is undervalued.
Source: Penn World Tables.

› Non-traded goods are goods that are not **traded** because of the absence of strong national cost advantages or because of high transport costs.

› **Relative PPP** states that the change in an exchange rate is equal to the difference in inflation rates between two economies.

Absolute PPP makes no sense if the reference baskets whose prices are compared in Eq. (5.13) are not the same. Price indices differ across countries and they include many goods and services that are not TRADABLE. In addition, even for perfectly homogeneous commodities, there are transactions costs, tariffs, and indirect taxes. It thus makes sense to translate absolute PPP from a statement about price and exchange rate levels, into one about price and exchange rate changes. This formulation is referred to as RELATIVE PURCHASING POWER PARITY.[14] If we write the absolute version of purchasing power parity, $P = EP^*$, in percentage form, then, the percentage change in the exchange rate between periods $t - 1$ and t, or $\Delta E / E = (E_t - E_{t-1})/E_{t-1}$, is given by,

$$\frac{\Delta E}{E} = \frac{\Delta P}{P} - \frac{\Delta P^*}{P^*} \tag{5.15}$$

On the right hand side of Eq. (5.15) is the difference between the domestic inflation rate, $\Delta P / P = (P_t - P_{t-1}) / P_{t-1}$, and the inflation rate abroad, $\Delta P^* / P^* = (P_t^* - P_{t-1}^*) / P_{t-1}^*$.

When countries calculate absolute price level estimates using reference baskets of commodities that differ in coverage and composition, and when factors causing deviations from absolute PPP are by and large stable over time, percentage changes in relative price levels (or differences in inflation rates) can still approximate percentage changes in exchange rates.

In monetary policy the relative version of PPP plays an important role. Many countries adopt a fixed exchange rate vis-à-vis the currency of a country with low inflation so that they can import that country's price stability. When the exchange rate is fixed, $\Delta E/E = 0$ in Eq. (5.15), and $\Delta P/P = \Delta P^*/P^*$ so that the country's inflation rate is aligned to the inflation rate of the country it pegs its exchange rate to.

Alternatively, proponents of a system of flexible exchange rates argue that countries can select their preferred national inflation rate, $(\overline{\Delta P/P})$, and then the exchange rate would compensate passively for the differential in inflation given that $(\Delta E/E) = (\overline{\Delta P/P}) - (\Delta P^*/P^*)$.

The empirical backing for the PPP theory is weak, both for its absolute and relative versions.[15] There are, of course, the transaction costs and restrictions to trade factors. Then, the price indices are based on different commodity

MACROFOCUS 5.2

Big Macs, iPods, and Professors' Salaries

Since 1986, the *Economist* magazine has published the Big Mac index which is based on the theory of purchasing power parity (PPP). This theory states that exchange rates should move towards levels that equalize the price of an identical basket of goods and services in any two countries. The Big Mac PPP rate, then, is the exchange rate that would leave burgers costing the same in America as elsewhere. In the middle of 2006, the Big Mac cost 10.5 yuan in China against an average price of USD 3.10 in the US. The two prices would be equal at an exchange rate of (10.5/3.10) or 3.39 yuan to a US dollar. The market exchange rate, however, at that time was 8.03 yuan per dollar. When the market determined value of the yuan is higher than that implied by PPP, it indicates that the local currency is "undervalued" against the dollar. We would then expect the yuan to appreciate relative to the dollar. Similarly, if the local currency exchange rate implied by PPP is lower than the market exchange rate, the local currency is "overvalued" relative to the dollar and we would expect it to depreciate.

A limitation of the Big Mac index is that burgers cannot easily be traded across borders and prices are distorted due to differences in local taxes, labour laws, and the cost of non-tradable inputs such as rents. In response to these limitations, economists at Commonwealth Securities (CommSec), a brokerage firm in Australia, have developed an iPod index. The key difference between the Big Mac and iPod index is that Big Macs are made in a host of countries whereas iPods are predominantly made in China. iPods can also be purchased over the internet so that if there were substantial price differences across locations, customers could switch their purchases to other countries. The CommSec iPod (for a 2 GB iPod nano) indeed reveals that it costs USD 149 to purchase an iPod in the US compared to USD 179.84 in China. Unlike the Big Mac index which would cause us to expect the yuan to appreciate, the iPod index indicates that the yuan should depreciate against the dollar. Again, if Apple sells iPods at different prices in different parts of the world (it gives volume discounts to retailers in the US for example) or if freight costs vary between countries, the PPP values of this index are distorted.

In recent times, professors have asked for higher salaries as it is not just higher commercial salaries, but also higher salaries overseas that is a barrier to attracting talent into academics. To test whether this is true, Ong and Mitchell (2000) argue that if a Big Mac costs USD 2.42 in the US and AUD 2.50 in Australia, then an academic would require a salary of 2.50 in Australia for every USD 2.42 earned in the US in order to purchase a similar lifestyle. In that case, they find that real academic salaries are highest in Hong Kong and Singapore, followed by Australia and the US. Canada and New Zealand are unattractive destinations by this measure for academics.

baskets, or if on the same reference basket of commodities, then, the number of commodities in this basket is limited and not fully representative of the production in the economy. The price indices also include services and NON-TRADABLE goods for which the law of one price does not hold. Many goods are not traded internationally because of prohibitive transportation costs. For example, if India were to export haircuts to the US it would require transporting an Indian barber to, say, New York every time a New York resident desired a hair cut. As transport costs prevent hair cuts from being traded internationally, the law of one price does not apply to this service.

› **Non-tradables** are goods and services where transport costs may be so large relative to the cost of production that they cannot be traded internationally at a profit. Examples are primarily agricultural land, highly perishable food, services such as the output of the construction industry with the exception of financial services provided by banks and brokerage firms.

Finally, over the last decade, capital flows have become so large that rather than passively accommodating inflation differentials, exchange rates have become an autonomous source for deviations from PPP. The principal weakness of absolute and relative PPP is that absolute and relative PPP focus solely on the international exchange of goods and services and do not consider the effect of financial flows and money stock on the exchange rate.

5.5 Choice of Exchange Rate Regimes

We have discussed the role that exchange rates play in affecting the trade balance and competitiveness of the asset markets. Exchange rates are also an area of concern because of the effect on macroeconomic management, particularly inflation, and due to the link between the exchange rate regime and vulnerability to currency crises. In fact, as Fischer (2001) points out, each of the major crises in the 1990s—Mexico in 1994; Thailand, Indonesia, and Korea in 1997; Russia and Brazil in 1998; and Argentina and Turkey in 2000—has involved a fixed exchange rate system. The advantage of a fixed exchange rate is that countries with a high propensity to inflation are able to import low inflation (Dornbusch, 2001, and the discussion in Section 5.4). Fixed exchange

MACROFOCUS 5.3

The Euro

The European Monetary Union is the latest step in a long movement that began during the mid 1980s towards integration of Western Europe with member countries agreeing to the abolition of internal barriers and the free movement of goods, persons, services and capital by 1992. In 1989, Jacques Delors, the president of the EU Commission (the executive body of the European Union) proposed a plan for the creation of a single currency to be issued by a European Central Bank (ECB). The proposal was adopted in the 1991 Treaty on European Union, often called the Maastricht Treaty. Under the terms of the treaty, countries wishing to join the European Monetary Union (EMU) must meet certain convergence criteria. There are four primary criteria:

1. Prices: For admission to the EMU the consumer price inflation rate of a country must be no more than 1.5 per cent above the average of those of the three EU member states with the lowest inflation rates.
2. Deficits: Actual and planned budget deficits should not exceed 3 per cent of GDP and government debt should not exceed 60 per cent of GDP. The budget should also be balanced in the medium run in that deficits should be counter balanced by surpluses in subsequent periods.
3. Interest rates: The long term interest rate must be, on average, no more than 2 per cent above the average of those of the three EU members with the lowest inflation rate.
4. Exchange rates: The country should have observed normal fluctuations in the exchange rate, without devaluing on its own initiative against the currency of another EU member.

The motivation for these criteria was to ensure that the single currency will be a hard currency. When an individual country runs into financial problems, it faces the consequence in terms of high interest rates, rising inflation, or even a run on its currency. When countries share a currency, the risks are spread and this can cause a country to take less care in tackling economic problems such as a fiscal problem as it escapes the full consequences of lack of action on its part. A profligate government with a loose fiscal policy also pushes up borrowing costs for all countries. The convergence criteria are meant to ensure that countries are sincere and committed to stable policies and are not free riders.

The euro was launched on 1 January 1999 with 11 member countries—Belgium, Germany, Ireland, Spain, France, Italy, Luxembourg, the Netherlands, Austria, Portugal, and Finland—fulfilling the criteria. Greece joined a couple of years later and Slovenia became the thirteenth member of the euro area in January 2007.

On 1 January 1999, national central banks of these countries became members of the European Central Bank and they operate in line with the ECB's guidelines and instructions. They carry out monetary policy operations such as providing central bank money to credit institutions and foreign reserve management operations as agents for the ECB.

On 1 January 1999, the nominal exchange rates at which member countries currencies were to be transferred into euro were fixed. The euro began as an electronic currency in which consumers held bank accounts and credit cards. National currencies were different expressions of what is economically the same currency and the ECB was obliged to exchange national banknotes against the euro at par. Cash appeared three years later on 1 January 2002. Banks and their ATMs after this date were to dispense only euros and retailers were to give change only in the single currency. After that, within two months, national notes and coins were to be withdrawn and cease to be legal tender. Bank notes prior to the Euro were adorned with images of Antoine de Saint-Exupéry (France), Vasco da Gama (Portugal), and René Margritte (Belgium). The Euro depicts the architectural style of seven periods in Europe's cultural history—classical, Romanesque, Gothic, Renaissance, baroque, and rococo, the age of iron and glass architecture, and modern twentieth century architecture—and shows three main architectural elements: windows, gateways, and bridges.

The nominal exchange rate of national currencies and the last date of their existence as legal tender are given in the following table: This is the first time that countries of this number, size or global economic weight, have collaborated to share a currency without a single government behind it. For the first time since the fall of the Roman Empire, does much of Western Europe have a single currency. Some have even called it the most momentous currency innovation since the establishment of the US dollar in 1792.

› **Table 1**

European Currencies and Exchange Rates Prior to the Introduction of the Euro

Country	National Currency Units Per Euro	End of Legal Tender for National Currency in 2002
Austria	13.7603	28 February
Belgium	40.3399	28 February
Finland	5.94573	28 February
France	6.55957	17 February
Germany	1.95583	31 December 2001*
Greece	340.750	28 February
Ireland	0.787564	9 February
Italy	1936.27	28 February
Luxembourg	40.3390	28 February
Netherlands	2.20371	28 February
Portugal	200.482	28 February
Spain	166.386	28 February

* Retailers will accept D-marks till 28 February 2002.
Source: European Central Bank, http://www.ecb.int/home/html/index.en.html

Even though the nominal exchange rates between the members of the euro area have been permanently fixed, their real exchange rates vary depending on differences in their rates of inflation. Between 1999 and 2006, for instance, Italy's real exchange rate has appreciated by more than 20 per cent relative to Germany's. From early 2002, the euro appreciated against the dollar, and that was believed to be bad news for the competitiveness of exports from Europe. However, German firms in that period improved productivity and clamped down on wage costs and this resulted in low inflation and a depreciated real exchange rate that allowed German exports to hold up strongly in world markets.

rates also reduce devaluation risk and thus lead to lower interest rates which stimulate investment. The fix in the exchange rate is maintained by means of changes in the country's foreign-exchange reserves—buying and selling foreign currency in order to balance supply and demand in the currency market to preserve the price of domestic currency vis-à-vis foreign currency.

To do this successfully a country generally requires foreign currency reserves equivalent to three to four months' worth of imports. When economic agents anticipate that reserves are inadequate and that the monetary authority will resort to devaluation, agents may launch speculative attacks based on a one-way bet that the peg will be abandoned leading to a currency crisis.

› When speculators expect that a devaluation is imminent they protect themselves against the expected loss in the value of the domestic currency by trading it in for foreign currency. The central bank in such a situation very quickly loses large amounts of its foreign-exchange reserves, which is known as a **speculative attack**. The monetary authority is then forced to abandon its exchange rate target and devalue the currency.

Due to the vulnerability of fixed exchange rates to SPECULATIVE ATTACKS, floating exchange rates are often advocated as an appropriate regime. However, floating exchange rate regimes, where the authorities do not intervene in the foreign-exchange market and do not set interest rates for the purpose of effecting the level or path of the exchange rate, do not insulate an economy from the adverse effects of international capital flows. Short-term capital flows seeking ARBITRAGE opportunities and quick return in anticipation of changes in the exchange rate under a currency float can affect the payment system especially when a country's financial sector is poorly regulated or lacks DEPTH. Volatility in a flexible exchange rate regime increases the currency risk which, in turn, increases the differential in the interest rates domestically and abroad. The corresponding higher domestic interest rate attracts hot money and also increases the likelihood of ORIGINAL SIN. When a national currency cannot be used by local firms or the government to borrow abroad, it suffers from original sin (Hausmann, 1999). In such a situation investors who find the country economically promising must borrow in a foreign currency such as the dollar or borrow short term because the domestic capital market lacks sufficient depth. When a firm borrows in dollars to finance a project that generates rupees, a subsequent depreciation can lead to bankruptcy. Investments suffer from a CURRENCY MISMATCH, and when firms see the domestic currency begin to deprecate, they may attempt to buy foreign currency to cover their exposure. This increase in demand for foreign currency causes the domestic currency to depreciate even further which increases the volatility of exchange rates.

› **Arbitrage** means "buy low – sell high" and indicates an activity through which individuals seek immediate profits based on price differentials. If exchange rate differences prevail in different markets forex traders purchase cheap and sell where the price is high to make a profit.

› A financial market is considered to have depth when participants can rapidly execute large volume transactions. The **depth** is the maximum amount or limit that a dealer stands ready to buy or sell at posted prices.

› When a country must borrow abroad in a foreign currency, it suffers from **original sin**. In such a situation, a depreciation of the currency could cause agents to purchase foreign currency to cover their repayments which, in turn, leads to further depreciation and volatility of the exchange rate.

Thus, the appropriate exchange-rate regime for a country depends on its exposure to international capital and the level to which its domestic financial sector has matured. Countries that are heavily exposed to global capital flows and which have a mature and well-regulated financial sector would find floating to be appropriate. Otherwise, countries would operate a fixed exchange rate regime. There are three types of fixed exchange rate regimes: currency boards, dollarization, and a currency union (Fischer, 2001, Obstfeld and Rogoff, 1995).

› A financial institution that chooses to borrow entirely in dollars and lend in rupees has a **currency mismatch** because if the value of the rupee were to depreciate its assets (rupees) would be the same, but its liabilities (dollars) in rupee terms would increase and the bank would lose money.

Currency Board: Under a CURRENCY BOARD, the stock of domestic money in circulation is backed by foreign currency reserves, and the monetary authority commits to buying or selling the domestic currency in unlimited quantities at some pre-announced exchange rate. The exchange rate is set by public law and the commitment to convert currency is limited to the domestic monetary base or reserve money, M_0, not the domestic money supply, M_3.

Hence,
$$M_0 = \lambda q Q_F$$

where, λ = degree to which domestic currency is backed by foreign currency
q = the exchange rate between the domestic currency and the foreign currency to which it is linked
Q_F = monetary authority's holdings of foreign currency

› Under a **currency board,** the exchange rate between the local currency and, say, the dollar is fixed by law and the monetary authority commits to buying or selling the domestic currency without any limit at this pre-announced exchange rate.

Occasionally, currency boards have less than 100 per cent backing unlike the textbook story where the domestic base is fully backed by foreign reserves and $\lambda = 1$. The Convertibility Law governing Argentina's currency board during 1991 to 2002, for instance, only required 80 per cent backing of the base.[16] A number of East European countries have adopted currency boards by linking their currencies to the Deutsche mark/euro—Estonia, Bulgaria, Lithuania, and Bosnia-Herzegovina. With the local currency completely equivalent to the foreign anchor currency at the fixed exchange rate, the currency board has no discretionary monetary powers and cannot extend credit if the domestic base is fully backed by foreign-currency reserves.

› Under **dollarization,** a country officially adopts a foreign currency as its legal tender. Dollarization removes a country's control over its monetary policy.

Dollarization: Under DOLLARIZATION (or euroization) a country officially adopts a foreign currency as its legal tender. To dollarise, two exchanges must be accomplished. First, the monetary base has to be exchanged for the adopted foreign currency at a predetermined conversion rate. Second, all contracts in the local currency must be transformed into contracts denominated in the adopted currency. Thus, local currency contracts would be redenominated and payable in, say, US dollars. Unlike a currency board arrangement, the local currency is completely replaced by the adopted foreign currency, rather than limited in quantity by the number of units of anchor currency held by the currency board. Again, there is no scope of independent monetary policy as the monetary policy would be determined by the US Federal Reserve Board, which is desirable if a country's monetary authorities are irresponsible. But it is undesirable if a country needs a more expansionary monetary policy. The dollarising country is also faced with the expense of buying dollars to swap with its national currency. It pays for these dollars either with its foreign reserves or with the money from a large dollar-denominated loan. In either case, the cost in terms of forgone interest payments on its reserves or new interest payments on its borrowings, could be significant. Argentina, for example, would be required to spend USD 15 billion to swap its peso currency notes for US dollars (Sachs & Larrain, 1999). Countries that are dollarised include Marshall Islands, Micronesia, Palau, and Panama—all small economies (except Panama)—most goods are used in international trade and most prices are set in dollars.

› In a **monetary union,** a group of countries share a common currency and jointly manage the currency through a common central bank.

Currency or Monetary Union: Dollarization is an asymmetric MONETARY UNION as one country adopts another country's currency as its own, but does not have any say in the management of that currency. In a symmetric monetary union, a group of countries share a common currency and jointly manage the currency through a common central bank. Under monetary union there is a regionalization as in the case of the euro rather than a dollarization of national currencies. With the responsibility for the exchange-rate policy and the balance of payments with the rest of the world assigned to a common central bank, there is a gain in terms of the reduction in transaction costs of doing business within the region. Also, the monetary policy is removed from the domain of populist national politics with a supranational central bank run by designated representatives from each of the participating countries. There are also savings unlike under dollarization. The countries who are party to the monetary union could print the common currency at a low cost and swap it for their outstanding currencies in circulation.[17] If they were to dollarise, they would sell interest earning dollar reserves or borrow new dollars at high interest rates to swap dollars for the existing currencies.

Monetary union is beneficial when countries have approximately the same economic structure, are subject to the same international shocks, and trade a lot with one another. By adopting a common currency, they fix their exchange rates with one another but remain flexible in relation to other major currencies such as the US dollar. If a country that is part of a monetary union is subject to an economic shock (such as a natural disaster and abrupt shifts in capital flows) that is not common to the union, then as it is deprived of exchange rate flexibility, it needs to adjust to the shock by other means such as wage and price flexibility, the mobility of labour and capital, and fiscal compensation. For example, suppose there is a sudden capital outflow from a country. Ordinarily this would have caused a depreciation of the currency. Since this option is foreclosed and the currency is overvalued, the alternative is that the country has to wait for the goods and labour markets to adjust such that nominal goods prices decline in order to clear the excess supply that results in the goods market. This process of adjustment could be protracted compared to the speed at which the exchange rate could change in response to the capital outflow. In practice, there are many political and cultural obstacles to the regionalization of national currencies. If that were not true, Argentina and Brazil would have established one by now.

5.5.1 Intermediate Exchange Rates

In between fixed and floating exchange rates there exist some intermediate exchange rate regimes such as a target zone, crawling pegs, basket pegs, and adjustable pegs.

Target zone or soft peg: In this case, the central bank announces a central parity or target for the exchange rate and margins around it. This regime is also referred to as a soft peg. Under a soft peg, the authorities adopt a particular target exchange rate and use monetary policy to prevent the market's straying too far from the target. "Too far" is operationalized by the announcement of a target rate and the width of a band around it. A target zone or soft peg with narrow bands is very much the equivalent of a fixed exchange rate. If the bands are wide then the exchange rate regime approaches a floating exchange rate regime. The central parity can be adjusted in line with inflation or the fundamentals of the economy.

Adjustable peg: Under an adjustable peg, the bands tend to be narrow—less than or equal to ±2.25 per cent—and the target rate is adjusted if the authorities perceive a discrepancy between the target exchange rate and the equilibrium rate. The target rate is adjusted infrequently and by large amounts (Kenen, 2001). The Bretton Woods system was an adjustable peg system where the official policy was that the peg will be adjusted if there is a fundamental disequilibrium.

Crawling peg: Under a crawling peg the authorities target a path for the exchange rate instead of a level. The bands tend to be somewhat wider than the bands around adjustable pegs as they must accommodate the crawling of the pegs. The target rate is altered frequently and by relatively small amounts with the aim being to offset inflation and prevent the currency from being overvalued in real terms (Kenen, 2001). Under a passive crawling peg, the exchange rate parity is adjusted for past inflation differentials as the goal is to offset inflation so as to keep the real exchange rate constant. An active crawling peg preannounces the rate of the crawl with the aim of influencing price expectations. The *tablita* is an active crawling peg where the preannounced rate of crawl is less than the inflation rate. This type of exchange mechanism was used by Argentina in the 1970s in an attempt to use the exchange rate to put downward pressure on inflation. Hungary, Israel, and Sri Lanka have crawling band exchange rate regimes.

Basket peg: Pegging to one currency means floating vis-à-vis other currencies. CROSS RATE FLUCTUATIONS can do serious damage to an economy, as was the case with the East Asian economies whose currencies were pegged to the dollar

› Arbitrage results in consistency of exchange rates across three or more currencies. For instance, you could buy USD 100 worth of British Pounds in New York, sell it in London for Indian rupees and then sell the rupees in Mumbai for dollars. If you end up with more (or less) than USD 100 the exchange rates are not consistent, and indeed, if you made a profit you would repeat this transaction till the market rates are consistent. Triangular arbitrage maintains consistency among bilateral cross rates. **Cross rate consistency** implies that the dollar/pound exchange rate times the rupee/dollar exchange rate must equal the rupee/pound exchange rate.

during the Asian financial crisis of 1997 (Corsetti, Pesenti, and Roubini, 1998). The sharp appreciation of the dollar vis-à-vis the yen simultaneously caused an appreciation of many East Asian currencies against the yen and resulted in their exports being priced out of foreign markets, paving the way for the crisis that followed. These countries had pegged to the dollar, though their external trade was quite diversified. Pegging to a single currency is not otherwise a problem for countries whose trade is geographically concentrated and who peg to the currency of that large trading partner. A way out of this difficulty caused by cross rate fluctuations is to peg to a weighted basket of currencies. However, if the weights used to calculate the basket are kept secret, then governments have a temptation to devalue under a basket peg which undermines the transparency and observability of monetary policy. If the weights used to calculate the basket are public information then there is also a need to change the weights in response to structural change that affects the trade pattern of a country. Basket pegs have been used by countries in the Middle East and some East Asian countries as well.

Managed float: Even when exchange rates are allowed to change due to market forces, central banks often intervene in the foreign-exchange market. In a managed float (also called a dirty float) the central bank influences the exchange rate by buying and selling foreign currency. In this regime there is no public commitment to a target exchange rate but the authorities may intervene in the foreign-exchange market and/or set interest rates to influence the exchange rate. The authorities' aim may be to smooth short term volatility that makes it difficult for firms operating in export markets to plan into the future, or to reverse sustained departure of the exchange rate from what they perceive as its equilibrium value (referred to as misalignment). Also countries with balance of payments surpluses are often averse to appreciation of their currency as it affects the sale of domestic businesses abroad. Such countries often intervene in foreign-exchange markets and sell their currency in exchange for foreign-exchange reserves. The managed float system operates in many countries including Britain, Japan, the Czech Republic, and Taiwan. When Japan intervened in the currency market in the 1980s to keep down the value of the yen, thereby boosting Japanese exports and restricting its imports, it was described as a dirty float.

5.5.2 Fixed Versus Float

Many countries attempt to run a monetary policy aimed at domestic economic conditions while intervening in the foreign-exchange markets to influence exchange rates. Often these goals are mutually incompatible, especially when a country has an open capital account and is a destination for capital flows. For instance, a country could attempt to correct a recession by an expansionary monetary policy that reduces domestic interest rates relative to international interest rates. With a pegged exchange rate, the lower interest rate reduces the relative return to foreign investors who will pull out their assets. The corresponding outflow of foreign currency will put pressure on the domestic currency and will require the use of the country's foreign-exchange reserves to defend the fixed exchange rate. Ultimately as reserves get depleted, the country will have to choose between abandoning the fixed exchange rate and abandoning its monetary policy by raising its domestic interest rate. This dilemma is referred to as the IMPOSSIBLE TRINITY—it is not possible for a country to have control over a fixed exchange rate, control over independent monetary policy (monetary autonomy) and a fully open capital account simultaneously. Thus, the necessary condition for a government to have both an exchange rate policy and an

› The **impossible trinity** refers to the dilemma that a country cannot simultaneously have control over a fixed exchange rate, control over monetary policy, and maintain an open capital account.

independent monetary policy in the short run is that it is imperfectly integrated with world capital markets.

Is there a link between macroeconomic performance and the exchange rate regime? Are output growth and inflation different depending on the exchange rate regime that prevails? Edwards (1996) found for a sample of 52 developing countries over the period 1980–1989 that countries with fixed exchange rates experienced lower inflation during the 1980s compared to countries with flexible exchange rate arrangements.[18] Ghosh, Gulde, Ostry, and Wolf (1996) examine the macroeconomic performance of 136 countries for the period 1960–1989. Their results indicate that countries with fixed exchange rates experience lower rates of inflation whereas when it comes to output growth there are no significant differences between fixed and flexible exchange rate economies. An IMF (1997) study found for a group of 123 developing countries during the period 1975–1996 that the rate of inflation in countries with pegged exchange rates has been consistently lower and less volatile than in countries with flexible exchange rates. This study also found that the inflation rate difference between pegged and flexible exchange rates has been decreasing throughout the 1990s. However, the output growth rate over the two decades that were examined in the study was not significantly different across exchange rate regimes. In the recent World Economic Outlook 2010, the IMF examines whether the choice of exchange rate regime[19] is important to understanding how 50 emerging market economies fared during the global financial crisis that peaked in September 2008. The finding is that economies with pegged regimes fared no better than those with floats and there is no difference in growth performance between pegs and floats (IMF, 2010, Chapter 1).

The debate over fixed versus floating exchange rates is still a wide open one. The International Monetary Fund too has shifted its recommendation according to circumstances. After the 1997 Asian Crisis, the IMF accused soft pegs, not of playing a part in the Asian meltdown, but of amplifying the cost of crisis. Pegged exchange rates encouraged growth of UNHEDGED foreign currency debt and currency mismatch of balance sheets. This pushed up the costs of devaluation for borrowers, triggering claims of bankruptcy and bank failures. These events, along with the huge losses incurred by the monetary authorities as they sought to defend their exchange rates from speculative attack, resulted in an even higher cost for the resolution of the crisis. This played a role in the ensuing IMF's doctrinal shift. From considering fixed exchange rates as a tool against inflation, the IMF turned to "corner" solutions based on hard pegs—dollarization or currency board or pure floats—in the late nineties (Fischer, 2001). However, there was another shift of doctrine, after the Argentine crisis in 2001–2002. Since that time, the IMF has stopped recommending currency boards as a credible solution and has switched to its current doctrine of floating arrangements with inflation targeting (Rogoff, Husain, Mody, Brookes and Oomes, 2003).

› When business is conducted across borders in a flexible exchange rate regime contracts are usually signed using the foreign-exchange rate deemed appropriate at that time. This foreign-exchange rate may not prevail at the time of the performance of the contract when currency is actually exchanged. **Hedging** is a way for a business entity to eliminate foreign-exchange risk. Two common hedges are forwards and options. A forward contract locks in the exchange rate at which the performance of the contract and the transaction in currency occurs in the future. An option sets the rate at which the business may choose to exchange currencies. If the current exchange rate is favourable the business entity will not exercise the option.

The advantage of fixed exchange rate as we saw is that (1) they reduce the transactions costs and uncertainty associated with exchange rates that those engaged in international trade in goods, services, and assets face and (2) when pegged to a major country's currency that is stable they induce an expectation of a low inflation rate in the home country as well. The cost of a fixed exchange rate regime is that, in a world where capital markets are highly integrated, the country loses the ability to pursue an independent monetary policy due to the impossible trinity. In contrast though flexible exchange rates restore monetary policy autonomy on the central bank of a country they have the downside that central banks that are free of the obligation to fix their exchange rate could embark on inflationary policies. Under flexible exchange rate regimes central banks are not disciplined by the exchange rate mechanism to a rate of inflation that prevails in the economy of the trading partner of the country.

In the mid-1990s, Obstfeld and Rogoff (1995) wrote an article titled "The Mirage of Fixed Exchange Rates," warning against fixed regimes. They argued that such systems last for a couple of years on an average and are regularly followed by a collapse in the exchange rate and a currency crisis. A fixed exchange rate often causes the real exchange rate to become overvalued which makes the regime vulnerable to a speculative attack. By the end of the decade Reinhart (2002) wrote an equally famous article titled "The Mirage of Floating Exchange Rates" where she argued that floating rates are even more of a delusion than fixed ones for the simple reason that they do not exist. Looking at a large sample of countries she demonstrated that no emerging country actually allows its exchange rate to float because the governments of those countries suffer from what Calvo and Reinhart (2002) dubbed the FEAR OF FLOATING. Fear of floating exists when a country claims to be pursuing domestic policy goals, such as price stability and full employment, that are independent of the exchange rate and yet that country repeatedly intervenes, directly or indirectly, to keep the exchange rate in check. This is distinguished from simple dirty floating by the predominant use of domestic monetary policy instruments—mainly the domestic interest rate and reserves—to "indirectly" influences the exchange rate.[20] The fear of floating derives from the actual or perceived cost of exchange rate volatility. For instance, currency fluctuations may adversely affect competitiveness, cause a ratcheting up of inflation (exchange rate pass-through), and adversely affect balance sheets and debt servicing burdens by raising the domestic currency value of foreign currency denominated debt. Due to these costs, policy-makers in emerging markets believe that the room to pursue an independent monetary policy and to be subject to exchange rate flexibility is, in practice, limited at best. As Calvo and Reinhart note, when it comes to exchange rate policy, discretion rules the day. However, it is worthy to note that even though no exchange rate system is best for all countries or for all times, no regime can act as a substitute for good policies or good institutions. The exchange-rate regime should be viewed as part of a coherent monetary order which is itself a part of a sound macroeconomic framework.

› A country exhibits **fear of floating** when it claims to let its exchange rate be determined in a float but yet it intervenes directly or indirectly to keep the exchange rate in check so as to dampen big movements in it.

SUMMARY

- A country's real exchange rate is the price of the average foreign good or service, relative to the price of the average domestic good or service, when this price are expressed in terms of a common currency.
- The real exchange rate—the nominal exchange rate adjusted for the relative price of foreign and domestic goods—is a measure of the competitiveness of a country's goods and services.
- A devaluation or depreciation of the real exchange rate improves a country's trade balance only when the Marshall–Lerner condition—the sum of the relative price elasticities of export and import demand exceeds unity—holds.
- In the short-run, the sum of the relative price elasticity of exports and imports almost always fail to sum to unity while in the long-run these elasticities almost always sum to greater than unity. This gives rise to a J-curve effect.
- The J-curve effect arises due to adjustment lags as quantity adjustments take long and the faster pass through of the exchange rate change into prices worsens the trade balance in the short run.
- A currency devaluation switches expenditures to the domestic market from imports and this expenditure could decline (Alexander) or rise (Laursen–Metzler) thereby causing the trade balance to improve or deteriorate.
- A devaluation can be contractionary in a developing country if it decreases the share of workers in national income or the increase in the import price of crucial inputs causes a contraction in supply.

- When foreign and domestic financial assets are perfect substitutes and there are no capital controls, equalization of the return on financial instruments domestically and abroad results in two types of interest parity conditions:
  - (a) Uncovered interest parity relates the interest differentials of the two countries to the expected change in the spot exchange rate between those countries
  - (b) Covered interest parity relates the difference between the interest rate domestically and abroad to the forward premium or discount.
- Purchasing power parity (PPP) states that if arbitrage across national borders in unhindered, the price of a good or service in one nation should be the same as the exchange rate adjusted price of the same good in another nation.
- Absolute PPP states that the domestic-price level should equal the foreign-price level times the spot exchange rate.
- Relative PPP states that the change in an exchange rate is equal to the difference in inflation rates between two economies.
- Fixed exchange rates enable countries to import low inflation but anticipation of devaluation due to dwindling reserves can lead to speculative attacks.
- Floating exchange rates, when a country's financial sector is poorly regulated or lacks depth, can result in greater volatility of exchange rates due to "original sin."
- When a country must borrow abroad in a foreign currency it suffers from original sin. In such a situation, a depreciation of the currency could cause agents to purchase foreign currency to cover their repayments, which leads to further depreciation and volatility of the exchange rate.
- Under a currency board the exchange rate between the local currency and, say, the US dollar is fixed by law and the monetary authority commits to buying or selling the domestic currency without any limit at this preannounced exchange rate.
- Under dollarization (or Euroization) a country officially adopts a foreign currency as its legal tender. Dollarization removes monetary policy from a country's control.
- In a monetary union a group of countries share a common currency and jointly manage the currency through a common central bank.
- Under a soft peg the monetary authorities adopt a particular exchange-rate target and use monetary policy to prevent the market's straying too far from the target.
- In a managed float there is no public commitment to an exchange-rate target but the authorities may intervene in the foreign-exchange market or the money market to influence the exchange rate.
- The impossible trinity refers to the dilemma that a country cannot simultaneously have control over a fixed exchange rate, control over monetary policy, and maintain an open capital account.
- A country exhibits fear of floating when it claims to let its exchange rate be determined in a float yet it intervenes directly or indirectly to keep the exchange rate in check.

NOTES

1. This is achieved statistically by calculating a weighted average of a country's bilateral exchange rates, using trade shares as weights. This trade weighted exchange rate is called the nominal effective exchange rate (NEER).
2. P^* is the consumer price index (CPI) for urban consumers in the US and P is the CPI for industrial workers in India. The real exchange rate is indexed with the base year 1993 value set equal to the nominal exchange rate that year for comparison purposes. The trade-weighted real exchange rate (REER) and nominal exchange rates (NEER) for India depict a similar pattern as seen in the Reserve Bank of India Handbook of Statistics on the Indian Economy.
3. The correlation between the percentage change in the exchange rate and the inflation differential between India and the US for this time period is 0.72.
4. In the national income accounts net exports is $NX = X - M$. In equation (5.2), $X = Q_X$ and $M = (EP^*/P)Q_M$. Multiplying by the real exchange rate converts Q_M which has dimension US goods per year to domestic goods per year.
5. Readers may take the extreme examples of a perfectly inelastic import demand curve and a perfectly elastic demand curve. In the perfectly inelastic demand case, the volume of imports do not decline but the value of those imports increases. In the perfectly elastic demand case, we have an opposite impact.
6. Krugman and Taylor (1978) argue that "In the short run the balance of payments deficit is 'structural', that is, both imports and exports are not very sensitive to price changes for a given level of domestic output."
7. Krugman-Taylor are discussing a nominal devaluation which due to the sluggishness with which prices change results in a real devaluation as well.
8. Of course current exchange rates affect future expected exchange rates, but here the focus is on a temporary change which is so transitory that it has no effect on the expected exchange rate.
9. The expected future exchange rate, E^e, will of course also be affected by a change in interest rates. We ignore that for now but note that a rise in the expected future price of

foreign currency in term of domestic currency shifts the downward slopping schedule in Figure 2.2 to the right and causes the spot rate to depreciate as foreign currency deposits offer a higher expected rate of return and individual seek to cash in on this by exchanging domestic deposit for foreign currency deposits.

10. The estimates are OLS estimates which are problematic as the data are non-stationary. Thus researchers prefer to estimate $E^e - E = F - E$ or $E_t(\Delta E_t) = F_t - E_t$ which leads to estimating $\Delta E_{t+1} = a + \beta(F_t - E_t) + \epsilon_{t+1}$. This yields bad results for the theory with a negative sign for β. This negative β is referred to as the 'forward premium puzzle' (Froot and Thaler, 1990).
11. For a history of PPP see Einzig, P. (1990).
12. In that case the homogeneous of degree one g (.) and f (.) functions are the same.
13. Of course, ignoring tariffs and transport costs.
14. This can be straight forwardly written taking the log of (5.13) which is $\log P = \log P^* + \log E$ and differentiating to obtain equation (5.15)
15. See Krugman, P. (1978).
16. Less than complete backing of the currency gives the central bank some leeway in case financial crises occur. The Central Bank can then act as a lender of last resort to stem the crisis.
17. As we will see later this is a saving achieved by not forgoing seigniorage – the income a monetary authority receives when the value of its currency exceeds the cost of producing the currency.
18. Edwards (1993) also found that the inflation rate is lower in countries with an exchange rate peg if the country has a history of price stability. Fixed exchange rate systems he finds also promote monetary discipline in the form of lower rate of growth of money and through that lower inflation.
19. Hard pegs with no separate legal tender or a currency board, pegs with horizontal bands, and crawling pegs were classified as pegged exchange rate regimes. Other exchange rate arrangements were classified as floats. Following the onset of the crisis there was a dip in the number of economies with pegs and this was mostly reversed by 2010. A similar shift towards flexibility of exchange rates was observed after the Asian crisis. Such economies may have switched to flexible exchange rates to increase their ability to respond to the crisis as exchange rate changes could then have been used as a means to adjust to external shocks and such economies that switched regimes were kept out of the study.
20. Countries can use domestic open market operation and thus the interest rate to stabilize the exchange rate, leading to the expectation that interest rate volatility will be higher under a fixed exchange rate regime than under a floating one. Similarly, foreign-exchange reserve variability would be higher under a fixed exchange rate regime than under a floating one. Hence countries claiming to be floaters under IMF classification but which exhibit high variability of interest rates and/or reserves are said to exhibit fear of floating.

TEST YOURSELF

1. What is the real exchange rate and why do we focus on it rather than on the nominal exchange rate in macroeconomics?
2. How does the real exchange rate affect the exports and imports of a nation? If the real exchange rate is devalued will there be an unambiguous impact on the trade balance?
3. What is the J-curve effect and how can one explain this phenomenon?
4. What are the channels apart from the real exchange rate through which devaluation affects output and prices in a developing country?
5. Explain what is uncovered and covered interest parity and in what way are they different from each other.
5. How does the exchange rate attain equilibrium under uncovered interest parity?
6. What is absolute and relative purchasing power parity and to what extent are they good explanations for exchange rate determination?
7. Can a country run an independent monetary policy to achieve domestic economic policy goals, if it is committed to the maintenance of a fixed exchange rate?
8. When is an exchange rate considered to be overvalued or undervalued? Suppose the exchange rate is overvalued and the policymakers wish to correct this by changing the domestic interest rate. What should they do?
9. Describe the various types of "corner" solutions advocated by the IMF for exchange rate regimes in the 1990s.

ONLINE APPLICATION

1. Go to the home page of the Reserve Bank of India. URL: www.rbi.org.in/home.aspx.
2. Click on the "DataBase" icon.
3. Then under the classification of Annual data, click on "Handbook of Statistics on Indian Economy."
4. Click on "Table 40: Consumer price index – annual average" and create a spreadsheet of data on the consumer price index for urban non-manual employees (UNME)—column 4 of Table 40—from 1993–1994 to 2009–2010. This column of data is the Indian consumer price index or $\text{CPI}_{\text{India}}$.
5. Then click on "Table 147: Exchange rate of the India rupee …." and create a data column in your spreadsheet on the exchange rate of the rupee corresponding to the US dollar from 1994 to 2010 (column 4 of Table 147). This is annual data on the nominal exchange rate.
6. Now go to the home page of the United States Department of Labor, Bureau of Labor Statistics. URL: http://www.bls.gov/.
7. Click on the "Subject Areas" icon.
8. Under Inflation and Prices click on "Consumer Price Index."
9. Scroll down to "CPI Databases."
10. Click on the icon "All Urban Consumers (current series)" and then click on "Tables."
11. Click on "Table containing history of CPI-U U.S.…1913 to Present."
12. Create a data column in your spreadsheet on the annual average consumer price index for all urban consumers (third last column—labeled Annual Avg.—of the data table you are viewing) from 1994 onwards till 2010. This column of data is the US consumer price index or CPI_{US}.
13. Divide the Indian CPI in a year by the United States CPI for that year to get the ratio $CPI_{\text{India}}/CPI_{\text{US}}$.
14. We want to create a relative price index. Hence, set the relative consumer prices in the two countries for the year 1994 at $CPI_{\text{India}}/CPI_{\text{US}} = 216/144.5 = 1.495 = 31.44$, where, 31.44 is the rupee–dollar nominal exchange rate in the year 1993.
15. For 1995 we index the relative prices accordingly. Thus with $CPI_{\text{India}}/CPI_{\text{US}} = 237/152.4 = 1.555 = 32.71$ for 1995 we have an index value of 32.71 for the year.
16. Calculate the index for the remaining years. The index of the ratio of CPIs between the two countries with the base 1994 ratio set equal to the actual nominal rate can be considered to be the PPP exchange rate between the two countries.
17. Now plot a graph of your calculated PPP exchange rate of the rupee versus the US USD with the actual nominal exchange rate for the time period. Is the exchange rate overvalued relative to PPP?
18. Is it possible that the RBI intervened in the foreign-exchange market to nominally devalue the currency in order to keep the exchange rate from straying away from its long-run fundamental PPP value?

Appendix 5.1 The Marshall–Lerner Condition

The trade balance (*TB*) when imports are measured in domestic output is given by:

$$TB = X - \frac{EP^*}{P} Q_M$$

Initially, prior to the devaluation or real depreciation the trade balance is (see Figure 5.4):

$$TB^0 = X^0 - \frac{E\bar{P}^*}{\bar{P}} Q_M^0 = X^0 - q^0 Q_M^0$$

where $q^0 = E\bar{P}^*/\bar{P}$ is the initial real exchange rate. After the change in real exchange rate, the trade balance is,

$$TB^1 = X^1 - \frac{E^1\bar{P}^*}{\bar{P}} Q_M^1 = X^1 - q^1 Q_M^1$$

Then, the change in the trade balance arising from a change in the real exchange rate is:

$$\Delta TB = TB^1 - TB^0 = (X^1 - q^1 Q_M^1) - (X^0 - q^0 Q_M^0)$$
$$= (X^1 - X^0) - q^1 Q_M^1 + q^0 Q_M^0$$

Add and subtract $q^1 Q_M^0$ on the right hand side:

$$\Delta TB = (X^1 - X^0) - q^1(Q_M^1 - Q_M^0) - (q^1 - q^0)Q_M^0$$

Let $X^1 - X^0 = \Delta X$ be the change in exports;
$Q_M^1 - Q_M^0 = \Delta Q_M$ be the change in the volume of imports;
$q^1 - q^0 = \Delta q$ be the change in the real exchange rate or the nominal exchange rate due to devaluation when prices are fixed.

Then,

$$\Delta TB = \Delta X - q^1 \Delta Q_M - \Delta q Q_M^0$$

Dividing throughout by Δq we obtain the response of a change in the trade balance to a change in the real exchange rate

$$\frac{\Delta TB}{\Delta q} = \frac{\Delta X}{\Delta q} - q^1 \frac{\Delta Q_M}{\Delta q} - Q_M^0$$

We now define the elasticities of export and import demand as the Marshall–Lerner condition is in terms of elasticities. Let the elasticity of export with respect to the real exchange rate be the proportionate change in exports ($\Delta X/X$) in response to a proportionate change in the real exchange rate ($\Delta q/q$). Then,

$$\eta_X = \frac{\Delta X / X}{\Delta q / q} = \frac{\Delta X}{\Delta q} \frac{q}{X}$$

From this, multiplying throughout by X/q,

$$\frac{\Delta X}{\Delta q} = \frac{X}{q}\eta_X$$

Similarly, the elasticity of import demand measured at the point corresponding to the real exchange rate prior to devaluation, q^0, is given by:

$$\eta_M = -\frac{\Delta Q_M / Q_M^0}{\Delta q / q^0} = -\frac{\Delta Q_M}{\Delta q}\frac{q^0}{Q_M^0}$$

We assume that the change in the real exchange rate is small by which we mean $q^1 \approx q^0$. Then, multiplying throughout the above by Q_M^0, we obtain,

$$\frac{-\Delta Q_M}{\Delta q} q^1 = Q_M^0 \eta_M$$

Substituting these into the $\Delta TB/\Delta q$ equation,

$$\frac{\Delta TB}{\Delta q} = \frac{X}{q}\eta_X + Q_M^0 \eta_M - Q_M^0$$

The trade balance was initially zero which means that $X^0 = q^0 Q_m^0$, allowing us to write X/q in the first term on the right hand side as Q_m^0:

$$\begin{aligned} \frac{\Delta TB}{\Delta q} &= Q_M^0 \eta_X + Q_M^0 \eta_M - Q_M^0 \\ &= (\eta_X + \eta_M - 1) Q_M^0 \end{aligned}$$

Then, $\Delta TB/\Delta q$ is positive provided that,

$$\eta_x + \eta_M > 1$$

This is the Marshall–Lerner condition that when the trade balance is initially zero, a real depreciation or devaluation of the currency results in a trade balance surplus if the sum of the elasticities of export and import demand with respect to the real exchange rate exceeds unity.

6

Demand for Money

CRITICAL QUESTIONS

- *What are the major functions of money?*
- *How do we determine the price of a bond?*
- *Why does macroeconomics consider money and bonds as the only two components of private-sector wealth?*
- *What is the difference between nominal and real interest rates, and how are they related?*
- *How is an individual's budget constraint affected by the holding of financial assets?*
- *How does a person decide on the amount of real money balances to hold?*
- *How do we decide on the allocation of a financial portfolio consisting of money and bonds?*
- *How does the government gain revenue (seigniorage) from the printing of money?*

6.1 Money, Bonds, and Private Wealth

Up to now, we have been focusing on the determinants of the various components of aggregate expenditures such as consumption, investment, and net exports. It is now time to transfer our attention from the goods market to the financial market, which is the market where financial assets such as money and bonds are traded. Macroeconomists get around the problem of specifying what money is by describing instead what properties something must have in order to be called money. The three major functions of money are as: (1) as a medium of exchange, (2) a unit of accounting, and (3) a store of value.

In a barter economy with no money, trading takes the form of the direct exchange of goods. However, finding someone who has the good you want and is, moreover, willing to exchange it for something you have can be very time consuming. Money makes searching for a trading partner unnecessary. By operating as a MEDIUM OF EXCHANGE—a device for making transactions—money allows people to trade with less time and effort.

› Money's most important function is as a **medium of exchange**—when it is used to purchase goods and services.

Besides, money is also a unit of accounting—the basic unit that is used to assess economic value. In India, for instance, all prices, wages, asset values, debts, and financial contracts are expressed in rupees. A single and uniform measure of value makes it straight forward to compare different goods and assets. As goods and services are exchanged for money—the medium of exchange function—it is also natural to express economic value in money terms—as a UNIT OF ACCOUNTING function.[1]

› As a **unit of accounting,** money is the yardstick for measuring economic value. It measures the value of goods, services, and assets and thereby enables a comparison of these based on their values.

The third function of money is as a STORE OF VALUE. Money can be used to buy goods not only today but also tomorrow and so it embodies and stands for future purchasing power. Money can thus be used as a store of value or a way of holding wealth. However, there are other assets—stocks, bonds, gold, real estate—that can be used as a store of value, and they typically outperform money in this role as they normally yield a higher rate of return than money. The distinguishing feature of money is thus its role as the medium. The holding of non-interest bearing currency and non-(or low) interest bearing checking deposits for use as a media of exchange in planned transactions. Any other commodity can serve as a medium of accounting without being a medium of exchange at the same time, and there are various non-money assets that are capable of serving as stores of value.

› As a **store of value** money is one way of holding wealth.

6.1.1 Bond Pricing

Money is needed to make purchases—it facilitates transactions. Without money you cannot buy groceries or pay rent and utility bills. With money—liquidity—you can obtain goods and services that you consume. Money is a financial asset held by households and firms. The other assets that the private sector holds are BONDS. There are many types of bonds in the financial market but it suffices for our purposes to focus on coupon bonds. A coupon bond pays the owner of the bond a fixed interest payment, also known as the coupon payment every year until the maturity date. The name "coupon bond" came from the fact that historically, the bond holder used to obtain the fixed interest, payment by clipping a coupon off the bond and sending it to the bond issuer, who then made the necessary payment to the bond holder. Even though this practice is not followed today, the name "coupon bond" has stuck. At the time of maturity of the coupon bond, a specified final value called the face value or par value of the bond is also repaid. A coupon bond with a face value of INR 5,000, for instance, could pay a coupon or interest payment of INR 250 per year for 5 years, and

› A **bond** is a legal promise to repay a debt. The principal amount or the amount originally lent is paid at some fixed date in the future called the maturation date. A bondholder receives regular interest or coupon payments, until the bond's maturation date.

at that maturity date, it would repay the face value amount of INR 5,000. The value of such a bond today is its present value—the sum of the present value of all the coupon payments plus the present value of the final payment of the face value of the bond. For the coupon bond that has just been considered with a face value of INR 5,000 and coupon payments of INR 250 per year for 5 years, the present value would be calculated as follows: At the end of the first year, there is an INR 250 coupon payment with a present value of INR $250/(1 + i)$, where i is a discount rate or interest rate. At the end of the second year, there is another coupon payment of INR 250 with a present value of INR $250/(1 + i)^2$. This continues till the maturity of the bond at the end of 5 years, when there is a coupon payment of INR $250/(1 + i)^5$ as well as the repayment of the face value of the bond with a present value of INR $5{,}000/(1 + i)^5$. Generally, a coupon bond that pays a coupon of INR C per period, has a face value of INR F at maturity, and which takes n years to mature, will have a present value of all the cash flow payments for such a bond, given by:

$$\frac{C}{(1+i)} + \frac{C}{(1+i)^2} + \frac{C}{(1+i)^3} + \dots \frac{C}{(1+i)^n} + \frac{F}{(1+i)^n}$$

There is a special type of coupon bond that is central to much of macroeconomics as its present value is easy to calculate and it captures the essence of the role that bonds play in financial markets. This bond is called a consol or perpetuity. A perpetuity is a non-maturing bond or a bond that has no final date of maturity and as a result they make no repayment of principal such as the INR F made on a standard coupon bond. Perpetuities were introduced by the British during the Napoleonic Wars in the early part of the nineteenth century. Perpetuities pay a fixed annual amount, or coupon return INR C, per year forever. A perpetuity that is purchased today will pay INR C next year, the year after that, and every other year into the future. That means the discounted present value of this bond, given a discount rate i, is the sum of the discounted present values of INR C, or the infinite sum

$$\frac{C}{(1+i)} + \frac{C}{(1+i)^2} + \frac{C}{(1+i)^3} + \dots \tag{6.1}$$

As this discounted sum is today's value of the coupon returns, the sum we ought to be willing to pay for the bond today should equal this discounted current value of coupon returns. Hence, the price of the perpetual bond, P_B, will be as follows:

$$P_B = \frac{C}{1+i} + \frac{C}{(1+i)^2} + \frac{C}{(1+i)^3} + \dots \tag{6.2}$$

Multiplying throughout by $(1 + i)$,

$$(1+i)P_B = C + \frac{C}{1+i} + \frac{C}{(1+i)^2} + \dots \tag{6.3}$$

Subtracting Eq. (6.2) from this one [Eq. (6.3)],

$$iP_B = C$$

› **Bond prices** and interest rates are inversely related.

Hence, the PRICE OF A PERPETUITY is:

$$P_B = \frac{C}{i} \tag{6.4}$$

This implies that, if nominal interest rates rise, bond prices will fall and people holding bonds will incur a nominal capital loss.

6.1.2 Private Sector Net Wealth

It may seem surprising that apart from money and bonds, households and firms in the private sector apparently hold no other financial assets and liabilities like mutual funds and common stock or equity. This is because the net wealth of the private sector consists of the sum of its assets minus the sum of its liabilities. Aggregating over individuals, the assets of a person or firm are, at the same time, liabilities of another person or business unit and thus cancel out. Common stock representing ownership in a firm are the assets of households and the corresponding liability of the firms that issue them. Hence, they cannot be part of the net worth of the private sector as both households and firms are entities within the private sector. Thus, the net wealth of the private sector consists of its net claims on agents outside that sector. It is only the outside financial wealth that we are concerned with, and there are two sources of such wealth—the government liabilities to the private sector on bonds it has issued and the central bank liabilities on money[2].

Let B_t be the stock of bonds outstanding at time t. Without loss of generality, we will assume that the coupon on the bond is INR 1, or, $C = 1$. Then, with bonds priced at $P_B = 1/i$, B_t/i_t is the nominal value of bonds held at time t. The composition of the net WEALTH OF THE PRIVATE SECTOR is then given by:[3]

› The net **wealth of the private sector** consists of its net claims on agents outside that sector—the stock of money and the stock of government bonds.

$$W_t = M_t + \frac{B_t}{i_t} \tag{6.5}$$

where W_t is the nominal wealth of the private sector in financial assets, M_t is the stock of money held by the private sector at time t, and B_t is the stock of bonds held at time t.

There are a couple of things to note regarding the stock of bonds that comprise the net wealth of the private sector. We can write:

$$B_t = B_{t-1} + (B_t - B_{t-1})$$

Multiplying throughout by (P_{Bt}) the price of bonds at time t,

$$P_{B,t}B_t = P_{B,t}B_{t-1} + P_{B,t}(B_t - B_{t-1})$$

The first term on the right hand side is the current value (P_{Bt}) of bonds that were held at the end of period $t-1$. The second term on the right hand side is the current value of the additional bonds ($B_t - B_{t-1}$) held between period $t-1$ and period t. We can write this first term on the right hand side as,

$$P_{B,t}B_{t-1} = P_{B,t-1}B_{t-1} + (P_{B,t} - P_{B,t-1})B_{t-1}$$

where the first term on the right hand side is the nominal value of bonds at the end of the period $t-1$, and the second term in brackets is the capital gains or losses incurred during the period t on the bond holdings from the previous period. Note that capital gains/losses are rightly treated as revaluations of wealth, rather than as a component of income. Hence, the value of bonds currently held is given by:

$$\frac{B_t}{i_t} = P_{B,t}B_t = P_{B,t-1}B_{t-1} + (P_{B,t} - P_{B,t-1})B_{t-1} + P_{B,t}(B_t - B_{t-1})$$

Then the bonds currently held comprise the value of the bonds that were held in the previous period ($P_{B,t-1}B_{t-1}$), the capital gains/losses on the bonds from the previous period [$(P_{B,t} - P_{B,t-1})B_{t-1}$], and the value of the additional bonds acquired during the current period [$P_{B,t}(B_t - B_{t-1})$].

The second thing to note is that as the value of the bonds at time t is $P_{B,t}B_t = B_t/i_t$, the amount of interest paid in period t by the government to the private sector is $i_t(B_t/i_t) = B_t$.

The interest rate being referred to in Eq. (6.5) is the nominal interest rate. Money differs from bonds in that the nominal price of money is always equal to one unit of money, e.g., USD 1, INR 1, JPY 1. In contrast, the nominal price of a bond can change over time as $P_B = 1/i$. An individual who owns a bond earns a capital gain if the nominal price of a bond increases over an interval of time. The person incurs capital loss if the nominal price of a bond falls. In contrast, a note of INR 1 has the same nominal value over an interval of time and agents cannot earn nominal capital gains or incur nominal capital losses if they hold all their financial assets as currency. As financial wealth is allocated between holdings of money and holdings of bonds—$W = M + B/i$—any change in holdings of bonds for a given stock of financial wealth must be offset by an equal change in money holdings in the opposite direction.[4] As a change in bond holdings requires a change in money holdings and because bonds earn a nominal interest return, it is not the real but the nominal interest rate that influences the desired holding of money.

6.2 Nominal and Real Interest Rates

When analyzing the demand for money as an asset, we refer to the nominal rate of interest, i. This is because, in most economies, contracts for borrowing and lending are denominated in the unit of account that is the currency of the economy. Assets such as money and bonds also represent future purchasing power as they enable goods which are to be produced in the future to be traded for goods that are currently produced. Underlying the nominal rate of interest, then, is the real rate of interest. Let us illustrate this with an example.

Suppose a farmer lent five sacks of rice to his poor neighbour under a stipulated contract that the neighbour is to repay with 6 sacks of rice a year later. This would translate into a real rate of interest of 20 per cent per annum. Instead of lending the commodity directly, if the farmer were to lend rupees, then assuming that a sack of rice cost INR 300, the farmer could have lent INR 1500, with a contract to repay INR 1800 a year later. This would amount to a nominal rate of interest of 20 per cent per annum. As long as the price of rice stays the same in each year, a loan denominated in units of the commodity is equivalent to a loan denominated in rupees. However, when the price of commodities changes from one time period to the next, the real rate of interest differs from the nominal rate of interest.

Let us assume now that the price of a sack of rice goes up to INR 350. In order to get back 6 sacks of rice the next year, the farmer would have to receive INR (350×6) = INR 2,100 from the person he lends the money to. He would then have to charge a nominal rate of interest,

$$i = \frac{2{,}100 - 1{,}500}{1{,}500} \times 100 = \frac{600}{1{,}500} \times 100 = 40 \text{ per cent}$$

Thus, it is only on charging a 40 per cent nominal rate of interest that the farmer receives the INR 2,100 that represents the purchasing power of six sacks of rice. In commodity (real) terms, the real rate of interest, however, is still $r = [(6 - 5)/5] \times 100 = 20$ per cent.

We can generalize this example. If at time t, the nominal rate of interest is i_t and the price is P_t, then the lender receives $P_t(1 + i_t)$ in the next period. The number of units of the commodity that can be purchased with this when the price of the commodity is INR P_{t+1} is $[P_t(1 + i_t)]/P_{t+1}$. Hence, the real rate of interest is given by:

$$1 + r_t = \frac{P_t(1 + i_t)}{P_{t+1}}$$

$$= \frac{1 + i_t}{P_{t+1}/P_t}$$

$$= \frac{1 + i_t}{1 + \pi_t}$$

where $\pi_t = (P_{t+1})/P_t) - 1$ is the rate of inflation.

Hence,
$$r_t = \frac{i_t - \pi_t}{1 + \pi_t} \quad (6.6)$$

Writing the expression in terms of i_t,

$$i_t = r_t + \pi_t + r_t\pi_t$$

In many practical situations, the real rate of interest and the rate of inflation have second decimal places (less than 10 per cent), so that the product $r_t \pi_t$ will have a third decimal place. In that situation, the term $r_t \pi_t$ is negligibly small and usually ignored so that we may write:

$$i_t = r_t + \pi_t \quad (6.7)$$

In other words, we can say that the NOMINAL INTEREST RATE is the real rate of interest plus the rate of inflation.

› The **nominal interest rate** is the real rate of interest plus the rate of inflation.

Alternatively, we may write,

$$r_t = i_t - \pi_t \quad (6.8)$$

This states that the real rate of interest is the nominal rate adjusted for a change in the purchasing power of money.

Equation (6.7) implies that nominal interest rates tend to be high when inflation is high and low when inflation is low. This tendency of nominal interest rates is referred to as the FISHER EFFECT after the economist Irving Fisher. This can be understood as the response of borrowers and lenders to the inflation they anticipate will continue in the future. Lenders can be expected to raise their nominal interest rate so that their real rate of return will not be affected. Borrowers will accept this raising of the nominal interest rate on the understanding that a higher nominal rate is a compensation to the lender for the fact that the loan will be repaid in currency of reduced real value. The cost of borrowing has not changed when the nominal interest rate and the inflation rate increase by the same amount. Thus, there will be a tendency for nominal interest rates to follow the pattern of the inflation rates in the economy.

› The **Fisher effect** describes the full adjustment of the nominal interest rate to a change in the inflation rate.

When the individual saves and allocates his savings to financial assets that earn nominal rates of return, it is the nominal rate of interest that becomes useful in describing the intertemporal budget constraint of the individual. We now examine how to construct this budget constraint.

6.3 Financial Assets and the Budget Constraint

In Chapter 2, Section 2.1, we have mentioned the expression for private disposable income as:

Private Disposable Income = GDP + NFI
+ Transfers from Abroad
+ Transfers Received from Government
− Taxes

For simplicity, we ignore the presence of NFI, transfers from abroad, transfers received from government, and taxes. Then, private disposable income is equal to GDP (Y).

Saving is the part of the disposable income that is not consumed. Alternatively, saving is nothing but an increase in the real wealth, $(\Delta W/P)$, of the private sector. Here $\Delta W/P$ denotes the addition to real wealth we will talk about real wealth later in the chapter. Hence,

$$Y - C = S = \frac{\Delta W}{P}$$

We have written wealth in real terms as income, consumption, and saving are all measured in real terms. It is the command over real goods and services that we are primarily interested in, and not the nominal incomes. In nominal terms, we may write this as:

$$PY - PC = PS = \Delta W$$

or,

$$PY = PC + \Delta W$$

The nominal wealth of the private sector constitutes its holdings of money and bonds [Eq. (6.5)] and a change in nominal wealth is the addition to the holdings of these assets, or,

$$\Delta W = (M_t - M_{t-1}) + \left(\frac{B_t}{i_t} - \frac{B_{t-1}}{i_{t-1}}\right)$$

We focus on a two period problem to enable us to draw graphs. If there are only two periods, then prior to the first-period, there are no assets such as money and bonds, and at the end of the second-period, nobody will be interested in holding money or bonds as there is no subsequent period in which these assets could be of any use. Individuals will then plan to have a zero holding of financial assets at the end of period 2. In a two-period set-up—such as when we looked at the intertemporal aspects of consumption—we may write for the first-period,

$$P_1Y_1 = \overbrace{P_1C_1}^{\text{Nominal Consumption}} + \overbrace{(M_1 - 0) + \left(\frac{B_1}{i_1} - 0\right)}^{\text{Nominal Savings}}$$

This is because the individual is taken, in a two-period set-up, to have no initial endowment of assets ($M_0 = 0, B_0/i_0 = 0$), and to end the second-period with no holding of assets either ($M_2 = 0, B_2/i_2 = 0$).

Thus, the first-period budget constraint of the individual in nominal terms is,

$$P_1Y_1 = P_1C_1 + M_1 + \frac{B_1}{i_1} \tag{6.9}$$

In the second-period, the individual earns an interest on the holdings of bonds given by $i_1(B_1/i_1) = B_1$ and the budget constraint in the second-period in nominal terms is:

$$P_2Y_2 + B_1 = P_2C_2 + (M_2 - M_1) + \left(\frac{B_2}{i_2} - \frac{B_1}{i_1}\right)$$

or, since this is a terminal period and the individual will plan not to hold any assets beyond this period,

$$P_2Y_2 + B_1 = P_2C_2 + (0 - M_1) + \left(0 - \frac{B_1}{i_1}\right)$$

$$P_2Y_2 + B_1 = P_2C_2 - M_1 - \frac{B_1}{i_1} \tag{6.10}$$

To get the lifetime budget constraint, we add together the first-period budget constraint [Eq. (6.9)] to the present discounted value of the second-period budget constraint [Eq. (6.10)].

As the budget constraints are in nominal terms, the present discounted value of the second-period budget constraint is achieved by discounting with the nominal interest rate. Hence, the present discounted value of the second-period budget constraint is,

$$\frac{P_2Y_2}{(1+i_1)} + \frac{B_1}{(1+i_1)} = \frac{P_2C_2}{(1+i_1)} - \frac{M_1}{(1+i_1)} - \frac{B_1}{(1+i_1)i_1} \tag{6.11}$$

Adding together Eqs (6.9) and (6.11) gives us,

$$(P_1Y_1) + \frac{P_2Y_2}{(1+i_1)} + \frac{B_1}{(1+i_1)} = \left(P_1C_1 + M_1 + \frac{B_1}{i_1}\right) + \frac{P_2C_2}{(1+i_1)} - \frac{M_1}{(1+i_1)} - \frac{B_1}{(1+i_1)i_1}$$

where, on substituting the relationship between the nominal and real interest rate we obtain, (see the derivation in Appendix 6.1):

$$Y_1 + \frac{Y_2}{(1+r_1)} - \frac{i_1}{(1+i_1)}\frac{M_1}{P_1} = C_1 + \frac{C_2}{(1+r_1)} \tag{6.12}$$

This is the TWO PERIOD BUDGET CONSTRAINT when we explicitly allow for the accumulation of assets between periods. This equation is the same budget constraint as written in the chapter on Consumption—see Eq. (3.8) in Chapter 3. The significant difference is that the term $i_1M_1/(1+i_1)P_1$ appears in the above equation. This is because holding money implies losing the interest that would have been earned if bonds were held in its place instead. The cost of holding money is the interest lost in the second-period which would have been the amount $i_1(M_1/P_1)$. This loss in the present value terms is obtained by discounting this by $1+i_1$ to obtain $i_1M_1/(1+i_1)P_1$. Holding money implies a cost in terms of the consumption that is foregone, and this cost increases

› The **two period budget constraint** with asset accumulation is the present value of income in the two periods less the discounted value of interest lost on account of holding money balances rather than bonds.

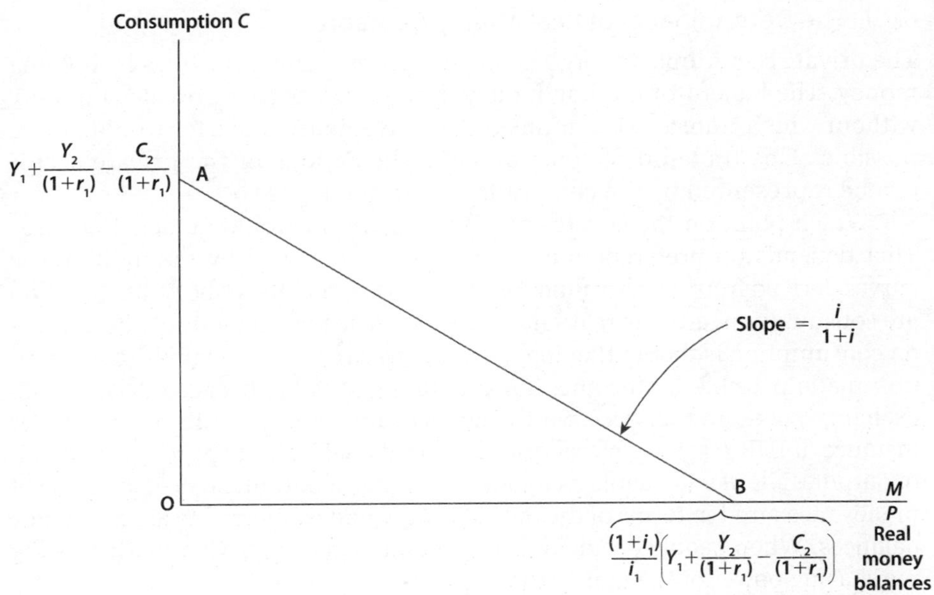

› **Figure 6.1**
Income Constraint When Allocating Savings to Money Balances. As an individual allocates his savings to money balances, he loses the implied interest income from bonds given in present value terms by $i_1M_1/[(1+i_1)P_1]$. As the individual transfers savings to bonds, he increases his consumption possibility. However at the same time decreases his liquidity in terms of money balances, as depicted by line AB.

with a rise in the nominal interest rate i_1, as $i_1/(1+i_1)$ increases with an increase in i_1. There is, thus, a trade-off between holding money and enjoying the consumption that is possible from the purchasing power of this money. This trade-off is depicted in Figure 6.1. We can rewrite Eq. (6.12) as:

$$C_1 = \left(Y_1 + \frac{Y_2}{(1+r_1)} - \frac{C_2}{(1+r_1)}\right) - \frac{i_1}{(1+i_1)}\frac{M_1}{P_1}$$

When the individual holds no money balances, then, with $M_1/P_1 = 0$, the consumption possibility in period 1 is given by:

$$C_1 = \left(Y_1 + \frac{Y_2}{(1+r_1)} - \frac{C_2}{(1+r_1)}\right)$$

This is depicted by point A in Figure 6.1.

The other case is where the individual does not consume in period 1 and saves the entire income in the form of money balances, $C_1 = 0$, and the lifetime budget constraint is:

$$\left(Y_1 + \frac{Y_2}{(1+r_1)} - \frac{C_2}{(1+r_1)}\right) - \frac{i_1}{(1+i_1)}\frac{M_1}{P_1} = 0$$

$$\frac{M_1}{P_1} = \frac{(1+i_1)}{i_1}\left(Y_1 + \frac{Y_2}{(1+r_1)} - \frac{C_2}{(1+r_1)}\right)$$

This is given by point B in Figure 6.1.

Joining points A and B gives us the budget line representing the various combinations of present consumption and holdings of real money balances that are possible over the life cycle.

The slope of the budget line is the ratio of the vertical distance OA to the horizontal distance OB, and is given by,

$$\text{Slope of Budget Line} = \frac{\{Y_1 + [Y_2/(1+r)] - [C_2/(1+r)]\}}{[(1+i_1)/i_1]\{Y_1 + [Y_2/(1+r)] - [C_2/(1+r)]\}} = \frac{i_1}{(1+i_1)}$$

6.3.1 The Determinants of Real Money Demand

The private sector opts to forgo an income from interest earnings by holding money. The benefit of holding money, however, is that it provides liquidity without which transactions minus the inconvenience of barter would not be possible. This trade-off of constraints on the actions of the private sector can be represented by the constraint line in the Figure 6.1.

Which point on the constraint AB in Figure 6.1 would an agent choose? That depends on preferences and, in turn, are depicted by the indifference curves derived from a utility function. The two arguments in the utility function are consumption[5] and the real value of money. The reason for utility depending on consumption is that in the final analysis, we are interested in the consumption made possible by income. Since money has value because it is used to exchange goods and services, we should measure money in units of output. For instance, if INR P is the general price level that enables us to purchase one unit of output, INR M will enable us to buy M/P units of output. Hence, the value of money measured in terms of the output is M/P and is referred to as real money balances. When people decide how much money to carry, what matters is the purchasing power of the money they hold.

Suppose, for instance, you decide to carry INR 30 to cover your intended purchases for lunch and tea during the day. Imagine, however, what happens if for some reason the price level doubles. The cost of lunch and tea is now INR 60. You will not be able to cover the cost of the lunch you planned to eat and you may have to forgo your cup of tea. The purchasing power of your cash of INR 30 is now half its previous value. To purchase the same meal and your favourite cup of tea you would have to double your nominal money balances to INR 60. A doubling of prices requires a doubling of nominal money balances to maintain the required purchasing power for the day's expenses. The utility function can accordingly be written as:

$$U = U\left(C, \frac{M}{P}\right) \tag{6.13}$$

This utility function generates standard indifference curves that are downward sloping. The aim of an individual agent is to maximize utility subject to the income constraint given in Figure 6.1. That is akin to finding the highest indifference curve that can be achieved, given the budget constraint as stated in Eq. (6.12) and depicted in Figure 6.1.

6.3.2 Parametric Changes on Money Demand

At this point, we are only interested in the agent's choice of money balances. The graphical solution is depicted in Figure 6.2 as the point E, where the highest indifference curve is tangential to the two period income constraint. The demand for real money balances at this point is given by M^{d*}/P. At point E, the slope of the income constraint is equal to the slope of the indifference curve.

Recall that the slope of the income constraint is the ratio of the vertical distance OA to the horizontal distance OB, or,

$$\text{Slope of Income Constraint} = \frac{\text{Distance OA}}{\text{Distance OB}} = \frac{i_1}{1 + i_1}.$$

What happens to the demand for money when there is a rise in the interest rate? An increase in the interest rate to i_1' makes the incomes constraint steeper, and the increased interest rate will result in an income constraint such as AB′ (Figure 6.3).

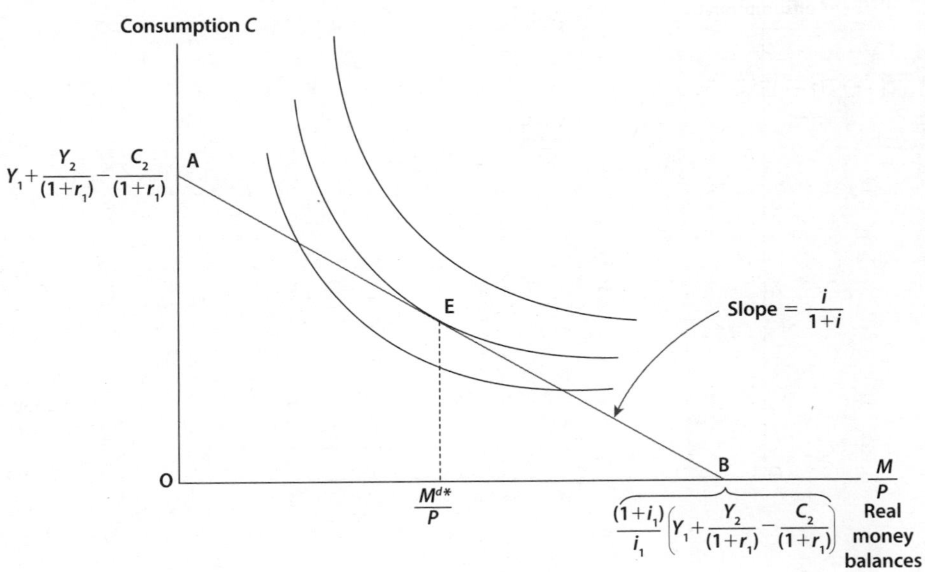

› **Figure 6.2 Equilibrium Money Balances Held.** The demand for real money balances—the value of money measured in units of commodities—is found by equating the preference for liquidity versus consumption as given by the slope of an indifference curve with the slope of the income constraint line.

› Figure 6.3
Effect of Rise in Interest Rate.
A rise in the interest rate causes an individual to reallocate savings from money to bonds thereby reducing the demand for real money balances.

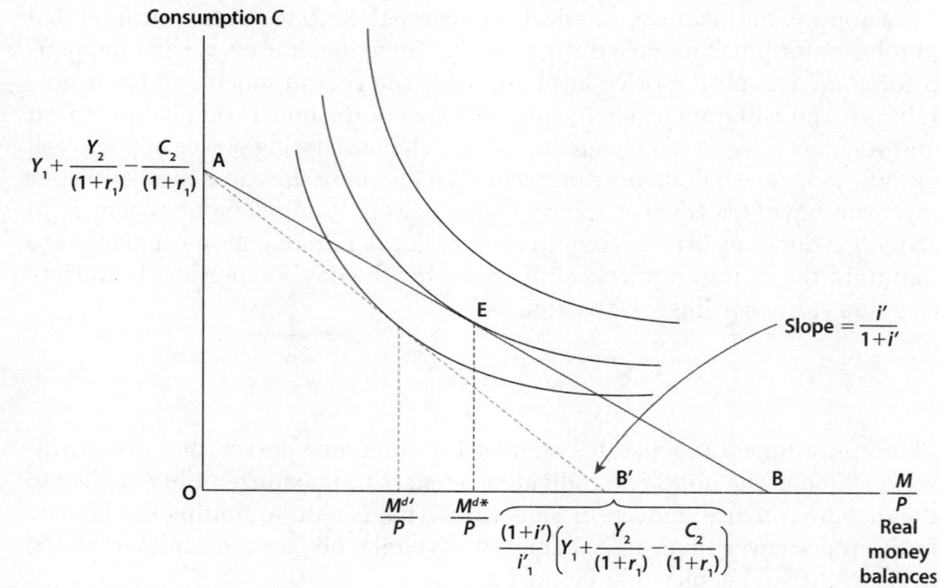

As depicted in Figure 6.3, the rise in the interest rate induces a decline in the demand for money balance to $M^{d'}/P$. The opportunity cost of holding money is the forgone interest on bonds. A rise in the interest rate induces agents to reallocate their portfolio of financial assets from money to bonds, so as to minimize the increase in forgone interest earnings.

What happens if the real income rises? A rise in real income (an increase, say, in Y_1) shifts the budget line outwards—parallel to itself. In Figure 6.4, this is depicted by the new income constraint A′B′. The rise in real income results in an increase in the demand for money to $M^{d'}/P$. A rise in income increases the volume of planned transactions in the economy which requires additional money balances.

It is conceivable that there is an increase in the demand for money with a rise in the interest rate, as depicted in Figure 6.5. That means that as the interest rate increases, there is a decrease in the proportion of bonds in the portfolio

› Figure 6.4
Effect of a Rise in Income.
A rise in income increases the requirement of liquidity for transactions and causes the individual to increase the demand for real money balances.

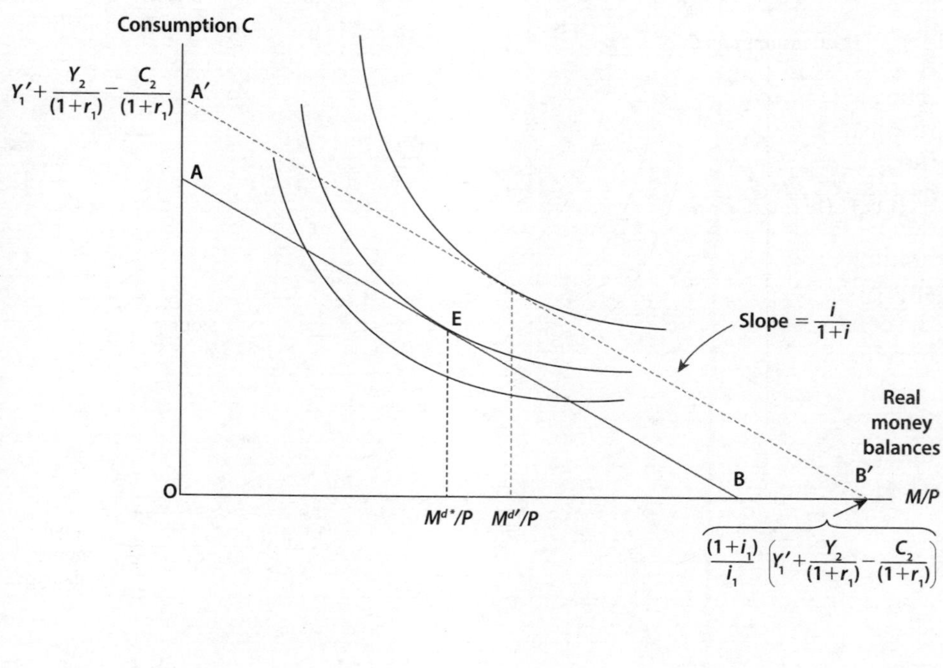

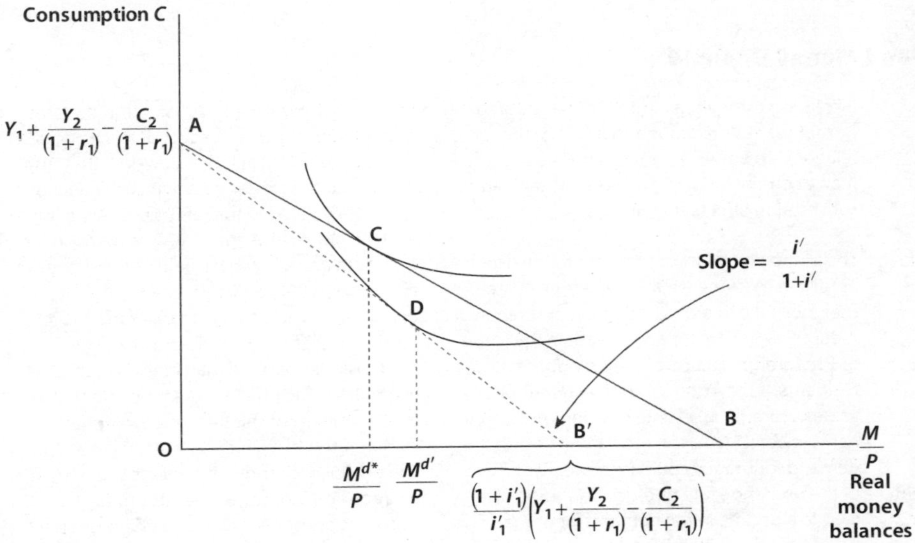

› **Figure 6.5**
Demand for Money Increasing with Interest Rates. At very high rate of interest, the individual can face significant capital losses, and will then reduce their holding of bonds despite the high-current return from bonds.

of net wealth of the individual. This is depicted in Figure 6.5 where the interest rate rise swivels the portfolio constraint from AB to AB′. The equilibrium portfolio composition shifts from point C to D, where the demand for money has increased and the share of bonds in the portfolio has declined. This is due to the standard substitution and wealth effects that operate when budget constraints change. In Figure 6.3, the substitution effect dominates the wealth effect and the demand for money decreases with a rise in the interest rate. With a rise in the interest rate, the interest rate increases from say i to i', or, since $P_B = 1/i$, the price of bonds declines from P_B to P'_B. The nominal value of bonds has now changed to $P'_B B_t$ from the earlier value of $P_B B_t$. We can write this value of bonds as,

$$P'_B B_t = P_B B_t + (P'_B - P_B)B_t$$

The first term on the right hand side is the value of the bonds before the change in the interest rate. The second term is the capital gain/loss incurred on the bond holdings with a change in the interest rate. As the price of bonds has declined to P'_B, this represents a capital loss. Keep in mind that money is a riskless asset with a nominal return of zero and bonds are risky assets whose return changes with interest rate variations. As the interest rates increase, the riskiness of the portfolio increases with the capital losses that are faced on the bonds being held. When this riskiness of the portfolio holding of money and bonds is significant, it triggers a response for a reduction in risk. This is done by reducing the proportion of bonds in the portfolio and increasing in the holding of money balances. In Figure 6.5, the wealth effect dominates the substitution effect and the individual trades off the increased risk by changing the composition of the portfolio as well as increasing the money holding so as to reduce the riskiness of the portfolio.

In general, we can write the demand for money balances as a function of the nominal interest rate and income in the economy. MONEY DEMAND decreases with a rise in the interest rate and increases with a rise in income. Thus,

› The **demand for real money** balances rises with income and declines with a rise in the nominal interest rate.

$$\frac{M^d}{P} = f(\underset{(-)}{i}, \underset{(+)}{Y}) \tag{6.14}$$

MACROFOCUS 6.1

Stock Markets, Exchange Rates, and Money Demand

Two Nobel laureates, Milton Friedman and Robert Mundell, have argued that the money demand, in addition to the standard variables—income and nominal interest rates—is also affected by stock market prices (Friedman, 1988) and the exchange rate (Mundell, 1963). Friedman observed a correlation between stock prices and money demand in the US economy and suggested a number of explanations for this phenomenon:
(1) Wealth effect—A rise in the stock prices is a rise in nominal wealth and higher wealth-to-income ratio will be reflected in a higher money-to-income ratio. (2) Substitution effect—The higher the real stock prices, the more attractive are the equities as a component of a portfolio that includes equities and money. (3) Risk considerations—A rise in stock prices is an increase in return from risky assets relative to liquid assets, which may be counterbalanced by increasing the weight of money in an aggregate portfolio. Friedman found that for US, the relationship between money and the stock market is time-varying, with both wealth and substitution effects showing up.

The Mundell (1963) conjecture is rationalized as follows. Assume wealth holders evaluate their portfolio in terms of domestic currency. A depreciation means an increase in the value of the foreign securities held by domestic residents. If the increased domestic currency value of foreign assets held by domestic residents is perceived as an increase in wealth, the demand for money could increase. The effect of the exchange rate depreciation could also lead to a decline in the demand for money. This is because the public expects further depreciation and, therefore, demands more of foreign currency and less of domestic currency.

Dua and Subramaniam (2005) found the presence of a strong wealth effect of stock prices on broad money (M_3) in India. However, they also found that the exchange rate has no effect on the money demand for 1980–2003. An increase in stock prices, thus, increases the demand for money in India. However, Bahmani-Oskooee and Tanku (2006) argue that in developing economies, where there is a black market for foreign exchange due to foreign exchange controls, it is the black market exchange rate rather than the official exchange rate which is a determinant of the demand for money. They find that the black market exchange rate and the official exchange rate affects the demand for money in countries like Argentina, Egypt, India, Indonesia, Mexico, and Philippines. Thus, money demand is a function of not just income and the nominal interest rate, but also stock market prices and the exchange rate.

The demand for real money balances is usually negatively related to the nominal rate of interest, which, in turn, (from the Fisher effect) is the sum of the real rate of interest and the rate of inflation. The demand for money, thus, represents a relation where the increase in the inflation rate means that there is a decline in the demand for real money balances. In developing countries, since the inflation rates are high, a substitution is induced not just between money and other financial assets such as bonds, but also between money and real assets such as gold and real estate that typically realize a rate of capital appreciation that is equivalent to, if not better than, the rate of inflation. When individuals expect that inflation is going to rise, they tend to choose such assets that are more inflation-proof and reduce their demand for money. In such cases, it is standard to include expected inflation as well as an explanatory variable in the demand for money function. Finally, as the demand for money is the demand for a stock of an asset, there is a period of adjustment before individual agents can achieve their desired stock of real money balances. It is, therefore, usual to have a one-period lag in real money stock as an explanatory variable to incorporate the partial stock adjustment in money balances. For the Indian economy, Manohar J. M. Rao (1997) estimated the following money demand function,

$$\log\left(\frac{M_t}{P_t}\right) = .48 + .73\log\left(\frac{M_{t-1}}{P_{t-1}}\right) + .38\log Y - .23i - .0043\log\pi^e \quad (6.15)$$

If we take a longer time period such as 1953–2003 [Bhaskara Rao and Singh (2006)], it still turns out that the money demand is positively related to income and negatively to the nominal interest rate, as predicted by the theory.

6.4 Velocity, Money, and Inflation

A different approach to the demand for money is based on the quantity theory of money. This approach is based on the concept of velocity, which measures the number of times a rupee has to change hands in a year in order to support the level of output and exchange that is represented by the nominal GDP. For example, a given rupee note passes from your hand to a shop keeper when you buy some merchandise such as a packet of sweets. The same rupee note then passes from the shop keeper to a cycle dealer when he purchases a cycle, and then from a cycle dealer to a barber in exchange for a hair cut. The more swiftly that money circulates from one person to the next, the higher is the velocity. VELOCITY, then, is the number of times per year the typical rupee in the money supply is utilized to purchase final goods and services. We can write the formula for velocity as

› **Velocity** is a measure of the speed with which money circulates in transactions involving final goods and services, and is the ratio of nominal GDP to the money stock.

$$\text{Velocity} = \frac{\text{Nominal GDP}}{\text{Nominal Money Stock}} = \frac{PY}{M}$$

Nominal GDP, which is a measure of the total value of transactions, is the price level p times the real GDP, Y. M is the money stock being considered, M_1 or M_3. The higher is velocity, V, the quicker is a typical rupee circulating.

Figure 6.6 shows the velocity of M_1 and M_3. The diagram reveals that the velocity of M_1 is higher than that of M_3. This is what we should expect as M_1 comprises mainly currency that is used more frequently for transactions. Each rupee of M_1, thus, changes hands more frequently than the typical rupee that comprises M_3. The velocity of both M_1 and M_3, however, are declining over time.

The ease of transacting in currency and financial innovation that involves new payment methods such as the introduction of credit cards affects how people hold money in the form of currency and deposits. In economies with few bank branches in rural areas and where lower-income groups are excluded from the formal banking system, people hold currency for transactions. As the financial system grows, cash is still accepted as a means of payment for transactions of small amounts, whilst the use of cheques is restricted to payments where the issuer's creditworthiness can be established, or where the delivery of goods can be delayed until after the clearance of the cheque through the banking system. With advances in payment technologies such as credit and debit cards, transactions rely even less on currency. We should, therefore, expect the velocity of M_1 to increase with time as the use of currency for transactions

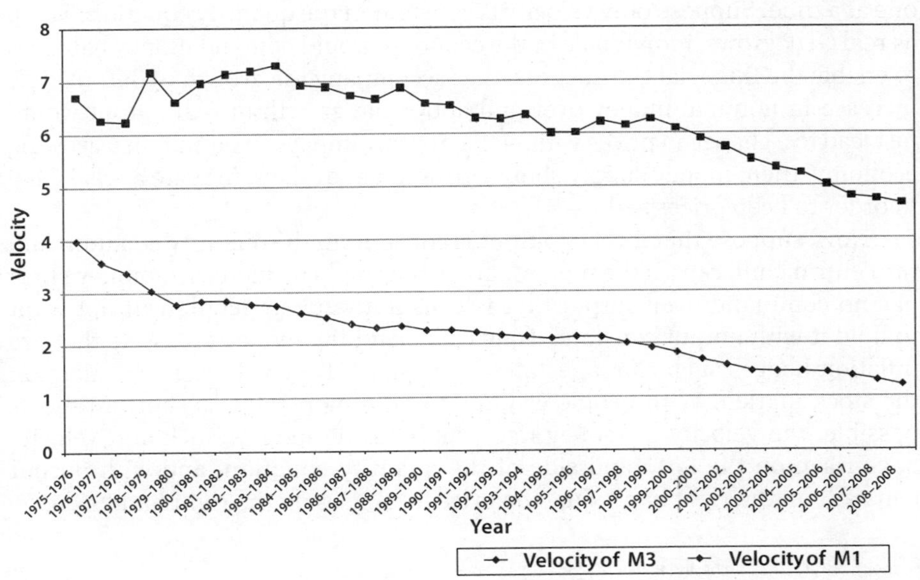

› **Figure 6.6**
Velocity of M_1 and M_3.
The typical rupee measured by M_1 and M_3 circulating in transactions involving final goods and services is declining over time.

purposes reduces with financial development. The decline in velocity in India is stemming more from the increase in financial intermediation and from a gradual reduction in financial exclusion. Financial exclusion is the lack of delivery of banking services at an affordable cost to disadvantaged and low-income groups. As larger sections of society are included in the provision of financial services such as savings, insurance, payments, and remittance facilities by the formal financial system, the provision of these new avenues to hold financial assets has increased the demand for money for transactions as compared to the nominal GDP. The provision has also reduced the velocity of money.

The definition of velocity is often rewritten by multiplying throughout by the nominal money stock to obtain,

$$MV = PY \tag{6.16}$$

› The **quantity equation** is the relationship between money times velocity or nominal aggregate expenditure and nominal aggregate output, as given by the price level times real output.

This equation, which states that money times velocity is equal to nominal GDP, is called the QUANTITY EQUATION in economics. *MV* measures nominal GDP in terms of aggregate expenditure on final goods and services, and *PY* measures the market value of the aggregate output of final goods and services. Irving Fisher (1911)* used this equation in the early part of the twentieth century to establish a link between money and prices. If velocity (which is determined by the nature of financial intermediation and current payment technologies) and real output constant at a full employment level is approximately constant over some period of time, then, we may write,

$$M\bar{V} = P\bar{Y}$$

where a bar over a variable denotes that the variable is constant. On the left hand side, the only variable that is not constant is the money supply, and on the right hand side, the only variable that is not constant is the price level. Thus, an increase in money supply will get reflected in a change in prices. The change in money supply cannot affect output (which is constant) and the increase in money supply leads people to bid up the prices of the fixed quantity of goods and services available. High rates of money growth will then be associated with high rates of inflation.

Of course, both real GDP, *Y*, and velocity, *V*, are not constant. Despite this, economists such as Friedman postulate a close link between the money circulating in the economy and the level of prices over long periods of time. To understand this, relax the condition that velocity and real output are constant one at a time. Suppose only velocity is constant in the quantity equation. Then, as real GDP grows, individuals in the economy would demand money balances to enable the financial transactions that accompany the growth of output. Any increase in nominal money over and above the growth of real output would just lead to a change in prices without having any impact on output. In a growing economy, then, money supply should grow at about the same rate as real GDP in order to keep prices stable.

Now, suppose that level of output is constant in the quantity equation and the central bank causes the money supply to grow. The increased money stock has no command over output that is constant, and so people will not want to hold it with output constant. They will spend the money on assets that are inflation hedges such as real estate or jewellery. They will even speculate on the stock market. With people wanting to hold money for as short a time as possible, the velocity of money rises. As both the money stock and velocity have risen on the left hand side of the quantity equation, and with output constant on the right hand side, the price level rises on the right hand side.

*Fisher, I. (1911) "The Purchasing Power of Money," New York: Macmillan.

Thus, any growth in money that is not absorbed by a growth in real output will lead to inflation in the absence of financial innovations. It will also lead to inflation in the absence of changes in financial intermediation that affect money demand, and thereby the velocity of money. Indeed, economies that have high rates of growth of money supply do experience high and sustained inflation. Over short periods of time, inflation can arise due to factors other than an increase in the supply of money, such as a bad harvest or an oil price increase. For long periods of time and more so for inflation that is high and persistent, there is a close relationship between the rate of inflation and the rate of growth of the money supply. This link is depicted in Figure 6.7 for a sample of countries between 1995 and 2006. The horizontal axis measures the average annual value of the growth in the money stock, and the vertical axis measures the average annual consumer price inflation between 1995 and 2006. The countries depicted include five developing countries from the western hemisphere (Argentina, Brazil, Colombia, Paraguay, and Uruguay), five developing countries from Africa (Ethiopia, Kenya, Nigeria, South Africa, and Zimbabwe),* five European countries in transition (Belarus, Bulgaria, Kazakhstan, Poland, and Turkey), China, and India. The trend line in Figure 6.7 indicates that countries with higher rates of money growth tend to have higher rates of inflation.

In 1956, Phillip Cagan studied hyperinflation during the period 1920 to 1946. A HYPERINFLATION was defined by Cagan as inflation in excess of 50 per cent per month for at least a year. Cagan found that during these hyperinflationary episodes in countries such as Russia, Germany, Poland, Hungary, and Greece, the rate of monetary growth was exceedingly high. Between 1947 and 1984, there were no hyperinflations in the world economy. Since 1984, there have been at least seven countries that have witnessed hyperinflationary episodes. The Nicaraguan hyperinflation, that occurred over a period of 58 months between June 1986 and March 1991, was the worst among these seven countries, with a cumulative inflation of 11,895 billion.**

› **Hyperinflation** is a situation in which the inflation rate is extremely high. Cagan defines it as inflation in excess of 50 per cent per month for at least a year.

The rapid increase in monetary growth that accompanies high inflation is usually due to large government budget deficits. When the government issues public debt to finance a deficit and the central bank buys up the new debt, it results in an increase in bank reserves and an injection of new money into

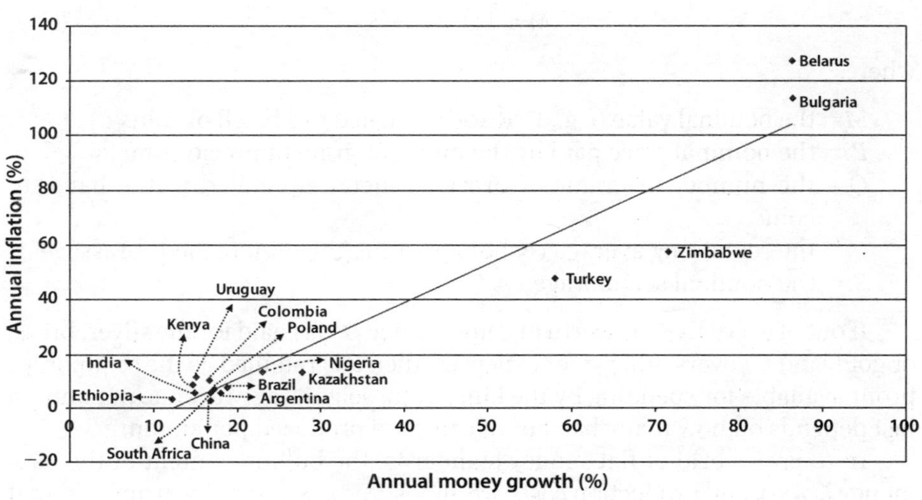

› **Figure 6.7 Inflation and Money Growth.** Higher rates of money growth are associated with higher rates of inflation.

*The data for Zimbabwe is up to 2002.

**See Fischer, Stanley, Ratna Sahay and Carlos A. Végh (2002) "Modern Hyper and High Inflations", Journal of Economic Literature, September, 837–880.

the economy. When the central bank accommodates deficit spending by the government in this manner, it monetizes the deficit. This occurs in countries that are suffering from war or political instability and governments are unable to raise revenues in the form of taxes. In these situations, governments are also unable to borrow directly from the public. The government then finds that the only alternative left to finance expenditures is to have its bills sent to the central bank for payment by having it purchase the government debt. When the central bank accommodates in a manner that results in a large increase in the nominal money stock, the result is inflation. Sargent* shows how, after World War I, Austria printed money at extremely high rates to finance its government deficit. Austrian notes in circulation increased by over 70 per cent from July to August 1922. This rapid increase in money creation led to annual inflation rates that approached 10,000 per cent per year.

6.5 Seigniorage

As real money yields direct utility, inflation affects the demand for money by reducing the purchasing power of money. The issuing authority, therefore, finds that there is an optimal rate at which it may issue money.

› The use of money creation as a revenue device by the government is called **seigniorage**.

The basic idea behind SEIGNIORAGE is that a government reaps profit when it produces new money at an expense less than the value of the money produced. The government finances additional expenditure by spending the new units of money. As new money is interchangeable with old money, the expansion of the money stock dilutes the value of existing money balances and implicitly taxes money holders. Seigniorage is the net revenue from producing money, or the difference between the exchange value of the produced money and the cost of producing and maintaining it in circulation.

The expression seigniorage dates from the time of the gold standard, when every citizen was entitled to have gold bars minted in the form of gold coin. A duty payable on this service was known as seigniorage since it was due to the ruler—the French seigneur or lord—who enjoyed the prerogative of money issue. If the coins were produced in a mint, then the mint operations were subject to the following accounting identity:

$$M = PQ + C + S \tag{6.17}$$

where,

M = the nominal value (e.g., INR 100) assigned to a batch of coins
P = the nominal price paid by the mint per gram of precious metal
Q = the number of grams of precious metal embodied in the batch of coins
C = the remaining average cost of operating the mint (called "brassage")
S = the nominal seigniorage.

If out of every INR, M worth of coins minted, PQ is paid for the silver, brass, or gold, and C covers other mint expenses, then S is retained as the seigniorage profit available for spending by the king. Total seigniorage revenue per annum just depends on how many batches of coins are produced per annum.[6]

In today's world of fiat-money standards, the bullion content of the base money is zero, and production costs are almost zero.[7] Setting $Q = 0$ and $C = 0$, it

*Sargent, Thomas J. (1986) "The End of Four Big Inflations", in Robert E. Hall (ed.) "Rational Expectations and Inflation", New York: Harper & Row.

follows that $M = S$. A government's nominal seignioage per annum is just the change in the stock of base money per year,

$$S = \Delta M_0 \tag{6.18}$$

where M_0 is the stock of base money (see Chapter 2). Real seigniorage is:

$$s = \frac{\Delta M_0}{P} \tag{6.19}$$

In Chapter 12, we will be looking at how government budgets are financed. We will also look at the impact of budget deficits or the excess of expenditures over revenues. At this juncture, it suffices to state that the budget constraint of a government that issues fiat money is,

$$G + B_{t-1} - T = \frac{\Delta B}{iP} + \frac{\Delta M_0}{P} \tag{6.20}$$

where, G is government expenditure, B_{t-1} is the interest payments on the debt, and T is the revenues of the government which includes tax revenues less subsidies, non-tax revenues such as user charges on public utilities like electricity, and revenues from disinvestment. Here, $\Delta B/i$ is the change in interest bearing debt held by the non-government public, and ΔM_0 is the nominal seigniorage or the change in fiat-base money held by the public. The left hand side of Eq. (6.20) is the deficit, which is the excess of expenditures over revenues, and the right hand side states that the deficit is financed by issuing more bonds or by increasing the liabilities of the central bank or the base money, M_0.

The budget constraint makes transparent the process of seigniorage—it helps to finance government spending with the central bank printing new notes to pay for the bills the government runs up. One way in which seigniorage is obtained is when the central bank expands the monetary base through an open-market operation. By purchasing ΔM_0 worth of government securities in the market, the central bank retires that much debt[8] and makes it possible for the government and the finance minister to finance a stream of new spending whose present value equals ΔM_0. Essentially, the central bank's open-market purchase increases M_0 and reduces B/i. The finance ministry issue of new debt brings B/i back up to its original level and finances a rise in G. The net impact is an increase in G financed by ΔM_0.

Seigniorage has a revenue implication in that the RATE of monetary expansion is not infinite. This is equivalent to the problem of profit maximization for a monopolist who has to take into account the decline in sales as he raises the price. In this case, the government is a monopoly producer of base money. The inflation rate is the 'price' of holding money. As the 'price' is increased because higher rates of growth of the money supply are associated with higher inflation rates (as depicted in Figure 6.7), the real quantity of the demanded base money shrinks. Hence, the revenue gained from monetary expansion is finite. Seigniorage can equivalently be thought of as the application of a tax rate on a tax base.

› As the government increases the growth **rate** of money in circulation, (the tax rate) individuals respond by reducing their holding of real money balances (the tax base) so that seigniorage does not increase without bound.

Write segniorage as:

$$s = \frac{\Delta M_0}{P} = \frac{\Delta M_0}{M_0}\frac{M_0}{P} \tag{6.21}$$

Here, $\Delta M_0 / M_0$ is the growth rate of base money and is taken to represent a "tax rate" whereas the real base money stock, M_0/P, represents the "tax base". Although the faster growth in base money (an increase in the tax rate) increases seigniorage, it reduces the real money supply held in an economy (a narrower tax base) as the resulting increase in inflation and nominal interest rates causes a decline in the holding of the money balances.

6.6 The Optimal Level of Seigniorage

Recall that the demand for money is inversely related to the nominal interest rate i, which in turn is the sum of the real rate of interest r and inflation π, or $i = r + \pi$. The demand for money is then inversely related to the rate of inflation. It is convenient to concentrate on the situation where the level of income Y is constant so that any increase in money supply has no medium of exchange function and individuals have no incentive to hold the increase in the stock of money.[10] As money supply increases, individuals extinguish their holdings of the increased money stock, and this results in a bidding up of prices such that the PERCENTAGE increase in prices equals the percentage increase in money supply, $\Delta P/P = \Delta M_0/M_0$. As a result, M_0/P is constant at the level required to meet the transactions associated with constant consumption and income. Simultaneously, an increase in the growth in money supply results in an equivalent increase in inflation and a reduction in the holding of real money balances because the demand for money is inversely related to the inflation rate. In fact, the relationship between inflation and real money demand is as depicted in Figure 6.8.

› When the **percentage** increase in prices equals the percentage increase in money, then the ratio M_0/P is a constant. When various quantities grow at constant rates, economists refer to it as a steady state.

The demand for real money balances—DD—as depicted in Figure 6.8, decreases as inflation increases. At high rates of inflation, as shown in the diagram, the demand for real money balances declines rapidly.

Abstracting from a fractional reserve banking system,[10] high-powered money or base money is equivalent to an increase in money stock, that is, $\Delta M_0 = \Delta M^S$. Real seigniorage is $s = (\Delta M^s/M^s)(M^s/P)$ from Eq. (6.21), that is, the product of the growth rate in the nominal money supply and the real money supply. For any given level of seigniorage, the product of $\Delta M^S/M^S$ and M^S/P is a constant—any given level (s_0) of seigniorage can be achieved both as a combination of a higher real money supply and a lower growth rate of money (point F in Figure 6.8 for $s = s_0$), and as a combination of a lower real money supply and a higher growth rate of money (point G in Figure 6.8 for $s = s_0$). Accordingly, the graph for seigniorage in Figure 6.8, Panel A is downward sloping.[11]

A higher level of seigniorage, $s > s_0$, is represented in this graph by combinations of real money supply and growth rate of money to the right of s_0.

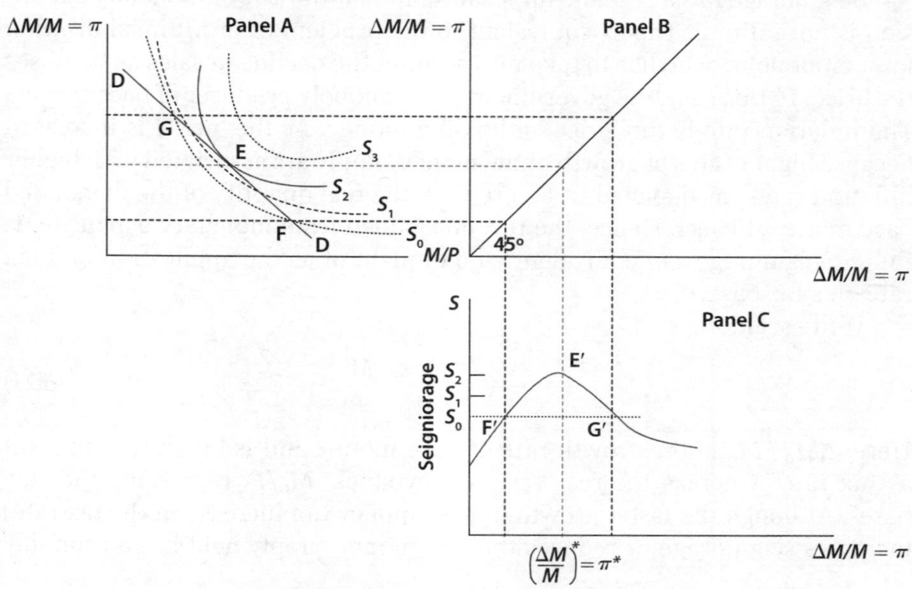

› **Figure 6.8**
Optimal Seigniorage and Inflation. An increase in the growth rate of nominal money supply increases the rate of inflation and results in a reduction in the demand for real money balances. At some point, depicted by point E in panel A and E in panel C, the reduction in the demand for money offsets the percentage increase in the money supply and reduces seigniorage.

In this way, various levels of seigniorage, s_0, s_1, s_2, … etc. can be represented by downward sloping curves as depicted in Figure 6.8, panel A. The real money demand function is depicted by the curve DD. For a given level of seigniorage s_0, money demand equals money supply at points F and G. Point F represents a lower growth of money supply compared to G, but both yield the same seigniorage revenue s_0. Using panel B, this information can be plotted in panel C of the diagram where points F′ and G′ correspond to points F and G in panel A. As depicted, higher levels of seigniorage are possible as we move along the money demand curve from point F towards E as the demand curve intersects successively higher seigniorage curves. After point E, as we move along the demand curve towards point F, we reverse this trend as the demand curve intersects successively lower seigniorage curves. This gives us the inverted U shaped seigniorage curve in panel C. The maximum seigniorage is the point of tangency of the demand curve for money and the seigniorage curve s_2 at point E in panel A–E′ in panel C.

A higher rate of monetary expansion has initially the direct effect of generating more seigniorage. However, it also increases inflation and reduces the demand for real money balances. This results in an offsetting effect. This offsetting effect grows larger and eventually exceeds the direct effect at points E and E′ as the rate of monetary base expansion is pushed up higher. The shape of the seigniorage curve in panel C suggests that a government trying to maximize its revenues should set a money supply expansion rate and corresponding inflation rate that is optimal for it at $(\Delta M / M)^* = \pi^*$. A government financing its expenditure via seigniorage would then achieve a constant rate of inflation given by π^*. When a government tries to finance a deficit by increasing the money supply at a rate that is higher than the seigniorage maximizing rate, the public adjusts by reducing its holding of real money balances. Sargent[12] showed how, after World War I in Austria, the increase in money creation led to annual inflation rates that approached 10,000 per cent per year as people responded by reducing their holding of real money balances drastically. Real money balances fell as the government resorted to increasing the notes in circulation since individuals expected inflation to rise and they sought to avoid capital losses on the holding of money balances.

MACROFOCUS 6.2

Saddam Dinars and Swiss Dinars

The most common reason advocated for people holding money is that it has the backing of a government and is a legal tender for the settlement of payments—the medium of exchange function. Yet, there have been currencies in existence, such as *cowrie* shells in India, which have had no government backing. Social convention, rather than monopoly issue by a government, often makes people willing to attribute a medium of exchange property to an asset. Mervyn King, the governor of the Bank of England, cites an interesting example of this (King, 2004).

After the Gulf War, southern Iraq was under Saddam's control and northern Iraq became a Kurdish protectorate. UN sanctions made Saddam resort to printing money to finance increasing fiscal deficits. In May 1993, the central bank of Iraq announced a three-week period during which citizens would have to exchange their old 25 dinar notes for new 'Saddam dinars' that bore his portrait. Saddam dinars were printed in abundance with the face value of the cash in circulation rising from 22 billion dinars towards the end of 1991 to 584 billion four years later, accompanied by an inflation averaging 250 per cent a year.

The Kurds had no opportunity to exchange their Swiss dinars—named because the notes had been printed by the company De La Rue on plates manufactured in Switzerland. The Swiss dinar was, therefore, in fixed supply unlike the Saddam dinar, and it became more valuable. Though there was no trade between northern and southern Iraq, both the currencies were traded against the dollar and the cross-exchange rate reveals that by 2003 it took 300 Saddam dinars to buy one Swiss dinar. King observes that by the fall of 2002, as it became more likely that the US would invade, the Swiss dinar became more valuable and began to appreciate. This was driven by expectations that the Swiss dinar would be honoured by future governments. That expectation turned out to be correct when, on 7 July 2003, the head of the Coalition Provisional Authority, Paul Bremer, announced the creation of a new Iraqi dinar that would be exchanged for the two existing currencies at a rate that implied that one Swiss dinar would be worth 150 Saddam dinars. Thus, expectations of changes in a policy regime can have a major impact on the demand for a currency quite independently of policies pursued by a current government.

Click's (1998) study of 90 countries for 1971–1990 found that only 10 depended on seigniorage for more than 20 per cent of government spending—countries such as Paraguay, Uganda, Burma, Israel, Argentina, and Yugoslavia. Most industrialized nations, including the USA, financed less than 3 per cent of government spending with seigniorage. The median country in the sample collected seigniorage equal to 1.7 per cent of GDP and 7.8 per cent of government spending.

India's position was slightly above the median situation in that it collected seigniorage equal to 1.72 per cent of the GDP and 11.8 per cent of the government spending. Moreover, inflation rates in most countries seem to be far lower than what a seigniorage maximizing government would resort to. Governments might want to keep in reserve the ability to raise seigniorage in a time period when there is a peak need for revenue, such as during a war or famine. The government in such circumstances encourages larger money holding and secures a larger tax base which can be taxed when there is a short-run need for revenues. For a seigniorage motivated government, there are limits to monetary expansion as the real base money stock accommodates itself to the real quantity of base money demanded through the adjustment of the price level. In a fiat-money system, according to the seigniorage approach, the equilibrium real money stock is determined entirely on the demand side where the real quantity of base money demanded falls as the rate of monetary expansion rises.

SUMMARY

- Money serves three functions—medium of exchange, unit of account, and store of value.
- The most important function of money is that of a medium of exchange—when it is used to purchase goods and services.
- Money, as a unit of account, is the yardstick for measuring the economic value of goods, services, and assets, and thereby enables a comparison of these based on their values.
- As a store of value, money is one way of holding wealth which can be compared with other ways of holding wealth such as stocks, bonds, or real estate.
- A bond is a legal promise to repay a debt. The principal amount or the amount originally lent is paid at some fixed date in the future called the maturation date. A bondholder receives regular interest or coupon payments, until the bond's maturation date.
- Bond prices and interest rates are inversely related.
- The net wealth of the private sector consists of its net claims on agents outside the sector—the stock of money and the stock of government bonds; $W_t = M_t + B_t / i_t$.
- The real interest rate is the percentage increase in the purchasing power of a financial asset.
- The nominal interest rate is the real rate of interest plus the rate of inflation.
- The Fisher effect is the tendency for nominal interest rates to be high when inflation is high and low when inflation is low.
- The two-period budget constraint—asset accumulation is allowed—implies that the lifetime income is the present value of income in the two periods less the discounted value of interest lost on account of holding money rather than bonds.

$$Y_1 + \frac{Y_2}{1+r} - \frac{i_1}{1+i_1}\frac{M_1}{P_1} = C_1 + \frac{C_2}{1+r}$$

- An individual decides on the amount of real money balances to hold by maximizing his preference for consumption and real money balances, subject to his intertemporal budget constraint.
- The demand for real money balances rises with income and declines with a rise in the interest rate.
- When trading off risk versus returns while deciding on the composition of the assets in his portfolio, the agent decreases his allocation to money as the interest rate rises up to an acceptable level of risk. As the risk keeps on increasing, at some point, the individual seeks to reduce exposure to risk by increasing the allocation to money even though the interest rates increase.
- The use of money creation as a revenue device by the government is called seigniorage; $s = \Delta M_0/P$.
- As the government increases the growth rate of money in circulation (the tax rate), individuals respond by reducing their holding of real money balances (the tax base) so that the rate of increase in seigniorage diminishes eventually.
- Seigniorage revenues can be enhanced by imposing reserve requirements on banks and putting restrictions on substitutes for base money.

NOTES

1. If all goods are expressed in terms of money, and money is the unit of account, then, only n different absolute prices for the different goods need to be recorded. If $P_i (i = 1, \ldots, n)$ denotes absolute price for good i, then the implied relatives prices are P_i/P_j. If there was no unit of account in an economy with n goods, we would need to record $n(n - 1)/2$ distinct relative prices which can be a fairly large number.
2. We are here ignoring another outside liability—the net borrowings from abroad by the private sector. Strictly speaking, also the deposits held as an asset by households and firms in the banking system are a liability of the banks in which they are held. Insomuch as banks are entities within the private sector, such deposits are not a part of the calculation of the net worth of the private sector. Such monetary assets that are the liability of banks within the private sector are sometimes referred to as inside money. Inside money should not, strictly speaking, be a part of the accounting calculation of the net worth of the private sector that includes only outside money—the monetary base that is a liability of the central bank. We shall be ignoring this distinction in what follows and treat money, both inside as well as outside, as part of the net wealth of the private sector.
3. The accumulation of financial wealth takes place by agents deciding to save rather than consume. Hence, $\Delta W/P = S = Y - C$. This is akin to stating that agents accumulate wealth by saving and adding to their stocks of money and bonds.
4. For W constant, $\Delta M + \Delta B/i = 0$ or $\Delta B/i = -\Delta M$.
5. In a general version of the transactions demand for money such as shopping cost models, utility is a function of consumption and leisure in each time period. Money reduces transaction cost associated with exchange and thus increases leisure [See McCallum, B. (1989)]. Feenstra (1986) demonstrated that there exists a functional equivalence between models with money in the utility function and models where money affects "liquidity costs" which in turn show up in the budget restriction.
6. Note that if it were a perfectly competitive minting industry competition would ensure price equals marginal cost or $M = PQ + C$, and $S = 0$. A royal mint can only earn seigniroage if it has a legally protected monopoly.
7. Well not quite. Printing costs are typically 2 to 3 per cent of smaller denominations of paper currency.
8. Interest on that debt now goes to the central bank which essentially rebates it back to the Ministry of Finance.
9. The result that we obtain in this sub-section then hold for all situations where the growth of money supply is larger than the growth rate of output and income. As income increases any increase in money supply is required for enabling financial transactions that support the increase in income. Once that purpose is accomplished, money is no longer required to be held and individuals will attempt to get rid of any additional money over and above what is required for transactions. That process generates inflation.
10. Otherwise, the money supply is the money multiplier times base money.
11. More technically, it is a rectangular hyperbola.
12. Sargent, Thomas, J. (1986). "The End of Four Big Inflations", in Robert E. Hall (ed.), "Rational Expectations and Inflation", New York: Harper & Row.

TEST YOURSELF

1. Prices were quoted in cowrie shells in medieval India for payments related to trade in food, clothing, and other services. How did cowrie shells fulfill the three functions of money?
2. You own a perpetuity that pays you INR 5,000 as coupon. You plan to sell the bond to finance a holiday. Can you expect to receive INR 5,000 in the bond market for the bond? Explain why.
3. How does the demand for money depend on the nominal interest rate and income?
4. The cash that you hold earns you no interest. What is the real rate of return to holding cash in your pocket?
5. Derive the two-period budget constraint for an individual whose wealth can be held in money or perpetual bonds.
6. Why is the demand for money stated in real terms (M/P) rather than in nominal terms?
7. How does an individual decide to allocate his portfolio between bonds and money when the latter yields a risky return?
8. Why does the government expand the stock of base money in the economy?
9. Explain the response of an individual's demand for real money balances when the government increases the rate of monetary expansion in the economy.
10. Why might a government not resort to increasing the money supply so as to achieve seigniorage maximizing revenues?

ONLINE APPLICATION

1. Go to the home page of the Reserve Bank of India. URL: www.rbi.org.in/home.aspx.
2. Click on the "DataBase" icon.
3. Under the classification of Annual data, click on the "Handbook of Statistics on Indian Economy."
4. Click on "Table 182: Yield of SGL Transactions in Treasury Bills for residual maturities". Look at the data for treasury bills with a term to maturity of 15–91 days. Create a spreadsheet of monthly data on yields for this maturity of treasury bills for the period April 2005–2006 to March 2009–2010. This data gives you the nominal interest rates for the period.
5. Then click on "Table 239: Wholesale price index—Annual variation" and create a data column with the data for all commodities for the period April 2005–2006 to March 2009–2010. This data is the inflation rate for the period.
6. Create a graph depicting the nominal interest rate available from the data in step 4 and the inflation rate available from the data in step 5. Do the nominal interest rate and the rate of inflation graphs have the same pattern? (You could find the correlation coefficient between the nominal interest rate and inflation as well to get a number that tells you the association between inflation and the nominal interest rate).
7. Are inflation and the nominal interest rate closely related? Why or why not?

Appendix 6.1 The Two-Period Budget Constraint

Derivation of Eq. (6.12):

Adding the first- and second-period budget constraint we obtained:

$$(P_1Y_1) + \frac{P_2Y_2}{(1+i_1)} = P_1C_1 + \frac{P_2C_2}{(1+i_1)} + \left[M_1 - \frac{M_1}{(1+i_1)}\right] + \left[\frac{B_1}{i_1} - \frac{B_1}{(1+i_1)} - \frac{B_1}{(1+i_1)i_1}\right]$$

or,

$$(P_1Y_1) + \frac{P_2Y_2}{(1+i_1)} = P_1C_1 + \frac{P_2C_2}{(1+i_1)} + \left[\frac{(1+i_1)M_1 - M_1}{(1+i_1)}\right] + \left[\frac{(1+i_1)B_1 - i_1B_1 - B_1}{(1+i_1)i_1}\right]$$

or,

$$(P_1Y_1) + \frac{P_2Y_2}{(1+i_1)} = P_1C_1 + \frac{P_2C_2}{(1+i_1)} + \frac{i_1M_1}{(1+i_1)}$$

Dividing throughout by P_1, we have:

$$Y_1 + \frac{P_2Y_2}{P_1(1+i_1)} = C_1 + \frac{P_2C_2}{P_1(1+i_1)} + \frac{i_1}{(1+i_1)}\frac{M_1}{P_1}$$

Now, recall that the real interest rate is given by:

$$1 + r_1 = \frac{P_1(1+i_1)}{P_2}$$

This implies that $P_2/[P_1(1+i_1)] = 1/(1+r_1)$ which we substitute into the above budget constraint to obtain:

$$Y_1 + \frac{Y_2}{(1+r_1)} = C_1 + \frac{C_2}{(1+r_1)} + \frac{i_1}{(1+i_1)}\frac{M_1}{P_1}$$

or,

$$Y_1 + \frac{Y_2}{(1+r_1)} - \frac{i_1}{(1+i_1)}\frac{M_1}{P_1} = C_1 + \frac{C_2}{(1+r_1)} \quad \text{(A.6.1.1)}$$

Appendix 6.2 The Inventory Demand for Money (Baumol–Tobin)

The demand for money for the purposes of transactions—people holding money because they want to use it for payments—was developed by Baumol (1952) and Tobin (1956). It derives the optimal money holdings for an individual who receives an annual income in installments which is then spent for the purchase of goods and services. Some individuals receive their income monthly, (12 installments) and some every fortnight (26 installments). In what follows, we presume (for simplicity) that the income is received annually. Typically, individuals receive their income in the form of a cheque which they then deposit into a bank in order that the amount may be credited to their bank account. The money stock in the bank account of an individual can command PY worth of goods and services in nominal terms. The choice problem the individual faces is that whilst all receipts and payments are made in money, money bears no interest. However, there is an alternative asset—bonds—that generates an interest income. The individual can convert his money into bonds and earn interest income, but there are transactions costs involved in exchanging money for bonds and vice versa. So the individual must choose the character and number of transactions involving the purchase and sale of bonds so as to maximize his interest receipts less the transactions costs to be paid. We introduce the following notation:

x: the number of transactions involving bonds, B—purchases or sales per payment period
c: fixed transaction cost per transaction in the purchase or sale of bonds

Transaction costs can be thought of as the costs of time spent in going to deposit and withdraw money from the bank, transport costs, and the various restrictions and penalties that may be imposed on withdrawal. Some of the transaction costs could also be psychic—nuisance value of dealing with brokers who purchase/sell bonds on your behalf—rather than explicitly pecuniary.

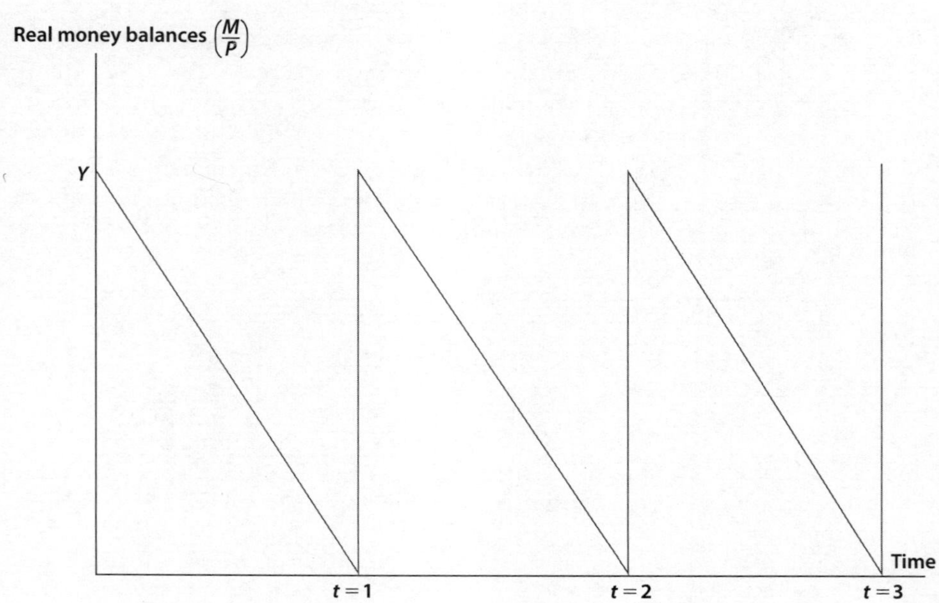

› Figure A6.2.1 Time Profile of Money Balances when $x = 0$. The individual receives an income held in the form of money balances at discrete regular intervals. With even and continuous expenditures within a time period, the money balances deplete at a uniform rate during each time interval.

Suppose $x = 0$, then the individual holds only money balances and no bonds. At regular time intervals, the individual receives Y of income which is then used to spend on goods and services. As in each time period, the individual will get paid his regular income and as we are assuming all income is for the purpose of expenditure, it makes perfect sense for the individual to deplete his cash balance to zero the moment before income is received. Thus, the cash balance is Y at the beginning of a time period and by the end of a time period, it is depleted to zero. With expenditures being even and continuous (a simplifying assumption made), the cash balances must be depleted in a smooth manner throughout any unit time interval. This results in the profile of money balances, M/P, as given in Figure A6.2.1. The average cash balance the individual holds in a time interval where he begins with real balances equal to Y and ends with real balances of zero is $(1/2)(Y + 0) = Y/2$.

Now, suppose the individual puts half his income receipt into bonds as soon as he receives the income. He is then left with half his cash balances to spend which as expenditure is even and continuous will deplete half way through the time interval. Requiring cash balances half way through the income payment interval he would sell his bonds purchased earlier in order to get the money balances that can be used for purchases of goods and services in the remainder of the time period. The number of transactions in bonds is then $x = 2$. At the beginning of the next income receipt period, he again sets half of the income aside to purchase bonds and continues with the same behaviour as in the previous period. The time profile of money balances is now that depicted in Figure A6.2.2. The average cash balance held by the individual when $x = 2$ is then given by $Y/4$.

If now the individual puts three-fourths of his cash balances into bonds, then he is left with real cash balances equal to $Y/4$. With even expenditures on goods he will run out of cash balances by the time one fourth of the time interval has elapsed. He then sells each quarter one-third of the bonds purchased earlier to finance his expenditure over each quarter period. In each time interval, he purchases bonds at the beginning of the interval and sells bonds thrice at the beginning of each second, third, and fourth quarter of the interval. Hence, $x = 4$. The time profile of money balances is that given in Figure A6.2.3. The average money balances held by the individual when $x = 4$ is then $Y/8$.

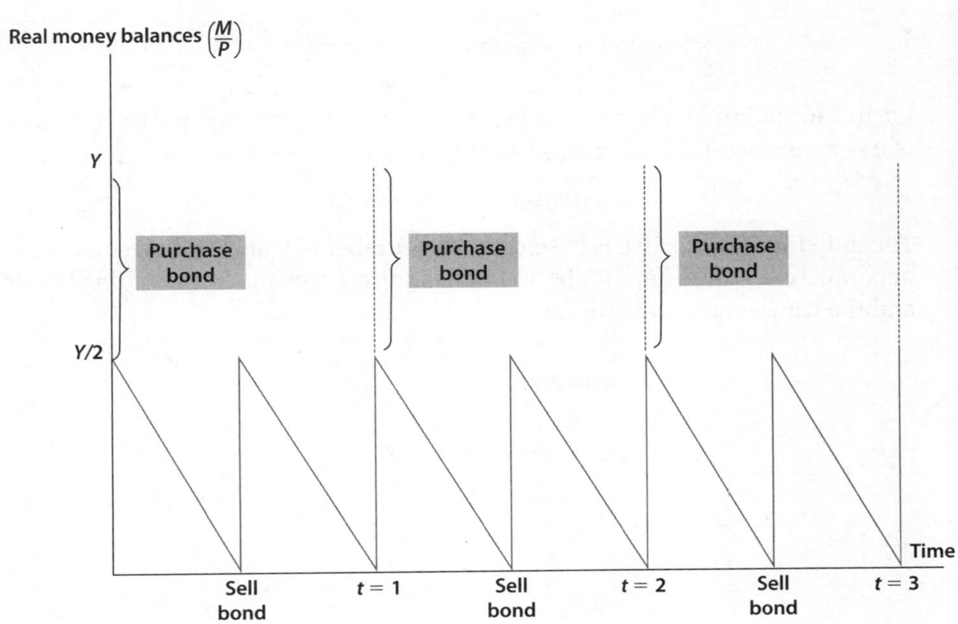

› **Figure A6.2.2**
Time Profile of Money Balances when $x = 2$. At the moment the individual receives his income he puts half of it into bonds. Half-way through the interval as money balances have depleted he sells the bonds to gain liquidity for the purposes of expenditures.

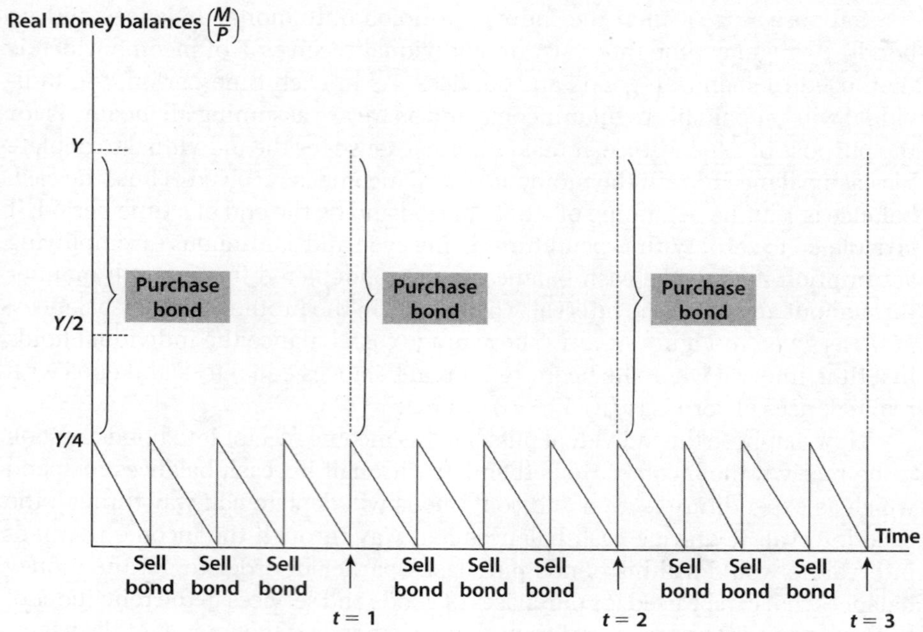

› Figure A6.2.3 Time Profile of Money Balances When $x = 4$. On receiving his income at the beginning of a time period, the individual puts three-fourths of it into bonds. Then each quarter he sells one-third of the bonds purchased in the beginning of the period to replenish his liquid money balances that have been depleted.

Generalizing, when x is an integer and $x \geq 2$, the average holding of money balances will be given by $Y/2x$. What about the average bond holding? Bonds are held whenever money is not required for transactions. Money required for transactions on average is $Y/2x$. Money held on average when bonds are neither purchased nor sold ($x = 0$) is $Y/2$. Thus,

$$\text{Average Bond Holding} = \frac{Y}{2} - \frac{Y}{2x}$$
$$= \frac{Y}{2}\left(1 - \frac{1}{x}\right)$$

With an interest rate i on bonds, the interest receipt on holding bonds on average is the average bond holding multiplied by the interest rate, or,

$$\text{Interest Receipts on Average Bond Holding} = \frac{iY}{2}\left(1 - \frac{1}{x}\right)$$

Each transaction in a bond—purchase or sale—is subject to a transaction cost of c per transaction. With x number of transactions, we have,

$$\text{Transactions Costs} = Cx$$

The individual's objective is to select x, the number of transactions in bonds, to maximize $\phi(x)$ the difference between the interest receipts from holding bonds and the transactions costs of those bond holdings,

$$\underset{\{x\}}{\text{Max}}\ \phi(x) = \frac{iY}{2}\left(1 - \frac{1}{x}\right) - Cx$$

Hence,
$$\frac{d\phi}{dx} = \frac{iY}{2}x^{-2} - C = 0$$

or,
$$x^{-2} = \frac{2C}{iY}$$

or, $$x^2 = \frac{iY}{2C}$$

or, $$x^* = \sqrt{\frac{iY}{2C}}$$

For example, if we take the estimated per capita national income at factor cost in 2005–2006 at 1999–2000 prices, it is INR 21,005. Let the transaction cost of buying bonds be INR 20 and the bond yield be 6 per cent per year. Then,

$$x^* = \sqrt{(.06)(21{,}005)/40} = 5.6$$

With the number of transactions an integer,

$$x^* \approx 6$$

An average income person then hardly transacts in bonds during a year.

As the second order condition is $\phi'' = -(iY/2x^3)$, the negative root can be disregarded. The average holding of money balances as we saw is $M/P = Y/2x$. Substituting the value of $x = x^*$ we obtain:

$$(M/P)^* = \frac{Y}{2\left(\sqrt{iY/2C}\right)} = \sqrt{\frac{CY}{2i}}$$

From the above equation, we can see the main results of the Baumol–Tobin approach to the demand for money. The demand for money depends differently in different situations:

1. It depends positively on real income. Note that the relationship is not proportional. In fact, real money demand grows less than real income which means that there are economies of scale in the holding of money balances.
2. It depends negatively on the interest rate on bonds.
3. It depends positively on transactions costs. In fact, when transactions costs fall drastically as the efficiency of financial transactions improves, the demand for money drops significantly.

7

The Labour Market

CRITICAL QUESTIONS

- *What are the determinants of the demand and supply of labour?*
- *How is the aggregate supply curve of output derived?*
- *When individuals are subject to money illusion, what form does the aggregate supply curve take?*
- *How does unemployment result when the aggregate supply curve is Keynesian?*
- *How does Friedman use the hypothesis of mistaken price expectations to generate an aggregate supply of output function?*
- *What is the natural rate of unemployment and what is cyclical unemployment?*
- *What is the Phillips Curve and what does it depict?*
- *How do inflation expectations affect the slope of the Phillips Curve?*

The supply of the economy deals with the production of output. To produce output, firms use factors of production like capital and labour. The production function summarizes this relationship:

$$Y = F(K, N) \tag{7.1}$$

where Y is output produced, and the two inputs are K and N. Here, K is the measure of the aggregate stock of land, machines, and other physical inputs, and N is the number of employee hours or man days hired by the firm. The number of employee hours is the product of the number of workers hired times the average number of hours worked per person. By writing the product N, rather than its two separate components, we are assuming the firm gets the same output from ten workers working eight hours per day, and twenty workers working four hours per day. In what follows, in the interests of simplicity, we ignore the distinction between the number of workers hired and the number of hours worked, and refer to labour input N as the number of workers hired by the firm.

7.1 Profit Maximization and Labour Demand

The firm produces that level of output where profits (Π) are maximum, where profits are total revenue less total costs, or,

$$\Pi = pY - wN - p^K(r + \delta)K$$

where p is the price at which the firm sells its output, w is the wage rate or the cost of hiring an additional worker, and $p^K(r + \delta)$ is the rental on capital. We assume the firm operates in a competitive environment so that the price of the output is unaffected by how much the firm produces and sells, and input prices are unaffected by how much labour and capital the firm hires.

Consider the situation faced by a profit maximizing firm in the short run—a time span that is sufficiently short that the firm cannot increase or reduce the size of its plant, or purchase machines and physical equipment that can immediately be pressed into producing an output. With capital stock fixed at some level $\bar{K}$, short-run profits are given by,

$$\Pi = pF(\bar{K}, N) - wN - p^K(r + \delta)\bar{K} \tag{7.2}$$

As the firm is competitive and input prices are fixed, $p^K(r + \delta)\bar{K}$ is akin to a fixed cost, and wN is the variable cost of the firm. The firm can, in the short run, affect profits by the number of workers it hires. It selects the number of workers as given by the profit maximization condition[1]:

$$pMP_N = w \tag{7.3}$$

MAXIMIZING PROFITS requires that the marginal cost of hiring an additional worker (w) equals the marginal gain from hiring that additional worker which is the value of the marginal product of labour (pMP_N). As the marginal product of labour declines with the hiring of more labour (because more and more workers added to a fixed capital stock reduces the gains from specialization) the profit maximization condition in Eq. (7.3) implicitly gives the number of workers to be hired[2] as N^{D*}, as depicted in Figure 7.1. Here pMP_N is the short-run demand curve for labour, and depicts how much labour the firm will hire at different wage rates.

› **Profit maximizing** firms hire workers up to the point where the wage equals the value of the marginal product of labour.

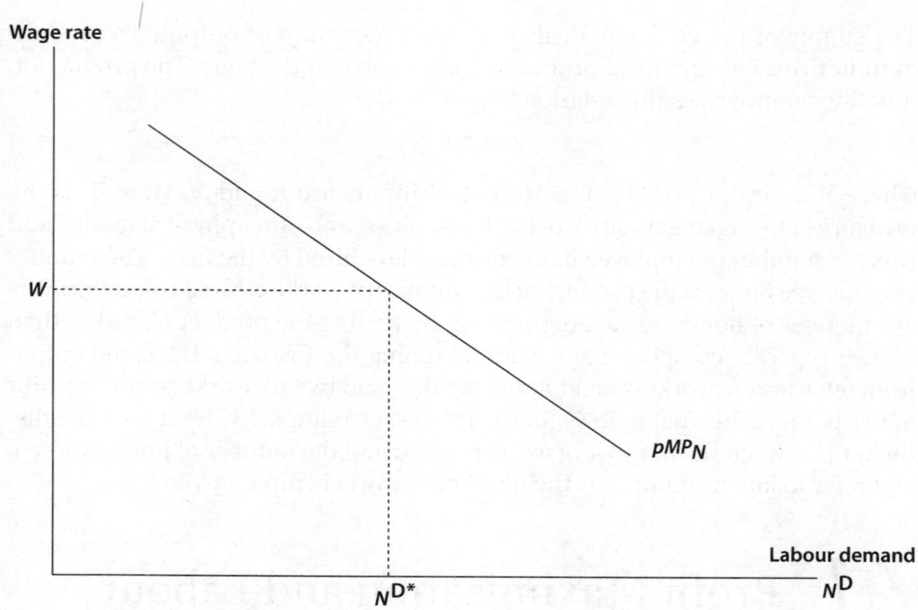

› **Figure 7.1**
Demand for Labour. The demand for labour is downward sloping, reflecting the diminishing marginal productivity associated with hiring additional labour. Firms hire labour up to the point where the revenue from hiring an additional unit of labour equals the nominal wage.

7.2 Utility and Labour Supply

The supply of labour is a decision made by individuals and that decision is a choice between labour and leisure. Of course, a person does spend some time on household activities, but in our simple set up, we assume that the person decides to allocate time between labour market and leisure activities. Moreover, the person receives satisfaction from the income received as it can be used for consumption of goods and services. The person also receives satisfaction from the consumption of leisure (l). The idea that the individual gets satisfaction from consuming goods and leisure is summarized by the utility function[3]:

$$U = U(C, l)$$

The consumption of goods and leisure are constrained by the individual's time as well as income. Let H be the number of hours after rest, sleep, and household activities, which the individual can allocate to the labour market. The individual allocates the H hours between supplying labour, N^S, and leisure, l. The time constraint then is,

$$H = N^S + l$$

In addition to a time constraint, an individual also faces a budget constraint. Part of a person's income is independent of how many hours he works. It can come from bequests, lotteries, dividends, and other asset incomes. This can be denoted as non-labour income V. The individual also gets an income by working at a real wage rate of w/p per hour for N^S hours. Hence, the consumption expenditure that is feasible for the individual is determined by the sum of the labour earnings and non-labour income[4]:

$$C = \frac{w}{p}N^S + V$$

We will combine the budget constraint and the time constraint by writing $N^S = H - l$ and plugging this into the income constraint to give:

$$C = \frac{w}{p}(H - l) + V$$

or,
$$\frac{w}{p}H + V = C + \frac{w}{p}l$$

The left-hand side is the income received if the individual spends all the time in the labour market working H hours. The non-labour income that is received is V. This income of $(w/p)H + V$ can be spent on INR C worth of consumption goods and the rest, $[(w/p)l]$, can be spent on leisure activities. Thus, each hour of leisure has a price or opportunity cost that is given by the wage rate w/p forgone. The budget line of the individual is given in Figure 7.2. Point E indicates that if the person decides not to work at all (all H hours devoted to leisure), his income is V. If the individual gives up all leisure activities, then his income is $(w/p)H + V$. From point E, as the individual moves up the budget line for every hour of leisure given up, he receives a real wage of w/p which is the slope of the budget line.

Which point on this budget line will the individual select? That will be determined by the individual's preferences for income that allows the consumption of goods versus leisure as given by the utility function. Formally, the individual maximizes utility subject to the budget constraint, or,

$$\underset{\{N^S\}}{Max}\, U(C,l)$$

such that,
$$C = \frac{w}{p}(H - l) + V \tag{7.4}$$

where $N^S = H - l$. The graphical solution to this is depicted in Figure 7.3, where the individual decides to supply N^{S^*} hours of labour and take $(H - N^{S^*})$ hours of leisure. The EQUILIBRIUM is where the slope of the budget line equals the slope of an indifference curve (the marginal rate of substitution of consumption for leisure, or, $MRS_{C,l}$), or,

› Workers maximize utility such that the last rupee spent on leisure activities yields the **same utility** as the last rupee spent on consumption.

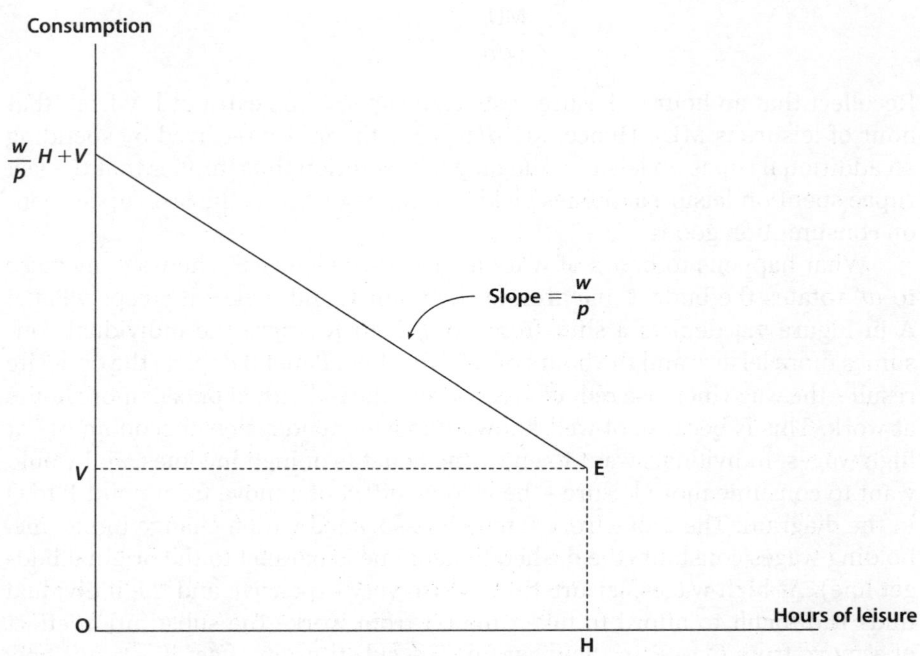

› **Figure 7.2**
Budget Line of Individual.
The budget line depicts the consumption possibilities, inclusive of the accounting for non-labour income V as the individual gives up leisure and works in the labour market at a real wage w/p.

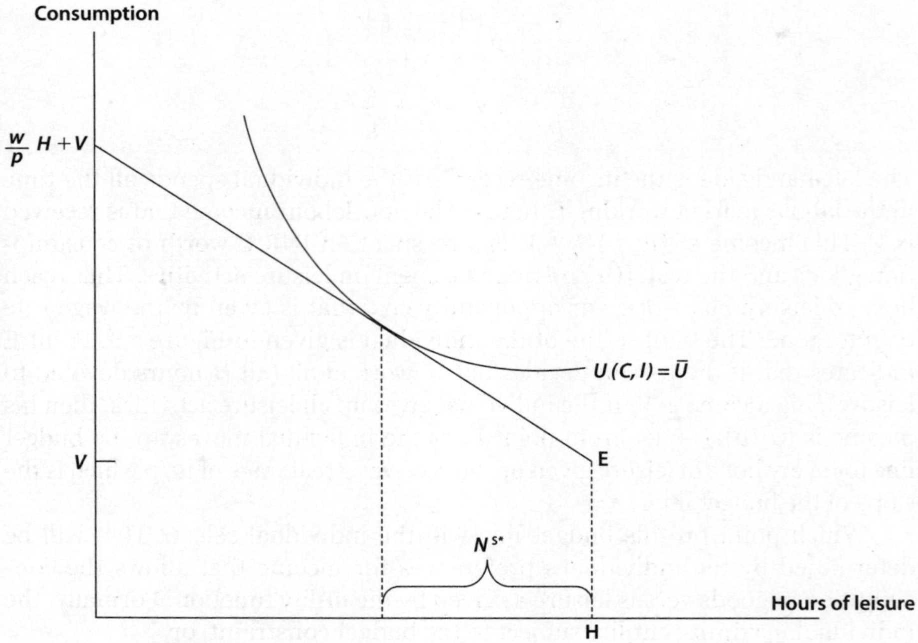

› **Figure 7.3**
Optimal Labour Supply. The optimal supply of labour is determined where the trade-off between consumption and leisure, as given by the slope of an indifference curve, equals the slope of the budget line.

$$\underbrace{MRS_{C,l}}_{\text{Slope of Indifference Curve}} = \underbrace{\frac{w}{p}}_{\text{Slope of Budget Line}}$$

or,

$$\frac{MU_l}{MU_C} = \frac{w}{p} \tag{7.5}$$

The slope of an indifference curve[5] is the ratio of the marginal utility of leisure to the marginal utility of consumption. The above condition can be written as,

$$\frac{MU_l}{w/p} = MU_C$$

Recollect that an hour of leisure costs w/p rupees. The extra utility from that hour of leisure is MU_l. Hence, $MU_l/(w/p)$ is the utility received by spending an additional rupee on leisure. The tangency solution thus implies that the last rupee spent on leisure activities yields the same utility as the last rupee spent on consumption goods.

What happens to hours of work as the wage changes? The wage increase to w' rotates the budget line around the point E and makes it steeper. Panel A in Figure 7.4 depicts a shift from point P to R where the individual consumes more leisure and the hours of work decline. Panel B depicts the opposite result—the wage increase reduces leisure and the individual puts in more hours at work. This is because of well-known opposing tendencies in economics—at high wages, individuals want to enjoy the benefits of high incomes, and would want to consume more leisure—the income effect of a move from point P to Q in the diagram. The move from P to Q is associated with a change in income, holding wages constant (the dashed budget line is parallel to the original budget line). At high wages, leisure time is also very expensive and the individual finds it difficult to afford to take time off from work—the substitution effect of a move from Q to R in the diagram. The substitution effect illustrates how

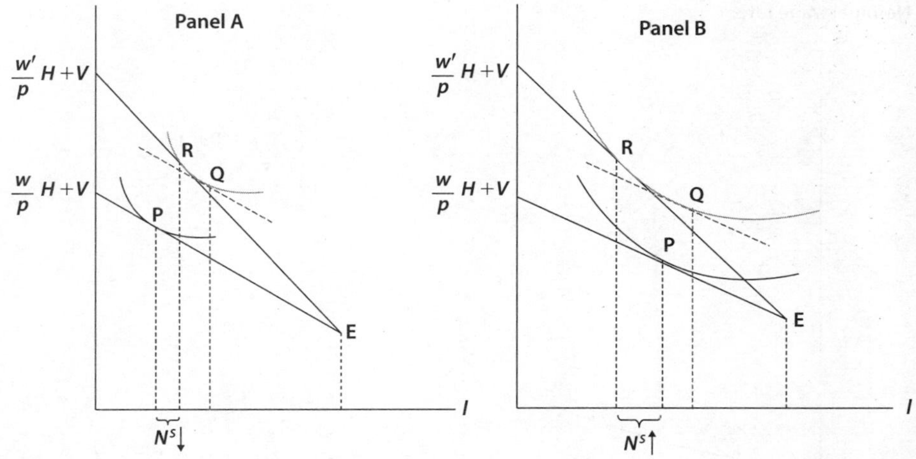

› **Figure 7.4**
Effects of a Wage Increase. An increase in the wage causes the budget line to rotate around the point E that depicts the non-wage income. This increases the demand for leisure (income effect). However, as leisure is now relatively more expensive than before, the individual is induced to substitute leisure for labour (substitution effect). In panel A, the income effect dominates and the supply of labour decreases. In panel B, the substitution effect dominates and the supply of labour increases.

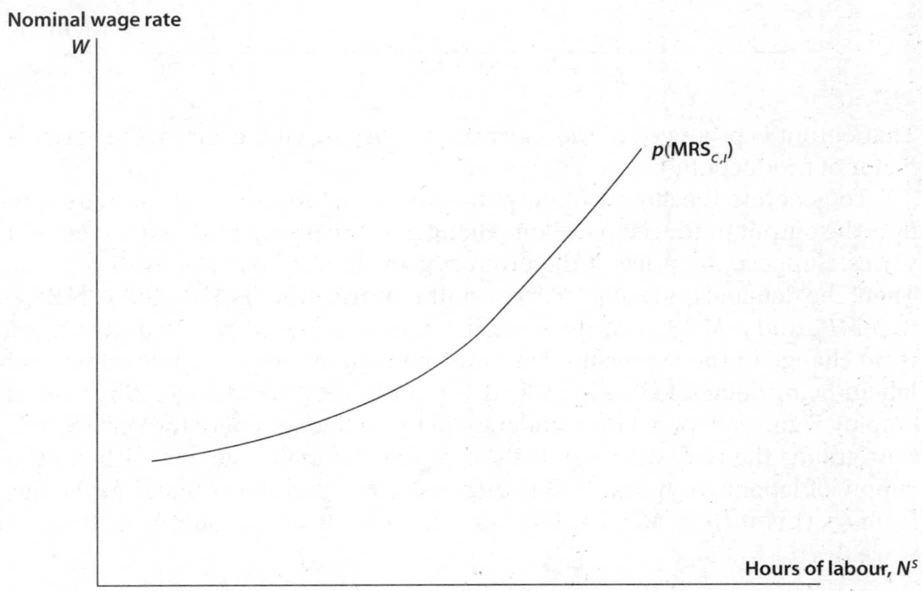

› **Figure 7.5**
Labour Supply Schedule. The supply of labour increases with the nominal wage rate as the individual responds to the increase in the wage by offering to work more and give up leisure.

consumption changes as the wage increases, holding utility constant along an indifference curve. In what follows, we will assume that the SUBSTITUTION EFFECT dominates the income effect—panel B of Figure 7.4—so that, as wages rise, individuals increase their supply of labour. Thus, the supply of labour schedule as given by Eq. (7.5), $w = p\text{MRS}_{C,l}$, is an upward sloping schedule as illustrated in Figure 7.5.

› An increase in the wages results in both an **income and substitution effect**. The labour supply curve is upward sloping when the substitution effect dominates.

7.3 Aggregate Supply with/without Money Illusion

By the familiar economic logic of demand equals to supply in the labour market, N^D equals N^S. Putting the demand and supply curves from Figures 7.1 and 7.5 together in Figure 7.6, we get the situation as depicted by point E. Recall that the reason for our exploration into the workings of the labour market is that we are interested in how firms produce the output that is to be sold in the market.

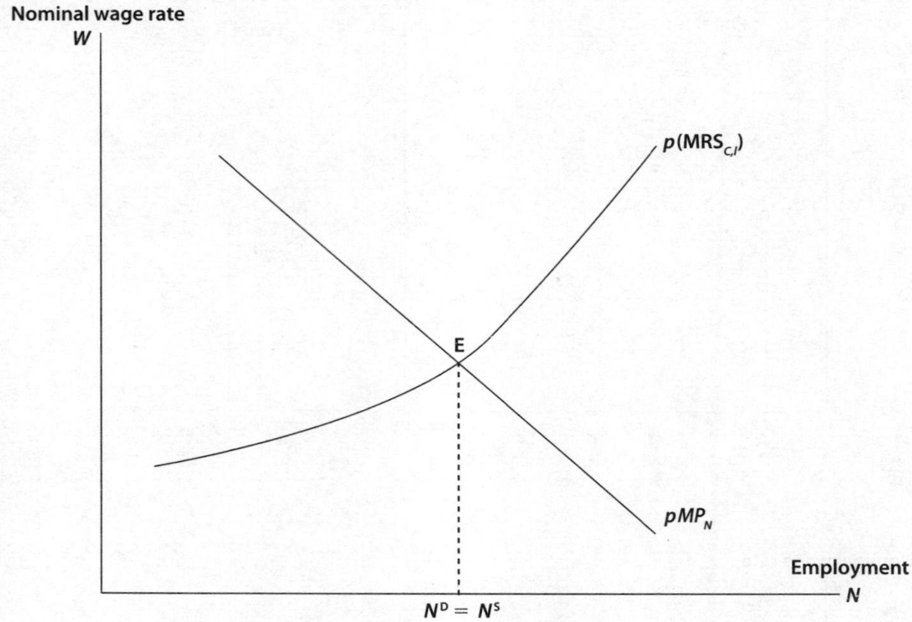

› **Figure 7.6**
Labour Market Equilibrium. The demand for labour by firms that are profit maximizers equals the supply of labour by individuals who maximize their preferences for consumption versus leisure at point E.

That output is produced in the short run by varying labour hired, the variable factor of production.

To generate the supply of output curve by the firm, we now inquire into how the output produced by labour changes as the price of the good to be sold varies. Suppose the price of the product goes up from p_0 to p_1, with $p_1 > p_0$. Then, the demand and supply curves shift upwards from p_0MP_N and $p_0\text{MRS}_{C,l}$ to p_1MP_N and $p_1\text{MRS}_{C,l}$, as depicted in panel A of Figure 7.7. As drawn there is no change in the labour market outcome with exactly the same amount of labour being demanded and supplied as prior to the price change. Why? Let us employ Figure 7.7, panel B, to understand this outcome where the vertical axis now graphs the real wage w/p instead of the nominal wage w as before. The supply of labour from Eq. (7.5) is $w/p = \text{MRS}_{C,l}$ and the demand for labour from (7.3) is $w/p = MP_N$. Labour demand equals labour supply at the real wage w_0/p_0.

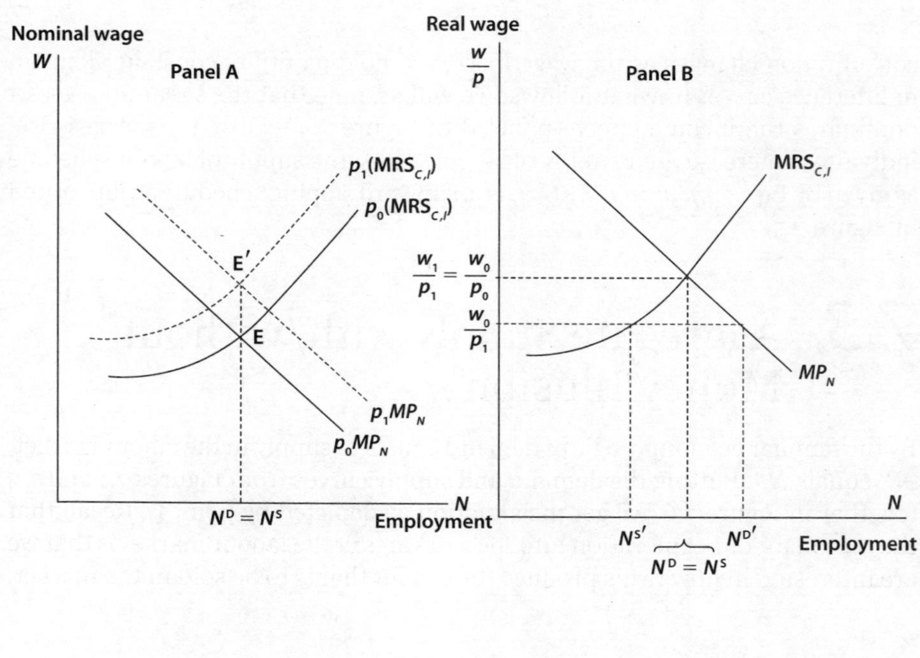

› **Figure 7.7**
Effect of Price Increase. An increase in the price results in an equal increase in the nominal wage (panel A) that results in a constant real wage (panel B). The change in price then has no effect on the employment in the labour market.

Essentially, the increase in the price reduces the real wage cost from w_0/p_0 to w_0/p_1. With a decline in the real wage, the cost of labour has become cheaper, and the firm responds by going down its demand curve MP_N and increasing the demand for labour to $N^{D'}$. The reduction in the real wage reduces the return to labour supply and individuals react by reducing their supply of labour to $N^{S'}$. At w_0/p_1, there is an excess demand for labour to the extent of $N^{D'} - N^{S'}$. As the firm faces a shortage of labour, the price of labour must be bid up so as to induce the required labour supply. Hence, the nominal wage rises up to w_1, the point where demand again equals supply, or, $w_1/p_1 = w_0/p_0$, and the equilibrium in the labour market is restored. This implies that the percentage increase in the price exactly equals the percentage INCREASE IN THE WAGE, or,

$$\frac{p_1 - p_0}{p_0} = \frac{\Delta p}{p} = \frac{\Delta w}{w} = \frac{w_1 - w_0}{w_0}$$

and the real wage is a constant as a result.

› If a change in price results in an equiproportionate **change in the money wage**, employment and output are unaffected. This is referred to as a situation of no money illusion—a situation where individuals do not ordinarily make mistakes in assessing nominal versus real changes.

The effect on output is depicted in Figure 7.8. Panel A of this diagram is the same as panel A of Figure 7.7. In panel B, the short-run production function $Y = F(\bar{K}, N)$ is graphed—the decline in the slope of this production function with an increase in N reflects the diminishing marginal productivity of labour. Panel C is just a 45° line in output that allows us to mirror the output changes in panel B to panel D, which traces the relationship between output produced and prices—the aggregate supply (AS) relationship. As the change in the price leads to no change in labour input as discussed above, there is no corresponding change in output. The aggregate supply curve is vertical. In effect, when both sides of the market—firms and workers—think in real terms, any increase in price is offset by an equal increase in money wages so that with no change in real income to individuals or real cost to firms, the real demand (MP_N) and supply ($MRS_{C,l}$) curves for labour are unchanged. This way there is also is no change in employment and output. When individuals think in real terms, they are said to be subject to no money illusion and the vertical aggregate supply curve is called a CLASSICAL SUPPLY CURVE.

› The **classical aggregate supply** curve is vertical and the quantity of output produced depends on real factors such as technology (productivity and labour demand) and preferences (labour supply), with no effect of nominal variables on output.

Now, suppose that individuals suffer from some degree of money illusion and do not formulate their labour supply decision on the basis of the real wage.

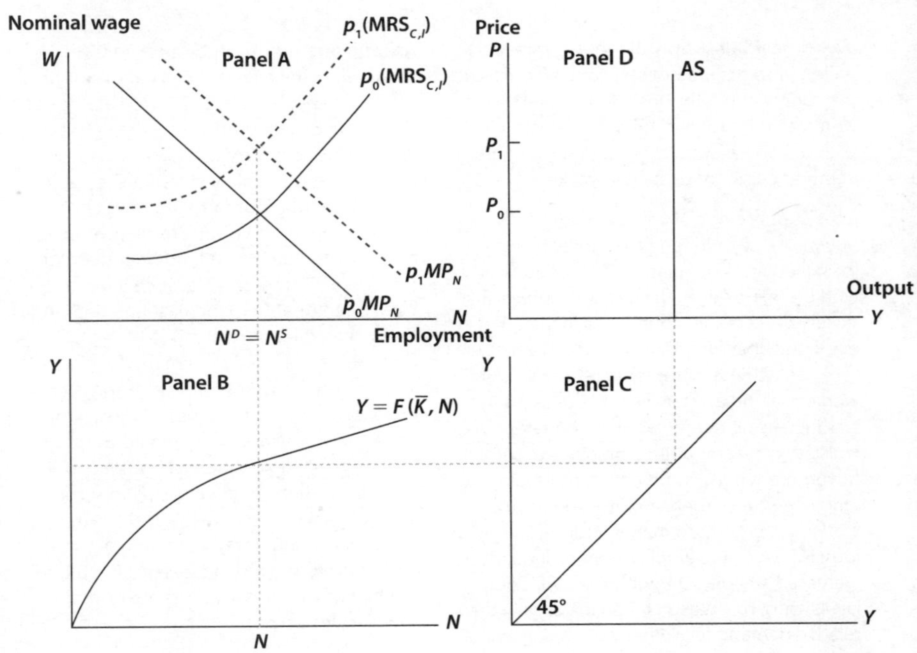

› **Figure 7.8**
Aggregate Supply (Real Wage). A rise in the price raises money wages by an identical amount when there is no money illusion (panel A). With no change in employment, output does not change (panel B). Output is, therefore, constant and the aggregate supply curve is vertical (panel D).

Suppose that rather than the real value of the good that the money wage can buy (w/p), they are interested only in their money wages (w) because they are more interested to compare their earnings position vis-à-vis the money earnings of others in the labour market. In that case, workers bargain with their employers, taking into account the nominal wages they receive vis-à-vis a reference group of workers with whom they make comparisons in terms of similarities in working conditions and job description. Employers, on the other hand, continue to make decisions about labour demand in terms of the real cost to them of any nominal wage they pay. An individual firm can observe its own price as well as the wage paid to its workers so that it can make decisions with respect to the real wage. In this case, the demand and supply curves for labour are given, respectively, by,

$$w = pMP_N$$

and

$$w = MRS_{C,l}$$

Figure 7.9 now depicts that when the price rises from p_0 to p_1, the aggregate supply curve is upward sloping like a standard supply curve. Hence, if workers suffer form some MONEY ILLUSION and make decisions about labour supply on the basis of nominal wages, the aggregate supply curve is upward sloping.

› When individuals formulate labour supply decisions on the basis of the money wage, they are subject to **money illusion**. The aggregate supply curve is then upward sloping.

7.4 Introducing Unemployment

By now, you would have noticed that in both diagrams—Figures 7.8 and 7.9—we have proceeded by equating the demand curve with the supply curve of labour. With $N^D = N^S$, there can never be any unemployment which is a characteristic of all economies. The early attempts to introduce unemployment into a macroeconomic framework introduced a friction, or rigidity, into the main model.

MACROFOCUS 7.1

Why Has Wage Inequality Increased?

In most countries around the world, the distribution of wages has become more unequal since the 1980s. In the US, for instance, most income groups faced a decline in real wages during the 1980s (Murphy & Welch, 1992). However, this widening of the wage distribution in the US is not a story of the rich getting richer and the poor poorer, as the wage of more skilled workers remained roughly constant while that of unskilled workers declined rapidly. In India, by contrast, during the 1980s and 1990s, even the workers in the lower end of the wage distribution gained in terms of real wage increases, with the accelerating wage inequality mainly in the upper half of the wage distribution (Kijima, 2006).

What causes wage inequality? One explanation is in terms of the simple supply–demand framework, with the added recognition that there are two types of workers in the labour market—skilled and unskilled. Then, the wages of skilled workers relative to the wage of unskilled workers would rise over time if the supply of labour curve for skilled workers did not shift out as much as the supply curve for unskilled workers. This would also happen if the demand curve for skilled workers shifted out by more than the demand curve for unskilled workers.

If the supply curve of college graduates shifts outwards, it would tend to reduce the wage for skilled workers relative to less educated workers. If, however, the demand curve for skilled workers shifts out by more than the demand curve for unskilled workers, an economy can witness increases in returns to skilled workers. In India, after the mid-1990s, there was increasing deregulation of job security legislation that required employers to seek government permission before dismissing an employee. Since then, about 15 per cent of workers in organized manufacturing lost their jobs. However, the employment of supervisors increased steadily. Deregulation of labour law is, thus, one reason for an increase in the relative demand for skilled labour.

As tariff and non-tariff barriers to trade reduced, many cheap imported goods also became available in India. These are goods that are typically produced in India in the small-scale sector by unskilled workers. However, small-scale industries are subject to a reservation policy that allows certain (mainly consumer) goods to be produced only if production is of limited scale. With restrictions on their scale, such industries have been unable to increase the demand for unskilled labour. Kijima (2006), thus, found that the relative demand for skilled workers grew faster than the supply, which increased inequality in India. Policies to decrease wage inequality would then require focusing on increasing the supply of skills through enabling access to secondary and tertiary (college level) education. Moreover, labour intensive manufactured export growth is also adversely affected to the extent that such exports are from the small-scale sector.

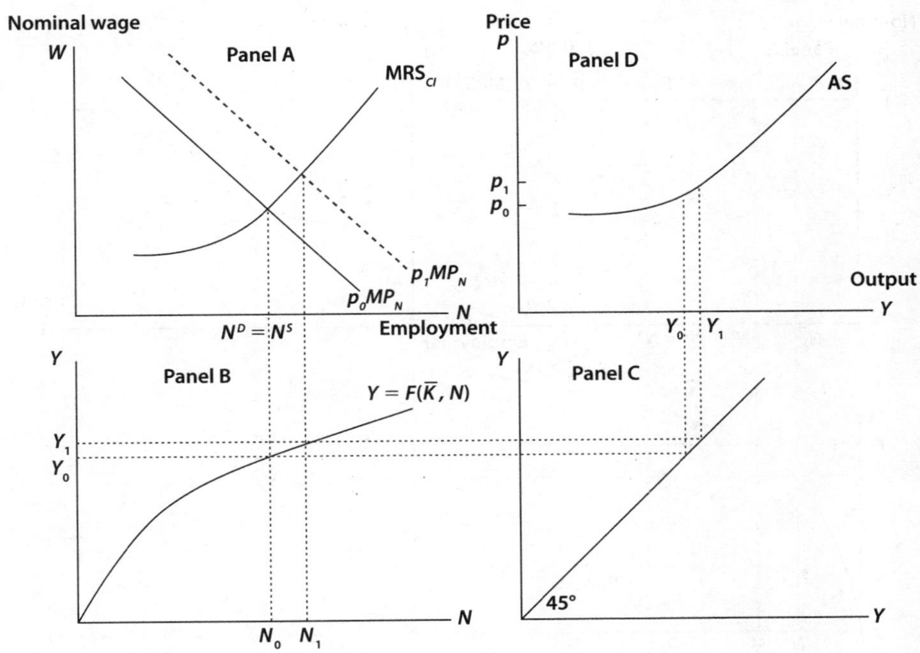

› **Figure 7.9 Aggregate Supply (Money Wages).** Individuals making labour supply decisions on the basis of money wages increase their supply of labour when firms increase their demand for labour due to an increase in the price of output (panel A). The increase in employment increases output (panel B). The price rise is then accompanied by an increase in the supply of output (panel D).

We now look at two such manipulations to the framework mentioned before[6]. The first is essentially the Keynesian approach in which money wages are treated as constant until the point where those who want to be employed at this constant wage find employment, after which the money wages are flexible upwards.[7] The second approach is due to Friedman, who argues that there is an asymmetry of information between workers and firms. Essentially, firms observe the actual value of their own price and the wage rate. Workers can observe their nominal wage, but it is inherently more difficult a task for them to estimate the prices of the whole basket of goods that they actually consume with their wage. Workers, therefore, form an estimate of the price level they will face for the goods in their consumption basket and the aggregate of these prices will be denoted by p^e, the price level they expect. Workers, in Friedman's view, supply labour on the basis of expected prices, whereas firms demand labour on the basis of actual prices. It is because workers have mistaken expectations that unemployment occurs in Friedman's analysis. Let us first derive the Keynesian aggregate supply curve.

7.4.1 Keynesian Aggregate Supply

Figure 7.10 derives the Keynesian aggregate supply curve. Let the initial price be p_0 and the fixed ruling money wage rate be $\bar{w}$. This results in a demand for labour of N_0^D and a supply of N_0^S with unemployment given by $N_0^S - N_0^D$. Even though more workers are willing to work, firms are not willing to offer them jobs as the wage cost is set high and it is not profitable to employ more than N_0^D workers. Actual employment is, thus, given by,

$$N = \min[N^D, N^S]$$

Given the level of employment determined in the labour market, $N_0^D = N_0$, we can, from the production function (panel B), determine the output Y_0 that is produced by these N_0 units of labour. Using the 45° line (panel C), this level of output Y_0 can be combined with the price associated with that output of p_0 as specified in panel A to give one point D on the aggregate supply curve.

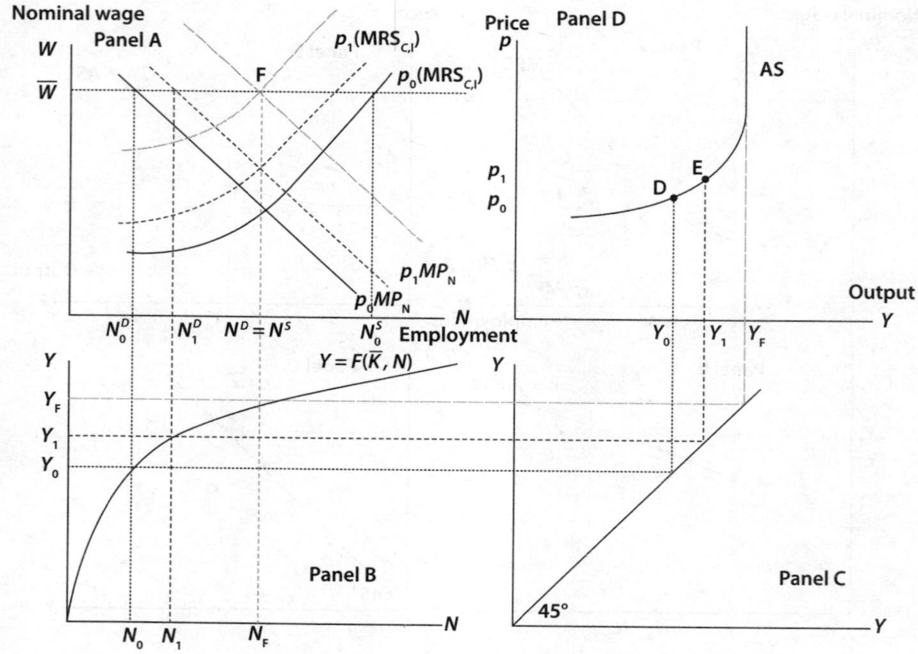

› **Figure 7.10**
Keynesian Aggregate Supply. With the money wage fixed, in the short-run firms are able to hire additional labour at fixed nominal costs when the price of the output increases up to the point of full employment F in panel A. The increase in employment raises output (panel B). The increased output that results when the price rises is the upward sloping aggregate supply (AS) curve in panel D. The AS curve is vertical at the point of full employment where the demand for labour equals the supply of labour.

› When money wages are fixed and employment is determined by the demand for labour, we obtain a Keynesian aggregate **supply curve** that is upward sloping till all those who offer to supply labour at the fixed money wage have been employed.

To derive the rest of the SUPPLY CURVE, let the price at which output is sold rise to $p_1 > p_0$. This causes the demand and supply curves to shift up, resulting in increased employment, $(N_1^D) = N_1$, as the real cost of labour has declined from $\bar{w}/p_0$ to $\bar{w}/p_1$, making it profitable to employ more labour. The resulting new output produced of Y_1 can be traced out from panels B and C to panel D where the new price output point of (p_1, Y_1) on the supply curve is given by point E. As price rises, the demand for labour rises. Thus more labour is hired, resulting in more output produced. The aggregate supply curve is, therefore, an upward sloping curve as long as $N^D < N^S$. Once $N^D = N^S$, as occurs at point F in panel A, all workers who are willing to work at that wage $\bar{w}$ have been fully employed and even if the firm advertises more vacancies, it will find no takers for those jobs. The level of employment at point F, N_F, is characterized by full employment and the output produced corresponding to this level of employment is the full employment level of output, Y_F. The Keynesian supply curve, thus, has an upward sloping portion that becomes vertical at full employment.[8]

7.4.2 Friedman on Mistaken Expectations

Another explanation of the labour market is that provided by Friedman who argues that workers on the supply side of the labour market are imperfectly informed about the aggregate price level of the typical basket of goods they consume. Thus, they form an estimate of the aggregate price level and on the basis of this, the supply of labour schedule is not given by $w = p\text{MRS}_{C,l}$. Rather it is defined in terms of the price level that they expect, p^e, so that,

$$w = p^e\text{MRS}_{C,l} \tag{7.6}$$

The demand for labour is still given by:

$$w = pMP_N \tag{7.7}$$

If $p^e = p$, that is, there are no expectational errors, then both sides of the market are making decisions in real terms and the outcome will be a vertical supply curve as in Figure 7.8. The level of employment and output produced when expectations are realized, that is, $p^e = p$, is called the NATURAL RATE OF EMPLOYMENT (N^*) and output (Y^*).

› When expected prices equal actual prices, then expectations are realized and the economy is at the **natural rate of employment** and output, with a vertical aggregate supply curve.

In Figure 7.11, we begin with an initial price of p_0 and let us assume that the expected price is also equal to this, that is, $p_0^e = p_0$. With workers making no expectational error, we can trace out the natural rate of employment and output, and the aggregate supply curve is the vertical curve given by AS($p^e = p$). Now, suppose the price increases to $p_1 > p_0$. The demand curve for labour shifts up. The expected price, however, is still p_0^e. The labour supply curve is, therefore, unchanged. The demand and supply curves for labour intersect at point A, where the nominal wage is w_1 and employment and output are given by $N_1 > N^*$ and $Y_1 > Y^*$. Tracing out through the labour input, product output, and 45° line panels, we get the point A′, which denotes the point (p_1, Y_1) in the price-output produced panel.

Employment and output have increased at point A because the actual real wage has declined making it profitable for firms to employ more workers. More workers accept to work because in their mental map, the expected real wage is the same. Workers have underestimated the price level $p_0^e < p_1$ and as a consequence, overestimated the real wage earnings $w_1/p_0^e > w_1/p_1$. If the actual price declines to $p_2 < p_0 < p_1$, the demand curve for labour shifts down to p_2MP_N. With unchanged price expectations the new demand and supply curves intersect at point B, where the nominal wage is w_2 and employment and output have declined to $N_2 < N^*$ and $Y_2 < Y^*$. Again tracing out through the two panels in the bottom half of the diagram, we get the point B′ which denotes the point (p_2, Y_2) in the price-supply of output space. With a decline in the price, the real cost of employing labour has increased and firms downsize. Workers have again overestimated prices, $p_0^e > p_2$, and underestimated their real wage earnings, $w_2/p_0^e < w_2/p_2$. Joining all points such as B′ and A′, we get the UPWARD SLOPING aggregate supply curve that traces out various price-supply of output combinations for constant price expectations p_0^e.

› When workers have mistaken expectations regarding the price of output, the aggregate supply curve for a given price expectation is **upward sloping**.

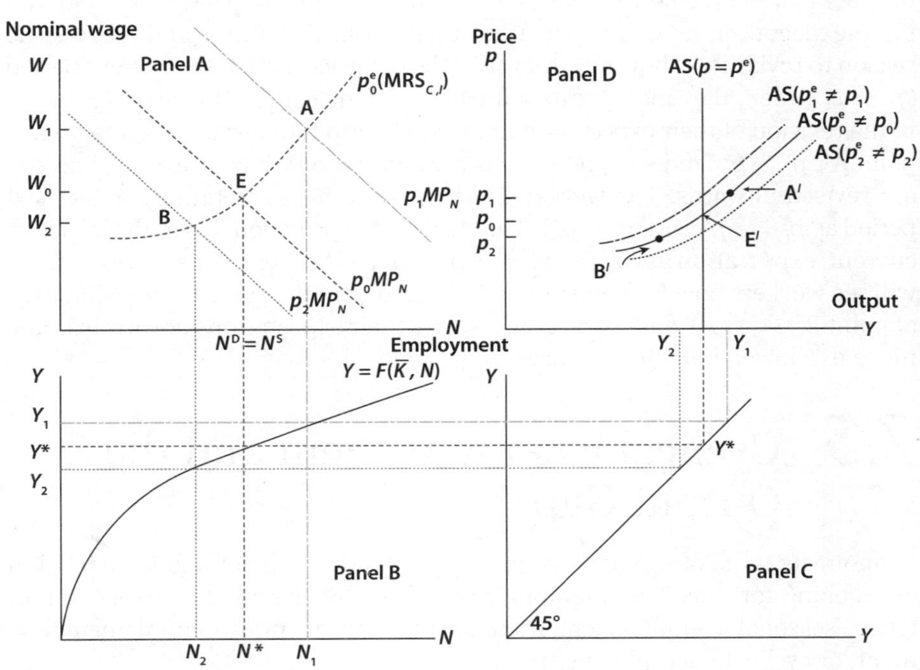

› **Figure 7.11**
Mistaken Expectations Aggregate Supply. When workers supply labour on the basis of expected prices, firms are able to employ more labour as the price of the output increases and employ less labour when the price falls (panel A). An increase in employment is associated with a rise in the output produced (panel B). The increase in output associated with the rise in the price results in an aggregate supply (AS) curve when price expectations are not realized AS($p^e \neq p$), that is, upward sloping. When price expectations are realized, the aggregate supply curve AS ($p^e = p$) is vertical.

For higher price expectations, $p_1^e > p_0^e$, it can be traced out that the aggregate supply curve will be higher everywhere, or, $AS(p_1^e) > AS(p_0^e)$. Similarly, for lower price expectations, $p_2^e < p_0^e$, the corresponding aggregate supply curve will be lower down, as given by $AS(p_2^e) < AS(p_0^e)$. There is, thus, a family of aggregate supply curves, each one corresponding to a given level of price expectation and resulting due to mistaken expectations on the part of workers, $AS(p^e \neq p)$. If expectations were always realized, $p^e = p$, then, the vertical aggregate supply curve would be the $AS(p^e = p)$ curve in the diagram. Friedman's aggregate supply curve can accordingly be labelled as the Mistaken Expectation Aggregate Supply Curve and the equation of this[9] curve can be written as,

$$Y = Y^* \left(\frac{p}{p^e} \right)^{\phi}, \phi > 0 \tag{7.8}$$

where $\phi > 0$ is a parameter that depends on the elasticities of demand and supply as well as the share of wages in output. When $p = p^e$ in Eq. (7.8), output is at its natural level, or, $Y = Y^*$. Similarly, when $p \neq p^e$, Eq. (7.8) gives the $AS(p \neq p^e)$ curve for each price expectation. Thus, if actual prices are greater than expected, $p > p^e$, Eq. (7.8) implies that $Y > Y^*$, as was derived in Figure 7.11 for point A′. If $p < p^e$, then, $Y < Y^*$ as derived in Figure 7.11 for point B′.

› Under **adaptive expectations,** individuals revise their price expectations every period to incorporate a fraction of the errors in expectation $(p - p^e)$ from the previous period.

Friedman is also of the view that price expectations change as individual workers realize that their expectations were mistaken. Specifically, Friedman advocated the ADAPTIVE EXPECTATIONS HYPOTHESIS where the expected price is given in the short run but moves slowly to correct for past expectational errors. This hypothesis may be stated as follows:

$$p_{t+1}^e = p_t^e + \lambda(p_t - p_t^e) \; 0 < \lambda < 1 \tag{7.9}$$

where λ represents the speed with which households update their price expectation. The lower λ, the more sluggish is the adjustment of expectations. If expectations regarding the price in the current period turn out to be correct, then, $p_t^e = p_t$. Equation (7.9) then reduces to $p_{t+1}^e = p_t$, which, since $p_t = p_t^e$, implies $p_{t+1}^e = p_t^e$. In other words, the individual continues with the current price expectation as this expectation turned out to be true and there is no reason to revise it. If, however, they mistake the price level in the current period $(p_t^e \neq p_t)$, then, they incorporate a fraction λ of the expectation error $(p_t - p_t^e)$ in the revision of their expectation in the next period. In terms of Figure 7.11, at point A′, $p_1 > p_0^e$, and so $\lambda(p_1 - p_0^e)$ is the amount by which price expectations are revised upwards. The worker will then set price expectation for the next period as $p_{t+1}^e = p_0^e + \lambda(p_1 - p_0^e)$. The change in expectation due to the mistaken current expectation is $p_{t+1}^e - p_0^e = \lambda(p_1 - p_0^e)$. The next time period, then, will see workers on a higher $AS(p \neq p^e)$ curve than the current one. Similarly, at point B′, $p_2 < p_0^e$, and workers will revise their expectations downwards and move to a lower $AS(P \neq P^e)$ curve.

7.5 Cyclical Unemployment and the Output Gap

Economists think of someone as unemployed if they are not holding a job, but are looking for one. The unemployed are broadly classified as being of four types—seasonal unemployment, frictional unemployment, structural unemployment, or cyclical unemployment.

Unemployment which varies predictably with the seasons is SEASONAL UNEMPLOYMENT. Workers in agriculture and tourism are regularly subject to seasonal unemployment. In the seaside state of Goa, for instance, tourism increases in the winter months and correspondingly the number of jobs that cater to tourists increase in these months. Agriculture in India is known to have peak demands for labour during the sowing season.

› **Seasonal unemployment** varies predictably with the seasons.

Seasonal unemployment follows a predictable pattern and is unlike other types of unemployment that affect workers as a part of a normal transition from one job to another. FRICTIONAL UNEMPLOYMENT, for instance, results when people are transitioning from one job to another or when they first enter the labour market to search for work. Though the labour market serves to match available jobs with available workers, this can be a time-consuming process because both jobs and workers are heterogeneous. Jobs, for instance, differ in the skills they require, in their working conditions, in their location, etc. Workers differ in their abilities and experience, in their willingness to travel and relocate as a job requires, in their career goals, etc. The short-term unemployment associated with the process of matching is called frictional unemployment. Frictional unemployment is not considered to be a burden for the economy to the extent that the process leads to a better match between a worker and a job. In that sense, it is actually productive in that the turnover of workers on such jobs would be lower and disruptions to output less frequent.

› **Frictional unemployment** is short term unemployment associated with matching workers with jobs.

STRUCTURAL UNEMPLOYMENT is a more long term and chronic form of unemployment than frictional unemployment and exists independently of the rate of output that is being produced in the economy. This often occurs in periods of economic change when the new jobs being created have requirements different from the old jobs being lost. In India, the textile industry declined for many years since the early 1980s as mills closed down. At the same time, the computer software industry has been growing rapidly. It would be ideal if textile workers who lose jobs could be gainfully employed in the software sector. However, textile workers lack the education and training that is a pre-requisite for working in the computer industry. With textile workers skills no longer being demanded, these workers enter into chronic or long-term unemployment that is structural. Structural unemployment also arises where there are labour market barriers to employment such as minimum wage laws, job security legislation, discrimination, and language requirements associated with jobs. Structurally, unemployed workers, unlike frictionally unemployed ones, are not involved in productive work for long spells. This represents a substantial economic loss.

› **Structural unemployment** is a long term unemployment that does not vary with the pace of economic activity.

CYCLICAL UNEMPLOYMENT is associated with reduction in real output during periods of recession[10]. Seasonal, frictional, and structural unemployment are always present in the labour market, even when the economy is operating normally. Cyclical unemployment, in contrast, occurs only during recessions.

› Unemployment associated with periods of low levels of economic activity is **cyclical unemployment.**

The sum of seasonal, frictional, and structural unemployment is called the NATURAL RATE OF UNEMPLOYMENT. Actual total unemployment in the economy is the sum of the natural rate of unemployment and cyclical unemployment. In practice, it is often very difficult to make sharp distinctions between the different categories of unemployment. However, the unemployment concept that is the FOCUS OF MACROECONOMICS is cyclical unemployment—the unemployment that increases when there is a slow down in economic activity and decreases when real output increases.

› The **natural rate of unemployment** is the sum of seasonal, frictional, and structural unemployment.

› **Macroeconomics focuses** on cyclical unemployment.

Emerging markets like India do not have statistics generated on the natural rate of unemployment. In the US, the Congressional Budget Office regularly provides estimates of the natural rate of unemployment[11]. The natural rate of unemployment changes over time due to such factors as changes in the age composition of the labour force. In the US, the natural rate has declined in the last 15 years. This is some times explained as due to the rising average age of US workers (Katz and Krueger, 1999). Older workers are not as likely to change jobs (a reduction in frictional unemployment) and also have greater experience and skills (a reduction in structural unemployment).

› **Full employment** is a state where cyclical unemployment is zero.

› **Cyclical unemployment** is the difference between total unemployment and the natural rate of unemployment.

In macroeconomics, FULL EMPLOYMENT occurs when there is no cyclical unemployment. There will still be the existence of seasonal, frictional, and structural unemployment when full employment prevails. CYCLICAL UNEMPLOYMENT, which is the difference between total unemployment and the natural rate of unemployment, is the unemployment that macroeconomics focuses on.

$$\text{Cyclical Unemployment} = \text{Total Unemployment} - \text{Natural Rate of Unemployment}$$

or,

$$\text{Cyclical Unemployment} = U - U^*$$

When economic activity decreases, actual unemployment exceeds the natural rate of unemployment and cyclical unemployment is positive. When there is an expansion in economic activity and real output, the actual unemployment rate is lower than the natural rate, and cyclical unemployment is negative.

It was Arthur Okun, US president John Kennedy's chief economic advisor, who suggested that there is a relationship between the cyclical unemployment in the economy and the output gap. The output gap is the difference between potential output and actual output. Potential output or the full employment output, Y^*, is what the economy would produce if labour were fully employed at normal levels of overtime, and plant and machinery were used at their normal rates of utilization. POTENTIAL OUTPUT, then, is the maximum sustainable amount of real GDP that can be produced. Real GDP can temporarily exceed its potential when individuals temporarily put in extra overtime. However, this is not sustainable as individuals cannot work overtime continuously, and even plant and machinery must be shut down for maintenance. Increases and decreases in potential output are then part of the reason for the rise or decline in economic activity. When factors of production such as capital and labour are not fully utilized, the actual output, Y, is below potential output, Y^*. This underutilization of factors of production constitutes a recession. When actual output exceeds potential output, factors of production are being utilized more than normal and this result in a boom. The percentage difference between potential and actual output is called the OUTPUT GAP.

› **Potential or full employment output** is the maximum sustainable amount of output that an economy can produce.

› The **output gap i**s the difference between potential output and actual output as a fraction of potential output.

$$\text{Output Gap} = \frac{\text{Potential Output} - \text{Actual Output}}{\text{Potential Output}} = \frac{Y^* - Y}{Y^*}$$

Okun (1970) pointed out that as an economy gets out of a recession, output increases by a greater percentage than the rise in employment. Similarly, when the economy heads into a recession, output decreases by a greater percentage than the reduction in employment. OKUN'S LAW, then, states that a one per cent increase in the unemployment rate results in about a 3 per cent increase in the output gap:

› **Okun's Law** states that each percentage point increase of cyclical unemployment is associated with a 3 per cent point increase in the output gap.

$$\frac{Y^* - Y}{Y^*} = 3(U - U^*)$$

Okun's Law allows us to link fluctuations in unemployment with fluctuations in the output gap. The unemployment rate by one measure (current daily status) increased by 1.2 per cent in India between 1994 and 2000, and was 7.3 per cent in that year. Suppose, the natural rate of unemployment is 6 per cent, then, cyclical unemployment is 7.3 minus 6 per cent, or 1.3 per cent. According to Okun's Law that would be associated with a $3 \times 1.3 = 3.9$ per cent negative output gap. Real GDP in the year 2000 was roughly INR 19,600 billion. Hence, a 3.9 per cent output gap means that the economy was producing 3.9 per cent of INR 19,600 billion, or INR 764.4 billion less than its potential. The lost output represents the opportunity[12] cost associated with the higher cyclical unemployment. A positive output gap implies that factors of production are not fully utilized and so output and employment are below maximum sustainable levels. A rise in cyclical unemployment, therefore, means the economy is not matching up to its potential and this cost can have drastic impacts on the popularity of policy makers and politicians. Similarly, a negative output gap is a situation where the utilization of factors of production is stretched beyond sustainable levels. This unsustainable situation is resolved through price increases that reflect the increased scarcity of capacity. Expansionary gaps, thus, result in inflation which also impacts adversely on the popularity of policy makers and politicians. Policy makers, therefore, attempt to eliminate output gaps and stabilize the economy. This process of aligning actual output with potential output is achieved, as we will see, through the usage of fiscal and monetary policies. Such policies by influencing total expenditure in the economy eliminate output gaps. Since a positive output gap (high cyclical unemployment) is associated with inflation, it implies a negative relationship between inflation and unemployment. This negative relationship was empirically established by the British economist A. W. Phillips and is called the Phillips Curve. Let us now examine how the analysis of the labour market by Keynes and Friedman can give us an insight into the Phillips Curve relationship.

MACROFOCUS 7.2

Unemployment and Wages in India

Data on employment and unemployment in India are available from the large sample surveys [National Sample Survey (NSS)], some of which were carried out in 1993/1994, 1999/2000, and 2004/2005. The 2009/2010 survey has also been conducted and at the time of writing the full data is still unavailable. The NSS sample is large in the sense that a sample of 10 households (12 households in the 1999/2000 round) per selected village/urban block is considered for canvassing the schedules. The NSS has evolved a system of capturing employment and unemployment through the time-use method. A worker is asked if he or she was working (a) last year (usual status), (b) last week (current week status), and (c) yesterday (current daily status). If the response to this question is Yes, then the worker is considered to be employed. If a worker has not been working, but sought or was available for work during the reference period, he or she is classified as part of the labour force but is deemed to be unemployed. The current weekly status basis for classification is the one that is predominantly used to capture the severity of unemployment. The labour force, then, is the sum of those employed (referred to as those participating in the labour force) and the unemployed. The sum of the labour force and those not in the labour force (either because they are acquiring skills or an education or are not part of the labour force due to other reasons such as adhering to social roles like taking care of the home or being past retirement age) is the total population of the economy. The categories employed, unemployed, etc. in the data is presented as per thousand populations.

› Table 1
Employment as Per Current Weekly Status as on June 2005 (Per Thousand Persons)

Activity	Rural Areas		Urban Areas	
	Male	Female	Male	Female
Employed	524	275	534	152
Unemployed	21	12	29	15
Labour force	545	287	563	167
Not in labour force	455	713	437	833
Population	1000	1000	1000	1000
Unemployment rate	3.8%	4.2%	5.2%	9.0%

(Continued)

The NSS data shows that the unemployment rates have gone up between 1994 and 2005. It is widely argued that countries like India suffer from widespread underemployment rather than open unemployment as it is hard for a person to remain unemployed without a formal and effective social security system. Unfortunately, there are no statistics on underemployment. However, as a rough measure, researchers take the difference between the weekly and daily unemployment status as a measure of underemployment. An estimate for underemployment on the basis of such a calculation is that 4.2 per cent and 2.3 per cent of males in rural and urban areas, respectively, were underemployed and the corresponding estimates for females was 4.5 per cent and 2.6 per cent.

What about wage rates? The real daily wage rates for various categories of workers are given below. As would be expected, urban wages are higher than rural wages, men get paid more than women, regular workers earn more than casual workers, and wages are higher in industry and services than in agriculture. Though we do not present the data here, it is also true that educated workers get paid more than illiterate workers.

› **Table 2**
Unemployment Rate (Per cent of the Labour Force Unemployed) as Per Current Weekly Status and Current Daily Status and Underemployment Rate as on June 2005

Unemployment/Underemployment rates	Rural Areas		Urban Areas	
	Male	Female	Male	Female
Current daily status unemployment	8.0%	8.7%	7.5%	11.6%
Current weekly status unemployment	3.8%	4.2%	5.2%	9.0%
Underemployment rate	4.2%	4.5%	2.3%	2.6%

› **Table 3**
Average Real Daily Wages (INR/Day at 1993/1994 Prices)

	Male		Female	
	1994	2005	1994	2005
Regular Salaried Workers				
Rural				
Agriculture	27.5	41.1	22.8	31.5
Non-agriculture	66.5	88.2	40.6	51.6
Urban				
Agriculture	51.4	52.1	46.7	39.6
Non-agriculture	79.2	101.4	62.7	76.5
Casual Workers				
Rural				
Agriculture	21.6	27.8	15.1	19.3
Non-agriculture	30.1	39.5	17.5	25.8
Urban				
Agriculture	25.5	28.1	16.5	17.2
Non-agriculture	33.8	38.2	19.5	23.7

Source: 61st Round of NSS Employment and Unemployment Survey.

7.6 The Static Phillips Curve

It is best to approach the Phillips curve—the tradeoff between the unemployment rate and inflation—via its static version that depicts the tradeoff between the price level and unemployment. In Figure 7.12, panel A represents the demand for labour given by the condition that the nominal wage equals the revenue generated from the productivity of the marginal unit of labour hired, or, $w = pMP_N$. The supply curve of labour is upward sloping, with the supply of labour increasing along with an increase in the expected price as individuals substitute labour for leisure, or, $w = p^e\text{MRS}_{c,l}$. Let the expected price be p_0^e and the demand and supply curves of labour intersect at point E. We know that point E represents an equilibrium in the labour market, where, with price expectations realized, $p_0^e = p_0$, the natural rate of employment prevails. Let the total labour force of the economy be given by $\bar{N}$. Those who are not employed in the labour market are considered to be unemployed so that:

$$\bar{N} = N + U$$

where U is the number of people who are unemployed. In panel B of Figure 7.12, we measure unemployment on the vertical axis and employment on the horizontal axis. At $U = \bar{N}$, everyone in the labour force is unemployed and at $N = \bar{N}$, there is full employment. Joining the points $U = \bar{N}$ and $N = \bar{N}$ gives us a locus of points, each of which informs us about the level of unemployment associated with a given employment determined in the labour market. Panel C, again, is a 45° line that transfers the level of unemployment from the vertical axis of panel B to the horizontal axis of panel D. Associated with the natural rate of employment N^*, when the price level in the economy is p_0, is the natural rate of unemployment U^* in panel D. The combination of p_0 and U^* in panel D at point E′ represents a combination of price level and unemployment that depicts one point among the possible tradeoffs between prices and unemployment.

If the actual price rises to p_1, then, for given price expectation p_0^e, the demand and supply of labour equilibrate at point A in panel A. Employment rises to N_1 (panels A and B) and unemployment declines to U_1 (panels B, C, and D). The lower unemployment U_1 is associated with the price level p_1 and point A′ in panel D represents another point on the static short-run Phillips Curve. In a similar vein, if the price level declined to p_2 for given price expectation p_0^e, employment declines to N_2 (panels A and B), and unemployment rises to U_2 (panels B, C, and D). Unemployment U_2 is associated with price p_2 and depicted as point B′ in panel D. Joining the points A′, E′, and B′ gives the inverse relationship between the price level and unemployment that is known as the STATIC PHILLIPS CURVE $PC(p_0^e \neq p_0)$.

› The **Static Phillip Curve** depicts a negative relationship between the price level and unemployment.

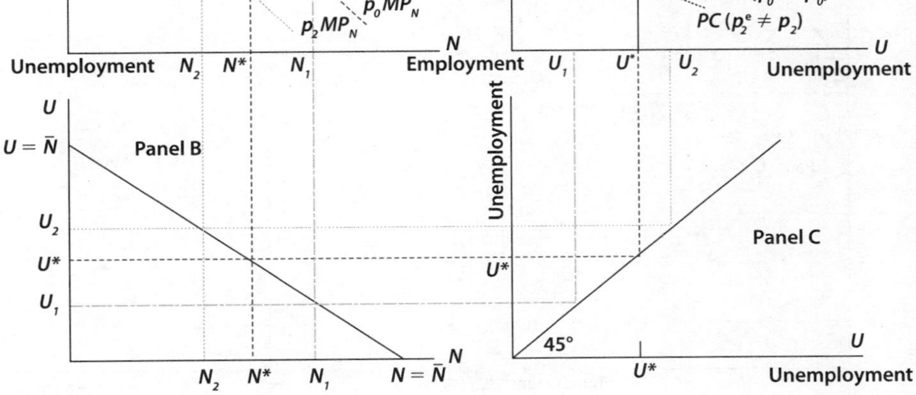

› **Figure 7.12**
Static Phillips Curve. When workers supply labour on the basis of the expected price, firms are able to employ more labour if the price of the output increases (panel A). The increase in employment reduces the unemployment in the economy (panel B). A reduction in unemployment is then associated with a rise in the price when workers supply labour on the basis of expected prices. This results in the inverse relation between price and unemployment, that is, the Static Phillip Curve PC($P^e \neq P$). When price expectations are realized, the static Phillips Curve PC($P^e = P$) is vertical (panel D).

What happens at a point such as A′ where prices are greater than expected? Recall that workers change their price expectation according to the adaptive expectations hypothesis. As $p_1 > p_0^e$, workers revise their price expectation next period by a fraction λ of the error in expectation $(p_1 - p_0^e)$. They then supply labour on the basis of their new expectation about the price level p_1^e, where $p_1^e > p_0^e$. This shifts up the supply curve of labour to $p_1^e \text{MRS}_{c,l}$ in panel A (not shown in the diagram) and the new short-run Phillips curve is $PC(p_1^e \neq p_1)$. Similarly, at point B′, price expectations are revised downwards resulting in a new short-run Phillips curve $PC(p_2^e \neq p_2)$. If price expectations are realized, we obtain the vertical Phillips curve $PC(p^e = p)$ at the natural rate of unemployment U^*.

Since panel A in Figures 7.11 and 7.12 are identical, it is but obvious that the panel D in Figures 7.11 and 7.12 are graphically stating the same thing in different ways. Figure 7.13 replicates both Figures 7.11 and 7.12 in one diagram. It is obvious that the factors resulting in points A′, B′, and E′ of Figure 7.11, panel D result in the outcomes depicted by points A′, B′ and E′ in Figure 7.12, panel D as well. In fact, if one were to place a mirror along the vertical axis of the farthest north-eastern quadrant of Figure 7.13—along the vertical axis of Figure 7.12, panel D—the Phillips curve would appear as a mirror image of the mistaken expectations aggregate supply curve. The Phillips Curve and the Aggregate Supply Curve are, therefore, interchangeable ways of stating the same—that there is a positive tradeoff between changes in price (or inflation) and output, or there is a negative tradeoff between changes in the price level and unemployment.

The Phillips Curve is usually stated in its dynamic form—the inverse relation between inflation (not price levels) and the unemployment rate. This dynamic version of the Phillips Curve can be derived in much the same way

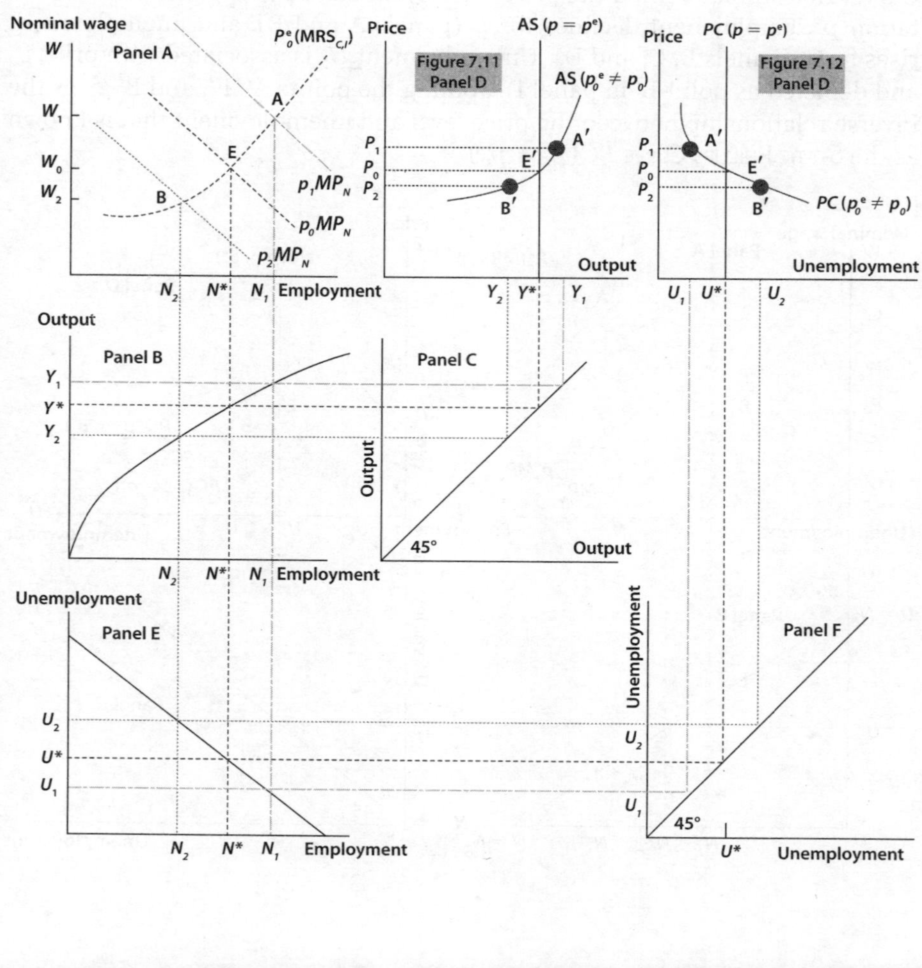

› **Figure 7.13**
Phillips Curve as Image of Aggregate Supply Curve. A rise in the price raises the demand for labour in panel A. This increase in employment raises the output produced in panel B and reduces unemployment in panel E. The increased output of panel B that accompanies the rise in the price is represented by the upward sloping aggregate supply curve $AS(p_0^e \neq p_0)$ that is a redoing of Figure 7.11, panel D. Similarly, the reduced unemployment that accompanies the rise in the price is represented by the downward sloping $PC(p_0^e \neq p_0)$ that is a redoing of Figure 7.12, panel D. The same price rise of panel A is then associated with an increase in output and a decline in unemployment that are depicted in panel D. The AS curve is therefore the mirror image of the PC curve.

as the static version. The dynamic aggregate supply curve with output supplied related to the rate of inflation will then form the basis for deriving the dynamic Phillips curve. Diagrammatically, this implies replacing p and p^e in Figure 7.12 with inflation and expected inflation respectively, and proceeding as before. Those readers interested in understanding the relationship stated in the dynamic Phillips curve can look up the reading on the same provided in the companion Web site of this book.

SUMMARY

- Profit maximizing firms hire workers up to the point where the wage equals the value of the marginal product of labour.
- Workers maximize their utility over consumption and leisure in such a way that the last rupee spent on leisure activities yields the same utility as the last rupee spent on consumption.

$$\frac{MU_l}{w/p} = MU_C .$$

- An increase in the wage results in both an income and a substitution effect. The income effect reduces labour supply while the substitution effect increases labour supply. The labour supply curve is upward sloping when the substitution effect dominates.
- When there is no money illusion an increase in the price of output results in an equiproportionate increase in the money wage and no change in employment and output. This results in a classical aggregate supply curve that is vertical.
- When individuals formulate labour supply decisions on the basis of the money wage they are subject to money illusion. The corresponding aggregate supply curve is upward sloping.
- The assumption that money wages are fixed and that employment is determined by the short side of the labour market which is usually the demand for labour side results in an upward sloping Keynesian aggregate supply of output up to the point where all those who offer to supply labour at the fixed money wage have been employed.
- When workers have mistaken expectations regarding the price of output the supply curve for a given price expectation is upward sloping.
- When expected prices equal actual prices then expectations are realized and the economy is at the natural rate of employment and output with a vertical aggregate supply curve.
- Under adaptive expectations individuals revise their price expectation in any period to incorporate a fraction of the error in expectation $(p - p^e)$ from the previous period.
- Actual unemployment in an economy is the sum of the natural rate of unemployment and cyclical unemployment.
- The natural rate of unemployment is the sum of seasonal, frictional, and structural unemployment that do not vary with the level of economic activity. In theory the natural rate of unemployment is that rate of unemployment that prevails when price expectations are realized.
- Cyclical unemployment is the unemployment associated with recessions and expansions in economic activity and equals the unemployment rate less the natural unemployment rate.
- Potential or full employment output is the maximum sustainable amount of output that an economy can produce.
- The output gap is the difference between potential output and actual output measured in relation to potential output.
- Okun's Law relates cyclical unemployment to the output gap. It states that each extra percentage point of cyclical unemployment is associated with a 3 per cent point increase in the output gap.
- The Phillips Curve depicts a negative relationship between the price level and unemployment. The Phillips Curve is the mirror image of the Aggregate Supply Curve.

NOTES

1. Maximizing (2) we obtain $\partial\pi/\partial N = p(\partial F/\partial N) - w = 0$ or $p(\partial F/\partial N) = pMP_N - w$.
2. In the long-run, the firm chooses both how many workers to hire and how much plant and equipment to invest in. If the two factors are cooperative in the sense that increasing one factor raises the marginal productivity of the other factor $F_{NK} = F_{KN} > 0$, the long run demand curve for labour will be more elastic than the short-run demand curve.
3. Firms and workers are connected in two different ways—through the goods market and through the labour market. Hence, behaviour in one market can affect behaviour in the other market. This creates a problem that demand variables are dependent on supply side variables and can result in circular reasoning. To avoid this, we assume that preferences are separable so that labour market variables do not affect money and goods market variables. See Appendix 1. How to deal with this issue is unresolved in macroeconomics?
4. We are, for simplicity, ignoring that some income is saved.
5. Differentiating $U(C, l) = \bar{U}$, we get

$$d\bar{U} = 0 = \frac{\partial U}{\partial C}dC + \frac{\partial U}{\partial l}dl$$

or, $$-\frac{dC}{dl} = \frac{\partial U/\partial l}{\partial U/\partial C} = \frac{MU_l}{MU_C}$$

6. See Modigliani (1944).
7. Later we will look at other explanations for unemployment as provided by the efficiency wage and insider–outsider frameworks.

8. Even though Keynesians believe that money wages decline in the face of unemployment and excess supply of labour, $N^S > N^D$, they conjecture that this occurs with a time lag due to the complexities of wage negotiations and so in the short-run money wages can be taken to be rigid.
9. See the Appendix 1 for the derivation of this equation.
10. Slowdowns in economic growth are called recessions. When the slowdown is severe as occurred in the period following 1929, it is called a depression.
11. This can accessed online at http://www.cbo.gov
12. The opportunity cost of an activity is the value of the next best alternative that must be forgone in order to undertake the activity.

TEST YOURSELF

1. Why is the demand curve for labour downward sloping?
2. How does a worker decide how many hours to allocate to the labour market?
3. What does it mean to say that an individual is subject to money illusion?
4. If workers are subject to money illusion, how is the aggregate supply of output curve derived?
5. Derive the aggregate supply curve when workers are subject to mistaken expectations about the price of output.
6. Define four types of unemployment and the causes for the same. Which type of unemployment is least costly for the economy? Why?
7. What is Okun's Law? Explain how it is possible for an economy to produce an output greater than potential output.
8. Why is there a tradeoff between unemployment and prices in the short run?
9. If unemployment is pushed below its natural rate what will happen to price inflation?
10. Suppose that individuals do not make mistakes in their forecasts of price expectations. What then is the slope of the tradeoff between prices and unemployment ?

ONLINE APPLICATION

1. The following is the data on the unemployment rate (as measured by the usual principal status) in India for some years:

Incidence of Unemployment: Usual Status	
1972–1973	1.6
1977–1978	2.6
1982–1983	1.9
1987–1988	2.7
1993–1994	1.9
1999–2000	2.8
2004–2005	3.1

Source: NSSO, Central Statistical Organisation, India.

2. Go the RBI website URL: www.rbi.org.in/home.aspx
3. Click on the "DataBase" icon
4. Then under the classification of Annual data, click on "Handbook of Statistics on Indian Economy"
5. Click on "Table 39: Wholesale Price Index—Annual Average". Calculate the inflation rate for all commodities for the years listed in the table above from this web page.
6. Create a scatter diagram between the inflation rate and the unemployment rate.
7. In this scatter diagram, note that when unemployment increased between 1982–1983 and 1987–1988 and again between 1999–2000 and 2004–2005, inflation increased rather than decreased contrary to what a Phillips Curve would predict.
8. Why would inflation increases have been accompanied by unemployment increases in the recent past? To try and understand the factors responsible for the rise in inflation in 2004–2005, read the relevant sections of the government's Economic Survey, 2005.
   - Go to URL: http://indiabudget.nic.in
   - Under "Previous Economic Surveys" click on "2005–2006"
   - Click on "Prices and Food Management"
   - Click on "Inflation"

Appendix 7.1 The Mistaken Expectations Aggregate Supply Curve

The demand and supply curves of labour are given by

$$w = pMP_N \tag{A7.1.1}$$

$$w = p^e \mathrm{MRS}_{Y,l} \tag{A7.1.2}$$

Taking logarithms of Eq. (A7.1.1) and differentiating,

$$\frac{\mathrm{d}w}{w} = \frac{\mathrm{d}p}{p} + \frac{\mathrm{d}(MP_N)}{MP_N} \tag{A7.1.3}$$

Now,
$$\mathrm{d}(MP_N) = \frac{\partial(MP_N)}{\partial N^D}\mathrm{d}N^D$$

Thus,
$$\frac{\mathrm{d}(MP_N)}{MP_N} = \frac{\partial(MP_N)/\partial N^D}{MP_N}\mathrm{d}N^D = \frac{\partial(MP_N)/MP_N}{\partial N^D/N^D}\frac{\mathrm{d}N^D}{N^D}$$

The wage elasticity of labour demand is defined as:

$$\varepsilon_D = -\frac{\partial N^D/N^D}{\partial(w/p)/(w/p)}$$

or,
$$\varepsilon_D = -\frac{\partial N^D/N^D}{\partial(MP_N)/(MP_N)}$$

Hence, we may write

$$\frac{\mathrm{d}(MP_N)}{MP_N} = -\frac{1}{\varepsilon_D}\frac{\mathrm{d}N^D}{N^D}$$

Substituting this result into Eq. (A7.1.3),

$$\frac{\mathrm{d}w}{w} = \frac{\mathrm{d}p}{p} - \frac{1}{\varepsilon_D}\frac{\mathrm{d}N^D}{N^D}$$

or,
$$\frac{\mathrm{d}N^D}{N^D} = -\varepsilon_D\left(\frac{\mathrm{d}w}{w} - \frac{\mathrm{d}p}{p}\right) \tag{A7.1.4}$$

Similarly, if we take the logs of Eq. (A7.1.2), totally differentiate, and define the wage elasticity of labour supply as:

$$\varepsilon_S = \frac{\partial N^S/N^S}{\partial(\mathrm{MRS}_{Y,l})/(\mathrm{MRS}_{Y,l})}$$

we obtain,
$$\frac{\mathrm{d}N^S}{N^S} = \varepsilon_S\left(\frac{\mathrm{d}w}{w} - \frac{\mathrm{d}p^e}{p^e}\right) \tag{A7.1.5}$$

Equilibrium in the labour market requires that $N^D = N^S$, or $\mathrm{d}N^D/N^D = \mathrm{d}N^S/N^S$. Equating (A7.1.4) and (A7.1.5),

$$\varepsilon_S\left(\frac{\mathrm{d}w}{w} - \frac{\mathrm{d}p^e}{p^e}\right) = -\varepsilon_D\left(\frac{\mathrm{d}w}{w} - \frac{\mathrm{d}p}{p}\right)$$

or,
$$(\varepsilon_S + \varepsilon_D)\frac{dw}{w} - \varepsilon_D\frac{dp}{p} = \varepsilon_S\frac{dp^e}{p^e}$$

Adding $-\varepsilon_S(dp/p)$ to both sides,

$$(\varepsilon_S + \varepsilon_D)\frac{dw}{w} - (\varepsilon_D + \varepsilon_S)\frac{dp}{p} = -\varepsilon_S\left(\frac{dp}{p} - \frac{dp^e}{p^e}\right)$$

or,
$$\frac{dw}{w} - \frac{dp}{p} = \frac{-\varepsilon_S}{\varepsilon_D + \varepsilon_S}\left(\frac{dp}{p} - \frac{dp^e}{p^e}\right) \tag{A7.1.6}$$

Substituting this result into the labour demand equation Eq. (A7.1.4) gives us:

$$\frac{dN}{N} = \frac{\varepsilon_D\varepsilon_S}{\varepsilon_D + \varepsilon_S}\left(\frac{dp}{p} - \frac{dp^e}{p^e}\right) \tag{A7.1.7}$$

The amount of labour employed produces the output defined by the production function $Y = F(\bar{K}, N)$. Totally differentiating the production function gives us:

$$dY = MP_N dN$$

Dividing throughout this expression by Y gives us:

$$\frac{dY}{Y} = \frac{MP_N}{Y}dN = \frac{MP_N N}{Y}\frac{dN}{N} \tag{A7.1.8}$$

Now, MP_N is the marginal product of labour which is set equal to the real wage – see Eq. (A7.1.1). Hence, $MP_N N$ is the total real wage bill, and, $MP_N N/Y = wN/pY$ is the share of wages in total output. Define this as,

$$\omega = \frac{MP_N N}{Y} = \frac{wN}{pY} \tag{A7.1.9}$$

Then, Eq. (A7.1.8) can be written as,

$$\frac{dY}{Y} = \omega\frac{dN}{N}$$

and on substituting in Eq. (A7.1.7) we obtain,

$$\frac{dY}{Y} = \frac{\omega\varepsilon_D\varepsilon_S}{\varepsilon_D + \varepsilon_S}\left(\frac{dp}{p} - \frac{dp^e}{p^e}\right) \tag{A7.1.10}$$

Define
$$\frac{\partial Y/Y}{\partial p/p} = \phi = \frac{\omega\varepsilon_D\varepsilon_S}{\varepsilon_D + \varepsilon_S} > 0 \tag{A7.1.11}$$

where ϕ is the inverse of the elasticity of the short-run aggregate supply curve in (p, Y) space when $p \neq p^e$. Higher values of ϕ represent flatter short run aggregate supply curves. If we integrate Eq. (A7.1.10) we can write it as,

$$Y = Y^*\left(\frac{p}{p^e}\right)^{\frac{\omega\varepsilon_D\varepsilon_S}{\varepsilon_D + \varepsilon_S}}$$

or,
$$Y = Y^*\left(\frac{p}{p^e}\right)^{\phi} \tag{A7.1.12}$$

where Y^* is the natural rate of output when price expectations are realized, or, $p^e = p$. That Eq. (A7.1.12) follows from Eq. (A7.1.10) and Eq. (A7.1.11) can be checked by taking the logs of Eq. (A7.1.12) and totally differentiating which will give us Eq. (A7.1.10). Eq. (A7.1.12) is the equation of Friedman's aggregate supply curve as noted in the text. Eq. (A7.1.12) can also be written as:

$$p = p^e \left(\frac{Y}{Y^*} \right)^{1/\phi} \tag{A7.1.13}$$

where $Y/Y^* < 1 \Rightarrow Y < Y^*$, or, there is a gap between actual output and the natural rate of output. This is akin to Okun's gap, which is a measure of unemployment.

8

The IS–LM Model

CRITICAL QUESTIONS

- » *What is Walras' Law and how is it applied in macroeconomics?*
- » *What is the difference between the nominal and the real rate of interest?*
- » *What is the* IS *curve and how does it represent the condition for equilibrium in the product market?*
- » *What are the parameters that cause the* IS *curve to shift? In which direction does the IS curve shift?*
- » *What is the* LM *curve and how does it represent the condition for equilibrium in the money market?*
- » *When is the* LM *curve elastic and when is it inelastic?*
- » *How does monetary policy affect interest rates and output in an* IS–LM *situation?*
- » *What is the impact of fiscal policy on interest rates and output?*
- » *What is crowding out and to what extent does it depend on the elasticity of the* IS *and* LM *curves?*
- » *What is Ricardian Equivalence?*

8.1 Walras' Law and the Relevant Interest Rate

By now, considerable insight has been gained into the determinants of consumption, investment, net exports, the demand and supply of money, and the demand and supply of labour. Our focus on these aggregate economic magnitudes was informed by the macroeconomic method of aggregating the economy up to four markets:

1. the output market
2. the money market
3. the bond market
4. the labour market

In macroeconomics, the output and financial markets (money and bond markets) are combined to derive the aggregate demand curve of the economy, whereas the labour market determines the output or the aggregate supply curve of the economy. Walras' Law is used to eliminate the explicit treatment of one of these markets. By convention, the market rendered implicit in the analysis is usually the bond market. The reason for this is the notion that if we have n number of markets and $n - 1$ are in equilibrium, then it must be true that the nth market is also in equilibrium. The reader interested in a formal statement of Walras' Law should see Appendix 8.1. Given that there are three markets on the aggregate demand side of the economy (goods, money, and bond markets) if any two of these are in equilibrium, the third must also be in equilibrium. We are then able to derive the aggregate demand of the economy by studying the determinants of the simultaneous equilibrium of the output and money markets. The equilibrium in the goods or output market, as we will soon see, is given by the IS relationship and the equilibrium in the money market is given by the LM relationship. As money and bonds constitute the two assets in the portfolio of savings of individuals, and since by holding money we are forgoing the interest earnings on bonds, the equilibrium in the money market is implicitly determining the equilibrium holding of bonds. Hence, even though we do not explicitly consider the bond market, it is always there in the background when the money market is being considered.

At the outset before proceeding further we need to differentiate between the nominal rate of interest and the real rate of interest. As we saw, in the money market the interest rate we referred to was the nominal interest rate as the opportunity cost of holding money was the forgone interest earnings on bonds which is a nominal return. In contrast, when we were analysing the determinants of real consumption and investment expenditure, the rate of interest that we used as a discount rate was the real rate of interest. As we are eventually going to combine the goods and money markets, we need to ensure that the interest rate referred to when goods market variables are being considered is the same as the interest rate that is referred to when the money market variables are being analysed. As we have already seen in the chapter on money demand, the REAL RATE OF INTEREST is the nominal interest rate minus the inflation rate (π),

› The **real rate of interest** is the nominal interest rate minus the rate of inflation.

$$r = i - \pi \tag{8.1}$$

The inflation rate π in Eq. (8.1) is the actual inflation rate. The trouble with an actual inflation rate is that it is known only in the future (after the current time period in which decisions are being made). For instance, if the interest rate is with reference to a loan that is being repaid now, the inflation rate is that which occurs over the life of the loan and is calculated as the percentage change in prices between the present when the loan is being repaid and the past when the loan was taken. As the inflation rate here is the actual inflation rate, the real interest rate in Eq. (8.1) is known as the *ex post* real rate, where *ex post* means "after the fact".

In actuality, the inflation rate is not known at the time when borrowers and lenders enter into commitments on the various aspects of the loan. Agents, thus, must form an expectation of the future inflation rate. This leads to a second definition of the real interest rate known as the *ex ante* real interest rate, r^e. This is the difference between the nominal interest rate and the expected inflation rate, π^e, where *ex ante* means "before the fact", that is, before inflation is known:

$$r^e = i - \pi^e \tag{8.2}$$

Comparing Eqs (8.1) and (8.2), we can see that the *ex post* real interest rate is the same as the *ex ante* real interest rate when agents have perfect foresight and can predict the future price level with certainty so that $\pi = \pi^e$. This makes it clear that the real interest rate that was used to discount the future value of income and consumption when analysing consumption behaviour, or to represent the opportunity cost of finance when analysing investment, is the *ex ante* real interest rate.

8.2 The IS Curve

With these preliminaries mentioned, we are in a position to analyse the equilibrium in the commodity market for a closed economy. The open economy equilibrium will be analysed in a subsequent chapter. In the closed economy, output equals expenditure, as given by:

$$Y = C + I + G$$

When looking at the determinants of consumption, we found that most approaches to consumption argued that consumption expenditure depends on income and the real interest rate:

$$C = C(\underset{(+)}{Y}, \underset{(-)}{r})$$

The signs under the variables on the right-hand side indicate that consumption increases with income and declines with a rise in the real interest rate that makes future consumption more attractive as compared to present consumption.[1]

We now work with a more appropriate definition of income for the consumption function, which is disposable income, Y^D. In reality, consumption can occur only with respect to that income which is in the hands of the individual after taxes (net of transfers)—T—have been paid to the government. Consumption is out of disposable income, Y^D, where[2],

$$Y^D = Y - T$$

The appropriate consumption function[2] may be written as:

$$C = C(\underset{(+)}{Y - T}, \underset{(-)}{i - \pi^e}) \tag{8.3}$$

The private savings then is the residual after deducting consumption expenditure from disposable income, or,

$$S_{pvt} = Y - T - C(\underset{(+)}{Y - T}, \underset{(-)}{i - \pi^e})$$

The private savings function may then be summarized as:

$$S_{pvt} = S_{pvt}(\underset{(+)}{i}, \underset{(+)}{Y}, \underset{(-)}{T}, \underset{(-)}{\pi^e}) \tag{8.4}$$

The private savings improve with an increase in the interest rate (i). This is because the return to savings in the form of the interest rate has gone up and makes future consumption more valuable compared to current consumption. An increase in income (Y) is partly spent as consumption and partly saved so that savings increases with income. An increase in imposed taxes reduces disposable income ($Y - T$). Consumption expenditure that is a fraction of disposable income reduces, and the remaining fraction of disposable income, i.e., savings also declines. Finally, an increase in expected inflation reduces the command that income in the future will have over real goods and services. This results in a rearrangement of consumption towards the present. As a result, with current consumption rising, savings will decline.

For those who prefer a more formal approach, we can, without much loss of generality, proceed with a linear version of the CONSUMPTION FUNCTION that we write as:

› **Consumption** is a positive function of aggregate disposable income and is negatively related to the nominal interest rate.

$$C = c_0 + c_1 (Y - T) - c_2 (i - \pi^e) \tag{8.5}$$

where c_0 is the autonomous consumption that is independent of income, and c_1 is the responsiveness of consumption to a change in disposable income. In Chapter 3, c_1 was called the marginal propensity to consume, or, the increase in consumption expenditure when disposable income increases by a rupee. c_2 is the responsiveness of consumption to a change in the nominal interest rate when inflation expectations are given, or, the response to the *ex ante* real rate of interest. In this chapter, we shall also not be concerned with inflation expectations and shall be considering macroeconomic outcomes that occur when inflation expectations are static and not changing. Inflation expectations, π^e, are taken to be a given in what follows.

Similarly, INVESTMENT EXPENDITURE was found to be positively related to the internal rate of return and negatively related to the *ex ante* real rate of interest. In linear terms, in Chapter 4, we stated this as Eq. (4.15) which we write here as:

› **Investment** is positively related to the productivity of capital and negatively related to the nominal interest rate.

$$I = a - b (i - \pi^e) \tag{8.6}$$

The parameter a is the value of the internal rate of return and it increases with an increase in the value of the marginal product of capital and decreases with an increase in the price of capital goods, the depreciation rate, and adjustment costs. Here, b is the parameter that summarizes by how much investment declines in response to an increment in the nominal interest rate for given inflation expectations, or, the response to changes in the *ex ante* real interest rate.

In what follows, we treat government expenditures to be EXOGENOUSLY determined. Whenever a factor that determines demand is outside the explanatory adopted framework, we treat it as an exogenous or autonomous change in demand. Government expenditures are determined in this fashion by some extraneous factors such as the desire to appease vote banks so as to increase the likelihood of being elected. Though government expenditures comprise both consumption and investment expenditure, we shall, in what

› An **exogenous** variable is a variable that is taken as given and is not explained within an economic model.

follows, treat government expenditure as of the consumption type and ignore public investment.[4] We write the government expenditure function as being exogenously determined at some level $\overline{G}$, so that:[5]

$$G = \overline{G} \tag{8.7}$$

The condition for equilibrium in the product market for a closed economy is given by:

$$Y = C + I + G$$

or, $$Y - C - G = I$$

Adding and subtracting taxes, T, on the left-hand side,

$$\underbrace{(Y - T) - C}_{\substack{\text{Private}\\ \text{Savings}}} + \underbrace{T - G}_{\substack{\text{Government}\\ \text{Savings}}} = I \tag{8.8}$$

The term $(Y - T)$ is disposable income, and disposable income less consumption expenditure constitutes private savings. Similarly, the subtraction of government expenditure from tax receipts constitutes government savings. EQUILIBRIUM IN THE PRODUCT MARKET, thus, requires that savings—private plus government savings—equals investment. Substituting for private savings from Eq. (8.4) and for the investment function from Eq. (8.6), we may write this equilibrium condition in the goods or output or product market as:

› **Equilibrium in the product market** is given by the condition that aggregate savings—private and public—equals investment.

$$S_{pvt}\left(\underset{(+)}{i}, \underset{(+)}{Y}, \underset{(-)}{T}, \underset{(-)}{\pi^e}\right) + S_{govt}\left(\underset{(+)}{T}, \underset{(-)}{G}\right) = I\left(\underset{(+)}{a}, \underset{(-)}{i}, \underset{(+)}{\pi^e}\right) \tag{8.9}$$

Savings by the government is $S_{govt} = T - G$, which increases with a rise in tax revenues [a positive sign under T in the government savings function in Eq. (8.9)] and declines with an increase in government expenditure (a negative sign under G in the government savings function). The signs under the arguments in the investment function in Eq. (8.9) follow the discussion of the determinants of investment that accompanied equation (8.6). We now combine the private and government savings function into an aggregate savings function, $S = S_{pvt} + S_{govt}$. This allows us to rewrite Eq. (8.9) as:

$$S\left(\underset{(+)}{i}, \underset{(+)}{Y}, \underset{(+)}{T}, \underset{(-)}{G}\,\underset{(-)}{\pi^e}\right) = I\left(\underset{(+)}{a}, \underset{(-)}{i}, \underset{(+)}{\pi^e}\right) \tag{8.10}$$

The signs associated with changes in the variables that accompany changes in aggregate savings follow from the reasoning that led to Eq. (8.9). The only variable that depicts an ambiguity is the impact of changes in taxes on aggregate savings, T. In Eq. (8.9), an increase in taxes reduces private savings but increases government savings. What, then, is the total impact on aggregate savings? To understand why the impact is for aggregate savings to increase as depicted in Eq. (8.10), recall that an increase in taxation reduces disposable income. A fraction of that reduction in disposable income translates into a reduction in private savings, with the remaining fraction translating into a decline in consumption. Thus, private savings decline by a fraction of the increase in taxation. This increase in taxation results in income being taken away from the private sector, and that taxed income is given to the government. The government obtains the full amount of the income that is taken away as additional taxation. Government savings, $S_{govt} = T - G$, increases by the full amount of the increase in taxation. Private savings, however, declines by a fraction of the increase in taxation. In the net, then, aggregate savings has increased as government savings increase by more than the amount by which private savings decline when taxation increases.

For those who are more inclined to think about this issue in a more formal manner with a bit of high school algebra (others may skip and go ahead to the second paragraph after Eq. (8.11) without in any way losing out on the economics of the argument), substituting for C and I from Eqs (8.5) and (8.6) in Eq. (8.8) gives us:

$$(Y - T) - c_0 - c_1(Y - T) + c_2(i - \pi^e) + (T - G) = a - b(i - \pi^e)$$

or, $$(1 - c_1)(Y - T) - c_0 + c_2(i - \pi^e) + (T - G) = a - b(i - \pi^e) \qquad (8.11)$$

Aggregate savings in the economy, the left-hand side, increases with the nominal interest rate (the coefficient c_2 appears with a positive sign). The aggregate investment, the right-hand side, decreases with the nominal interest rate (the coefficient b appears with a negative sign).

The graphs of savings, S, and investment, I, as a function of the nominal interest rate and for given values of $\{Y, T, G, \pi^e\}$ are depicted in Figure 8.1.

In Figure 8.1, the nominal interest rate is measured on the vertical axis, and savings and investment are measured on the horizontal axis. The savings schedule is upward-sloping as an increase in the nominal interest rate is associated with an increase in savings. The investment schedule is downward-sloping as an increase in the interest rate increases the cost of capital and reduces investment expenditure.

Note that aggregate income Y's value is what we are trying to determine whereas T, G, π^e are exogenous variables. An increase in Y increases disposable income and increases the savings out of disposable income, which shifts the savings curve to the right in Figure 8.1A. This is the motivation for the POSITIVE SIGN UNDER THE VARIABLE Y in the savings function.

› An increase in income increases disposable income and **aggregate savings.**

An increase in taxes (ΔT) reduces disposable income of the private sector by ΔT and increases the tax receipts of the government by ΔT. The private sector, as stated earlier, would have spent a fraction ($c_1\Delta T$) on consumption and saved a fraction $[(1 - c_1)\Delta T]$ of this income that is now transferred to the government.

For the government, on the other hand, the entire amount of the increase in taxes (ΔT) is an addition to receipts. For a fixed government expenditure, this results in an increase in government savings (by ΔT). There is, in consequence,

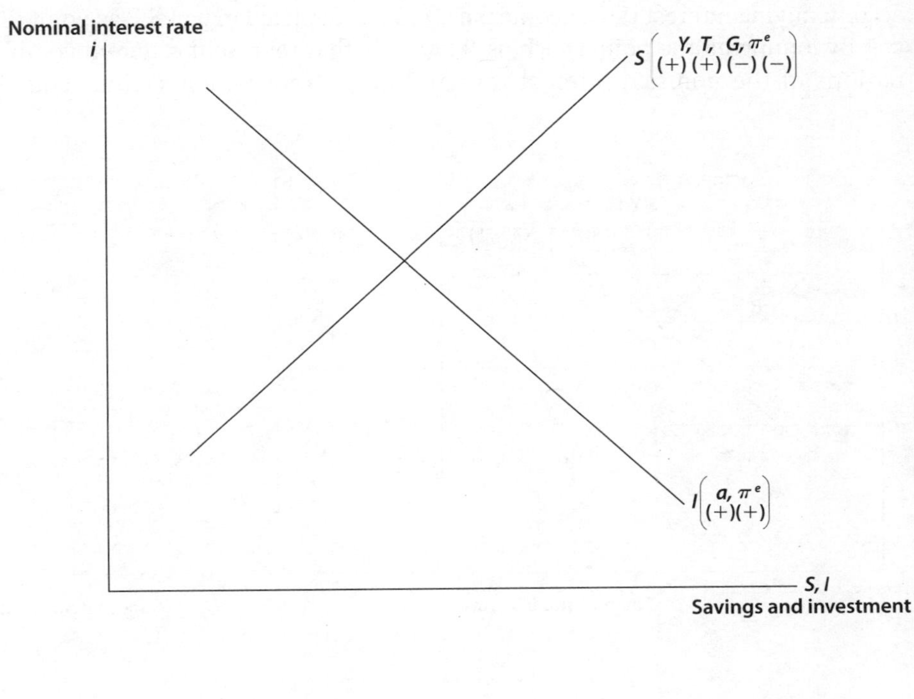

› **Figure 8.1**
Aggregate Investment and Savings. An increase in the interest rate increases aggregate savings because the relative return to future consumption has risen. An increase in the interest rate reduces aggregate investment because of the decline in investment opportunities.

› An increase in taxes reduces private savings but **increases government savings,** with the net effect being a rise in aggregate savings.

› An **increase in the expected rate of inflation** reduces the real interest rate and makes savings for purposes of future consumption less attractive.

a NET ADDITION TO AGGREGATE SAVINGS $\Delta T - (1 - c_1)\Delta T$ [given by $\Delta T - (1 - c_1)\Delta T$ or $c_1\Delta T$], justifying the positive sign under the variable T in Figure 8.1.

Similarly, an INCREASE IN GOVERNMENT EXPENDITURE corresponds to a reduction in government saving, $(T - G)$, and the S schedule shifts to the left when this occurs. An INCREASE IN EXPECTED INFLATION reduces the real interest rate, which makes savings for the purposes of future consumption less attractive and reduces savings. This, in turn, shifts the savings schedule to the left (see Figure 8.1).

The investment schedule in Figure 8.1 shifts to the right with an increase in productivity (increase in a) that improves investment opportunities. Also, an increase in expected inflation reduces the real interest rate and rental on capital, thereby making it profitable to increase investment which shifts the investment schedule up and to the right.

We are now set up to derive the IS curve. This is the curve that plots combinations of the interest rate and income along which equilibrium prevails in the product market. Equilibrium in the product market is where income equals expenditure, or, aggregate savings—private plus government—equals investment, as written in Eq. (8.8). Since investment (I) equals saving (S) at every point on the curve, it is termed the IS curve. The IS curve is easily derived in Figure 8.2. Suppose the savings schedule in (i, S) space is drawn for a particular income level Y_0 and this savings equals investment at point P in Figure 8.2, panel A. The nominal interest rate, when savings equals investment at P, is, thus, associated with an interest rate–income combination (i_0, Y_0). This combination is plotted in (i, Y) space in panel B as point P′. P′ is an interest rate–income combination where SAVINGS EQUALS INVESTMENT.

› The IS curve is downward-sloping in **nominal interest rate—aggregate income space**, as a rise in income raises the supply of savings to the capital market and causes the interest rate to decline.

Suppose income increases to $(Y_2 > Y_0)$. Then, savings increases with the increase in income and the savings schedule shifts down to intersect the investment schedule at point Q where the interest rate is i_2. The increased saving at higher incomes increases the supply of savings to the capital market, and the increased supply of funds pushes down the interest rate to i_2. Again, the interest rate–income pair (i_2, Y_2), when savings equals investment at point Q, is depicted as point Q′ in panel B.

Analogously, if income declines from Y_0 to Y_1—the change in income is $(Y_0 - Y_1)$—there is an accompanying decline in savings that shifts the savings schedule up and to the left. Savings is now equal to investment at point R and the accompanying interest rate-income pair (i_1, Y_1) is depicted in panel B as point R′.

By joining all the points such as P′, Q′, R′—that represent different combinations of the nominal interest rate and income for which savings equals

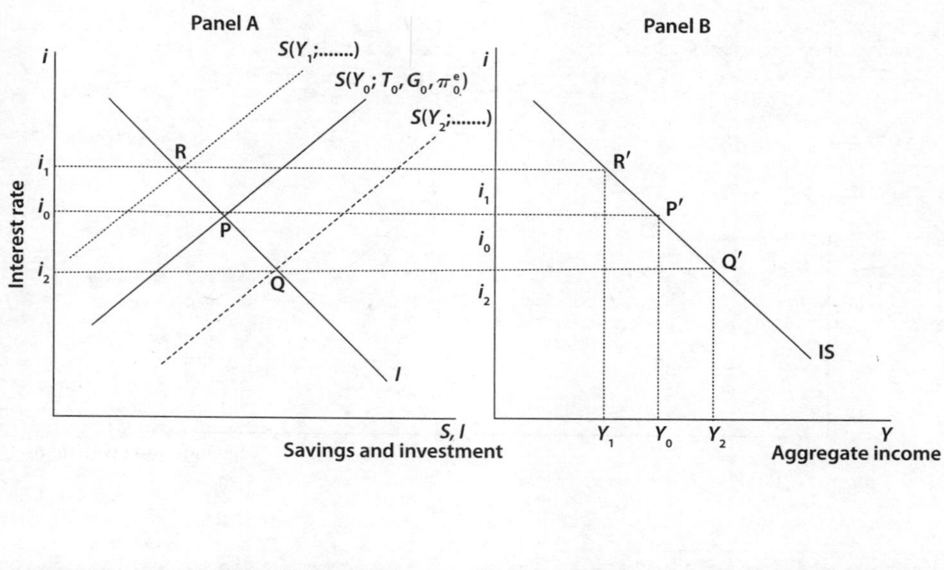

› **Figure 8.2**
The IS Curve. The IS curve depicts combinations of the interest rate and aggregate income that are associated with aggregate investment (I) equal to aggregate savings (S).

investment—we obtain the IS curve for the economy along which the goods market is in equilibrium. The IS curve is downward-sloping because an increase in income increases savings, the increased supply of which reduces interest rates. A reduction in interest rates makes investment projects more profitable and investment rises to match the increased savings.

8.2.1 Parametric Shifts of IS Curve

We now look at how parametric changes affect the IS curve. First, we analyse the impact of an increase in government expenditure. An increase in government expenditure to $G_1 > G_0$ corresponds to a decline in government savings $(T-G)$. The decline in savings shifts the savings schedule upwards to the left and savings now equals investment at point Q (where the interest rate has risen to i_1 from i_0) in Figure 8.3.

The INCREASED GOVERNMENT EXPENDITURE in the absence of any change in taxes is financed by a sale of bonds by the government to the private sector. The increased supply of bonds pushes down the price of bonds, which, in turn, raises the interest rate [see the price formula for bonds given by Eq. (6.4) in Chapter 6 on the demand for money]. Essentially, the government competing with the private sector for the funds of savers drives up the interest rate. The interest rate at the original income level Y_0, and indeed at all income levels, is now higher, and the IS curve shifts out to the right.

› The IS curve shifts to the right with an **increase in government expenditure,** as the increased supply of bonds causes bond prices to decline and the interest rate to rise.

What if TAXES INCREASE? Then, as we saw earlier, the private sector would have saved a fraction of the increase in taxes, whereas the government's receipts, which accrue as savings, increase by the entire increase in taxes. Hence, aggregate savings increases. The savings schedule shifts to the right in Figure 8.4 where taxes are now higher at T_1, up from the earlier value of T_0, and the increased supply of savings pushes down the nominal interest rate. In fact, it is now lower at the original and indeed at all levels of income, causing the IS curve to shift to the left.

› An increase in **taxes increases** aggregate savings and the nominal interest rate declines. This shifts the IS curve leftwards.

If firms come up with a new technology that INCREASES PRODUCTIVITY, they will undertake investments to exploit this technology. Expectations about the future profitability of a technology shifts the investment schedule to the right—an increase in the parameter a in Eqs (8.6) and (8.11). Again, the increased demand for the funds supplied by savers bids the interest rate up, and the IS curve shifts to the right (see Figure 8.5). We could also interpret the parameter a as the expectations of future profitability due to the mass psychology around business conditions that characterizes entrepreneurs and business persons—what Keynes referred to as animal spirits.

› An **increase in the productivity** of capital increases the demand for investment and the interest rate, thereby shifting the IS curve out to the right.

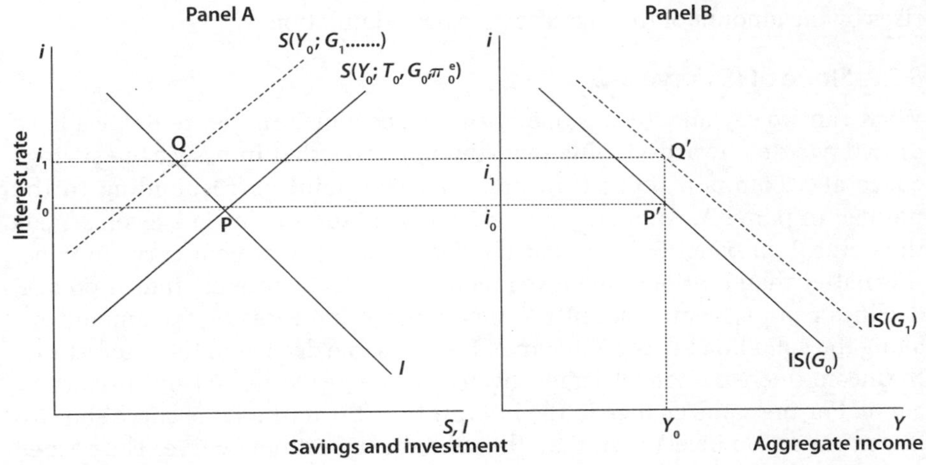

› **Figure 8.3 Increased Government Expenditure.** An increase in government expenditure reduces the savings of government (panel A) and shifts the IS curve to the right (panel B).

› **Figure 8.4**
Increase in Taxes. An increase in taxes increases aggregate savings (panel A) and shifts the IS curve to the left (panel B).

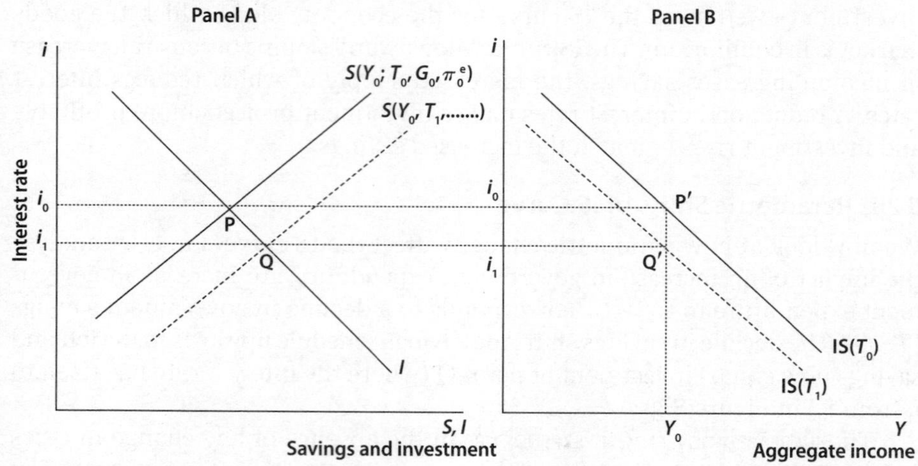

› **Figure 8.5**
Increase in Productivity. An increase in productivity increases investment (panel A) and shifts the IS curve to the right (panel B).

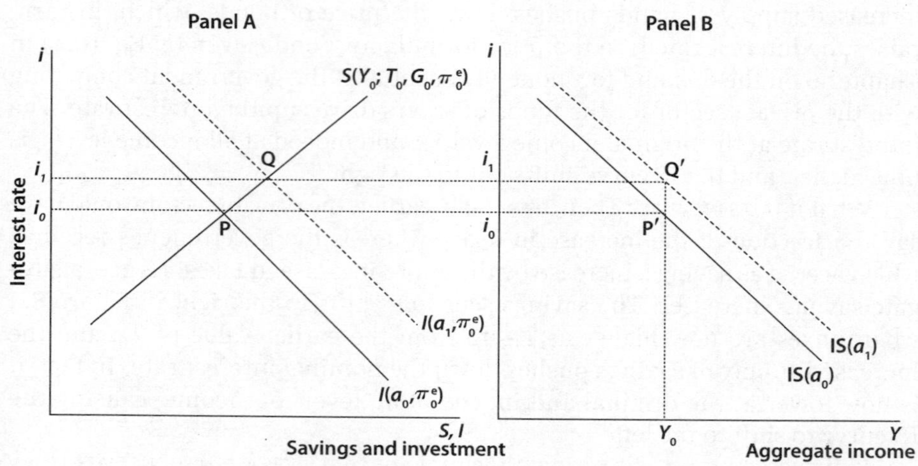

› An increase in **expected inflation** leaves aggregate savings and investment unchanged, but shifts the IS curve out to the right as the nominal interest rate rises.

Finally, if there is an increase in the EXPECTED INFLATION (say, because of the current nominal rate seeming low in terms of the surge in production and accompanying constraints on capacity that will occur in the future) the IS curve shifts to the right (see Figure 8.6).

As savings and investment are conducted in real terms, the reference interest for decisions regarding these variables is the *ex ante* real interest rate. With no change in the *ex ante* real interest rate, there is no change in savings and investment, which stays at $S_0 = I_0$. However, the nominal interest rate rises by the amount of the increase in expected inflation.

8.2.2 Slope of IS Curve

What can we say about the slope of the IS schedule? In Figure 8.7, we have drawn two downward-sloping investment curves that intersect the savings curve at a common point P in panel A. The point corresponding to the point P in panel A, where the interest rate is i_0 and the income level is Y_0, is the point P′ in panel B. Note that the dashed line investment curve in panel A is flatter than the solid line investment curve. If the interest rate at point P declines from i_0 by an amount PA, then income increases by the amount AB along the solid line investment curve. For the same decline in the interest rate the income increase is much larger, given by AC along the dashed line investment curve. For the same change in the interest rate, the dashed line curve shows a larger impact on investment than the solid line investment curve. The dashed

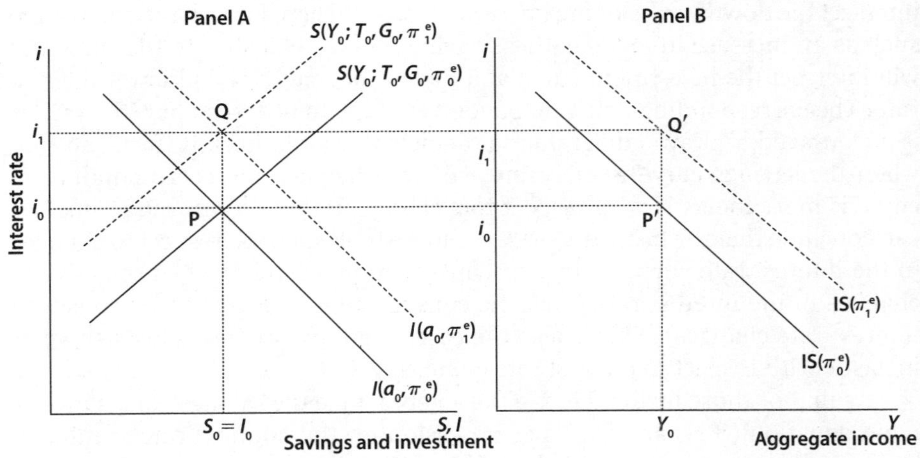

› **Figure 8.6**
Increase in Expected Inflation. An increase in expected inflation raises the nominal interest rate but does not affect the real rate of interest. Savings and investment in real terms are unaffected (panel A) and the IS curve shifts out to the right (panel B).

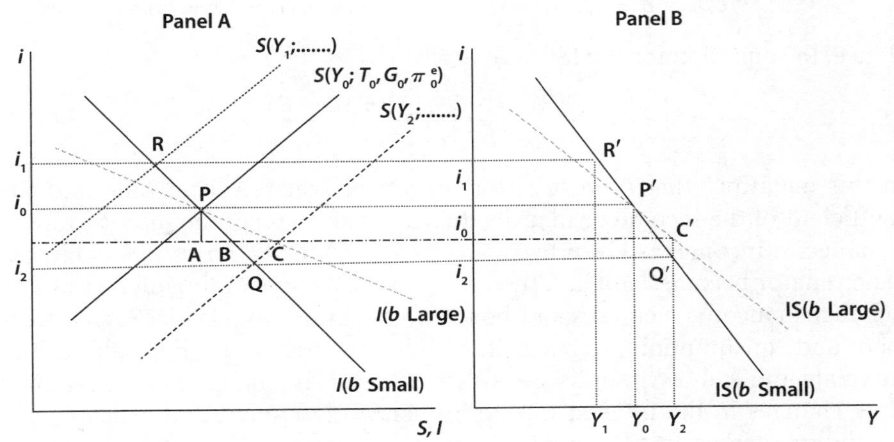

› **Figure 8.7**
IS Curve when Investment Sensitivity to Interest Rate is Low and High. If investment is not very sensitive to interest rates (*b* small), the demand for investment curve is inelastic (steep)—panel A. This results in a steep IS curve—panel B. The IS curve is flat when investment is sensitive to interest rate changes (*b* large).

line curve is, thus, more sensitive to changes in the interest rate. Thereby it is a more elastic investment curve. The solid line investment curve is relatively more inelastic with respect to changes in the interest rate.

If income increases to Y_2, savings equals investment at (i_2, Y_2) along the solid line investment curve that is interest inelastic: point Q in panel A corresponds to point Q′ in panel B. Joining points P′ and Q′ in panel B and extending it to include declines in income such as to Y_1 that results in the interest rate–income combination given by point R′, we obtain the IS curve that corresponds to the interest inelastic investment curve of panel A.

For the same increase in income to Y_2, the dashed line interest elastic investment curve in panel A intersects the savings curve at point C and the corresponding point in panel B is C′. In panel B, if we join points P′ and C′ and extend the line, we obtain the dashed line IS curve that corresponds to the interest elastic dashed line investment curve of panel A. We can see that when the investment is interest inelastic—the solid line investment curve in panel A—the corresponding IS curve in panel B is also inelastic. We can then conclude that the slope of the IS curve is, therefore, steeper. Alternately, the IS curve is more inelastic when investment is more inelastic to changes in the rate of interest.

The other interest sensitive variable in panel A of the diagram is of course savings—which is the residual of disposable income after consumption. Just as we have done for investment, it is possible to draw two upward sloping savings curves—one steeper and so inelastic and the other flatter and so elastic—to intersect the downward-sloping investment curve. Then, for a change in income such as an increase in income, these savings curves will shift to the right and will intersect the investment curve at a higher income level and lower interest rate. The corresponding points in panel B could then be traced out (the reader is encouraged to draw a diagram that depicts this situation). It turns out that when the savings curve is more inelastic (or steeper), the corresponding IS curve is more inelastic with respect to a change in the interest rate. Thus, we can conclude that the IS CURVE IS STEEPER or more inelastic with respect to changes in the interest rate when savings or consumption are relatively insensitive to changes in the interest rate (inelastic consumption and savings responses to interest rate changes). This is also the case when investment is insensitive or inelastic with respect to interest rate changes.

› The **IS curve** is steeper or inelastic when the responsiveness of aggregate investment and consumption expenditure to a change in the interest rate is low.

Again, for those inclined to see the algebra, take the savings equals investment equation (8.11) and find the expression for the nominal rate of interest by first taking the terms in *i* on the left-hand side:

$$(b + c_2)i = a + c_0 - (1 - c_1)(Y - T) - (T - G) + (b + c_2)\pi^e$$

Hence, the equation for the IS curve is given by,

$$i = \frac{a + c_0 - (1 - c_1)(Y - T) - (T - G)}{b + c_2} + \pi^e \tag{8.12}$$

In this equation, the interest rate is negatively related to income and the coefficient of the income term gives the responsiveness of the interest rate to a change in income, as given by $(1 - c_1)/(b + c_2)$. If the term $(b + c_2)$ in the denominator becomes smaller, then the responsiveness of the interest rate to a change in income increases, or, the IS curve is interest inelastic. So, if investment and consumption are insensitive to interest rates ($b + c_2$ small), the IS curve algebraically written as Eq. (8.12) is steep. In such a case, it requires large changes in the interest rate to influence investment and consumption expenditures in order to have a large impact on income. If, on the other hand, the parameters b and c_2 are large, then the IS curve is flat and small changes in the interest rate have a large impact on income.

8.3 LM Curve

The LM curve depicts combinations of the nominal interest rate and income that represent equilibria between the supply of and demand for money. In deriving the LM curve, it is assumed that the entire money supply is an exogenous variable directly under the control of the central bank. Realistically, the central bank's ability to control the money supply in circulation is imperfect. This is because changes in interest rates induced by money supply changes cause banks to respond by altering the amount of deposits they issue.[6] Nevertheless, it is worth simplifying by assuming that the central bank can supply any quantity of nominal money balances it desires in the form of non-interest bearing cash and deposits. The quantity of supplied money that is independent of the nominal interest rate is then given by:

$$M^s = \bar{M} \tag{8.13}$$

The real purchasing power of money is what matters to individuals, and so a central bank would find it desirable to have control over the quantity of real money balance directly. However, central banks are not in a position to set prices, which are determined in the markets for goods and services.

At best, central banks can conduct policies that influence the price level. But price levels can change without any policy action being initiated by a central bank. Hence, the supply schedule for real money balances M^S/P is affected by both the nominal money stock and the price level.

The demand for real money balances has already been derived as Eq. (6.14) in Chapter 6 as $M^d/P = f(Y, i)$, where it was shown that real money demand is positively related to aggregate income and inversely related to the nominal interest rate. In linear form, we may write this as:

$$\frac{M^d}{P} = h + nY - ei \tag{8.14}$$

where h, n, and e are fixed parameters. The demand for real money balances is, therefore, inversely related to the nominal interest rate. This relation is because a rise in the interest rate represents income forgone from holding alternative financial assets like bonds that induce people to give up the liquidity associated with money. Alternatively, a rise in interest rates, which is a decline in the price of bonds for given expectations, makes individuals anticipate increased capital gains on bond holdings and allocate more of their portfolio to bonds.

The demand and supply schedules for real money balances is depicted in Figure 8.8 for a given price level, P_0. The two schedules intersect at a point where all individuals in the economy are satisfied holding the nominal money stock supplied by the Central Bank, M_0, deflated by the current price level, P_0. The nominal interest rate adjusts to achieve equilibrium where real money demand equals real money supply. To understand how equilibrium is achieved, consider what transpires if the interest rate happened to be i_1. At the higher interest rate i_1, the quantity of real money supplied exceeds the demand for real money balances. People wishing to hold smaller real money balances than the Central Bank has supplied will attempt to get out of money and hold more bonds in its place. They already hold the money balances required for transacting in goods and services at Y_0, and so, instead of spending in the goods market, they acquire bonds. The additional demand for bonds cause bond prices to rise

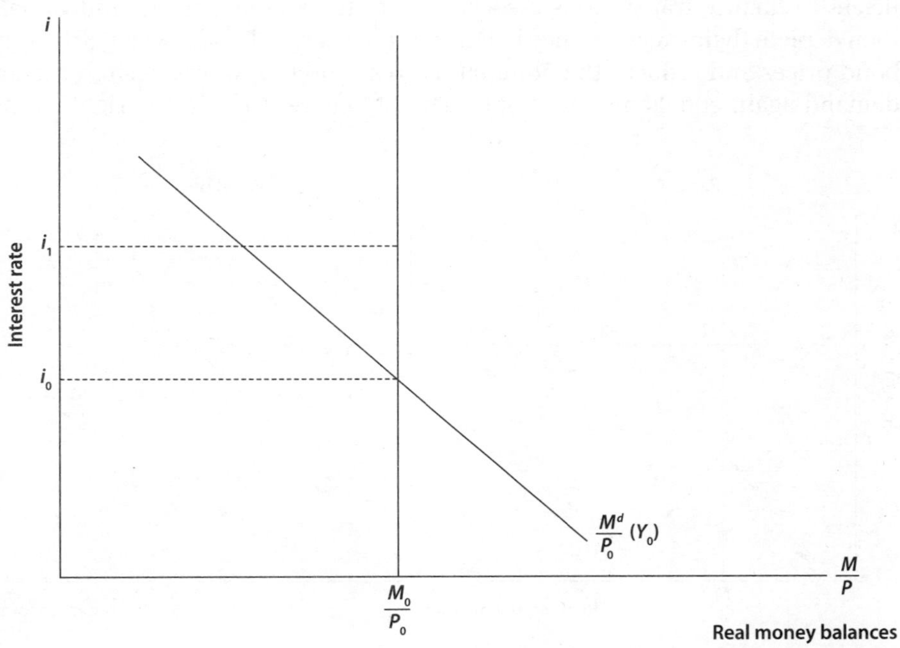

› **Figure 8.8 Equilibrium Real Money Balances.** The demand for real money balances (M^d/P_0) is inversely related to the nominal rate of interest. The supply of money (M_0/P_0) is independent of the interest rate and is a vertical curve. In equilibrium, the demand equals the supply of money and the nominal interest rate is determined.

and as there is an inverse relation between the price of bonds and the nominal interest rate, the interest rate falls towards the equilibrium rate i_0.

We can now derive the LM curve by asking what the relation between the nominal interest rate and income is, when the demand for real money balances equals the supply of real money balances. If income increases to Y_1, then, there is an increase in the demand for money required for transactions purposes[7]. Thus the demand for money schedule shifts to the right—Figure 8.9.

With fixed money supply, how is the demand for money going to be met? Essentially, individuals rebalance their portfolio of financial assets by selling bonds in order to acquire the money balance required to finance the higher transactions associated with income Y_1. The increase in the supply of bonds, in turn, causes the price of bonds to fall. It also causes the nominal interest rate, which is inversely related to the price, to rise till i_1 where demand and supply for real money balances are again equal. We plot the combinations of nominal interest rate and income such as (i_0, Y_0) and (i_1, Y_1), where money demand equals money supply in panel B of Figure 8.9. The graph of these combinations of real income and nominal interest rate, where money demand equals money supply, is called THE LM CURVE. The name LM follows a notation introduced by John Hicks in 1937, where he referred to the demand for money as desired liquidity *L*. Setting desired liquidity equal to the supply of real money balances, *M*, that is, $L = M$, results in a schedule where the money market is in equilibrium called the LM schedule. The LM curve is upward-sloping because an increase in real income increases the demand for real money balances, which is satisfied by selling bonds that causes a decline in bond prices and a corresponding rise in the nominal interest rate.

› **The *LM* curve** is upward-sloping in nominal interest rate—aggregate income space as an increase in income raises the demand for real money balances which results in a rise in the interest rate.

8.3.1 Impact of Varying the Money Supply

What if the Central Bank manipulates the money supply? Manipulation of the money supply with a view to influence endogenous variables such as the interest rate or the level of income is referred to as *monetary policy*. The increase in nominal money supply from $\bar{M}$ to $\bar{\bar{M}}$ shifts the money supply curve to the right as depicted in Figure 8.10, panel A.

There is now an EXCESS SUPPLY OF MONEY, as $\bar{M}/P_0$ real money balances are sufficient to finance transactions associated with the real income Y_0. Individuals then deplete their excess money balance by purchasing bonds, which drives up bond prices and reduces the nominal interest rate to i_1 where desired money demand again equals money supply. The LM curve shifts to the right as the

› The LM curve shifts to the right if there is an **increase in the money supply** as interest rates decline in response to individuals rebalancing their financial portfolio by purchasing bonds when this occurs.

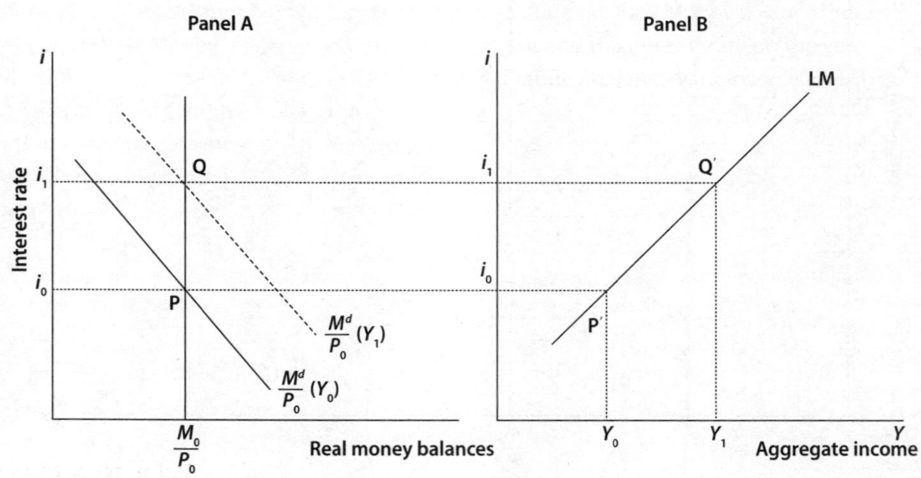

› **Figure 8.9**
The LM Curve. An increase in income shifts the demand for money curve to the right and raises the interest rate in the money market (panel A). An increase in income results in a new money demand and supply equilibrium that is associated with an increase in the interest rate. Tracing out such points, where money demand equals money supply at various levels of income, gives the LM curve (panel B).

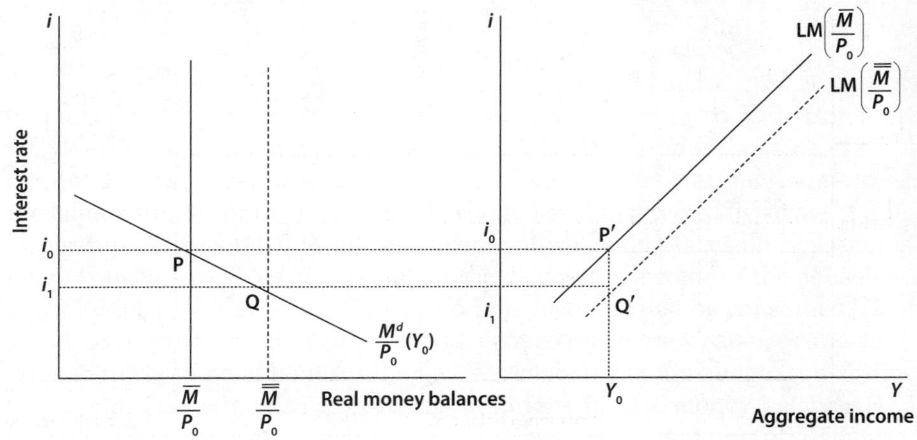

› **Figure 8.10**
Effect of Increase in Money Supply. An increase in money supply shifts the money supply curve to the right—the dashed line in panel A—and results in a decline in the interest rate in the money market. The decrease in the interest rate associated with a higher money supply shifts the LM curve to the right (panel B).

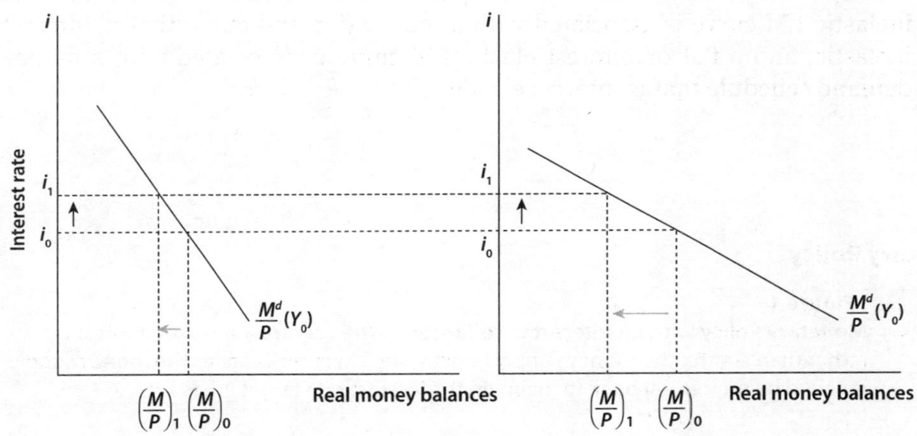

› **Figure 8.11**
Interest Elasticity of Money Demand. When the demand for money is not sensitive to the interest rate (interest inelastic), the curve is steep (panel A). When the demand for money is sensitive to interest rate changes, (interest elastic) the curve is flat (panel B).

nominal interest rate associated with any level of real income is lower—as depicted in Figure 8.10 panel B.

8.3.2 Slope of LM Curve

What can be said about the slope of the LM schedule? In Figure 8.11, the interest sensitivity of real money demand is low for the curve in panel A—an *interest inelastic* money demand schedule.

A small rise in the nominal interest rate from i_0 to i_1 causes a relatively small reduction in the quantity of real money balances demanded. In contrast, the interest sensitivity of real money demand is high for the curve in panel B of Figure 8.11—an *interest elastic* money demand schedule. Here, a small rise in the nominal interest rate from i_0 to i_1, induces a relatively large decline in the quantity of real money balances demanded—from $(M/P)_0$ to $(M/P)_1$.

In Figure 8.12, panel A, suppose we begin at the point P where money demand associated with real income Y_0 equals money supply, and this results in a nominal interest rate, i_0. Suppose the relevant money demand curve is the interest inelastic solid curve and there is an increase in income to $Y_1 > Y_0$. The money demand curve then shifts out, resulting in interest rate $i_1|_{\text{inelastic}}$ associated with Y_1.

The ***LM*** CURVE corresponding to this money demand curve is also relatively interest inelastic as seen in panel B. If the relevant money demand curve is the dashed interest elastic one in panel A, then, an increase in real income

› The ***LM* curve** is inelastic (elastic) when the demand for money is interest inelastic (elastic).

› **Figure 8.12**
Interest Elasticity of the LM Schedule. When the demand for money is sensitive to changes in the interest rate (interest elastic dashed curve) an increase in the demand for money for transactions that accompanies an increase in income does not result in a large change in the interest rate (panel A). The resulting LM curve (dashed line) is also relatively flat—panel B. If the demand for money is interest inelastic—solid curve—the LM curve is steep.

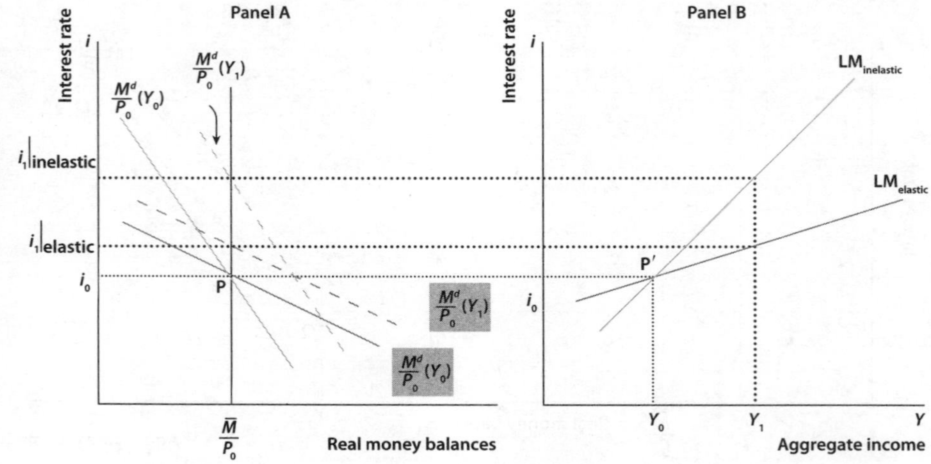

to Y_1 results in a smaller rise in the nominal interest rate to $i_1|_{\text{elastic}}$ and the corresponding LM schedule is relatively more elastic. Hence, a steep or interest inelastic LM curve is associated with a money demand curve that is interest inelastic, and a flat or interest elastic LM curve is associated with a money demand schedule that is interest elastic.

MACROFOCUS 8.1

Interest Rate Targets and Monetary Policy

Monetary policy involves the variation in money supply by monetary authorities with a view to achieving a given level of income. However, in many economies, setting interest rates is much more common among central banks than fixing the money supply. For instance, in the US, the Federal Reserve through open market operations—the purchase and sale of government securities—strives to achieve a target for the Federal Funds interest rate. In this case, the LM curve is flat at the targeted level of the interest rate. The difference arises because, for an upward-sloping LM curve, the supply of money is fixed. As a result, when incomes rise (or fall) and the demand for money for transactions purposes along with it, the interest rate rises (or falls) so as to keep the demand for money at the constant level of the money supply. A rise (or fall) in income is, thus, associated with a rise (or fall) in the interest rate and the LM curve is upward-sloping. In the case of an interest rate target, however, the money supply fluctuates so as to maintain a given level of the interest rate and there is no relationship between and i—the LM curve is flat. In this case, the monetary authorities change the price of holding money balances in a way that induces people to want to hold that amount of money. When the monetary authorities use an interest rate target, then an expansionary monetary policy involves reducing the target level of the interest rate (from i_0 to i_1 and the impact on the economy is very much the same as for the case of increasing the money supply in an upward sloping LM case—output rises (and the interest rate declines) as the economy moves down its IS curve. In a sense, the distinction between using money supply targets and interest rate targets is of significance only when the demand for money schedule is not stable, and so the corresponding position of the LM curve is also variable (see Chapter 15).

› **Figure 1**
Monetary Policy with an Interest Rate Target When central banks set interest rates rather than control the money supply directly, the LM curve is flat as the money supply is varied by the central bank to maintain the interest rate target it has set.

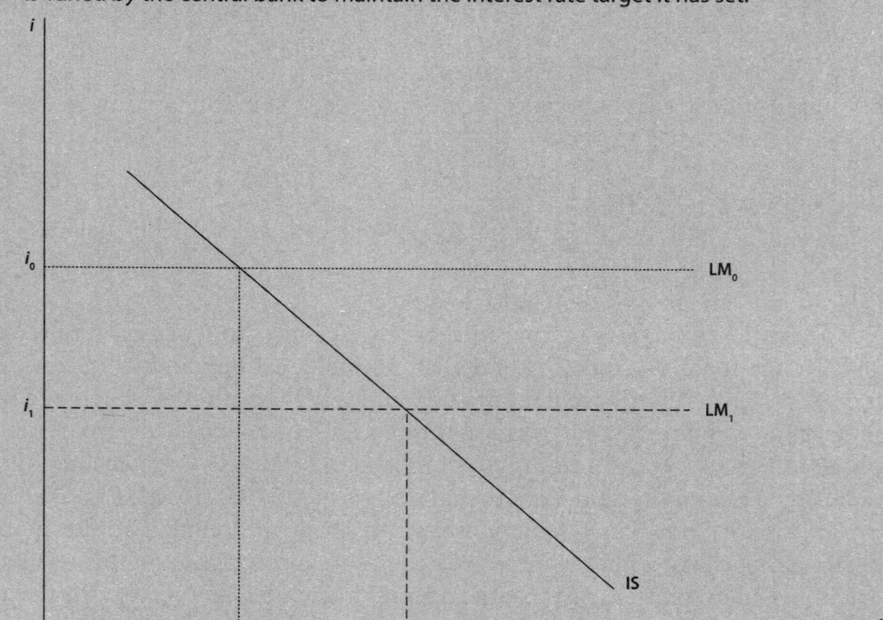

8.4 IS and LM—Fiscal and Monetary Policy

Combining the IS and the LM schedules in a diagram enables us to find a single combination of real income and the nominal interest rate that is simultaneously equilibrium in the commodities market and in the market for real money balances.

Figure 8.13 combines the IS and LM schedules in a single diagram. The two schedules intersect at point E which is an IS–LM equilibrium, where real income and the nominal interest rate simultaneously achieve goods market and money market equilibrium. At any point other than E in the diagram, three conditions can occur:

1. The goods market is not in equilibrium (any point other than E on the LM curve).
2. The money market is not in equilibrium (any point other than E on the IS curve).
3. Both markets are not in equilibrium (points off the IS and LM curve).

In that case, interest rates and expenditure must change to re-attain the real income–nominal interest rate combination that concurrently achieves equilibrium in the goods and money markets.

We now analyse the effect of monetary policy in an IS–LM set up. Monetary policy results in a change in the nominal money stock and a corresponding change in the real money supply (when the price level is unchanged). The IS–LM MODEL allows us to understand the immediate impact of monetary and fiscal policy actions under the assumptions that:

› The **IS–LM model** is appropriate for the short run where wages and prices do not change and there is underutilization of the capacity to produce output.

1. Wages and prices are fixed
2. Resources such as labour and capital are not fully utilized.

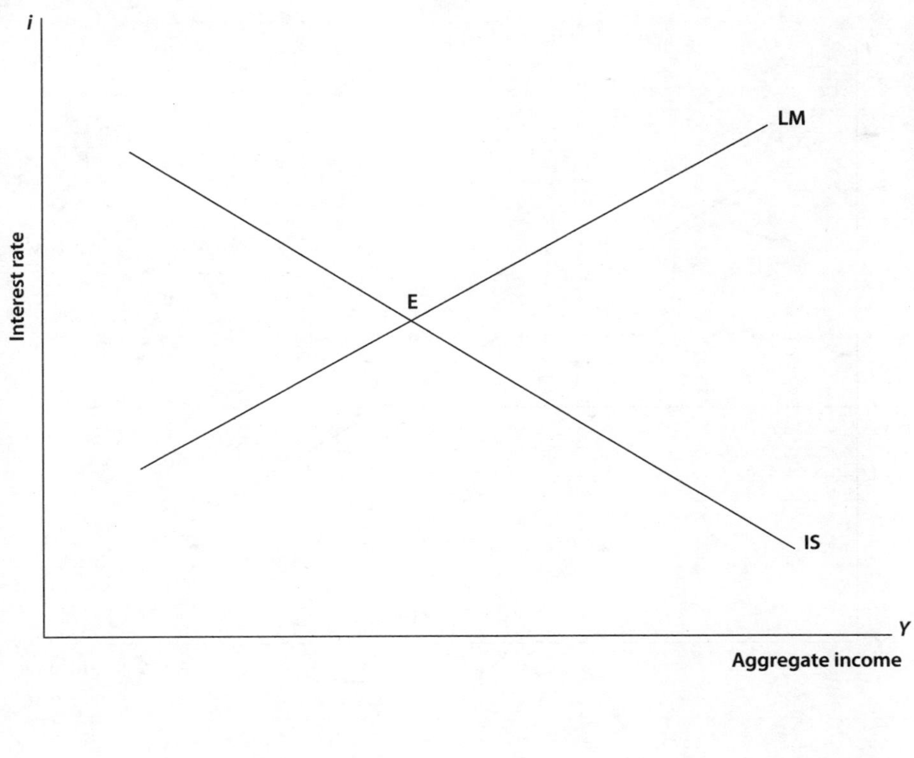

› **Figure 8.13**
IS – LM Equilibrium. The IS and LM curves intersect at a point E and result in a nominal interest rate and real income outcome where simultaneously the goods market (IS) and the money market (LM) are in equilibrium.

In such a set up we can ignore the labour market and the supply of output, and firms are thought of as not having supply constraints on the production of goods. Rather, the constraint on output is the lack of demand. Any additional demand results in firms increasing output, and a reduction in demand leads them to reduce output.

› An **expansionary monetary policy** in the IS–LM model results in a portfolio rebalancing with an increase in the demand for bonds, a reduction in the interest rate, and an increase in income. This happens as interest-sensitive components of expenditures such as consumption and investment increase.

Suppose, now, the central bank increases the nominal money stock. Then, as we know from Figure 8.10, this shifts the LM curve to the right. This is depicted in Figure 8.14 as the dashed LM curve. The immediate impact of the INCREASE IN MONEY SUPPLY is that at the initial real income Y_0, the increased money balances are not required for transactions purposes. Thus individuals give up this liquidity in favour of interest earnings on bonds.

The increase in the demand for bonds increases the price of bonds, or what amounts to the same thing, the interest rate declines to i_2. The decline in the interest rate, in turn, induces two effects. One effect is that individuals prefer to consume now rather than later, and consumption expenditure increases. This is because of present savings earning a lower return with a decline in interest rates.

Second, the reduction in the interest rate makes more investment projects, which earlier were unprofitable at the higher interest rate, profitable and investment expenditure increases. This increased expenditure on consumption and investment is reflected in a movement along the IS curve from *E* towards *E′*, and causes a rise in real income. With increased expenditure and incomes, the demand for real money balances rises for facilitating transactions. This causes the interest rate to rise to i_1 with goods and money market equilibrium at E′.

In all, the rise in the nominal stock of money causes a reduction in the equilibrium nominal interest rate and an increase in equilibrium real income. The extent of the increase in real income depends on the interest elasticity of the LM schedule as we discuss in the next section.

8.4.1 Fiscal Policy and Crowding Out

What if the government decides to use fiscal policy by, for instance, increasing government expenditure? As we know from Figure 8.3, the IS curve shifts outwards to IS(G_1) as depicted in Figure 8.15.

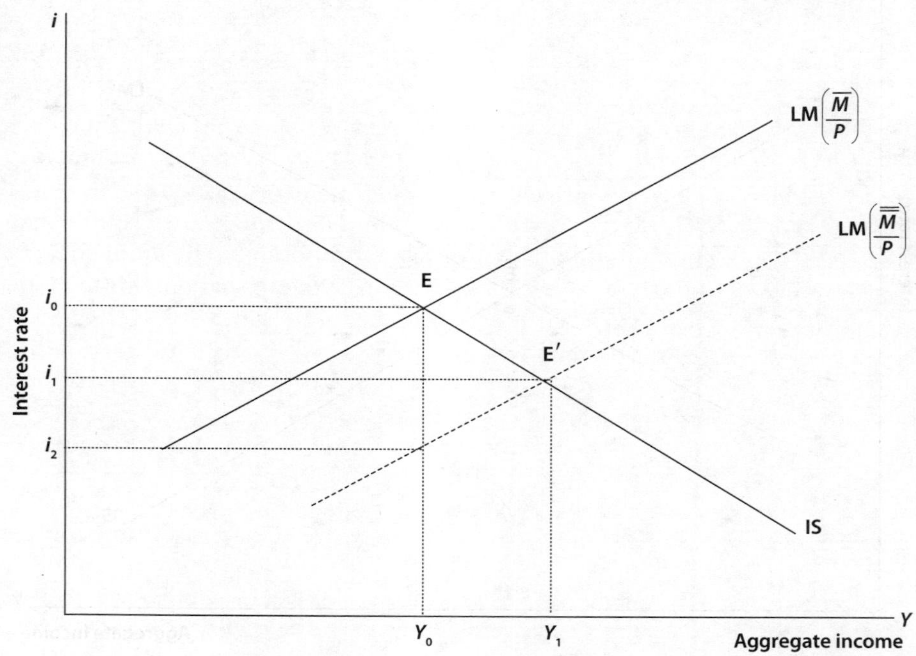

› **Figure 8.14**
Increase in Nominal Money Stock. An increase in money supply induces individuals to shift their portfolio towards bonds, and the interest rate declines to i_2. This stimulates investment and consumption expenditure in the goods market, which raises the demand for money and results in the interest rate ultimately settling at i_1. An increase in money supply, therefore, reduces the interest rate and increases aggregate income.

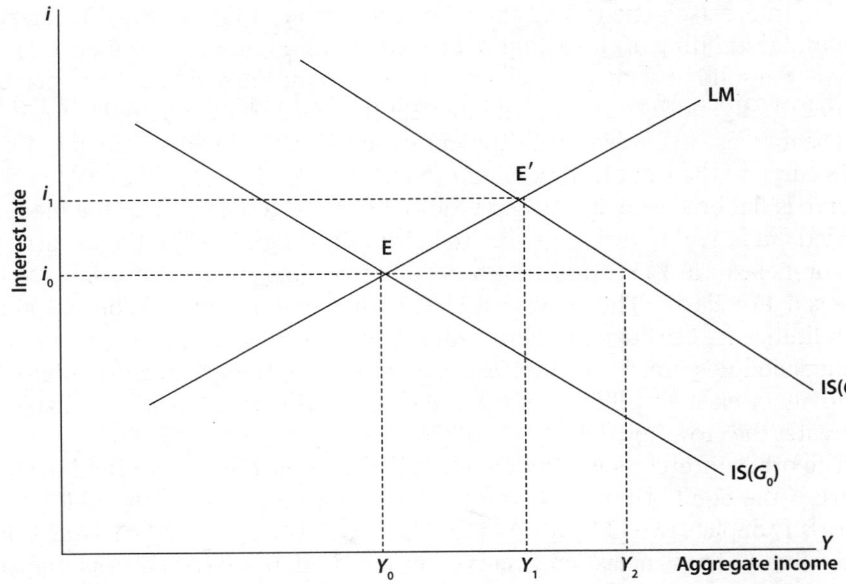

› **Figure 8.15**
Increase in Government Expenditure. An increase in government expenditure shifts the IS curve to the right. It increases income and the demand for money for transactions purposes. The increased demand for money results in an increase in the interest rate in the money market. The rise in the interest rate crowds out—reduces—some interest-sensitive private expenditures on investment and consumption.

The increased government expenditure raises real income to Y_2 initially. The increased income causes a rise in the demand for money for transaction purposes. In the face of a fixed supply of money, the increased money demand [see Figure 8.9] causes the interest rate to rise from i_0 to i_1. The rise in the interest rate induces a decline in investment expenditure due to a decline in the present value of investment projects [Eq. (8.6)]. It also induces a decline in the interest-sensitive component of current consumption expenditure [Eq. (8.4)] as the attractiveness of future consumption increases.

The decline in the interest-sensitive elements of private expenditures reduces income from Y_2 to Y_1 in Figure 8.15. In the process, despite the rise in interest rates which choke off some investment and consumption, the final equilibrium level of income is higher after the increased government spending. The rise in income from Y_0 to Y_1 also induces an increase in the income-sensitive component of consumption expenditure as consumption increases with income. The constrained increase in income—Y_0Y_1 in Figure 8.15—can then be thought of as the net outcome of:

1. An expansion of income arising from the increase in government spending
2. A decline of income arising from the induced decline in investment and that part of consumption which is sensitive to interest rates, and
3. An expansion in income arising from an induced increase in consumption expenditure as income rises.

The induced reduction in consumption and investment, which offsets the effect of the increase in government spending, is referred to as CROWDING OUT. The tendency for the stimulative effects of fiscal policy to be offset by an induced decline in private expenditures as the interest rate increases is called crowding out.

› **Crowding out** occurs when the stimulative effects of fiscal policy are offset by a reduction in interest-sensitive consumption and investment due to a rise in the interest rate.

What determines the extent of crowding out? Since crowding out occurs due to the decrease in expenditures caused by the rise in the interest rate, it is intuitive that the extent of crowding out will be determined by the interest-sensitivity of various components of aggregate expenditures. In the goods or output market, the interest rate affects consumption and investment expenditures. The IS curve, which represents equilibrium in the output market, is elastic or flat when these interest-sensitive components of expenditures are also interest-elastic (recall the discussion around Figure 8.7). To arrive at an understanding of the extent of crowding out, Figure 8.16 depicts two IS curves—the solid line steep or inelastic curve, and the dashed line flat or elastic curve. Initially, both these curves intersect the LM curve at the point E.

The increase in government expenditure at the initial interest rate of i_o shifts the IS curve to the right to IS(G) and expands income from Y_o to Y_3. When the IS curve is flat or elastic, it intersects the LM curve at a point where the income crowded out is $Y_1 Y_3$, which is greater than the crowding out when the IS curve is steep or inelastic at $Y_2 Y_3$. This informs us that crowding out is larger when the IS curve is flat or elastic. The IS curve is elastic when investment and consumption expenditures are sensitive to interest rate changes, or when the investment and saving schedules are flat or interest elastic. Hence, the greater the interest-sensitivity or elasticity of investment and consumption to interest rate changes, the greater the crowding out.

The other interest-sensitive function is the money demand function that is part of the equilibrium in the money market as depicted by the LM curve. Figure 8.17 depicts two LM curves—the solid line flat or elastic LM curve and the dashed line steep or inelastic LM curve. Initially both these LM curves intersect the IS curve at point E. The increase in government expenditure at the initial interest rate of i_o shifts the IS curve to the right to IS(G) and expands income from Y_o to Y_3. The steep or inelastic LM curve intersects the IS(G) curve at a point where the income crowded out is $Y_1 Y_3$, which is greater than the crowding out when the LM curve is flat or elastic at $Y_2 Y_3$. Crowding out is then larger if the LM curve is inelastic. Recall the discussion surrounding Figure 8.12 where it was shown that the LM curve is inelastic when the demand for money is inelastic. Hence, crowding out is larger when the demand for money is interest inelastic.

To summarize, then, crowding out is larger (or the impact of a fiscal policy of increased government expenditure on aggregate income is smaller) when:

1. Investment is sensitive to interest rate changes or the investment schedule is interest elastic
2. Consumption is sensitive to interest rate changes or the consumption function is interest elastic

› Figure 8.16
Crowding out Effect of Interest Sensitivity of Aggregate Expenditures. When investment is not sensitive to interest rates—the solid IS line—crowding out, or the decline in investment caused by an increase in government expenditure, is smaller than when investment is sensitive to interest rate changes—the dashed IS line.

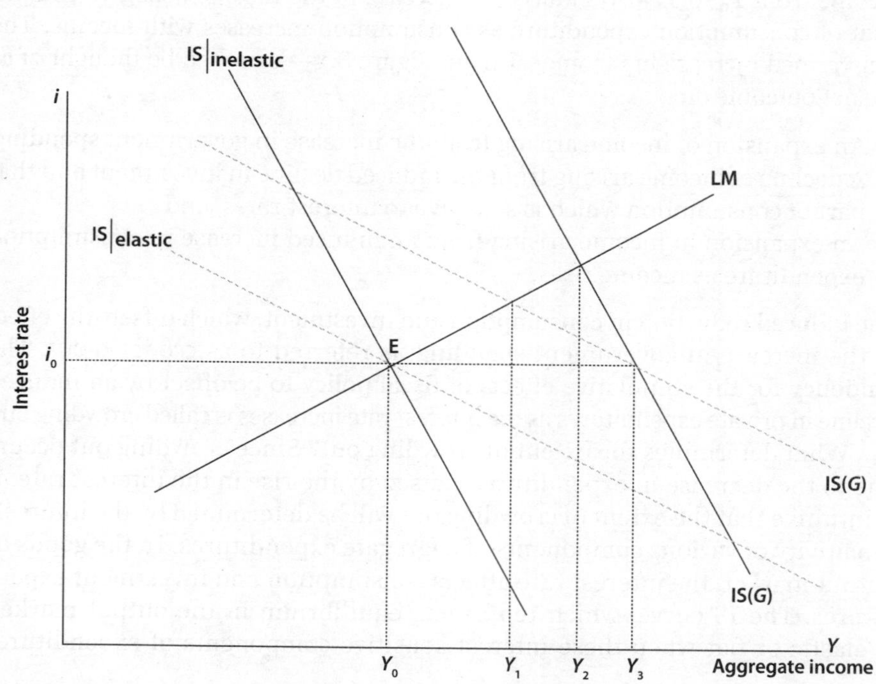

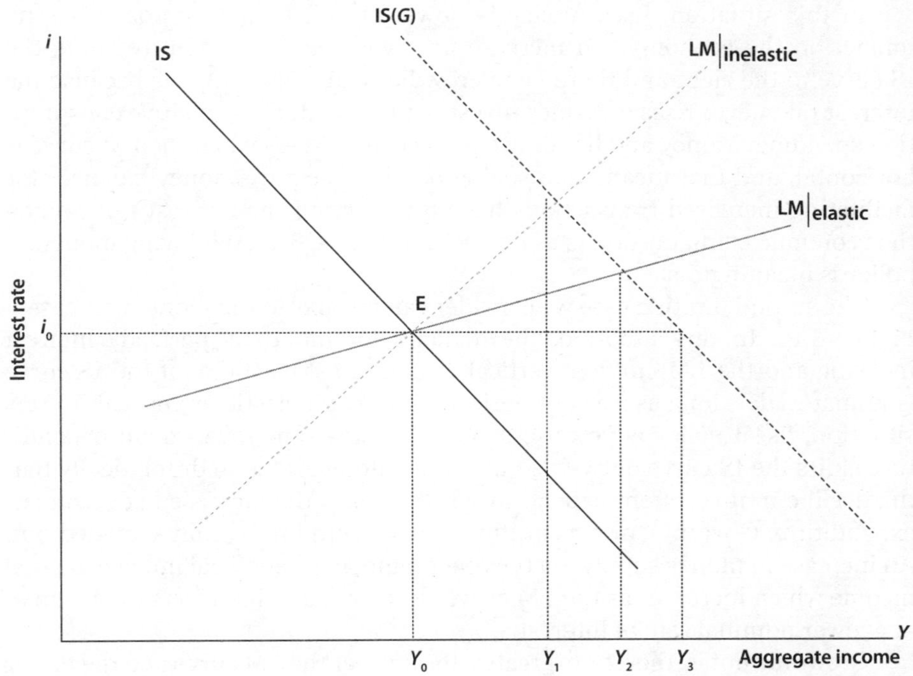

› **Figure 8.17**
Crowding out Effect of Interest-Sensitivity of Money Demand. When an increase in the interest rate does not have much effect on the demand for money, the LM curve is steep or interest inelastic. The interest rate must then rise by a relatively large amount so as to induce individuals to sell bonds and shift their portfolio towards money that is required for transacting the expenditures at higher incomes. This crowds out—reduces—private expenditures to a larger extent than when the LM curve is flat, as there the interest rate need not increase as much to induce a reduction in bond holdings.

3. The demand for money is relatively insensitive to interest rate changes or the demand for money is interest inelastic.

8.4.2 Fiscalist and Monetarist Intervention

It is useful to consider two special cases which help in summarizing the discussion on fiscal and monetary policy. In the first instance that we label the Fiscalist case, investment is totally insensitive to interest rates and the IS curve is vertical. Also, the demand for money is very sensitive to the interest rate and is interest elastic. When the money demand is perfectly interest elastic, the LM curve is horizontal [see Figure 8.18].

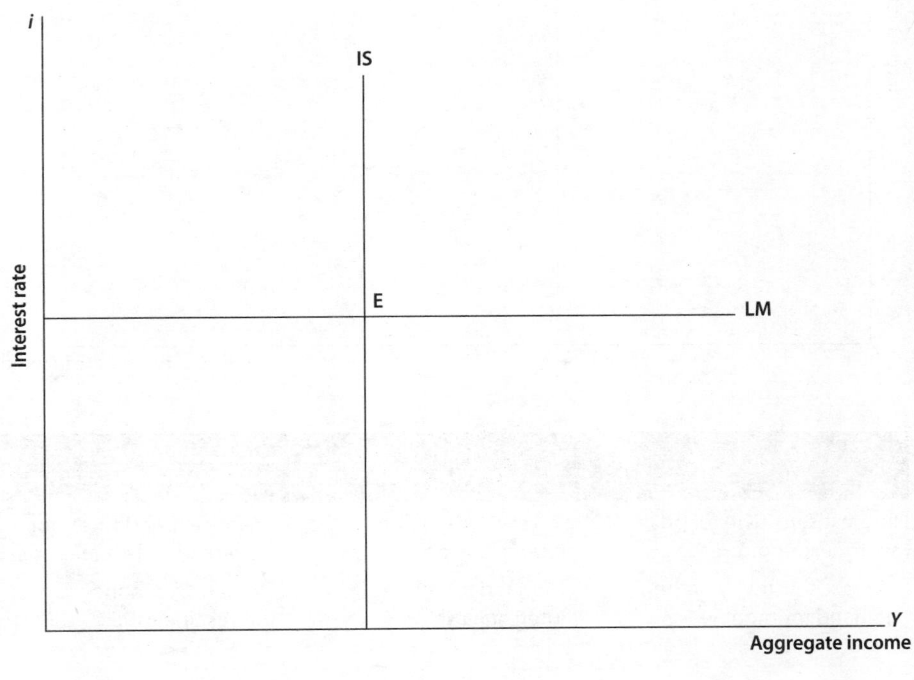

› **Figure 8.18**
Fiscalist Case. When investment is not sensitive to interest rates, the IS curve is vertical. When the demand for money is very sensitive to interest rates, the LM curve is horizontal. In this case only fiscal policy can influence the level of aggregate income—a Fiscalist scenario.

In this situation, fiscal policy is powerful and monetary policy has no impact on the economy. An increase in government expenditure shifts the IS curve to the right and there is no crowding out. This happens because the interest rate never rises to reduce investment and interest-sensitive consumption spending. Money and bonds are perfect substitutes when the LM curve is horizontal, and that means that selling bonds to acquire money balances for facilitating increased transactions has no impact on the interest rate. When the economic configuration is as depicted in Figure 8.18, deploying monetary policy is meaningless.

The second limiting case we consider can be labeled the monetarist case—Figure 8.19. In this situation, the demand for money is perfectly interest inelastic and the LM curve is vertical. The interest elasticity of the IS curve is immaterial as long as it is not perfectly interest inelastic or vertical. In this situation, fiscal policy is powerless, as any increase in government expenditure shifts the IS curve outwards but raises interest rates so dramatically that the decline in investment expenditure fully offsets the increased government expenditure. Government expenditure is considered to be fully crowded out. An increase in money supply, on the other hand, has beneficial impacts on real income which increases as the LM curve shifts out, and intersects the IS curve at a lower nominal rate of interest.

Crowding out is, therefore, greater, the steeper the LM curve and the flatter the IS curve—the monetarist case.

Conversely, when crowding out is smaller, the LM curve is flatter, and the IS curve is steeper—the fiscalist case. These results are summarized in Table 8.1.

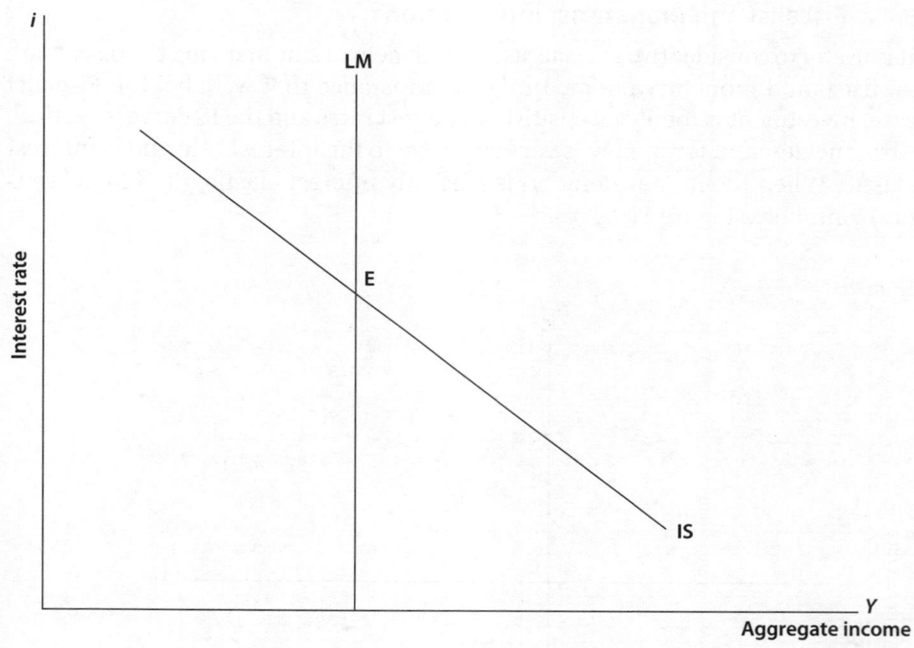

› Figure 8.19
Monetarist Case. When the demand for money is not at all sensitive to interest rates, the LM curve is vertical. In this case, monetary policy is very effective in influencing the level of aggregate income.

› Table 8.1
Effectiveness of Fiscal and Monetary Policy

	Fiscal Policy Effective	Monetary Policy Effective
Interest sensitivity of private sector expenditures	Private expenditures interest inelastic	Private expenditures not perfectly interest inelastic
Interest sensitivity of the demand for money	Demand for money interest elastic	Demand for money interest inelastic

MACROFOCUS 8.2

Zero Interest Rates and Macro Policy in Japan

The Japanese economy experienced a period of deflation and slow growth after the stock and real estate markets collapsed in the late 1980s. During the 1980s, the Japanese economy was allowed to overheat with real estate speculation combined with a loose lending policy by banks. In 1987, capital gains from securities and real estate transactions were 40 per cent larger than GDP (Bigsten, 2005). By 1989, the Bank of Japan started to dampen the speculation by raising interest rates and introducing lending regulations for real estate. This speeded up the burst of the speculative bubble and the Nikkei index fell from 38,915 in December 1989 to 7,000 in early 2003. It has been estimated that the decline in wealth was equal to two yeas of GDP. The decline in asset prices resulted in a massive deflation. During the 1990s, the recession in Japan resulted in a decline in goods prices. However, this was insufficient to restore the demand for goods. The deflationary episode in Japan was broad-based as prices for all major items including food, clothing, transportation, and durable goods declined. The year-on-year consumer price inflation rate has been negative for about six years since the second quarter of 1998. In an effort to stimulate the economy, the Bank of Japan board made a decision on 12 February 1999 to lower it to be "as low as possible". The overnight call rate in the money market has been virtually zero since this decision. When the nominal interest rate is zero, the economy is said to be in a liquidity trap. When prices start falling (a deflation), nominal interest rates begin to decline but the real cost of taking out loans rise and investment decline. With prices falling, real interest rates—nominal interest rates minus inflation—are high. Even though the nominal interest rate is 0 per cent, loans are expensive in real terms and businesses find interest payments high. With falling prices, consumers also tend to delay purchases and this reduces demand further. A decline in consumption is a decline in the demand for goods produced by firms and this further reduces firm profitability and the incentive to invest. This leads to a vicious spiral because banks realizing that business profitability is in doubt would be reluctant to lend, and in any case with low lending rates and zero lower bound on deposit rates, the profit margins on commercial lending are exceedingly low.

The interest rate offered by banks or for government bonds cannot be set below zero, as in that case, everyone would hold cash which has a nominal interest rate of 0 per cent, and nobody has an incentive to hold financial instruments with a negative nominal return. Monetary policy is then incapable of stimulating the economy when the zero bound has been reached. Can fiscal expansion be the solution? Since the bubble burst in 1990, the Japanese government has spent in excess of 120 trillion yen on more than 12 different programmes aimed at stimulating economic activity (Yu, 2003). Tax revenues declined with the burst of the bubble and fiscal deficits rose. Government expenditure also increased as part of a counter-cyclical fiscal package. Government debt accumulated to 108 per cent of GDP by 1999 and the deficit was (0 per cent of GDP (Ihori, Nakazato, and Kawade, 2003). Yet the economy did not recover from the deflationary spiral. Why? The Japanese had been saving a little more than 30 per cent of GDP, which had financed investment when the collapse of the 1990s occurred. With the decline in domestic investment demand by firms, the excess savings were placed abroad (a current account surplus) and they financed the fiscal deficit (a reduction in public savings). However, when the government borrows money, individuals realize the loans have to be paid back one day. The expectations of higher taxes in the future mean that expected lifetime post-tax earnings are lower and this induces lower consumption. Also, Japan has a large segment of old persons concerns about rising health burdens, and an anxiety regarding nursing care has caused the elderly to increase their savings. From 1990, therefore, household savings rates have gradually risen (Nakagawa, 1999) and fiscal policy has been ineffective in raising aggregate income.

8.5 IS–LM in India

Prior to the liberalization of the Indian economy over the 1990s, fiscal policy was the dominant tool of macroeconomy policy and monetary policy played a subservient role.[8] Increases in government expenditure—fiscal policy—prior to the 1990s were financed through two main mechanisms. The increased government borrowing was accommodated by hikes in the STATUTORY LIQUIDITY RATIO (SLR) imposed on commercial banks. This allowed the placement of government securities with commercial banks at below market rates of interest. By 1990, the SLR was 39 per cent. Second, the residual funding required was accommodated by the central government unilaterally accessing the central bank (the RBI) through the medium of 'ad hoc' TREASURY BILLS. This mechanism was routinely used in the 1980s to meet the government's requirement of funds. This resulted in a monetization of the deficit, which, in turn, expanded reserve money—the changes in net RBI credit to the central government accounted for 93 per cent of the variation in reserve money in the 1980s (Rangarajan, 1995). Such an automatic monetization of the deficit severely circumscribed the scope for discretionary monetary policy.

› The **statutory liquidity ratio** specifies the required holding of government securities as a fraction of the assets of the commercial bank.

› A **Treasury bill** or T-bill is a government bond with a maturity period not exceeding one year.

The growing fiscal deficit raised concerns about its SUSTAINABILITY and impact on the economy. Fiscal adjustment that proved difficult to sustain over the 1990s was finally sought to be achieved through the enactment of the Fiscal Responsibility and Budget Management Act in 2003 that institutionalized

› The **sustainability** of fiscal deficits is analysed in Chapter 12.

› An **open market operation** is a purchase (or sale) of government bonds from (to) the public by the central bank for the purpose of increasing (decreasing) the supply of bank reserves and the money supply.

› **Discretionary monetary policy** results form deliberate and conscious choices by the central bank on money supply (or the interest rate) so as to influence output and prices in the economy.

fiscal consolidation by a legislative mandate (see Chapter 12). Similarly, the autonomy of monetary policy was instituted through the phasing out of ad hocs and shifting government borrowing towards market rates of interest. As the suppression of the allocative role of interest rates in the money market was removed, the central bank could begin to conduct OPEN MARKET OPERATIONS. This raised the ability of the central bank to influence liquidity and removed the constraint on DISCRETIONARY MONETARY POLICY.

Figure 8.20 depicts the trends[9] in the fiscal deficit, real money supply, and output (GDP) growth, as well as the real interest rate over the period 1995–1996 to 2009–2010. The IS–LM approach informs us that the interest rate rises when the IS curve shifts to the right (fiscal policy). Also, an increase in income (output) raises the demand for money for transactions purposes and raises the interest rate in the money market as well. The interest rate declines, however, if there is an increase in real money supply that shifts the LM curve to the right (monetary policy).

Figure 8.20 reveals that from 1995–1996 to about 2000–2001, both fiscal and monetary policy were expansionary with a rise in the fiscal deficit and an increase in the real money supply growth rate. However, the impact of fiscal policy was larger than that of monetary policy in this period. The fiscal deficit (the extent of government borrowing) grew at a trend rate of 18.1 per cent during 1995–1996 to 2000–2001, compared to the real money supply trend growth rate of 10.3 per cent. In contrast, during 2001–2002 to 2005–2006, the fiscal deficit growth rate decelerated by a significant factor to a figure of -0.4 per cent, whereas real money supply growth decelerated marginally to 9.1 per cent. The large government borrowing programme in the period up to 2000–2001 shifted the IS curve more than the rightward shift of the LM curve and raised the real interest rate of the economy from 4.7 per cent in 1995–1996 to 7.4 per cent by 2000–2001. The high interest rate dampened the output increase in the period with a trend deceleration in output growth (Figure 8.20). In the period from 2001–2002 to 2005–2006, government borrowing retreated, whereas the expansionary character of monetary policy was not curtailed extensively. During this period, the LM curve shifted more to the right than the rightward shift of the IS curve. As a result, an interest rate decline accompanied the rise in output. Moreover, this is the period when improvements in the technology of financial transactions (such as credit and debit cards) reduced the demand for money for transactions purposes. The demand for money then grew at a

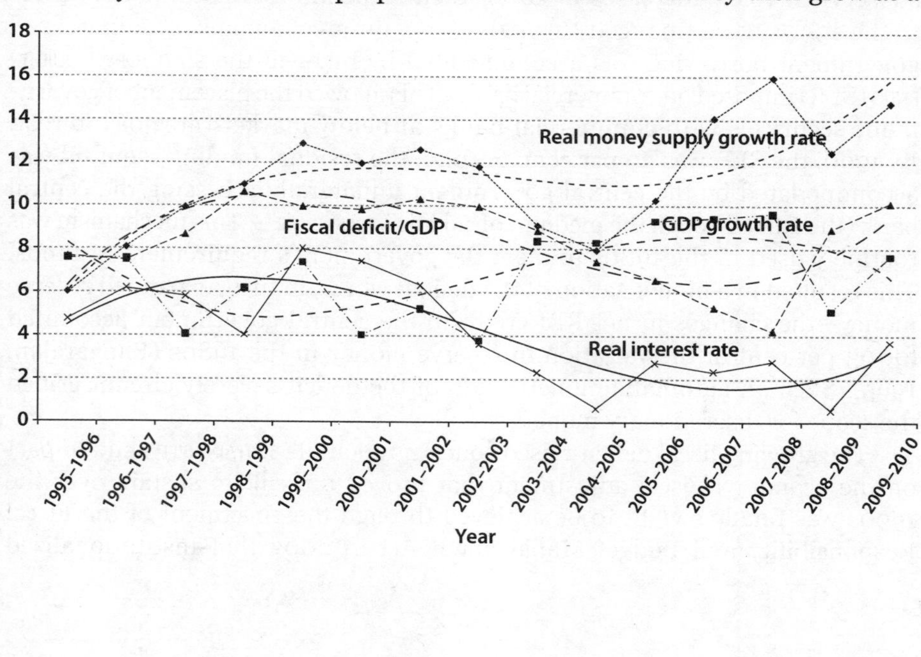

› **Figure 8.20**
Trendlines—Macroeconomic Policy Stance. During 1995 to 2000 fiscal policy was more expansionary than monetary policy and was accompanied by a rise in the interest rate and a diminishing rate of increase in income (GDP). From 2000 to 2005, monetary policy was more expansionary resulting in a decline in interest rates and an increase in the rate of growth in income. Again from 2006 onwards even though monetary policy was expansionary, fiscal policy was even more expansionary, causing interest rates to rise and GDP growth to moderate.

smaller pace despite the swifter growth in output and the LM curve shifted rightwards. An easy monetary policy that accommodated the output increases and a gradual reigning in of fiscal policy has, thus, accompanied the BOOM in the Indian economy from 2001 to 2006.

From 2006–2007 to 2009–2010, real money supply growth again picked up from the 9.1 per cent of the earlier period to a higher growth rate of 13.3 per cent. However, during this period the fiscal deficit—which had been seeing incremental reductions, began to increase rapidly and grew at the trend rate of 39.5 per cent from 2006–2007 to 2009–2010. As a result, the real interest rate again began to increase during the recent past. During this period the growth rate of GDP also moderated compared to the period from 2001 to 2006 (see the trendline for the GDP growth rate in Figure 8.20).

› During the first half of this decade, the LM curve shifted out to the right to a larger extent than the rightward shift of the IS curve. The Indian economy witnessed a decline in interest rates and an increase in output.

› During the latter half of the decade, even though the LM curve shifted to the right with a large growth rate of money supply than in the previous period, the IS curve shifted out significantly. Interest rates increased and GDP growth moderated.

Consistent with this explanation, Dua and Pandit (2002) found that the money supply and government expenditures have an impact on the interest rate in the Indian economy as predicted by IS–LM theory. However, as they emphasized, the interest rate is not only affected by domestic factors but also by external factors. In fact, they show how deviations of the domestic interest rate from the interest rate abroad such as $i > i^*$ leads to a capital inflow as predicted by the interest rate parity approach. In fact, capital inflows have become such a dominant component of money supply that the Economic Survey, 2002–2003, of the Government of India remarked that "from 9.1 per cent as at end March 1991, the share of net foreign exchange assets in reserve money ... became 100.7 per cent on 24 January 2003, which is close to a currency board situation" (Para 1.9). It is this extent of capital flows that has been the major factor behind the robust increase in money supply in the Indian economy. Managing capital flows has, therefore, become a predominant concern of monetary policy—an issue we examine in Chapter 11.

8.6 Ricardian Equivalence

One of the implications of the IS–LM analysis is that bond financing of government expenditures is more expansionary than tax financing of government expenditures. We have already seen that bond financing initially increases real income by $\Delta Y = \Delta G$ and the increased real income induces a further rise in consumption expenditure of $c_1 \Delta T$, where c_1 is the marginal propensity to consume out of an increase in income. The horizontal rightward shift of the IS curve is then equal to $\Delta Y = \Delta G + c_1 \Delta Y$, or, $\Delta Y = \Delta G/(1 - c_1)$.

In contrast, if the increase in government expenditure is financed by raising tax revenues, $\Delta G = \Delta T$, the initial increase in real income due to the increase in government expenditure like before induces an increase in consumption expenditure given by $c_1 \Delta Y$. However, now there is an offsetting effect due to a decline in consumption expenditure, as the increased taxes reduce disposable income available for spending.

From the consumption function (8.5), the reduction in consumption when taxes are increased is given by $c_1 \Delta Y$, which is equal to $c_1 \Delta G$ as $\Delta T = \Delta G$. Then, the rightward shift of the IS curve, when increased government expenditures are tax-financed, is given by:

$$\Delta Y = \Delta G + c_1 \Delta(Y - T)$$
$$= \Delta G + c_1 \Delta Y - c_1 \Delta G$$

or,
$$\Delta Y(1 - c_1) = \Delta G(1 - c_1)$$

or, $$\Delta Y|_{\text{tax}} = \Delta G < \frac{\Delta G}{1 - c_1} = \Delta Y|_{\text{bonds}}$$

The rightward shift of the IS curve is larger under bond financing than under tax financing. So, bond financing of government expenditure is more expansionary than tax financing. This occurs because bond financing does not reduce disposable income that is available for spending, whereas tax financing does reduce disposable income and lowers aggregate expenditure.

› **Ricardian equivalence** is the proposition that it is irrelevant in terms of the impact on aggregate income, whether increased government expenditure is financed by taxes or bonds.

The RICARDIAN EQUIVALENCE proposition, named after the classical economist David Ricardo (1772–1823), argues that the above reasoning is faulty and that essentially the impact on real income is the same whether government expenditure is tax financed or bond financed. In other words, the rightward shift of the IS curve is identical when government expenditures are tax financed or bond financed.

Ricardo's reasoning, which was resurrected in an influential article by Robert Barro (1974), is as follows. A government that issues bonds to finance an increase in expenditure must, in the future, pay interest, on these bonds. To pay this interest, taxes will eventually have to be increased. Far-sighted tax payers realize that the government has substituted a current tax, that it could have imposed to finance its expenditures, with a future tax. Thus, rational, self-interested individuals will respond by saving the implicit tax cut of bond financing until the future, when the government increases taxes to pay back the debt. At that time, the savings will be used to pay the increased taxes. As a result, government financing by borrowing has the equivalent impact as financing by taxation. This is because far sighted individuals save an amount that is equivalent to the future taxation by the government.

› **Ricardian equivalence** occurs when the government budget is intertemporally balanced, and individuals are forward-looking with perfect foresight about the future consequences of current actions.

For RICARDIAN EQUIVALENCE TO HOLD, two assumptions are required:

1. Individuals are forward looking and have perfect foresight
2. The government budget is intertemporally balanced

Both assumptions imply that when the government finances a given level of expenditures by selling bonds, households, recognizing that the budget is intertemporally balanced, will have the foresight that higher taxes will be levied in the future to pay back the borrowings on the bonds sold today. Hence, the tax burden for individuals who have foresight is not just current taxes, but rather current taxes plus the present value of the taxes in the future that will be required to pay the interest on current bond sales.

For simplicity, assume that the government does not resort to money financing and each government bond pays a coupon of INR 1 per annum. Then, the market price of a bond is:

$$P_B = \frac{1}{i}$$

Let ΔB be the number of bonds sold to finance the increased government expenditures. Then, the nominal value of these bonds is:

$$\text{Value of Bonds} = P_B \Delta B = \frac{\Delta B}{i}$$

The annual interest payments on the bonds sold will be:

$$\text{Interest Payments on the Bonds} = i\left(\frac{\Delta B}{i}\right) = \Delta B$$

The government will have to make interest payments of INR ΔB in each period and it will make these payments by increasing taxes. Hence, the present value (PV) of implied future taxes is:

$$\begin{aligned}\text{PV (Future Taxes)} &= \text{PV (Interest Payments)}\\ &= \frac{\Delta B}{1+i} + \frac{\Delta B}{(1+i)^2} + \dots\\ &= \frac{\Delta B}{i}\end{aligned}$$

The real present value of implied future taxes will then be $\Delta B/iP$. Thus, the current period tax burden on individuals who have perfect foresight and realize the intertemporal nature of the budget—individuals who follow the propositions of Ricardian Equivalence (RE)—is:

$$T_{RE} = T + \frac{\Delta B}{iP} \tag{8.15}$$

The current period government budget equation states that current government expenditure is financed by current taxes and the real value of debt issued to finance current expenditures, given by $P_B \Delta B/P = \Delta B/iP$.

The current period budget constraint of the government can then be written as:

$$G = T + \frac{\Delta B}{iP} \tag{8.16}$$

But the right-hand side of this government budget constraint is none other than the current period tax burden experienced by individuals subject to Ricardian equivalence as evinced by the previous equation. This makes the appropriate definition of disposable income when Ricardian Equivalence propositions, hold as:

$$Y^d_{RE} = Y - T_{RE} = Y - G \tag{8.17}$$

In the IS–LM approach described earlier, the current burden of the government is the current taxes levied, T, that affects the amount of disposable income in the hands of individuals. In the Ricardian approach, the *current burden of government*, by contrast, as given in Eq. (8.17) is the goods and services it absorbs, G. Accordingly, equilibrium in the goods market can be rewritten as:

$$\begin{aligned}Y &= C + I + G\\ &= c_0 + c_1(Y - G) - c_2(i - \pi^e) + I + G\end{aligned}$$

or,

$$Y(1 - c_1) = c_0 + G(1 - c_1) - c_2(i - \pi^e) + I \tag{8.18}$$

This leads to two propositions.

Proposition I: It is irrelevant whether increased government expenditure is financed by taxes or bonds.

From Eq. (8.18),

$$\frac{\Delta Y}{\Delta G} = \frac{1 - c_1}{1 - c_1} = 1$$

or,

$$\Delta Y = \Delta G$$

Hence, the IS curve under Ricardian Equivalence shifts out by the same distance, irrespective of whether government expenditures are tax financed or bond financed. This is because bond sales impose the same burden on individuals as the taxes that could have been imposed in their place.

Proposition II: A tax cut financed by bond sales has no effect on output.

This is due to the bond sales having the implication that higher future taxes will have to be levied to pay back the interest on the bonds. The present value of the higher future taxes is equal to the present tax cut. Moreover, disposable income, as defined in Eq. (8.17), has not changed and the IS curve has consequently not shifted out. Recall that the disposable income measured in a standard way is used for consumption expenditure or saved:

$$Y^d = Y - T = C + S$$

or,
$$S = Y - C - T$$

Under Ricardian equivalence, $C = C(Y - G, i - \pi^e)$ rather than Eq. (8.4), so that,

$$S = Y - C(Y - G, i - \pi^e) - T$$

With G unchanged when current taxes are substituted by debt,

$$\Delta S = -\Delta T$$

The change in taxes, thus, has an equal and opposite effect on savings. Tax cuts are saved completely, unlike in conventional IS–LM theory where a tax cut ($\Delta T < 0$) increases disposable income by the amount $(Y - \Delta T)$, and a fraction $c_1 (Y - \Delta T)$ of this is spent by individuals. This shifts the conventional IS curve outwards.

In the Ricardian Equivalence approach, governments should not bother too much about deficits financed by debt. This is because, in macroeconomic terms, what the government dissaves, the private sector saves and aggregate savings in the economy do not get altered. People just save to pay for higher anticipated future taxes when the government dissaves.

Two reasons advocated as to why this proposition may not hold are myopia and liquidity constraints. Keynesians, in particular, argue that those who advocate Ricardian equivalence give people too much credit for looking far ahead into the future. Most people are shortsighted and myopic and the time horizon of their decision making is about a year or so. Moreover, most people face constraints on the availability of credit to meet spending needs at various points of time in their lives.

Instead of saving the proceeds of a tax cut, individuals who are subject to liquidity constraints may allocate the tax cut to higher consumption that they are compelled to curtail due to constraints on the availability of credit. For these and other reasons[10], many economists hold the view that Ricardian Equivalence holds true only to a limited extent, and that budget deficits and the mode of their financing do indeed matter.

In developing countries, where financial systems are underdeveloped, capital markets lack depth and are subject to financial repression, and there is considerable uncertainty regarding the incidence of taxes, the Ricardian propositions may not hold. Haque and Montiel (1989) were unable to find evidence of debt neutrality for 15 out of a group of 16 developing countries. Veidyanathan (1993), using a larger sample of 60 countries and data covering three decades, was unable to detect any significant effects of public sector deficits on private savings, and attributed this to individuals in these countries being subject to borrowing constraints. However, though individuals may not have perfect foresight, they are indeed forward-looking, as any policy maker who is smart realizes fast on the job. Individuals anticipate policy, figure out if they are credible, and take offsetting action if necessary.

SUMMARY

- Walras' Law states that the sum of the excess demand for money, bonds, and current output must equal zero.
- Walras' Law allows macroeconomics to explicitly analyse the markets for goods output and money and ignore the bond market.
- The nominal interest rate is the sum of the real interest rate and the expected rate of inflation.
- Consumption is a positive function of aggregate income and is negatively related to the *ex ante* real interest rate.
- Investment is positively related to the productivity of capital and negatively to the *ex ante* real interest rate.
- Equilibrium in the product market is given by the condition that savings—private plus government savings—equals investment.

$$[(Y - T) - C] + (T - G) = I$$

- An increase in income increases disposable income and aggregate savings.
- An increase in taxes reduces private savings by a fraction but increases government savings by the extent of the increase in taxes with the net effect being a rise in aggregate saving.
- An increase in expected inflation reduces the real interest rate and makes savings for the purpose of future consumption less attractive.
- An increase in government expenditure reduces public savings and aggregate savings.
- The IS curve is downward sloping in nominal interest rate-aggregate income space as a rise in income raises the supply of savings to the capital market and causes the interest rate to decline.
- The IS curve shifts to the right with an increase in government expenditure as the increase in government bonds causes bond prices to decline and the interest rate to rise.
- An increase in taxes increases aggregate savings and the nominal interest rate declines, thereby shifting the IS curve leftwards.
- An increase in the productivity of capital increases the demand for investment and the interest rate thereby shifting the IS curve out to the right.
- An increase in expected inflation leaves aggregate savings and investment unchanged but shifts the IS curves out to the right as the nominal interest rate rises.
- The IS curve is steeper the lower is the responsiveness of aggregate investment to the interest rate.
- The LM curve is upward sloping in nominal interest rate—aggregate income space as an increase in income raises the demand for real money balances which results in a rise in the interest rate.
- The LM curve shifts to the right if there is an increase in the money supply as interest rates decline in response to individuals rebalancing their financial portfolio by purchasing bonds when this occurs.
- The LM curve is inelastic (elastic) when the demand for money is interest inelastic (elastic).
- The IS–LM model is appropriate for the short run where wages and prices do not change and there is underutilization of capacity.
- An expansionary monetary policy in the IS–LM is more effective the more interest inelastic is the demand for money as long as private expenditures on consumption and investment are not interest inelastic.
- An expansionary fiscal policy in the IS–LM model is more effective the more interest inelastic are private investment and consumption expenditures and the more interest elastic is the demand for money.
- Crowding out occurs when the stimulative effects of fiscal policy are offset by a reduction in consumption and investment due to the rise in the interest rate.
- Crowding out is larger the larger is the interest sensitivity of investment and consumption expenditure, and the smaller is the interest sensitivity of money demand.
- Ricardian equivalence is the proposition that it is irrelevant in terms of the impact on aggregate income whether increased government expenditure is financed by taxes or bonds.
- For Ricardian equivalence to hold the government budget must be inter-temporally balanced and individuals should be forward looking with perfect foresight about the future consequences of current actions.

NOTES

1. We are therefore assuming the substitution effect dominates the income effect—see the section on Effects of interest rates in the chapter on consumption.
2. The lifetime budget constraint will then be $C_1 + C_2/1+r = (Y_1 - T) + (Y_2 - T)/1+r$. Also, we are not considering private.
3. For simplicity taxes in this chapter are lump-sum taxes. This assumption does not affect the basic results.
4. If some government expenditure is investment expenditure such as on infrastructure, then, that can increase the productivity of private investment expenditure. We would then write $a = a$ (government investment) in (12). It is well known that infrastructure expands market opportunities and results in gains to the economy in terms of increasing the scale and efficiency of production and output.

5. In this chapter, we also do not model expectations endogenously. Expectations will be deemed to be exogenous and do not alter in response to specific policy changes. Expected inflation is therefore treated as exogenous.
6. Recall from Chapter 2 that $M^s = C^P + D_R$, or money supply is currency in circulation plus deposits.
7. The increase in the demand for money also follows directly from Eq. (8.14).
8. These issues are further discussed in Chapters 12 and 14.
9. These trend lines in Figure 8.20 are the result of fitting a polynomial to each data series.
10. For instance, the tax changes considered in the theory are lump-sum tax changes such as tax rebates. Changes in marginal tax rates, however, influence decisions on production and the supply of labour.
11. Alternatively we could obtain equation (A8.2.7) by setting the interest rate in the IS equation (A8.12) equal to the interest rate in the LM equation (A8.2.4) and solving that expression for Y. Then, (A8.2.7) follows directly from this solution to the IS–LM model for Y.

TEST YOURSELF

1. What is Walras' Law and how does macroeconomics employ it to eliminate the explicit treatment of the bond market?
2. Why is the IS curve a depiction of equilibrium in the product market? What factors cause the IS curve to shift and in what direction (outwards or inwards)?
3. Why is the LM curve a depiction of equilibrium in the money market? What causes the LM curve to shift to the right or left?
4. What makes the IS curve and the LM curve steeper—that is, more inelastic, and why?
5. What factors restrict the effectiveness of using fiscal policy as a means to increasing aggregate income? When is fiscal policy most effective?
6. Under what circumstances is fiscal policy more effective in influencing the level of income in the economy than monetary policy and vice versa?
7. "Tax financing of government expenditure is less expansionary than bond financing". Examine the conditions under which this proposition is true.
8. Demonstrate using the IS–LM model whether it may be necessary to have negative interest rates in order that the economy achieves a given level of income that policy makers seek.
9. Suppose that in an economy with a balanced budget the government in order to increase citizen voter support decides to temporarily reduce tax rates. After a year the tax rate will return to its original level. Meanwhile the government issues perpetual bonds to cover the cost of the tax cut. What would be the impact of the tax cut on domestic saving and consumption?
10. In the IS–LM set up suppose that the responsiveness of investment and consumption to the interest rate reduces. In order to have the same final impact on aggregate income would the change in the interest rate be required to be larger or smaller?

ONLINE APPLICATION

1. Go to the home page of the Reserve Bank of India. URL: www.rbi.org.in/home.aspx.
2. Click on the "DataBase" icon.
3. Then under the classification of Annual data, click on "Handbook of Statistics on Indian Economy."
4. Click on "Table 172: Components of the Money Stock" and create a spreadsheet of monthly data on Narrow Money (M1) for the period April 2006 to June 2010.
5. Then click on "Table 169: Wholesale Price Index—Monthly Average" and in your spreadsheet insert monthly data on the wholesale price index from April 2006 to June 2010.
6. The wholesale prices are in the form of indices. To create an indexed data series of real money balances index the data you inserted in Step 4. For example, let the M1 data for April 2006, INR 8517.53 billion, equal the index value of 1000. In that case the index for May 2006 for INR 8160.97 billion is 958.14, and so on.
7. Divide the index for M1 by the price index of the Wholesale Price Index in that month to obtain an index for real money balances.
8. Next go back to the RBI Handbook of Statistics on Indian Economy. Click on "Table 179: Weighted Average Call Money Rates". Take data for the corresponding period April 2006 to June 2010 on the average call money interest rate each month.
9. Create a graph depicting the Real Money balance index on the horizontal axis and the interest rate on the vertical axis. Does the real money balance vary inversely with the interest rate?
10. You would have noticed that there is no clear cut relationship between the money balances and the interest rate. Create a graph between the change in the interest rate in a year and the change in the real money balances in that year and fit a linear trend to that graph. Do you would observe a negative relationship between changes in money balances and changes in the interest rate.
11. Give reasons as to why the relationship between real money balances and the interest rate may not be strictly negative.

Appendix 8.1 Walras' Law

To understand Walras' Law, consider the income and expenditure statement of households, firms, and government. The expenditure of an agent is income left over after deducting necessary payments. For a household, income is obtained in the form of wages from the labour market [the real wage times the labour supply, or $(w/p)N$] 'and distributed profits received by virtue of their ownership in firms (Π_d). From this income, if we deduct taxes on households' net of transfers received, T_h, we obtain the disposable income of the household given by $(w/p)N + \Pi_d - T_h$. This disposable income must be consumed, C, or saved. Savings will be in the form of additions to real money balances and additions to the holding of bonds. When we were looking at the budget constraints Chapter 6, we defined savings as the additions to real money balances and bonds because we were focusing on the private sector which comprises households and firms together. In that case, the liabilities of firms such as their equity issued is the asset of a household. The savings of one entity—households—is a source of funds or liability for the other entity—firms. We are here following that account by disregarding the use of funds by households such as in deposits at banks, which are loaned to firms or put in to the equities of firms. We can then define the savings of the household (S_h) as the additions to the holdings of real money balances and bonds:

$$S_h = \left(\frac{M^d}{P} - \frac{M}{P}\right) + \left(\frac{B^d}{iP} - \frac{B}{iP}\right)$$

or,

$$S_h = (m^d - m) + (b^d - b)$$

where $m^d = (M^d/P)$ is the real demand for money balances, $m = (M/P)$ is the holding of real money balances at the beginning of the period, $b^d = (B^d/\, iP)$ is the real demand for bonds, and $b = (B/iP)$ is the bonds held at the beginning of the period. The budget constraint of the household, then, is, disposable income equals consumption plus savings of the household, which is:

$$(w\,/\,p)N + \Pi_d - T_h = C + S_h = C + (m^d - m) + (b^d - b)$$

The constraint of the firm can be specified as follows. The revenues received by the firm from sales of their products less taxes to be paid by them (net of transfers), T_f, must equal the sum of payments made to workers, payments made for adding to their capacity to produce (investment), and payments as a return to the holders of equity in the firm (distributed profits). Firms do hold money balances as well, which we are not including here for simplicity—in essence we have counted private sector holdings of money balances to be done by households on behalf of households and firms. Also, liabilities of firms such as the stock of equity are not being considered as these are a corresponding asset of a private sector agent—the household. The revenues the firm receives come from the sale of products to households for consumption, to other firms for investment, and to government. The revenues equals payments constraint the firm faces may then be written as:

$$C + I + G - T_f = (w/P)N + I + \Pi_d$$

Then, retained profits of the firm (Π_r) that is used to finance investment expenditure the is given by:

$$\Pi_r = C + I + G - T_f - (w/P)N - \Pi_d = I$$

Since in a closed economy, $Y = C + I + G$, we may write this as:

$$\Pi_r = Y - T_f - (w/P)N - \Pi_d = I$$

Finally, the third agent—apart from households and firms—is government. Government receives revenues from taxes (net of transfers) on households (T_h), and taxes (net of transfers) on firms (T_f). The expenditure of the government is G, and if this expenditure is greater than revenues, there is a deficit which must be financed. The government deficit is financed by issuing new bonds, b^s-b, or issuing new money, m^s-m. The government budget constraint then is:

$$G - T_f - T_h = (m^s - m) + (b^s - b)$$

We now write the three constraints associated with the three agents in the economy together:

Households: $$(w/p)N + \Pi_d - T_h = C + (m^d - m) + (b^d - b)$$

Firms: $$Y - T_f - (w/P)N - \Pi_d = I$$

Government: $$(m^s - m) + (b^s - b) = G - T_f - T_h$$

If we add these three constraints together and cancel terms, we obtain,

$$(m^s - m^d) + (b^s - b^d) + (Y - C - I - G) = 0$$

› **Walras' Law** states that the sum of the excess demand for money, bonds, and current output must equal zero.

This is WALRAS' LAW—the sum of the excess demand for money, bonds and current output must equal zero. We could rearrange this as:

$$(b - b^d) = -(Y - C - I - G) - (m - m^d)$$

This states that the excess demand for bonds (the left-hand side) must correspond to an excess supply of some other quantity—current output and/or money (the right-hand side).

Hence, once we have specified the workings of the output and the money market, the specification of the bond market becomes superfluous. This is why there is an explicit treatment of the markets for commodities (or output) and money in modern macroeconomics, and the bond market is ignored.

Appendix 8.2 The Algebra of Crowding Out

The increased government expenditure as a result of expansionary fiscal policy raises real income initially to Y_2. The increased income causes a rise in the demand for money for transaction purposes. In the face of a fixed supply of money, the increased money demand [see Figure 8.9] causes the interest rate to rise. In symbolic form, the increase in the interest rate in what follows will be written as Δi. The rise in the interest rate induces a DECLINE IN INVESTMENT EXPENDITURE ($\Delta I|_{\Delta i}$)—see Eq. (8.6)—due to a decline in the present value of investment projects, and a decline in the interest-sensitive component of consumption expenditure ($\Delta C|_{\Delta i}$)—see Eq. (8.5)—as the attractiveness of future consumption increases.

› The **change in variable *V*** that occurs as a result of a change in the interest rate is written as $\Delta V|_{\Delta i}$

The decline in the interest-sensitive elements of private expenditures reduces income from Y_2 to Y_1 in Figure 8.15. In the process, despite the rise in interest rates which choke off some investment and consumption, the final equilibrium level of income is higher after the increased government spending. This rise in income induces an increase in the income-sensitive component of consumption expenditure ($\Delta C|_{\Delta Y}$)—see Eq. (8.5). The constrained increase in income—Y_0Y_2 in Figure 8.15—can then be thought of as the net outcome of:

1. An expansion of income arising from the increase in government spending—ΔG
2. A decline of income arising from the induced decline in investment and that part of consumption which is sensitive to interest rates—$\Delta I|_{\Delta i}$, $\Delta C|_{\Delta i}$
3. An expansion in income arising from an induced increase in consumption expenditure as income rises —$\Delta C|_{\Delta Y}$.

Hence,

$$\Delta Y = \Delta G + (\Delta I|_{\Delta i} + \Delta C|_{\Delta i}) + \Delta C|_{\Delta Y} \quad \text{(A8.2.1)}$$

From Eq. (8.5),

$$\Delta C|_{\Delta Y} = c_1 \Delta Y$$

Substituting this expression into (A8.2.1),

$$\Delta Y = \Delta G + (\Delta I|_{\Delta i} + \Delta C|_{\Delta i}) + c_1 \Delta Y$$

Taking the terms in ΔY on the left-hand side we can write:

$$\Delta Y = \frac{\Delta G}{1 - c_1} + \frac{\Delta I|_{\Delta i} + \Delta C|_{\Delta i}}{1 - c_1} \quad \text{(A8.2.2)}$$

The first term on the right-hand side of Eq. (A8.2.2)— $\Delta G/(1-c_1)$—is the unconstrained increase in income due to a rise in government expenditure—Y_0Y_2 in Figure 8.15. The second term on the right-hand side of Eq. (A8.2.2) is the induced fall in investment and consumption expenditure when the interest rate increases—Y_1Y_2 in Figure 8.15.

The rise in interest rates discourages investment spending as investment is inversely related to the interest rate. It discourages consumption spending as well because future consumption (or savings) becomes more attractive with a rise in the interest rate. The decline in investment and consumption is given from Eqs (8.5) and (8.6) by:

$$\Delta I|_{\Delta i} = -\, b\Delta i$$

$$\Delta C|_{\Delta i} = -\, c_2\Delta i$$

The induced decline in investment and consumption is, therefore,

$$\Delta C|_{\Delta i} + \Delta I|_{\Delta i} = -(c_2 + b)\Delta i \tag{A8.2.3}$$

What is the extent of the rise in interest rates? The initial increase in income at Y_2 induced an increase in the real demand for money for transactions purposes. With unchanged money supply, this demand is met through the sale of bonds which reduces the price of bonds and raises the interest rate. With money supply given as $M^s = \bar{M}$ and money demand as in Eq. (8.14), we have,

$$\frac{M^d}{P} = \frac{\bar{M}}{P} = h + nY - ei$$

or,

$$i = \frac{h + nY - (\bar{M}/P)}{e} \tag{A8.2.4}$$

Hence, the rise in the rate of interest when income rises by ΔY is:

$$\Delta i = \frac{n}{e}\Delta Y \tag{A8.2.5}$$

This rise in the interest rate is represented by the distance i_0, i_1 in Figure 8.15. Substituting Eq. (A8.2.5) into Eq. (A8.2.3) gives us the decline in consumption and investment that results from a rise in the interest rate as:

$$\Delta C|_{\Delta i} + \Delta I|_{\Delta i} = -(c_2 + b)\frac{n}{e}\Delta Y \tag{A8.2.6}$$

Substituting the expression (A8.2.6) into (A8.2.2), we obtain,

$$\Delta Y = \frac{\Delta G}{1 - c_1} - \frac{(c_2 + b)(n/e)}{1 - c_1}\Delta Y$$

Multiplying throughout by $(1-c_1)$,

$$(1 - c_1)\Delta Y = \Delta G - (c_2 + b)\frac{n}{e}\Delta Y$$

or,

$$\Delta Y\left[(1 - c_1) + (c_2 + b)\frac{n}{e}\right] = \Delta G$$

or,

$$\Delta Y = \frac{\Delta G}{(1 - c_1) + (c_2 + b)(n/e)} \tag{A8.2.7}$$

This represents the distance Y_0, Y_1 in Figure 8.15.[11] Even though the rise in government expenditure caused real income to rise initially by a multiple amount, $1/(1-c_1)$, the induced rise in the interest rate caused investment and consumption expenditures to decline by a multiple amount $[(c_2 + b)(n/e)\Delta Y/(1 - c_1)]$.

› **Crowding out** occurs when the stimulative effects of fiscal policy are offset by a reduction in interest-sensitive consumption and investment due to a rise in the interest rate.

The induced reduction in consumption and investment, which offsets the effect of the increase in government spending, is referred to as CROWDING OUT. The tendency for the stimulative effects of fiscal policy, to be offset by an induced decline in private expenditures, is called crowding out. As can be seen from Eq. (A2.2.7), CROWDING OUT IS LARGER (the final impact on income is smaller),

› **The larger the crowding out**, the larger is the interest-sensitivity of investment and consumption expenditure, the larger is the income-sensitivity of money demand, and the smaller is the interest sensitivity of money demand.

1. The larger is b—(the interest-sensitivity of investment is large)
2. The larger is n—(the income-sensitivity of money demand is large)
3. The smaller is e—(the interest-sensitivity of money demand is relatively small)
4. The larger is c_2—(the interest-sensitivity of consumption expenditure is large)

Appendix 8.3 IS–LM in Japan

The LM curve is depicted as upward-sloping because, as the interest rate rises, the demand for money falls and equilibrium in the money market that brings the demand for money in line with the available money supply is obtained by an increase in income. Consider the situation in the money market where the demand for money schedule at a level of income Y_0 is given by $M^d(Y_0)/P_0$, as shown in panel A of Figure A8.3.1. The supply of money is given by the supply schedule (M_0/P_0). Then, the demand for money equals the supply of money at a nominal rate of interest, that is zero. This interest rate of zero and income level of Y_0 combination is depicted in panel B of the diagram along the horizontal axis where the interest rate is zero at the point Y_0.

If income increases to Y_1, then there is an increase in the demand for money for transactions purposes, and the demand for money schedule shifts to the right to $M^d(Y_1)/P_0$. For a given money supply, the increase in the demand for money causes an increase in the interest rate to i_1. This combination of an interest rate of i_1 and an income level of Y_1 is depicted in panel B as the point (i_1, Y_1). Similarly, if the level of income in the economy increases further to Y_2, there is a further requirement of money in order to transact in those increased incomes. Now, the money demand schedule shifts even further to the right in panel A to $M^d(Y_2)/P_0$. The interest rate rises to i_2 and the combination of this interest rate and income is depicted as the point (i_2, Y_2) in panel B. Joining the interest rate–income combinations in panel B that depict various points of equality between money demand and supply in panel A as the level of income varies, gives us the LM curve. In panel B, the LM curve has a flat segment along the horizontal axis up to the level of income Y_0. Along this flat segment, the economy is considered to be in a LIQUIDITY TRAP.

› When the money market situation is such that the nominal rate of interest is zero, the economy is said to be in a liquidity trap. This term originates from the fact that in this situation any increase in money supply or **liquidity** is trapped or willingly held by the public as the alternative financial asset, bonds, gives an equivalent return.

Recall that the nominal return on money is zero, whereas the return on a bond is inversely related to its price. With a known coupon (say INR 1) on the bond, the return on the bond is given by $i = 1/P_B$, where P_B is the price of the bond. Hence, the interest rate is the return on bonds. When the interest rate is zero, then the nominal return on bonds ($i = 0$) and on money (0) are identical. With both bonds and money paying the same nominal interest rate—zero—people are indifferent about whether to hold their financial wealth as money or bonds. This is the liquidity trap.

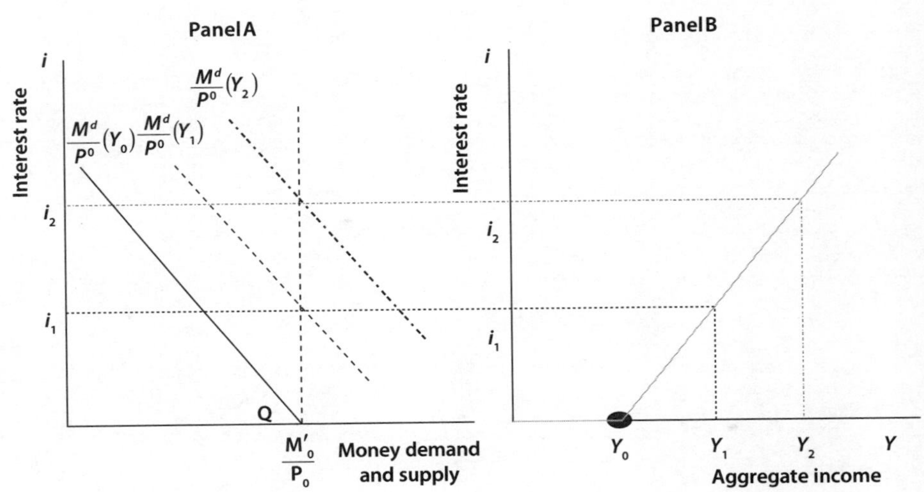

› **Figure A8.3.1**
The LM Curve with a Liquidity Trap. When the nominal interest rate is zero, individuals hold enough money for transactions purposes. They are also willing to hold any increase in money supply as both bonds and money yield the same nominal return of zero. When this occurs, the LM curve is horizontal along the income axis and the economy is in a liquidity trap.

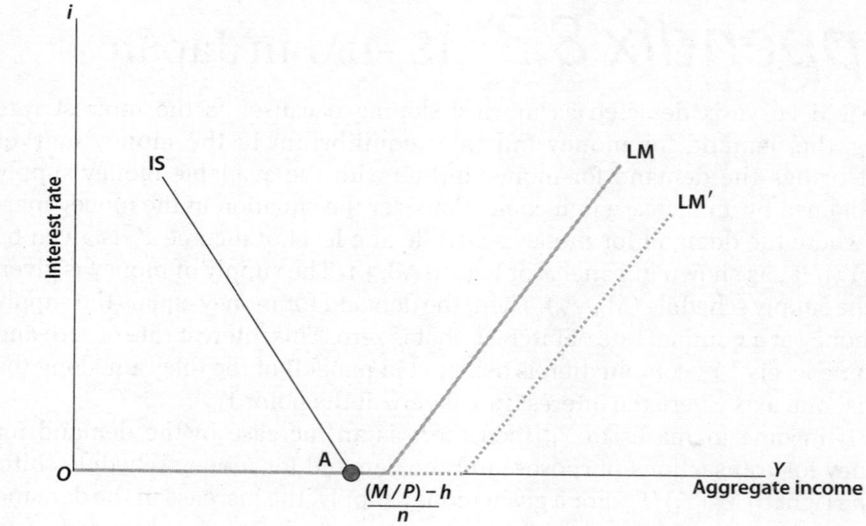

› Figure A8.3.2
Monetary Policy in a Liquidity Trap. In a liquidity trap, expansionary monetary policy that shifts the LM curve to the right has no impact on income as individuals willingly hold the extra money and there is no impact on the interest rate. Interest-sensitive private expenditures such as investment expenditures are, thus, unaffected. Aggregate income does not change.

Now, suppose the IS and LM curves intersect at point A in Figure A8.3.2. If the central bank increases the money supply, the LM curve shifts out rightwards to LM′. The IS and LM curves still intersect at the same point A and the expansionary monetary policy has had no effect on output. So, a central bank is powerless in a liquidity trap to affect output. This arises because the additional money is readily held by individuals at an unchanged interest rate of zero—there is no sense in reallocating the portfolio to purchase bonds with the increased money balances, as the return on bonds is also zero.

Even though the central bank may attempt to cut interest rates (the implication of an expansionary monetary policy) prices declined at a faster rate in Japan (see Macrofocus box 8.2), leading to deflation. A rise in deflation shifts the IS curve to the left—see the discussion around Figure 8.6—and output declines. A combination of a liquidity trap and deflation led the Japanese economy into a recessionary phase in the 1990s.

9

Aggregate Demand and Aggregate Supply

CRITICAL QUESTIONS

» *What is aggregate demand?*

» *How are the equilibrium output and price level determined when the aggregate supply is Keynesian and when they occur as a result of mistaken expectations?*

» *How does the presence of policy lags affect activist (discretionary) policymaking?*

» *Who are real business cycle theorists and why do they privilege real supply side shocks over demand shocks in understanding business cycles?*

9.1 The Aggregate Demand (AD) Curve

We use the IS–LM model to develop the aggregate demand (AD) for the economy as a whole. The IS–LM model relates the nominal interest rate to output, whereas AD relates the price level to output. The IS–LM model is useful for examining the effect of various shocks on the interest rate and on variables such as savings and investment that depend on the interest rate.

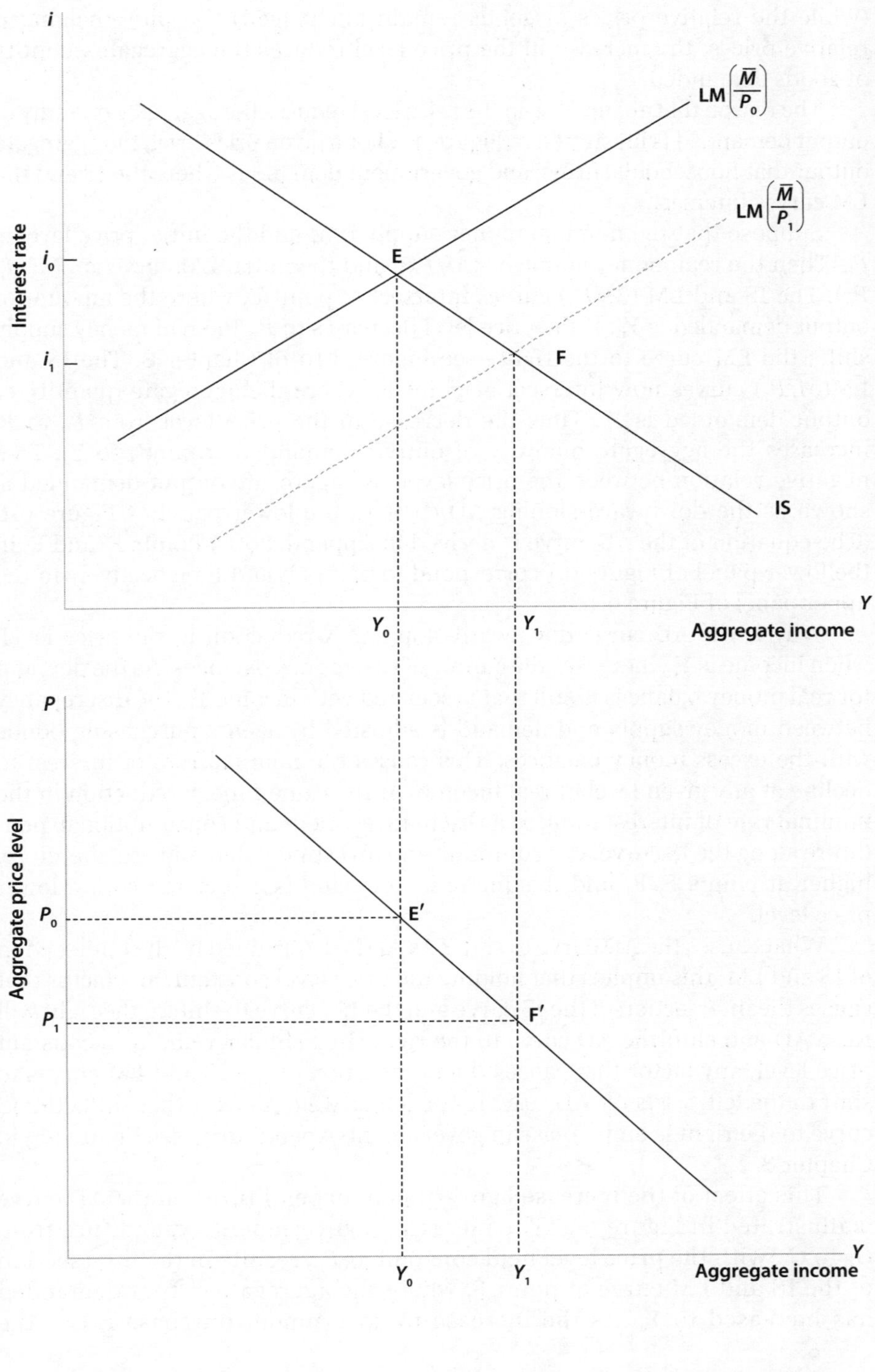

› **Figure 9.1**
The Aggregate Demand Curve. A reduction in the price level increases the money supply and shifts the LM curve to the right (the upper panel). The reduction in the price is, therefore, associated with an increased aggregate income (the lower panel).

However, when discussing issues related to the price level or inflation and relating that to unemployment, using an AD and supply framework is more convenient.

› The **aggregate demand (AD) curve** is the relationship between the real quantity demanded of final goods and services and the general price level.

The AD CURVE depicts the relation between the aggregate quantity of goods demanded,[1] $C + I + G$, and the price level, P. Though the AD curve slopes downward like the curve for a single product, the AD curve relates the aggregate quantity of output demanded to the general price level, whereas the demand for a single good relates the demand for that good to the price of that good as compared to the prices of other goods. Thus, when the prices of all goods increase by five per cent, the price level, P, also increases by five per cent (while the relative prices of goods remain unchanged). Despite unchanged relative prices, the increase in the price level reduces the aggregate quantity of goods demanded.

The reason that an increase in the price level reduces the aggregate quantity of output demanded is illustrated in Figure 9.1. For a given price level, the aggregate output that households, firms, and government demand is where the IS and the LM curves intersect.

Suppose that the nominal money supply is $\bar{M}$ and the initial price level is P_0. Then the real money supply is $(\bar{M}/P_0)$, and the initial LM curve is LM($\bar{M}/P_0$). The IS and LM ($\bar{M}/P_0$) curves intersect at point E, where the amount of output demanded is Y_0. If the price level decreases to P_1, the real money supply shifts the LM curve to the right—see Figure 8.10 of Chapter 8. The IS and LM($\bar{M}/P_1$) curves now intersect at point F, where the aggregate quantity of output demanded is Y_1. Thus the decrease in the price level from P_0 to P_1 increases the aggregate quantity of output demanded from Y_0 to Y_1. This negative relation between the price level and aggregate output demanded is shown as the downward-sloping AD CURVE in the lower panel of Figure 9.1. (The equation of the AD curve is derived in Appendix 9.1.) Points E′ and F′ in the lower panel of Figure 9.1 correspond to points E and F respectively in the upper panel of Figure 9.1.

› The aggregate demand **curve** relates a given price level to the demand for output and is derived from simultaneous equilibrium in the goods (IS) and money (LM) markets.

Why is the AD curve downward-sloping? A reduction in the price level, when income is Y_0, increases the supply of real money balances. As the demand for real money balances is still that associated with income Y_0, the discrepancy between money supply and demand is adjusted by agents purchasing bonds with the excess money balances. This causes the nominal rate of interest to decline at any given level of real income. At the same time, a reduction in the nominal rate of interest induces a rise in investment and consumption expenditure along the IS curve. Consumption and investment demand are, therefore, higher at points F, F′ and this increased demand is associated with a lower price level.

What causes the AD curve to shift? As AD is determined by the intersection of IS and LM, this implies that holding the price level constant, any factor that causes the intersection of the IS curve and the LM curve to shift to the right will raise AD and shift the AD curve to the right. In a similar vein, for a constant price level, any factor that causes the intersection of the IS and LM curves to shift to the left, SHIFTS THE AD CURVE to the left as well. A factor that shifts the IS curve to the right is an increase in government expenditure—see Figure 8.3 in Chapter 8.

› Changes in any variable other than the price level that shift the IS and LM curves, such as fiscal and monetary policy, consumption spending, or investment expenditure, **shift the aggregate demand curve.**

This effect of the increased government expenditures on the AD curve is illustrated in Figure 9.2. The increase in government expenditure from G_0 to G_1, with the price level held constant at P_0, results in the intersection of the IS and LM curve at point F, where the aggregate output demanded has increased to Y_1. As the increase in government purchase raises the

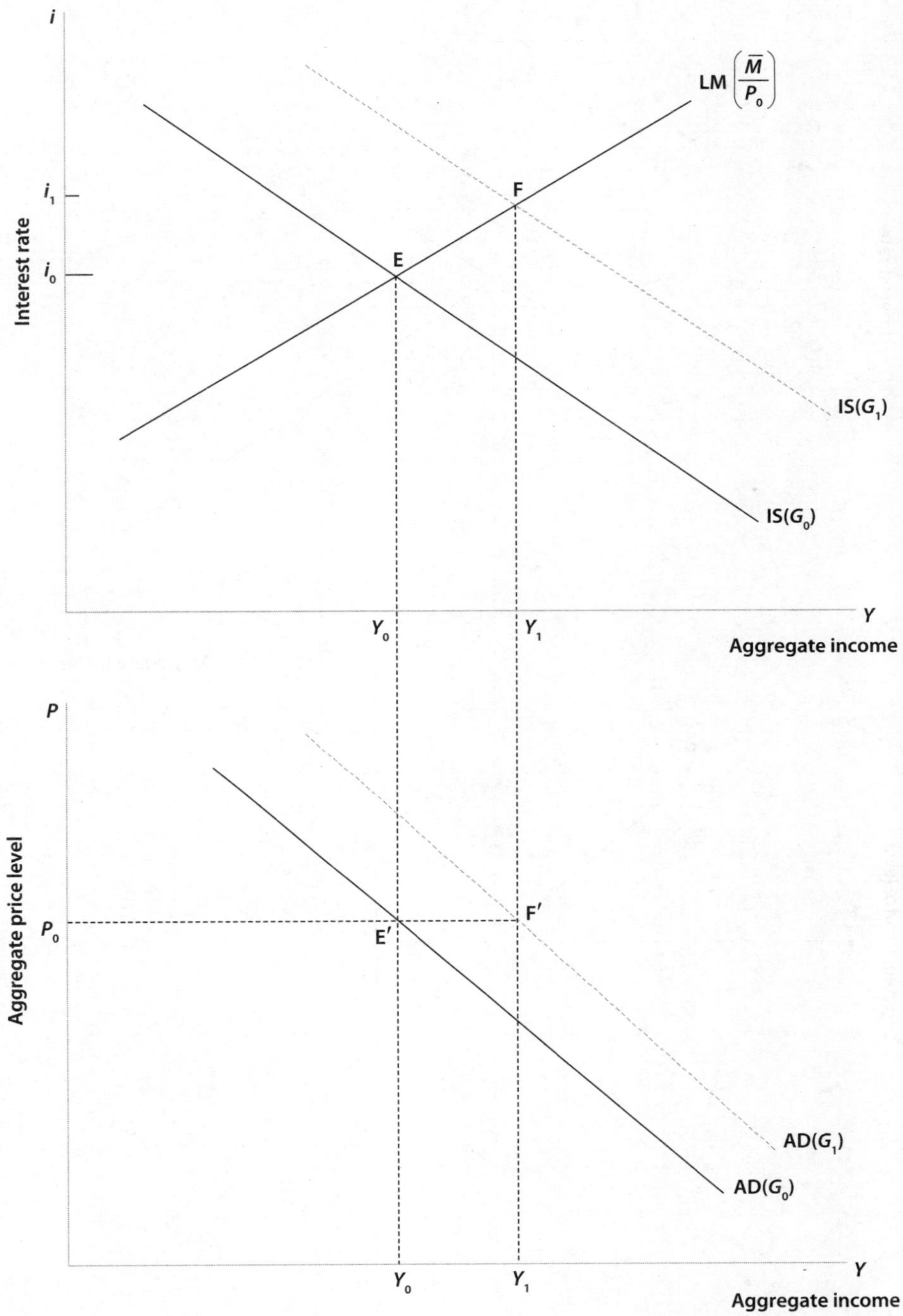

› **Figure 9.2**
An Increase in Government Expenditure. An increase in the government expenditure at a given price level, shifts the IS curve out to the right and increases the aggregate income and output (upper panel). At the given price level, the increased government expenditure shifts the AD curve to the right (lower panel).

output demanded at any price level, the entire AD curve shifts to the right to AD (G_1).

If the central bank increases the nominal money supply to $\overline{\overline{M}}$, this is associated with a rightwards shift of the LM curve (see Figure 8.10 of Chapter 8). The new IS–LM equilibrium, with the price level constant at P_0, is at the point F in Figure 9.3. The AD curve at P_0 and at any price level, shifts to the right in response to the increased nominal money supply. With Figures 8.3 to 8.6 as well as 8.10 in Chapter 8 as references, we summarize the factors that shift the AD curve in Table 9.1.

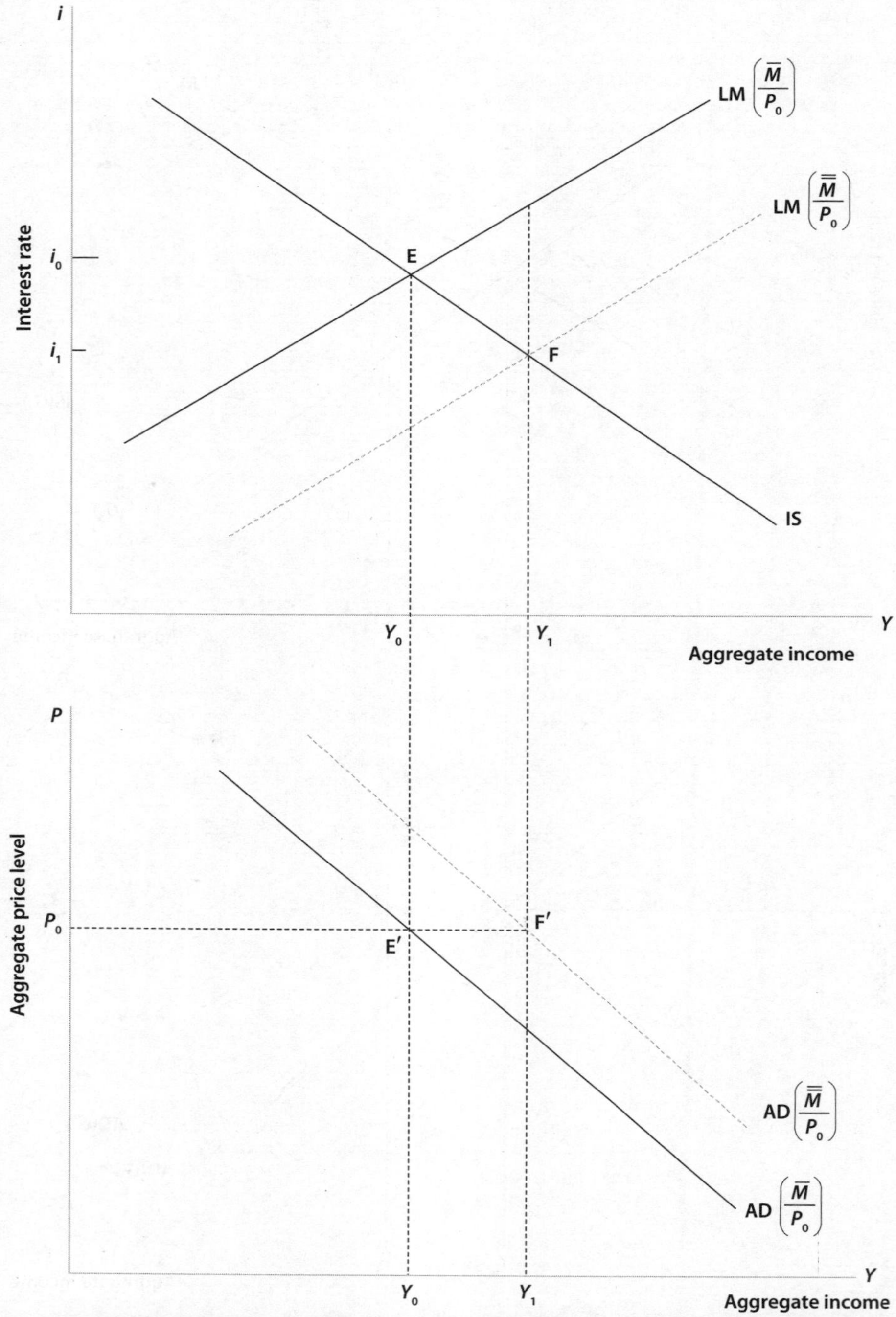

› **Figure 9.3**
An Increase in Nominal Money Supply. An increase in money supply by the central bank at a given price level shifts the LM curve to the right and increases the aggregate income and output (upper panel). At the given price level, the increase in money supply shifts the AD curve to the right (lower panel).

› **Table 9.1**
Factors that shift the AD Curve

Factor	Direction of Shift
1. An increase in government expenditures	IS and AD shift to the right
2. Increase in taxes	IS and AD shift to the left
3. Increase in the productivity of capital	IS and AD shift to the right
4. Increase in expected inflation	IS and AD shift to the right
5. Increase in expected future output (rise in permanent income)	IS and AD shift to the right
6. Increase in nominal money supply	LM and AD shift to the right
7. Reduction in real demand for money due to increased use of credit cards[2]	LM and AD shift to the right

9.2 Equilibrium Output and Price When the Aggregate Supply (AS) Curve Is Keynesian

As we saw in the chapter on labour markets, the AS CURVE derives from workers and firms pursuing their rational self-interest. Workers seek to maximize their preference for income and leisure, whereas firms seek to maximize profits. In the Keynesian set up, money wages are inflexible or sticky at $\overline{w}$. There are many possible reasons for this.

› The **aggregate supply (*AS*) curve** is the relationship between the real quantity of final goods and services produced in an economy and the general price level.

One possibility is that there exist minimum-wage laws that result in an artificial floor to the wages that firms can pay. Another possibility is that organized groups of workers seek to keep their nominal wage at levels they think to be appropriate as compared to other occupations—workers seek to maintain their position in the job ladder hierarchy. Yet another possibility is that workers and firms adopt implicit contracts. This is a tacit agreement that firms will not reduce workers' wages during an economic downturn and in return, workers won't demand a raise in wages when business conditions improve. This is an insurance scheme with workers paying an insurance premium in the form of lower than feasible wages in good times in return for insurance coverage in the form of higher than feasible wages in bad times. Keynesians who argue that nominal wages are inflexible, offer one of these rationales in support of their position. When wages are sticky, we derived the KEYNESIAN AS CURVE in Chapter 7, Figure 7.10. This AS curve is upward-sloping as long as there is an excess supply of labour, $N^D < N^S$. Once $N^D = N^S$, there is full employment and the AS curve becomes vertical.

› The **Keynesian aggregate supply curve** in the short run is drawn for a fixed money wage and is upward-sloping up to the point where full employment occurs where it is vertical.

The AD and the Keynesian AS schedules are depicted in a single diagram now, illustrating the market for real output (see Figure 9.4). The equilibrium price level and real output are at the intersection of the AD and AS schedules at point E. As point E is on the AD schedule, the economy is at a point where IS

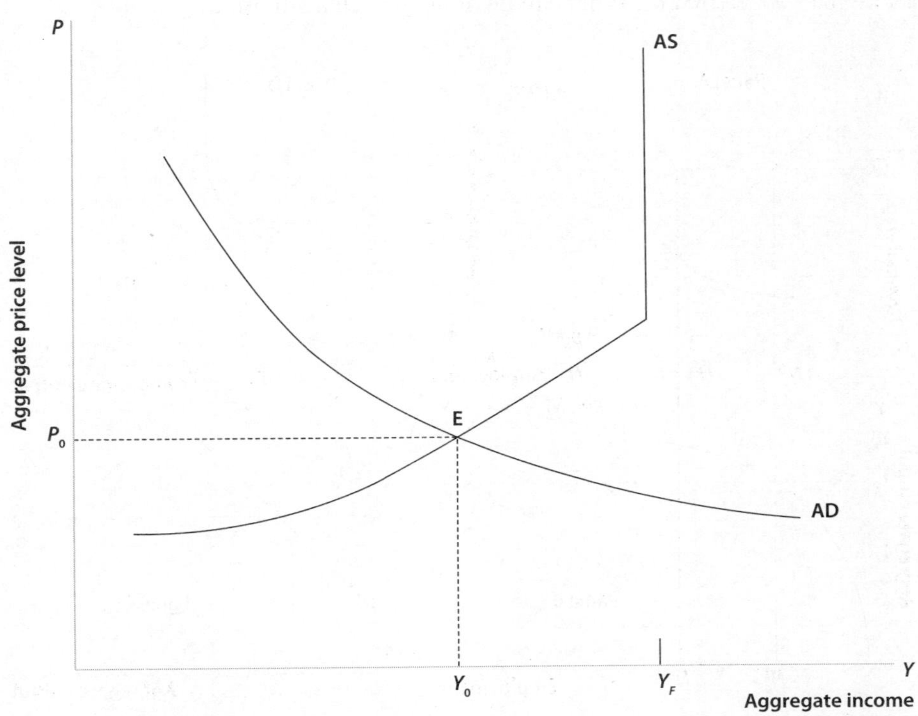

› **Figure 9.4**
The Market for Real Output (Keynesian). The AD curve representing equilibrium in the goods and money markets intersects the Keynesian AS curve at point E, which determines the equilibrium in the goods, money, and labour markets, and the aggregate price level and output/income.

equals LM. Thus, at price level P_0 in Figure 9.4 aggregate expenditure is equal to output (IS equilibrium), and the quantity of real money balances demanded equals the real value of nominal money balances supplied (LM equilibrium). As point E is on the aggregated supply schedule, workers and firms in pursuit of their rational self-interest produce the level of output Y_0 at the price level P_0. Of course, point E results from the given stationary levels of all those variables that result in the given position of the AD curve, as summarized in Table 9.1. A change in any of the factors listed in Table 9.1, such as government expenditure or the nominal money stock, will shift the AD curve in Figure 9.4 and result in a different equilibrium in the market for real output. Note also that AD does not intersect the AS curve on its vertical portion. Point E is, thus, an equilibrium where unemployment prevails.

The complete Keynesian system may accordingly be written[3] as:

$$\left.\begin{aligned} \text{IS Curve: } & Y = C(\underset{(+)}{Y - T}, \underset{(-)}{i - \pi^e}) + I(\underset{(-)}{i - \pi^e}) + G \\ \text{LM Curve: } & \frac{M^s}{P} = L(\underset{(+)}{Y}, \underset{(-)}{i}) \end{aligned}\right\} \text{AD Curve}$$

$$\left.\begin{aligned} \text{Labour Supply: } & \frac{w}{P} = MRS_{C,l} \\ \text{Labour Demand: } & \frac{w}{P} = MP_N \\ \text{Output Supply: } & Y = F(\bar{K}, N), \quad N = \min[N^D, N^S] \\ \text{Nominal Wage Ridigity: } & w = \bar{w} \end{aligned}\right\} \text{AS Curve}$$

These six equations together determine the six macroeconomic variables of interest—w, N^D, N^S, i, P, Y. This represents a complete macroeconomic description of the closed economy. In diagrammatic terms, the solution to the equations above is depicted in Figure 9.5.[4] As depicted, the equilibrium outcome results in unemployment as $N_0^D < N_0^S$. $(N_0^S - N_0^D)$ individuals are willing to work at the going wage, but there are no job offers forthcoming—a situation referred to as INVOLUNTARY UNEMPLOYMENT. What can be done in such a situation?

› **Involuntary unemployment** refers to a situation where the workers are willing to work at the going wage and yet firms do not employ them.

› **Figure 9.5**
Aggregate Demand and Supply in the Keynesian System. The nominal wage results in the demand for labour that is less than the supply of labour (panel A). Employment is determined by the demand side of the market and the level of employment determines the aggregate output produced (panel B). The price level at which the firm determined its demand for labour is associated with the output produced as a point on the AS curve in panel D. The AD curve intersects the AS curve on its upward-sloping part in panel D, resulting in involuntary unemployment.

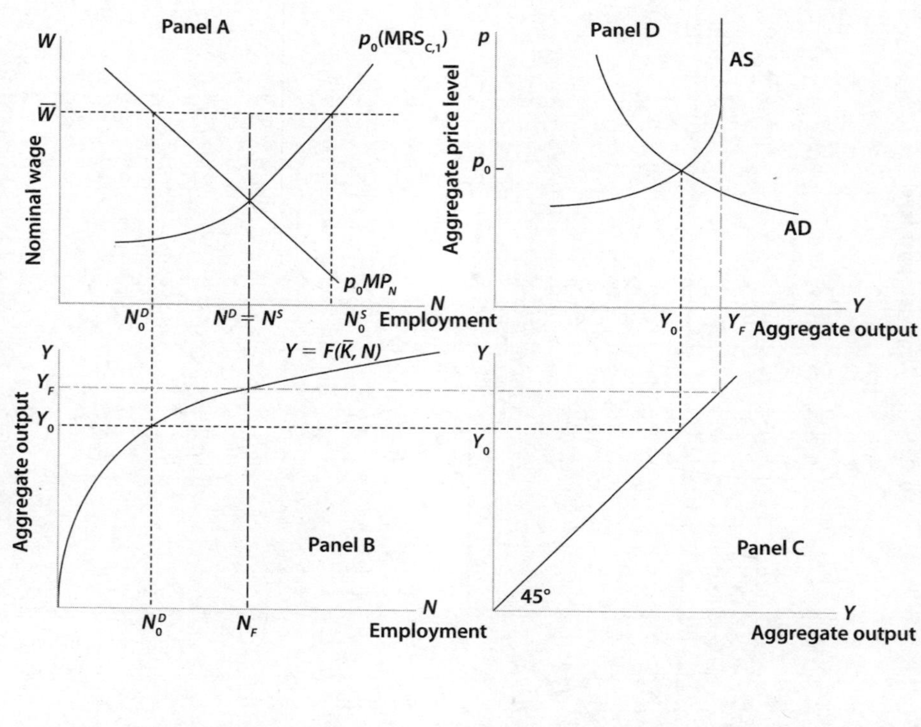

MACROFOCUS 9.1

Fiscal Policy and Working Capital

In developing countries, working capital finance is crucial to doing business. It is required to make payments in advance for the services of inputs once a production process is initiated. Suppliers of inputs to firms are often financially constrained and cannot wait for payments to be made after the production cycle has been completed.

If inputs uniformly precede outputs by a period of *T* units of time, labour services and capital stock that are introduced into the production process at time *t* will account for a finished output at time $t + T$. Workers, then, have to be paid in advance of the sale of output, and working capital expenses involve the borrowing costs at time *t* when production is initiated. These working capital funds are tied up till the firm receives a cash flow when the finished output is sold. In such a situation, the firm hires labour up to the point where the cost or the wage equals the present value of the benefit—the discounted revenue received from the output sold by the labour hired, or, $pMP_N/(1 + i)^T$. [Recall from Chapter 7 (Section 7.1) that when revenues and expenditures are synchronized, the demand for labour is described by the present cost equals present benefit condition, $w = pMP_N$.] If the interest rate rises, then, the present value of the benefit of hiring labour declines and firms reduce their demand for labour. If the price of output increases, the present value of the benefit of hiring labour rises and firms increase their demand for labour. With employment determined by the demand for labour (the short side of the market), the AS of output will accordingly increase with the price, but will decrease with a rise in the interest rate.

The AS curve is upward sloping but shifts to the left with a rise in the interest rate as this increases the cost of working capital required to hire inputs like labour. Similarly, a decrease in interest rates shifts the AS curve out to the right as the cost of financing working capital inputs decreases. Figure 1 illustrates the impact of fiscal policy when the AS responds to the interest cost of working capital finance.

An expansion in government spending, that shifts the AD curve to AD_1, initially increases output to Y_1 along the AS curve AS_0. Fiscal policy, however, involves some crowding out and the interest rate rises. This makes working capital costly and the AS curve shifts leftwards to AS_1. Output then decreases to Y_2. If the interest-sensitivity of AS is strong, Y_2 can even be to the left of Y_0 and increased government expenditure can contract the economy. Higher interest rates due to fiscal policy, in addition to crowding out private investment on the demand side, also make working capital more costly and reduce AS. In economies with poor infrastructure and underdeveloped financial systems, the production and distribution of goods and services takes time—requiring firms to make large advances for working capital. Expansionary fiscal policy has a cost-push effect that causes firms in these countries to reduce output.

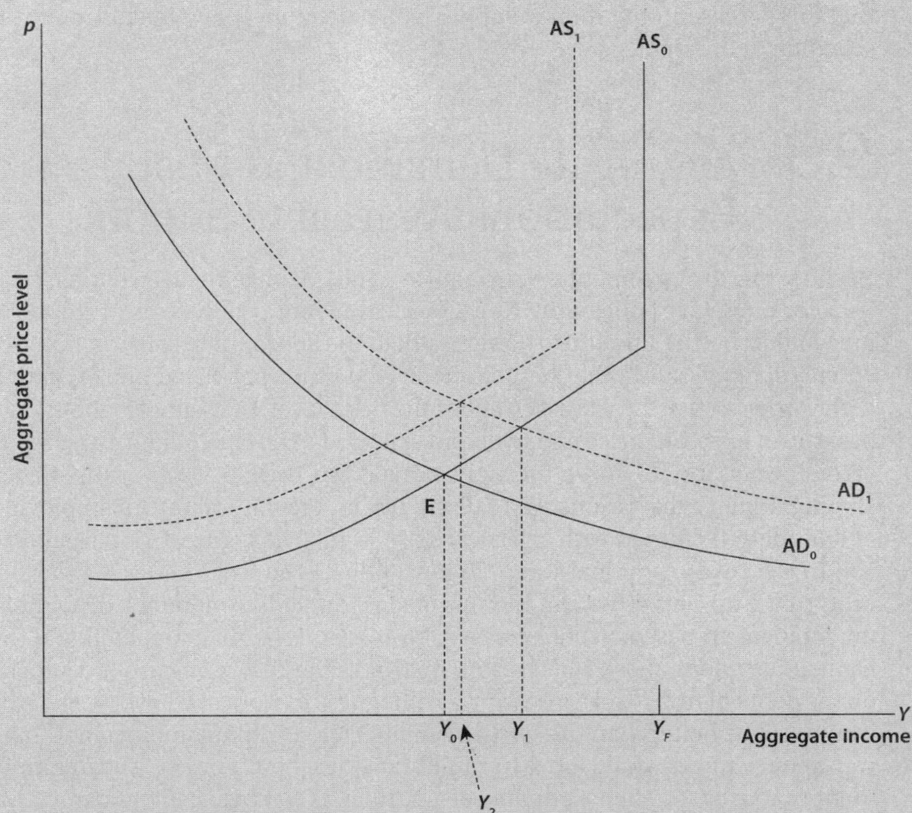

› **Figure 1**
Employment and Insider-Outsider Effects.

Source: D. R. Shaller, "Working Capital Finance Considerations in National Income Theory", *American Economic Review* 73, no. 1 1983: 156–165; L. Taylor, *Structuralist Macroeconomics—Applicable Models for the Third World* (New York: Basic Books, 1983).

Keynesians are of the view that the low AD is due to low confidence of investors regarding the future prospects of the economy.[5] Investment demand is thought by the Keynesians to be unresponsive to the rate of interest and the IS curve is considered to be steep[6], implying that crowding out of private expenditures would be low (see Figure 8.16 in Chapter 8). The Keynesians accordingly advocate FISCAL POLICY to reduce the involuntary unemployment that exists. Keynes had taken this position after considering the facts of the Great Depression when the stock markets declined by 85 per cent between September 1929 and June 1932. Between 1929 and 1933, gross national product (GNP) in the US economy fell by nearly 30 per cent and the unemployment rate rose from 3 to 25 per cent. Net investment was negative from 1931 to 1935.

› Keynesians advocate the use of **fiscal policy** to reduce involuntary unemployment as they believe that crowding out of private investment expenditures is low.

The view that the Great Depression was due to a leftward shift of the AD curve is accepted by Keynesians and Monetarists alike. However, whereas Keynesians emphasize a leftward shift in the IS curve due to a collapse of investor confidence, the Monetarists emphasize a leftward shift of the LM curve. As the interest rates in the economy declined and depositors' confidence in the economy declined, they rushed to withdraw cash from their bank accounts. With everyone rushing to withdraw money before other depositors, banks were unable to meet depositor demand for cash and many banks failed. The increase in the desired currency-deposit ratio resulted in a reduction in the money multiplier,[7] which reduced the money stock. The money stock declined by 26.5 per cent between 1929 and 1933. Friedman and Schwartz fault the Federal Reserve Board in the US for failing to increase the money supply and offsetting the decline in AD. Monetarists argue that the LM curve is steep and that an increase in the money supply is the effective policy in shifting the AD schedule to the right.

9.3 Aggregate Demand and Mistaken Expectations Aggregate Supply

Besides the disagreement regarding demand management—whether to use fiscal or monetary policy—the New Classical economists such as Milton Friedman and Robert E. Lucas also disagree about the appropriate construction of the AS curve. As we saw in the chapter on the labour market, Friedman argued that with workers IMPERFECTLY INFORMED about the price level, they supply labour on the basis of an expected price and hence an expected real wage. When expectational errors occur, the AS curve for a given expected price AS($p^e \neq p$) is upward-sloping. When expectations are realized, $p = p^e$, the natural rate of employment and output is achieved with a vertical AS($p = p^e$) (see Figure 7.11 in Chapter 7).

› The Mistaken Expectations AS curve is upward-sloping when the **expected price diverges** from the actual price. When expectations are realized, the natural rate of output is achieved with a vertical aggregate supply curve.

In the 1960s, nominal wages in most OECD countries showed great flexibility in the upward direction, and this made it difficult to maintain an analysis of unemployment based on sticky wages. Moreover, Friedman argued that if there is unemployment, those who are unemployed should be going around knocking on the doors of firms and expressing a willingness to work at a lower wage, which would still be better than the zero wages associated with unemployment. In this way, money wages would move to equilibrate the labour market. The unemployment that exists in the Friedman set-up, then, is not because the money wage has been fixed at a level where labour demand is less than labour supply, but is due to mistaken expectations. As individuals revise their expectations in the light of errors in past expectations—an adaptive process—they reach the natural rate of output (Y^*).

When expectations are wrong, however, the market can equilibrate at a different level of employment from the natural rate temporarily. Suppose in this Friedman mistaken expectations framework AD intersects the AS curve when price expectations are p_0^e at point M to the left of the natural rate of output Y^* (see Figure 9.6, panel D). At point M, workers have expected a price higher than the realized price, $p_0^e > p_1$, and they realize a nominal wage w_1 (depicted in panel A) that is lower than what would have been realized (w_0) if expectations had been correct. With mistaken expectations, employment and output are lower than the natural rate of employment and output, $Y_1 < Y^*$.

As workers adapt to this outcome, they will revise their expectation of prices downwards and the supply of labour will shift down. This results in pushing the money wage down as well. Initially, the downward revision of price expectations from p_0^e to, say, p_i^e, where $p_i^e < p_0^e$, will result in the operative labour supply function $p_i^e(\text{MRS}_{C,l})$, which is not depicted in panel A so as not to clutter up the diagram. The corresponding mistaken expectation AS function $AS(p_i^e \neq p_i)$ is shown in Figure 9.6, panel D. However, workers are still expecting a price level above the one that actually obtains at the intersection of $AS(p_i^e \neq p_i)$ and the AD curve in panel D. There is also a continued presence in the labour market of individuals who are volunteering to work at lower wages. The revision of prices will, therefore, continue until price expectations are again consonant with experienced prices—$p_n^e = p_n$—and the operative mistaken expectations AS curve is $AS(p_n^e \neq p_n)$. The adaptive expectations mechanism restores employment to its natural rate and there is NO NEED FOR GOVERNMENT INTERVENTION in the form of AD management. If, in this New Classical set-up, the government manipulated AD and shifted the AD curve to the right, it would push the price level up exactly at a time when workers are revising their expectation of prices in the reverse direction, downwards. An expansionary demand policy would cause workers to revise their price expectations upwards and shift the mistaken expectation AS curve up—resulting in an offset

› In the Mistaken Expectations set up aggregate demand, management could end up destabilizing the economy. Given enough time, the economy tends to self-correct and return to the natural rate of employment and output **without changes in monetary and fiscal policy**.

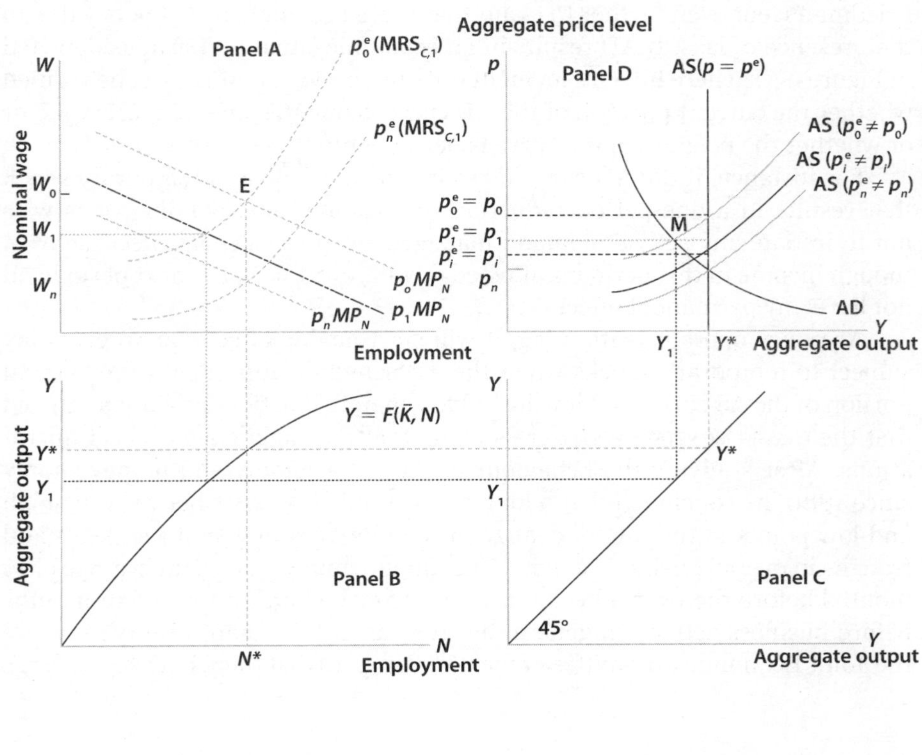

› **Figure 9.6**
Mistaken Expectations and AD–AS. The AD equals the mistaken expectation AS at point M in panel D when workers expect prices to be p_0^e. Tracing out through panels C and B to panel A, the realized nominal wages at w_1 are lower than what was expected (w_0), and, in panel D, the expected price is higher than that realized, $p_0^e > p_1$. This makes workers revise their expectations regarding prices downward, until the expectations are realized at $p_n^e = p_n$.

to the direction set by AD policy. Demand management is counterproductive in this framework. Friedman's macroeconomic system can be summarized as follows:

$$\left.\begin{aligned} &\text{IS Curve: } Y = C(\underset{(+)}{Y - T}, i - \underset{(-)}{\pi^e}) + I(i - \underset{(-)}{\pi^e}) + G \\ &\text{LM Curve: } \frac{M^s}{P} = L(\underset{(+)}{Y}, \underset{(-)}{i}) \end{aligned}\right\} \text{AD Curve}$$

$$\left.\begin{aligned} &\text{Labour Supply: } \frac{W}{P^e} = MRS_{C,l} \\ &\text{Labour Demand: } \frac{W}{P} = MP_N \\ &\text{Output Supply: } Y = F(\bar{K}, N), \quad [N^D = N^S] \\ &\text{Price Expectations: } P^e_{t+1} = P^e_t + \lambda(P_t - P^e_t) \end{aligned}\right\} \text{AS Curve}$$

The essence of the Keynesian–Monetarist debate, then, is not so much about whether fiscal policy is more appropriate than monetary policy. Rather, it is about whether governments should intervene by manipulating AD judiciously in order to achieve full employment (see Figure 9.5), or market forces should be relied on to eventually bring about the necessary adjustment of the real and nominal wage (see Figure 9.6). Should states intervene or should markets be left to adjust and solve the problem of unemployment?

Macroeconomists prefer state intervention if their prior belief is that money wages are sticky and respond only sluggishly or with large inertia to the excess supply in the labour market. In such a situation, it is expedient to manipulate demand. Otherwise, if markets self-correct with reasonable accuracy and speed, it is expedient to allow markets to solve economic problems such as employment.

9.4 Policy Lags

Friedman went even further to claim that there are limits to AD policy due to the presence of lags. If AD results in an economic situation (such as depicted in Figure 9.5), where full employment does not prevail, it must first be verified whether the current position of the AD curve is due to some temporary factor or whether the position of the curve is permanent.

For instance, if the AD curve takes its position due to a temporary shock that results in a one-period reduction in consumption spending, it is wise not to initiate any activist demand management policy. This is because even though income in this period is affected, it will revert back the next period and not have any permanent effect.

› **Policy lags** can make attempts to fine-tune the economy and reduce the impact of business cycles counterproductive.

As policy operates with a lag, it will start having effects on an economy subject to temporary shocks when the AD schedule approaches the vertical portion of the AS curve, and it will tend to generate inflation. Friedman[8] argued that the LAGS IN MONETARY POLICY are so long that they aggravate cyclical fluctuations. After studying the behaviour of the US economy and money supply since 1880, he concluded that a long and variable lag exists between the high and low points in the rate of change in the money supply and the peaks and troughs in overall business activity. The money supply peaked an average of 16 months before the over-all economy, and troughed an average of 12 months before business activity in general did the same. Friedman[9] observed before the Joint Economic Committee of the 86th Congress that there have been a large number of occasions "on which major fluctuations have been a consequence of changing and at times erratic governmental policies with respect to money".

On this basis, he urged to keep monetary changes from being the costly destabilizing force they have been through much of history. Friedman identified the inside and outside lags, which are important for activist policymakers. INSIDE LAGS in macroeconomic policy refer to the delay between the time a policy change is needed and the time the policy change is implemented. The inside lag comprises three types of lags:

› **Inside lags** refer to the delay between the time a policy change is needed and the time the policy change is implemented.

1. Data lag
2. Recognition lag
3. Implementation lag

The data lag involves the time taken before the data that indicates the state of the economy becomes available. For instance, GDP data is available with a time lag. Quick estimates are revised and eventually become available as actual figures, and this process can take a couple of years for annual data in India.

After the data is available, a recognition lag comes into effect. This is the time period it takes policymakers to recognize that a disturbance, which requires action on their part in terms of stimulating or restraining aggregate spending, has occurred Kareken and Solow[10] showed that, on average, the recognition lag is approximately five months. This lag was found to be a bit longer when restrictive policy was necessary and a bit shorter when expansionary policy was required.

The implementation lag is the delay between the recognition of the need for action and the policy decision. Here, monetary policy has a much shorter decision lag. Even though there are quarterly monetary policy reviews, central bank officials can and do meet on a daily basis to discuss and decide on policy. Fiscal policy that requires changes in government spending and tax programmes has to be passed in the parliament. This occurs mainly during its budget session. Thus, many months can pass before fiscal policy changes are put into effect. The inside lag for monetary policy is, therefore, substantially shorter than the inside lag for fiscal policy.

After implementation, a policy is subject to an OUTSIDE LAG—the time required for a change in policy to affect the economy, or, an effectuation lag.

› The **outside lag** is the time required for a policy change to affect the economy.

Fiscal policy, despite having a larger inside lag than monetary policy, has a shorter outside lag. Changes in government spending have immediate impact on real output by adding to or subtracting from AD, and individuals respond to tax changes by varying consumption expenditures immediately. Monetary policy, by affecting the money supply and interest rate, affects investment expenditure, which responds slowly to such a change. This is because the interest rate is just one of many factors that influence the decision to order new capital equipment, and it takes time for the capital-goods sector to begin to produce for new items on its order books. Even though monetary policy may face shorter implementation delays, its initial impact could be small and empirical studies show that the significant impact of the policy change on output and income builds up only gradually over a few quarters.

Since stabilization policy has potential destabilizing effects on the economy due to the presence of lags, some macroeconomists like Friedman advocated that policy should not respond to fluctuations. With no role for countercyclical policy, Friedman argued that money supply should rather grow at a constant rate.[11] Advocates of stabilization policy, on the other hand, argue that lags are unimportant and that the government should maintain a high and stable level of AD.

MACROFOCUS 9.2

Nominal Anchors and Intertemporal Policy Constraints

The power of producing good or bad economic effects is often attributed to policymakers. Yet these policymakers are distinct—fiscal policy is the responsibility of the Ministry of Finance and monetary policy is under the jurisdiction of the central bank (the Reserve Bank of India). However, they are connected through the arithmetic of the government budget constraint. In each period, the government must finance its expenditure plans. To do this, it can use taxation, the sale of new government bonds, or print money. When it sells bonds, the government accumulates public debt that is the stock of government bonds sold to the printed sector. It must pay interest, on this debt so that the government budget constraint is (see Chapter 12):

Government Expenditure + Interest on Public Debt = Tax Revenues Net of Transfers + New Bonds + New Money

The money referred to here is base money. What is important for the economy, therefore, is the net impact of monetary and fiscal policy—not the impact of either in isolation, as has been our focus. Suppose the Finance Ministry, for instance, increases its spending by issuing bonds to the central bank and spending the newly issued money. If this rightward shift of the AD curve kicks up inflation, the central bank may need to offset this and pull in the opposite direction by engaging in restrictive monetary policy. However, if the growth of currency is controlled with a view to stabilizing the price level, other elements of the budget constraint must be adjusted. Either government expenditures must be scaled down or tax collections or the net proceeds from new issues of interest-bearing debt must be stepped up to compensate for the loss of a source of revenue.

As a result, printing new money to finance government expenditure is ruled out by the constitution of the central bank in many countries. This denial of money financing of the government expenditures allows monetary policy to provide the nominal anchor for the economy. If agents in the economy are confident that the central bank will not change its announced policy about the target inflation rate, their expectations of future inflation are unaffected by any temporary changes in the inflation rate. This is described as a case of anchored inflationary expectations, where people believe that the central bank will act to ensure that any temporary inflation will be reversed. This belief allow them to not change their expectation of the future inflation even though the current inflation has risen. When expectations do not change, workers, for instance, will not press for wage increases, and firms will not be pushed to raise prices. As a result, future inflation will be controlled and the short-run AS curves will not drift in response to inflation, allowing output to return to the natural rate more quickly.

The fiscal authorities must somehow manage their affairs without seigniorage so that the fiscal deficit (Government Expenditure + Interest on Debt − Net Tax Revenues) equals the net proceeds from new debt. This would require that the government have a fiscal policy satisfying the condition that the present value of the government's net of interest surplus equals the current stock of interest bearing government debt (see Chapter 12).

The government must balance any current deficits with the prospect of future surpluses, sufficient to service the debt created by those deficits. These longer-run effects of fiscal and monetary policy are distinct from their short-run impact on AD where both can be used to expand or contract AD in the short run.

9.5 Real Business Cycles

The repeated sequence of economic expansion giving way to a decline in economic activity followed by recovery is known as the business cycle. When an economy goes through a downturn, many sectors experience declining sales and production. Workers are laid off or forced to work only part time. Should policymakers respond to such cyclical fluctuations?

The Keynesians argue that, because wages and prices adjust slowly, disturbances in spending or production can drive the economy away from a better utilization of productive resources for long periods of time. The Keynesian view is that, due to this sluggishness in market response, government should intervene to smooth business cycle fluctuations. The Monetarists, on the other hand, do not see much need for government intervention to counteract economic fluctuations. They have greater faith in the equilibrating power of market forces.

There are three types of impulses or shocks that result in economic fluctuations. One is policy shocks that follow from decisions made by policymakers. These affect the demand side of the economy. These policy impulses include changes in the money supply, the exchange rate, and fiscal policy.

A second type of shock is private demand shocks, such as modifications in consumption and investment spending, which are influenced by expectations about the future course of the economy.

Finally, there are supply shocks that affect the production side of the economy, which include natural disasters, climatic change, and innovations in technological knowledge.

Both KEYNESIANS and MONETARISTS tend to emphasize the fluctuations in economic activity as being determined by demand shocks, such as a collapse of investor confidence, a change in consumption spending as consumers become more optimistic or pessimistic about the future, a change in government expenditure, or changes in money supply. However, the two oil price increases during the 1970s made macroeconomists more aware of the importance of supply side factors in explaining macroeconomic fluctuation. Supply shocks result in a relationship between the price level and output (or inflation and growth) that differs from the relationship between these variables when demand shocks occur.

› **Keynesians** and **Monetarists** emphasize that fluctuations in economic activity are determined by demand shocks, such as a collapse of investor confidence, a change in consumer spending, or changes in the government expenditure and money supply.

In panel A of Figure 9.7, an adverse demand shock is depicted as a leftward shift of the AD curve from AD_0 to AD_1, resulting in a decline in price and output. In panel B of Figure 9.7, an adverse supply shock, say, due to a drought or oil price hike, reduces the production possible from given levels of labour and capital (the production function shifts inwards) and shifts the AS curve up from AS_0 to AS_1.

If we trace out the effects of pure demand shocks in panel C of Figure 9.7, the data would depict a positive relation over time between price and output. If most shocks in a period are supply shocks, however, the observation between price level and output would be a negative one—as traced out in panel D of Figure 9.7. The Great Depression resulted in data observations as in panel C of Figure 9.7. During the decade of the 1970s and 1980s, however, the data show price levels (or inflation) and output (or growth) moving together, as in panel D, Figure 9.7. These decades were predominantly noted for their supply shocks.

In the 1970s and 1980s, a group of economists—who came to be called REAL, BUSINESS CYCLE THEORISTS—suggested that real shocks may be far more important than monetary shocks in explaining the path of aggregate output overtime.[12] Real business cycle theorists argue that nominal variables, such as the money supply and the price level, have no role in explaining fluctuations in real variables such as output and employment.

› **Real business cycle theorists** emphasize that real shocks to supply, such as oil price hikes, changes in government regulations, and productivity changes stemming from technological changes are far more important in explaining economic cycles.

Edward Prescott[13] of the University of Minnesota does state that the claim is not that monetary institutions never matter, for he admits that periods of

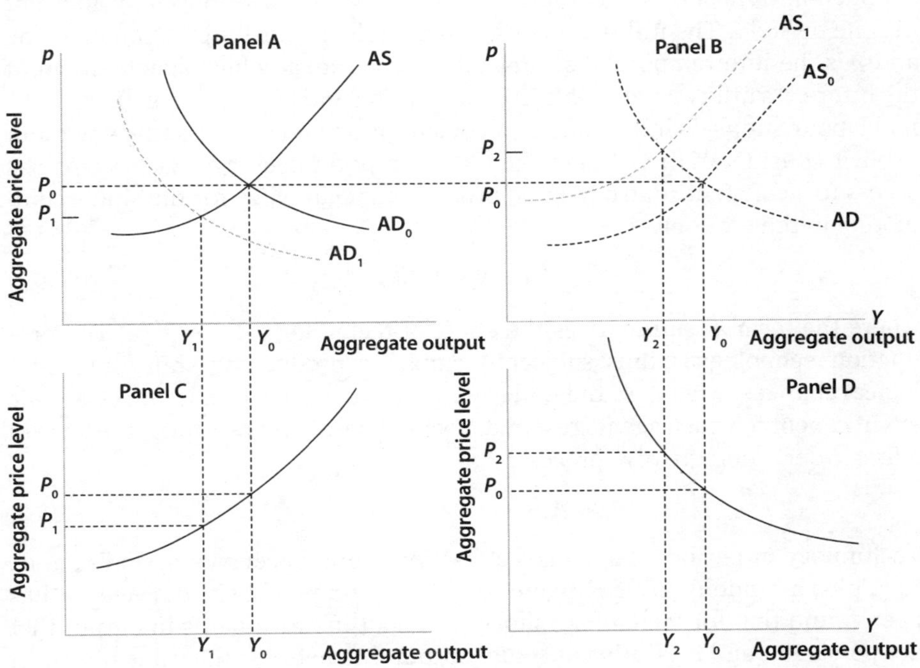

› **Figure 9.7**
Demand and Supply Shocks. An adverse demand shock shifts the AD curve to the left (panel A) and results in a decline in the price level and output. Tracing out shifts in the AD curve due to shocks gives us the relationship between the price level and the output, as depicted in panel C. An adverse supply shock reduces the output at each price level and shifts the AS curve to the left (panel B). The decline in the output is accompanied by a rise in the price level. Tracing out shifts in the AS curve due to shocks gives us the relationship between the price level and output, as depicted in panel D.

financial breakdown such as the Great Depression are not accounted for by real business cycle models. Rather, his argument is that postwar macroeconomic time series can be represented without explicit attention to monetary institutions.

The supply side shocks that the real business cycle theorists refer to include:

1. Unfavourable developments in the physical environment which adversely affect output. This type of shock would include natural disasters such as earthquakes, droughts, and floods.
2. Significant changes in the price of energy such as the oil price hikes of 1973 and 1979, and the subsequent reduction in 1986.
3. War, political upheaval, or labour disputes, which disrupt the existing performance and structure of the economy.
4. Government regulations such as import quotas, which damage incentives and divert entrepreneurial talent towards rent-seeking activities.
5. Productivity shocks generated by changes in the quality of the capital and labour inputs, new management practices, the development of new products, and the introduction of new techniques of production.

› **Real Business Cycle theorists** assume that individuals maximize intertemporal utility and firms maximize profits and there are no market imperfections. As a result, market equilibrium is efficient and there is no need for government intervention.

Apart from stressing productivity shocks stemming from technological progress, REAL BUSINESS CYCLE THEORISTS also view aggregate economic variables as the outcomes of the decisions made by many individual agents acting to maximize their utility—subject to production possibilities and resource constraints. Real business cycle models, thus, have an explicit and firm foundation in microeconomics. Typically, the economy is populated by many identical long-lived agents. In what follows, we simplify and adopt our standard two-period framework. Each agent has a utility function over the consumption and leisure they expect to enjoy over their lifetime of two periods.

$$U = U(C_1, H - N_1) + \frac{U(C_2, H - N_2)}{1 + \rho} \tag{9.1}$$

where H is the fixed time endowment of the individual and N_i is the labour supplied in time period i. Thus, $H - N_i = l_i$ is the leisure enjoyed by an agent in time period i. The utility function is separable in consumption and leisure, and ρ is the intertemporal discount rate or the rate at which agents discount the future. As utility is separable in consumption and leisure (labour), the optimal labour supply is independent of consumption and can be derived without explicit consideration of the optimal consumption decision. Each agent has access to a constant return to scale production technology for the single commodity in the economy.

$$Y_t = F(K_t, N_t) = A_t K_t^{1-\alpha} N_t^{\alpha} \tag{9.2}$$

where the term A_t summarizes the effect of technological progress. The production technology is, thus, subject to temporary productivity shifts or technological changes, which are the underlying source of variation in the economic environment to which agents respond. Technological progress takes the form of a first order autoregressive process:

$$A_t = a + \theta A_{t-1} + \varepsilon_t \tag{9.3}$$

Technology in period t, A_t, equals a fraction θ of its previous period's value, A_{t-1}, plus a random term, ε_t. In empirical work on real business cycles, it has been found that for technology shocks to result in movements in output that are persistent and indicative of actual output fluctuations, the value of θ must be large—usually above 0.95. ε_t is a random variable that is independently and identically distributed. Finally, the model involves an identity and a behavioural equation. The identity is that the capital stock evolves through time according to:

$$K_{t+1} = (1 - \delta)K_t + I_t \tag{9.4}$$

where $0 < \delta < 1$ is the rate of depreciation. The identity that the sum of consumption and investment equals to output allows us to substitute $I_t = Y_t - C_t$ into Eq. (9.4):

$$K_{t+1} = (1 - \delta)K_t + Y_t - C_t \tag{9.5}$$

With aggregate consumption as the difference between aggregate output and savings, $C_t = (1 - s)Y_t$, where s is the marginal propensity to save, we can write equation (9.5) as:

$$K_{t+1} = (1 - \delta)K_t + sY_t$$

or,

$$K_{t+1} = (1 - \delta)K_t + sA_tK_t^{1-a}N_t^a \tag{9.6}$$

The agent's problem then boils down to choosing how to allocate hours between work and leisure, and how to allocate the supply of the good between investment and consumption by maximizing the utility function subject to the constraints [Eqs. (9.3) and (9.6)] and subject to the lifetime budget constraint [Eq. (9.7)], written as:

$$C_1 + \frac{C_2}{1+r} = \omega_1 N_1 + \frac{\omega_2 N_2}{1+r} = Y_{\text{lifetime}} \tag{9.7}$$

where ω is the real wage, (w/p). Under most specifications of preferences and production functions, it is not possible to solve analytically this maximization problem. Accordingly, business cycle theorists compute approximate solutions to the choice problem in the neighbourhood of the steady state.

We will proceed, however, by teasing out the economic intuition underlying the resulting optimal decisions. Since the utility function has, as one of its arguments, leisure and not directly labour,[15] we recast the budget constraint in terms of leisure. The intertemporal budget constraint, then, is:

$$\omega_1(H - l_1) + \frac{\omega_2(H - l_2)}{1+r} = Y_{\text{lifetime}}$$

Multiplying throughout by $(1 + r)$,

$$(1 + r)\omega_1(H - l_1) + \omega_2(H - l_2) = (1 + r)Y_{\text{lifetime}}$$

or,

$$(1 + r)\omega_1 H + \omega_2 H - (1 + r)Y_{\text{lifetime}} = (1 + r)\omega_1 l_1 + \omega_2 l_2$$

As usual there are two polar situations:

1. The agent does not enjoy leisure in period 1, $l_1 = 0$.

   Then, $$l_2 = \frac{(1 + r)\omega_1 H + \omega_2 H - (1 + r)Y_{\text{lifetime}}}{\omega_2} = \frac{\Psi}{\omega_2}$$

   where Ψ is the numerator of the expression for l_2.[16]
2. The agent does not enjoy leisure in period 2, $l_2 = 0$, in which case,

$$l_1 = \frac{(1 + r)\omega_1 H + \omega_2 H - (1 + r)Y_{\text{lifetime}}}{(1 + r)\omega_1} = \frac{\Psi}{(1 + r)\omega_1}$$

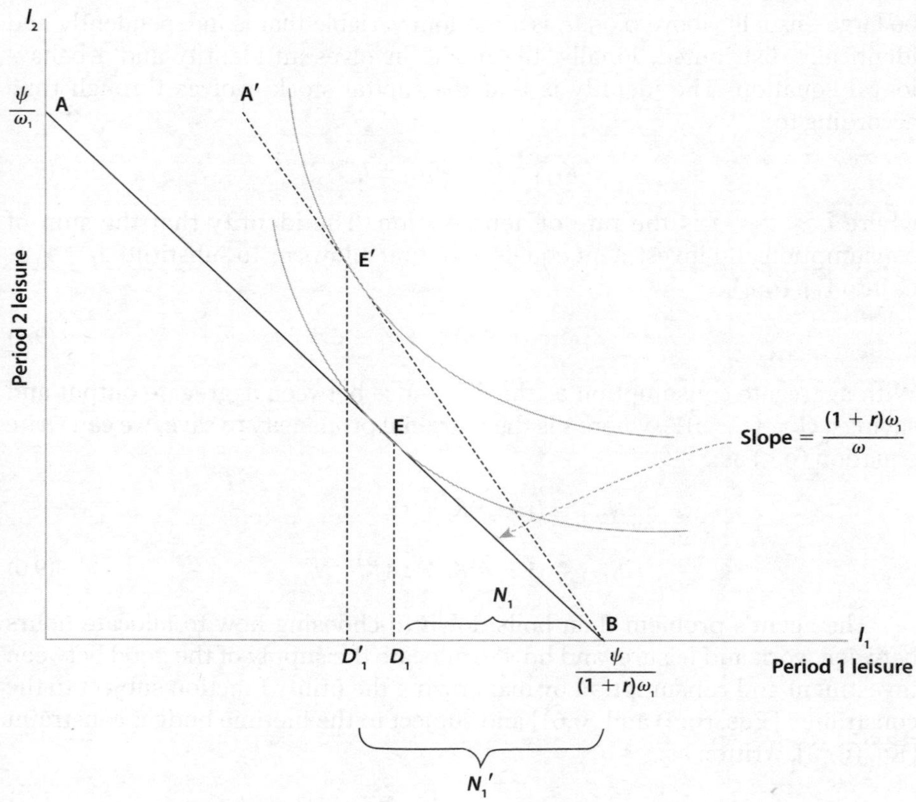

› **Figure 9.8**
The Intertemporal Labour Supply Decision. In real business cycle theory, individuals trade work in one period for work in another period, or leisure in one period for leisure in another, as depicted by the budget constraint AB. An increase in the wage in period 1 makes period 1 leisure more expensive and the budget constraint A′B operates with the increase in the wage in this period. The individual then takes less leisure or works more, $N_1' > N_1$, in response to the increased wage in period 1. Less leisure today is substituted for more leisure in the future.

These corner situations, $l_1 = 0$ and $l_2 = 0$, are represented by points A and B in Figure 9.8. Joining points A and B gives the budget constraint for leisure. The slope of this constraint is the ratio of the vertical to horizontal distance, or,

$$\text{Slope of Budget Line AB} = \frac{\text{Distance OA}}{\text{Distance OB}}$$

$$= \frac{\Psi/\omega_2}{\Psi/(1+r)\omega_1} = \frac{(1+r)\omega_1}{\omega_2}$$

Which point on the lifetime constraint AB will the agent choose? Optimality demands that the agent select that point on AB which is tangential to an indifference curve, reflecting the preferences of the agent for leisure (and, therefore, labour) in the two time periods, as described in the utility function. This occurs at point E in Figure 9.8. The agent then enjoys OD_1 hours of leisure and spends $N_1 = D_1B$ hours in work in period 1. Suppose the first period wage, ω_1, increases. Then, the slope of the budget constraint AB becomes steeper—the dashed line A′B. As is usual, there are substitution and income effects. Current productivity and income is high, which encourages intertemporal substitution of current for future work.[15] On the other hand, lifetime income is higher and that acts to reduce current and future work effort. Real Business Cycle theorists demonstrate that, for plausible parametrizations of the model, the substitution effect dominates so that current labour supplied rises. $N_1' = D_1'$ B hours are now worked in response to the higher current wage. Similarly, any other factor that increases the slope of the budget constraint, such as a rise in interest rates, will result in an increase in current labour supply. The labour supply function can then be written as:

$$N^S = N^S\left(\underset{(+)}{\frac{\omega_1}{\omega_2}}, \underset{(+)}{r}\right) \tag{9.8}$$

The demand for labour arises from the standard profit maximization condition[17] and labour is demanded upto the point where the real wage equals the marginal product of labour:

$$\omega = \text{MP}_N$$

We know that labour is subject to diminishing marginal productivity, giving us a downward-sloping demand curve[18] for labour:

$$N^D = N^D(\text{MP}_N) \tag{9.9}$$

The demand and supply curve for labour are drawn in panel B of Figure 9.9 for an instant of time where the capital stock and technology are constant at $K_t = \bar{K}$, $A_t = \bar{A}$, making output $Y = \bar{A}\bar{K}^{1-\alpha}N^{\alpha} = \bar{A}F(\bar{K}, N)$ a function of labour input. This production function is drawn in panel A of Figure 9.9, where the gradually

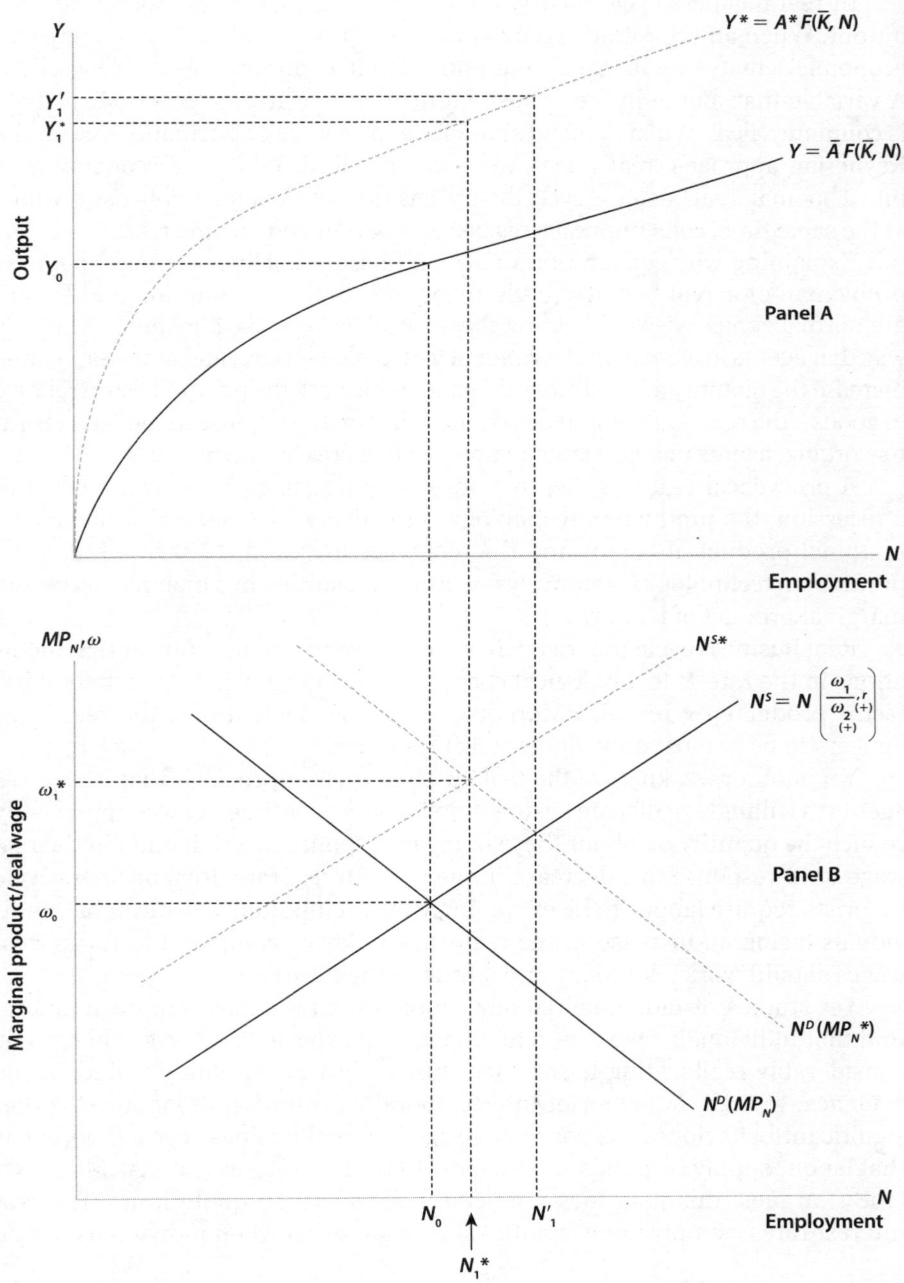

› **Figure 9.9 Employment and Wages in Real Business Cycle Models.** A favourable technological shock shifts the production function outwards, with more output produced per unit of labour (panel A). The increased productivity of labour shifts the demand for labour curve out to the right in panel B. This results in a rise in the real wage. However, due to the increase in income and savings, the interest rate declines and reduces the return to the current labour supply. The supply of labour curve then shifts to the left in response to this reduced return to the labour in panel B. The reduction in the labour supply increases the real wage further. An improvement in the productivity is, therefore, associated with a rise in real wages.

diminishing slope of the production function reflects the diminishing marginal productivity of labour.

Now, suppose there is a beneficial technological shock that shifts the production function outwards to $Y^* = A^* F(\overline{K}, N)$. Improvements in technology enable more product or output to be produced with the same inputs. As the productivity of labour goes up with this beneficial technological shock, the demand curve for labour shifts out to $N^D(MP_N{}^*)$. With the increased demand for labour raising the current wage, individuals supply more labour[19] in response to the productivity shock at N_1'. However, now that output and income have increased from Y_1 to Y_1', this increase in output raises savings and the rise in savings, in turn, lowers the interest rate. This shifts the labour supply curve up and to the left—a reduction in the interest rate increases the present value of future income and makes the return from current labour supply unattractive. The output and income, thus, finally increase to $Y_1{}^*$ and the real wage increases to $\omega_1{}^*$.

› Real business cycle theorists assert that the supply of labour has strong positive relation with transitory movements in the **real wage** rate. They also asset that the real wage rate is procyclical.

In real business cycle theory, the REAL WAGE is, therefore, procyclical with output. When an economic variable moves in the same direction as aggregate economic activity—up in expansions and down in contractions—it is procyclical. A variable that moves in the opposite direction to aggregate economic activity is countercyclical. When demand shocks are the source of fluctuations, as in the Keynesian approach, real wages are countercyclical. When the economy goes into a boom in real business cycle theory, leisure falls (labour supply rises) while, at the same time, consumption rises because output and income rise.

Explaining why consumption rises and leisure declines during a boom is problematic for real business cycle theory—as both consumption and leisure are normal goods, we would expect these variables to move together.[20] The only way that agents in a boom find it rational to decrease leisure, and at the same time increase the quantity of goods they demand, is because the price of leisure relative to goods—the real wage—increases during a boom. In response to the high return to working, agents increase labour supply and decrease leisure.

A procyclical real wage is, therefore, only possible in two ways: (a) If in a recession, the production technology is relatively adverse, which makes the marginal product of labour and the real wage low; and (b) If in a boom the production technology is relatively favourable, resulting in a high real wage and marginal product of labour.

Real business cycle theorists, therefore, have to assume substantial fluctuations in the rate of technological change—which is not what the data on total factor productivity reveal.[21] Moreover, in actual fluctuations, the real wage appears to be at most only moderately procyclical.

Yet another weakness of the real business cycle approach is that it requires agents to willingly reallocate leisure (and labour) over time. Agents appreciably reduce the quantity of labour they supply in response to a reduction in the real wage or in response to a decrease in the real interest rate. Real business cycle theorists require labour to be exceedingly intertemporally substitutable. Individuals facing an increase in the real wage today as compared to future real wages should work a lot today and a little in the future.

Yet studies of individual labour supply over time have not been able to find that individuals take action in response to expected real wage changes by considerably reallocating leisure over time.[22,23] A recent study,[24] finds some evidence, though, in favour of intertemporal substitution of labour. Another significant behavioural response envisaged by real business cycle theorists is that labour supply responds significantly to the real interest rate. As Mankiw[24] (1989) argues, this just does not seem believable. To quote him, "The real interest rate is simply not a significant consideration when individuals decide to leave their jobs or to accept new employment. While economists can easily convince laymen and students that the quantity of apples depends on the price of apples, it is much harder to convince them that labour supply depends on the real interest rate".

Perhaps the most disturbing feature of real business cycle theory is that, by portraying work and leisure to be highly substitutable over time, it treats fluctuations in employment as reflecting voluntary changes in the number of hours people want to work. Any unemployment that we see around us is, thus, voluntary and, to the extent that it is the outcome of optimizing behaviour, there is no room for any corrective policy or state intervention. The invisible hand of the market results in outcomes such as employment and unemployment and the outcome is PARETO-EFFICIENT—that is, any intervention designed to improve someone's lot can only be at the expense of someone else's lot. Prescott's[26] statement that "economic fluctuations are optimal responses to uncertainty in the rate of technological change", builds on the premise that markets are complete and that information asymmetries are non-existent. In this world, however, individuals are never rationed out of jobs involuntarily, which is not plausible.

› **Pareto efficiency** or optimality is a condition in which no change in outcome is possible that will make some members of society (such as the unemployed) better off, without making some other members of society (such as the employed) worse off.

It is useful to document that real shocks effect the economy differently from nominal stocks. However, then, to allow real shocks to result in optimal outcomes for the economy with no role for stabilization policy through state intervention is to develop a world of art.

SUMMARY

- » The AD curve is the relationship between the real quantity demanded of newly produced final goods and services and the general price level. It is a downward sloping curve.
- » The AD curve is derived from the equilibrium conditions in the goods (IS curve) and the money market (LM curve).
- » Changes in any variable other than the price level that shift the IS and LM curves, such as fiscal and monetary policy, consumption spending or private investment, shift the AD curve.
- » The AS curve is the relationship between the real quantity supplied of newly produced final goods and services in an economy and the general price level.
- » The Keynesian AS curve in the short-run is drawn for a fixed money wage and is upward sloping up to the point where full employment ($N^D = N^S$) occurs. At this point, it is vertical.
- » Involuntary unemployment refers to a situation where workers are willing to work at the going wage rate and yet firms do not employ them.
- » Keynesians advocate the use of fiscal policy to reduce involuntary unemployment as they believe that crowding out of private investment expenditures is low.
- » The Mistaken Expectations Short-Run AS curve is upward sloping when the expected price diverges from the actual price ($p^e \neq p$). When expectations are realized ($p^e = p$), the natural rate of output is achieved with a vertical AS curve.
- » In the Mistaken Expectations set up AD management could end up destabilizing the economy since with a revision of expectations, employment reverts to its natural rate. According to Friedman, given enough time, the economy tends to self-correct and return to the natural rate of employment and output without changes in monetary or fiscal policy.
- » Even when it is recognized that policy changes are needed policy lags can make attempts to fine-tune the economy counterproductive. The inside lag is the time required to recognize a need for a policy change and then to implement that policy change. It is shorter for monetary policy due to shorter implementation lags associated with it. The outside lag is the time required for the change in policy to affect the economy and is shorter for fiscal policy.
- » Keynesians and Monetarists emphasize that fluctuations in economic activity are determined by demand shocks such as a collapse of investor confidence, a change in consumer spending arising from changes in confidence regarding the state of the economy, or sudden unanticipated changes in government expenditure or money supply.
- » Real business cycle theorists emphasize that real shocks to supply such as oil price hikes, changes in government regulations, and productivity changes stemming from technological progress are far more important in explaining economic cycles.
- » Real business cycle theorists assume that individuals maximize intertemporal utility and firms maximize profits and there are no market imperfections. As a result market equilibrium is efficient and there is no need for government intervention.
- » Real business cycle theorists assert that the supply of labour is strongly and positively related to transitory movements in the real wage rate—the intertemporal substitution hypothesis—and that the real wage rate is procyclical.

NOTES

1. We are restricting ourselves to a closed economy for the time being.
2. This is a reduction in the parameter h in Eq. (8.18) of Chapter 8.
3. L in the LM curve represents the real demand for money or the demand for liquidity.
4. Figure 9.5 depicts the equilibrium values of w, N^D, N^S, P and Y. Panel D of this diagram depicts equilibrium output as Y_0 and this information can be used in Figure 9.1.
5. To derive the equilibrium nominal interest rate from the intersection of the IS and LM curves.
6. This can be interpreted as a low value of the parameter a in the investment function.
7. The parameter b in the investment function also assumes a low value.
8. See Chapter 2 on the money multiplier.
9. M. Friedman, "A Monetary and Fiscal Framework for Economic Stability", in "Essays in Positive Economics", Chicago University Press, Chicago, 1953.
10. M. Friedman, "Employment, Growth, and Price Levels", 86th Congress, First Session, 25–28 May 1958, pp. 609.
11. J. Kareken and R. Solow, "Lags in Monetary Policy", in *Stabilisation Policies*, Commission on Money and Credit, (Prentice Hall, 1963). Is this a book? Or Report? Insufficient information.
12. See M. Friedman, "The Role of Monetary Policy", American Economic Review, (March 1968).
13. The seminal paper is that of C. R. Nelson and C. I. Plosser. C. R. Nelson and C. I. Plosser, "Trends and Random Walks in Macroeconomic Times Series: Some Evidence and Implications", *Journal of Monetary Economics* 10 (September 1982): 139–162.
14. E.C. Prescott, "Theory Ahead of Business Cycle Measurement", Federal Reserve Bank of Minneapolis, *Quarterly Review*, (Fall 1986): 9–22.
15. This is because it allows the drawing of standard convex to the origin indifference curves. Labour in the utility function would provide negative utility.
16 When $l_1 = 0$, we still have $0 \leq l_2 \leq H$, that is, it does not necessarily imply that in period 2 the agent must spend all the hours in leisure just because he spent all the time working in period 1 ($l_1 = 0$). If $l_2 = H$, then, the expression for

$$Y_{\text{lifetime}} = w_1N_1 + \frac{w_2N_2}{1+r} = w_1(H - l_1) + \frac{w_2(H - l_2)}{1+r} = w_1H$$

Then,

$$l_2 = \frac{\Psi}{w_2} = \frac{(1+r)w_1H + w_2H - (1+r)w_1H}{w_2} = H$$

Hence,

$$l_2 = \frac{\Psi}{w_2} \text{ is the general expression for } 0 \leq l_2 \leq H$$

17. Simultaneously there will also be an intertemporal substitution of current consumption for leisure that we are not foregrounding right now.
18. Real Profits are given by $\pi = q - wN - (r + \delta)K$, where, $q - AK^{1-a}N^a$
19. With $Y = AK^{1-a}N^a$ we have $MP_N = a(Y/N)$. The average product of labour (Y/N) diminishes as employment increases resulting in a downward sloping MP_N curve.
20. If productivity shocks are persistent and long-lived there would be less incentive for agents to increase current labour supply because future output would also rise and increase the income effect while reducing the substitution effect.
21. N. G. Mankiw, "Real Business Cycles: A New Keynesian Perspective", *Journal of Economic Perspectives*, (Summer 1989): 79–90.
22. Ibid.
23. J. G. Altonji, "Intertemporal Substitution in Labour Supply: Evidence from Micro Data," *Journal of Political Economy* Part 2 94 (June 1986): S176–S215.
24. L. Ball, "Interpersonal Substitution and Constraints on Labour Supply: Evidence from Panel Data", *Economic Inquiry*, 28 (October 1990): 706–724.
25. C. B. Mulligan, "Substitution over Time: Another Look at Life Cycle Labour Supply", NBER Macroeconomics Annual 13, 1998.
25. Ibid.
26. E. C. Prescott, "Theory Ahead of Business Cycle Measurement," Federal Reserve Bank of Minneapolis, *Quarterly Review*, (Fall 1986): 21.

TEST YOURSELF

1. What is AD and how is it determined?
2. How can fiscal and monetary authorities affect the position of the AD curve of an economy?
3. Suppose the AS curve of the economy is Keynesian. How does monetary and fiscal policy affect the level of investment in the economy? As investment adds to capacity, comment on the possible long-run impacts.
4. Draw a Mistaken Expectations AD–AS diagram with the economy away from the natural rate of output. Describe how the economy gets to long-run equilibrium over time.

5. How does the presence of lags inherent in the policy process affect the use of monetary versus fiscal policy?
6. It is often argued that active policymaking is unnecessary as the economy has a tendency to self-correct. Elaborate on the pros and cons of this view.
7. What are the main channels through which monetary policy may affect economic activity?
8. What are shocks? What differential impacts do demand and supply shocks have on the economy?
9. Explain how productivity shocks affect real wages in the real business cycle model.
10. The real business cycle approach to macroeconomics ignores the demand side of the economy and portrays business cycles as a pure supply-side phenomenon. What is the advantage of this approach to macroeconomics?

ONLINE APPLICATION

1. Go to the home page of the Reserve Bank of India URL: www.rbi.org.in/home.aspx
   b. Click on the "DataBase" icon
2. Then under the classification of Annual data, click on "Handbook of Statistics on Indian Economy"
3. Click on "Table 114: Combined Deficits of Central and State Governments" and create a spreadsheet of annual data on the fiscal deficit of the nation from 1981–1982 to 2009–2010.
4. Then click on "Table 1: Macro-economic aggregates (at *current* prices)" and in your spreadsheet insert annual data on GDP at market prices (base 1999–2000) from 1981–1982 to 2009–2010.
5. Finally click on "Table 2: Macro-economic aggregates (at *constant* prices)" and in your spreadsheet insert annual data on GDP at market prices (base 1999–2000) from 1981–1982 to 2009–2010.
6. Find the inflation rate as implied by the GDP price deflator. The GDP price deflator is the GDP at current market prices divided by the GDP at constant market prices and the result so obtained multiplied by 100. For instance, the GDP at current prices in 1980–1981 is INR 1,453.70 billion and at constant prices it is INR 6,953.61 billion. The GDP deflator for 1980–1981 is $(1453.70/6953.61) \times 100 = 20.91$. Similarly, the GDP deflator for 1981–1982 is 23.17. The implied inflation rate between 1980–1981 and 1981–1982 then is $[(23.17 - 20.91)/20.91]* 100 = 10.85$ per cent.
7. Now create an index of the growth in real fiscal deficit. First find the growth rate of the fiscal deficit per period. The fiscal deficit in 1980–1981 was INR 107.8 billion and in 1981–1982 it was INR 106.08 billion. The growth rate then is $[(106.08 - 107.8)/107.8]* 100 = -1.6$ per cent. For each period subtract the growth rate for the nominal fiscal deficit by the inflation rate you calculated in Step 6 above. The inflation rate in 1981–1982 was 10.85 per cent. Hence, the real growth in the fiscal deficit in 1981–1982 is $-1.6 - 10.85 = -12.45$ per cent. Let the real value of the growth in fiscal deficit in 1980–1981 have an index value equal to the value 2. Then, the index in 1981–1982 is equal to $2 \times [1 + (-12.45/100)] = 1.75$. Similarly, calculate the index of the growth in real fiscal deficit per period.
8. Now, create an index of output. Let the output at constant prices in 1980–1981 of INR 6,953.61 billion have an index value of 5.33. Then, the index value of 1981–1982 output at constant prices of INR 7,370.78 billion will have an index value of $(5.33 \times 7370.78/6953.61) = 5.65$.
9. Finally create an index of the price level of the economy. The inflation rate as measured by the GDP deflator in 1980–1981 was 11.49 per cent. If the price level in 1979–1980 is indexed at 5.5, then, the price index in 1980–1981 is $5.5 \times [1 + (11.49/100)] = 6.13$.
10. Now, create a graph with the index of the growth of fiscal deficit on the horizontal axis and the index of the price level and output on the vertical axis. What does your graph depict about the impact of the fiscal deficit on the aggregate price level and aggregate output in the economy?
11. For the graph you created in Step 10, note that the linear trend line of the impact of the fiscal deficit on prices is higher than that on output. In fact, as the fiscal deficit increases it has a larger impact on prices and does not impact as much on output. If you closely analyse the slopes of the linear trends you will find that a unit increase in the index of the fiscal deficit increases the index of prices by 3.2 (the slope is 3.2) while it increases the index of output by 1.9. Why does the increased government expenditure that is financed by borrowing (the fiscal deficit) result in a larger increase in prices than on output in the Indian economy?

Appendix 9.1 The Aggregate Demand Curve

The AD curve is the outcome of equilibrium in the goods and financial markets. Hence, the AD curve is derived by considering the determinants of the variables that influence the equilibrium in these markets. In the goods market for a closed economy, we have the familiar income equals expenditure identity:

$$Y = C + I + G \tag{A9.1.1}$$

Consumption expenditure depends on disposable income and the interest rate as given by Eq. (8.5) in Chapter 8:

$$C = c_0 + c_1(Y - T) - c_2(i - \pi^e) \tag{A9.1.2}$$

We have taken direct taxes to be a lump sum but now we allow them to vary with income:

$$T = t_0 + t_1 Y \tag{A9.1.3}$$

where t_0 is the autonomous component of taxes that does not vary with income and t_1 is the marginal tax rate. Of course, $0 < t_1 < 1$.

Investment is inversely related to the rate of interest, as given by Eq. (8.6) in Chapter 8:

$$I = a - b(i - \pi^e) \tag{A9.1.4}$$

Government expenditure is exogenous, $G = \overline{G}$. Substituting Eqs. (A9.1.2), (A9.1.3), and (A9.1.4) into Eq. (A9.1.1), we obtain,

$$\begin{aligned} Y &= c_0 + c_1(Y - t_0 - t_1Y) - c_2i + c_2\pi^e + a - bi + b\pi^e + G \\ &= c_0 - c_1t_0 + a + G + (b + c_2)\pi^e + c_1(1 - t_1)Y - (b + c_2)i \end{aligned}$$

Solving for the interest rate,

$$i = \frac{c_0 - c_1t_0 + a + G - [1 - c_1(1 - t_1)]Y}{(b + c_2)} + \pi^e \tag{A9.1.5}$$

Similarly, equilibrium in the money market is given by the condition that money demand equals money supply. The supply of money is controlled by the central bank and is given by [Eq. (8.13) of Chapter 8]:

$$M^S = \overline{M} \tag{A9.1.6}$$

The demand for money is inversely related to the interest rate and directly related to aggregate income [see Eq. (8.14) of Chapter 8]:

$$\frac{M^d}{P} = h + nY - ei \tag{A9.1.7}$$

Equating (A9.1.6) and (A9.1.7) gives us,

$$\frac{\overline{M}}{P} = h + nY - ei$$

or,

$$i = \frac{h + nY - (\overline{M}/P)}{e} \tag{A9.1.8}$$

Equating the interest rates in Eqs. (A9.1.5) and (A9.1.8),

$$\frac{c_0 - c_1t_0 + a + G - [1 - c_1(1 - t_1)]Y}{(b + c_2)} + \pi^e = \frac{h + nY - (\bar{M}/P)}{e}$$

Taking terms in Y on the left-hand side,

$$Y\left[\frac{n}{e} + \frac{1 - c_1(1 - t_1)}{(b + c_2)}\right] = \frac{c_0 - c_1t_0 + a + G}{b + c_2} + \pi^e - \frac{h - (\bar{M}/P)}{e}$$

or,
$$Y\left\{\frac{(b + c_2)n + [1 - c_1(1 - t_1)]e}{(b + c_2)e}\right\} = \frac{c_0 - c_1t_0 + a + G}{b + c_2} + \pi^e - \frac{h - (\bar{M}/P)}{e}$$

Multiplying throughout by the inverse of the coefficient of Y,

$$Y = \frac{c_0 - c_1t_0 + a + G}{b + c_2}\,\frac{(b + c_2)e}{(b + c_2)n + [1 - c_1(1 - t_1)]e} + \pi^e\frac{(b + c_2)e}{(b + c_2)n + [1 - c_1(1 - t_1)]e}$$
$$+ \frac{(\bar{M}/P) - h}{e}\,\frac{(b + c_2)e}{(b + c_2)n + [1 - c_1(1 - t_1)]e}$$

We may write this as:

$$Y = [c_0 - c_1t_0 + a + G]\frac{e}{(b + c_2)n + [1 - c_1(1 - t_1)]e}$$
$$+ \pi^e\frac{(b + c_2)e}{(b + c_2)n + [1 - c_1(1 - t_1)]e}$$
$$+ [(\bar{M}/P) - h]\frac{(b + c_2)}{e}\,\frac{e}{(b + c_2)n + [1 - c_1(1 - t_1)]e}$$

Alternatively,

$$Y = [c_0 - c_1t_0 + a + G]\frac{1}{(b + c_2)(n/e) + [1 - c_1(1 - t_1)]}$$
$$+ \pi^e(b + c_2)\frac{1}{(b + c_2)(n/e) + [1 - c_1(1 - t_1)]}$$
$$+ [(\bar{M}/P) - h]\frac{(b + c_2)}{e}\,\frac{1}{(b + c_2)(n/e) + [1 - c_1(1 - t_1)]}$$

To solve this equation for P, take the term in real money supply to the left-hand side:

$$[(\bar{M}/P) - h]\frac{(b + c_2)}{e}\,\frac{1}{(b + c_2)(n/e) + [1 - c_1(1 - t_1)]}$$
$$= Y - [c_0 - c_1t_0 + a + G]\frac{1}{(b + c_2)(n/e) + [1 - c_1(1 - t_1)]}$$
$$- \pi^e(b + c_2)\frac{1}{(b + c_2)(n/e) + [1 - c_1(1 - t_1)]}$$

Then, the expression for $\bar{M}/P$ is given by:

$$\frac{\bar{M}}{P} = Y\frac{e}{(b + c_2)}\left\{(b + c_2)\frac{n}{e} + [1 - c_1(1 - t_1)]\right\}$$
$$- [c_0 - c_1t_0 + a + G]\frac{e}{(b + c_2)} - e\pi^e + h$$

Then, the expression for *P* is:

$$P = \frac{\bar{M}}{Y[e/(b+c_2)]\{(b+c_2)(n/e) + [1-c_1(1-t_1)]\} - (c_0 - c_1 t_0 + a + G)[e/(b+c_2)] - e\pi^e + h} \tag{A9.1.9}$$

This is the equation of the AD curve, where *P* and *Y* are inversely related, and, thus, give a downwardly sloping curve. By observing the signs of the parameters in this equation, we can write the effect of a change in a parameter on the position of the AD curve as:

$$P = f\left(\underset{(-)}{Y}; \underset{(+)}{M}, \underset{(+)}{G}, \underset{(-)}{t_0}, \underset{(-)}{t_1}, \underset{(+)}{\pi^e}, \underset{(+)}{a}\right) \tag{A9.1.10}$$

The AD curve—the relation between *P* and *Y*—shifts to the right when:

1. The money supply increases—*M* increases
2. Government expenditure increases—*G* increases
3. There is an increase in inflation expectations—π^e increases
4. There is an increase in business confidence or productivity—*a* increases

The AD curve shifts to the left when either the marginal income tax rate t_1 or the base rate of tax t_0 increases.

10

More on Unemployment

CRITICAL QUESTIONS

- *What accounts for the fact that wages are higher than the market-clearing level?*
- *What are efficiency wages?*
- *How do efficiency wages improve a firm's productivity?*
- *How is the aggregate supply curve related to efficiency wages in the short run and in the long run?*
- *Why are wage contracts staggered over time?*
- *Who are insiders and outsiders in the labour market?*
- *How does the presence of insiders generate unemployment?*

10.1 Shirking and Efficiency Wages

In any economy, there are always unemployed people who are available for work and are, in fact, seeking work. Up to now, we have looked at two explanations for this aggregate unemployment or excess supply of labour. One has been that the money wage has been set above the equilibrium rate and, as actual employment is determined by the short side of the labour market (the demand side), this results in unemployment.

The other explanation argues that workers form mistaken expectations about prices, and when expected prices are higher than actual prices, wages are set too high which again results in unemployment. What is the basis of this non-market-clearing wage that results in the outcome of unemployment? There are two approaches that explain this.

Keynes argued that employees were more concerned with relative, rather than real wages, and that various institutional factors kept the wage rates high. Friedman argued that workers are imperfectly informed about prices, and with adaptive expectations, revise the nominal wage as the information about prevailing prices becomes available.

But with nominal wages set too high—either because workers are concerned about their relative position in the labour market or because workers expect prices to be high, what prevents unemployed workers from knocking on the doors of firms and offering to work for lower wages? And what prevents the firms from hiring such workers, thus bidding down the wage and balancing supply and demand? After all, a worker who is otherwise identical to the firm's current workers, and who offers to work for less than what the firm currently pays its workers, should be acceptable to a firm that seeks any opportunity to increase profits. The efficiency wage theory explains why firms may not find it profitable to hire more workers at reduced wages.

It is the hallmark of the efficiency wage approach that even if workers offer to work for lower wages, firms do not want to reduce wages. In fact, firms pay higher wages because it is beneficial to them. Firms are willing to PAY MORE than the market clearing wage in order to recruit good workers, to discourage quitting, or to stimulate employees to work effectively.[1] Not just that, in developing countries, higher wages increase workers' food consumption, thereby causing them to be better nourished and more productive. Higher wages can allow workers to afford a more nutritious diet as well as be better nourished, healthier, and more productive, which is beneficial to the firm. Thus, the increase in labour costs, in terms of higher wages, can be compensated for by a greater increase in the productivity of the work force.[2] The efficiency wage is that wage where the marginal cost of increasing the wage exactly equals the marginal gain in the productivity of the firm's workers. The source of efficiency wages that we focus on here, however, is not nutrition or a reduced turnover of workers, but the fact that firms have a limited ability to monitor workers. This causes them to provide workers with an incentive to exert effort. This approach is due to a famous paper by Shapiro and Stiglitz.[3]

› Firms **pay higher** than market-clearing wages to elicit effort, reduce turnover, recruit better workers, and improve worker morale.

A problem arises when firms CANNOT EASILY MONITOR WORKERS' EFFORTS at their jobs as monitoring activities are expensive. Workers can shirk and spend time on activities unrelated to the position for which they have been hired to—such as reading the newspaper, updating their gossip from the tabloids, or sending texts to their friends. Shirking workers result in a loss of productivity for the

› When firms have difficulty **monitoring employees,** they have an incentive to offer a wage-employment package that deters workers from shirking on the job.

firm, which would like to offer a wage-employment package that encourages workers not to shirk at all.

Let there be $\bar{N}$ workers in the labour market, and let the labour supply curve be inelastic. Workers are either employed or unemployed. If w/p is the real wage and e is the workers' effort, the instantaneous benefit to a worker is:

$$B = \begin{cases} \dfrac{w}{p} - e & \text{If Employed} \\ 0 & \text{If Unemployed} \end{cases}$$

There are only two possible efforts levels. Thus, either the worker exerts effort, e, or the worker shirks, $e = 0$. Hence,

$$B_{\text{employed}} = \begin{cases} \dfrac{w}{p} - e & \text{If Effort is Expended} \\ \dfrac{w}{p} & \text{If Shirks} \end{cases}$$

At any moment, a worker could then be: (1) employed and exerting effort; (2) employed and shirking; or (3) unemployed.

Let μ be the probability of unemployment. Unemployment occurs because firms detect workers who are shirking and detection occurs with probability μ. Workers who are caught shirking are fired.[4] Those who become unemployed may eventually find a new job. For simplicity though, we will assume that the probability of unemployment is equal to the probability that a shirking worker is detected and, accordingly, fired. The basis of this could be because once a person is fired for shirking, the word gets out to the labour market as to the person's attributes and firms are then reluctant to hire them. What is the net benefit gained by the employee by cheating on the job?

$$\begin{aligned} \text{Net Benefit of Shirking} &= B\,(\text{Shirking}) - B\,(\text{Exerting Effort}) \\ &= \frac{w}{p} - \left(\frac{w}{p} - e\right) \\ &= e \end{aligned}$$

The downside to cheating on the job is that the worker will be detected with probability μ and that will result in his being fired and the loss of his income. The expected loss from shirking is, therefore, the probability that the cheating is detected, (μ), times the loss of income from being fired, (w/p).

$$\text{Expected Loss of Shirking} = \mu\frac{w}{p}$$

The expected loss of wages from cheating is, therefore, equal to the gain from cheating, when,

$$\mu\frac{w}{p} = e$$

or,

$$\frac{w}{p} = \frac{e}{\mu} \quad \text{[No Shirking Condition (NSC)]}$$

This equation is the no shirking condition (NSC), which gives the wage the firm must pay to ensure that workers do not shirk. If the unemployment rate is high—μ is large—shirking is costly for a worker. This is because once a shirking worker gets caught and fired, he faces a long unemployment spell. Firms can

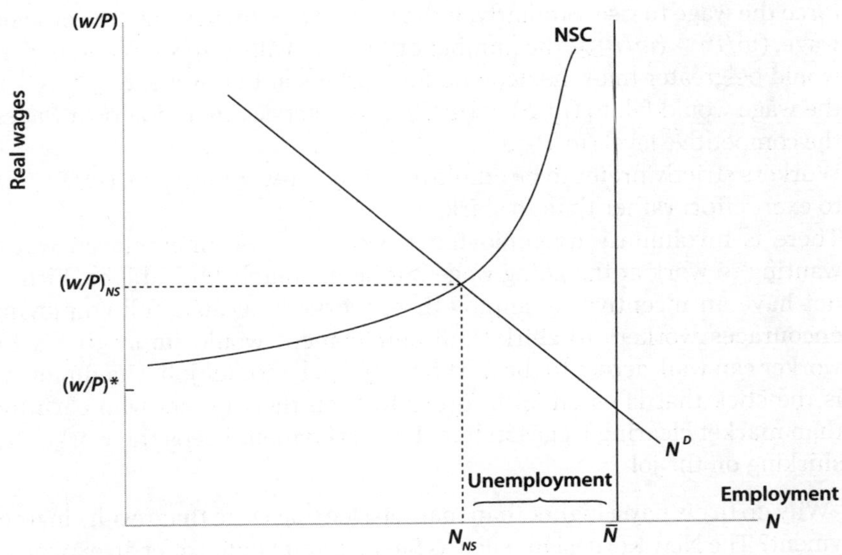

› **Figure 10.1**
Unemployment in a Shirking Model. There are $\bar{N}$ workers offering to work in the labour market. Firms seek to deter shirking workers. When the rate of unemployment is high, the firm can pay close to competitive wages, (w/p)*, and deter shirking. As the unemployment rate falls, higher wages have to be paid to deter shirking. This results in the upward-sloping NSC. The demand for labour is given by the downward-sloping marginal productivity of the employment curve. Equilibrium unemployment is determined at the point where the NSC curve intersects the demand-for-labour curve.

pay a relatively low wage in such a situation and will still be able to attract workers who will not shirk.

On the other hand, if the unemployment rate is low—μ is small—shirking workers who are caught face a low chance of an unemployment spell that is not too costly for them, and firms must offer a relatively high wage in order to make shirking costly for such workers. This generates an upward sloping—no shirking supply curve in Figure 10.1. As the probability of unemployment declines, that is, as we move closer to the full employment level $\bar{N}$, the firm must pay a higher no shirking wage to deter workers from shirking.

Firm behaviour is otherwise unchanged—seeks to maximize profits. With e as the effort per employee and N the number of employees who are exerting effort, its workforce measured in efficiency units is eN. Its output is given by[5]:

$$Y = F(eN)$$

With S the number of employees who are shirking, the firm's profits are:

$$\Pi = F(eN) - \frac{w}{p}(N + S)$$

Profit maximization results in a downward-sloping demand for labour curve N^D depicted in Figure 10.1, along which the wage is equal to the marginal product of employment (eMP_{eN}), or,

$$\frac{w}{p} = eMP_{eN}$$

The equilibrium wage is where the no shirking supply curve and the labour demand curve intersect. At this equilibrium, $(w/P)_{NS}$ is the EFFICIENCY WAGE and N_{NS} workers will be employed, leaving $\bar{N} - N_{NS}$ WORKERS UNEMPLOYED.[6] If there was perfect monitoring, equilibrium would occur at the intersection of N^D and $\bar{N}$. It is because of imperfect monitoring that equilibrium occurs at the intersection of the labour demand curve and the NSC. Three interesting implications arise:

› **Efficiency wages** are the wages that maximize firm profits when workers may work or shirk.

› Efficiency wages are higher than the competitive market wage and generate **involuntary unemployment.**

1. There is no market pressure to bid the wage down to the competitive wage $(w/P)^*$ by unemployed workers. If firms paid less than $(w/P)_{NS}$, that is, $(w/P) < (w/P)_{NS}$, the number of workers willing to work and not shirk will be less than the number of workers demanded, or, $N_{NS} < N^D$, and this would

force the wage to rise. Similarly, if the wages were higher than the efficiency wage, $(w/P) > (w/P)_{NS}$, the number of workers willing to work and not shirk would be greater than the demand for workers at that wage, $N_{NS} > N^D$, and the wage would fall to $(w/P) = (w/P)_{NS}$. Workers cannot bid down wages to the competitive level $(w/P)^*$.

2. Workers strictly prefer to be employed at the prevailing wage, $(w/P)_{NS}$, and to exert effort rather than to shirk.
3. There is involuntary unemployment with $\overline{N} - N_{NS}$ unemployed workers wanting to work at the going wage but being unable to find jobs. Firms do not have an incentive to employ these workers because full employment encourages workers to shirk. Full employment would imply that a fired worker can walk across to the next firm and get another job. Unemployment is the stick that is essential in order to keep the workers who earn more than market clearing wages in line. Unemployment keeps the worker from shirking on the job.

Why do firms pay a higher than market-clearing wage that results in unemployment? The New Keynesians such as Shapiro and Stiglitz offer an explanation of unemployment which emanates from the demand side of the labour market. They argue that firms choose to pay a wage higher than the market clearing wage because of their limited ability to detect shirking on the job, and that the higher wage is intended to provide an incentive to workers to exert more effort and raise the output of the firm. Even if workers, in Friedman fashion, offer to work for lower wages, the efficiency wages approach argues that firms do not want to reduce wages. In the Friedman version of why wages may be higher than market-clearing levels, it is the workers who set them that way to neutralize the expected cost of living increases. The nominal wage is chosen by workers in the Friedman model, whereas it is chosen by firms in the New Keynesian model. In the classical model, by contrast, the firm chooses employment to maximize profit, taking the real wage as given.

10.2 The Long-Run and Staggered Wage Setting

Efficiency wages account for the existence of unemployment in equilibrium just as the Friedman mistaken expectations model does. However, it does not result in an upward-sloping supply curve of output[7] and to get this type of outcome the Keynesians assume that nominal wages are chosen less frequently than employment is chosen by the firm. The nominal wage is said to be STICKY. The firm sets its wage rate less frequently than it hires or fires workers.

› The New Keynesians argue that nominal wages are **sticky** in the short run.

Let the initial nominal wage and price be such that the real wage is w_0/P_0, and let unemployment be at the natural rate where U^* individuals are unemployed (see Figure 10.2, panel A).

Now, suppose the price level increases to P_1. As nominal wage adjustment takes time, in the short run the wage will remain at its nominal level w_0. In real terms, the nominal wage has declined to w_0/P_1, and the firms respond by recruiting more labour lower down on their demand-for-labour curve. Unemployment declines to U_1 and so output rises, as traced out via the production function part of the diagram (see Figure 10.2, panel B). Conversely, if there is a decline in the price, the real wage rises, firms employ less, and there is a rise in unemployment along with a decline in output. In the short run then,

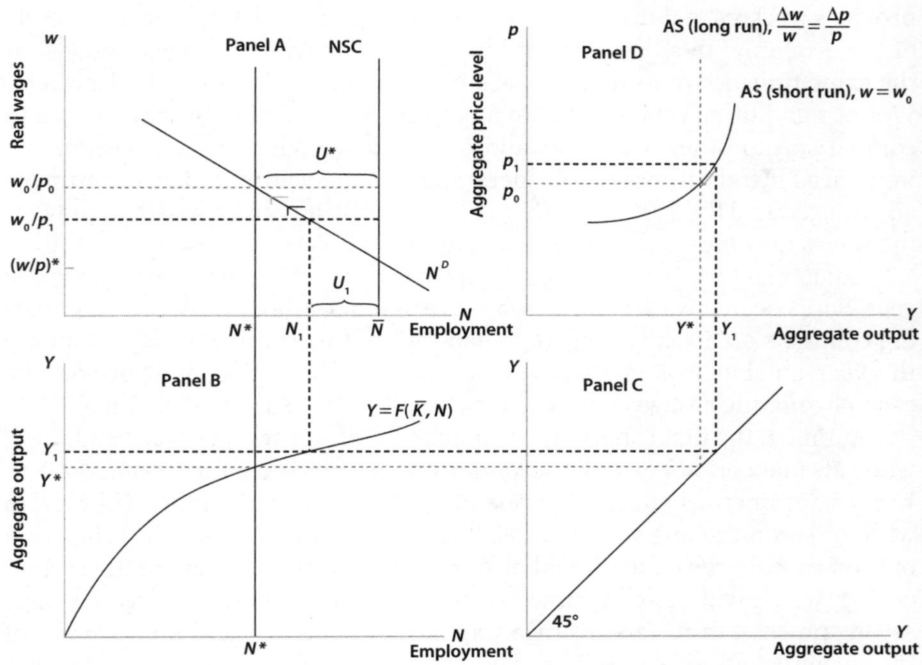

› **Figure 10.2 The New Keynesian Supply Curve.** Unemployment is at its natural rate U^* at the prevailing real wage w_o/p_o in panel A. With sticky nominal wages, firms increase their demand for labour from N^* to N_1 when the price level rises to p_1 in panel A. The increase in employment increases the output in panel B. The higher price level p_1 is associated with an increased output Y_1 in panel D. As prices rise, the output increases resulting in the upward-sloping, AS (short-run) curve in panel D. Over the long run, as the nominal wages adjust, employment and output move towards the natural rate as given by the vertical AS (long-run) curve.

we have an upward-sloping supply curve, which results due to nominal wage stickiness, AS($w = w_o$).

When the real wage equals the efficiency wage w_o/P_o, unemployment is at its natural rate, $\bar{U}^*$, and the quantity of output produced is the natural rate of output, Y^*. New Keynesians attempt to differentiate themselves by referring to point (w_o/P_o, N^*) in Figure 10.2, panel A, as the QUASI-EQUILIBRIUM RATE OF UNEMPLOYMENT (QERU). It is an equilibrium because the point is a solution to the profit maximization and NSC equations, and the "quasi" term comes about because there is aggregate excess supply of labour. Such a quasi-equilibrium point is the only point at which the demand for labour is consistent with wage setting behaviour that deters shirking. With deference to the New Keynesians, we refer to the point as the Keynesian natural rate of unemployment. This natural rate of output is an outcome of the fundamentals of the economy—preferences, endowments and technology—and is unaffected by the money supply or any other factor that affects aggregate demand.

› The New Keynesian natural rate of unemployment is an **equilibrium** labour market outcome where wages deter shirking behaviour, firms maximize profits, and there is an excess supply of labour.

Suppose the price level is P_1 and unemployment is below the natural rate. The New Keynesians assume that adjustment begins with some fraction of firms adjusting their nominal wages over any given period of time.

10.2.1 Staggered Wage Contracts

As emphasized by Taylor,[8] contract decisions are STAGGERED in that all wage contract decisions in the economy are not made at the same point in time. First, wages are set for a predetermined length of time (contract period) because the cost of frequent adjustments to wages and salaries is high. Firms set wages by keeping in mind labour productivity and forecasts of revenues in the near future. It would be prohibitive to frequently review worker's performance and seek information about wages paid elsewhere and renegotiate wage contracts. Second, wage setting is also staggered, decisions on wages across the economy are not synchronized or coordinated and workers in different industries set and adjust wages at different points in time. There is an informational benefit to this process, as the staggered wage setting

› The New Keynesians argue that the nominal wage setting is **staggered**, so that wages are sticky in the short run.

provides workers and firms information about wages and prices in other parts of the economy. In a decentralized market economy, if all wages were set at the same time, there would be a lack of information about wages elsewhere. Workers and firms would not be in a position to know what their wages are in comparison to other industries and occupations. When wage decisions are influenced by relative wage considerations, a non-sychronized wage setting is advantageous. This is because, then, the wage setting can be based on prevailing wages in comparable reference industries.

Adjustments to wage contracts are generally staggered throughout the year. Suppose that wage contracts last a year and decision dates for renegotiating contracts are evenly staggered—half the contracts, say, are set in January this year, and half in January next year. There are then two cohorts of workers, each negotiating a wage contract for two periods in a staggered manner.

At time t, the first cohort sets its nominal wage for two periods, t and $t + 1$, while at time period $t + 1$, the second cohort sets its wage for $t + 1$ and $t + 2$. In such a framework, the first period of the firm cohort's contract will overlap with the second cohort's contract set at time $t - 1$. Furthermore, the last period of the first cohort's contract will also overlap with the contract of the second cohort, which will be set at time $t + 1$. In such a two-period staggered wage setting process, firms face average wage costs[9] given by the simple average of the current contract wage (X_t) signed in period t and previous contract wages signed in period $t - 1$ (X_{t-1}), or,

$$w_t = \frac{1}{2}(X_{t-1} + X_t)$$

where X_i is the contract wage settlement signed in period i. The contract wage set in a period need not be a function of just currently observed variables. If agents are forward looking, they will estimate the average wage in the next period as well as the tightness of the labour market as given by future unemployment. If workers expect wage settlements in the next period $t + 1$ to be moderate, they will also attempt to conclude moderate wage settlements in period t. Also, if there is an expectation that the economy will enter into a downturn next period, which raises future unemployment, there will be a tendency to restrain wage increases this period.[10]

10.2.2 Wage Adjustment

If wage contracts were *synchronized* rather than *staggered*, it would allow aggregate wage responses to be induced faster when prices change. With all firms responding quickly to price changes, it would be akin to a classical supply curve. As firms adjust their wages, they will also adjust their employment levels. As time passes, more firms adjust their nominal wages and the economy-wide average wage slowly SHIFTS BACK TO EQUILIBRIUM. The sequences of events are illustrated by the arrows in the Figure 10.2. A similar sequence of adjustment occurs when the prices declines and the real wage temporarily rises.

› In the long run, as wages adjust, the **labour market moves towards the natural rate of employment** and output.

Firms renegotiate nominal wages when the unemployment rate moves away from the natural rate. This is because at a real wage less than that ($w/P < w_0/P_0$), there are fewer workers who are willing to work than the number demanded by firms in the industry which would lead to a rise in wage. Similarly, if the wage was higher than the efficiency wage, there would be more workers willing to work and not shirk than are being demanded and the wage would fall. The efficiency wage, after all, is set above the market-clearing wage so as to make it costly for workers to shirk. Unemployment, to reiterate, is a disciplining device that keeps employed workers in line.

MACROFOCUS 10.1

Henry Ford and Efficiency Wages

The Ford Motor Company, that was founded in 1903, had a highly skilled workforce. Ford began by assembling, rather than manufacturing, cars and the parts were produced by outside machine shops with low tolerances. This required a lot of shaping and fitting to get them together properly, which in turn required skilled metal-working craftsmen. Ford then decided in 1908 to make the Model T where one automobile would be just like another automobile. He decided to do this by having parts made to high tolerances so that skilled fitting would no longer be required. The workshop was also redesigned to reduce unnecessary movements of workers and parts. The scale of production increased tremendously from 450 employees in 1908 to 14,000 in 1913, and the output increased 25-fold over this period.

In the process, tasks got routinized and the work became menial. The requirement for workers to be in lockstep so that the assembly line moved smoothly increased the pressure on them. By 1913, workers' dissatisfaction and turnover increased drastically so that Ford hired 50,448 men in the course of the year to maintain the average labour force at 13,623. In January 1914, Ford announced a reduction in the working day from nine to eight hours and a rise in daily payments from USD 2.34 to USD 5.00 a day. He also made it clear that inefficient workers would be discharged and that if the company fortunes dipped, then it would not be bound to continue such wage payments.

Soon after the announcement there were long queues for jobs outside the plant and the crowd had to be managed with water cannons. Excess supply of labour seeking jobs became the norm at Ford. There was a pronounced decline in absenteeism and the turnover rate of 370 per cent declined to 16 per cent. Productivity per worker increased by over 40 per cent and profits by about 20 per cent. Fifteen per cent more cars were produced per day in the span of a year.

Thus, the wage hike was sufficient to ensure that it exceeded workers' opportunity cost of working and allowed Ford to ration jobs. It provided substantial productivity benefits as well. An increase in the wage reduced turnover among workers and extracted more productive effort from them. Ford derived the benefits of paying efficiency wages.

Source: D.M.G. Raff and L.H. Summers, "Did Henry Ford Pay Efficiency Wages?" *Journal of Labour Economics* 5, no. (4), Part 2, (1987): 557–585.

10.3 The Insider–Outsider Approach

In the efficiency wage approach, it is not in the interest of the firm to reduce wages. In the insider–outsider approach, it is not in the interest of incumbent workers to do so. Insider–outsider theories argue that various types of labour turnover costs create rents and market power for incumbent workers in existing firms, who are called the insiders. This allows insiders to push their wages above the market-clearing wage without them losing their jobs.[11] INSIDERS are experienced incumbent employees whose positions are protected by labour turnover cost. Outsiders are taken to be the unemployed. Rather than use the descriptive terms employed and unemployed, the terms insider and outsider are used as analytical categories. These highlight the asymmetric position of incumbent workers who have market power emanating from labour turnover costs. This is unlike the unemployed, who lack market power.

› **Insiders** are incumbent employees who have market power in the determination of wages. This market power arises from the insiders' ability to exploit turnover costs of hiring and firing in the wage bargain compared to outsiders.

The traditional labour turnover costs are the costs associated with hiring and firing labour. Hiring costs include the costs of searching, screening, negotiating with, and training newly hired workers. Firing costs include costly firing procedures and severance pay that are often part of a job security legislation. Labour turnover costs also arise when insiders refuse to cooperate with outsiders who try to get jobs by underbidding the wages of insiders. If an unemployed worker offers to work for a lower wage, insiders can THREATEN NOT TO COOPERATE with the underbidder. Since output is only possible when workers coordinate their activities with each other, a worker who can't get cooperation is unable to contribute adequately towards production. This makes his productivity so low that the firm does not find it worthwhile to hire him. Apart from making it unprofitable to the firm to hire someone who offers to work at a lower wage, incumbents can also make life disagreeable for the underbidder by harassing him for breaking into the firm by underbidding. Outsiders then face less favourable working conditions than insiders do and these discriminatory conditions result in a disinclination on the part of outsiders to engage in

› Insiders can also **refuse to cooperate** with outsiders who attempt to underbid prevailing wages and thereby reduce labour productivity. Firms then find outsiders unattractive to hire.

› **Harassment** also raises the opportunity cost of employment and deters outsiders from offering their labour services.

underbidding if outsiders underbid, the insiders would HARASS them and raise the cost to them of accepting employment with the firm.

Let N_I and N_E represent the labour input of the insider and the entrant, and their real wage be given by ω_I and ω_E. The production function of the firm[12] is given by $F(N_I + N_E)$. Standard demand for labour curves are downward-sloping curves representing the marginal product of labour. For the case of an insider's demand curve (IDC), the demand for labour will be the sum of the marginal product of labour, MP_N, and the marginal cost of firing (F) that labour, MC_F. Similarly, the demand curve for entrants (EDC) is the marginal product of entrants, MP_N, minus the marginal cost of hiring (H) workers, MC_H. Thus,

$$\text{IDC} = MP_N + MC_F$$

$$\text{EDC} = MP_N - MC_H$$

If there were no labour turnover costs, $MC_F = MC_H = 0$, and the traditional demand curve for labour would be given by MP_N, which lies in between the IDC and EDC curves in Figure 10.3.

Let the wages of entrants be equal to their reservation wage,[13] $\omega_E = R$, as given by the horizontal line in the upper-half of the diagram.[14] What is the maximum wage, above the reservation wage of entrants, that the insiders can demand without losing their jobs?

The maximum wage that insiders may obtain, without being replaced by outsiders, is the entrant wage plus the sum of the marginal costs of hiring and firing labour, $\omega_E + MC_H + MC_F$. Any insider wage above this makes it profitable for the firm to replace insiders by outsiders. We can refer to $\omega_E + MC_H + MC_F$ as the relative profitability constraint (RPC), or, the maximum wage insiders may obtain without being replaced by outsiders.

Let the number of insiders at the time of analysis be m^*. Instead of bargaining over the rents with firms, assume that insiders acquire the entire rent generated

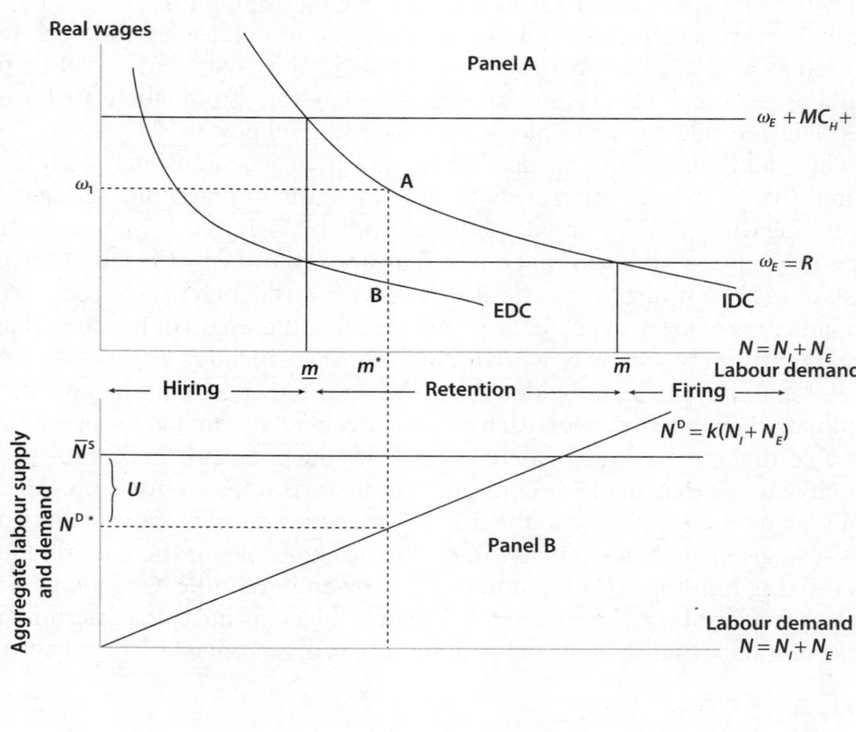

› **Figure 10.3**
Employment with Insiders and Outsiders. The EDC is the marginal productivity of labour minus the marginal cost of hiring in panel A. The IDC is the marginal productivity of labour plus the marginal cost of firing. With reservation wage rate ω_E for an entrant, incumbents are profitable to the firm and will not be replaced by entrants up to a wage given by ω_E plus the marginal costs of hiring and firing in panel A. In this case, insiders will retain their jobs (between $\underline{m}$ and $\overline{m}$). When the productivity of insiders falls below the reservation wage rate (after $\overline{m}$), it is profitable for the firm to fire them. Hiring will occur to the left of $\underline{m}$. The employment per firm at m^* multiplied by the number of firms gives the aggregate demand for labour in panel B. Subtracting the aggregate demand from the aggregate supply N^S gives the extent of unemployment.

by the marginal turnover costs ($MC_H + MC_F$). With m^* insiders, the wages that they are able to demand will be given by ω_1, giving point A on the IDC. At this wage all insiders get to keep their jobs and no entrants find jobs. This is because their marginal productivity at point B, after deducting for labour turnover costs, is below the entrant wage ω_E.

Hence, if there are any unemployed workers between $\underline{m}$ and $\overline{m}$, they will remain unemployed.

Another case could be that if the number of insiders currently in the firm is smaller than $\underline{m}$, the firm will hire more workers—a hiring situation.

Finally, if the number of insiders currently in the firm is greater than $\overline{m}$, some insiders will be fired even if they accept an entrant's wage. This is because their productivity, as given by the IDC, will be below ω_E—a firing situation. For any initial employment level between $\underline{m}$ and $\overline{m}$, the number of employees will remain unchanged—a retention situation.

MACROFOCUS 10.2

Macroeconomic Policy with Insiders

What macroeconomic policy is appropriate when employment is determined by insider–outsider effects? Suppose there is a supply-side shock—a sudden increase in the prices of intermediate imported inputs such as oil, or a natural disaster such as a drought—that adversely affects the marginal productivity of labour. This shifts the marginal productivity IDC to the left, the dashed IDC curve. If the shock occurs after insider wages have been set, employment declines at the constant insider wage to point C. Insiders, who, if their initial number is m^*, would normally negotiate wages on the basis of market power and obtain wage rate ω_1.

Suppose the shock occurs prior to wage-setting by insiders. Then, insiders could all club together out of anxiety that they may lose their jobs and they would accept a wage reduction to ω_2—point B where employment is still m^*.

The other extreme possibility is that insiders insist on maintaining the wage prior to the shock, ω_1. Some workers lose their jobs. If there is a seniority system that governs firing decisions, then it would be common knowledge as to who the laid-off workers would be. If a majority of workers continue to be employed at an unchanged wage, this outcome is likely. Laid-off workers are not in a position to save their job by bidding for lower wages as insiders would threaten not to cooperate with them. This would, in turn, reduce their productivity and attractiveness to the firm. The creation of a hostile work environment for those who underbid also raises the reservation wages of laid-off workers who underbid.

If later a favourable supply-side shock occurs, the labour market scenario might return to that depicted by the curve IDC. In that case, if insiders exploit the improved labour market situation and push for higher wages, they can attain wage rate ω_3 without being displaced by other workers. This is point D in Figure 1 where the employment increase is modest. A favourable shock, may not increase employment while an unfavourable shock reduces employment. Wages, however, show an upward trend over time, even as employment reduces.

In such a situation, reducing the barriers to entry of firms may be an important correlate of demand management policy. Lower barriers to entry by firms in the US as compared to firms in Western Europe could be a reason for the recovery in US employment from the recession in the late 1970s and early 1980s, as compared to European employment. (An increase in the number of firms k in Figure 10.3 reduces unemployment.) Also, government expenditures on infrastructure by raising the marginal productivity of labour could have a larger impact on the labour market than spending by governments. The latter does not have such supply side effects such as the transfer payments that have increasingly dominated European government budgets.*

› **Figure 1**
Employment and Insider-Outsider Effects.

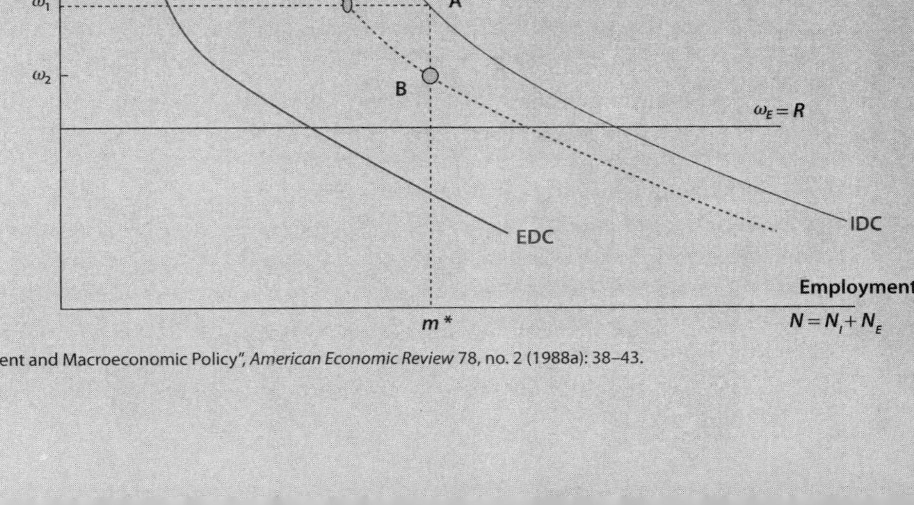

* A. Lindbeck and D. J. Snower, "Long-Term Unemployment and Macroeconomic Policy", *American Economic Review* 78, no. 2 (1988a): 38–43.

Let us look at an aggregate level now. The simplest way to represent the situation is to assume that there are k identical firms so that the aggregate demand for labour is given by $N^D = k\,(N_I + N_E)$. At the labour demand m^* of the individual firm, aggregate labour demand will be N^{D*}, which can be seen in the lower-half of Figure 10.3. With aggregate labour supply in the economy given by $\overline{N}^S$, unemployment is given by $U = \overline{N}^S - N^{D*}$.

› Established firms that set wages on an insider-outsider basis are susceptible to competition from **new firms** which have no insiders and can employ workers at lower reservation wages.

› The rate of **unemployment** is dependent on the barriers to entry faced by new firms in the economy.

The insider–outsider theory provides an alternative explanation for why underbidding of wages by the unemployed may not find them gaining entry into the labour market. It is not in the interests of incumbents since they exploit the rents generated in connection with the turnover costs to keep potential entrants out. However, the insider–outsider theory neglects to account for NEW FIRMS, which, having no insiders, could hire unemployed workers at their reservation wages, and undersell established firms. The potential entry of a new firm could then cause insiders to lose their jobs and lead them to temper their wage demands and shift the IDC curve to the left. However, such entry may not be able to ALLEVIATE UNEMPLOYMENT substantially if there are obstacles to the entry of firms, such as limited entrepreneurial skills, risk aversion, and credit rationing, which restricts the availability of equity capital and borrowed funds. Apart from the entry of new firms, established firms may go in for plants at other locations and pit the insiders in one plant against those in another location. They can do this by making an offer that the plant that settles for a lower wage would remain open while the other would shut down if their insiders insist on keeping their wages. Of course, firms lose out on economies of scale if they split production across various units of small size, and centralized unions operating above the level of individual plants could prevent any wage concessions sought by the firm in this manner.

SUMMARY

- Firms pay higher than market clearing wages to elicit effort, reduce turnover, recruit better workers, and improve worker morale.
- When firms have difficulty monitoring employees, they have an incentive to offer a wage—employment package that deters workers from shirking on the job.
- Efficiency wages are the wages that maximize firm profits when it is difficult to monitor whether workers work or shirk.
- Efficiency wages are higher than the competitive market wage and generate involuntary unemployment.
- The New Keynesian natural rate of unemployment is an equilibrium labour market outcome where wages deter shirking behaviour, firms maximize profits, and there is an excess supply of labour.
- The New Keynesians argue that nominal wage setting is staggered so that wages are sticky in the short run.
- In the long run as wages adjust the labour market moves towards the natural rate of employment and output.
- Insiders are incumbent employees who have market power in the determination of wages. This market power arises from insiders' ability to exploit turnover costs of hiring and firing in the wage bargain compared to outsiders.
- Insiders can also reduce labour productivity by refusing to cooperate with outsiders who attempt to underbid prevailing wages. Firms then find outsiders unattractive to hire. Harassment by insiders also raises the opportunity cost of employment and deters outsiders from offering their labour services.
- Established firms setting wages on an insider–outsider basis are susceptible to competition from new firms who have no insiders and can employ workers at lower reservation wages.
- The rate of unemployment is dependent on the barriers to entry faced by new firms in the economy when insider effects prevail in the labour market.

NOTES

1. L. Katz, "Efficiency Wage Theories: A Partial Evaluation", NBER Macroeconomics Annual, Cambridge: MA, 1986, pp. 235–276.
2. H. Leibenstein, "The Theory of Underemployment in Backward Economies", *Journal of Political Economy* 65 (April 1957): 91–103.
3. C. Shapiro and J. E. Stiglitz, "Equilibrium Unemployment as a Worker Discipline Device", *American Economic Review* 74 (1984): 433–444.
4. When firms want to hire workers they choose at random from the pool of unemployed workers. Since workers are

considered to be identical, the chance of finding a job does not depend on how workers become unemployed, or on how long they are unemployed.

5. The marginal product is positive and subject to the usual condition of diminishing marginal productivity.
6. We have presented the results as a result of a decision by one firm. This is for ease of exposition that we have concentrated on employment per firm. The number of workers unemployed is the number of firms times the number unemployed per firm.
7. Since efficiency wages are real efficiency wages, an increase in the price would be consistent with a rise in the nominal wage such that all real variables are the same. Any price change in the efficiency wage model can result in no change in the employment and output, a vertical supply curve.
8. J.B. Taylor, "Staggered Wage Setting in Macro Model", *American Economic Review* 69, no. 2 (1979): 108–113.
9. Taylor argues that the average real contract wage is increasing in the level of real economic activity, and uses it to argue further that inflation dynamics in an economy is influenced by the interaction of staggered contracts apart from the well know expectations mechanism.
10. Wage settlements in period t can then be written as $X_t = (1/2)\{[(1/2)(X_{t-1} + X_t)] + [(1/2)(X_t + X_{t+1})]\} - (\theta/2)$ $[(U_t - U^*) + (U_{t+1} - U^*)]$ where θ is the sensitivity of wages to unemployment, and U^* is the natural rate of unemployment. Solving for X_t, $X_t = (1/2)(X_{t-1} + X_{t+1})$ $- \theta[(U_t - U^*) + (U_{t+1} - U^*)]$. Hence, wages may be determined on a forward looking basis.
11. A. Lindbeck and D. Snower, *The Insider–Outsider Theory of Employment and Unemployment*, Cambridge, MA: MIT Press, 1988; Also A. Lindbeck, and D. Snower, "Interactions between the Efficiency Wage and Insider-Outsider Theories", *Economics Letters* 37, (1991):193–196.
12. Insiders can be presumed to be more productive than outsiders without any damage to the basic results.
13. The reservation wage is the minimum increase in income that makes a person indifferent between working and not working. A person will not work at all if the market wage is less than the reservation wage and the person will enter the labour market if the market wage exceeds the reservation wage.
14. We do not deal with the cooperation-harassment version of the theory. However, lack of cooperation with outsiders who try to underbid wages keeps down their productivity and shifts the EDC curve to the left. Similarly, harassing underbidders is akin to pushing up the reservation wage of outsiders.

TEST YOURSELF

1. Briefly outline the various approaches to explaining the phenomenon of involuntary unemployment.
2. Why do firms pay efficiency wages and what prevents the market from clearing in an efficiency wage labour market?
3. Why are nominal wages sticky in the short run? How would the aggregate supply curve differ in the situation when the wage adjustment is slow as compared to the case where the wage adjustment is fast?
4. What is staggered wage setting and why is it prevalent?
5. Why is the long-run aggregate supply curve inelastic even though the short-run aggregate supply curve is elastic?
6. Differentiate between insiders, entrants, and outsiders in the labour market.
7. What sort of market power do insiders wield and how does it impact on employment in the firm?
8. Distinguish between the hiring, retention, and firing phases of employment within a firm that is subject to insider power.
9. How does a supply shock affect the relationship between wages and employment in an insider–outsider model?
10. How successful would aggregate demand management be in dealing with unemployment when firms pay efficiency wages or wage setting is influenced by insider power?

ONLINE APPLICATION

This chapter has argued that the labour market cannot be exclusively identified with productive relations due to the complexity of what is being exchanged in this market. For instance, the cooperation offered by senior workers to new employees plays a crucial role in inducting new workers into a firm and affects its productivity. Insider power has many manifestations. One such example is the implicit understanding in many public-sector institutions in India that the child or the spouse of an employee should be hired in his/her place in case of death, injury, or retirement. If the public sector is subject to insider–outsider effects, then there could be limits to its ability to generate employment. To understand this more, try the following:

1. (a) Go to the home page of the Reserve Bank of India URL:www.rbi.org.in/home.aspx
   (b) Click on the "DataBase" icon
   (c) Then under the classification of Annual data, click on "Handbook of Statistics on Indian Economy"
2. Click on "Table 14: Employment in Public and Organized Private Sectors" and create a spreadsheet of data on public sector and organized private sector employment for the

years 1983–1984, 1987–1988, 1993–1994, 1999–2000, and 2004–2005.

3. From the National Sample Survey Employment-Unemployment Surveys and the National Commission for Enterprises in the Unorganized Sector (NCEUS) Report on Conditions of Work and Promotion of Livelihoods in the Unorganized Sector (http://nceus.gov.in/) we have the following data on total employment:

Year	Employment in Millions
1983	303
1987–1988	324
1993–1994	374
1999–2000	397
2004–2005	457

4. Subtract the data on organized sector employment, as obtained in Step 4, from total employment to obtain the estimate of unorganized employment in India. The unorganized sector is an enterprise-based concept and is defined as "all unincorporated private enterprises owned by individuals or households engaged in the production and sale of goods and services operated on a proprietary or partnership basis and with less than ten total workers". (The NCEUS argues that an enterprise based definition is insufficient as it does not reflect the characteristics of jobs. For instance, some workers in the organized sector may not enjoy employment security (casual workers), and may not be eligible for paid sick/annual leave or other social security benefits. The Commission argues that though organized sector employment increased during 1999–2000 and 2004–2005, the entire net increase of 8.5 million employment was due to workers without social security benefits. Thus the organized sector may have informal employment, an issue we sidestep for now.)
5. Estimate (a) the share of the public sector and unorganized sector employment in total employment and (b) the growth rate of employment between 1983–1984 and 2004–2005 for the public sector and the unorganized sector. What do these statistics reveal about the structure of employment in India? Could the relatively faster growth of public sector employment of the 1980s, which decelerated subsequently compared to unorganized sector employment, be due to insider-outsider effects?
6. Recall that in Chapter 1 we had found that the contribution of the public sector to GDP was about 25 per cent. Can you explain the very low employment contribution compared to that in output that occurred in the public sector?

11

Open Economy: The Mundell–Fleming Model

CRITICAL QUESTIONS

» *How does an open economy change the nature of* IS–LM *analysis?*

» *How do controls on capital affect the balance of payments?*

» *What is the impact of monetary policy under fixed and flexible exchange rates?*

» *What is the impact of fiscal policy under fixed and flexible exchange rates?*

» *How can an economy deal with capital inflows?*

11.1 Accounting for an Open Economy

We now turn to the determinants of output and income when we have an open economy. Let us first recall some macroeconomic accounting that we had done initially. For an open economy, aggregate output can be written as:

$$Y = C + I + G + X - M \tag{11.1}$$

In Section 2.1, we had added net factor incomes earned by residents of the country from abroad (NFI) and transfers from abroad (mainly remittances) to both sides of the income equals expenditure equation [Eq. (11.1)] to obtain:

$$Y + \text{NFI} + \text{Transfers from Abroad} = C + I + G + X - M + \text{NFI} + \text{Transfers from Abroad}$$

However, since the current account surplus (CA) is the last four terms in the previous expression—the sum of exports less imports ($X - M$), NFI, and transfers from abroad, we could rewrite this expression as:

$$Y + \text{NFI} + \text{Transfers from Abroad} - C - G = I + \text{CA} \tag{11.2}$$

We then showed in Section 2.1 that the left-hand side of Eq. (11.2) is the expression for the sum of private savings (S_{pvt}) and public savings (S_{govt}). We can then rewrite Eq. (11.2) as:

$$S_{\text{pvt}} + S_{\text{govt}} = I + \text{CA}$$

Taking the current account term on the left-hand side, we obtain:

$$S_{\text{pvt}} + S_{\text{govt}} - \text{CA} = I \tag{11.3}$$

The current account surplus, from its definition in the national income accounts, is the sum of the following:

1. Balance of merchandise trade in goods
2. Net receipts from non-factor incomes—services or invisibles—such as travel, transport, insurance, and software exports
3. Net receipts from factor incomes from abroad—net investment income earned by domestic residents from abroad as well as compensation to employees from abroad
4. Transfers—official transfers between governments and private transfers such as remittances

The sum of the first two components of the current account—the balance of merchandise trade and NFI—is the definition of the net exports, ($X - M$), of an economy. In Chapter 5, we have studied how the real exchange rate is an important variable that influences the net exports of an economy. In contrast, we have not investigated the decisions that lead to domestic factors of production such as capital and labour being deployed abroad which result in factor incomes to residents of a country. It also leads to remittances being made by family members across national borders. The study of such decisions has not yielded robust evidence[1] and it does not significantly affect the analysis of the macroeconomy if we ignore these components of the current account.[2] We will accordingly ignore these components of the current account, which means that the current account is equal to the net exports of the economy for the purposes of this chapter. Equation (11.3) may then be written as:

$$S_{pvt} + S_{govt} - NX = I$$

where the net exports is given by $NX = X - M$. In Chapter 8, we had combined private and government saving into national savings, written as $S = S_{pvt} + S_{govt}$. The income equals expenditure Eq. (11.1) may then be written as:

$$S - NX = I \qquad (11.4)$$

› The investment equals savings condition for an **open economy** is where aggregate savings (private, government, and foreign) equals investment, or $S - NX = I$.

In a closed economy, the goods market was in equilibrium when income equals expenditure or savings (S) equals investment (I). Savings, in a closed economy, is the sum of private saving and government saving. In an OPEN ECONOMY, the investment equals savings or IS equation is where national savings (private savings plus government savings) plus foreign savings (a deficit of net exports) equals investment. Eq. (11.4) is the equation for the open economy IS curve.

The net exports of an economy are influenced by changes in two macroeconomic variables—the real exchange rate and income. In Chapter 5, we have studied how, as the real exchange rate, $(EP^*)/P$, depreciates, exports become cheaper. Simultaneously, imports become more expensive so that net exports increase with a rise in the real exchange rate.[3] The real exchange rate, being the price of foreign goods in terms of domestic goods when both are valued in the same currency, is a summary measure of how price-competitive the domestic economy's goods are as compared to goods produced abroad. Apart from this relative price that indicates the cheapness of domestic goods, the other major factor affecting the demand for goods is the income of the economy. We had seen how an increase in income that relaxes individual budget constraints increases consumption expenditure. The increase in income in an open economy will result in an increase in expenditure not only on domestic goods, but also on foreign goods or imports.

Hence, the imports of an economy will be influenced not only by how cheap imports are, as measured by the real exchange rate, but also by how large is the budget available for expenditure, as measured by aggregate income. The demand for exports from an economy will also be affected by the relative cheapness of domestic goods abroad (as measured by the real exchange rate) and the size of expenditure budgets abroad or the aggregate income of the country to which goods are being exported. From the perspective of the exporting economy, the aggregate income abroad is not a variable that may be significantly affected by domestic policy actions, and so the effect of aggregate income abroad on exports is not considered in what follows.[4] The net exports of an economy then increase with a rise in the real exchange rate of the economy, $(EP^*)/P$, as this makes domestic goods relatively more cheaper than goods abroad. The net exports of an economy also decline with a rise in income. This is because some of this increase in income is spent on imports which results in a decline in net exports since $NX = X - M$. This is summarized as follows:

$$NX = NX\left[\underset{(-)}{Y}, \left(\underset{(+)}{EP^*/P}\right)\right]$$

› The Mundell–Fleming focuses on the **short run** where prices are fixed. With fixed prices, the reference real exchange rate is the nominal exchange rate, and the reference interest rate is real interest rate.

where a negative (positive) sign under a variable indicates that an increase in that variable reduces (increases) net exports.

The IS–LM analysis focuses on a period of time known as the short run, during which prices are treated as given. In the SHORT RUN, the price P in domestic currency, for the output which is to be exported, and the foreign price P^*, at which goods are imported into an economy, are constant. This means that the real exchange rate $E\overline{P}^*/\overline{P}$ can vary only when there is a change in the nominal exchange rate E. Without any loss in generality, and so as to simplify the exposition, we scale the domestic and foreign price levels so that $P = P^* = 1$. The exchange rate that affects net exports is then the nominal exchange rate E which equals the real exchange rate, since $P = P^* = 1$. Since the price level is fixed, the rate of change in prices or inflation is zero, and the reference interest rate in this chapter is the real interest rate, r, which is the nominal exchange rate minus inflation. Given our focus on the short run, the net export function may be written as:

$$NX = NX\left(\underset{(-)}{Y}, \underset{(+)}{E}\right) \tag{11.5}$$

The determinants of national savings and investment in Eq. (11.4) have already been investigated in Chapter 8. There, we had written the determinants of savings as (see Section 8.2):

$$S = S\left(\underset{(+)}{i}, \underset{(+)}{Y}, \underset{(+)}{T}, \underset{(-)}{G} \underset{(-)}{\pi^e}\right) \tag{11.6}$$

Savings rise with an increase in the interest rate (i) as the return to savings in the form of the interest rate has gone up, and that makes future consumption more valuable compared to current consumption. An increase in income (Y), is partly spent as consumption and partly saved so that savings increases with income.

An increase in taxes (T) reduces private savings but increases government savings. Government obtains the full amount of the income that is taken away. This is because additional taxation and government savings, $S_{\text{govt}} = T - G$, increase by the full amount of the increase in taxation. Private savings, however, declines by a fraction of the increase in taxation. In all, then, aggregate savings has increased as government savings increase by more than the amount by which private savings decline when taxation increases.

Savings by the government is $S_{\text{govt}} = T - G$, which declines with an increase in government expenditure (a negative sign under G in the savings function).

Finally, an increase in expected inflation reduces the command that income in the future will have over real goods and services, which results in a rearrangement of consumption towards the present. As a result, with current consumption rising, savings will decline.

The aggregate investment function for an economy is given by:

$$I = I\left(\underset{(+)}{a}, \underset{(-)}{i}, \underset{(+)}{\pi^e}\right) \tag{11.7}$$

The parameter a is the value of the internal rate of return and it increases with an increase in the value of the marginal product of capital and decreases with an increase in the price of capital goods, the depreciation rate, and adjustment costs—as was emphasized in Chapter 4. An increase in the nominal interest rate raises the user cost of capital and reduces investment. Finally, an increase in expected inflation reduces the real interest rate and rental on capital, thereby making it profitable to increase investment.

Inserting Eqs (11.5), (11.6), and (11.7) into the open economy, savings equals investment [Eq. (11.4)], we may write:

$$S\left(\underset{(+)}{i}, \underset{(+)}{Y}, \underset{(+)}{T}, \underset{(-)}{G}, \underset{(-)}{\pi^e}\right) - NX\left(\underset{(-)}{Y}, \underset{(+)}{E}\right) = I\left(\underset{(+)}{a}, \underset{(-)}{i}, \underset{(+)}{\pi^e}\right) \tag{11.8}$$

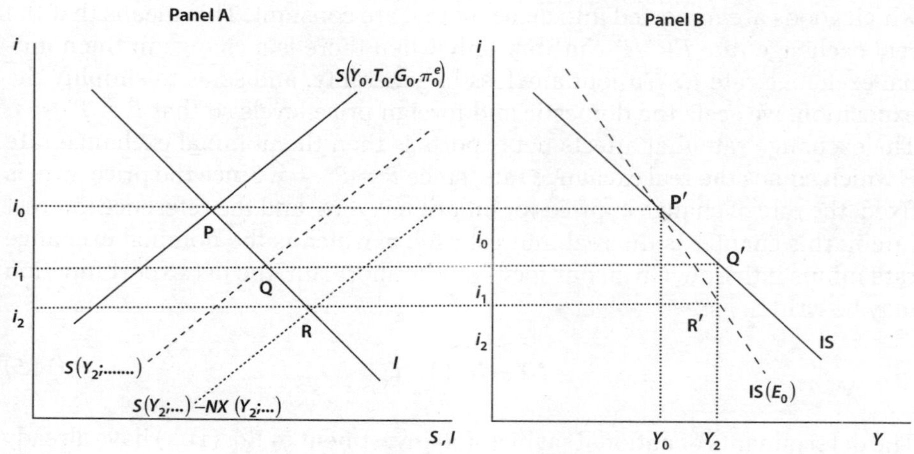

› **Figure 11.1 The Open Economy IS Curve.** In an open economy, the savings ($S - NX$) increase more with a rise in aggregate income as foreign savings finance the trade or current account deficit. Investment must, therefore, be higher in an open economy which requires the interest rate to decline by a larger amount. The open economy IS(E_0) curve is steeper than the closed economy IS curve.

This equation is graphed in Figure 11.1 for given initial values of aggregate income (Y_0), taxation (T_0), government expenditure (G_0), inflation expectations (π_0^e), exchange rate (E_0), and internal rate of return (a_0). For given values of these variables, saving is an increasing function of the interest rate and depicted as an upward-sloping $S(Y_0; T_0, G_0, \pi_0^e)$ saving curve in panel A of Figure 11.1. Investment is a downward-sloping function of the interest rate and depicted by the I curve in panel A of Figure 11.1. Aggregate saving equals investment at the point P. The nominal interest rate, when savings equals investment at P, is, thus, associated with an interest rate–income combination (i_0, Y_0). This combination is plotted in (i, Y) space in panel B as point P′.

Suppose income increases to ($Y_2 > Y_0$). First, take the case of a closed economy as analysed in Chapter 8. Then, national savings (sum of private and government savings) increases with the increase in income and the savings schedule shifts to the right to intersect the investment schedule at point Q, where the interest rate is i_1. The interest rate–income pair (i_1, Y_2), when savings equals investment at point Q, is depicted as point Q′ in panel B.

Now, take the case of an open economy. In this situation, the increase in aggregate income results in an increase in expenditure on imports which reduces net exports, *NX*. The increase in imports, without any commensurate increase in exports, creates a deficit that is financed by resorting to foreign savings. Then, the deficit of net exports raises aggregate savings given by $S - NX = S(Y_2, T_0, G_0, \pi_0^e) - NX(Y_2, E_0)$, which results in an open economy savings curve that intersects with the investment curve at point R in panel A. The interest rate–income pair (i_1, Y_2), when savings equals investment in an open economy at point R, is depicted as point R′ in panel B.

By joining all the points such as P′, Q′, that represent different combinations of the nominal interest rate and income for which savings equals investment for a closed economy, we obtain the IS curve for the closed economy along which the goods market is in equilibrium. Similarly, by joining the points P′, R′, that represent different combinations of the nominal interest rate and income for which national and foreign savings equals investment for an open economy, we obtain the dashed line IS (E_0) curve for an open economy along which the goods market is in equilibrium.

The decrease in net exports in an open economy when income increases, raises the value of $S - NX$ as compared to what it would be—S—if we were dealing with a closed economy. Hence, the reduction in the interest rate for a given increase in income must be larger when we consider an open economy,

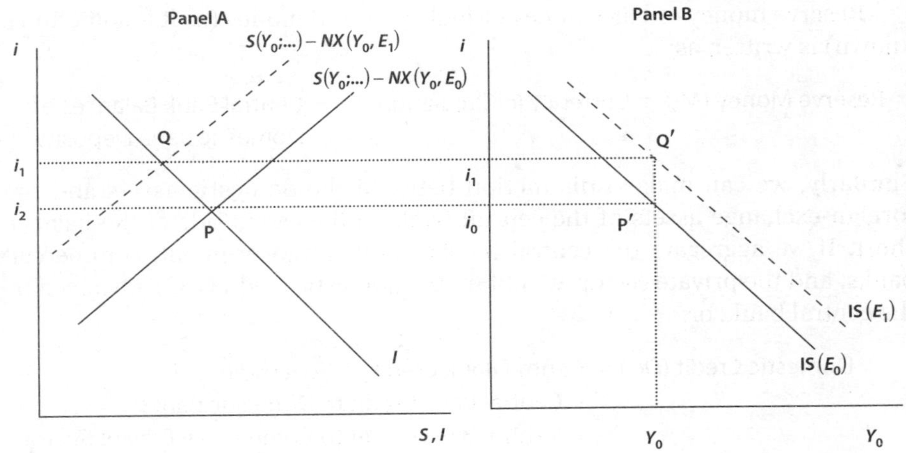

› **Figure 11.2**
Depreciation of the Exchange Rate. A depreciation of the exchange rate to E_1 increases the competitiveness of exports and raises net exports. National plus foreign savings, given by $S - NX$, declines and the IS(E_0) curve shifts right to IS(E_1).

so that the rise in $S - NX$ is matched by a corresponding rise in I. Notice that the decline in the interest rate, when income increases to (i_2), is larger for an open economy so as to induce a larger increase in investment that matches the larger savings as compared to the closed economy. The IS CURVE has a steeper slope for an open economy than a closed economy.[5]

› The open economy **IS curve** is steeper than the closed economy *IS* curve.

The IS curve of an open economy is also drawn with reference to a given exchange rate. Consider now what happens when, from an initial exchange rate E_0, the exchange rate depreciates to E_1. The depreciation makes exports from the economy more competitive and increases net exports from $NX(Y_0, E_0)$ to $NX(Y_0, E_1)$. The sum of national savings and foreign savings, ($S - NX$), then declines and shifts the $S(Y_0, T_0, G_0, \pi_0^e) - NX(Y_0, E_0)$ curve to the left to $S(Y_0, T_0, G_0, \pi_0^e) - NX(Y_0, E_1)$ in panel A of Figure 11.2. Savings now equals investment at point Q in Figure 11.2, panel A where the interest rate has risen to i_1 from i_0.

The interest rate at the original income level Y_0, and indeed at all income levels, is now higher and the IS (E_0) curve shifts out to the right to IS (E_1) in panel B of Figure 11.2. The depreciation of the currency by increasing the aggregate expenditure on exports has increased the earnings or aggregate incomes earned in the domestic economy, which is depicted by the rightward shift of the IS curve.

The money market or LM curve for an open economy is given by the equality between money demand and money supply. Again, let us recall some of the accounting associated with the money supply. The money supply is the outcome of the interplay between the central bank and the private sector. The balance sheet of the central bank, as we discussed in Table 2.2 of Chapter 2, is replicated in Table 11.1.

› **Table 11.1**
A Central Bank Balance Sheet

Assets	Liabilities
Advances (credits) to commercial private sector	Currency in circulation
Central Bank Credit to Government = Holdings of Government Debt (Including Loans to Government) *Less* Government Deposits	Central bank balances of domestic bank deposits
Credit to domestic banks	Net non-monetary liabilities of central bank
Foreign-exchange assets FE_{CB}	

Reserve money or base money or high-powered money (as it is sometimes known) is written as:

$$\text{Reserve Money } (M_0) = \text{Currency in Circulation } (C) + \text{Central Bank Balances of Domestic Bank Deposits}$$

Similarly, we can make a distinction between the domestic assets and the foreign-exchange assets of the central bank on the assets side of the balance sheet. If we aggregate the central banks' credit to government, commercial banks, and the private sector, we obtain the domestic credit (DC) advanced by the central bank, or:

$$\begin{aligned}\text{Domestic Credit } (DC) = {} & \text{Central Bank Credit to Government} \\ & + \text{Central Bank Credit to Domestic Banks} \\ & + \text{Central Bank Credit to Commercial Private Sector}\end{aligned}$$

Hence, ignoring the non-monetary liabilities of the central bank, the balance sheet of the central bank may be written as is given in Table 11.2:

› **Table 11.2**
Alternative Exposition of Central Bank Balance Sheet

Foreign exchange assets (FE_{CB})	Reserve money (M_0)
Domestic credit advanced (DC)	

› **Reserve or base money** in an open economy is the sum of domestic credit advanced by the central bank and its foreign-exchange assets.

› **Money supply** is the money multiplier times reserve money.

Hence, $M_0 = FE_{CB} + DC$ is an alternative expression for RESERVE OR BASE MONEY. In a fractional banking system, the MONEY SUPPLY, as we saw in Chapter 2, is a multiple of the stock of high powered or reserve money. In fact, when m is the money multiplier, then,

$$M^s = mM_0 = m(FE_{CB} + DC) \quad (11.9)$$

Thus, any increase in the country's net foreign-exchange assets with the central bank raises the extent of base money in the economy, and through the operation of the deposit multiplier, increases the money supply. The central bank can, of course, sterilize the increase in its holdings of foreign-exchange assets. This involves a countervailing reduction in its domestic assets, either by reducing its DC to government or by decreasing credit to the commercial private sector. For instance, it could sell its holdings of government bonds through an open market sale which reduces its stock of domestic assets, DC.

The money demand function is unchanged in an open economy and is as given by Eq. (6.14) in Chapter 6. There, it was shown that real money demand is positively related to aggregate income and inversely related to the nominal interest rate, or $M^d/P = f(Y, i)$. A rise in the interest rate reduces the demand for money, as bonds become more attractive with higher interest earnings on them. A rise in income increases the demand for money for transactions purposes. Money market equilibrium is given where money demand equals money supply, or,

$$M^s = m(FE_{CB} + DC) = f(Y, i) = M^d \quad (11.10)$$

The LM curve, that depicts the relationship where money demand equals money supply, is upward-sloping as before.[6] For the purposes of this chapter which deals with an open economy, we should keep in mind that the changes in the stock of net foreign assets of the central bank changes the money supply.

11.2 Capital Mobility and the Balance of Payments

We need to know how financially open an economy is before we look at open economy IS–LM issues. To do that, we consider the balance of payments (*BP*) of an open economy. We follow the Mundell–Fleming model[7] where the current account balance is determined independently of the capital account so that the achievement of overall balance requires adjustment in the domestic economy. The current account, which we take to be the net export function as already described, depends positively on the exchange rate and negatively on income. What are the determinants of net capital flows on the capital account? In Chapter 5, we have studied (Section 5.3.1) how capital flows to the destination where it obtains the highest rate of return. Net capital inflows (NKIs) into an economy occur when the domestic interest rate there is higher than the interest rate abroad, inclusive of the per cent by which the exchange rate is expected to depreciate, or, when:

$$i > i^* + \frac{E^e - E}{E}$$

This was the basis of the interest parity condition which resulted from capital flows to the economy with the higher interest rate, resulting ultimately in an equalization between the rates of return in the two countries. From now on, for ease of expression, we will write the right-hand side of the above inequality as i^*, where it is to be understood that i^* is the exogenously given FOREIGN INTEREST RATE that includes the expected depreciation of the domestic currency. Then, the NKI will be an INCREASING FUNCTION of the extent to which the domestic interest rate is greater than the one ruling abroad, inclusive of any depreciation expected in the value of the domestic currency. We may write,

› i^* denotes the **foreign interest rate** that is taken to be given, and is inclusive of the expected depreciation of the domestic currency.

› Capital flows to destinations that offer higher returns. The net capital flows to an economy is, therefore, an **increasing function** of the extent to which the domestic interest rate is greater than the interest rate abroad (inclusive of expected depreciation of the domestic currency).

$$\text{Net Capital Inflow} = \text{NKI}(\underset{(+)}{i - i^*}) \tag{11.11}$$

We assume that the exchange rate expectations are static.[8] If NKI is positive, it means that domestic residents are selling more financial assets, such as bonds, to foreigners than they are buying from them.

We now distinguish between three regimes of financial openness or capital mobility. Many countries impose capital controls to influence the capital flows into or out of the country. Capital controls may affect (a) the foreign direct investment of residents and non-residents, (b) portfolio investments by residents and non-residents, (c) borrowing and lending between residents and non-residents through financial institutions, and (d) other capital transactions such as controls over resident holdings of foreign currency deposits and real estate investments.

Capital controls have been introduced in countries through the use of direct or administrative measures and market-based or indirect measures. Direct controls place restrictions on the movement of capital and the associated payments and transfers of funds through outright prohibitions, explicit quantitative limits on such capital flows, or the requirements that they be subject to approval procedures. Indirect or market-based controls seek to discourage capital flows by making them more costly to undertake. Such controls include:

1. Explicit taxation of external financial transactions. For example, countries may mandate that taxes are to be paid only on short-term inflows, with the

intention of changing the composition of capital inflows towards those that are more enduring.

2. Indirect taxation of cross-border flows, such as requiring residents to DEPOSIT AT ZERO INTEREST RATES a proportion of the flows at the central bank.
3. A dual or multiple exchange rate system where different exchange rates apply to different types of transactions.

› Countries requiring that a proportion of cross-border flows be compulsorily placed in a reserve or **deposit** that is non-interest bearing are said to have an unremunerated reserve requirement (URR) for capital flows.

Chile, as a country, introduced controls on capital flows in 1991 that were a mixture of direct and indirect controls. The indirect control was the requirement that a percentage of foreign borrowing be left in an unremunerated reserve requirement (URR) or a non-interest bearing deposit at the central bank for up to one year. Additionally, there was a direct control that required all FDI to stay in the country for at least one year. Capital controls may be absolute in that a country does not allow any capital to flow in or out of an economy (capital immobility). The other polar extreme is when there are no restrictions on capital flows (perfect capital mobility). In between these polar cases is the situation where a country places some restrictions on the inflows and outflows of capital (imperfect capital mobility). We now distinguish between these regimes of capital controls.

1. Capital immobility—a country that has capital controls and completely restricts the mobility of capital is in a regime of capital immobility. A change in the domestic interest rate, *i*, vis-à-vis the foreign interest rate, *i**, has no impact on foreign capital flows in such an economy. In such an economy, the international transactions are restricted entirely to the export and import of goods and services that get recorded on the current account. The capital account is closed. This system, where capital is immobile and does not respond to variations in the domestic interest rate, is depicted in Figure 11.3, panel A. In the diagram, no matter what the domestic interest rate, the amount of NKIs is constant. The diagram does not show NKIs as zero as there may be current account deficits that require external financing. The country will then go in for an external loan that requires some debt servicing which will get reflected as a fixed amount of a capital inflow that is unvarying with changes in the domestic interest rate.
2. Perfect capital mobility—a country that does not place any restrictions whatsoever on the flow of capital is in a regime of PERFECT CAPITAL MOBILITY and this is depicted in panel B of Figure 11.3. In such a case, capital flows to the location where it earns the highest return. With domestic and foreign financial assets being perfect substitutes, portfolio adjustment is instantaneous

› **Perfect capital mobility** results in a domestic interest rate equal to the foreign interest rate, $i = i^*$, and a horizontal NKI curve.

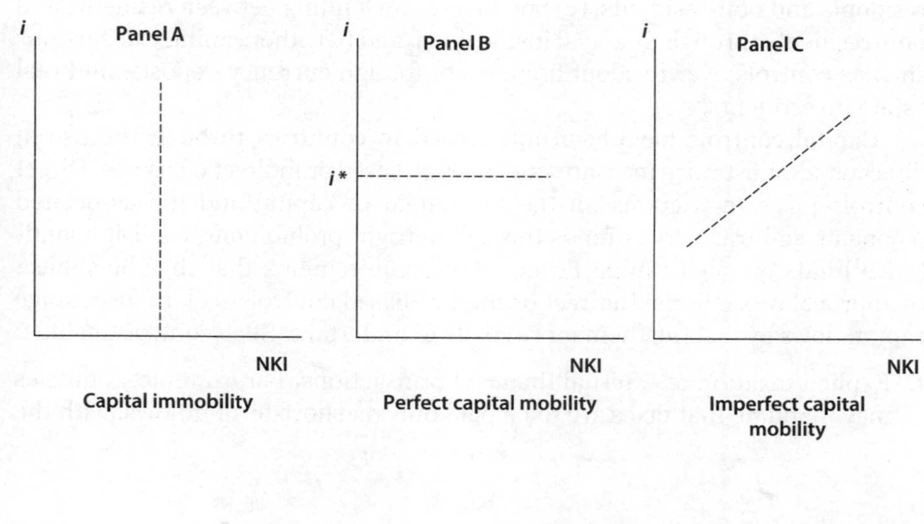

› **Figure 11.3**
Capital Mobility. Net capital inflows (NKI) do not respond to changes in the interest rate (i) when capital controls completely restrict the flow of capital (panel A). When there is perfect capital mobility (panel B), even a small deviation of domestic interest rates from that abroad (*i**) results in a large net capital inflow. Finally, when capital is imperfectly mobile (panel C), then a change in domestic interest rates induces finite changes in net capital inflows.

in response to deviations of domestic and foreign rates of return and rates of return are equated across the world. With arbitrage in the capital markets and capital flows ensuring that $i = i^*$, perfect capital mobility implies large flows of capital for even a small deviation of i from i^*. This would be the situation of a typical advanced economy.

3. Imperfect capital mobility—in a regime of IMPERFECT CAPITAL MOBILITY, international interest rate differentials result in finite flows into or out of a country. In this case, small deviations from interest rate parity, $i \neq i^*$, do not result in a potential flood into or out of a country. Imperfect capital mobility arises due to capital controls, a limited supply of arbitrage funds, or where risk aversion results in a risk premium that increases with the flow of funds into the home country. This is the situation of developing and emerging market economies in which capital flows are not as elastic with respect to changes in interest rate differentials as in advanced market economies. This regime is depicted in panel C of Figure 11.3 by a less elastic NKI response to variations in domestic interest rates.

› **Imperfect capital mobility** results in finite flows in and out of a country due to interest rate differentials and an upward-sloping NKI curve.

In INTERNATIONAL TRANSACTIONS on the capital account, an issue we have just considered is the openness of the capital account. The other issue to consider is whether the international transactions are taking place in an economy that keeps the exchange rate fixed, or allows it to float. The *BP* is the sum of the current account and the capital account. Since we ignore international transfers and NFI, the current account coincides with net exports, $CA = NX$, and we can write,

› In the macroeconomics of **international transactions,** two issues need to be considered. One is the degree of openness of the capital account—the extent of mobility of capital. The second is the nature of the exchange rate regime. The two polar cases here are a country operating in a fixed exchange rate regime and a country in a flexible exchange rate regime.

$$BP = NX(Y, E) + NKI(i - i^*) \tag{11.12}$$

BP equilibrium in a floating exchange rate regime obtains when the flow of capital is just sufficient to finance the current account deficit or absorb the surplus. Under a pure floating exchange rate regime, the sum of the surplus on capital and current account must be zero, a surplus on one account must be balanced by a deficit on the other. A pure float, thus, requires the following to hold true at all times:

$$NX(Y, E) + NKI(i - i^*) = 0 \tag{11.13}$$

In a fixed exchange rate regime, the central bank sets the exchange rate and absorbs any excess of foreign-exchange if the supply of foreign-exchange by exporters and capital inflows into the economy exceeds the demand for foreign-exchange by importers and capital outflows from the economy. If, on the other hand, the demand for foreign-exchange exceeds the supply of foreign-exchange, the central bank provides for the excess demand from its holding of foreign-exchange reserves. In a fixed exchange rate regime, then, the *BP* would be given by:

$$NX(Y, E) + NKI(i - i^*) = \Delta FE_{CB} \tag{11.14}$$

where the change in foreign-exchange reserves of the central bank, ΔFE_{CB}, occurs in response to excess demand or supply in the market for foreign currency.

We reproduce the *BP* diagram of Chapter 2 as Figure 11.4. To recapitulate the notation,

D_M: demand for foreign-exchange by importers
S_X: supply of foreign-exchange by exporters
X_K: demand for foreign-exchange due to a capital outflow
M_K: supply of foreign-exchange due to a capital inflow

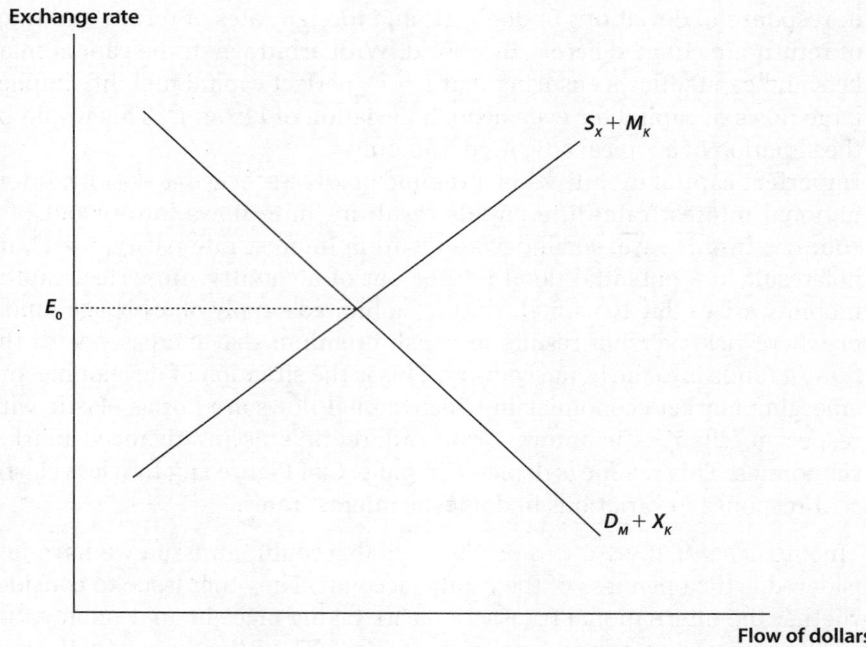

› **Figure 11.4**
Exchange Rate Determination.
The demand for dollars is by importers, D_M and due to capital outflow or the export of capital from the economy, X_K. The supply of dollars is by exporters S_X and due to capital inflows or the import of capital, M_K. The exchange rate is determined at E_0, where the demand for dollars equals the supply of dollars.

In a freely floating exchange rate regime, the exchange rate is market determined. The demand for foreign-exchange is by importers (D_M) and by those seeking to hold assets abroad, or from an export of capital, or capital outflow (X_K). The supply of foreign-exchange is by exporters (S_X) and by agents from abroad who want to hold assets in the domestic economy, or from an import of capital, or capital inflow (M_K). In Figure 11.4, the demand for foreign currency equals the supply of foreign currency at an exchange rate given by E_0. With demand equal to supply, at exchange rate E_0, we have,

$$D_M + X_K = S_X + M_K$$

This may be rearranged as,

$$S_X - D_M = -(M_K - X_K)$$

The left-hand side is exports minus imports or net exports. The right-hand side term in brackets is capital inflows minus capital outflows or NKIs. Thus, with demand equals supply at exchange rate E_0,

$$NX = -\text{NKI}$$

Taking the NKI term on the left-hand side and writing in explicitly the variables that determine net exports and NKIs, we have,

$$NX(Y, E) + \text{NKI}(i - i^*) = 0$$

This is Eq. (11.13), which is the *BP* equation for an economy with a floating exchange rate. We can depict the situation for a fixed exchange rate regime, as written in Eq. (11.14), by fixing the exchange rate at some level other than E_0 in Figure 11.4. If, for example, the exchange rate is fixed at some level above E_0, then, the supply of foreign-exchange is greater than the demand for foreign-exchange and this results in the central bank absorbing the excess supply of currency by increasing its holding of foreign-exchange reserves (ΔFE_{CB}).

Figure 11.4 is one way of depicting the *BP* of an economy. However, Figure 11.4 is unable to relate the *BP* which represents the condition in the foreign currency market with the equilibrium in the goods and money markets. We know that the equilibrium in the goods and money markets is given by the combination of the interest rate and aggregate income, where savings equals investment (IS curve) and the demand for liquidity equals the supply of money (LM curve). To relate the *BP* to the goods and money markets, we would have to depict the *BP* equation for a flexible or fixed exchange rate situation in a diagram where the interest rate is on the vertical axis and aggregate income is on the horizontal axis. We turn to that now.

We derive the graph of the *BP* equation for a flexible exchange rate economy given by $NX(Y, E) + \text{NKI}(i - i^*) = 0$. The balance of payment equation has three unknowns—i, Y, E. To graph the equation, we would require a three-dimensional diagram or we would have to take combinations of two variables each in three quadrants and then relate those quadrants. That is somewhat complicated. An easier way is to keep one of the variables fixed and depict the relationship between the other two. Then, by changing the value of the fixed variable, we can trace out how the *BP* relationship gets altered. As we want to relate the *BP* to the goods and money markets, it is best to temporarily keep the exchange rate fixed and draw out the *BP* curve for variations in the interest rate and aggregate income. We, therefore, plot combinations of i and Y that are consistent with the *BP* equilibrium for a given value of the exchange rate E.

In Figure 11.5, begin by assuming that the *BP* of an economy for a given value of the exchange rate is at point A, where the interest rate of the economy is i_0 and the aggregate income/expenditure in the economy is Y_0. Let the aggregate income of the economy then increase to a level higher than Y_0. Then, for the *BP* to be in equilibrium at the given value of the exchange rate, will the interest rate increase or will it decrease? To arrive at the answer, note that as income increases there is a growth in import demand which reduces net exports, *NX*. As $NX(Y, E) = -\text{NKI}(i - i^*)$ from the *BP* equilibrium given by Eq. (11.13), preservation of equilibrium requires that to offset the decline in net exports, the capital account must improve. This is achieved if domestic interest rates rise and there is an increase in NKIs. Hence, starting at point A, an increase in aggregate income will be associated with an increase in the interest rate on the *BP* curve. The *BP* curve, for a given value of the exchange rate, $BP(E)$, is upward sloping in Figure 11.5.

By how much does the interest rate rise when aggregate income increases? That is to say, how steep or how elastic is the *BP* curve? The amount by which interest rates rise in order to offset a rise in income [the slope of the $BP(E)$ line] depends on the sensitivity of NKIs to interest rate changes. If NKIs were perfectly mobile (panel B of Figure 11.3), then, a marginal change in the interest rate is sufficient to induce a sufficiently large increase in capital inflows that

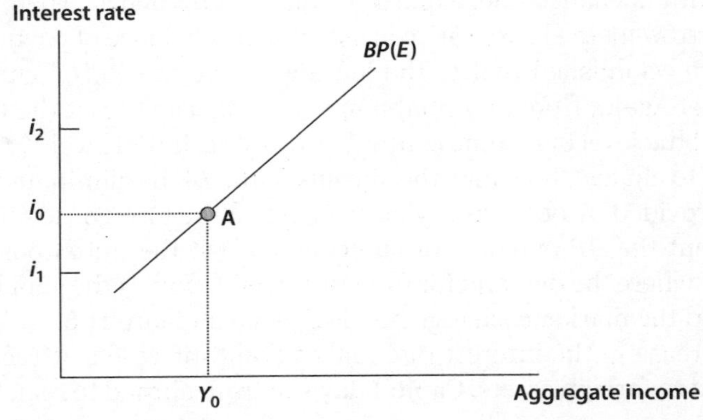

› **Figure 11.5**
The Balance of Payments. The balance of payments curve is drawn for a given exchange rate, *E*, and labeled *BP*(*E*). It is upward-sloping as an increase of the interest rate induces an increase in net capital inflows. To bring the balance of payments back into balance, the increase in net capital inflows must be offset by a decrease in net exports. This occurs via a rise in imports when aggregate income rises.

offset the decline in net exports arising from the increased aggregate income. The less sensitive that capital inflows are to interest rate changes [the more imperfectly mobile are NKIs (such as in panel C of Figure 11.3)] the more would interest rates require to change in order to offset the decline in net exports and keep the *BP* in equilibrium.

If there were perfect capital mobility, a marginal interest rate increase is sufficient to stimulate an infinite flow of capital (panel B of Figure 11.3) and the *BP*(*E*) line is completely flat. If there were imperfect capital mobility (panel C of Figure 11.3), the *BP*(*E*) curve slopes upwards. The slope of the *BP*(*E*) curve in Figure 11.5, then, depends on the slope of the NKI curve with respect to changes in the interest rate in Figure 11.3. In Figure 11.5, we have drawn the *BP*(*E*) curve as upward-sloping as our concern is with developing and emerging economies which have capital controls in place and the capital flows are imperfectly mobile.

› **A depreciation of the currency** increases net exports and shifts the *BP* curve down and to the right. An appreciation of the currency reduces net exports and shifts the *BP* curve up and to the left.

The next question we ask is about the impact on the *BP*(*E*) curve when the exchange rate changes. If the EXCHANGE RATE DEPRECIATES, net exports increase as domestic goods become cheaper for foreigners. This must be offset by a decline in capital inflows, as $NX = -\text{NKI}$, which requires a lower interest rate. A rise in *E* (a depreciation of the currency) is then associated with a decline in the interest rate, and this requires the *BP*(*E*) line to shift down and to the right. The exception is in the case of perfect capital mobility where the *BP*(*E*) line is flat and unaffected by changes in the exchange rate.

Analogously, an appreciation of the currency makes imports cheap as compared to domestic goods. This results in a reduction in net exports. This requires an improvement in capital inflows to bring the *BP* into equilibrium and that requires that there be an increase in the interest rate. An appreciation of the currency (a reduction in the value of *E* or a decline in the rupees that may be exchanged per dollar) is then linked with the *BP*(*E*) line shifting up and to the left.

› **Points to the left of and above** the *BP* curve represent a balance of payments surplus.

Finally, we identify the external economic configuration for an economy, that, for some reason, is at a point off the *BP* curve. We can see that POINTS TO THE LEFT OF AND ABOVE THE *BP*(*E*) curve are consistent with a balance of payment surplus. For instance, let the economy be at point A in Figure 11.5, where the level of income is Y_0 and the interest rate is i_0. Let the level of income continue to be Y_0 and allow the interest rate to rise to $i_2 > i_0$. Then there will be a capital inflow. As income has not changed and the exchange rate is given, there will not be any change in net exports. The increase in capital inflow with net exports unchanged results in a *BP* surplus.

Similarly, from an initial position at point A, let the interest rate decline to i_1, and let the level of income remain unchanged at Y_0. Now, there will be a capital outflow as assets abroad offer more attractive rates of return. Income is unchanged and, for a given exchange rate, so are net exports. The capital outflows combined with unchanged net exports, results in a *BP* deficit. Then, POINTS TO THE RIGHT OF AND BELOW THE *BP*(*E*) curve are consistent with a balance of payment deficit.

› **Points to the right of and below** the *BP* curve represent a balance of payments deficit.

We have established that to the left and above the *BP*(*E*) curve, there is a *BP* surplus. Again, from an initial point A in Figure 11.5, let the interest rate rise to i_2 and the level of income continue to be at its initial level Y_0. If income is not allowed to change, how may the surplus in the *BP* be eliminated? The short answer is provided by observing what happens in the foreign currency markets that represent the *BP* outcome of an economy. Let the initial position of the economy be where the demand for foreign currency equals the supply of foreign currency and the market exchange rate is E_0—as in Figure 11.6.

The increase in the interest rate makes domestic assets attractive to hold as compared to foreign assets. Capital flows in from abroad to reap the benefits

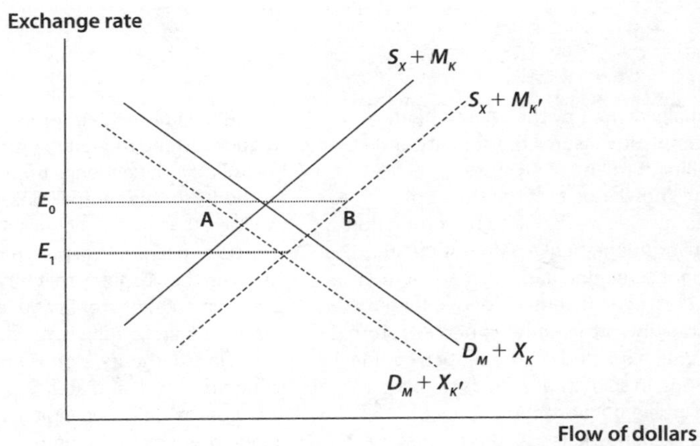

› **Figure 11.6**
Exchange Rate Determination (2). An increase in the differential between interest rates domestically and abroad, $i - i^*$, increases is the inflow of capital to M_K' and reduces is the outflow of capital to X_K'. There is an excess supply of foreign currency in the market given by distance AB. The exchange rate appreciates to E_1 in order to clear the market.

of the higher returns in the domestic market and the capital inflows increase from M_K to $M_{K'}$, shifting the supply of foreign currency curve to the right to $S_X + M_{K'}$. Residents, finding that the domestic market is offering better prospective gains, will reduce their holding of financial assets abroad too, reducing capital outflows from X_K to $X_{K'}$. The demand for foreign currency curve will then shift leftwards to $D_M + X_{K'}$. At the original exchange rate E_0, there is an excess supply of foreign currency or a *BP* surplus given by distance AB in Figure 11.6. The currency appreciates in response to this excess supply or *BP* surplus, and eventually the exchange rate E_1 will prevail in the market for foreign-exchange.

What if, from the initial point A in Figure 11.5, the income of the economy decreased while the interest rate continued to be at its initial level i_0? Again, the market for foreign currency provides the answer. A decrease in income will reduce the demand for imports. In Figure 11.6, the demand for foreign currency curve will shift to the left. Again, at the original exchange rate, there is an excess supply of foreign currency or a *BP* surplus, and the currency must appreciate in value so as to clear the market. We have, thus, been able to show that at all points to the left of and above point A on the *BP*(*E*) curve, the currency is appreciating. What is true of point A is also true of all other points on the *BP*(*E*) curve. We may then conclude that if the ECONOMY IS INITIALLY at a point on the *BP*(*E*) curve, and the economic configuration gets shifted to a point to the left of and above this curve (where there is a *BP* surplus), then, the currency will appreciate. Using a similar line of reasoning, it is easy to show that when the economy is initially at a point on the *BP*(*E*) curve, and the ECONOMIC CONFIGURATION gets shifted to a point to the right of and below this curve representing a *BP* deficit, the currency will depreciate:

› When the **configuration of the economy** moves from an initial point on the *BP*(*E*) curve to one to the left of and above this curve where there is a balance of payments surplus, the exchange rate appreciates.

› When the **configuration of the economy** moves from an initial point on the *BP*(*E*) curve to one to the right of and below this curve where there is a balance of payments deficit, the exchange rate depreciates.

Let us summarize the main points:

1. The *BP* curve is drawn for a given exchange rate and is an upward-sloping curve in interest rate–income space. The slope of the curve depends on the extent of capital controls or the extent to which there is imperfect capital mobility.
2. A depreciation of the currency increases net exports and shifts the *BP*(*E*) curve down and to the right. An appreciation of the currency reduces net exports and shifts the *BP*(*E*) curve up and to the left.
3. Points to the left of, and above, the *BP*(*E*) curve represent a *BP* surplus. Points to the right of, and below, the *BP*(*E*) curve represent a *BP* deficit.
4. When there is a *BP* surplus, the exchange rate appreciates so as to diminish the surplus. When there is a *BP* deficit, the exchange rate depreciates so as to diminish the deficit.

These results are important inputs to the study of the effect of macroeconomic policy in an open economy, towards which we now turn our attention.

MACRO FOCUS 11.1

Capital Account Convertibility

If capital flows freely across national borders, interest rate differentials would be minimal, reducing the cost of capital and making investment more efficient. So why are there capital controls? All advanced economies have open capital accounts. Most developing countries do not. Due to government policy, developing countries have pervasive distortions in markets. If the removal of these distortions is not practical, then it could be beneficial to have an additional distortion in the international capital market. Important policies in developing countries that impede the removal of capital controls include:

1. Protection and Subsidies: If certain industries are protected from global competition, it increases the price domestic producers receive as compared to world prices. A liberal capital account would then attract investment into these protected industries, where the value of investment at world prices is negative. A similar argument applies for sectors that are subsidized.
2. Government Ownership: In economies where there is substantial financial repression, the banking system is substantially owned by the government. This implicitly insures the stability and viability of the banking system. Secure in the knowledge that the threat of bankruptcy is weak due to the protection of government, bankers do not pursue efficient screening and risk management. This creates an incentive for overlending and overinvestment (i.e., expected return less than expected cost). An open capital account, in such a case, leads to greater than efficient investment.
3. Fixed Exchange Rates: A country that uses fixed exchange rates will have its inflation moderated by the inflation abroad. An economy that employs monetary policy to regulate economic cycles cannot have an open capital account and fixed exchange rates. This is the impossible trinity of fixed exchange rates, independent monetary policy, and capital mobility (Chapter 5). Opening the capital account and continuing the practice of discretionary monetary policy requires letting go of pegging the exchange rate. This requires that inflation expectations, which were influenced by the inflation rate abroad during a pegged regime, now have to be anchored in the credibility of the central bank and its monetary policy (Chapter 13). This, in turn, requires strong monetary institutions, including independence from the fiscal authority for the central bank. Government policies, that are subject to short-term effects due to political pressures, impose costs on the economy that forward-looking capital markets factor in and respond to via inflows and outflows. An independent monetary authority, along with a well supervised and regulated financial system, ensures that macroeconomic policy is not jeopardized by the scrutiny of forward looking capital markets. Capital account liberalization, the move to a floating exchange rate, and reforms for strong monetary institutions must be pursued at the same time.

For a review of capital account convertibility in the Indian context, go to the RBI's website—http://www.rbi.org.in/home.aspx

Click on "Publications."

Click on "Reports."

Click on "Report of the Committee on Fuller Capital Account Convertibility", submitted in July 2006, under the chairmanship of S. S. Tarapore.

Source: E. D'Souza, "Prudential Regulation in Indian Banking," in S. Arumugam (ed.) Indian Capital Markets—Modern Perspectives and Empirical Evidence (Mumbai: Allied Publishers, December 2001) pp. 486–511.

11.3 Monetary Policy under Flexible Exchange Rates

Essentially, the Mundell–Fleming model is the open economy extension of the Keynesian model. It deals with a demand constrained economy where the supply of output adjusts passively to meet the requisite demand. We can then study the open economy Mundell–Fleming model by resorting to an extension of the IS–LM analysis.[9] To the IS–LM diagram, add in the *BP* curve of Figure 11.5. The Mundell–Fleming approach to the open economy may then be called the IS–LM–*BP* approach.

The starting point of the analysis of an open economy is one of equilibrium where the IS–LM–*BP* curves intersect, so that the goods market, money market, and foreign-exchange market are in equilibrium. We then isolate a policy variable—monetary or fiscal—and ask ourselves the question as to what will occur when this policy variable is changed. A change in monetary or fiscal policy is a shift in the LM curve or the IS curve and has an immediate impact on the interest rate in the domestic financial market. The analysis, therefore, proceeds by identifying the direction of change in the interest rate in the money market as a result of the change in the policy variable.

We know that a change in the interest rate affects the differential returns between domestic and foreign financial assets, $i - i^*$, and this influences capital flows. The capital flows, in turn, have an impact on the foreign-exchange market. If, for instance, NKIs increase, then the supply of currency in the market for foreign-exchange increases and causes an excess supply of foreign currency. To know the total impact in the market for foreign currency, however, we will need to consider that in addition to capital flows, this market is also affected by any changes in net exports.

The policy change also affects the level of economic activity in addition to the interest rate changes we have just discussed. A change in aggregate income due to the policy change (change in government expenditure or money supply) results in a changed demand for imports and net exports. The change in demand for imports affects the demand for foreign-exchange and also has an impact on the foreign-exchange market. If, for instance, aggregate income decreases due to the policy change, then there will be a decrease in the expenditure on imports. This reduces the demand for foreign currency and causes an excess supply of foreign currency. The second part of the analysis, then, combines the effect of the policy change on NKIs and net exports in order to arrive at an understanding of whether the *BP* has been made surplus or whether a deficit has emerged.

In the third part of the analysis, the impact of a change in the *BP* is considered and this depends on whether the economy operates a fixed exchange rate or a flexible exchange rate system. If exchange rates are fixed, then, if there is an excess demand (or supply) for foreign exchange in the foreign currency market, it will be provided for (or absorbed) by the central bank through decreasing (or increasing) the stock of foreign-exchange reserves it possesses. This, in turn, changes the base money in the economy and affects the money supply. If the economy operates with flexible exchange rates, then the exchange rate will change in response to the change in the balance of payments.

Finally, the change in the *BP* or foreign-exchange market impacts the goods or money market. If the exchange rate changes as in a flexible exchange rate regime, then this affects the competitiveness of exports and shifts the open economy IS curve. If the economy is operating a fixed exchange rate regime, then, foreign-exchange assets of the central bank must change in response to the change in the *BP* and this, in turn, changes the money supply and shifts the LM curve. The final part of the analysis then identifies the impact of the change in policy on the goods or money market and the corresponding final equilibrium.

We begin the analysis of monetary policy when exchange rates are flexible, with an initial equilibrium in Figure 11.7 at point P, where the IS, LM, and *BP* curves intersect indicating equilibrium in the goods, money, and foreign currency markets. The initial level of real money supply is M_0, and, at the initial equilibrium, the exchange rate is E_0. The $BP(E_0)$ and IS(E_0) curves at point P, then, represent the equilibrium between the demand and supply of foreign currency that clears the foreign currency market at exchange rate E_0, and the equilibrium between aggregate expenditure and income, respectively.

We now consider the case of expansionary monetary policy that raises the money supply to M_1. Since the price level is fixed in the IS–LM analysis, an increase in the nominal money stock is equivalent to a rise in the real money stock. The LM curve shifts down and to the right to LM(M_1) as a result of the increase in money supply, and the interest rate declines to i_2 where the IS(E_0) and LM(M_1) curves intersect. At point M, interest rates have declined (resulting in a drop in NKIs) and there is a higher level of economic activity with income higher than Y_0 (resulting in a higher level of imports and a deficit in net exports). Hence, at point M, the economy is facing a balance of payment deficit. We showed in the previous section that when there is a deficit in the *BP*, the currency depreciates. In terms of Figure 11.4, the increased import demand

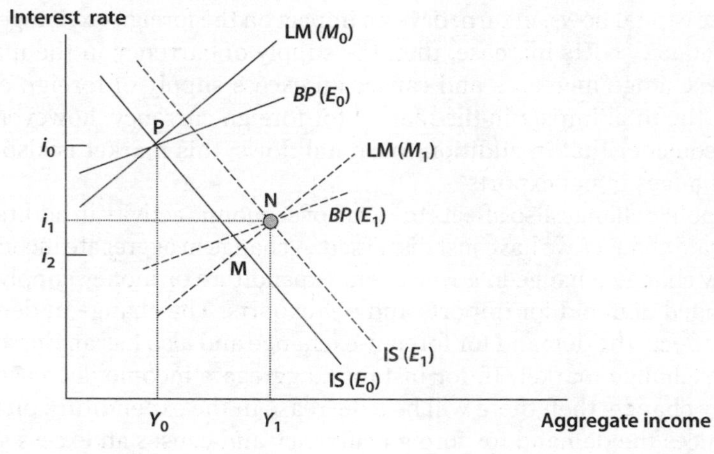

› **Figure 11.7 Monetary Policy with Flexible Exchange Rates.** The goods (IS), money (LM), and foreign-exchange (*BP*) market are initially in equilibrium at point P. An increase in money supply shifts the LM curve to the right, with temporary equilibrium at point M. The reduction in the interest rate reduces capital inflows and the increased income increases imports and results in a deficit in net exports. The *BP* is, therefore, in deficit and this causes a depreciation of the currency to E_1. The *BP* curve shifts downwards in response to this depreciation of the currency and the IS curve shifts to the right to IS(E_1) as competitiveness improves with currency depreciation. Final equilibrium, then, is at point N.

and the reduction in capital inflows causes the $D_M + X_K$ curve to shift to the right and the $S_X + M_K$ curve to shift to the left, resulting in a depreciation of the currency from E_0 to E_1. As the depreciation of the currency occurs, the *BP* curve, $BP(E_0)$, which is drawn for a given exchange rate, shifts down and to the right to $BP(E_1)$.

The exchange rate depreciation improves the competitiveness of the domestic economy, and exports increase. The IS curve shifts to the right to IS(E_1) as additional exports increase the aggregate income earned in the economy. The additional demand from export markets pushes interest rates, that had declined to i_2, part of the way back to their original level at i_0. Finally, the economy settles at point N where the interest rate is i_1 and the *BP* is back in balance along the line $BP(E_1)$.

At point N, the *BP* is again in equilibrium at a more depreciated exchange rate. Since the interest rate has declined, NKIs must have declined. Therefore, with *BP* equilibrium given by the sum of NKIs and net exports equal to zero for a flexible exchange rate regime, it must be the case that net exports have increased at point N. The increase in income and imports decreases net exports, and the depreciation of the currency increases net exports, with a net outcome for net exports that appears ambiguous. However, from the *BP* equilibrium outcome, we are able to conclude that net exports actually increases. This means that the exchange rate effect on net exports is larger than the income effect on imports. THE INCREASE in money supply in a floating exchange rate regime with imperfect capital mobility, thus, results in:

› **Expansionary monetary policy**, under floating exchange rates, causes a depreciation of the exchange rate, an increase in income, a decline in the interest rate, and an improved current account balance.

1. A depreciation of the exchange rate
2. An increase in income
3. A decline in the interest rate
4. An improvement in the current account balance

11.4 Fiscal Policy under Flexible Exchange Rates

Again, let the economy be at an initial equilibrium at point P where the IS(E_0), LM(M_0), and $BP(E_0)$ curves intersect. A fiscal expansion results in an increase in government expenditure from G_0 to G_1, and shifts the IS(E_0) curve to the right to IS(G_1, E_0) (see Figure 11.8). The initial impact is to raise both the interest

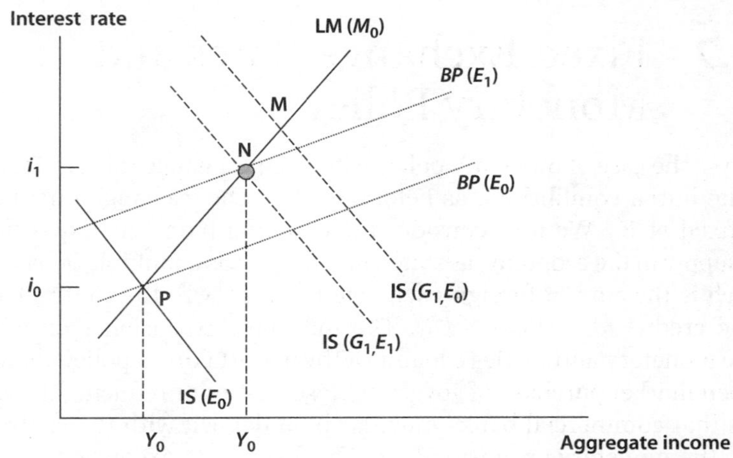

› **Figure 11.8**
Fiscal Policy with Flexible Exchange Rates. The goods (IS), money (LM), and foreign exchange (*BP*) market are initially in equilibrium at point P. A fiscal expansion shifts the IS curve to the right and there is a temporary equilibrium at point M. The increase in the interest rate results in a capital inflow, and the increase in income increases imports and causes a deficit in net exports. The capital inflow is greater than the deficit in the trade balance and the *BP* is in surplus, causing the exchange rate to appreciate to E_1. The *BP* curve then shifts up as the currency appreciates and the IS curve shifts to the left as the competitiveness of the economy is adversely affected. Final equilibrium is at point N.

rate and aggregate income to the level where the IS(G_1, E_0) and LM(M_0) curves intersect at point M. Again, the increase in the interest rate will increase NKIs and push the *BP* into surplus. On the other hand, the increase in income will increase imports and result in a deficit on the current account that pushes the *BP* towards a deficit. The net impact on the *BP*, then, seems to be ambiguous. Recall from our earlier discussion, however, that when the economy is above the *BP*(E_0) curve such as at point M, there is a *BP* surplus. A *BP* surplus is a situation where the supply of foreign currency exceeds the demand for foreign currency, and the currency appreciates.

The appreciation of the exchange rate ($E_1 < E_0$) makes domestic goods more expensive to foreigners and reduces exports. It, thus, shifts the IS curve down and to the left to IS(G_1, E_1) and reverses some of the rise in the interest rate. With the appreciation of the currency, the *BP*(E_0) curve is no longer the relevant *BP* curve. A new curve associated with *BP* equilibrium, when the exchange rate appreciates to E_1, becomes the appropriate curve to focus attention on. The currency appreciation shifts the *BP* to *BP*(E_1). The economy finally achieves equilibrium at point N.

On the trade front, there is a current account deficit at point N due to the decline in exports from an appreciation of the currency, and a rise in expenditures on imports induced by a rise in income. In contrast to a closed economy, where the rise in interest rates crowds out some investment expenditure, in an open economy, there is an additional CROWDING OUT from the appreciation of the currency which crowds out spending by foreigners on domestic goods and reduces net exports. The ultimate expansion of demand is, therefore, smaller than that in a closed economy.

› A fiscal expansion in an open economy results in two types of **crowding out**: (a) crowding out of private investment and (b) crowding out of exports.

THE INCREASE in government expenditure in a floating exchange rate regime with imperfect capital mobility, thus, results in:

1. An appreciation of the exchange rate
2. An increase in income
3. A rise in the interest rate[10]
4. A deterioration in the current account balance.

› **Expansionary fiscal policy** in a floating exchange rate regime causes an appreciation of the currency, a deterioration of the current account, a rise in income, and a rise in the interest rate.

It can be concluded that for a floating exchange rate regime, when capital is imperfectly mobile, the MONETARY POLICY is more expansionary than fiscal policy because fiscal policy is associated with a deterioration of the current account balance. We would expect, therefore, that countries with a floating exchange rate regime would concentrate on monetary policy and de-emphasize fiscal policy in economic policy making for managing economic cycles.

› In a flexible exchange rate regime, **monetary policy** is more effective than fiscal policy in influencing aggregate income.

11.5 Fixed Exchange Rates and Monetary Policy

We analyse the case of monetary policy with fixed exchange rates in Figure 11.9, where the initial equilibrium, as before, is at P. The exchange rate, however, is now fixed at E_0. We now consider the case of a monetary expansion. The money supply in the economy, as stated in Eq. (11.9), is a multiple of base money, M_0, which is the sum of foreign-exchange reserves with the central bank and domestic credit, $M_0 = FE_{CB} + DC$. The monetary expansion then will occur when the monetary authorities expand DC by undertaking a policy change such as an open market purchase of government securities or reducing the required reserves that commercial banks must keep on deposit with the central bank. Suppose the monetary expansion takes the form of an expansion of DC from DC_0 to DC_1.

This shifts the LM curve to the right to LM($DC_1 + FE^0_{CB}$). The decline in the interest rate to i_1 reduces NKIs and pushes the capital account into deficit, whereas the increase in income to Y_1 causes a deterioration in the current account, which goes into deficit with the increase in imports that accompany an increase in income. There results an overall *BP* deficit. However, the exchange rate is not flexible and cannot depreciate in response to an excess demand for foreign currency that accompanies a *BP* deficit. With exchange rates fixed, the excess demand for foreign currency requires to be financed, and this financing comes from a running down of foreign-exchange reserves with the central bank.

As the central bank finances the *BP* deficit, its stock of foreign-exchange reserves diminishes and the foreign-exchange component of the monetary base reduces from the initial value of FE^0_{CB}. This diminishes the money supply, and the LM curve begins to shift back to its original position—as indicated by the arrows along the IS curve in the diagram. Equilibrium is restored when the economy is back at point P. The money supply expansion has been totally reversed and the final stock of money in the economy is exactly at the level it was at before the expansion in the money supply. Reserve money, before the monetary expansion, was $M_0 = DC_0 + FE^0_{CB}$. After the monetary policy change, it has the same value of M_0. The only difference is that the composition of reserve money has now changed to $M_0 = DC_1 + FE^1_{CB}$. In the new equilibrium, there is a greater quantity of domestic financing of assets ($DC_1 > DC_0$), and a lower quantity of foreign-exchange reserves, $FE^1_{CB} < FE^0_{CB}$, such that, $DC_1 - DC_0 = FE^0_{CB} - FE^1_{CB}$.

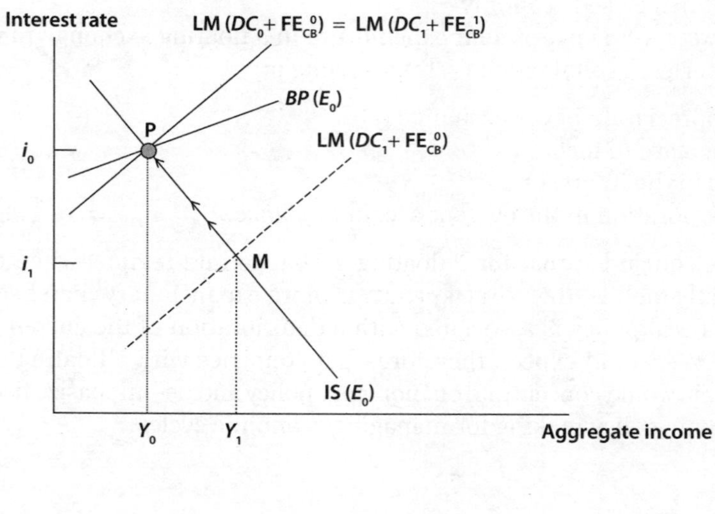

› **Figure 11.9**
Monetary Policy with Fixed Exchange Rates. The goods (IS), money (LM), and foreign-exchange (*BP*) market are initially in equilibrium at point P. A monetary expansion shifts the LM curve to the right and there is a temporary equilibrium at point M. The interest rate has declined, which results in a decline in capital inflows. The increase in income induces additional imports and a deficit in net exports. The *BP* is, accordingly, in deficit at point M. This deficit is financed by running down foreign-exchange reserves at the central bank. The reduction in forex reserves results in a decline in money supply and the LM curve shifts leftwards. Finally, the economy achieves equilibrium back at point P where the IS, LM, and *BP* curves intersect.

Of course, the central bank may attempt to prevent the money supply from declining at point M by further expanding *DC*. This is called sterilization—the process of neutralizing the effect of a *BP* deficit (surplus) by creating (retiring) enough *DC* to offset the fall in foreign-exchange reserves. It achieves this by purchasing domestic government bonds to add to its stock of domestic assets, and prevents the decline in its asset base as a result of the erosion in foreign-exchange reserves. However, this cannot be continued indefinitely, as with reserves declining, currency markets will build expectations as to whether the central bank has adequate reserves to defend the exchange rate or will resort to devaluation of the currency and such expectations have destabilizing effects on the economy. Hence, a MONETARY EXPANSION in a fixed exchange rate regime results in:

› **Monetary expansion** in a fixed exchange rate regime has no impact on macro-variables such as the interest rate or income in the long run.

1. A decline in the interest rate, an increase in income and a deterioration in current and capital accounts of the *BP* in the short run
2. A decline in foreign-exchange reserves with no change in the interest rate, income, or the *BP* in the long-run.

11.6 Fixed Exchange Rates and Fiscal Policy

We analyse the case of fiscal policy with fixed exchange rates in Figure 11.10, where the initial equilibrium, as before, is at P. The exchange rate is fixed at E_0. Consider an increase in government expenditure or an expansionary fiscal policy that shifts the IS curve up and to the right, as in Figure 11.10. The interest rate and income have both increased to point M where the new IS curve IS(G_1, E_0) intersects the unchanged LM(DC_0 + FE_{CB}^{0}) curve. Again, the increase in the interest rate will increase NKIs and push the *BP* into surplus, whereas the increase in income will increase imports and result in a deficit on the current account that pushes the *BP* towards a deficit. Though the net impact on the *BP* seems to be ambiguous, we know from our earlier discussion, that when the economy is above the *BP*(E_0) curve such as at point M, there is a *BP* surplus.

Hence, at point M, the higher interest causes the capital account to improve by a greater amount than the deterioration in the current account. However, the exchange rate is not flexible and cannot appreciate in response to an excess supply of foreign currency that accompanies a *BP* surplus. With exchange rates fixed, the excess supply of foreign currency requires to be absorbed and this

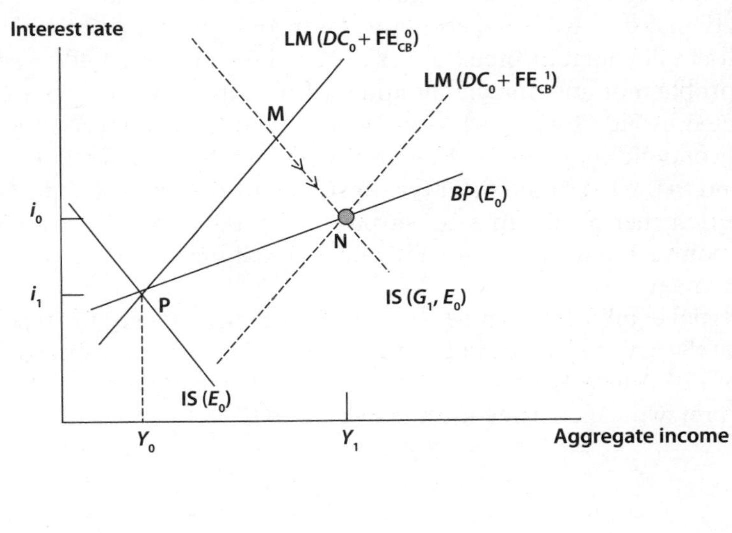

› **Figure 11.10**
Fiscal Policy with Fixed Exchange Rates. The goods (IS), money (LM), and foreign-exchange (*BP*) market are initially in equilibrium at point P. An expansionary fiscal policy shifts the IS curve to the right and there is a temporary equilibrium at point M. The increase in the interest rate induces capital inflows, and the increase in income results in a deficit in net exports. However, the increased capital inflows more than offset the increased trade deficit, and the *BP* is in surplus. This results in an accumulation of foreign-exchange reserves at the central bank and the LM curve shifts to the right as indicated by the arrows. Eventually, the final equilibrium is at point N where IS, LM, and *BP* intersect.

takes place with the central bank taking in the excess foreign supply and adding to its stock of foreign-exchange reserves, FE_{CB}. The money supply in the economy, as stated in Eq. (11.9), is a multiple of base money, M_0, which is the sum of foreign-exchange reserves with the central bank and *DC*, $M_0 = FE_{CB} + DC$. With the monetary authority absorbing the excess supply of foreign-exchange there will be an expansion of the money supply.

As the money supply increases, the LM curve shifts to the right in the direction of the arrows in the diagram towards LM($DC_0 + FE^1_{CB}$). Eventually, the LM curve settles at point N. As aggregate income, Y_1, is higher at point N, there is a deficit on the current account. The deficit on the current account is financed by a capital inflow that is induced by a relatively high domestic interest rate, i_1. Hence, a FISCAL EXPANSION in a fixed exchange rate regime results in:

› **Expansionary fiscal** policy in a fixed exchange rate regime increases foreign-exchange reserves and results in the long run income level to be even higher than the short run impact of the policy.

1. A rise in the interest rate and income and a surplus in the *BP* in the short run
2. A further increase in income and a decline in the interest rate from its short-run level with no change in the overall *BP*, that is accompanied by a current account deficit and an expansion in foreign-exchange reserves in the long run.

If you compare monetary policy (Figure 11.9) with fiscal policy (Figure 11.10) in a fixed exchange rate regime where there is imperfect mobility of capital, you will note that FISCAL POLICY IS MORE EXPANSIONARY than monetary policy and that it is associated with a current account deficit.

› In a fixed exchange rate regime, **fiscal policy is more effective** than monetary policy in influencing aggregate income.

11.7 Capital Flows and Macro Policy

We would expect countries with a fixed exchange rate to keep fiscal policy in the forefront of economic policymaking for managing economic cycles. However, IS, LM, and *BP* passing through a common point only ensures goods market, money market, and *BP* equilibrium. The aggregate demand at this point, however, may be associated with unemployment. Economic policy is required to deal with *demand deficiency* in addition to *BP disequilibria*.

If the three curves do not intersect at a common point, which is highly likely in a fixed exchange-rate regime, then the disequilibrium that results is likely to be concentrated most in that market which bears the least influence on the rate of interest and the level of income. Thus, if *BP* is not likely to be as much income and interest rate determining as IS and LM, then, the intersection of the IS and LM curves is the point towards which i and Y will strongly gravitate towards. Given a demand constrained economy, let income be at a point which is less than full-employment income,[11] $Y < Y_f$. Then, the economy could be subject to a dual-problem of unemployment and a surplus in the balance of payments, as depicted in Figure 11.11, which may be argued to characterize the current Indian economic conjuncture. In Figure 11.11, the IS and LM curves intersect above and to the left of the *BP* curve—resulting in an income and interest rate combination that results in a *BP* surplus. Simultaneously, IS and LM intersect (at point A) to the left of the full employment income line Y_f, resulting in unemployment.

External equilibrium can be restored via a contractionary fiscal policy that shifts the IS curve to pass through point B, which decreases income from point A′ to point B′. Alternatively, an expansionary monetary policy restores external equilibrium while increasing income from A′ to C′.

MACROFOCUS 11.2

The Pressure on China to Float

Protectionism in the US has been increasingly targeting China in an attempt to get it to revalue its currency. In fact, the US Senate is considering a bill that would require the Treasury to identify undervalued currencies and allow US firms to ask for protective anti-dumping duties if such countries do not revalue. This follows the infamous Schumer–Graham bill (which was withdrawn in 2006) that had proposed a 27.5 per cent tariff on all Chinese goods to offset the yuan's alleged undervaluation.

The US argues that China has been artificially depreciating its currency and causing the US trade deficit to increase. China's trade surplus with the US last year accounted for approximately 30 per cent of the US trade deficit. For a decade or so, China had pegged the yuan to the dollar. In July 2005 it abandoned this policy. However, since then the yuan has appreciated by less than 10 per cent against the dollar because the dollar itself has weakened since then. The yuan is still undervalued—China's foreign-exchange reserves, which are in excess of USD 1.2 trillion, are the highest in the world. This indicates a massive purchase of dollars by the People's Bank of China to keep the currency from appreciating. Many people believe that a revaluation of at least 25–40 per cent is required. The current Chinese economy predicament is depicted in the accompanying diagram.

It is hoped that a large revaluation will shift the BP curve to BP_1, reduce the *BP* surplus, and control the overheating of Chinese economy (the fastest growing economy in the world in the past decade). The revaluation, however, has second-round effects. Currency appreciation reduces net exports and shifts the *IS* curve leftwards to IS_1. The reduction in foreign-exchange reserves reduces money supply and shifts the LM curve leftwards to LM_1. The economy overcorrects and the *BP* surplus continues. This requires further revaluation.

If the government engages in small revaluations at irregular intervals, it could introduce speculation regarding the currency and increase volatility. Controlling outcomes in an economy is made difficult by second round effects and by expectations that agents form.

In 2005, when China unexpectedly declared a 2.1 per cent revaluation and its change from the dollar peg to a basket peg with a managed trading band, it disturbed market expectations and induced speculation. Markets overreact to unanticipated changes in policy. Transparency of a policy reform process is important in avoiding destabilizing expectations.

› **Figure 1**
China's Macroeconomic Quandary

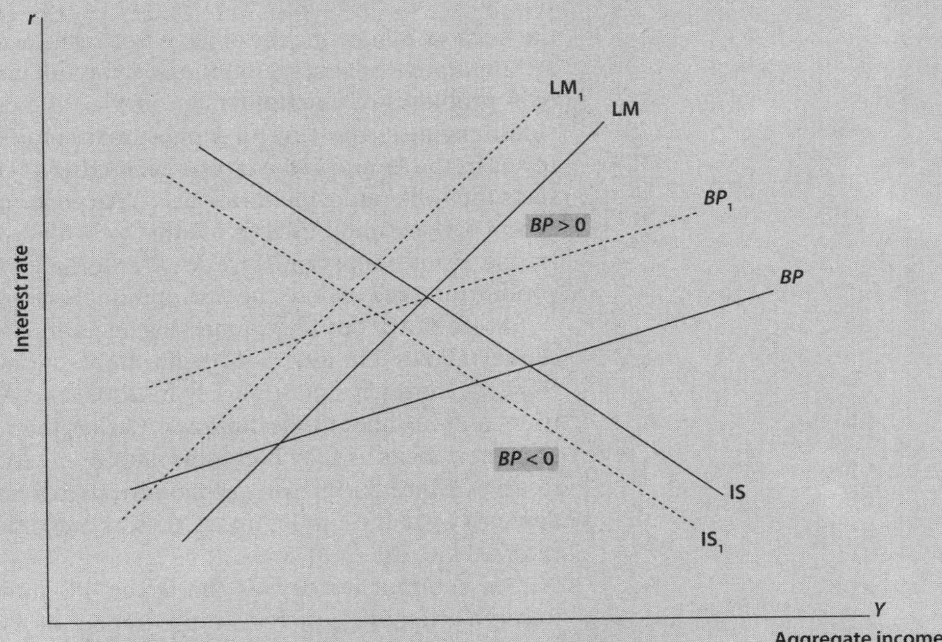

Suppose, however, that full employment (and not external equilibrium), is the primary policy goal. Then, expansionary monetary policy restores full employment at point C″ but causes a *BP* deficit. Expansionary fiscal policy restores full employment at point B″ while simultaneously making the initial *BP* surplus even larger. In short, monetary policy that was effective in meeting the external equilibrium objective is not as effective for meeting the full-employment goal. MONETARY POLICY, thus, has a comparative advantage over FISCAL POLICY for

› In an economy experiencing demand deficiency and a balance of payments surplus, **monetary policy** is better able to achieve the objective of balance of payments equilibrium, whereas **fiscal policy** is better able to achieve the objective of attaining full employment.

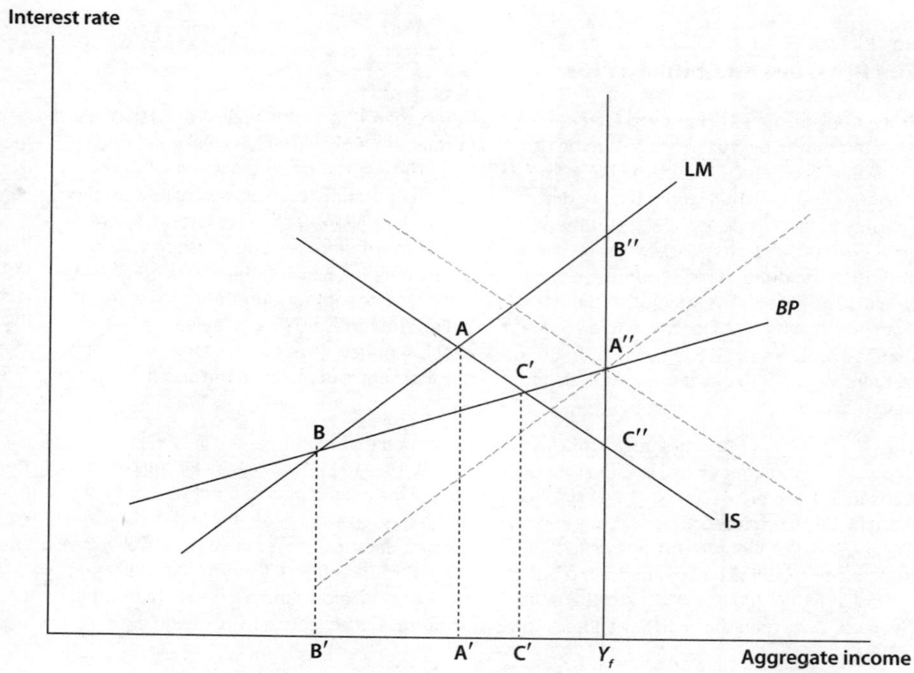

› **Figure 11.11**
Demand Deficiency and a Payments Surplus. If the economy is at point A where the goods and money market are in equilibrium, there is, nevertheless, a *BP* surplus as A is above the *BP* line. The output at A is also below the full employment income level Y_f. The economy is characterized by demand deficiency and *BP* disequilibrium. Demand deficiency can be overcome by an expansionary fiscal policy that shifts the IS curve rightwards to pass through point B″. However, this further improves the *BP* situation. Expansionary monetary policy can overcome the demand deficiency by shifting the LM curve rightwards to pass through point C″, but this worsens the *BP* situation.

the purpose of meeting the objective of external equilibrium but fiscal policy has a comparative advantage of meeting the full employment goal. Of course, the twin problems of unemployment and a payments surplus can be resolved by simultaneously applying an expansionary monetary and fiscal policy. This will result in the IS and LM curves intersecting at the same point where *BP* intersects the full employment line at A″. An economy must of course be willing to accept lower capital inflows for this to be an acceptable policy situation. Otherwise, the economy must trade-off external equilibrium and full employment equilibrium and choose the mix of monetary and fiscal policy accordingly.

From 2002 onwards, emerging markets began to be favoured with huge capital inflows. The lessons of the East Asia crisis of 1997, and of similar currency crises in Russia in 1998, Turkey in 2001, and Argentina in 2002, made countries cautious about these inflows. Rather than use it to finance huge current account deficits as they had previously done, they used the inflows to build up reserves. Since 2002, many economies have found themselves in a position like depicted by point A in Figure 11.11. This outcome was the result of internal and external factors.

An external factor was the fall in US interest rates due to the Federal Reserve attempting to reduce the impact of a recession in the US economy. This increased the interest rate differential ($i - i^*$) and encouraged capital flows to emerging markets, which caused an appreciation of the exchange rate and pushed the *BP* curve up and to the left.

An internal factor responsible for the emergence of the economic configuration, as shown by point A, was the increase in aggregate spending following liberalization in these countries. As controls were removed and financial markets liberalized, consumption increased in response to the availability of a variety of goods and the easy availability of finance. Investment also increased as the climate of investment improved. The increase in aggregate spending resulted in an outward shift of the IS curve to a point like A from a point like B. As we have already mentioned, many economies used these capital inflows to build up reserves. As reserves have built up, however, there is an increasing pressure on policymakers to contain the capital inflows and remove the disequilibrium in the economy as depicted by point A. There are four strategies advocated to deal with the inflow problem:

1. Sterilization: Recall that the monetary base comprises foreign-exchange reserves plus *DC* advances. Sterilization involves an equal sized decline in *DC* advances via an open market sale of government securities so as to maintain an unchanged monetary base. A purchase of foreign-exchange by the central bank involves an increase in its assets which requires an increase in its liabilities or a decline in some other asset. When the central bank sells government securities, it is reducing its stock of domestic assets (stock of government bonds) and the total assets of the central bank remain the same. As the central bank reduces its stock of domestic government bonds, it would require to replenish its stock of domestic assets in order to continue with sterilized intervention.

   In India, as the central bank lost its asset base from sterilization, the government added to the stock of the bank's domestic assets by introducing the Market Stabilization Scheme (MSS) in 2004. Under the MSS, the government issues securities to mop up rupee liquidity and then parks the proceeds in a separate cash account maintained and operated by the Reserve Bank of India. These funds are then used to redeem or buyback securities issued under the MSS. This results in a decline in the RBI credit to government, which nullifies the impact of the increased stock of foreign-exchange assets with the RBI due to capital inflows.[12] To induce the commercial banks and public to hold these bonds, the central bank must pay a high interest rate on these bonds—often an interest rate higher than its returns on the holding of international reserves.[13] For instance, the central bank payment of interest on these sterilization bonds amounted to INR 296.9 million in 2004–2005.

   Sterilization allows the economy to remain at point A in Figure 11.11 without a corresponding increase in the money supply. The inflationary pressure that increased money supply causes is, thus, curtailed. This advantage, however, is counterbalanced by the cost of open market operations.
2. Appreciation of the Currency: Allowing the currency to appreciate in response to a capital inflow is another policy response to inflows. This makes exports more costly and reduces net exports and shifts the IS curve to the left to point B and restores *BP* disequilibrium. This reduction in demand makes governments hesitate in implementing such a policy. However, when inflation is caused due to high import prices (such as when oil prices are high) this is an attractive option to governments as it reduces the price of imports and curtails inflationary pressure.
3. Allow the Inflow of Money: As reserves increase, the central bank could just allow the increase in assets to result in an increase in its liabilities. It could also allow the money supply to increase. The LM curve shifts outwards towards point C in Figure 11.11. The *BP*, as we saw, reverts to equilibrium in such a situation. However, an increase in the money supply can cause inflationary pressure to build up over time—especially if the economy is close to the Y_f curve. Given the lags in monetary policy, the increase in money supply tends to result in inflation over a longer period of time. Thus, the achievement of *BP* equilibrium comes at the cost of inflation.
4. Capital Controls: The imposition of capital controls results in a steeper *BP* curve. As the slope of the *BP* curve increases—say, a rotation counterclockwise around a point below A—it can result in a curve that goes through point A where there is no *BP* surplus. However, the cost here is that interest rates are higher and the economy is financing investment at high cost.

Clearly, policymaking is a matter of trade-offs. That involves hard choices about what to do when faced with a situation such as that represented in Figure 11.11.

11.8 Aggregate Demand and Supply in an Open Economy

The Mundell–Fleming model, with its focus on the goods market, the financial market, and the *BP* is a short run model that focuses on the demand side of the economy on the assumption that there is underutilized capacity and prices and wages are fixed. However, once we allow prices to vary in an open economy, as in an aggregate demand–aggregate supply analysis, then we must distinguish between two prices—the price of the domestic good, *P*, and the price of the foreign good in domestic currency, EP^*. The price level in the economy, $\tilde{P}$, is then a weighted average of the price of domestic goods and the price of imports. We may write,

$$\tilde{P} = aP + (1 - a)EP^* \tag{11.15}$$

where a indicates the relative importance of domestic goods in total domestic expenditures in the home country.[14] We will continue to assume that the price of the foreign good (P^*) is exogenous. The exchange rate will, of course, continue to be determined by the demand and supply of foreign currency in the foreign-exchange market. The average price level of the economy can then vary with a change in the domestic price or with a change in the nominal exchange rate.

An implication of this distinction (of the price of domestic goods from foreign goods in an open economy) is that the real money supply is now defined with reference to the average price level of the economy, $\tilde{P}$, rather than with reference to the domestic price level, *P*. The equation for the LM curve of the economy, as written in Eq. (11.10), then needs to be rewritten as:

$$\frac{M^S}{\tilde{P}} = f(Y, i) \tag{11.16}$$

Interestingly, even though the IS curve for an open economy, IS(E_0), is steeper than that for a closed economy, IS, the open economy aggregate demand curve is flatter than that for a closed economy. This is explained with the help of Figure 11.12. As in Figure 11.1, begin with an initial position where the aggregate income of an economy is Y_0 and savings (S) of an economy equals investment (I) at the interest rate i_0. From this initial position, allow the aggregate income of the economy to increase to Y_2. Then, if the economy were closed, the savings schedule would shift to the right to S', whereas if the economy were open then it would shift further to the right to $S' - NX_0$ as the increase in imports has increased the sum of national plus foreign savings. As in Figure 11.1, the closed economy IS curve is less steep than the open economy IS(E_0) curve.

Now, suppose that the price of domestic goods declines to P_1. This results in a depreciation of the real exchange rate, EP^* / P, which increases the net exports from the economy to NX_1. Consequently, there is a decline in foreign savings and the aggregate savings schedule of the open economy shifts to the left to $S' - NX_1$. The interest rate rises to the point where the $S' - NX_1$ schedule intersects the investment curve I. The savings equals investment, or, IS curve of the economy then shifts up[15] by the extent of this increase in the interest rate. The new open economy IS curve, after the decline in the price of domestic

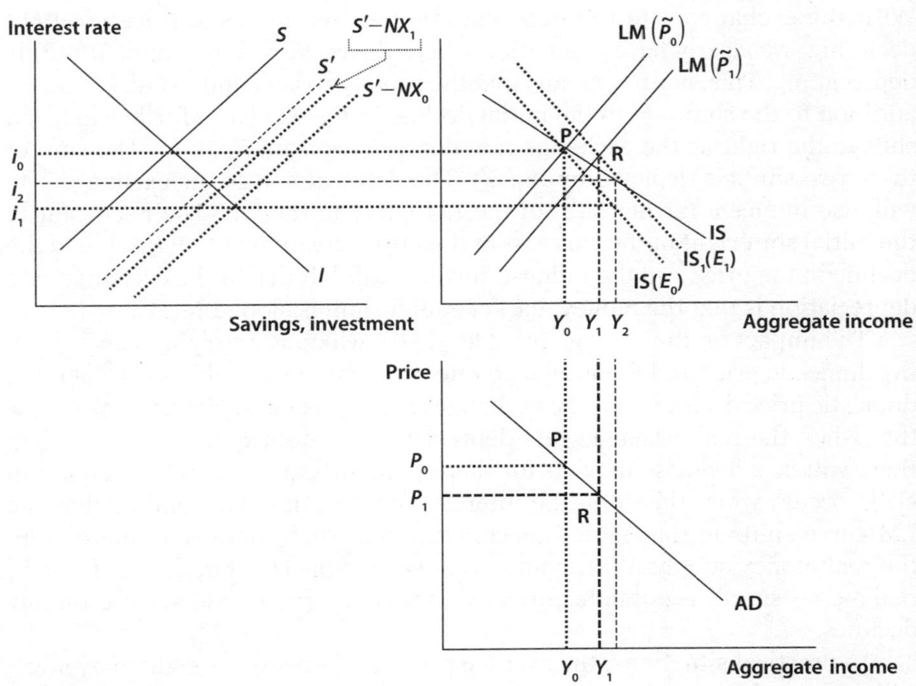

› **Figure 11.12**
Aggregate Demand in an Open Economy. From an initial income of Y_0, suppose income rises to Y_2. Then the closed economy goods market equilibrium is along the IS curve, while the open economy curve is the steeper IS(E_0) where investment equals $S' - NX_0$. When the price level declines to P_1, the sum of national and foreign savings declines to $S' - NX_1$ as net exports have risen from NX_0 to NX_1. The goods market curve shifts to $IS_1(E_1)$. The decline in the domestic price also shifts the money market curve to the right to LM($\tilde{P}_1$) and goods and money market equilibrium is at point R. With net exports increasing, *BP* equilibrium requires NKIs to decline, which comes about with a decline in the domestic interest rate. The interest rate at point R is then below the interest rate at point P. In the bottom half of the diagram, the points P and R represent goods, money, and foreign-exchange market equilibrium. The open economy aggregate demand curve *AD* is flatter than the closed economy curve because, in addition to the increased consumption and investment expenditure that takes place when the interest rate has declined in the closed economy, there is additional net exports in the open economy due to the depreciation of the real exchange rate.

› In a closed economy the IS curve does not shift in response to a change in the price level. In the **open economy,** the IS curve shifts to the right because a decline in the price causes a real depreciation of the currency that increases net exports.

goods, is $IS_1(E_1)$.[16] In a closed economy, a change in domestic prices does not change the position of the IS curve. However, in an OPEN ECONOMY it results in a shift of the IS curve as it changes the expenditure on net exports.

The decline in the price of domestic goods also changes the position of money market equilibrium in addition to the goods market equilibrium of the rightward shift of the IS curve. A decline in domestic prices reduces the average price level of the economy, $\tilde{P}$, and increases the real money supply. The increase in real money supply shifts the LM curve to the right—from LM($\tilde{P}_0$) to LM($\tilde{P}_1$). The IS and LM curves of the economy, which intersected at point P, now intersect at point R. The price level $\tilde{P}_0$ at point P was associated with income level Y_0. This combination of price and aggregate income, at which the goods and money markets are in equilibrium, is also denoted as point P in the lower half of Figure 11.12. Similarly, the price and aggregate income combination associated with simultaneous equilibrium in the goods and money markets at point R is also depicted in the lower half of the diagram. Note that the intersection of $IS_1(E_1)$ and LM($\tilde{P}_1$) at R is to the right of the intersection of the closed economy IS curve and LM($\tilde{P}_1$), indicating that the aggregate income is higher and the aggregate demand curve is more elastic in an open economy.

By now you may be wondering what happened to the *BP* curve of the Mundell–Fleming approach to the open economy. We have not drawn it in to avoid a cluttering up of an already overcrowded diagram. The *BP* curve would intersect the IS and LM curves at point P. Eventually, there would also be a *BP* curve that is passing through point R, which is to the right of and below the *BP* curve, through point P. If the real depreciation increased net exports, then, for *BP* equilibrium there will occur a decrease in NKIs which takes place when the domestic interest rate decreases. From the interest parity condition, the interest rate differential is equal to the percentage change in the exchange rate. If the interest rate differential declines, then, the exchange rate should depreciate. In turn, this implies that since the exchange rate is depreciating, the new *BP* curve through point R is below the one that passes through point P.

With the exchange rate (E) depreciating and the domestic price level (P) declining, we clearly have a situation where the real exchange rate (EP^*/P) is depreciating. This, in turn, means that the goods market equilibrium curve—in addition to the shift due to the initial decline in P—also has a further induced shift to the right as the exchange rate depreciates from E_0 to E_1. The sum of these two shifts is depicted by $IS_1(E_1)$. The depreciation of the exchange rate will also induce a further shift of the LM curve to the left. The net result of the initial shift right of the curve from the initial position at $LM(\tilde{P}_0)$ due to the decline in the price and the induced further shift left due to the exchange rate depreciation is that the money market equilibrium is along $LM(\tilde{P}_1)$.

The impact on the average price level ($\tilde{P}$), which is a weighted average of the domestic price and the exchange rate, is *prima facie* ambiguous when the domestic price declines and the exchange rate depreciates. However, we know that when the real exchange rate depreciates and net exports increase, then there will be a decrease in NKIs for there to be *BP* equilibrium. A decrease in NKIs occurs when the domestic interest rate declines. This entails that the LM curve shifts to the right. This comes about when there is an increase in the real money supply. With nominal money supply constant, an increase in real money supply is possible, provided the average price level of the economy declines.

In practical situations, the average price level—being a weighted average, will decline when the share of imports in domestic expenditures is sufficiently small—$(1 - a)$ small in Eq. (11.15). Then, the weight given to the depreciation of the exchange rate is insufficient to offset the impact of the decline in domestic prices, and the average price level will decline. Suppose, for instance, that the share of domestic goods in domestic expenditures is a realistic $a = 0.8$. Then, if the domestic price level declines by 10 per cent (a rare occurrence) and the exchange rate depreciates by 20 per cent (also a rare occurrence), the average price level of the economy will decline by 4 per cent. In addition, we can be sure that the average price level will decline for the case when there is perfect capital mobility and the *BP* curve is horizontal. Then, an interest rate differential can only be accommodated by a large capital outflow that brings the interest rates back to equality along the horizontal *BP* curve. Then, final equilibrium will only be achieved between the goods, money, and foreign-exchange market if the LM curve shifts to the right to intersect the $IS_1(E_1)$ curve that has shifted right along the horizontal *BP* curve. This is possible only if the average price level has declined and the real money supply has increased.

› The decline in the price level in a closed economy increases the real money supply, reduces the interest rate, and increases consumption and investment. In an **open economy,** it additionally increases the real exchange rate and net exports. The aggregate demand curve for an open economy is thereby more elastic than that for a closed economy.

The difference between the aggregate demand curve for a closed and an OPEN ECONOMY is that in the latter there is an additional component of expenditure—net exports. A decline in the price by increasing the real money supply and decreasing the interest rate increases the interest-sensitive component of domestic expenditures—consumption and investment. When the decline in price is associated with a real depreciation of the exchange rate, then an additional component of expenditure—net exports—increases and this adds to the expenditure by residents. Aggregate expenditure and aggregate income, then, increase by a larger amount in an open economy than in a closed economy when the domestic price level declines. This is the source of the higher elasticity of the open economy aggregate demand curve.

What causes the aggregate demand curve to shift? All the factors that shifted the aggregate demand curve of the closed economy (as listed in Table 9.1) will still be operative and will shift the aggregate demand curve of the open economy in the same direction.[17] In an open economy, the additional variable to take into account is the exchange rate.[18] Note that a depreciation of the exchange rate shifts the IS, LM, and *BP* curves as in Figure 11.12, but will get reflected in the aggregate demand curve as a movement down and along the curve.

What about the aggregate supply curve in an open economy? This depends on conditions in the labour market. There are two extreme cases that span the range of possibilities in this market.[19] One is that the nominal wage is fixed. The other is that the nominal wage increases in line with the price level so that real wages are fixed. Take the intermediate situation where wages adjust slowly to the growth rate of the average price level. This generally occurs because wage contracts are usually staggered (see Chapter 10, Section 10.2). Then, nominal wages are more sticky than the average level of prices ($\tilde{P}$), and rise by less than the change in the average price level.[20] When the average price level changes, a fraction of firms renegotiate with workers and change the nominal wage as wage contract decisions in the economy are staggered. This means that, initially, only a fraction of the losses in real purchasing power due to changes in the average price level are offset with an increase in nominal wages in the labour market—the nominal wage changes by less than the change in the average price level. As more and more contracts get renegotiated as time goes by after the initial rise in the average price, the average nominal wage in the labour market slowly catches up with the initial price rise and eventually equals the average price level increase. This is the New Keynesian view of the labour market. However, all that we are about to discuss can easily be adapted to the New Classical view of Friedman–Phelps–Lucas where wages adjust when price expectations are not equal to actual prices.

The logic by which wage determination and output are connected is different in an open economy from that in a closed economy. This is because in the open economy the average price level is a weighted average of domestic and foreign prices. The average price level can then change to reflect changes in the exchange rate even when the domestic price level is unchanging. The average price level affects the command over real goods and services by workers and wage negotiations will be influenced by changes in the average price level. However, the revenues to domestic firms is in terms of the domestic price and the output supply of firms will be determined by the amount of labour they employ to produce that output. Firms demand labour when the marginal benefit in terms of the value of the additional output that the marginal employee produces [the revenue received from the marginal product of labour, or $P(MP_N)$] equals the cost of hiring the additional employee (the nominal wage, or w). Labour demand then is in terms of domestic prices and given by the condition $w = P(MP_N)$. The reference price for firms in an open economy is the domestic price whereas the reference price for workers is the average price level of the economy.

Labour supply is determined by the condition depicted in Figure 11.13 where the real wage equals the ratio of the marginal utility of leisure to the marginal utility of consumption, or the marginal rate of substitution of consumption for leisure, $\text{MRS}_{c,l}$. The supply of labour is then given by the relation $w = \tilde{P}\text{MRS}_{c,l}$ and is depicted in panel A of Figure 11.13. The demand for labour is given by the condition that the marginal product of labour equals the real wage. This condition for the demand for labour may be stated as $w = P(MP_N)$ and the relation is depicted in panel A of Figure 11.13.

Suppose the domestic price is P_0 and the relevant demand and supply curves of labour are P_0MP_N and $\tilde{P}_0\text{MRS}_{c,l}$, respectively. Demand is equal to supply at point E at employment N^* which in panel B results in an output Y^*. Using the 45° line in panel C, we obtain the price output combination (P_0, Y^*) as point E' in panel D. Suppose the initial nominal wage is at w_0 when the

› **Figure 11.13**
The Labour Market and Aggregate Supply in an Open Economy. In the open economy, the demand for labour is with reference to domestic prices, whereas the supply of labour is with reference to the average level of domestic and foreign prices. The nominal wage, then, changes when there is a change in the average price level. If the exchange rate depreciates the average price level increases and the supply of labour in panel A moves up to the dashed line. The demand for labour is along the initial domestic price demand curve which is the solid line in panel A. The nominal wage is renegotiated when the average price level rises and increases to a level such as w_1. The demand for labour then declines to point F in panel A where the demand equals the new wage w_1. As a result, the aggregate supply of labour in panel D shifts to the left from point A′ to point F′ and the new short run aggregate supply of output curve is *AS*(w_1). As long as the nominal wage change is less than the change in the average price level, the aggregate supply curve is upward-sloping. When the nominal wage change is equiproportionate to the change in the average level of prices, the aggregate supply curve is the vertical *AS* curve

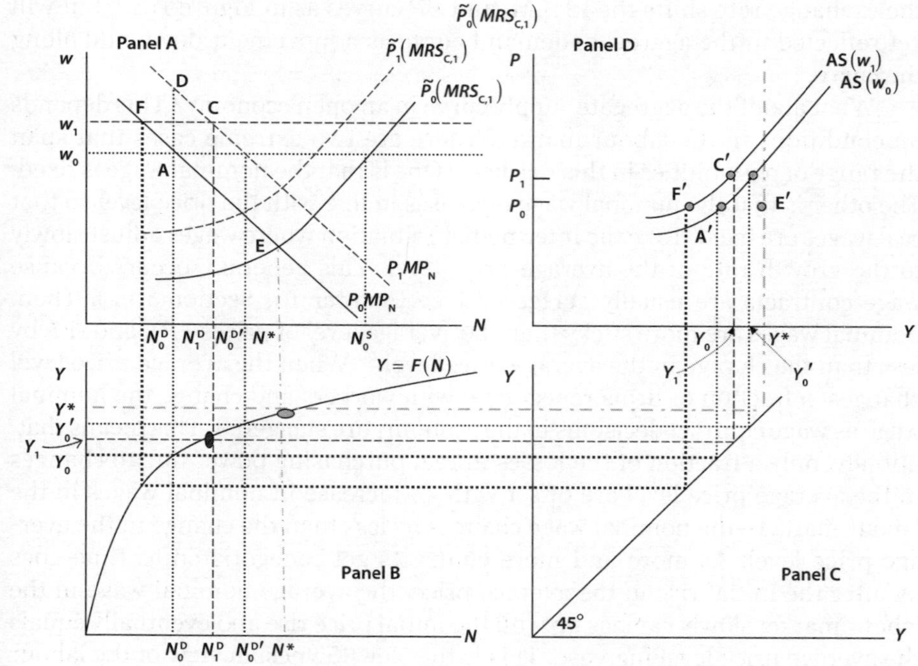

prevailing domestic price is P_0. At this wage-price combination the demand for labour is N_0^D and the supply of labour is N_0^S. With $N_0^D < N_0^S$ there is unemployment.

The rationing rule[21] is that when the labour market does not clear it is the short side of the market which determines the level of employment (N), $N = N_0^D$. The production function in panel B allows us to trace out that the output produced is Y_0 from this employment by the firm. Using the 45° line in panel C, we obtain the point A′ in panel D which represents the information depicted by point A in panel A in the price output space of panel D as A′.

Suppose the domestic price rises to P_1 and the exchange rate is unchanged. Then, the demand and supply curves for labour shift upwards and are depicted by the dashed lines in panel A. At the initial wage w_0 the demand for labour has increased to $N_0^{D\prime}$ which results in output Y_0' (panel B) and the price output combination of (P_1, Y_0') in panel D. By varying the price we can then trace out the aggregate supply of output that is depicted by AS(w_0) when the nominal wage is fixed at w_0. The average price level which is a weighted average of domestic and foreign prices will rise with a rise in the domestic price to P_1. Wages, however, adjust sluggishly to average price changes as discussed above. The nominal wage will then rise by a distance less than AD as given by w_1 in panel A. The demand for labour has increased to N_1^D as the decline in the real wage has made it profitable for the firm to employ more labour. The output associated with the employment N_1^D is Y_1 in panel B and the price output combination (P_1, Y_1) is depicted by the point C′ in panel D. For a fixed nominal wage of w_1 if we allow the price to vary we can trace out the aggregate supply of output AS(w_1) when the nominal wage is fixed at w_1. Notice that AS(w_1) lies above AS(w_0).

› The **aggregate supply curve** is upward-sloping in the short run when nominal wages do not change. Nominal wages are renegotiated when there is a change in the domestic price or in the price of foreign goods caused by changes in the exchange rate. As nominal wages increase, the short run aggregate supply curve shifts upwards.

Each nominal wage then is associated with an upward-sloping AGGREGATE SUPPLY CURVE and there will accordingly be a family of aggregate supply curves where a higher nominal wage will be represented by an aggregate supply curve that is above the one depicting the supply of output at a lower nominal wage. With the nominal exchange rate constant, and $\tilde{P} = aP + (1 - a)EP^*$, a change in the average price level $\tilde{P}$ is exactly equal to a change in the domestic price level, P.

If nominal wages rise equiproportionately to the domestic or average level of prices[22] then the demand and supply curves of labour will intersect at higher nominal wages but will result in the same level of employment N^* in panel A. This is because with the proportionate change in the nominal wage equal to the proportionate change in the average price level, real wages are constant. With real wages constant there is no change in the demand for labour by firms from or in the supply of labour. As a result, employment is unchanged even though nominal wages and prices have changed. With employment at N^*, output is Y^*, and panel D depicts the vertical AGGREGATE SUPPLY curve AS where as the domestic price changes, the output stays constant at Y^*. Y^* is the natural level of output and N^* is the natural level of employment. The natural level of output is an outcome of the fundamentals of the economy—preferences, budget constraints, and technology—and is unaffected by factors that influence aggregate demand. Panel D of Figure 11.13 depicts the aggregate supply of the economy which is the New Keynesian view of the supply side in an open economy.

› When the nominal wage rises equiproportionately with the domestic price level, as occurs in the long run when all wage contracts in the economy have been renegotiated, then the aggregate supply curve of the economy is vertical.

Again, return to the initial nominal wage w_0 and let the initial domestic price be P_0. Let the domestic price continue at this initial level but now allow the price of the foreign good to rise because of a depreciation of the exchange rate from E_0 to E_1. As a result of this the average price level of the economy rises say to $\tilde{P}_1$. Now, the supply of labour is given by the dashed $\tilde{P}_1\text{MRS}_{c,l}$ curve in panel A. The domestic price level is unchanged and the demand for labour is given by the solid downward sloping curve labeled as P_0MP_N. With the price of the reference basket of goods for workers having changed renegotiations for changes in nominal wages will begin so as to neutralize cost of living increases and with staggered wage setting the nominal wage will rise initially by less than the distance between $\tilde{P}_1$ and $\tilde{P}_0$. Suppose the nominal wage rises in response to the change in the average price level to w_1 as shown in panel A of Figure 11.13. With demand for labour given by the P_0MP_N curve, the employment in the economy will move from point A to point F in panel A. The counterpart of point F in panel A is point F′ in panel D. The aggregate supply curve of the economy has then moved from passing through point A′ to passing through point F′ which is to the left of A′ along a horizontal price line beginning from the price axis at P_0 in panel D. We can then CONCLUDE THAT a depreciation of the exchange rate shifts the aggregate supply curve of the economy to the left. The depreciation of the exchange rate has raised the cost of living which resulted in a higher renegotiated nominal wage. Firms find that the cost of an additional employee has risen, whereas the benefit of the price received from the output produced by that employee has remained unchanged, (P unchanged at P_0). Firms then reduce their demand for labour and reduce the output supplied in order to cut costs in line with reduced revenue. The aggregate supply curve of the economy shifts up and to the left. If aggregate demand is unchanged when the exchange rate depreciates, then the shift upwards of the aggregate supply curve will reduce equilibrium output and increase the domestic price level.

› A depreciation of the exchange rate results in a shift of the aggregate supply curve to the left. Firms reduce output at any given domestic price because the cost of labour has risen whereas they still receive the same revenue for the supply of output.

SUMMARY

» The aggregate output equals expenditure IS condition for an open economy is given by $S - NX = I$, that is, aggregate savings [private, government, and foreign (NX)] equals investment.

» Given any combination of interest rate and income where aggregate savings equals investment, $S - NX = I$, if there is a rise in the interest rate, the accompanying decline in income is smaller for an open economy as net exports increase. The open economy IS curve is therefore steeper than the closed economy IS curve.

» Reserve or base money in an open economy is the sum of DC advanced by the central bank (to government, the commercial private sector, and commercial banks), and foreign-exchange assets (FE_{CB}). Money supply is a multiple of reserve money given by $M^S = m[FE_{CB} + DC]$.

- » Capital flows to destinations that offer higher returns. The NKIs to an economy is therefore an increasing function of the extent to which the domestic interest rate is greater than the interest rate abroad – $NKI = K(i - i^*)$ – where i^* is inclusive of expected depreciation of the domestic currency.
- » The *BP* schedule is the set of interest rate—income combinations that are consistent with a *BP* equilibrium in which the current account balance and capital account balance sum to zero or result in a change in the foreign-exchange assets held by the central bank.
- » Capital controls are legal restrictions on the ability of citizens to hold and exchange assets denominated in the currencies of other nations. This affects capital mobility—the degree to which finance can flow across a country's borders.
- » The extent of capital mobility affects the slope of the *BP* curve. When capital is completely immobile the *BP* curve coincides with equilibrium on the current account.
- » Perfect capital mobility results in a domestic interest rate equal to the foreign interest rate, $i = i^*$ (the uncovered interest parity condition), and a *BP* curve that is horizontal.
- » Imperfect capital mobility results in finite flows in and out of a country due to interest rate differentials and an upward sloping *BP* curve.
- » Points to the right of the *BP* curve represent a *BP* deficit. Any point to the south-east of a point on the *BP* curve depicts a lower interest rate-higher income combination. The lower interest rate reduces NKIs and the higher income reduces net exports. $BP = NX + NKI$ must then be in deficit at this point off and to the right of the *BP* curve.
- » Points to the left of the *BP* curve represent a *BP* surplus, $BP > 0$.
- » A depreciation of the currency increases net exports and aggregate income and shifts the *BP* curve down and to the right.
- » An appreciation of the currency reduces net exports and aggregate income and shifts the *BP* curve up and to the left.
- » A monetary expansion under flexible exchange rates results in:
  1. a depreciation of the currency
  2. an increase in income
  3. a decline in the interest rate
  4. an improvement in the current account balance.
- » A fiscal expansion under flexible exchange rates results in two types of crowding out: (a) Crowding out of private investment as the interest rate increases and (b) crowding out of exports as the currency appreciates.
- » A fiscal expansion under flexible exchange rates results in:
  1. an appreciation of the currency
  2. an increase in income
  3. a rise in the interest rate
  4. a deterioration in the current account balance.
- » In a flexible exchange rate regime monetary policy is more effective than fiscal policy in influencing aggregate income.
- » An expansionary monetary policy under fixed exchange rates and no sterilization of the foreign-exchange assets accumulated results:
  1. in the short run in
     - (a) a decline in the interest rate
     - (b) an increase in income
     - (c) a deterioration in the current and capital accounts of the balance of payments.
  2. in the long run in
     - (a) no change in the interest rate, income, or the balance of payments
     - (b) a decline in foreign-exchange reserves.

  An expansionary fiscal policy when the exchange rate is fixed results:
  1. in the short run in
     - (a) a rise in the interest rate
     - (b) a rise in income and
     - (c) a surplus in the balance of payments
  2. in the long run in
     - (a) a further decline in the interest rate
     - (b) a further rise in income
     - (c) no change in the overall balance of payments
     - (d) a current account deficit and
     - (e) an expansion of foreign-exchange reserves
- » In a fixed exchange rate regime, fiscal policy is more effective than monetary policy in influencing aggregate demand.
- » In an economy experiencing demand deficiency and a *BP* surplus, monetary policy is better able to achieve the objective of *BP* equilibrium whereas fiscal policy is better able to achieve the objective of attaining full employment.
- » The recent capital inflows to emerging markets are the result of internal factors such as liberalization of the economy and external factors such as the low rates of return in advanced economies such as the US which went through a recession.
- » Capital inflows can be managed by (1) sterilization, (2) allowing the currency to appreciate, (3) allowing money supply to increase, and (4) imposing capital controls. Sterilization maintains the inflow episode at the cost of high interest rates and/or the introduction of sterilization bonds that have an interest cost. Appreciation of the currency can solve the *BP* disequilibrium at the cost of reducing aggregate demand as net exports decline. Increasing the money supply runs the cost of increasing inflation. Imposing capital controls has the opportunity cost that it makes the economy a high cost economy. Each response to capital inflows involves tradeoffs that make policy making no clear cut exercise.

NOTES

1. See the excellent work here by Devesh Kapur. Kapur, D. (2010)—"Diaspora, Development, and Democracy–The Domestic Impact of International Migration from India", Oxford University Press, New Delhi.
2. In 2009–2010, the sum of net factor incomes and transfers from abroad was 3.4 per cent of the GDP.
3. The presumption here is that the Marshall–Lerner condition holds.
4. In the final chapter where we study how the financial crisis that began in the advanced economy affected emerging economies such as India we will have occasion to bring in the impact that a change in incomes abroad have on a domestic economy.
5. $\partial r/\partial Y|_{\text{open economy}} = [(1 - A_Y) - NX_Y]/A_r < (1 - A_Y)/A_r = \partial r/\partial Y|_{\text{closed economy}}$ where $A = C + I + G$ is absorption.
6. Since the price level is constant and has been set equal to unity real money demand and supply are the same as nominal money demand and supply as written in Eq. (11.10).
7. See R. A. Mundell, "The appropriate use of monetary and fiscal policy under fixed exchange rates", IMF Staff Papers, no. 9 (1962): 70–77; Also see J. M. Fleming, "Domestic financial policies under fixed and floating exchange rates", IMF Staff Papers no. 9 (1962): 369–377. As Mundell himself once stated, "I am not quite sure when the term 'Mundell–Fleming model' first appeared in the literature.... (my work) preceded his (Fleming's) in publication but not necessarily in conception". See R. A. Mundell, "Notes on the Development of the International Macroeconomic Model", in A. Arnon and W. Young (eds.), *The Open Economy Macromodel: Past, Present and Future* Kluwer (Boston, M.A.: Academic Publishers, 2002), pp. 1–16.
8. The Dornbusch sticky price model looks at the expectation mechanism with respect to exchange rates. See R. Dornbusch, "Expectations and exchange rate dynamics", *Journal of Political Economy* 84 (1976): 1161–1176.
9. In the IS–LM model as well as the Mundell–Fleming model of the open economy the period of analysis is a short period where the price level is taken as given. Earlier in the chapter we had normalized the price level to $P = 1$. In terms of the aggregate demand and supply analysis this implies that the *AS* curve is flat at the given price level.
10. With perfect capital mobility the *BP* curve is flat and the whole of the increase in government expenditure is offset by the fall in exports making crowding out complete. This is because with the interest rate determined in the international capital market, $i = i^*$, the burden of adjustment is borne entirely by the exchange rate which has to appreciate to an extent such that the current account deficit that results is as great as the increase in fiscal spending. The whole of the increase in government expenditure is therefore funded by external borrowing.
11. We can also think of Y_f as the point of potential output where expectations are realized as in the Friedman–Lucas approach.
12. See RBI Annual Report, Box III.3, 2004–2005, pp. 110.
13. When the central bank pays a higher interest rate on sterilization bonds than it receives on the holdings of international reserves it is said to incur a quasi-fiscal deficit.
14. In fact, a is the share of domestic goods in total domestic expenditures and may then be stated as $a = (C + I + G)/(C + I + G + M)$.
15. As usual we are presuming that the indirect effect of the real exchange rate on net exports is smaller than the direct effect. The indirect effect is that when net exports rise with an increase in the real exchange rate it increases aggregate income which in turn results in an additional increase (the indirect effect) in imports. The indirect effect reduces net exports but by a smaller amount than the initial increase in net exports from the direct effect.
16. Note that even though the upward shift of the IS curve is by the extent of the increase in the interest rate, the rightward shift is more than by the initial increase of aggregate income from Y_0 to Y_2 because now in addition net exports have increased which in turn further increases aggregate income.
17. A new factor that emerges is that when there is an increase in government expenditure for instance, it raises the interest rate and causes a *BP* surplus. This requires the exchange rate to appreciate which reduces the average price level of the economy. As a consequence there is an increase in the real money supply and the LM curve shifts to the right. The double crowding out due to appreciation of the currency is then reduced due to the outward shift of the LM curve. However, the aggregate demand curve still shifts to the right.
18. The exchange rate is an endogenous variable that is determined by the *BP* equilibrium. As it is not an exogenous variable a change in this variable does not result in a shift of the aggregate demand curve but rather in a movement along the curve.
19. In the chapter on the labour market we saw that there is the Classical view where individuals think in real wage terms and then there is the more modern Keynesian or Friedman–Phelps view where there is some money illusion either because money wages are fixed or because of imperfect information there is a deviation of expected prices from actual prices and the aggregate supply curve is upward sloping. The exploration of macroeconomic policy

when alternative wage regimes are involved is examined in Jeffrey Sachs (1980), "*Wages, Flexible Exchange Rates, and Macroeconomic Policy*", The Quarterly Journal of Economics, Vol. 94, No. 10, June, pp. 731–747.

20. Technically, this is the situation where the percentage change in wages is a fraction of the percentage change in the average price level of the economy. That is, $\Delta w/w = \theta(\Delta\tilde{P}/\tilde{P})$, where, $0 \leq \theta \leq 1$. See Errol D'Souza (2009), "*A Consistent Macroeconomic Model*", India Macroeconomics Annual 2009, Sage Publications, pp. 13–27.
21. This rationing rule as discussed in the chapter on the labour market is $N = \min(N^D, N^S)$.
22. Since the average level of prices is a weighted average of domestic and foreign prices, an equiproportionate change in domestic prices equals an equiproportionate change in the average price level provided there is no change in the exchange rate (for a given price of output of goods from abroad, P^*). Then nominal wages will rise equiproportionately with domestic prices if $\theta = 1$ in the equation for wage adjustment given in endnote 19.
23. The slope of the *BP* line is given by $\Delta i/\Delta Y|_{E\text{ given}} = -(\Delta NX/\Delta Y)/(\Delta \text{NKI}/\Delta i)$.
24. $(\Delta i/\Delta Y)|_{LM} = -(\Delta M^d/\Delta Y)/(\Delta M^d/\Delta i)$.
25. $(\Delta \text{NKI}/\Delta i) > |\Delta NX/\Delta Y|$ and $|\Delta i| < |\Delta Y|$ for a reduction in *i* and *Y*.

TEST YOURSELF

1. What is the *BP* schedule for an open economy? What determines its slope? What causes shifts in the *BP* curve?
2. Suppose an economy maintains a fixed exchange rate and its monetary policy involves no sterilization. How does a contractionary monetary policy affect the *BP* and aggregate income?
3. Suppose an economy with a fixed exchange rate allows capital flows without any controls. What is the impact of a contractionary fiscal policy on the economy?
4. Suppose an economy with a flexible exchange rate has perfect capital mobility. Explain how a contractionary fiscal policy affects the value of its currency and the composition of the balance of payments.
5. An economy with a flexible exchange rate and perfect capital mobility is expanding too fast and is overheating. Should the monetary or the fiscal authority take the lead in attempting to contain income growth?
6. As an economy increasingly integrates with the world economy during this era of globalization should it maintain fixed or floating exchange rates? Why?
7. Currently the US economy is subject to a consumption boom which has increased it trade balance substantially. Suppose capital mobility is perfect and the dollar-renminbi exchange rate floats. The US government is trying to prevail upon Beijing to reduce government spending. Is this good policy from the US point of view?
8. An economy's exchange rate is fixed and it has imperfect capital mobility. Analyze the effect on the economy in the short and long runs of a reduction in taxes.
9. What results in the LM curve becoming endogenous in the case of fixed exchange rates and the IS curve becoming endogenous in the case of flexible exchange rates?
10. Suppose there is an increase in the price level in an open economy with flexible exchange rates. What happens to the nominal exchange rate and to the real exchange rate? Can an appreciation of the nominal exchange rate be associated with a depreciation of the real exchange rate?

ONLINE APPLICATION

1. a. Go to the home page of the Reserve Bank of India URL: www.rbi.org.in/home.aspx
   b. Click on the "DataBase" icon.
   c. Then under the classification of Annual data, click on "Handbook of Statistics on Indian Economy."
2. Click on "Table 114: Combined Deficits of central and state Governments" and create a spreadsheet of annual data on the fiscal deficit of the nation from 1993–1994 to 2009–2010.
3. Then click on "Table 128: India's foreign trade—rupees" and in your spreadsheet insert annual data on the trade deficit from 1993–1994 to 2009–2010.
4. Finally click on "Table 156: Foreign Exchange Reserves" and in your spreadsheet insert annual data on foreign currency reserves in Indian rupees from 1993–1994 to 2009–2010.
5. Now index the various data series. Let the base value of the fiscal deficit be INR 646.84 billion = 100. Then, the index of the fiscal deficit in 1993–1994 of – INR 707.2 billion is $[(707.2 \times 100)/646.84] = 109.33$. Calculate the index value for subsequent years.
6. Similarly, let the base value of the trade deficit of INR 45.6951 billion be 100. Then, the index of the trade deficit in 1993–1994 of INR 33.496 billion is [(33.496 × 100)/

45.6951] = 73.30. Calculate the index value for subsequent years.

7. The base value of the foreign-exchange reserves can be set at INR 430.306 billion equals to an index value of 100. Accordingly the index of foreign-exchange reserves of INR 604.20 billion in 1993–1994 is [(604.20 × 100)/430.306] = 140.41. Calculate the index value for subsequent years.
8. Now, create a graph with the index of the fiscal deficit on the horizontal axis and the index of the trade deficit and foreign-exchange reserves on the vertical axis. You will notice that fiscal policy has a positive impact on the trade deficit—a linear trend will depict that a unit increase in the index of the fiscal deficit increases the index of the trade deficit by 15.4 units. The impact of the fiscal deficit on foreign-exchange reserves is much smaller—a unit increase in the index of the fiscal deficit increases the index of foreign-exchange reserves by 3.92 units. In the text we had concluded that fiscal policy results in a deterioration of the trade balance and an expansion of foreign exchange reserves if the exchange rate is fixed. Relate your graph to the conclusions of the text.
9. Exchange rate flexibility in India gradually increased after 1993–1994. Prior to this year the financial system was administered. The text had argued that under flexible exchange rates fiscal policy should result in an appreciation of the currency. Insert data on the real (effective trade weighted) and nominal exchange rates from 1993–1994 onwards (base year 1993–1994 =100) by clicking on "Table 149: Indices of Real Effective Exchange Rate (REER) and Nominal Effective Exchange Rate (NEER) of the Indian rupee (36 country bilateral weights". If you create a graph from this you will see that the real and nominal exchange rates appreciate mildly with increases in the fiscal deficit. A unit increase in the index of the fiscal deficit reduces the real exchange rate index by –0.0083 units while the nominal exchange rate index diminishes by –0.014 units. Explain this apparent lack of relationship.

Appendix 11.1 Slopes of *BP* and LM Curves

The *BP* curve has a positive slope, as has the LM curve, and the *BP* curve has been drawn flatter than the LM curve throughout the chapter. The absolute slope of the *BP* curve is the ratio of the responsiveness of net exports to the level of income and the responsiveness of NKIs to the rate of interest.[23] The absolute slope of the LM curve is the ratio of the responsiveness of the transactions demand for money to the level of income and the responsiveness of the asset demand for money to the rate of interest.[24] There is no way we can *a priori* state a generalization that one of these ratios exceeds the other for all economies. We need a justification for the slopes as drawn. One such justification is to consider an intersection of LM and *BP* at some point J, resulting in (i_0, Y_0) in the accompanying Figure A11.1.1.

We then consider what would happen if a recession that shifts the IS curve to the left from point J (to pass through points F and G) were to occur without this being anticipated by the monetary and fiscal authorities. There would be a decline in income and the interest rate. We would expect portfolio readjustment to be rapid as financial markets react fast to economy-wide conditions, and individuals would adjust their holdings of money vis-à-vis other financial assets (bonds) so that the lower (i, Y) combination pushes them lower down on the LM curve. What would happen to the external equilibrium in the balance of payments? We could expect that international capital markets react faster to information regarding a recession, and that the market for international trade, takes time to renegotiate contracts and delivery schedules. Thus, the recession's interest rate effect of decreasing NKIs outweighs its income effect of increasing the net export of goods and services.[25] This being the case, it means the new interest rate is too low (point G is lower than point F) and the new income too high (at point G income is higher than at point F) to prevent a payments deficit. The *BP* curve thus lies above the LM curve for income values to the left of the intersection of *BP* and LM. Similarly, in an unanticipated boom, one would expect a *BP* surplus to develop—implying that the *BP* curve lies below LM for values of Y to the right of the intersection of *BP* and LM.

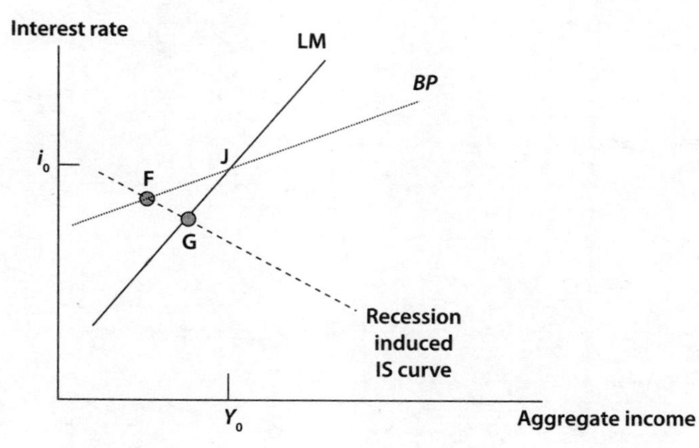

› **Figure A11.1.1**
Slopes of the LM and *BP* Curves. A recession that was not forecast by monetary and fiscal authorities shifts the IS curve to the left. Speedy portfolio readjustment in the money market ensures an interest rate prevailing at the intersection of IS and LM. With trade in goods involving a longer adjustment period than capital flows, the *BP* should be in deficit. This implies that the *BP* curve is flatter than the LM curve.

12

Stabilization and Government Deficits

CRITICAL QUESTIONS

- *What are the roles of automatic stabilizers and discretionary fiscal policy?*
- *How does the long-run goal of fiscal policy constrain discretionary fiscal policy?*
- *What is the intertemporal government budget constraint?*
- *When is the government deficit sustainable?*
- *What are the measures adopted to cut fiscal deficits?*

12.1 Limits to Discretionary Policy

Until 1990, the concept of the fiscal deficit was absent from official government documents such as the budget and the Economic Survey.[1] It was only after the economic crisis of the early 1990s that fiscal consolidation made the fiscal deficit a focus of policy discussions. Before 1991, government borrowing to finance the deficit was accommodated by hikes in the STATUTORY LIQUIDITY RATIO imposed on banks, which allowed the placement of government securities at rates below market rates of interest. With financial liberalization, the move to market-determined rates of interest, when government securities are bought and sold, requires the fiscal deficit to be sustainable so that interest payments and deficits do not run out of control.

› The **statutory liquidity ratio** specifies the required holding of government securities as a fraction of the assets of a commercial bank.

In India, the government formalized an agreement with the Reserve Bank of India (RBI) in 1994 to phase out *ad hoc* TREASURY BILLS over a three-year period. Prior to this, the government used to finance its deficits routinely through the issue of *ad hoc* Treasury Bills that provided it unrestricted access to RBI credit and enabled it to monetize its deficits. With the delinking of budget deficits from their monetization, any fiscal shock had to per se be absorbed through variations in borrowings. Fiscal reforms, therefore, became associated with making fiscal deficits sustainable.

› The government requirement for funds to finance expenditure above the level mandated by the holding of government securities (statutory liquidity ratio) was met by the government unilaterally accessing the RBI by issuing **T-bills** or bonds with a maturity not exceeding one year. The RBI monetized these T-bills and increased reserve money.

As we saw in Chapter 8, fiscal policy refers to changes in government expenditures and taxes—with a view to achieving policy goals such as full employment output. There are, in practice, two ways by which fiscal policy contributes towards macroeconomic policy goals—automatic stabilizers and discretionary fiscal actions. AUTOMATIC STABILIZERS are government expenditures that automatically increase or taxes that automatically decrease when the pace of economic activity diminishes. Direct taxes such as income taxes are a good example of automatic stabilizers. As incomes decrease, individuals have to pay less taxes to the government. This limits the decrease in consumption spending that accompanies a decline in income. Let us take an example.

› **Automatic stabilizers** are expenditures that automatically increase, or taxes that automatically decrease when aggregate income and output decline.

With a marginal tax rate of 30 per cent when income reduces by INR 1000, your tax bill reduces by INR 300. Of the remaining INR 700 (the amount by which your disposable income has been reduced), with a marginal propensity to consume of 0.65, you would have consumed INR 455 and saved INR 245. So, your consumption expenditure declines by INR 455. Without the income tax in place, you would have decreased your consumption spending by a much larger amount—0.65 × INR 1000, or INR 650.

As taxes rise and fall with income, they reduce the variation in consumption spending and result in more stable expenditures in the economy. In advanced economies, transfer payments such as unemployment benefits also act as automatic stabilizers. A decline in economic activity, accompanied by a rise in unemployment, results in a rise in government transfers via unemployment benefit programmes. This income support, to those affected by a downturn in the economy, limits the decline in consumption spending that would otherwise have occurred and stabilizes expenditures.

Automatic stabilizers affect the slope of the aggregate demand curve—the inverse relationship between the price level and aggregate income/expenditure. A rise in the price level reduces real money supply and raises the interest rate. This, in turn, reduces investment expenditure and aggregate income. Tax payments, along with income, decline and this limits the decline in consumption spending. Hence, without income taxes, the decline in consumption expenditure would have been greater. Thus, the AGGREGATE DEMAND CURVE with automatic stabilizers has a STEEPER slope than one without such stabilizers in existence.[2]

› Automatic stabilizers result in a **steeper aggregate demand curve** and reduce the variability of output arising from shocks to aggregate demand.

Automatic stabilizers also cushion the impact of shocks—unanticipated sudden changes—on the economy. A reduction in business confidence, for instance, shifts the aggregate demand curve to the left. The magnitude of this shift is, however, reduced by the presence of automatic stabilizers. Such smaller shifts of the aggregate demand curve reduce the variability of economic fluctuations.

› **Discretionary fiscal policy** results form deliberate and conscious choices by the government on public expenditure and taxes so as to achieve macroeconomic goals.

DISCRETIONARY FISCAL POLICY is the deliberate and conscious use of government expenditure and tax decisions to influence the course of the economy. This aspect of fiscal policy is subject to long inside lags of recognition and implementation, which reduces its effectiveness in helping to stabilize the economy. To stabilize the economy, fiscal policy must, therefore, work through automatic stabilizers. This means that as the economy expands, tax revenues increase and the government's budget deficit declines. By contrast, if the economy goes into a downturn, the budget deficit increases. In addition to such cyclical impacts, the budget deficit may increase or fall as fiscal policy is used to provide an additional discretionary stimulus to steer the economy towards an equilibrium level of output.

So far, we proceeded to analyse fiscal policy in the IS–LM model as an exogenous change in government spending or taxation that causes a shift in the IS curve. At that point, we did not consider the financing of these changes in fiscal policy explicitly. A change in government expenditure for a given taxation and borrowing from the central bank (SEIGNIORAGE) must be financed through borrowing and an increase in public debt. This imposes an obligation on the government to pay interest on the debt and eventually to repay the principal amount. Once we recognize this intertemporal aspect of fiscal policy, it is natural to ask ourselves as to whether the repayment of debt places limits to government borrowing that affects its ability to engage in discretionary fiscal policy. Only if the public debt is sustainable, in the sense of the government being able to repay the debt, does a government have the fiscal space to increase borrowings to finance increases in public expenditure. The discretionary element of fiscal policy is, therefore, limited by the sustainability of the government's debt.

› When the government finances its expenditure with the use of new money that is created for the purpose, it resorts to money creation as a revenue device. This process, where the central bank accommodates the expenditure of the government with new currency, is known as **seigniorage.**

Fiscal policy, which was associated with its short-run role of using government expenditure and tax policy to stabilize output over the business cycle, has an objective for a longer run as well. This is the objective of fiscal discipline or debt sustainability, which we address in this chapter.

Until now, we have explored the role of fiscal policy as a short-run output stabilization tool. Two concerns that we faced in using this tool were that the impact of fiscal policy can be rather slow and that the impact is also rather uncertain. The lags in fiscal policy action arise because such actions must be approved by a central organization, e.g., the Indian parliament. This could result in the loss of precious time before action is initiated. Discretionary fiscal policy is usually carried out with annual budgets, which is a major hurdle as this results in long lags. For discretionary fiscal actions to be useful as a countercyclical device, the decision and implementation lags need to be sharply reduced. This is a difficult task, however, as fiscal policy decisions on expenditure or taxation have redistributive impacts, and such actions in a democratic set-up should be subjected to parliamentary oversight. Monetary policy, on the contrary, has a faster speed of reaction and can be implemented in a short time as it is not subject to as much *ex ante* political control, with the monetary authorities shielded much more from political influence.

Fiscal policy, which had been used as a short-run tool in the pursuit of stabilizing the business cycle in a liberalized economic environment, is increasingly being asked to deliver over time in the longer run on fiscal discipline. Fiscal discipline means that the government faces an intertemporal budget constraint and any fiscal action taken by the government does not violate this constraint. This does not require the doing away of deficits altogether. Some deficits may be caused by government expenditure that is an investment expenditure, which is growth promoting and so may well pay for itself through the taxes garnered from the increase in output. Such deficits are not a hazard and it is difficult to label them as problematic for long-term fiscal discipline.

Similarly, a few years of deficits are not antithetical to fiscal discipline provided they are followed by a few years of surpluses. However, when future action to reverse a sequence of deficits is not predictable, a government may be seen as not respecting its intertemporal budget constraint and thereby reneging on fiscal discipline. Moreover, as governments are in office for limited time spans and they cannot commit to deficit reduction on behalf of their successors, there is a built-in bias for deficits. The reason for this is that the burden of the deficit is not faced by the incumbent government currently. Hence, it is important that while governments have the short-run flexibility to stabilize the economy, they also respect the long-run objective of fiscal discipline as given by their intertemporal budget constraints.

12.2 The Government Budget Constraint and Debt Dynamics

The intertemporal budget constraint of the government is:

$$G_t - (T_T + T_N + T_D)_t + rB_{t-1} = (M_t - M_{t-1}) + (B_t - B_{t-1})$$

where the subscript t indicates the time period, and

G: public expenditure—current plus capital expenditure
T_T: tax revenue (net of non-debt related transfer payments such as subsidies)
T_N: non-tax revenues such as user charges on public utilities
T_D: revenues from disinvestment
B_t: end of period stock of domestic public debt which bears interest rate r
M_t: stock of reserve money allocated by the central bank

Let $T = T_T + T_N + T_D$ be the total government revenue. In what follows, we restrict ourselves to debt financing of deficits so that we may write the budget constraint as:

$$\Delta B = (B_t - B_{t-1}) = G_t - T_t + rB_{t-1}$$

The left-hand side of the above equation is the FISCAL DEFICIT. The PRIMARY DEFICIT is the non-interest component of the fiscal deficit:

$$\text{Primary Deficit} = G_t - T_t = D_t$$

Another way of expressing the government budget constraint is to write the budget constraint of the government in the following way:

$$\Delta B = B_t - B_{t-1} = rB_{t-1} + (G_t - T_t)$$

or,

$$B_t = (1 + r)B_{t-1} + D_t$$

› The **fiscal deficit** is government expenditure that is not related to the repayment of the debt, G, plus repayment of the debt, rB, less government revenues, T.

› The difference between the fiscal deficit and interest payments is the **primary deficit**.

where D_t is the primary deficit. Dividing throughout by GDP, Y_t, we obtain:

$$\frac{B_t}{Y_t} = (1 + r)\frac{B_{t-1}}{Y_{t-1}}\frac{Y_{t-1}}{Y_t} + \frac{D_t}{Y_t}$$

Let $b_t = B_t/Y_t$, the debt/GDP ratio, $d_t = D_t/Y_t$, the primary deficit/GDP ratio and the one-period growth rate of GDP be $g = (Y_t - Y_{t-1})/Y_{t-1} = (Y_t/Y_{t-1}) - 1$ or $1 + g = Y_t/Y_{t-1}$. Then, we can rewrite the above as

$$b_t = \frac{1+r}{1+g}\, b_{t-1} + d_t$$

› The **debt/GDP ratio** increases (1) as the government issues new debt to cover a primary deficit and (2) to pay interest on the existing debt. An increase in the growth rate of the GDP reduces the debt/GDP ratio.

The DEBT/GDP RATIO grows for two reasons. First, the government issues debt to cover a primary deficit—the term d_t. Second, the government must pay interest on existing debt. This is reflected in the expression $(1 + r)/(1 + g)$.

To understand this second expression, consider what happens when the primary deficit is zero. In that case, two factors affect the expression for the debt/GDP ratio, $b_t = [(1 + r)/(1 + g)]b_{t-1}$. The government must increase debt by a factor of $(1 + r)$ to pay the interest on existing debt. This causes a rise in the debt/GDP ratio. But, GDP is itself increasing at the rate of $(1 + g)$, which increases the tax revenues of the government as taxes increase with GDP. This factor causes a decline in the debt/GDP ratio. The net effect of the two factors is given by the ratio $(1 + r)/(1 + g)$. If $g > r$, the debt/GDP ratio will not increase and in that sense, the debt-GDP ratio is sustainable.

To analyse the dynamics of the debt and the government budget constraint, the previous difference equation can be further analysed. If we graph b_t as a function of b_{t-1}, it is a straight line with an intercept equal to d_t and a slope equal to $(1 + r)/(1 + g)$. This graph appears in Figure 12.1.

Now, consider the steady-state solution of the difference equation. A steady-state solution is a value for the debt/GDP ratio that satisfies the

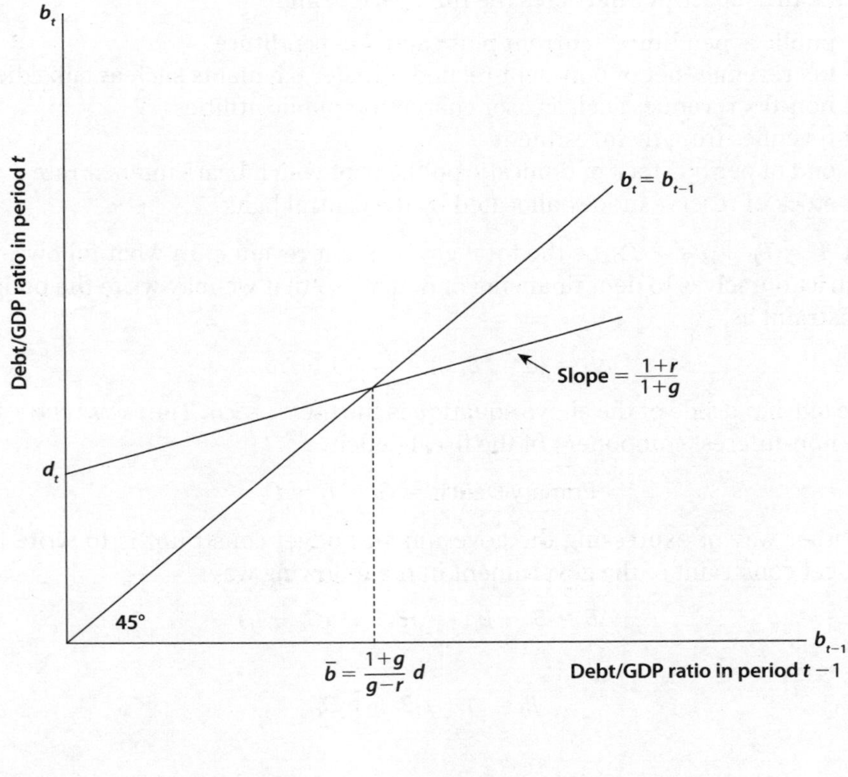

› **Figure 12.1**
The Evolution of Debt/GDP. The debt/GDP ratio in period t, b_t, is the sum of two components. The first is the primary deficit/GDP ratio, b_t. The second is the ratio of one plus the interest rate to one plus the growth rate of GDP times the debt/GDP ratio of the previous period, $t - 1$. The steady-state debt/GDP ratio that does not change with time is given by $\bar{b}$.

government budget equation and that is independent of time.[3] A STEADY STATE, $b_t = b_{t-1} = \bar{b}$, is a solution that gives that value of b which if attained will not change without a shock to the system. The $b_t = b_{t-1} = \bar{b}$ line is the 45° line from the origin and the steady-state value is given by

› The **steady-state** debt/GDP ratio is that value of the debt/GDP ratio that satisfies the government budget constraint and is independent of time.

$$\bar{b} = \frac{1+r}{1+g}\bar{b} + d$$

or,

$$\bar{b}\left(\frac{g-r}{1+g}\right) = d$$

or,

$$\bar{b} = \frac{1+g}{g-r}d$$

12.2.1 Primary Deficits and Stability

We now examine a property of steady states called stability. In the two panels in Figure 12.2, the intercepts, d, is the same number in both the graphs. However, the slopes of the graphs in the two panels are different.

› A **steady state** is **stable** if the debt/GDP ratio moves closer towards the steady-state value of the debt/GDP ratio over time, regardless of where it starts from. This occurs when $r < g$.

In panel A, the slope is less than unity—$[(1 + r)/(1 + g)] < 1$, or $r < g$, and this depicts the situation of a STABLE STEADY STATE. The debt/GDP ratio at any time t, b_t, moves closer to the steady-state value $\bar{b}$ over time, regardless of which value it starts from.

In panel B, the slope is greater than unity—$[(1 + r)/(1 + g)] > 1$, or $r > g$, and this depicts an UNSTABLE STEADY STATE. The debt/GDP ratio, b_t, moves further away from the steady-state value $\bar{b}$ over time, for any starting value of b_t other than ($\bar{b}$) the steady-state value itself. (Note that we are, for simplicity, assuming $[(1 + r)/(1 + g)] > 0$, which is assured if $r > -1$, $g > -1$.)

› A **steady state** is **unstable** if the debt/GDP ratio moves further away from the steady-state value of the debt/GDP ratio when we look at its trajectory starting from any point other than the steady-state point itself. This occurs when $r > g$.

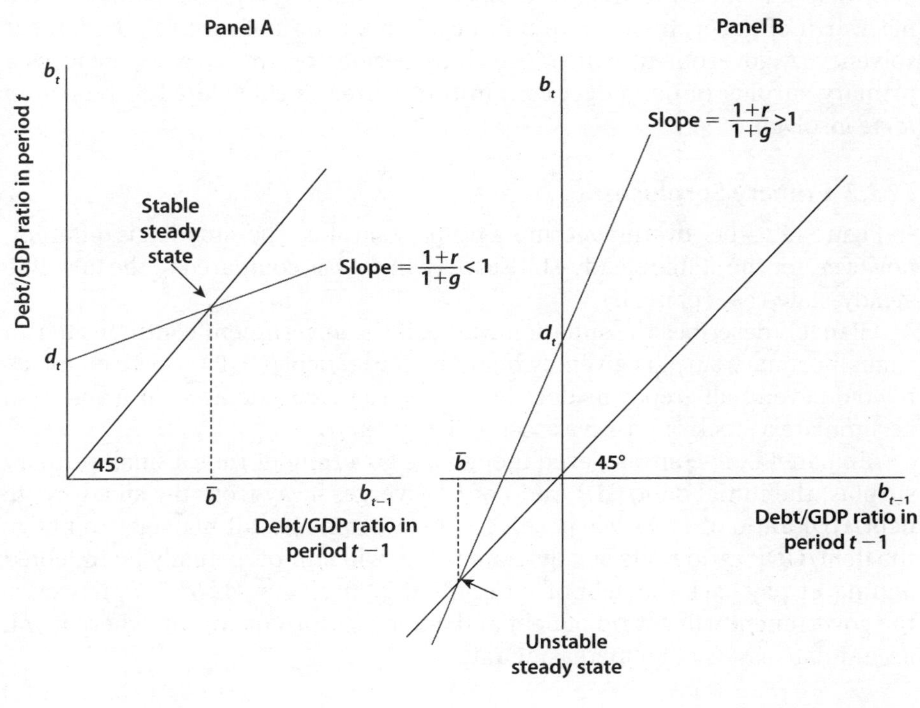

› **Figure 12.2**
Stability of Debt/GDP.
When the interest rate is less than the growth rate of GDP, as in panel A, the steady-state level of debt is stable in that if the economy, at any moment of time, has a debt/GDP value other than $\bar{b}$, it will gravitate towards $\bar{b}$. On the other hand, if the interest rate is greater than the growth rate of GDP (as in panel B), the steady-state level of debt is unstable and if the economy at any moment of time has a debt/GDP value other than $\bar{b}$, it will, over time, achieve a value of debt/GDP that recedes away from $\bar{b}$.

From panel A of Figure 12.2, we can see that if the growth of GDP exceeds the interest rate, the economy would eventually settle into a steady state with a debt/GDP ratio that is constant at $\bar{b}$. A constant debt/GDP ratio is not unduly worrying to policymakers and politicians. However, a perpetual constant value of the debt/GDP ratio implies that the debt will never be repaid and b_t will not tend to zero. Instead, the debt/GDP ratio will tend towards $\bar{b}$, $b_t \rightarrow \bar{b}$, and the government would be insolvent in the sense that it never repays the principal sum of debt borrowed.

In the case of panel B in Figure 12.2, where $r > g$, the GDP is growing at a slower rate than the interest rate and the debt/GDP ratio increases over time. Eventually, debt will be larger than GDP and it will be so large that the entire GDP will be insufficient to pay the interest on the debt. The government will eventually become bankrupt. In practical terms, as the government's tax revenues are substantially less than GDP, bankruptcy occurs well before the interest on the debt is larger than the GDP. The steady-state debt, however, is negative. A negative debt implies the government must lend to the private sector instead of borrowing from it. A policy that describes this involves increasing taxes above government expenditures and using the revenues to first pay off the existing government debt and then purchase financial assets from the private sector.

To sustain the positive primary deficit d, the government must accumulate enough assets, and this is obtained by running large primary surpluses for many years with an average value of $\bar{b}$. This is politically not an easy objective to attain. Instead, governments often strive for an easier alternative. They try to continue the existing level of debt and to raise enough revenue to service the interest on it. This is a policy of pursuing budget balance. Under this balanced budget policy, the government would attempt to set its fiscal deficit as close to zero and in the limit to equal zero. If $(G - T) + rB = 0$, then, because the interest payments on debt are positive, $rB > 0$, we must have $(G - T) < 0$—the government runs a primary surplus.

Primary surpluses generate the revenues that pay off the interest on the debt that was raised to finance deficits. They make the present value of the net worth of government more non-negative but do not ensure government solvency. A government which, over long periods of time, never generates a primary surplus in its budget can, in this sense, be considered to be *prima facie* insolvent.

12.2.2 Primary Surpluses

In Figure 12.3, the government runs a primary surplus. The situation is different, however, for the stable steady-state case (panel A) as compared to the unstable steady-state case (panel B).

Panel A describes the situation where, if the government continues to run a small primary surplus given by d and its initial debt/GDP ratio given by b^*, it would eventually repay its debt (as the zig zag arrow depicts). It would also accumulate a stock of positive assets/GDP given by $\bar{b}$.

In panel B, in contrast, even though the government runs a small primary surplus, the initial debt/GDP ratio of b^* diverges away from the steady-state debt/GDP ratio of $\bar{b}$. As $\bar{b}$ is positive, the government, if it manages to nudge the debt/GDP ratio to its steady-state value, will still perpetually be indebted and never pay back the debt of $\bar{b}$ raised—it is insolvent. (If $b^* < \bar{b}$, however, the government will get rid of debt and enter the third quadrant, where it will accumulate assets at an increasing rate.)

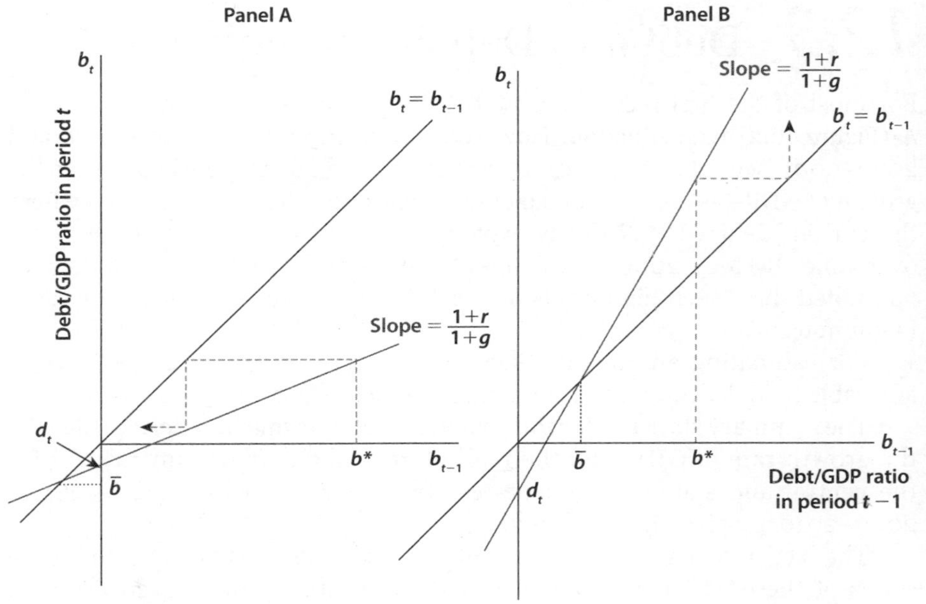

› **Figure 12.3**
Primary Surpluses. For the case of primary surpluses, $dt < 0$, when the interest rate is less than the growth rate of GDP—as in panel A, the steady-state level of debt is stable and if the economy at any moment of time has a debt/GDP value other than $\bar{b}$, it will gravitate towards $\bar{b}$ where the debt is repaid and the government has accumulated a stock of financial assets that earn it a return. On the other hand, if the interest rate is greater than the growth rate of GDP—as in panel B, the steady-state level of debt is unstable and if the economy at any moment of time has a debt/GDP value other than $\bar{b}$, it will over time achieve a value of debt/GDP that diverges away from $\bar{b}$.

MACRO FOCUS 12.1

Fiscal Surpluses

"The budget has been to our era what civil rights, communism, the depression, industrialization, and slavery were at other times.*"

Deficit reduction has become a major priority for governments and has captured many policymakers' attention. Those championing fiscal restraint were, at one time, at the margins, and intellectual forces championing higher spending and lower taxes dominated the policy discourse. Over the previous decade, however, there have emerged economies that have moved from reducing deficits, in order to bring the budget into balance, and toward sustaining surpluses. Surpluses are harder to find support for because it typically follows a painful period of deficit reduction, during which expenditures are cut and taxes raised and citizens begin to question whether further surpluses are needed at all. Instead, it is natural for demands to be present for new spending and tax cuts following a period of restraint. Yet, some economies have managed to sustain surpluses over many years.

Norway is one country that has set itself a macro goal of continued budget surpluses in order to build up the savings required to address long-term economic concerns arising from an aging population and declining petroleum revenues. Projections by the Norwegian government show a doubling of retirement benefits from 7 per cent of the GDP in 2001 to about 15 per cent of GDP by 2030. Oil revenues are also projected to decline from about 8 per cent of GDP to less than 1 per cent during the same period. In the mid 1990s, Norwegian decision makers reached a consensus to save surpluses to pay for future budget needs and since 1994, the country has been maintaining a surplus. The government created the Government Petroleum Fund in which surpluses were deposited to help pay for future pension costs and the funds' assets were invested in foreign stocks and bonds to help reduce inflation and depreciation pressure on the exchange rate for the krone.

In New Zealand, the public debt reached a peak of nearly 65 per cent of GDP in 1992. This led to a loss of investor confidence in the early 1990s and a credit downgrade. Keenly aware of the need to sustain foreign and domestic investor confidence in the nations' economic and fiscal policies, the Fiscal Responsibility Act (FRA) was passed in 1994 with a goal of reducing the country's net debt to between 20 and 30 per cent of the GDP. Under the FRA, New Zealand policymakers must consider the impact of fiscal policy on variables such as debt burden and national wealth. The entire budget surplus was committed to debt reduction, with a promise to cut taxes once the debt target was achieved. When the debt target was attained, a tax cut was enacted and the government then reset its debt target to 20 per cent of the GDP and further lowered it to 15 per cent in 1998. This occurred during a period of coalition government. The minority partner in the coalition was an advocate of social spending, and the larger National Party was an advocate of continued debt reduction. The parties agreed to implement a spending package which allowed for continued surpluses. Even when the Asian economic crisis occurred in 1997, which would have resulted in a budget deficit, the government enacted a package of spending cuts while scaling back previously promised spending increases.

Both these countries justified surpluses by expressing a clear set of fiscal targets and making changes to the budget process.** In Norway, the budget was usually the outcome of the aggregate of spending decisions on individual items of expenditure. This was changed to a top-down approach where the Parliament agrees first on an overall fixed-expenditure limit and ceilings on 23 spending and two income areas at the beginning of the budget process. All spending and revenue proposals must then fit within these ceilings. In New Zealand, the policymakers began to focus on its balance sheet, assets, and liabilities. This made them aware of long-term unfunded liabilities. For instance, the insurance premiums on the accident insurance programme, were increased to fully fund the programme. These examples prove that going beyond zero balances and towards fiscal surpluses are achievable goals.

*J. White and A. Wildavsky, *The Deficit and the Public Interest* (Berkeley, CA: University of California Press, 1990).
**P. L. Posner and B. S. Gordon, "Can Democratic Governments Save? Experiences of Countries with Budget Surpluses", *Public Budgeting and Finance* (Summer 2001): 1–28.

12.3 Debt and Deficits in India

For most of the first-half of the 1990s, the Indian economy was in a panel A (Figure 12.2) type situation. However, during 1997–1998, 1999–2000, and 2000–2001 (see Table 12.1), the interest rates shifted up and were higher than the growth of GDP—as depicted in panel B of Figure 12.2. This is a situation where the current debt/GDP is slowly exploding as the debt/GDP ratio increases over time. By May 2000, the RBI's Monetary and Credit Policy Statement had noted that "such high levels of fiscal deficit are not sustainable over the medium term".

For estimating an equation such as $b_t = [(1 + r)/(1 + g)]b_{t-1} + d_t$, it is advisable to look at a data period longer than just a decade.

The summary statistics for the debt/GDP ratio, primary deficit/GDP ratio, the growth rate of GDP, and the real interest rate on government debt for the central and state governments combined for the period 1980–1981 to 2009–2010 are given in Table 12.2.

The accompanying diagrams—Figures 12.4–12.6—chart out the time series of these variables. As can be seen, the interest rate on government securities has been below the GDP growth rate for most of the period. Only in the early part of the decade beginning in 2000 has the real interest rate exceeded the growth rate of GDP (an unstable situation). As Table 12.2

› Table 12.1
Debt and Primary Deficits in India
Source: Reserve Bank of India, Handbook of Statistics on Indian Economy.

Year	Debt Liabilities of Government as Ratio of GDP	Actual Primary Deficit as % of GDP	Growth Rates of GDP	Real Interest Rates on Government Securities
1990–1991	0.59	5.02	5.53	0.74
1991–1992	0.58	2.27	1.06	–1.94
1992–1993	0.58	2.12	5.48	3.58
1993–1994	0.60	3.23	4.77	2.97
1994–1995	0.58	1.90	6.65	2.00
1995–1996	0.57	1.56	7.57	4.72
1996–1997	0.55	1.24	7.56	6.17
1997–1998	0.58	2.13	4.05	5.70
1998–1999	0.59	3.65	6.19	3.97
1999–2000	0.63	3.81	7.39	8.00
2000–2001	0.67	3.57	4.03	7.43
2001–2002	0.73	3.69	5.22	6.36
2002–2003	0.78	3.09	3.77	3.58
2003–2004	0.79	2.07	8.37	2.25
2004–2005	0.79	1.35	8.30	0.61
2005–2006	0.77	0.99	9.32	3.22
2006–2007	0.74	–0.01	9.27	1.52
2007–2008	0.71	–1.15	9.82	2.39
2008–2009	0.72	3.49	4.93	1.04
2009–2010	0.69	4.73	9.10	–0.11

Note: The interest rates on government securities is the weighted average of interest rates on Central and state government securities less the inflation rate as measured by the GDP deflator.

› **Table 12.2**
Summary Indicators of Debt and Deficits

	Primary Deficit/GDP 1980–1981 to 2009–2010	Debt/GDP 1980–1981 to 2009–2010	GDP Growth Rate 1980–1981 to 2009–2010	Real Interest Rate on Government Securities 1980–1981 to 2009–2010	Real Interest Rate on Government Securities 1992–1993 to 2009–2010
Average	0.0327	0.61	6.18	2.50	3.63
Standard deviation	0.02	0.11	2.17	2.89	2.35

Note: The trend growth rate for the real interest rate is quadratic (inverse U shape) with a maximum around 1996–1997 for the entire sample, and a maximum in 1999–2000 for the period 1992–1993 to 2009–2010. On a trend basis, then, interest rates rose over the period up to the latter half of the 1990s, and then began to decline. Similarly, on a trend basis, the primary deficit/GDP peaked around 1985–1986 before declining till 2004–2005 after which it began to rise again.

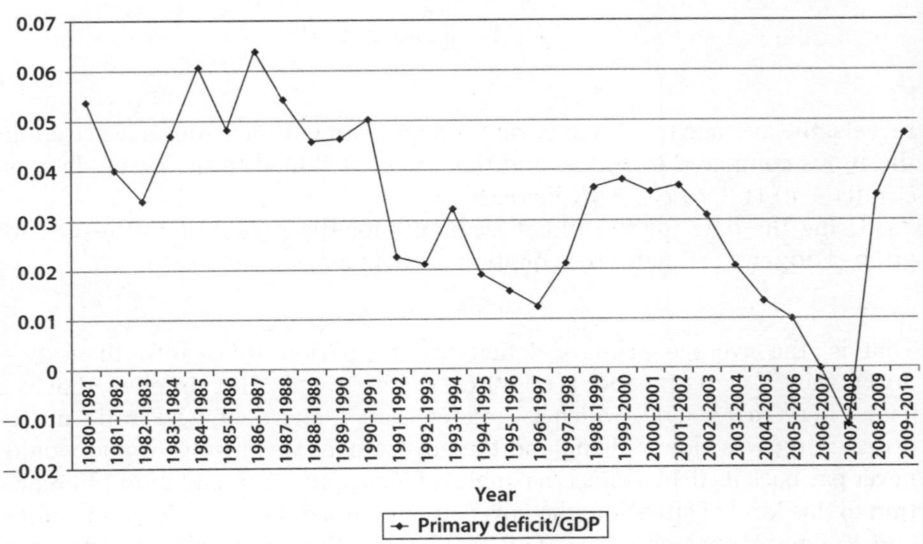

› **Figure 12.4**
Primary Deficit to GDP Ratio. The primary deficit has, on an average as a ratio of GDP, been 0.0327. It increased on a trend basis till 1986–1987, before declining till 2007–2008. Since then, it has been increasing again.

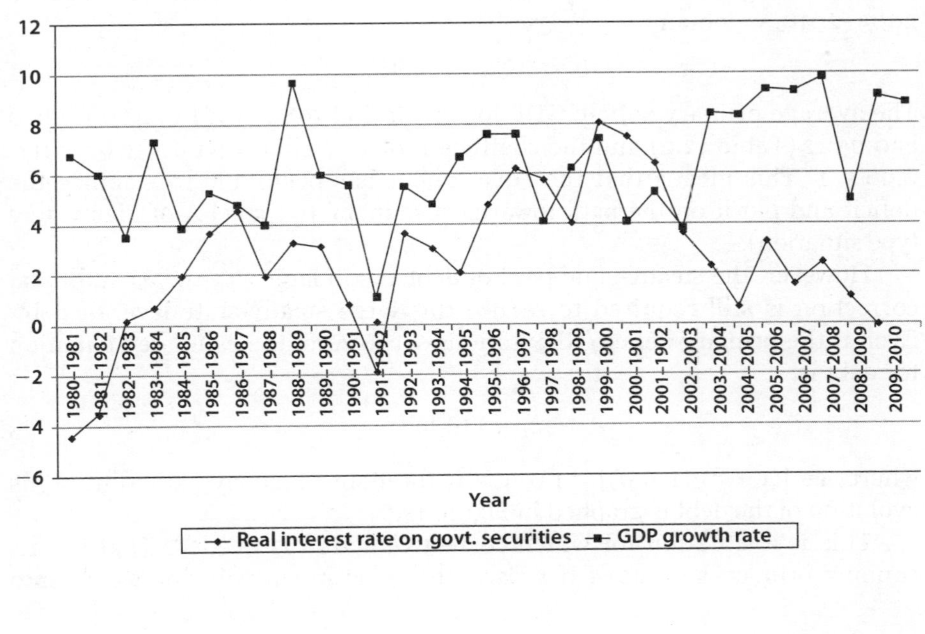

› **Figure 12.5**
GDP Growth Rates and Real Interest Rates. Except for some time periods such as 1997–1998, and 2000–2001 till 2002–2003, the growth rate of GDP has been higher than the interest rate. The trend growth rate of GDP is 6.18 per cent and the interest rate has been subject to an increasing trend growth till the end of the 1990s, after which it has been on a declining trend growth path.

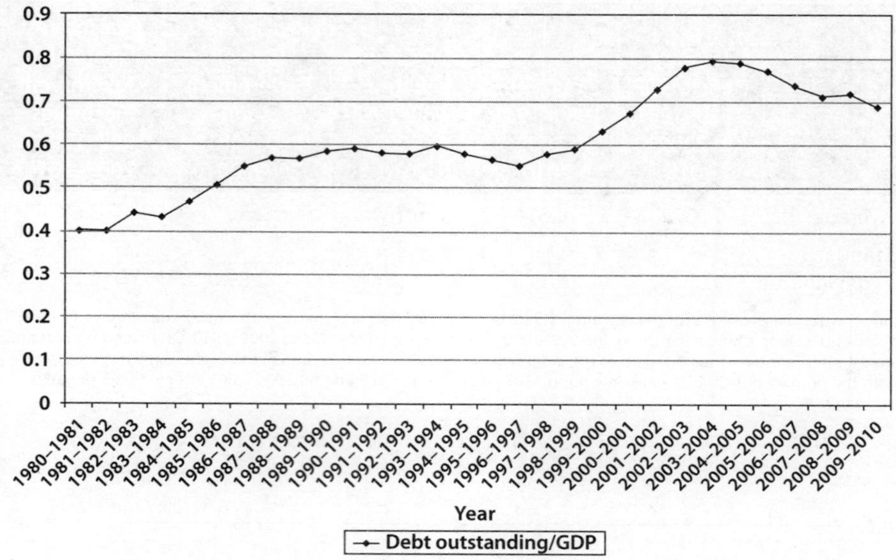

› Figure 12.6
Government Debt/GDP Ratio.
The debt/GDP ratio has, on an average, been 0.61 and its trend growth rate has been 2.02 per cent from 1980–1981 to 2009–2010.

reveals, the average real interest rates on government securities have risen in the 1990s compared to 1980s, and this has contributed to the rising debt as $b_t = [(1 + r)/(1 + g)]b_{t-1} + d_t$ increases with r.

Using the data for the Indian economy for the period of 1980–1981 to 2002–2003, we estimate[4] the equation for debt as[5]:

$$b_t = 0.0377 + 5.97b_{t-1}$$

That is, the average primary deficit for the period 1980–1981 to 2002–2003 was $d = .0377$ and $[(1 + r)/(1 + g)] = 5.97$.[6] This implies that as $[(1 + r)/(1 + g)] = 5.97$, which is greater than 1, the debt/GDP ratio up to 2002–2003 was slowly rising and the government was insolvent and would never pay back its debt. (This is a panel B of Figure 12.2 type situation.) In reaction to this kind of situation, the government passed the Fiscal Responsibility and Budget Management Act (FRBMA) that stipulated numerical targets for the reduction of the deficit. Since then, the primary deficit reduced (see Figure 12.4) till 2007–2008. After that, the financial crisis hit and it began to rise once again. If we re-estimate the equation for debt from 1980–1981 to 2009–2010, we obtain:

$$b_t = 0.0327 + 0.96b_{t-1}$$

The average primary deficit/GDP for the period 1980–1981 to 2009–2010 is 0.0327 (Table 12.2) and the coefficient of b_{t-1} is now $[(1 + r)/(1 + g)] = 0.96 < 1$. This means that the government has been able to stabilize the deficit and put it on the path towards sustainability (panel A of Figure 12.2 type situation).

However, the steady-state level of debt is still large ($\bar{b} = 0.74$) and fiscal correction is still required to reduce this large steady-state level of debt. Even if the primary deficit/GDP ratio is set to zero, the estimated equation for debt is:

$$b_t = 1.013b_{t-1}$$

where, as $[(1 + r)/(1 + g)] = 1.013 > 1$, the debt is slowly exploding. This evolution of the debt is graphed in Figure 12.7.

This is a situation for which corrective action is needed. That means running primary surpluses. If r rises, the government will sink slowly into

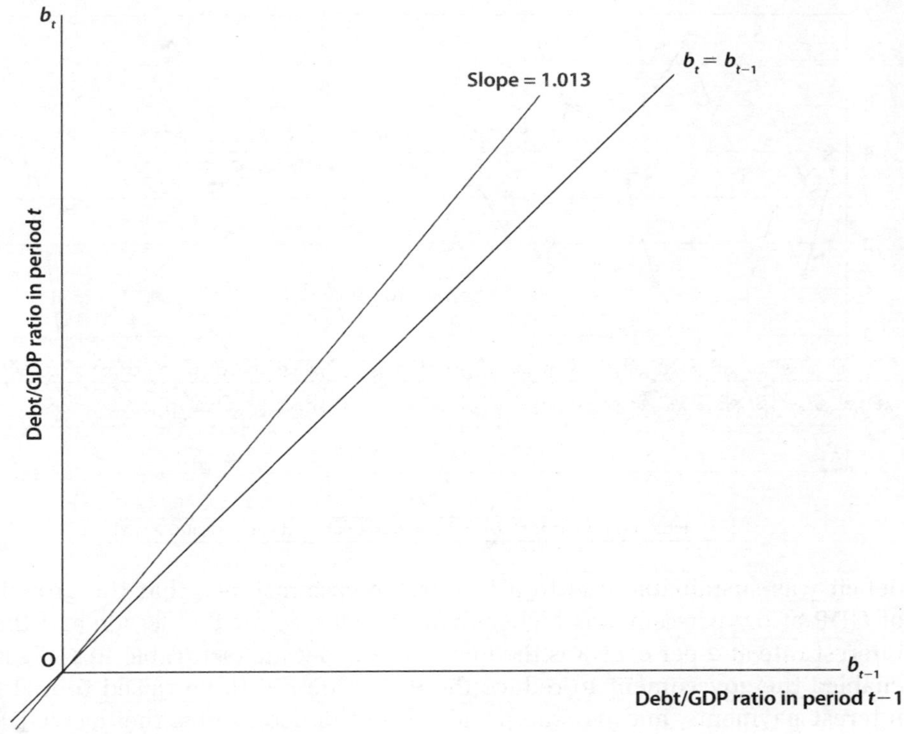

› **Figure 12.7**
Zero Primary Deficit and Evolution of Debt. A strategy of reducing the primary deficit to GDP ratio to zero will still not result in stabilizing the debt/GDP ratio, which will increase over time as the steady state associated with this strategy is unstable.

bankruptcy. From the present point of view, however, the government, as of today, is insolvent. This is because it will never repay its debt. It can and does roll over debt to repay interest on the debt, and the growth in GDP enables it to pursue this strategy and put off repayments of the principal on the debt for a future government to pursue.

12.4 Sustainable Primary Deficits

Another way to analyse the long-term debt and deficit scenario is to ask at any point in time that, if the historically given debt at that time is to be continued at that constant level forever, and if there is no change in interest rates and the growth of GDP, (the current configuration of the economy continues to prevail) what is the primary deficit that can sustain this time path of the economy? The answer is derived from the debt equation:

$$b_t = d_t + \frac{1+r}{1+g} b_{t-1}$$

or,

$$\left[1 - \frac{1+r}{1+g}\right] b_{t-1} = d_t \quad \text{when } b_t = b_{t-1}$$

or,

$$d_t = \frac{g-r}{1+g} b_{t-1}$$

This gives the primary deficit/GDP ratio that is required in order to sustain the existing level of debt in the economy. The Figure 12.8 denotes that the sustainable primary deficit/GDP ratio has been below the actual primary deficit/ GDP ratio for most of the 1980s and the 1990s. In 1994–1995, the primary

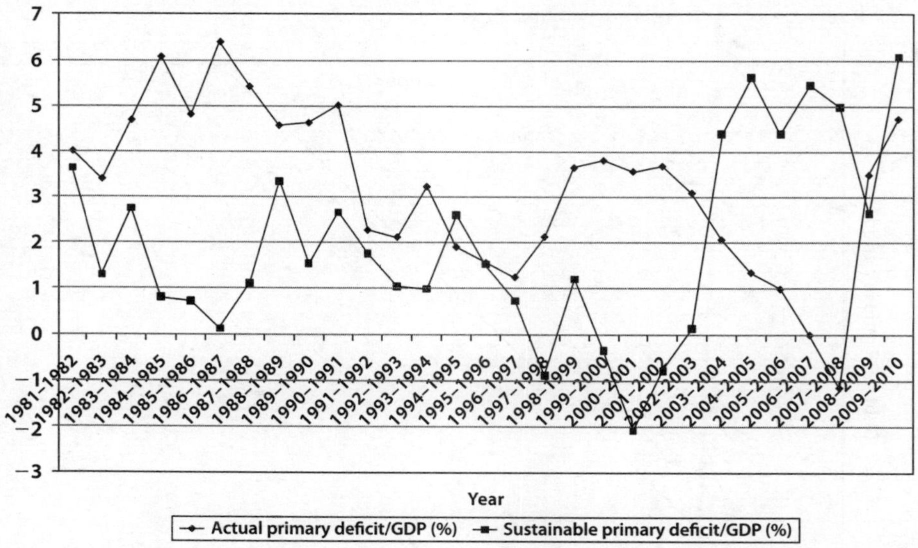

› Figure 12.8 Actual and Sustainable Primary Deficits. The sustainable primary deficit indicates that the current debt/GDP ratio can be financed indefinitely, given the continuation of the current interest rate and growth rate regime. Apart from 1994–1995, only in the recent past (from 2003–2004 to 2007–2008 and again in 2009–2010) have the primary deficit to GDP ratios of the government been sustainable—as indicated in the diagram.

deficit was sustainable due to a favourable circumstance that the growth of GDP at 6.7 per cent was higher than the average for the decade and the interest rate at 2 per cent was the lowest in the decade (see Table 12.1). This enabled the government to reduce the debt required to be raised to make interest payments, and pay the principal on the debt. Thus, the debt/GDP ratio reduced in the next year, 1995–1996.

In fact, the primary deficit/GDP ratio should be below 2.1 per cent of GDP (the average sustainable primary deficit since the beginning of the 1990s) if current levels of debt are to be continued indefinitely. A fiscal correction cannot be delayed indefinitely. As the graph shows, there was a sharp fiscal correction in 1990–1991, after which, except for the solitary year 1993–1994 there was a decline till 1996–1997 in the primary deficit ratio. After 1996–1997, however, till 2002–2003, the fiscal situation worsened again and the increased primary deficits during this period required substantial fiscal correction policy initiatives afterward. Since 2008–2009, fiscal stress is again visible, with the actual primary deficit close to the value required for sustainability.

12.5 Fiscal Rules for Adjustment

Before expounding on the constituents of a fiscal correction, it should be mentioned that, apart from debt, the deficit is financed by money creation. Thus,

$$(M_t - M_{t-1}) + (B_t - B_{t-1}) = rB_{t-1} + G_t - T_t$$

where M_t is domestic base money.[7] Hence,

$$(B_t - B_{t-1}) = rB_{t-1} + (G_t - T_t) - (M_t - M_{t-1})$$

and debt creation is smaller to the extent that some of the deficit is financed by money creation. In a growing economy, some extra real money balances are demanded to finance the growing level of transactions. Beyond that, the demand for nominal money expands only to the extent that inflation erodes the purchasing power of existing real balances. To restore real balances, the public adds at least partially to nominal money holdings. In this way, inflationary finance automatically creates a demand for the money issue that finances the deficit. The inflation tax in India is estimated to be 1.5 per cent of GDP.[8]

This means that the sustainable primary deficit/GDP ratio for 2000–2001, when we account for the inflation tax, is (−2.07 + 1.5) or −0.57 per cent of the GDP and not −2.07 per cent of the GDP, as Figure 12.8 depicts.

The analysis of the dynamics of the debt makes clear that a few years of debt decline is not enough to attain sustainability. What may be needed is a procedure that guarantees that the debt-to-GDP ratio is stabilized year after year. There are two important points to note about the intertemporal budget constraint of the government.

First, it is NOT A BEHAVIOURAL EQUATION, and so, is silent on the question of which of the government's revenue and expenditure variables should be adjusted in the face of disequilibrium. After this, we indicate what sort of changes in government expenditure and tax revenues can be initiated to bring the deficit under control. However, these policy recommendations are independent of the long-term discipline required for fiscal sustainability.

› The **intertemporal budget constraint** is an accounting identity that does not recommend how adjustments to budget balance should be made.

Second, the intertemporal budget constraint is also silent on the QUESTION OF THE TIMING of any required adjustment and simply specifies that an adjustment must occur, sooner or later. In practice, this keeps open the possibility of delay in undertaking what could be a costly adjustment programme for the government, and deficits may just balloon up. To keep out this possibility, governments have been enacting rules that set strict limits on the size of deficits. Chile and Brazil, for instance, have set strict limits on the budget deficit.

› The intertemporal budget constraint is silent about the **timing** of any required adjustment to the budget.

In Chile, the rule, in fact, calls for a structural surplus of 1 per cent of GDP. The Brazilian rule establishes that the Congress sets limits to spending on personnel over a three-year horizon, while the government commits to a pre-announced primary budget balance.

12.6 Fiscal Rules in India

In India, the Parliament passed the FRBMA in August 2003, which requires the fiscal deficit of the central government to not exceed 3 per cent of GDP by 2007–2008. It also requires that the deficit on the revenue account be eliminated by the same date. The specified annual reductions in the two measures are 0.5 percentage point of GDP or more for the revenue deficit, and 0.3 percentage point of GDP or more for the fiscal deficit. The FRBMA was amended in July 2004 to shift the terminal date for achieving the numerical targets pertaining to the fiscal indicators by a year to 2008–2009. The act also disqualifies the RBI from subscribing to government paper after 31 March 2006.[9]

› A **fiscal rule** is a restraint on fiscal policy, defined in terms of an indicator of overall fiscal performance. In India, the rule is defined in terms of the fiscal deficit (3 per cent of GDP by 2008–2009) and a public-debt rule disqualifying borrowing from the central bank.

In February 2004, the government constituted a task force to devise a strategy for implementing the FRBMA. The recommendations of the task force were made public in July 2004. The task force made recommendations to enhance direct taxes by 2 per cent points of GDP and to shift the revenue base of indirect taxes to include a greater share of services. In addition to the central government, several states in India have passed FRAs. Karnataka was the first to enact such legislation in 2002. It was followed by Kerala, Tamil Nadu, Punjab, Uttar Pradesh, and Maharashtra.

In all these cases, the common trend has been to include an imposition of quantitative and time-bound targets for fiscal consolidation. Most states have stipulated a reduction in the fiscal deficit as a per cent of the State Domestic Product (SDP) to 3 per cent by 31 March 2010.

In all of the cases, whether at the centre or at the level of the states, the limits to the deficit are self-imposed and there are no sanctions when the deficit limits are reached. As the rules are generally non-binding, there are chances that they will be set aside when economic and political expediency are required. This has already occurred in India in 2005–2006, when the target for the revenue deficit was put into a "pause" mode by the finance minister on account of a higher demand on resources arising out of the award of the Twelfth Finance Commission.

A problem with rules for deficits, then, is that they are not flexible enough in the face of unexpected events. This debilitates the discipline that the FRBMA is designed to deliver. Rules like the FRBMA work to promote the long-run quest for discipline in spending, but at the cost of ignoring short-run exigencies. The limit of 3 per cent of GDP on the fiscal deficit is also somewhat arbitrary and seems to have been selected from the same limit put for European Monetary Union membership in the EU's Stability and Growth Pact.[10]

This means that it is considered alright if public investments, presumed to average 3 per cent of GDP, are financed through borrowing. Thus deficits are tolerated as long as they do not exceed the size of public-investment spending.

There is no guarantee, however, that public investments generate a rate of return that matches the cost of borrowing. Also, there is no economic rationale for what, in budgetary accounting, is referred to as public investment. Education is classified as public consumption expenditure, while the building of new government offices is considered an investment. However, public spending on education is likely to be far more socially productive than building a new government building. Similarly, defence and police expenditures are treated as government consumption expenditures, while arguably they may be considered

MACROFOCUS 12.2

Are Fiscal Rules a Good Way to Bind Policymakers?

A fiscal rule is a restraint on fiscal policy and is typically defined in terms of an indicator of overall fiscal performance.* Among the various types of fiscal rules that have been adopted are the following:

1. Expenditure-limiting rules, that cap the level or growth in total government expenditure or specific categories of government spending. For example, Brazil has a rule that limits spending on the government wage bill and Argentina has a limit on primary expenditure. The US also has a rule that limits discretionary expenditures.
2. Current balance rules stipulate that current government spending should not exceed current government revenue. This amounts to a rule that states that governments may not borrow to finance current expenditure. Such rules apply in Brazil and the UK.
3. Overall balance rules prescribe limits to the extent of the budget deficit. Such rules are in force in India, Chile, Peru, and the European Union. The Chilean rule specifies, in fact, a structural surplus of 1 per cent of GDP on an annual basis.
4. Public debt rules limit the extent of the public debt, and in some cases, prohibit borrowing from sources like the central bank. Such rules are in force in India, Indonesia, the UK, the European Union, and the CFA franc zone.

In practice, governments find it easy to circumvent, suspend, or even abandon fiscal rules. A good example is the Balanced Budget and Emergency Deficit Control Act—the Gramm–Rudman–Hollings Legislation—introduced in the US in 1985. This act set targets to reduce the projected budget deficit to zero by 1991, which was later extended to 1993. The act applied to a projected deficit and not an actual deficit. The authorities used this to generate optimistic forecasts and projections that met the targets even though the actual deficits consistently exceeded the limits.

Even in the European Union, the Maastricht Treaty, which came into force in 1993, stipulated a condition that entry into the EU requires overall fiscal balances not exceeding 3 per cent of GDP. During 1993–1999, this fiscal balance rule was followed, but thereafter, many countries breached the rule. By the end of 2003, for instance, France and Germany (which were in a recession) had breached the deficit limit for the third year running but did not implement the remedial measures suggested by the European Commission. Even though the rules stipulated that both countries should be fined heavily, in November 2003, the majority of the EU finance ministers voted not to impose fines.

Rules may not bind governments to sound fiscal policies. The sanctions for non-compliance such as reprimands by courts or financial penalties on officials (elected or appointed) are too weak to deter governments. Also, the policymakers often have limited control over fiscal outcomes. In the short run, a GDP shock that impacts tax revenues is not amenable to be controlled by changing tax rates due to the inside lags associated with policy.

Cowen, Glazer, and Zajc**, in fact, suggest that when the durability of rules is in doubt, discretionary policy regimes are better. This is because, when there is a pre-conceived mistrust by economic actors that government may not follow the rule, then, the existence of a rule prevents a government from demonstrating its underlying preference for sound policies. A government with discretionary powers can actually signal its commitment to prudent policy and establish a reputation for sound policy that makes its policy credible. Hence, rules-based policy cannot be credible unless buttressed by a pre-existing reputation of responsible policymaking.

*G. Kopits and S. Symansky, "Fiscal Policy Rules", IMF Occasional Paper No. 162, (Washington, D.C.: IMF, 1998).

**T. Cowen, A. Glazer, and K. Zajc, "Credibility may require discretion, not rules", *Journal of Public Economics* 76, (2002): 295–306.

as an investment in security. Rules, meanwhile, do not leave room for flexibility in the face of unexpected events. Such was the case in 2005–2006 and such instances can occur again if there is a contingency such as a war or external threat and prolonged economic downturn. In fact, the financial crisis that began in 2007–2008 is another instance where the rule has been sent into the background. Also, rules do not matter much if they are not backed by an enforcement mechanism. This leaves the task of deficit containment in the face of unsustainable levels of debt to the presence of competent and dedicated policymakers and politicians who have good judgement and know when to exercise discretion and when to press for fiscal discipline. Of course, that is a tall order.

12.7 Fiscal Restructuring

Two questions are really raised in budget balancing as an element of adjustment policy. The first has already been answered before: How large a deficit is consistent with stability? The second question is: How are deficits to be cut down to the required size?

FISCAL ADJUSTMENT involved expenditure restructuring and the introduction of a productive tax structure. Prior to reforms, the Indian income-tax laws, for instance, had resulted in various distortions, such as the exclusion of perquisites, the exemption of income up to a certain level from taxation and from particular sources such as agriculture. It treated certain items of income, such as capital gains, to a lower tax rate. This eroded the BASE OF THE INCOME TAX and it became necessary to have higher rates of tax to raise a given volume of revenue. High rates of tax adversely affect economic incentives as the after-tax returns are reduced. They even induce evasion when enforcement by the authorities is weak. Tax reforms accordingly aimed at securing a broad tax base, without exemptions, and only a few rates of tax. The 1991 Tax Reforms Committee has laid the agenda for this. Some of the unfinished issues here are an extension of the tax net to the agricultural and services sectors, reductions in the corporate and personal income tax exemptions (such as for the export and small-scale sectors), strengthening tax administration to reduce corruption and evasion so as to increase compliance and reduce the undermining of the collection of taxes, and moving to a full-fledged VAT with some surcharges for luxuries.[11] Extension of the tax net has been significant, but improvements in fiscal administration still have a long way to go.

› **Fiscal adjustment** to meet a rule requires expenditure restructuring and the introduction of a productive tax structure.

› Taxes are collected by applying a rate structure to a **tax base**. Income, consumption, and wealth are the major tax bases.

The third important aspect of a productive tax structure is absence of significant subsidies of any form and establishment of efficient public utility rates. The economic approach advocated is for public sector prices to be set on the basis of microeconomic efficiency considerations. Income distribution consequences of prices set in this manner should be resolved through the general tax structure. During times of financial instability, public sector pricing is a contentious issue. When inflation is high, policymakers go slow on public sector price increases so as to reduce inflation. This results in a deficit which creates financial problems that are then resolved by raising public sector rates. For instance, the government in India subsidizes kerosene and domestic LPG, as these are deemed to be consumed by economically weaker sections of society. Oil marketing companies cannot adjust retail selling prices of these products in line with international prices. The restraint on this pass through of international prices to domestic consumers affected the margins of oil marketing companies adversely, as international oil prices began to rise from late 2003. Rather than allow these companies to raise prices, the government issued oil bonds to them to help tide over their financial problems. To repay these bonds in the future, the government will have to raise domestic prices, and if international prices do not soften the inflationary impact on the economy, could be substantially larger than if prices were raised today.

This see-sawing is bad for the economy and, stead, public utility rates should be indexed on a regular basis even when more indexation implies greater vulnerability to inflation. Inflation should be tackled by budget balance and not by temporary freezes on public sector price increases. The aim of government should be to eliminate all subsidies as far as possible. The resulting revenue gains should be partly deployed to restore fiscal balance and reduce inflation which, as inflation is a regressive tax, raises the real incomes of the poor. Part of the revenue gains should be used for targeted food and employment programmes for poor groups.

Currently, the central bank's "quasi-fiscal" deficit should also be made part of the fiscal accounting so as to make the accounting system transparent. Quasi-fiscal deficits arise from loans by the central bank at subsidized rates, losses on foreign-exchange operations in the form of guarantees, and subsidized credit that is not strictly an investment subsidy, but rather a production subsidy that finances wages and profits.

On the expenditure side, a number of reforms that are important are:

1. Cuts in public sector employment—civil service reforms are needed to reduce the public sector wage bill and improve efficiency. These include the 30 per cent staff cuts recommended by the Fifth Pay Commission, increases in the retirement age to address long-term pressures on pension budgets, and improvements in mechanisms to adjust pay scales. These are difficult issues as employment in the public sector is bloated due to patronage as well as poor accountability.
2. A second important issue on the expenditure side is *privatization* and the closing of public sector firms. Privatization is advocated for three reasons. First, the public sector often does not have the managerial capacity to administer in a cost-effective and quick response manner. Second, there is a scarcity of resources with the public sector and it does not have the capital resources to provide all public services well. The provision of public and merit goods could be privately provided, and the degree of public funding of this provision could be worked out, in the interests of promoting equity. Third, privatizations are often delayed because of the perceived low prices received from privatization. However, if failure to privatize and obtain resources results in fiscal precariousness and inflationary pressures, then even lower prices may be obtained from a delayed privatization programme. The downsides of privatization are that they often result in job losses, require retraining of workers, and are accompanied by the loss of subsidies to the poor. A reduction of state subsidies often translates into higher prices for goods and services and triggers popular unrest. A successful privatization policy requires governments to guard against replacing a public monopoly with a private one, and this necessitates the development of effective regulatory institutions.
3. Maintenance and investment expenditures on social and economic infrastructure—the fiscal problem is not just about firing public sector employees and privatization. There is an urgent need to restructure public sector spending from consumption to investment and productive services.

Most spending should be diverted to infrastructure, health, and social services for poorer groups. Available resources should be diverted to sectors in which private initiative is less willing or able to function. Infrastructure spending on telephone companies, steel mills, and airlines which need not be in the public sector is a misallocation when it is at the expense of spending on health and education.

The extent and manner of fiscal adjustment is but one element of an adjustment programme. Other elements include an appropriate MONETARY POLICY and an appropriate level of the EXCHANGE RATE. In some countries with hyperinflation, there is a fourth pillar of adjustment programmes, incomes policy that becomes important. We discuss these other pillars of stabilization policy in a summary fashion.

› Fiscal adjustment must be accompanied by a **monetary policy** that keeps real interest rates low. Real **exchange rates** should also not be overvalued as this reduces competitiveness which affects aggregate demand. In high inflation economies, an incomes policy that indexes wages is also important to control inflation expectations.

4. Monetary policy—tight monetary policy is not a substitute for balancing the budget which is the essential aspect of stabilization. Monetary policy does not, however, play an independent role in adjustment—it is dictated by the budget and exchange rate policy. Tight monetary policy, which results in high real rates of interest, is more a signal of serious misalignments in the budget, the real exchange rate, or both. Real interest rates should be low (the US interest rates plus, say, 3 per cent) and such a situation is sustainable if fiscal and real exchange rate policies are sound. Following stabilizations, real interest rates are usually high and debtors often go into distress due to these high real interest rates. Many argue that some monetary expansion is required to reliquify the economy. Reliquification is, however, best done by monetizing reserve inflows rather than by deficit finance or domestic credit creation.
5. Exchange rate policy—this plays a strategic role in adjustment. "When fiscal austerity reduces demand, full employment growth requires an offsetting mechanism for crowding in. A competitive real exchange rate does provide such a mechanism".[12] Competitiveness requires reduced inflation and adjustment programmes that are undertaken during high inflation would do well to fix the exchange rate. The downside of this is that, if inflation does not end soon, the government will have to abandon the fixed rate and signal its acceptance of inflation as inevitable—which has expectational effects. Governments, therefore, prefer a floating exchange rate, but as they are concerned then with targeting low inflation, there is a tendency for this to be accompanied by a tight monetary policy which raises interest rates sharply, attracts capital inflows, and leads to a real appreciation of the currency which becomes overvalued. The high-interest rate increases debt servicing and worsens the budget, and overvaluation creates an expectation of devaluation. If there is political resistance to the devaluation, policymakers are forced to defend the overvalued exchange rate through tight money—which puts pressure on the fiscal budget. If the government cannot absorb the fiscal pressure, it succumbs by allowing the exchange rate to adjust, which is just as well, because it is better to remove pending problems such as large fiscal deficits rather than to create new ones like an overvalued exchange rate that generates speculative expectations of reversal of tight monetary policy and an eventual collapse of the exchange rate. Real exchange rates should not be overvalued from the start of the adjustment programme as that sacrifices competitiveness and delays the onset of growth.[13]
6. Incomes policy—in periods of high inflation, without an income, policy adjustment has lower chances of success. As inflation accelerates, contracts

shorten as people seek to protect their real incomes. The shortening of contracts causes inflation to accelerate. If built-in inflation expectations are prevalent in contracts through indexation clauses, then it is important to break the inflation inertia that prevails due to the indexation. Under wage indexation, an increase in inflation results in an increase in wage costs that are often passed on into higher prices. Current inflation, accordingly, is tied to the past inflation in the economy. Exchange rate depreciation, a positive value of $E_{t+1} - E_t$, also has pass-through impacts on domestic prices as imports become costlier. Finally, inflation is also responsive to the tightness in the labour market or the unemployment rate (u)—the Phillips curve. Current inflation, π_t, can then be considered to be a weighted average of past inflation, exchange rate depreciation, and the unemployment rate.

$$\pi_t = \tau\pi_{t-1} + (1 - \tau)(E_{t+1} - E_t) - \phi u_t$$

In the previous equation, τ and $(1 - \tau)$ are the weights given to past inflation and exchange rate depreciation, while ϕ is the weight attached to the unemployment rate. With current inflation linked to past inflation and depreciation of the currency, and incomes indexed to inflation, current inflation cannot break away from past inflation unless the government intervenes and controls the exchange rate depreciation and disallows renegotiation of wages and incomes. It is only in an economy where individuals are entirely forward-looking, and wages and prices are fully flexible, that income freezes are not required as individuals will expect lower prices (presuming they believe the stabilization programme is credible) in the future and not renegotiate nominal incomes. However, this may be an extreme assumption to make for an economy, and as long as people are not all that forward-looking, incomes policy has a role to play in shifting wages and prices to a new regime. However, incomes should not just be frozen. Indexation on a periodic annual basis should be part of incomes policy. Without explicit indexation, the government is under pressure to grant wage increases, and the income setting process becomes politicized, with the chances of large wage increases being sanctioned by the government. Indexation helps establishing the expectation of a low inflation.

There are two other points that need to be kept in mind in the context of large fiscal deficits. One is that large fiscal deficits are seen to generate pressure on the current account as the increased income is spent abroad (in the form of higher imports), and the higher inflation rate domestically relative to inflation abroad also adversely impacts on the current account. Higher fiscal deficits exacerbate the double crowding out that takes place as the exchange rate appreciates in response to the higher government expenditure. The second issue concerns the financial sector (a supply side structural policy issue). High fiscal deficits in developing countries, till recently, were accompanied by controlling the interest rates of depository financial institutions. Apart from interest rate limitations, these institutions have also been required to hold reserves or government debt at controlled rates. This affected the efficiency of financial intermediation, whereby savings were not allocated efficiently among alternative investment projects. Financial sector reforms are, thus, tied to stabilization efforts. A more holistic view of the impact of stabilization policy needs to keep in mind changes in the current account and financial liberalization as well.

SUMMARY

- Automatic stabilizers are expenditures that automatically increase or taxes that automatically decrease when aggregate income and output decline.
- Automatic stabilizers result in a steeper aggregate demand curve and reduce the variability of output arising from economic shocks to aggregate demand.
- Discretionary fiscal policy results from deliberate and conscious choices by the government on public expenditure and taxes so as to achieve its macroeconomic goals.
- The fiscal deficit is government expenditure that is unrelated to the repayment of debt, G, plus interest payments on the debt, rB, less government revenues, T. Fiscal deficit $= G - T + rB$.
- The difference between the fiscal deficit and interest payments on the debt is the primary deficit. Primary deficit $= G - T$.
- The fiscal deficit is financed by increasing the stock of debt related government securities, $B_t - B_{t-1} = \Delta B$.
- The debt/GDP ratio increases as (1) the government issues new debt to cover a primary deficit as well as (2) to pay interest on the existing debt. An increase in the growth rate of the GDP reduces the debt/GDP ratio.
- The steady-state debt/GDP ratio is that value of the debt/GDP ratio that satisfies the government budget constraint and which is independent of time, that is, $b_t = b_{t-1} = \bar{b}$, where, $\bar{b} = [(1+g)/(g-r)]\, d$.
- A steady state is stable if the debt/GDP ratio moves closer towards the steady-state value of the debt/GDP ratio over time, regardless of where it starts from. This occurs when $r < g$.
- A steady state is unstable if the debt/GDP ratio moves further away from the steady-state value of the debt/GDP ratio when we look at its trajectory starting from any point other than the steady state point itself. This occurs when $r > g$.
- The intertemporal budget constraint is an accounting identity that does not recommend how adjustments to budget balance should be made.
- The intertemporal budget constraint is also silent about the timing of any required adjustment.
- A fiscal rule is a restraint on fiscal policy defined in terms of an indicator of overall fiscal performance. In India, the rule is defined in terms of the fiscal deficit (3 per cent of GDP by 2008–2009) and a public debt rule disqualifying borrowing from the central bank.
- Fiscal adjustment to meet a rule requires expenditure restructuring and the introduction of a productive tax structure.
- Fiscal adjustment must be accompanied by a monetary policy that keeps real interest rates low. Real exchange rates should also not be overvalued as competitiveness gets reduced which affects aggregate income. In high inflation economies an incomes policy that indexes wages is also important to control inflation expectations.

NOTES

1. See Shankar Acharya, "Macroeconomic Management in the Nineties", *Economic and Political Weekly* (20 April 2002): 1515–1538.
2. Note that the tax payment term in Eq. (A1.9) in Appendix 9.1 of Chapter 9 that results in tax revenues varying with income is given by t_1. This appears with a positive sign in the denominator on the right-hand side. If there were no income taxes, $t_1 = 0$, the denominator would have been smaller, thus making the inverse relationship between P and Y steeper.
3. We are taking the position here that the intertemporal budget constraint is satisfied if the debt/GDP ratio converges without specifying its target value. Some authors (Buiter and Patel, 2006) take sustainability to be the case when the debt/GDP ratio returns to its initial level which is a stronger condition that requires that a government that has outstanding debt must run future surpluses on the primary budget sooner or later. See Willem Buiter and Urjit Patel, "Excessive Budget Deficits, a Government-Abused Financial System, and Fiscal Rules", in Suman Bery, Barry Bosworth, and Arvind Panagariya (eds.) *India Policy Forum*, No. 2 (New Delhi: Sage Publications, 2006).
4. Strictly speaking, the algebraic expression for debt should be estimated in a structural time series framework. The estimate from such a framework results in a policy conclusion that replicates the one from regression analysis and so we do not report those estimates here.
5. The actual estimate is $b_t = 0.000232 + 1.0306 b_{t-1}$ but we have estimated the regression for an intercept of 0.0377 equal to the average primary deficit/GDP ratio for the data period. The coefficients are significant and $R^2 = .93$ which indicates a good fit.
6. Note how the graph of the real interest rate in Figure 12.5 is increasing. If we draw a trend line through the points, we obtain an upward sloping straight line with a slope of 0.35. By contrast, a trend line for the growth rate of GDP is mildly negative with a slope of –0.01. This indicates why the ratio of the real interest rate to the growth rate of GDP is greater than unity.
7. We could also break up the debt into its domestic (B) and foreign (B^*) components so that with a spot exchange rate of E_t, we would have $(M_t - M_{t-1}) + (E_t B_t^* - E_{t-1} B_{t-1}^*) + (B_t - B_{t-1}) = rB_{t-1} + r^* E_{t-1} B_{t-1}^* + G - T$. In the data above

we have not included the external debt liabilities of the government as part of the debt/GDP ratio.

8. M.J. Manohar Rao and Raj Nallari, *Macroeconomic Stabilization and Adjustment* (New Delhi: Oxford University Press, 2001).
9. However, borrowing from the RBI to cover temporary excess of cash disbursements over receipts—ways and means advances—is permitted.
10. See Willem Buiter and Urjit Patel, "Excessive Budget Deficits, a Government-Abused Financial System, and Fiscal Rules", in S. Bery, B. Bosworth, and A. Panagariya (eds.) *India Policy Forum*, No. 2 (New Delhi: Sage Publications, 2006).
11. See Parthasarathi Shome, "India: Tax Policy for the Ninth Five Year Plan", Report of the Working Group on Tax Policy of the Steering Group on Financial Resources, New Delhi, 1997; and the Kelkar Committee Report.
12. Rudiger Dornbush, "Policies to Move from Stabilization to Growth", *Proceedings of the World Bank Annual Conference on Development Economics*; 1990.
13. Many Latin American countries in order to tackle the real appreciation problem resorted to crawling pegs where the exchange rate is depreciated at a pace that maintains external competitiveness.

TEST YOURSELF

1. Distinguish between automatic and discretionary fiscal policy.
2. Define the intertemporal budget constraint of the government. How is it related to the sustainability of the debt?
3. Why is the level of debt not as suitable a measure as the debt/GDP ratio of a country's debt obligations?
4. What is the difference between the fiscal deficit and the primary deficit? Which is a more appropriate measure of the deficit of the government and why?
5. Define a steady state. When is a steady state stable and when is it unstable? What condition must be satisfied to ensure that the debt/GDP ratio results in a stable steady state?
6. India is said to be experiencing a "demographic dividend" in that a large section of the population is in the labour force. What is the likely impact of this on future deficits?
7. In the case where the debt/GDP ratio is on an unstable steady-state path, what should the government do to reduce the debt?
8. Discuss the deficit and debt scenario in India between 1980–1981 and 2002–2003. In what way would a FRBMA alter the debt and deficit position of the government?
9. What are fiscal rules and how effective are they in restraining the growth of government debt?
10. What correlated macroeconomic policy is required to sustain a fiscal adjustment?

ONLINE APPLICATION

1. (a) Go to the home page of the Reserve Bank of India URL: www.rbi.org.in/home.aspx
   (b) Click on the "DataBase" icon
2. Then under the classification of Annual data, click on "Handbook of Statistics on Indian Economy".
3. Click on "Table 114: Combined Deficits of Central and State Governments" and insert data into a spreadsheet on the Gross Fiscal Deficit and the Gross Primary Deficit from 1982–1983 to 2009–2010.
4. Then click on "Table 1: Macro-economic Aggregates (at current prices)" and insert data on GDP at market prices (Base 1999–2000) for the period 1982–1983 to 2009–2010.
5. Calculate the Primary Deficit and Fiscal Deficit as a percentage of GDP for each year. For the year 1982–1983, for instance, the primary deficit was INR 64.82 billion and the GDP was INR 1910.59 billion. The primary deficit as a per cent of GDP in 1982–1983 then was $(64.82/1910.59)^* 100 = 3.39$. In a similar way, the fiscal deficit as a per cent of GDP in 1982–1983 was $(111.16/1910.59)^* 100 = 5.82$.
6. Create a graph of the primary deficit and fiscal deficit as a percentage of GDP for the years 1982–1983 to 2009–2010.
7. Insert a trend line for each of the two line graphs that you created in Step 7.
8. What do you notice about the trend of the primary deficit and the fiscal deficit over the period? Do the primary deficit and fiscal deficit diverge over time? If so, what is the root cause of the phenomenon that the difference between the fiscal deficit and the primary deficit increases over time?
9. The text demonstrated that the primary deficit in the recent past between 2003–2004 and 2007–2008 and again in 2009–2010 has been sustainable. Notice that the slope of the trend line of the fiscal deficit is mildly positive whereas the slope of the trend line of the primary deficit is negative. What policy decision(s) can result in a reduction of the fiscal deficit over time so that its trend has a negative slope?
10. If the policy objective is to attain the sustainability of deficits which definition of the deficit—fiscal or primary—is more meaningful and why? Why then do you think are targets for fiscal responsibility fixed in terms of the fiscal deficit and not the primary deficit?

13

Monetary Policy Objectives and Targets

CRITICAL QUESTIONS

- *What are the goals of monetary policy?*
- *Why do central banks use intermediate targets while attempting to achieve their ultimate objectives?*
- *Which intermediate target—interest rate or money stock—is effective when there are real aggregate demand shocks and money demand shocks?*
- *Which intermediate target is effective in the presence of supply shocks to the economy?*
- *What is time inconsistency and do monetary policymakers have an incentive to deviate from a pre-announced policy?*
- *How do individuals with rational expectations react to announcements of monetary policy when policymakers have the discretion to change policy?*

13.1 Goals of Monetary Policy and Intermediate Targets

Apart from attempting to understand how the aggregate economy functions, macroeconomics is also concerned with the goals that policymakers may appropriately engage with. The goals of macroeconomic policymaking are usually the following:

1. *Output*—Several theories point out that there is little scope for monetary and fiscal policy to have long-run effects. However, in the short run, unexpected changes in the growth rate of the money stock can have an effect on real output. This makes the prevention of spikes in output fluctuations as compared to its natural, full-information level one of the goals of macroeconomic policy. Such a POLICY GOAL also alleviates business cycles.
2. *Inflation*—Inflation redistributes resources from creditors to debtors by reducing the real value of debt, and redistributes incomes from the private sector to the government as it pushes people into higher nominal tax brackets. Moreover, inflation variability induces uncertainty about the future gains from sinking resources into a new project and results in reductions in investment and economic growth. These costs of inflation provide good reasons for policymakers to attempt to keep inflation rates low and to limit the variability in inflation rates.

› The goals of monetary **policy** are to keep output and inflation as stable as possible, with output stabilized around the potential or natural rate of output and a low rate of inflation.

Some policymakers are also burdened with demands to prevent significant unemployment in the economy, especially when workers are a significant vote bank. However, in the short run, with a trade-off between inflation and unemployment—as depicted by the Phillips curve, there could be conflicts among macroeconomic objectives. In the face of conflicting goals, how should monetary and fiscal policies be conducted? Moreover, due to the time lags associated with policymaking, as pointed out by Friedman, a policymaker focusing on ultimate objectives may not react with the instruments at its disposal until a disturbance has already occurred.

As a way around this problem, economists suggest an indirect management of the ultimate target by means of an intermediate target. In fact, typically, most central banks have sought to achieve intermediate targets of monetary policy. An INTERMEDIATE TARGET is a macroeconomic variable that a central bank attempts to control because it is of the view that doing so is consistent with its ultimate objectives. Intermediate targets serve as proxies for ultimate objectives.

› An **intermediate target** is a macroeconomic variable that the central bank can influence with some predictability, and which is related to its ultimate objectives.

There are two reasons for using intermediate targets when conducting monetary policy. The first is that there are a variety of theories about how monetary policy affects inflation and output. Given that individual policymakers may subscribe to different theoretical outlooks on the economy, it can be difficult to reach a consensus on the best way to attain the policy objectives. In such a situation, pursuing an intermediate policy target is a compromise when it is difficult to agree about how to achieve ultimate objectives directly. For instance, even though there is disagreement about the extent of the effect of changes in the money stock on output, most theories point out that a change in the nominal quantity of money has an effect on the price level. In that case, CENTRAL BANK OFFICIALS might resolve to pursue a money stock growth rate objective as it is an approximation to the ultimate goal, on which a consensus exists.

› Intermediate targets are used in monetary policy as a compromise in the absence of complete agreement among policymakers about how best to achieve ultimate objectives and because policymakers possess limited current information about their ultimate policy goals such as output and inflation.

Second, even if policymakers can agree on how policies influence economic activity, they typically possess limited information about the economy. Current information about ultimate policy goals—inflation and real output—is available only with a lag, and even then, the estimates of these variables is revised in the period following their initial release. By contrast, interest rates, money stock, and credit data are on hand for inspection and use at any given moment. By pursuing an intermediate target defined around such financial variables, the central bank can infer whether the eventual outcome for the economy is in the direction of its eventual policy objectives, rather than having to wait to make such an assessment.

The choice of a macroeconomic variable that is to serve as an intermediate target is usually made on the basis of the following considerations[1]:

1. *Frequent Observability*—It must be readily observable with little or no lag which is the rationale for preferring to use intermediate targets rather than focusing on ultimate goal variables. For instance, the price level as measured by the wholesale price index is observable at monthly intervals and real GDP at quarterly intervals but with a lag in the availability of the data. Hence, the central bank must choose an intermediate target variable that can be observed more frequently—say, weekly, if not daily.
2. *Consistent with Ultimate Goals*—The policies resulting in the target variables taking on certain values must in turn result in the ultimate goal variables taking on certain values. A CENTRAL BANK successfully meeting values for the intermediate target should at the same time meet its goals for inflation and output.
3. *Controllable*—An intermediate target variable should be one whose value the central bank can rapidly influence so that on attaining the intermediate target, the ultimate objective is also eventually achieved.

› Macroeconomic variables selected as intermediate targets must be frequently observable, consistent with ultimate goals, and controllable.

› Central banks have a range of options from which to select **intermediate targets** – monetary or credit aggregates, interest rates, and nominal GDP.

The ALTERNATIVE INTERMEDIATE TARGET VARIABLES that central banks have adopted included the following:

1. *Monetary or Credit Aggregates*—The rationale for targeting monetary aggregates bunch as *M*1 or *M*3 has been that the quantity of money determines aggregate demand and influences the price level. Also, monetary aggregates are controllable by central banks and frequently observable as well as their values are known weekly or at most fortnightly. Many countries including Japan (1975–1994), the UK (1976–1994), and Germany (1975–2001) have used monetary aggregates as intermediate target variables. Financial innovations, however, began to affect the stability of money demand in the 1980s as new forms of money-like assets have emerged and a given stock of money has been able to service a larger volume of transactions. The 1999 Bank of England survey of monetary frameworks reported 43 out of 50 central banks as viewing monetary aggregates as relevant intermediate targets while 7 central banks preferred the interest rate as intermediate targets.

   Another financial aggregate that has been emphasized in China and Russia is a credit aggregate or the volume of lending. In India, the RBI had traditionally used credit—aggregate as well as sectoral—as an intermediate target of monetary policy. This adherence to credit targeting went hand in glove with the concept of development banking that accompanied the planning process in India. As inflation was considered to be structural, selective credit controls were used to regulate bank advances to sensitive commodities so as to influence production outlays and curb speculation. Over time as deficit financing of public investment leaked out into inflation, the focus of monetary management shifted to the management of demand

MACROFOCUS 13.1

Evolution of Operating Instruments of Monetary Policy in India

In an emerging market such as India, the availability of credit is often an important dimension of policy because of the reliance of small and medium enterprises (that dominate the economy) on bank credit. In the 1990s, with the opening up of the economy, the linkages between money, credit, and output began to weaken. Until the mid 1990s, banks surrendered the foreign currency they raised via non-resident deposits and current account transactions. Thus, there was a direct link between the process of money and credit creation. As the external account got liberalized, banks could increasingly invest their foreign currencies abroad and as domestic credit demand was weak, they resorted to this measure. Between 1995–1996 and 2003–2004, bank credit to the commercial sector grew at a trend rateof 14.2 per cent, whereas their foreign currency assets grew[3] at 20 per cent. The Reddy Working Group accordingly re-emphasized the importance of monitoring credit aggregates as there was a substantial accretion to net foreign assets of the banking sector.* In the absence of a clear connection between intermediate targets and final objectives, the RBI has turned to a multiple indicator approach. The RBI has shifted from direct to indirect instruments of monetary control in consonance with macroeconomic outcomes. It now modulates market liquidity to steer monetary conditions to the desired trajectory. This is achieved via a mix of policy instruments, including changes in reserve requirements and standing facilities and open-market (including repo) operations which affect the quantum of liquidity. It also includes changes in policy rates, such as the bank rate and repo rate, which influence the price of liquidity.** The Liquidity Adjustment Facility is used by the RBI to manage liquidity on a daily basis and to transmit interest rate signals to the market. It has emerged as a principal indirect operating instrument of monetary policy.

*Reddy, Y. V. (2003) " Parameters of Monetary Policy", RBI Bulletin, February.
**RBI (1998) "Report of the Working Group on Money Supply: Analytics and Methodology of Compilation, Chairman: Dr. Y. V. Reddy", June 1998, Mumbai.

rather than the regulation of supply. The Chakravarty Committee recommended a monetary targeting framework to target inflation in line with output growth.[2] Monetary targeting was successful as a tool of monetary policy in the late 1980s and early 1990s as inflation was driven by excessive monetary expansion.

2. *Interest Rates*—The price of credit or the nominal interest rate is another intermediate monetary policy target. Central bank policy actions have direct effects on nominal interest rates and interest rates can be observed daily. However, the relationship between interest rates and economic activity is not necessarily obvious directly. Though lower interest rates stimulate capital investment, it is also the case that increases in aggregate income raise the demand for credit and push up interest rates. While the operating procedures of central banks in developed economies can be described as interest-rate targeting, there are significant differences in implementation. Many countries target the interest rate with refinancing facilities[4] but some countries have a preference for open-market operations. The operating target can also relate to the rate for overnight money or the money market rate for longer maturities such as the three-month rate. There is also a difference regarding the precision with which the money market rate is controlled—whether a specific interest rate level is targeted or fluctuation within a given interest rate band in permissible. Interest rate targeting does not involve keeping the money market rate constant over long periods of time but rather aims to exert an effect over economic events via a money market rate. The Federal Reserve deployment of this operating procedure, in the US, demonstrates that there can be phases when the money market rate is noticeably stable as in the second half of the 1990s as well as phases involving rapid and abrupt interest rate changes as occurred during 1972–1975.
3. *The Nominal GDP*—In recent times, the nominal GDP has been advanced as an intermediate target. As the nominal GDP is equal to the real GDP times, the GDP price deflator, minimizing the nominal GDP helps contain the volatility in either of the ultimate goal variables—real output and the price level.

13.2 Choosing Intermediate Targets in Case of Demand Shocks

The analysis of the merits of interest rate targeting and monetary targeting goes back to Poole.[5] In the context of a deterministic macromodel, Poole argued that the "policy prescription may be in terms of either the interest rate or the money stock; it makes no difference which instrument is selected".

› In a deterministic environment, it is irrelevant whether the interest rate or the money stock is targeted.

In Figure 13.1, the equilibrium income level Y^* is reached either by the monetary authorities setting the interest rate of i^*or by setting the money stock at some level M* that makes the LM function intercept the IS function at Y^*. From A POLICY PRESCRIPTION VIEWPOINT, THE CHOICES ARE EQUALLY SERVICEABLE.

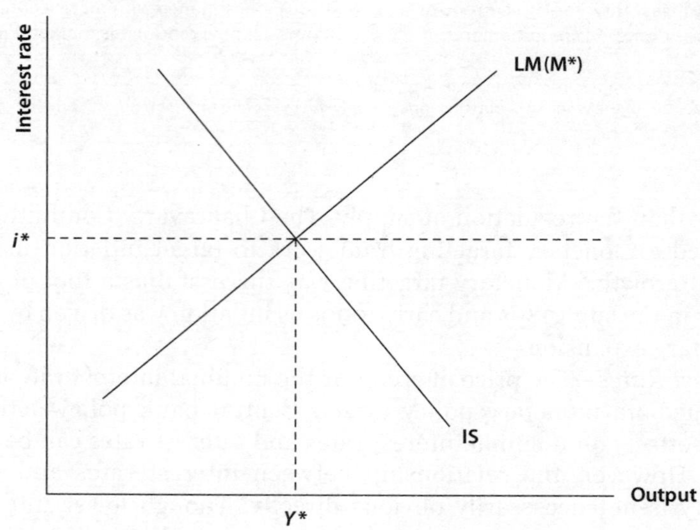

› **Figure 13.1**
Equivalence of Instruments in a Deterministic Environment. The equilibrium income level Y^* can be achieved by the monetary authorities setting an interest rate of i^*, or controlling the money supply at a level M^* that ensures that the LM curve intersects the IS curve at Y^*. Both instruments give an identical result.

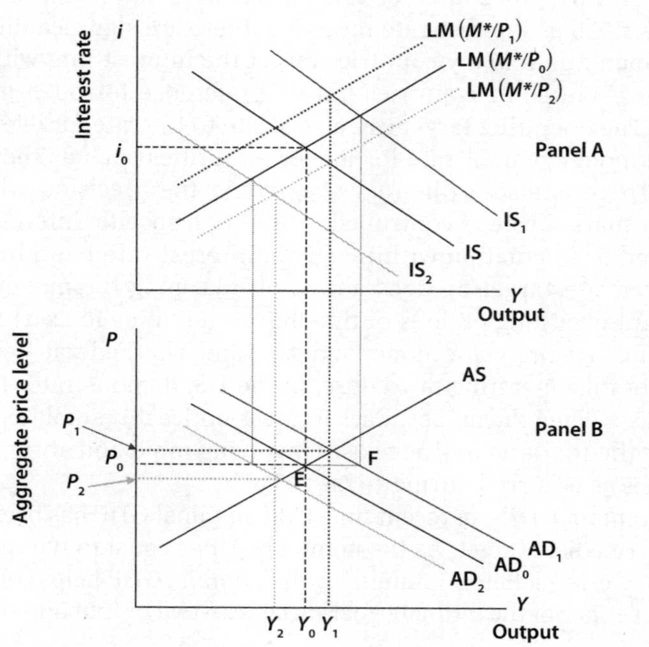

› **Figure 13.2**
Shocks to IS Curve. A positive shock to the IS curve shifts it rightwards to IS_1 in panel A and the aggregate demand curve to AD_1 in panel B. The excess demand for goods given by distance EF increases the price to P_1 in panel B and reduces the real money supply which shifts the LM curve in panel A to LM (M^*/P_1). Similarly a negative shock to the IS curve results in a price P_2 and a rightward shift of the LM curve to LM (M^*/P_2) . Output fluctuates between Y_1 and Y_2 and the price fluctuates between P_1 and P_2.

Poole then went on to show that such is not the case when the IS and LM functions are subject to random shocks. We study such stochastic shocks which we consider to be in the form of variations in the additive error terms that are added to the money demand and aggregate expenditure equations (IS equation) of the model. We abstract from shocks that affect the slopes of the curves in the macroeconomic model. Poole's analysis neglected the impact of shocks on the price level. We extend his approach to an aggregate demand–supply model with flexible prices and also examine the effects of the supply shocks, which are important in a development context.

13.2.1 IS Curve Shocks

We begin with shocks such as changes in autonomous consumption, investment, government spending, export or import spending, or net taxes that cause a multiple change in the equilibrium real income and result in a shift of the IS curve. A shift in the IS curve to IS_1 causes the aggregate demand curve to shift to AD_1 Figure [13.2(B)]. At the initial price level P_0, there is an excess demand for goods (distance EF), which results in a rise in the price level. In turn, the increase in the price reduces the real money supply to $M^*/P_1 < M^*/P_0$ and the LM curve shifts to the left in Figure 15.2(A). The price rises till the excess demand is eliminated, $P = P_1$ and $AD_1 = AS$. Similarly, a leftward shift of the IS curve to IS_2 will result in an excess supply of output at the initial price P_0 causing the price level to decline to P_2 and the LM curve to shift rightward to $LM(M^*/P_2)$. The excess supply is eliminated at $P = P_2$ and $AD_2 = AS$. Under monetary targeting, the central bank keeps the money supply fixed at M^*. In such a situation, fluctuations in the IS curve result in the real output fluctuating between Y_1 and Y_2 and the price level varying between P_1 and P_2.

If the central bank targeted the interest rate, it would adjust the money supply in such a way that the LM curve intersects the IS curve at the desired interest rate i^*. When there is an occurrence of a positive shock to the IS curve which shifts right to IS_1, then the IS_1 and LM curve intersect at an interest rate greater than the targeted i^*. The central bank now has to resort to expanding the nominal money supply so as to shift the LM curve rightwards and achieve i^*.

In Figure 13.3, the increase in the money supply to $M_1 > M_0$ reinforces the expansionary effect of the shift in the IS curve and increases the pressure on the price level as excess demand at the original price level P_0 is now even greater at EG. As a result, the aggregate demand curve under interest rate targeting $AD_1|_i$ is even further to the right of the aggregate demand curve under money supply targeting, $AD_1|_M$. As depicted in Figure 13.3, the real output and price level variation is higher under interest rate targeting than monetary targeting with $Y_1|_i - Y_0 > Y_1|_M - Y_0$ and $P_1|_i - P_0 > P_1|_M - P_0$.

If a restrictive IS shock occurs, which pushes the IS curve leftwards to IS_2, the monetary authority in an attempt to achieve i^* will have to restrict nominal money supply which in turn reinforces the contraction due to the negative IS shock [Figure 13.4(C and D)].

If the central bank selects an intermediate target[6] on the basis of minimizing the distance of the actual income (such as Y_1, Y_2), from a desired level of income (such as Y_0), then if the economy is subject to real shocks to the IS curve, it is clear that MONETARY TARGETING [Figure 13.4(A and B)] is superior to interest rate targeting [Figure 13.4(C and D)]. This is independent of whether the ultimate objective is to stabilize prices or output. Using the money stock as an intermediate, target is preferable to targeting the nominal interest rate which could result in a much wider variation in real output and prices.

› If the economy is subject to real shocks that shift the IS curve, then, money stock **targeting** results in less output and price variability than interest rate targeting.

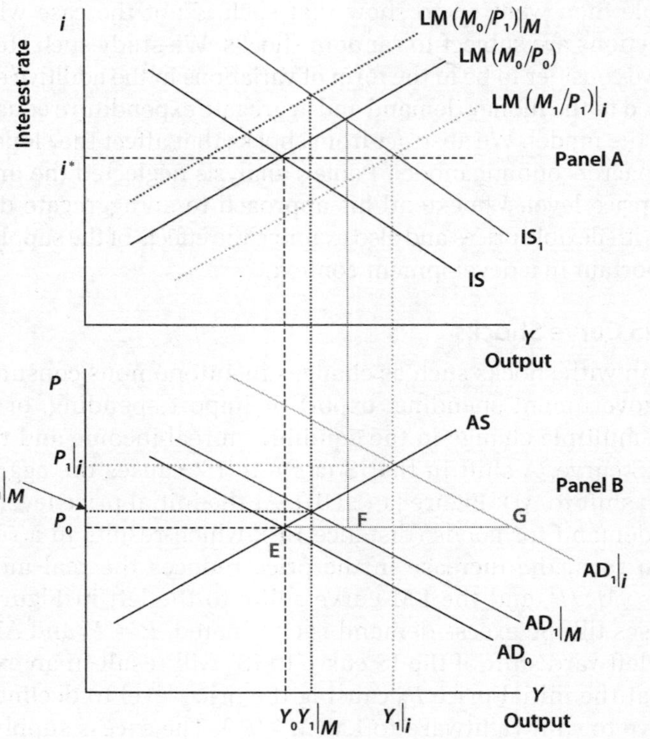

› **Figure 13.3**
Monetary and Interest Rate Targeting under IS Shock.
A positive shock to the IS curve shifts it to IS_1 in panel A. With the central bank targeting an interest rate of i^* it increases money supply to M_1 that shifts the LM curve to LM $(M_1/P_1)|_i$. The rightward shift of the IS and LM curves causes the AD curve to shift to $AD_1|_i$ in panel B and the price to rise to $P_1|_i$. Compared to money supply targeting, which was dealt with in Figure 15.2, the price and the output variation is higher under interest rate targeting.

13.2.2 LM Curve Shocks

Shocks to the LM curve can occur through variations in the demand for money that arise from changes in the technology by which people make payments, and not from any change in real income. In Figure 13.5, we examine the case where the central bank maintains a nominal interest rate target i^*.

To achieve this intermediate target,[7] the central bank will have to make sure that the supply of real money balance (M_o/P_o) intersects the demand curve for real money balances $(M^d/P_0)(Y_0)$ at the interest rate i^* in panel A. This results in the LM(M_0) curve in panel B, which intersects with the IS curve and results in a real income equal to Y_0. In turn, the accompanying aggregate

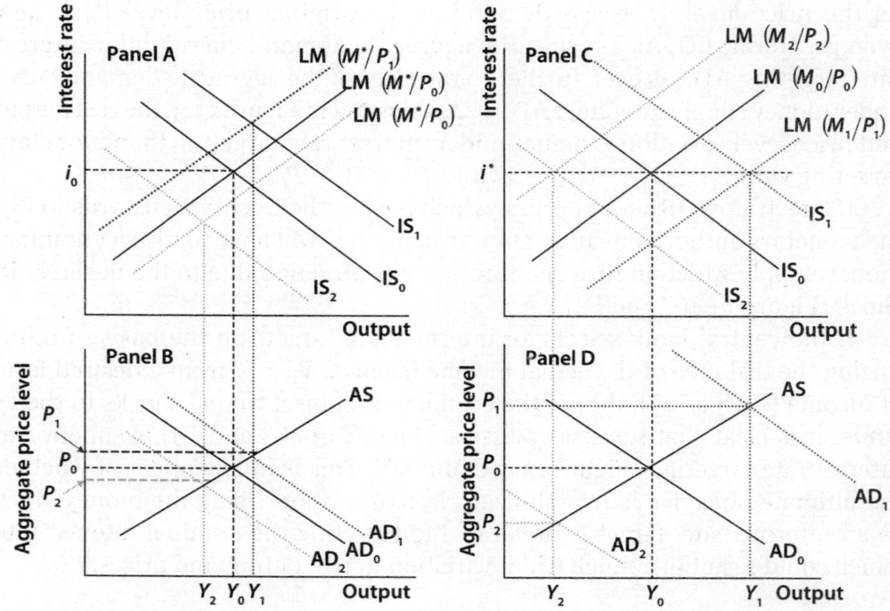

› **Figure 13.4**
Variability under Monetary and Interest Rate Targeting for IS Curve Shocks. Under money supply targeting, which was analysed in Figure 13.2, the shocks to the IS curve cause it to vary between IS_1 and IS_2 as depicted in panel A. This results in the aggregate demand curve varying between AD_1 and AD_2 in panel B. Under money supply targeting the output varies between Y_1 and Y_2 and the price level varies between P_1 and P_2 in panel B. Under interest rate targeting which was analyzed in Figure 13.3 the shocks to the IS curve are accompanied by corresponding shifts to the LM curve as shown in panel C where the monetary authority targets an interest rate of i^*. The combined effect of the shifts of IS and LM results in the AD curve shifting left to AD_2 or right to AD_1 in panel D. Under interest rate targeting the output variation and price variation in panel D is much higher than the variation in panel B.

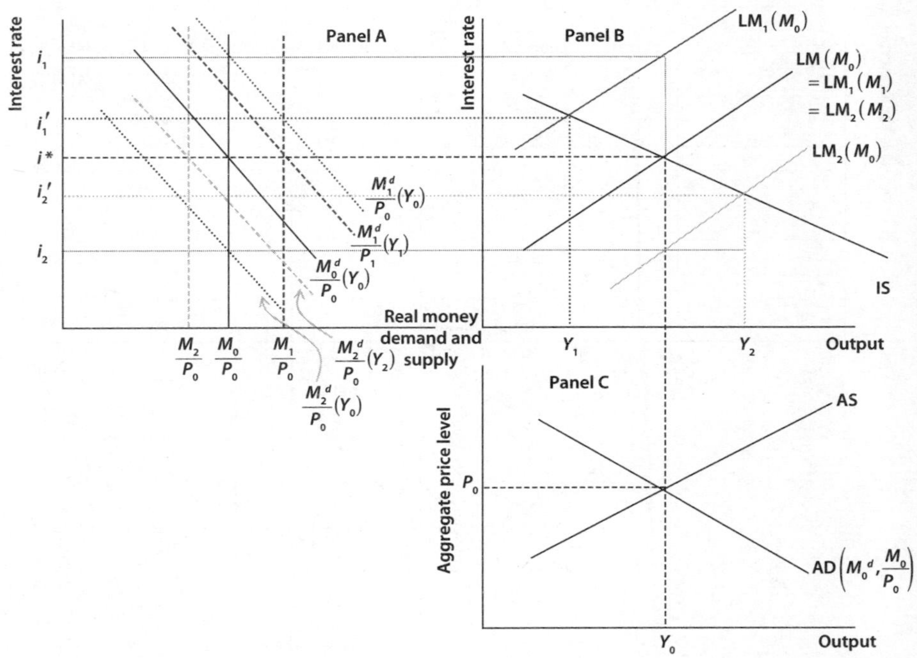

› **Figure 13.5**
Interest Rate Targeting under Shock to Money Demand.
When money demand is given by M^d_0/P_0, the central bank that targets the interest rate of i^* must fix the money supply at M_0/P_0 in panel A. This results in the LM curve given by LM (M_0) in panel B that intersects the IS curve to give the aggregate demand curve depicted in panel C that results in output Y_0 and price level P_0. An increase in the demand for money due to a shock shifts the money demand curve to M^d_1/P_0 and raises the interest rate to i_1 in panel A. The LM curve shifts left to $LM_1(M_0)$ in panel B and income declines to Y_1, whereas the interest rate moves to i_1' at the intersection of the IS curve with $LM_1(M_0)$. The demand for money for transactions reduces to $(M^d_1/P_0)(Y_1)$ in panel A. The monetary authorities now increase money supply to M_1/P_0 in panel A to intersect the demand for money at the target rate of interest, i^*. The new LM curve is given by $LM_1(M_1)$ in panel B, which takes the same position as the original LM curve before the shock. The level of output and price are therefore unaffected in the goods market in panel C. A similar outcome occurs for a negative shock to money demand.

demand curve AD[M_0^d, (M_0/P_0)] and aggregate supply curve AS intersect at (P_0, Y_0) in panel C. An increase in the demand for real money balances due to financial innovation to $(M_1^d/P_0)(Y_0)$ causes the equilibrium nominal interest rate in the money market to rise to i_1 in panel A. The LM schedule will accordingly shift upward by the vertical distance $i_1 - i^*$ in panel B. The rise in interest rate leads to a decline in real investment in the goods market (movement upwards along the IS curve) and the real income will fall to Y_1.

As the real income declines, it is accompanied by a reduction in the demand for money for transactions purposes and the interest rate settles at i_1' where the IS and $LM_1(M_0)$ curves intersect.[8] The interest rate is now above the targeted interest rate, $i_1' > i^*$, and the central bank will respond by raising the quantity of money to M_1. This increase in the supply of money in panel A will shift the $LM_1(M_0)$ curve in panel B to $LM_1(M_1)$ and the original IS–LM equilibrium will be re-attained. This monetary disturbance is offset by an adjustment in the money supply, the LM curve does not change its position, and real output and the price level remain unchanged at P_0, Y_0.

If, instead, the money demand falls from $(M_0^d/P_0)(Y_0)$ to $(M_2^d/P_0)(Y_0)$, there is a reduction in the interest rate to i_2' (up from the initial decline to i_2 because of the subsequent increase in the money demand for transaction as the investment expenditure and real income increase). As the interest rate has declined as compared to the target rate, the monetary authority will respond by reducing the money supply to M_2, shifting the LM curve back to the left in panel B to $LM_2(M_2)$ until the original equilibrium is re-attained. As a result, the real output and the price level remain unchanged at P_0, Y_0.

What if the central bank targets the nominal money supply at M^*? In Figure 13.6, the initial equilibrium where the demand and supply of real money balances is equal occurs at interest rate i_0, which results in the price and output level P_0 and Y_0, respectively. Suppose that now there is an increase in the demand for money that is not caused by a change in the real income. The increase in money demand to $(M_1^d/P_0)(Y_0)$ results in a rise in the interest rate to i_1 in Figure 13.6(A) and shifts the $LM(M^*)$ curve leftwards to $LM_1(M^*/P_0)$. The aggregate demand curve also shifts leftward to $AD(M_1^d)$ in Figure 13.6(C) and at price P_0 there is now an excess supply of goods, which pushes the price level down.

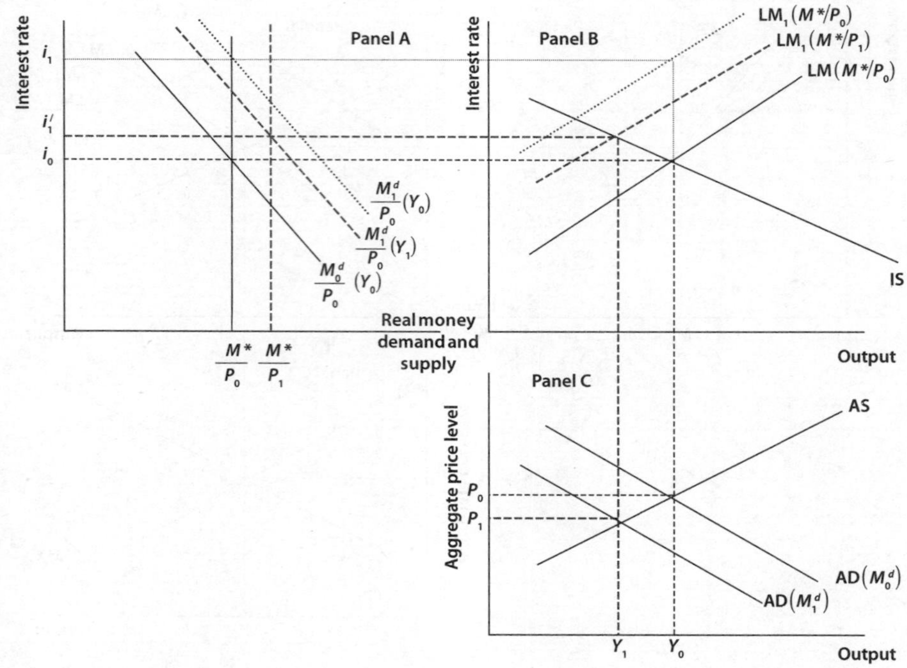

› **Figure 13.6**
Positive Shock to Money Demand When Money Stock is Targeted. With the central bank targeting the nominal money supply at M^* the intersection of money demand and supply results in the interest rate i_0 in panel A. The LM curve is given by LM (M^*/P_0) in panel B and the aggregate demand curve representing IS and LM equilibrium is AD (M_0^d) in panel C. Aggregate demand and supply intersect to give output Y_0 and price level P_0. A positive shock to money demand shifts the demand for money curve to the right in panel A and raises the interest rate to i_1. The LM curve shifts to the left in panel B to LM_1 (M^*/P_0) and results in the aggregate demand curve shifting to the left in panel C to AD (M_1^d). The price level declines to P_1 and the income also declines to Y_1. This is associated with a shift to the left of the money demand curve in panel A to the dashed downward sloping curve, and a rightward shift of the LM curve in panel B to LM_1 (M^*/P_1). Both price and output have declined.

The rise in the interest rate reduces investment expenditure and real income, which shifts $(M_1^d/P_0)(Y_0)$ to the left in panel A. At the same time, the reduction in the price shifts the money supply curve M^*/P_0 to the right. The intersection of the new money demand $(M_1^d/P_0)(Y_0)$ and money supply curve M^*/P_1 results in interest rate i_1' and this is accompanied by a price–output combination P_1, Y_1 in panel C.

Suppose, there is a decrease in the demand for money that is unrelated to the level of income. In this case, the decline in real money demand to $(M_2^d/P_0)(Y_0)$ results in a decline in the interest rate to i_2 in Figure 13.7(A) and shifts the LM(M^*) curve rightwards to $LM_2(M^*/P_0)$. The aggregate demand curve shifts rightwards to AD(M_2^d) and the excess demand for goods causes the price to rise. The decline in the interest rate spurs investment expenditure and increases real income which shifts the money demand curve in panel A to the right. The rise in price reduces the real money supply and shifts the M^*/P_0 curve to the left in panel A. The final equilibrium occurs where the money demand and supply intersect at interest rate i_2', which is accompanied by a price output combination given by P_2, Y_2 in panel C.

When the central bank pursues a policy of monetary targeting the aggregate demand curve fluctuates between AD(M_1^d) in Figure 13.6 and AD(M_2^d) in Figure 13.7. The result is a fluctuation in the output between Y_1 and Y_2 and in the price level between P_1 and P_2. As a result, an economy confronted with SHOCKS IN MONEY DEMAND will face less variation in output and prices if it targets the interest rate—Figure 13.5—rather than if it targets the nominal money supply—Figures 13.6 and 13.7. Monetary targeting is fruitful only when there is a stable money demand.

› If the economy is subject to **shocks to the demand** for money, interest rate targeting results in less variation in output and prices than money stock targeting.

13.3 Choosing Intermediate Targets in the Case of Supply Shocks

So far, the shocks considered were those due to monetary disturbances or due to shifts in the demand for goods. Poole did not consider supply shocks that

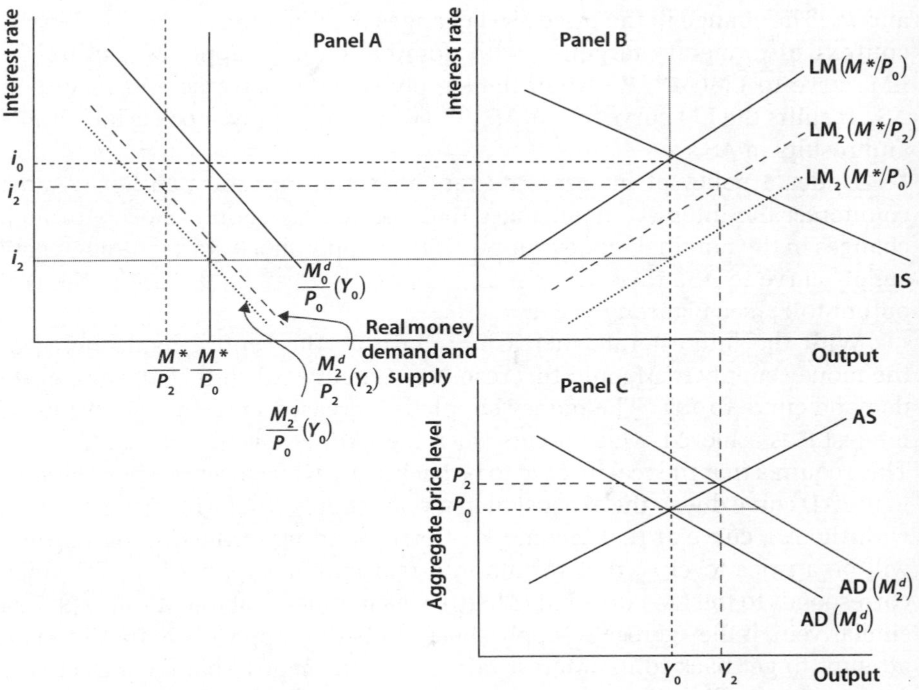

› Figure 13.7 Negative shock to money demand when Money Stock is targeted. With the central bank targeting nominal money supply at M^* the intersection of money demand and supply results in the interest rate i_0 in panel A. The LM curve is given by LM (M^*/P_0) in panel B and the aggregate demand curve representing IS and LM equilibrium is AD (M_0^d) in panel C. Aggregate demand and supply intersect to give output Y_0 and price level P_0. A negative shock to money demand shifts the demand for money curve to the left in panel A and reduces the interest rate to i_2. The LM curve shifts to the right in panel B to LM_2 (M^*/P_0) and results in the aggregate demand curve shifting to the right in panel C to AD (M_2^d). The price level increases to P_2 and income also rises to Y_2. This is associated with a shift to the right of the money demand curve in panel A to the dashed downward sloping curve and a leftward shift of the LM curve in panel B to LM_2 (M^*/P_2). Both price and output have risen.

could arise say due to a rise in nominal wages arising from trade union activity that causes an upward shift in the aggregate supply curve. Similarly, a rise in oil prices or a drought could result in the aggregate supply curve shifting up. Fluctuations in the supply curve lead to fluctuations in both the output level and the price level in the economy.

If the aggregate supply fluctuates between AS_1 and AS_2, as depicted in Figure 13.8(B), the intersection of the aggregate supply and demand curves determines the equilibrium incomes Y_1 and Y_2 and price levels P_1

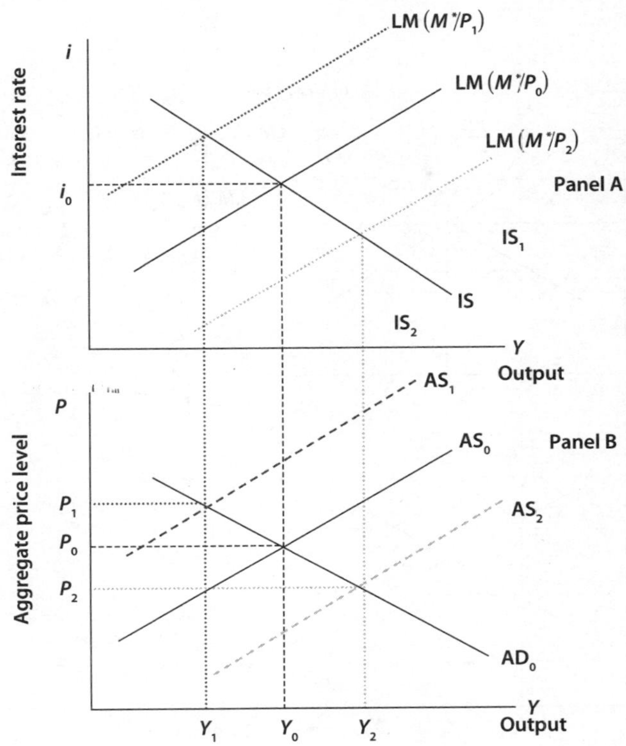

› Figure 13.8 Supply Shock under Monetary Targeting. An adverse supply shock shifts the aggregate supply curve upwards to AS_1 in panel B and raises the price and reduces output. With the central bank targeting the money supply at M^* the higher price and lower output shifts the LM curve to the left to LM (M^*/P_1) and the interest rate increases as depicted in panel A. A favourable supply shock shifts the aggregate supply curve downwards to AS_2 in panel B and reduces price whilst increasing output. With the central bank targeting the money supply the LM curve shifts to the right to LM (M^*/P_2) in panel A. Under monetary targeting supply shocks result in prices varying between P_1 and P_2 and output varying between Y_1 and Y_2.

and P_2. The change in the price level changes the real money stock and in the context of monetary targeting with nominal money supply M^*, shifts the LM curve to LM(M^*/P_1) when the supply shock is adverse and results in AS_1. It shifts the LM curve to LM(M^*/P_2) when the supply shock is favourable and results in AS_2.

Under a policy of interest rate targeting, the monetary authority must counteract the interest rate changes that accompany supply shocks through changes in the nominal money supply. If the supply shock shifts the aggregate supply curve to AS_1, there is a rise in the price to P_1 and a decline in the real output to Y_1 [see Figure 13.9(B)].

With the interest rate increasing above i^*, the central bank increases the money supply to M_1, and this results in an outward shift of the aggregate demand curve to AD_1. The money supply is increased until the target rate of interest i^* is achieved, which occurs when the LM curve is back at LM (M_0/P_0). This requires that the real income to be back at Y_0, which occurs when the shift in the AD curve due to the expansion in money supply results in an intersection with the AS_1 curve at real income Y_0. Corresponding to the output Y_0 there will be a price level P_3 that results in a real money supply of M_1/P_3 which corresponds to the LM curve LM (M_1/P_3), which is identical to LM (M_0/P_0). In a similar vein, if the aggregate supply shock shifts the supply curve to AS_2, in an attempt to get back to its interest target of i^* the central bank contracts the money supply till the real money supply M_2/P_4 results in the LM curve given by LM (M_2/P_4) = LM (M_0/P_0).

› If the economy is subject to a supply shock then money stock targeting results in less variation in prices than **interest** rate targeting. However, interest rate targeting results in less variation in the output than does money stock targeting.

Comparing Figures 13.8 and 13.9, we can see that monetary targeting results in a smaller variability of prices (P_1 to P_2) COMPARED TO INTEREST rate targeting (P_3 to P_4). On the other hand, interest rate targeting results in a smaller variability of the real output (Y_0) compared to monetary targeting (Y_1 to Y_2).

The effectiveness of monetary versus interest rate targeting can be summarized in Table 13.1.

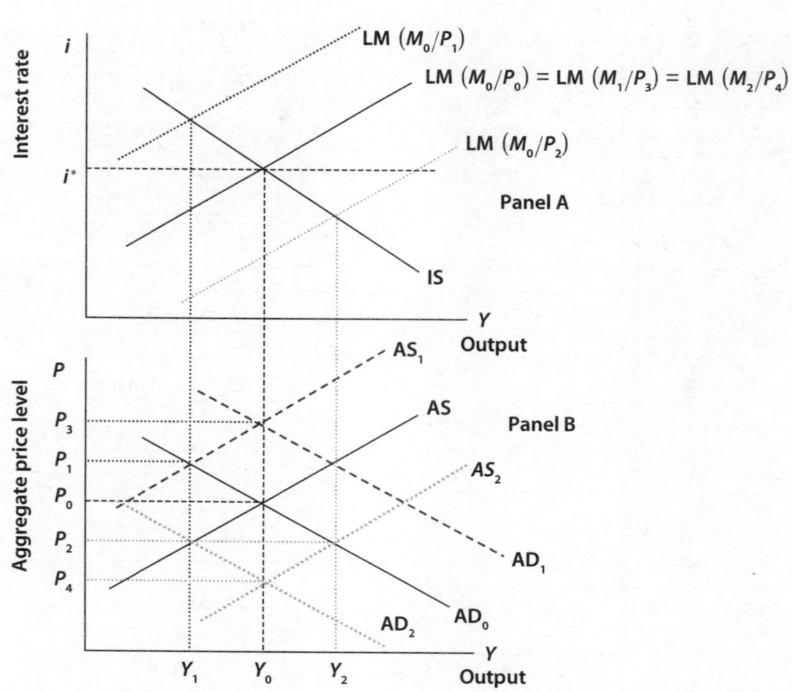

› **Figure 13.9**
Supply Shock under Interest Rate Targeting. An adverse supply shock shifts the *AS* curve up to AS_1 in panel B. The price rises to P_1 and the output declines to Y_1 resulting in the LM curve shifting leftwards to LM (M_0/P_1) in panel A. With the central bank targeting the interest rate at i^* it increases the supply of money to M_1 which causes the LM curve to shift to the right in panel A till it intersects the IS curve at i^*. The rightward shift of the LM curve is accompanied by a rightward shift of the aggregate demand curve in panel B to AD_1 that results in the price rising further to P_3 and the output returning to the pre shock level of Y_0. Similarly, a favourable supply curve shock shifts the AS curve to AS_2 and results ultimately in a reduction of the price to P_4 and the output returning to the pre shock level of Y_0.

	Effective Intermediate Target	
Type of Shock	Interest Rate	Nominal Money Stock
Demand shock	Money demand shock	Real aggregate demand shock
Supply shock	If real output target is the ultimate objective of the central bank	If price level target is the ultimate objective of the central bank

› **Table 13.1**
Effectiveness of Intermediate Targets

13.4 Targeting the Nominal GDP

An alternative policy to money stock or interest rate targeting is to target the nominal GDP. Interest rate and monetary targeting are effective when the source of variability is on the demand side of the economy, either shocks to IS, or to money demand and LM. This is because demand shocks move prices and output in the same direction and so any policy that offsets price changes will also offset the real output simultaneously. This does not occur with supply shocks as we saw. Under a supply shock interest targeting stabilizes output but prices vary considerably. Also, for monetary targeting a supply shock stabilizes prices better but at the cost of output variability. This is because under supply shocks, prices, and output change in opposite directions. An adverse supply shock, for instance, reduces the output and results in a rise in the price level.

When the position of an economy's aggregate supply schedule varies from time to time due to labour militancy, energy price changes, or drought, the nominal GDP can be an attractive intermediate target. To understand the theoretical case for nominal GDP targeting, we need to flesh out the macroeconomic framework we have adopted up to now. So far we have drawn the aggregate supply curve as upward sloping, which is a reflection of the Keynesian argument that nominal wages are set in a staggered manner, or set by agreement for a fixed period of time and the amount of employment is determined by the employer. Alternatively, the aggregate supply curve could be upward sloping because of mistaken expectations on the part of workers. In both scenarios, nominal wages adjust slowly to unexpected changes in the economic environment. The aggregate supply curve which

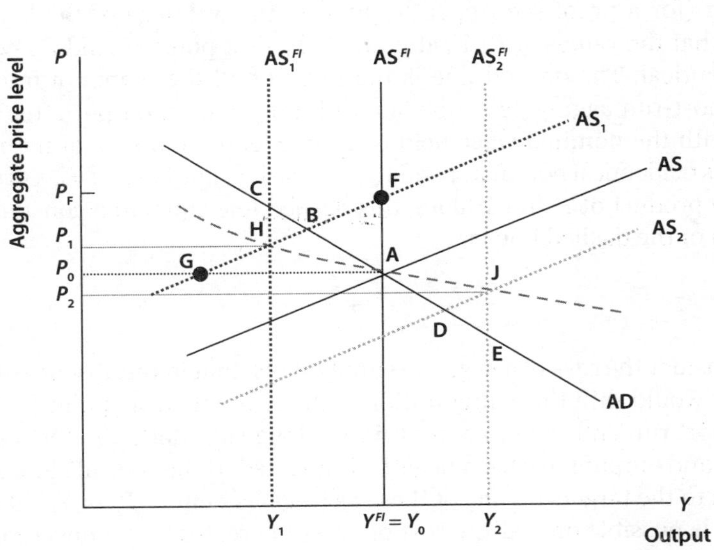

› **Figure 13.10**
Nominal GDP Targeting. Initial equilibrium is at point A where aggregate demand intersects the short run aggregate supply curve AS and the long run full information aggregate supply curve AS^{FI}. An adverse supply shock shifts the short-run AS curve to AS_1 and the long-run curve to AS_1^{FI}. In the short run equilibrium is at point B where as prices have risen workers renegotiate contracts and the short run curve shifts upwards further till it intersects the long run curve at point C. Similarly a favourable supply shock will result in short run equilibrium at point D where the aggregate demand curve intersects the AS_2 curve and long run equilibrium at point E. The initial short run curve after the shock and the corresponding long run AS^{FI} curves result in the same level of nominal spending as at point A. Joining these points of intersection such as points H, A, and J, results in the dashed downward sloping curve giving the locus of points along which nominal spending is the same. A central bank that targets output after an adverse supply shock that results in AS_1 will have to increase money supply and shift the aggregate demand curve to pass through point F where the price rises further to P_F. If it targets prices, then it will have to reduce aggregate demand so that it passes through point G and output declines further than Y_1. Nominal GDP targeting at point H avoids these extremes and the effect of the supply shock is distributed between the objectives of price and output stabilization.

takes into account expected changes in the environment when nominal wage accords are made can be labelled the full information aggregate supply curve AS^{FI}, which takes into account changes in the economic environment that are expected to occur when wage agreements are endorsed by workers and employers. For expected changes, the applicable supply curve as we know is vertical at the output level Y^{FI}, indicating no direct relationship between the price and output as the expected changes regarding the economic milieu have been factored into the decision making regarding wages and employment and thereby output. Thus expected changes in the price level will be compensated for by adjustments in nominal wages when workers and firms negotiate wage agreements.

The initial macroeconomic equilibrium, when we include expected changes in the analysis, is at point A in Figure 13.10 where AD and AS intersect the AS^{FI} curve. Supply shocks, which are unexpected changes in supply, are different from demand shocks as they shift both the short run and the full information aggregate supply curves. For example, a negative supply shock shifts both the long run and short run aggregate supply curves to the left to AS_1^{FI} and AS_1. In the short run aggregate demand and short run aggregate supply AS_1 intersect at point B. As prices have risen workers renegotiate their nominal wages upward, which shifts the short-run supply curve leftward again until it intersects the full information aggregate supply curve AS_1^{FI} at point C. The FULL INFORMATION LEVEL OF output has declined because the adverse supply shock has reduced the productive capacity of the economy and by definition the full information aggregate supply is that output which is produced when the economy has completely adjusted to any shock so that there are no unexpected changes in the economic environment affecting economic decisions that impinge on output. The reduction in the full information aggregate supply can be temporary in which case the full information output level will return to AS^{FI} after the shock disperses. In such a case, the decline in potential output is transitory.

› The **full information** aggregate supply curve is vertical and established at the level of output where expectations are realized and the economy has completely adjusted to any shocks.

The situation for a positive supply shock is symmetric with the full information level of output and the short run aggregate supply curve shifting to the right. As the shock is unexpected, the initial equilibrium is at point D and after wage adjustments have been made, the economy produces at the full information level of output at point E. The intersection of the short run aggregate supply and full information output curves occurs at the same level of nominal spending (for a proof see Appendix 13.2 on the webpage of the book). This implies that the values of $P_0\ Y_0$ at point A, $P_1\ Y_1$ at point H, and $P_2\ Y_2$ at point J are identical. The dashed line is the locus of all the points of intersection of the short-run aggregate supply and full information output after a supply shock, with the nominal wage held constant. As these points of intersections are points of identical nominal spending, this dashed line is a RECTANGULAR HYPERBOLA. With the product of P and Y along this dashed line equal to a constant, k, the equation of the dashed line is:

› If the product of two variables, *x* and *y*, is a constant, i.e., *xy* = constant, then, the graph of this equation is called a **rectangular hyperbola**.

$$P = \frac{k}{Y}$$

Now, consider the case of a negative supply shock that in the absence of a policy response would shift the configuration of the economy from point A to point B in the short run and then to point C in the long run. Both ultimate objectives for price and output have been negatively affected. If the central bank attempts to return to the targets on one of these aggregates—either P_0 or Y_0—it will find that this is possible only at the cost of an even greater target deviation on the other aggregate. An expansionary monetary policy, for instance, may restore the output to Y_0 by shifting the aggregate demand curve to the right to pass through point F but this will cause the price level to rise sharply to P_F. As the rise in prices is a surprise to workers, they will bargain for a nominal wage hike and the rise in input prices will cause the short run aggregate supply curve to shift to the left again. If monetary policy perseveres with getting the economy back to the real output level Y_0, prices will keep spiralling upwards. If the monetary authority pursues a price level target instead, then, it will pursue a restrictive monetary policy and reduce the demand curve to pass through point G to keep the price level at P_0. However, this leads to a further decline in output from that due to the initial supply shock and even more undershooting from the target output Y_0. Going further, the decline in output results in a rise in unemployment which pushes down nominal wages and shifts the short-run aggregate supply curve to the right, where it intersects with the full information aggregate supply curve at an even lower price level. The economy may be pushed towards deflation.

> › **Nominal GDP targeting** in response to variations in aggregate supply stabilizes output and minimizes the inflationary effects of such variations.

NOMINAL GDP TARGETING represents a compromise between these two extremes as it distributes the negative effects of the supply shock equally between the two ultimate objectives. With nominal GDP targeting the intersection of short run aggregate supply and full information output after a supply shock results in the product of price and output—P_1Y_1, being at the same level of nominal spending as their intersection before the occurrence of the shock, $P_0Y_0 = P_1Y_1$. Thus, nominal GDP targeting requires the economy after a shock to be on the dashed locus of points given by HAJ. This means the central bank must pursue a slightly restrictive monetary policy that is enough to move the economy from point B after the occurrence of the supply shock to point H. As a consequence, the rise in the price level is less sharp and the fall in output ensures that it is at the new full information long-run output level that is achievable by the economy after the shock has dissipated. The advantage of the nominal income rule can be visualized by noting that the negative supply shock results in the nominal wages that had been agreed before the shock had been realized having become too high. If the central bank allows a temporary increase in the price level, a partial reduction in real wages results so that the decline in output is mitigated. If the central bank holds the price level constant the correction to nominal wages would then take place in the next round of wage negotiations and that means a higher real output loss in the present. If policy is aimed at keeping the real output at the full information level, then nominal GDP targeting is superior in responding to supply shocks in comparison to price level or output targeting.

What about shocks to aggregate demand? A negative demand shock, say, due to falling autonomous investment leads to an unexpected decline in the aggregate demand and lower prices and output on the short-run aggregate supply curve to point B in Figure 13.11. Because of the decline of the price level from P_0 to P_1 the real money supply increases and shifts the LM curve to $LM_1(M_0/P_1)$. In this situation, if there is no policy response workers and firms will react to the unexpected decline in prices by adjusting nominal wages downwards until the full information level of output point C is achieved and the relevant LM curve is $LM_2(M_0/P_2)$. On the other hand, if the central bank pursues a nominal GDP target then it must expand the money supply and cause the aggregate demand curve to shift upwards until it again intersects the supply curve at the supply curve's point of intersection with the nominal GDP rectangular hyperbola given by $P = k/Y$. This requires an expansion in the money supply till the LM curve shifts to $LM_3(M_1/P_0) = LM_2(M_0/P_2)$, the aggregate demand

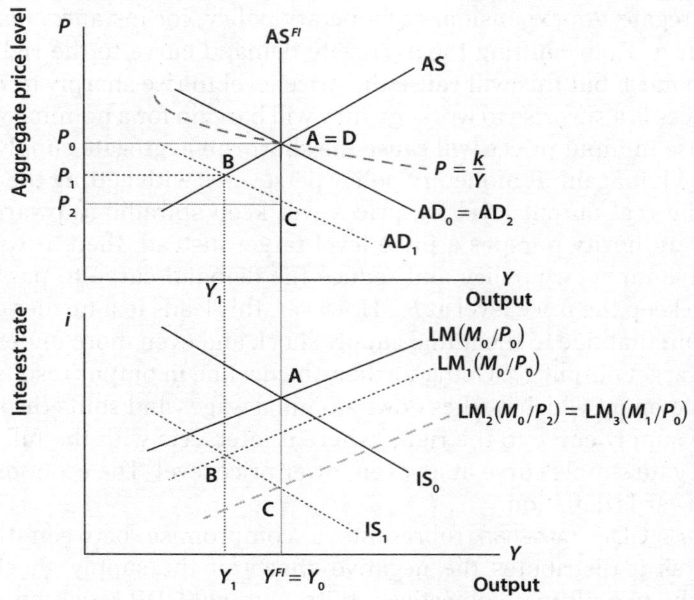

› Figure 13.11
Demand Shock and Nominal Income Targeting. The economy is initially in equilibrium at point A in the upper panel where aggregate demand intersects the short run and long run full information aggregate supply curves. An adverse demand shock shifts the AD_0 curve to the left to AD_1. The price declines to P_1 and output declines to Y_1 and this results in the LM (M_0/P_0) curve shifting to the right to LM_1 (M_0/P_1) in the lower panel. In response to lower prices at point B, workers will revise downwards their nominal wage demands and the short run aggregate supply curve will shift downwards over time to eventually intersect the AS^{FI} curve at point C in the upper panel. The lower price will cause the LM curve to eventually settle at LM_2 (M_0/P_2). Alternatively, the central bank pursuing a nominal GDP target expands the nominal money supply to M_1 and shifts the LM curve to LM_3 (M_1/P_0) in the lower panel. This shifts the aggregate demand curve in the upper panel to AD_2 where it passes through point D which is identical to point A which was the pre shock equilibrium.

› Nominal GDP targeting is superior to price level targeting when an **economy is subject** to variations in aggregate demand and/or supply.

› Nominal GDP targeting is difficult to achieve due to the absence of **good forecasts** for nominal GDP.

› Shocks to the economy say emanating from expectational errors could wrongly be attributed to a **monetary policy** that targets nominal GDP.

curve shifts out to $AD_2 = AD_0$ at point D, and there is a restoration of the original price and output level P_0 and Y_0, respectively.

If the central bank followed a price level target or an output level target monetary policy would have been required to respond in an identical manner as in the case of a nominal GDP target. Thus, a central bank that is obliged to target, say, the price level in the short run, is automatically obliged to target the real output and also the nominal income. There would be no conflict between the output and employment objectives and the goal of price level stability when an economy is subject to shocks to demand unlike the situation where supply shocks occur. Under a supply shock, however, price level targeting leads to further deviations away from the pre-shock equilibrium position, and nominal income targeting is superior in meeting the ultimate objectives. Thus for an ECONOMY SUBJECT to demand and supply shocks nominal income targeting demonstrates a clear advantage over a price-level target. It results in the same performance as in the situation of a demand shock and allows a more flexible reaction in the situation of a supply shock.

Given its advantage, it seems attractive to prescribe a stable nominal income as the short-run goal of monetary policy and continuing to have price stability as a long-term goal. Despite its theoretical advantage there are implementation difficulties, however. First, a short-run nominal income target can be met with precision if monetary policy is able to react to changes in the economy, which, in turn requires SUFFICIENTLY PRECISE FORECASTING values of nominal GDP. The technical skills of the central bank would have to be of a high order to provide the information at an early stage so that the monetary authority can act on it. Otherwise, instead of fine-tuning the nominal GDP the central bank will end up aggravating cyclical fluctuations. Second, monetary policy is liable to be held responsible for mistakes in other areas of economic policy that cause a decline in the growth of the real GDP. For the case of a negative supply shock caused by negotiated wage increases that are not in consonance with the underlying fundamentals of the economy, MONETARY POLICY would have to take on some of the blame for fluctuations in output and employment while workers and firms would be discharged of their responsibility for actions that led to such an outcome in the first place.

In practice, therefore, most central banks do not explicitly announce a short-term nominal income target but act to accommodate supply shocks in the short run. Rather than being tied to an explicit nominal income target it gives a central bank the discretion to decide on the short-run orientation of its monetary policy. However, this results in the risk that a central bank may use its discretion to cause surprises in inflation in an attempt to grow the economy. Economic agents realizing this incentive of the central bank will expect an even higher rate of inflation which is welfare reducing. We now turn to this issue of whether it is better to have rules or to give discretion to monetary authorities.

13.5 Rules versus Discretion in Monetary Policy

If any rule can be adopted by discretion it seems natural to think that discretion should be superior to rules. After all with discretion there is flexibility available to policymakers to choose and one such choice is to choose to do what a rule would oblige policymakers to do. The rule is, therefore, a subset of the policy choices under discretion. The concept of dynamic inconsistency that was introduced into macroeconomics in the rules versus discretion context by Finn Kydland and Edward Prescott[9] and further elaborated by Robert J Barro and David B Gordon,[10] however, showed that a monetary authority which operates under a discretionary regime can be trapped by its own good intentions and generate excessive inflation, which has no offsetting benefit.

DYNAMIC OR TIME inconsistency occurs when a future policy decision that forms part of an optimal plan formulated at an initial date is no longer optimal from the viewpoint of a later date, even though no new information or event has appeared in the meantime. An academic example provides some initial insight into the nature of the problem.

› A policy that is optimal from the vantage point of the announcement date may not subsequently be optimal from the vantage point of a later date and the policymaker then has an incentive to deviate from it. This is **dynamic or time** inconsistency.

As is well known in academic institutions the purpose of an examination apart from ranking students' abilities, is to induce students to learn and study. At the beginning of a term it is, therefore, optimal to announce that there will be a final exam. In anticipation of this exam, students will study and learn more. On the exam day, students arrive to the exam having put in effort towards absorbing the study material. The purpose of pre-announcing the exam which was to get students to study has been achieved. Everyone is now better off if the professor cancels the exam and gives each student some satisfactory grade—students are spared the anxiety of giving an exam and can use the exam time for something else and the professor is spared the hassle of evaluating exam papers. With students having studied, the time-inconsistent behaviour by the professor in cancelling the exam is optimal. However, students with rational expectations who know that a professor has discretion will realize that he has an incentive to cancel the exam at the end of the term and so may not put in adequate effort into their studies. Discretion then is a trap and it may be better if the announced exam must take place—as a rule no exam can be cancelled.

13.5.1 The Social Welfare Function of Policymakers

To demonstrate the advantage of rules, we follow the Barro and Gordon[11] approach which describes the strategic interaction between the central bank and the private sector. The model assumes that the central bank has the instruments to perfectly manage the economic process and its decisions are based on a social welfare function that corresponds to the preferences of private individuals. The social welfare function is formulated as a cost or loss function. Social loss, L, is considered to be a weighted average of the deviation of inflation (π) from the target level of inflation which is taken to be zero, and the deviation of unemployment from the target unemployment rate. Thus,

$$L = \pi^2 + b(u - ku_n)^2, \quad b > 0, 0 < k < 1 \tag{13.1}$$

Social costs are due to two factors:

1. The unemployment rate deviates from a target unemployment rate ku_n, where u_n is the natural rate of unemployment. This gives rise to social costs irrespective of whether the deviation is positive or negative. The deviation is squared in Eq. (13.1) because both positive and negative deviations are costs. Also, squaring of the deviation implies that large deviations are weighed more heavily than small ones. When the unemployment rate is too high it implies that output is too low[12] and this results in a loss in social welfare. Too low an unemployment rate is also evaluated negatively because this implies mistaken expectations about prices. As the natural rate of unemployment can be too high due to allocative distortions it is not considered as a target value for policy to achieve. k is referred to as an "efficiency criterion" by Barro and Gordon.[13] They argue that the imposition of taxes or payment of unemployment benefits makes labour supply more expensive relative to consumption goods and individuals will respond by consuming more leisure. The aggregate supply of labour is lower than it would be without the corresponding state intervention in the labour market.[14] Alternatively, as argued by Canzoneri,[15] the labour supply curve includes only union members and wage setters' behaviour and systematically excludes other workers. In such a situation, the real wages are too high because of the power of trade unions and, therefore, employment is too low compared to the level regarded as desirable by all workers who are represented in the loss function.
2. The actual inflation rate (π) deviates from the target inflation rate assumed to be zero. Positive inflation is an inflation tax on money balances and negative inflation impairs the unit of account function of money which requires adjustments to all nominal magnitudes. Wage and salary settlements have to be renegotiated, and firms have to post new prices (menu costs).[16]

Social costs will be minimal and welfare maximal when neither of the two deviations with respect to target unemployment and inflation occurs. However, deviations from the unemployment target are weighted differently from those associated with deviations from the inflation target—$b > 0$. When b is large a high priority is given to the unemployment target and low values of b indicates a high preference for price stability.

The Eq. (13.1) in graphical terms results in ellipsoids in (π, u) space—Figure 13.12. The target unemployment and inflation rate is measured by the "bull's-eye" point. Ellipses around this point (0, ku_n) represent social indifference curves with curves further away from the target (0, ku_n) representing higher social losses or costs. Social costs increase with the distance from (0, ku_n). The weighting factor b will determine the actual shape of the indifference curve. The more the weight that is given to deviations from the desired unemployment rate (ku_n)—the larger is b—the closer to the origin will the points of intersection of the indifference curves with the X-axis lie.[17]

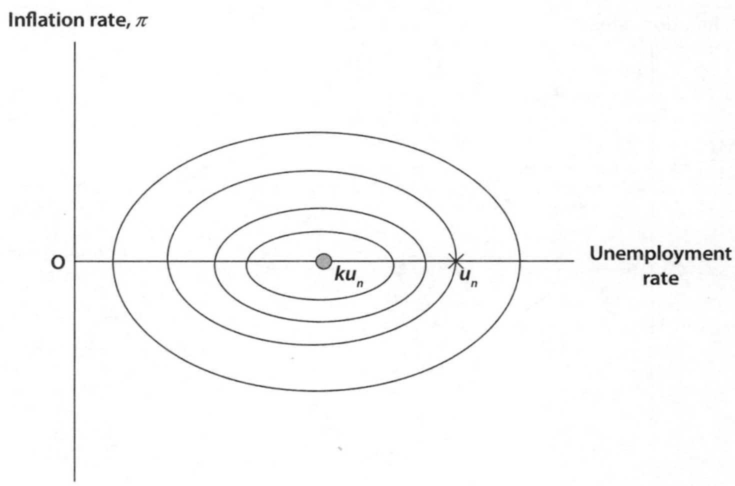

› **Figure 13.12**
Loss Function of Policymaker/ Individual Agents. Policymakers target an unemployment rate given by kU_n and an inflation rate of zero which is the bull's eye point on the horizontal axis. The ellipses around this point are social indifference curves. Along any one ellipse or social indifference curve the social loss of trading off inflation and unemployment that is not on target is constant. Social indifference curves further away from the bulls eye represent higher social losses.

13.5.2 The Private Sector and Central Bank Policy

The conditions of interaction between policymakers and private agents may now be specified. Private individuals form their expectations regarding inflation and on the basis of this nominal wage settlements are made, which they cannot renegotiate till the end of the game of strategic interaction. The monetary authority, however, has discretion at all times. In the labour market (see Section 7.6) when prices are above those that were expected then firms find the real wage to be low and employ more persons. Higher employment for a given labour force is equivalent to lower unemployment. Hence, prices above the price expectations of the workers are associated with reductions of unemployment from the natural rate of unemployment. This is the logic of the Phillips Curve where due to expectational errors of wage setters there are deviations of unemployment from the natural rate which we may write as[18]:

$$\pi - \pi^e = a\,(u_n - u) \tag{13.2}$$

Once individual agents form their inflation expectations and commit to a nominal wage, on the basis of this, the policymaker deploys the policy instrument, which is the growth rate of the money supply. Under a simplifying assumption that there are no lags in the effect of money supply growth on inflation, the policymakers have direct and continuous control over the inflation rate.[19] This correspondence between the inflation rate and the growth rate in money supply ($\Delta M/M$) implies:

$$\frac{\Delta M}{M} = \pi$$

The ultimate target (π) being identical to the intermediate target ($\Delta M/M$) implies no distinction between a rule geared to the ultimate target and a rule geared to an intermediate target. Thus, we can treat the inflation rate itself as an instrument.

The Phillips Curve $\pi - \pi^e = a\,(u_n - u)$ is depicted in Figure 13.13. When $\pi = \pi^e$, we have $u = u_n$ in Eq. (13.2). That is, the natural rate of unemployment is that rate where inflation expectations are realized and there is no unexpected inflation. The condition $u = u_n$ when $\pi = \pi^e$ is also the description of the long-run Phillips Curve (LRPC) which is depicted in Figure 13.13 as the vertical curve passing through $u = u_n$. The expected rate of inflation, π^e, associated with any short-run Phillips curve (SRPC) is then the Y-coordinate of the point

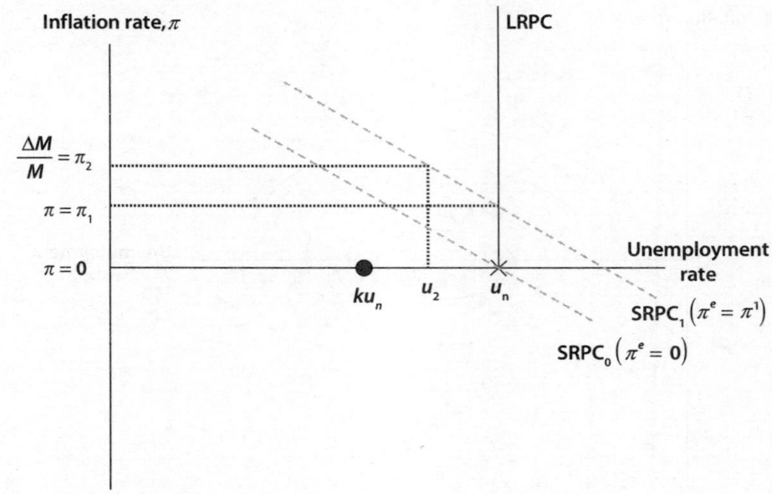

› **Figure 13.13**
Phillips Curves. The SRPC for a given expected inflation is an inverse relationship between inflation and the unemployment rate. Higher expected inflation, $\pi^e = \pi_1 > \pi^e = \pi_0$ shifts the SRPC to the right. In the long run the Phillips curve is vertical at LRPC and passes through the natural rate of unemployment U_n. Policymakers control the inflation rate which is equal to the growth in money supply. If the monetary authority selects a growth of money supply equal to an inflation rate of π_2 when the agents are on the short-run Phillips Curve $SRPC_1$, then the unemployment rate is given by U_2.

at which the SRPC described by Eq. (13.2) crosses the vertical LRPC. Thus, when private agents expect the inflation rate to be $\pi^e = \pi_1$, the relevant short-run Phillips Curve is $SRPC_1$ ($\pi^e = \pi_1$). When the expected inflation rate is zero, $\pi^e = 0$, the relevant short-run Phillips Curve is $SRPC_0$ ($\pi^e = 0$).

Given the public's expectations of a particular rate of inflation the monetary authority and the public realize, due to perfect information, which SRPC the economy is operating on. The monetary authority can then choose an inflation rate π (equal to money supply growth rate) and as a result the associated unemployment rate. For instance, if expected inflation is $\pi^e = \pi_1$ and the private sector is operating along $SRPC_1$ ($\pi^e = \pi_1$) the monetary authority can select an inflation rate of π_2 and by doing so will obtain an outcome for unemployment given by u_2 (see Figure 13.13).

13.5.3 Discretion and Surprise (Unanticipated) Inflation

Now consider what happens in a discretionary regime. Suppose the central bank announces a policy target of zero inflation and private individuals go by this announcement and expect inflation to be zero, $\pi^e = 0$. They then set wages on the basis of an expected inflation of $\pi^e = 0$ and the economy is on the short-run Phillips Curve $SRPC_0$ ($\pi^e = 0$). The central bank, however, has complete discretion at all times, it has a free hand to maximize social welfare (minimize L) at each point in time, while treating past events as given. Given that the private

› **Figure 13.14**
Surprise Inflation. The central bank announces a policy of targeting zero inflation and agents set wages so that they are on the short-run Phillips Curve $SRPC_0$. The central bank which has discretion over policy making then finds that it can target an inflation rate $\pi_s > 0$ which puts it on a lower indifference curve representing lower social loss that is tangential to $SRPC_0$ where inflation expectations are unchanged. The higher inflation rate reduces real wages and unemployment declines to U_s. The central banks original announcement of zero inflation as a target is time inconsistent.

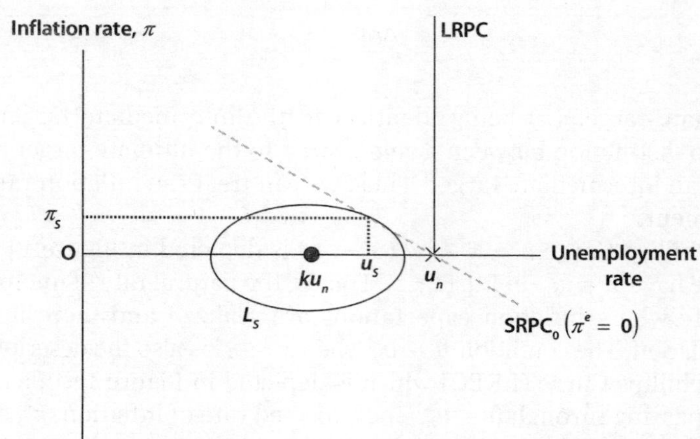

sector is locked in to operate along $SRPC_0$ ($\pi^e = 0$), the central bank will find that though it had originally announced to target $\pi = 0$, it can achieve a lower value of the loss function as given by the indifference curve L_s that is tangential to $SRPC_0$ ($\pi^e = 0$) (see Figure 13.14).

The central bank exploits the lock-in as the private sector can only renegotiate wage contracts with a lag and so it surprises the private sector by increasing the money supply and inflation to $\Delta M/M = \pi_s > 0$ in order to generate an economic boom—the demand for labour increases with inflation as real wages declines—and reduce the unemployment rate to u_s. The central bank's original announcement of an inflation rate of zero is, therefore, time inconsistent and it has an incentive to surprise the economy by changing the inflation target to a higher level π_s subsequently.

However, the private sector has perfect information and knows the central bank's loss function as well as the unemployment-inflation trade-offs as given by the Phillips Curve. They will then set their inflation expectations as *rational expectations* and equal to the central bank's optimal inflation rate of $\pi^e = \pi_s$ in the next time period despite an announcement of $\pi = 0$ now. This means that they will not take the central bank's announcement that it is targeting to achieve an inflation rate of zero as CREDIBLE. Having set $\pi^e = \pi_s$ the new short-run Phillips Curve $SRPC_s(\pi^e = \pi_s)$ will be what the private sector will aim to operate on—Figure 13.15.

› A policy announcement is **credible** if the agents in the economy believe that the central bank will keep to its pre-announced policy promise of targeting low inflation even if doing so may result in foregoing short-run economic benefits or imposing short-run costs.

However, when it chooses to operate on $SRPC_s$ ($\pi^e = \pi_s$) the private sector will rationally expect the central bank to select the indifference curve L_s' as with surprise inflation π_s' the central bank can inflate the economy and achieve a lower unemployment rate u_s' than with the natural rate. The private sector with rational expectations will, of course, foresee the incentive of the central bank to surprise the economy and so in order not to be caught in such a situation will set inflation expectations as rational expectations. They then set π^e equal to the central bank's optimal inflation rate from which it has no incentive to deviate and surprise the economy. This occurs at $\pi^e = \pi_{rat}$ at which inflation rate the central bank has no incentive to deviate from the expected rate of inflation (and by consequence also from the natural rate of unemployment). Under discretion, then, the private sector will thwart the attempt by the central bank to renege on its initial announced target of zero inflation with a subsequent upward revision to get to point B by operating along $SRPC_{rat} = \pi^e = \pi_{rat}$ Point B is the only point that is both consistent with[20]:

1. The correct expectations by the private agents (along the LRPC where $\pi = \pi^e$) and

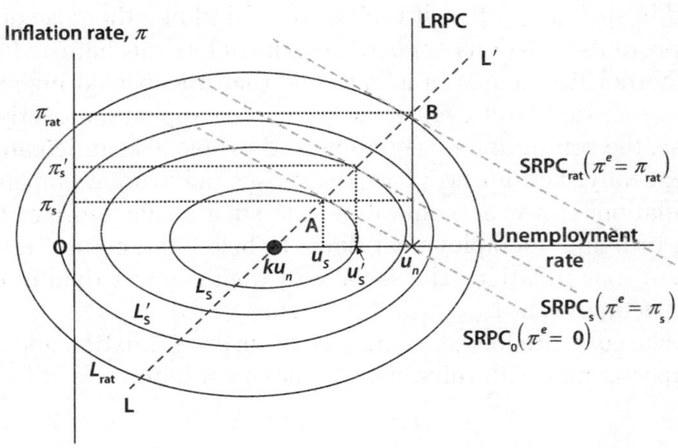

› **Figure 13.15 Rational Expectations Outcome.** When the central bank announces an inflation target of zero private agents will expect it to renege on this announcement and will expect instead an inflation rate of π_s given by the tangency between the short-run Phillips curve $SRPC_0$ and the central bank's indifference curve representing a social loss of L_S. With inflation expectations $\pi^e = \pi_s$ the new SRPC will be $SRPC_S$. At this expectation of inflation private agents can expect the central bank to again surprise them and select an inflation rate of π_s' given by the tangency between $SRPC_S$ and the central bank indifference curve representing a social loss of L_S'. Only at point B will the central bank have no incentive to deviate from the inflation rate given by π_{rat} as the social indifference curve is tangential to the SRPCs at a point through which the LRPC also passes. At such a point, inflation expectations are correct and the central bank cannot surprise agents by choosing a different policy target. Point B represents the rational expectations equilibrium.

2. The social cost minimizing welfare level that the central bank can achieve given that the private sector is operating for a given expectation of inflation along a SRPC (that is along the dashed line *LL′*).

At any point in time the policymaker is motivated to generate unexpected inflation in order to stimulate the economy. But the private agents understand these incentives in advance and, therefore, form high expectations of inflation. The policymaker then must choose a high rate of inflation just to stay even—that is, in order for the unexpected inflation to be zero. Overall then two conditions must be satisfied in equilibrium. First, the private agents' expectations of inflation are correct on average—a rational expectations condition. This occurs along the vertical LRPC. Second, although monetary authorities retain the power to fool private agents via inflation surprises, they are not motivated to exercise this power. This occurs along the dashed *LL′* line.

Monetary authorities will not indulge in surprise inflation when inflation is high enough so that the marginal cost of inflation (a higher inflation rate than expected) equals the marginal benefit from inflation surprises (a lower unemployment rate than the natural rate of unemployment). Only at point B is the marginal cost equal to the marginal benefit of surprise inflation with no incentive for the monetary authority to deviate from this outcome. At this point the inflation rate is high ($\pi = \pi_{rat}$) but there is no surprise to this high inflation rate. The economy bears the cost of this high inflation and does not receive rewards, in the form of lower unemployment, which would arise from unexpected inflation. The inflation rate at π_{rat} is higher than with surprise inflation π_s. Also with a correct anticipation by private agents of the inflation rate it is not possible to reduce the unemployment rate below the natural rate. Both the rational inflation rate and the natural unemployment rate will be higher at B than the case of surprise inflation, which is at point A. The social costs at B given by L_{rat} are accordingly higher than the social costs at point A given by L_s.

13.5.4 Commitment to a Policy Rule

Barro and Gordon demonstrate that with rational expectations the social costs can be reduced by subjecting the monetary authority to a strict rule that the inflation rate (and also the growth rate in the nominal money supply) must equal the target value of zero:

$$\pi_{rule} = 0$$

Thus, the policymaker must commit *ex ante* to low inflation. The rule must be formulated in such a way that it is absolutely binding—there is some mechanism that prevents violations *ex post*. There must be a mechanism for tying the monetary authorities' hands in advance so that unexpected higher inflation cannot be generated later even if such a choice appears attractive *ex post*. In that case, the commitment is credible and people also anticipate low inflation. Consequently, there are no inflation surprises and so no accompanying social costs to inflation. However, commitment to such a rule deprives the central bank from bringing unemployment down to below the natural rate as is the case with surprise inflation. The social cost then is lower than in the case of rational expectations, or $L_{rule} < L_{rat}$ (see Figure 13.16).

The social costs are lowest in the case of surprise inflation and highest for rational expectations, with rules being a midway solution:

$$L_s < L_{rule} < L_{rat}$$

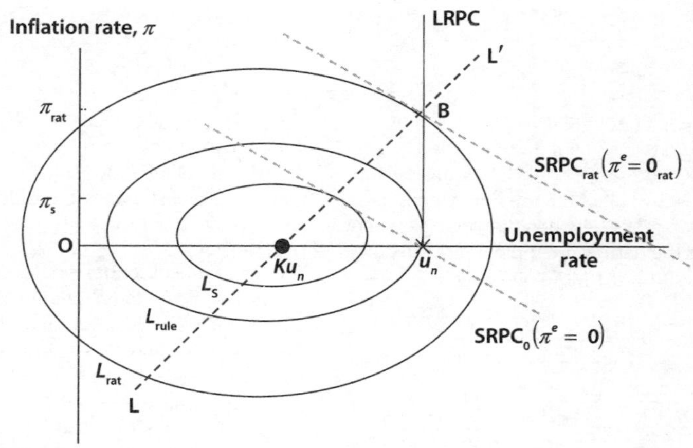

› **Figure 13.16**
Commitment to a Rule. If the policymaker can commit to a policy rule of zero inflation and it is credible to agents in the economy that there will be no incentive to deviate from this announcement then inflation expectations will be set equal to zero and the SRPC on which the economy will operate will be $SRPC_0$. The social loss from such a commitment to a rule is lower than the loss from rational expectations due to discretion with the policymaker, or $L_{rule} < L_{rat}$.

The Barro–Gordon model points to the conclusion that an exogenous monetary rule is a preferred policy arrangement even when in principle optimal conditions exist for a discretionary policy. As Barro and Gordon note inflation has historically been higher since central banks abandoned the rules of the gold standard, despite the reality that fiat money central banks have the means to produce the same, or lower inflation.

In his description of central banking Blinder[21] who was a former vice chairman of the Federal Reserve Board argues that the descriptions of policy-making in the Barro–Gordon model bears little resemblance to the process of formulating monetary policy in the US and many other countries. He argues that the whole inflation bias depends on $0 < k < 1$ or an unemployment target of monetary policy $ku_n < u_n$. According to Blinder, who has been a practicing central banker as well as an academic, monetary policy is not viewed in terms of the temptation to move up the SRPC in order to lower the rate of unemployment below the natural rate. In fact, central banks are extremely concerned about the potential inflationary consequences of pushing unemployment too low. A more accurate description is that the central bank targets the natural rate of unemployment and so the problem of time inconsistency flowing from a target below the natural rate does not arise.

However, this is true for central banks that are insulated from the political process where there is no pressure for monetary policy to follow an activist employment policy. If myopic politicians who are bothered about voter behaviour during elections have a say in monetary policy, $k < 1$ is an effective description of economic reality. In fact many central banks in emerging markets are under a very tight control by the government. In such a situation the Barro–Gordon and Kydland–Prescott setups provide an important insight into why central bank independence is required in order to pursue time-consistent policies that keep inflation in check. A central bank is independent when it is better able to take a long-term view of the economy and need not pursue policies that may be temporarily beneficial, such as reducing unemployment below the natural rate. A central bank is considered to be independent if:

1. Its actions are not subject to frequent interference by the legislature or the executive branch of government,
2. If it does not have the obligation to finance the government's deficit, and
3. Central bankers are appointed for long terms and cannot be replaced at the whims of the executive or legislature.

MACROFOCUS 13.2

Monetary Policy Rules

A good monetary policy is one that is successful in stabilizing inflation around a low average level. It also stabilizes output around potential output. This is referred to as flexible inflation targeting in the monetary policy literature. How can these goals be achieved? Many economists argue that they are best achieved when central banks follow a simple policy rule. Friedman had advocated following a rule prescribing a fixed growth rate for the money supply, but the growing instability of money demand in the 1980s caused interest in this rule to wane. Since then there has been a search for alternatives. Some academics have advocated a policy that targets the growth of nominal GDP.* Yet others** have advocated a "Taylor rule" in which interest rates are adjusted in response to movements in output and inflation.

John Taylor of Stanford University, who served as the Treasury Undersecretary for International Affairs under President George W. Bush, focused on the Federal funds rate—which is the interest rate banks charge each other when they loan funds they have on deposit at the Fed. Taylor's rule states that the monetary authority (the Fed) should raise the real interest rate, $i - \pi$, (i is the nominal interest rate and π is the rate of inflation), by 1/2 of the excess of the annual rate of inflation over 2%—($\pi - 0.02$). However, the monetary authority should also lower the real rate by half of the GDP gap [the difference between potential and actual output expressed as a percentage of potential output (Y^*)], that is, by [(1/2) (Y − Y*/Y*)] Alternatively, the monetary authority should lower the real rate of interest by half of the unemployment gap or the difference between the unemployment rate and the natural unemployment rate, that is, by $(1/2)(u - u_n)$. More precisely,

$$i - \pi = .02 + \frac{1}{2}(\pi - 0.02) - \frac{1}{2}(u - u_n)$$

$$\text{or } i = .02 + \pi + \frac{1}{2}(\pi - 0.02) - \frac{1}{2}(u - u_n)$$

If inflation is $\pi = .02$ or 2 per cent, and unemployment is at the natural rate ($u = u_n$), then, the real interest rate should be $i - \pi = .02$, or 2 per cent and the nominal rate $i = .02 + \pi = 0.04$, or 4 per cent. If inflation rises to 3 per cent, that is, by a percentage point, the Taylor rule requires the monetary authority to put the brakes on the economy and to increase the real interest rate by $(1/2) \times 0.01 = 0.005$, or by 0.5 percentage points, and the nominal interest rate by $i = 0.2 + (1/2) + \pi\ (\pi - 0.02)$ or 5.5 per cent.

Hence, it is not enough for monetary policy to raise the nominal interest rate when inflation threatens—it must raise the nominal rate by more than the rate of inflation so that the real cost of borrowing increases. This is because, when inflation increases and the central bank wants to decrease spending and output, it must increase the real interest rate, which is the rate that matters for spending.

The Taylor rule also prescribes that if unemployment has increased by 2 per cent but the rate of inflation remains unchanged, then, the nominal interest rate should be lowered by 1 per cent.

The Taylor rule describes what central banks have been doing for long as "leaning against the wind" or attempting to slow the economy when it is expanding too rapidly, and stimulating it when it is chugging along at a slow pace.

In contrast to the expanding literature on rules, no central bank has explicitly adopted a rule and announced it as a guideline. Monetary reform in many countries has focused, instead, on formulating explicit and precise objectives for monetary policy and creating an institutional setting where the central bank is strongly committed to achieving those objectives. There has been a commitment to objectives rather than to rules.[†] Also, central banks in the pursuit of output and inflation stability collect and process large amounts of information, such as on credit aggregates and asset prices, and exercise considerable judgement in analyzing this large number of variables before making decisions on monetary policy. Yet, the Taylor rule has been found to be a good description of monetary policy behaviour not only in the US, but in many other countries as well. It, thus, has usefulness as a benchmark to assess policy decisions.

*Hall, R. E. and N.G. Mankiw (1994), "Nominal Income Targeting", in N. Gregory Mankiw (ed.), "Monetary Policy", University of Chicago Press, Chicago; McCallum. B.T. (1993), "Specification and Analysis of a Monetary Policy Rule for Japan", Bank of Japan, Monetary and Economic Studies, 11, pp. 1–45.
**Krugman, P. (1996), "Stable Prices and Fast Growth: Just Say No", The Economist, August 31, pp. 15–18;
[†]Svensson, L. E. O. (2003), "What is Wrong with Taylor Rules? Using Judgment in Monetary Policy through Targeting Rules", *Journal of Economic Literature*, June, 426–477.

13.5.5 Achieving Credibility

Another important aspect of the Barro–Gordon framework is its identification of credibility as an important determinant of the real economic effects of monetary policy. Monetary policy announcements are regarded as credible by private agents to the extent that they base their inflation expectations on them. If a central bank lacks credibility as we saw the economy will move to point B in Figure 13.15 where there is high inflation and monetary policy is incapable of influencing the unemployment rate. This would be a case of stagflation, a phenomenon that affected many economies in the first half of the 1980s. A central bank can regain lost credibility by its own endeavour by pursuing a policy of disinflation over a long period of time. Thus, despite positive inflation expectations, $\pi^e > 0$, the central bank must engage in a policy of price stability, $\pi = 0$. With $\pi < \pi^e$ from Eq. (13.2), $u_n < u$ or there is a decline in output and employment demanded as real wages have risen substantially.

This requires the central bank to provisionally consent to a rise in unemployment to u_{dis} (see Figure 13.17) in order to convince private agents[22] that

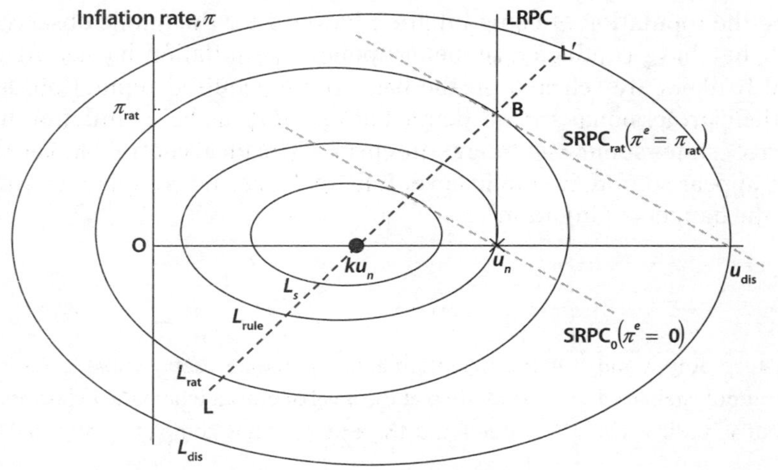

› Figure 13.17 Achievement of Credibility. To signal that it is serious about bringing down inflation in the economy the policymaker can select to operate at an exceedingly low rate of inflation that is associated with very high unemployment such as U_{dis}. Agents immediately see that by deliberately choosing a level of social loss that is higher than rational, $L_{dis} > L_{rat}$ the policymaker is attempting to regain credibility that it is willing to accept a high social cost to signal that it intends to not indulge in surprises. This will result in agents to revise downwards their expectations of inflation.

its announcement of a policy of price stability is to be taken seriously by them. By doing so the central bank adopts the indifference curve L_{dis} and when private agents acknowledge that this high cost of $L_{dis} < L_{rat}$ is being done with a view to invest in credibility, the monetary authority regains its credibility.

Of course, the reinstatement of credibility is a long drawn out process requiring the pursuit of a disinflationary policy, $\pi < \pi^e$, for many periods of time. There are other methods a CENTRAL BANK can adopt to convince private agents of its sincerity in controlling and targeting low inflation. One radical and extreme approach has been currency reform, where a currency that has lost its value through inflation is entirely withdrawn from circulation with the anticipation that a new currency will be subject to significantly lower inflation expectations. The German currency reforms of 1923 and 1948 showed that this is possible but similar reforms in Latin America and the Ukraine did not eliminate inflation expectations.[23]

› Credibility can be achieved by (1) withdrawing an existing currency and issuing new notes in circulation, (2) monetary union with countries whose central banks have credibility, and (3) making monetary policy transparent by allowing **central bank** independence and appointing central bankers who are hawkish about low inflation.

Another quicker way to achieve credibility is monetary union with a country or group of countries whose central bank has the benefit of a high degree of credibility. The former German Democratic Republic managed for instance to replace the unpopular East German mark with the globally revered Deutschmark almost in a matter of days. However, often there will be resistance by countries with a stable currency to form a common currency area with countries that have shown themselves to be incapable of controlling their domestic economy.

However, a less drastic way to achieve credibility is to make monetary policy more transparent for private agents so as to enable them to identify a policy of surprise inflation more rapidly and reduce the possible advantage a central bank can derive from such a policy. This is brought about by giving a central bank independence to set its own targets and appointing a central banker who is conservative—who places a great weight on the losses from deviations of inflation from the optimal rate.[24] Such central bankers have a reputation for pursuing price stability with reputation being an indicator to private agents of the expected future policy based on the perceived characteristic of the central banker and his actions observed in the past. In the final analysis credibility is achieved by performance and a central bank's performance is in some measure dependent on its reputation as being an inflation hawk or an inflation dove. An INFLATION HAWK is a central banker who is committed to a successful record of maintaining low inflation even if it comes at the cost of a reduction in employment and output. In contrast an inflation dove is a central banker who does not have a strong commitment to a realization of low inflation. Central bankers

› An **inflation hawk** is a central banker who is committed to the realization of a low rate of inflation even at the cost of a reduction in output and employment. An inflation dove is a central banker who is not committed to achieving and sustaining a low rate of inflation.

acquire the reputation of being inflation hawks after the public observes that in fact they have conducted monetary policy like inflation hawks. At times, central bankers are selected on the basis of an acquired reputation derived from their professional and academic backgrounds as being inflation hawks. As Barro[25] states somewhat tongue-in-cheek, "The ideal central banker should always appear sombre in public never tell any jokes and complain continually about the dangers of inflation".

SUMMARY

- The goals of macroeconomic policy are to keep output and inflation as stable as possible with the output stabilized around the potential or natural level of output and with a low rate of inflation.
- An intermediate target is a macroeconomic variable that the central bank can influence with some predictability, and which is related to its ultimate objectives.
- Intermediate targets are used in monetary policy as a compromise in the absence of complete agreement among policymakers about how best to achieve ultimate objectives and also because policymakers possess limited current information about their ultimate policy goals such as output and inflation.
- Macroeconomic variables selected as intermediate targets must be frequently observable, consistent with ultimate goals, and controllable.
- Central banks have a range of options from which to select intermediate targets: Monetary or credit aggregates, interest rates, and nominal GDP.
- In a deterministic environment, it is irrelevant whether it is the interest rate or the money stock that is targeted.
- If the economy is subject to real shocks that shift the IS curve, money stock targeting results in less output and price variability than interest rate targeting.
- If the economy is subject to shocks to the demand for money, interest rate targeting results in less variation in output and prices than money stock targeting.
- If the economy is subject to a supply shock, money stock targeting results in less variation in prices than interest rate targeting. However, interest rate targeting results in less variation in the output than does money stock targeting.
- The full information aggregate supply curve is vertical and established at the level of output where the expectations are realized and the economy has completely adjusted to any shocks.
- Nominal GDP targeting in response to variations in aggregate supply stabilizes output and minimizes the inflationary effects of such variations.
- Nominal GDP targeting is superior to price-level targeting when an economy is subject to variations in aggregate demand and/or supply.
- Nominal GDP targeting is difficult to achieve due to the absence of good forecasts for nominal GDP.
- Shocks to the economy, say, emanating from expectational errors could wrongly be attributed to a monetary policy that targets nominal GDP.
- A policy that is optimal from the vantage point of the announcement date may not subsequently be optimal from the vantage point of a later date, and the policymaker then has an incentive to deviate from it. This is dynamic or time inconsistency.
- A policy announcement is credible if the agents in the economy believe the central bank will keep to its pre-announced policy promise of targeting low inflation even if doing so may result in foregoing short-run economic benefits or imposing short-run costs.
- Credibility can be achieved by: (1) withdrawing an existing currency and issuing new notes in circulation; (2) monetary union with countries whose central banks have credibility; and (3) making monetary policy transparent by allowing central bank independence, and appointing central bankers who are hawkish about low inflation.

NOTES

1. Thomas R. Saving, "Monetary Policy Targets and Indicators", *Journal of Political Economy* 75, no. 4 (1967): 446–456.
2. RBI, "Report of the Committee to Review the Working of the Monetary System", Chairman: S. Chakravarty, Mumbai (1985).
3. Calculated from *Handbook of Monetary Statistics of India*, (Mumbai: RBI, 2006).
4. A central bank refinancing facility can be thought of as an overdraft facility whereby it grants to each credit institution a generous credit line (at a given interest rate) which it can draw on as and when it needs to. Access to this facility is dependent on banks complying with supervisory regulations in force.

5. William Poole, "Optimal Choice of Monetary Policy Instrument in a Simple Stochastic Macro Model", *Quarterly Journal of Economics* 84, no. 2 (May 1970): 197–216.
6. The objective of the central bank can be described as minimizing an expected loss function given by $L = E(Y - Y_0)^2 + E(P - P_0)^2$
7. In Figure 13.5, the intermediate target i^* is selected to achieve the ultimate policy objective of a GDP equal to Y_0.
8. There will also be price effects as the leftward shift of the LM curve will result in *AD* shifting left and the decline in the price increases real money supply which will shift LM_1 to the right again. We have ignored this detail and drawn LM_1 as the final curve after the intermediate price changes have occurred.
9. Finn E. Kydland and Edward C. Prescott, "Rules rather then Discretion: The Inconsistency of Optimal Plans", *Journal of Political Economy* 87 (June 1977): 473–492.
10. Robert J. Barro and David B. Gordon, "A Positive Theory of Monetary Policy in a Natural Rate Model", *Journal of Political Economy* 91 (August 1983): 589–610.
11. Ibid.
12. Alternatively, we could write $L = a\pi^2 + (Y - kY^*)^2$ where Y^* is the natural rate of output or can also be interpreted as full employment output.
13. Barro and Gordon, op. cit.
14. The assumption here is that while deciding on the supply of labour the individual does not take account of the related increase (in the case of income tax) or decrease (in the case of unemployment benefit) in the supply of public goods.
15. Matthew B. Canzoneri, "Monetary Policy Games and the Role of Private Information", *American Economic Review* 75 (December 1985): 1056–1070.
16. The term menu costs originates from the fact that in inflationary conditions restaurant menus need to be reprinted more often and as this entails fixed costs high inflation rates increase the incentive to change prices quickly.
17. The point of intersection of elliptical indifference curves for loss level L_0 with the X-axis is $kU_n + \sqrt{L_0/b}$. The indifference curve intersects the Y-axis at $\sqrt{L_0}$ which is independent of b. If $b = 1$ we get circular indifference curves.
18. See Eq. (7.22) of the Section 7.7 of Chapter 7 that is on the webpage of the book. Note that this is in another form of the output supply function $Y = Y^* + b(\pi - \pi^e)$.
19. We are also abstracting from the temporary effect of a change in money growth on real income. The economy is always on its long-run money demand curve and the inflation rate equals its steady state equilibrium value. These are useful abstractions that lay bare the essential ingredient of time inconsistent behaviour.
20. In game theory parlance point B is the Nash equilibrium. This is akin to a prisoner's dilemma game where the strategies that are optimal for the central bank and the private sector leads to an outcome detrimental to both of them.
21. Alan S. Blinder, *Central Banking in Theory and Practice*, (Cambridge, MA: MIT Press, 1998).
22. The subscript in U_{dis} stands for disinflation.
23. Michael Bruno, *Crisis, Stabilization and Economic Reform: Therapy by Consensus*, (Oxford: Clarendon Press, 1993).
24. Kenneth Rogoff, "The optimal Degree of Commitment to an Intermediate Monetary Target", *Quarterly Journal of Economics* 100, no. 4 (1985): 1169–1189.
25. Robert J. Barro, *Getting it Right-Markets and Choices in a Free Society*, (Cambridge, MA: MIT Press, 1996), p. 58.

TEST YOURSELF

1. What are intermediate targets of monetary policy and why are they employed by monetary authorities?
2. What are the alternative intermediate targets of monetary policy that have been suggested and used by central banks?
3. Why are the choices of money stock and the interest rate irrelevant as intermediate targets in a deterministic environment, and which is superior in a stochastic environment subject to demand shocks?
4. When supply shocks prevail, is it better to target the interest rate or the money supply and why?
5. What is nominal GDP targeting and in what way does it smoothen out the conflict between the ultimate price level and output targets?
6. What is time inconsistency? In what way is it an outcome of discretionary policymaking?
7. What are the properties of the social welfare function that form the basis of the central bank policy?
8. In what way may a central bank attempt to inflate an economy once the private sector forms its expectations when there is discretion in monetary policy?
9. How do rational expectations account for surprise inflations engineered by a central bank?
10. In what way is commitment to a policymaking rule beneficial when rational expectations prevail? How can a policymaker achieve credibility that a rule will be adhered to?

ONLINE APPLICATION

1. (a) Go to the home page of the European Central Bank: URL: http://www.ecb.int
   (b) Click on the icon "Monetary Policy" on top of the page.
2. Under the Background heading click on "Objective of Monetary Policy".
3. What are the objectives of monetary policy of the European Central Bank? Can the objectives be broken up into a primary objective and secondary objectives?
4. Read the sections on "Benefits of Price Stability", "Scope of Monetary Policy", and "Monetary Policy Implementation".
5. Now, go to the home page of the Federal Reserve of the US: – URL: http://www.federalreserve.gov/
6. Click on the icon "About the Fed" on top of the page.
7. Click on "The Federal Reserve Board".
8. Click on "Purposes and Functions".
9. Click on "Monetary Policy and the Economy".
10. What are the objectives of monetary policy of the US Federal Reserve? Does the Federal Reserve have two primary goals as opposed to the European Central Bank's one primary objective? Does the presence of two goals affect the ability of a central bank to influence economic activity?
11. Read the sections on "How Monetary Policy Affects the Economy", "Limitations of Monetary Policy", and "Guides to Monetary Policy".
12. Now go to the home page of the Reserve Bank of New Zealand: URL: http://www.rbnz.govt.nz/
13. Click on the icon "Monetary Policy" and read the Introduction that states the objective of monetary policy.
14. Click on the icon "About Monetary Policy" and then on "Explaining Monetary Policy".
15. Go to the section on "Monetary Policy Implementation in New Zealand" and read more about the objectives of monetary policy in New Zealand that explains what is called the "Policy Targets Agreement" in New Zealand, which binds the Governor of the Reserve Bank to keep inflation between 1 to 3 per cent per year on average. Also read the last section on "Other Roles for Monetary Policy".
16. Next click on the icon "Monetary Policy accountability and monitoring". Read the section titled "The Statutory Provisions". What does this state about the accountability of the Governor of the Reserve Bank of New Zealand? Can he be sacked for non-performance with regard to a target set down in the Policy Targets Agreement?
17. Put together the reading you have done on these three central banks. Are the goals of monetary policy different across these central banks? Why would this be the case? Are some central banks more independent of the legislatures of their countries and of political interference? How much discretion do central banks have and what are the means by which they seek to achieve their objectives?

Appendix 13.1 Derivations of the Equations in Section 13.5 on Rules versus Discretion

Derivation of the Surprise Inflation and Discretion Situation

$$L = \pi^2 + b(u - ku_n)^2 \quad b > 0 \tag{A13.1.1}$$

$$\pi - \pi^e = \alpha(u_n - u) \tag{A13.1.2}$$

or,

$$\alpha u = -(\pi - \pi^e) + \alpha u_n$$

Hence,

$$u = u_n - \frac{1}{\alpha}(\pi - \pi^e) = u_n - a(\pi - \pi^e)$$

where $a = 1/\alpha$.

Under discretion the policymakers sets π and the expected inflation is taken as given. Substituting (A13.1.2) into (A13.1.1):

$$L = \pi^2 + b[u_n - a(\pi - \pi^e) - ku_n]^2$$

$$= \pi^2 + b[(1-k)u_n - a(\pi - \pi^e)]^2$$

The central bank would calculate the optimal inflation rate by differentiating the above loss function in terms of π and setting the first-order condition equal to zero:

$$L = \pi^2 + b(1-k)^2 u_n{}^2 + ba^2(\pi - \pi^e) - 2ab(1-k)u_n(\pi - \pi^e)$$

Hence,

$$\frac{\partial L}{\partial \pi} = 2\pi + 2a^2 b(\pi - \pi^e) - 2ab(1-k)u_n$$

Setting this equal to zero,

$$2\pi + 2a^2 b\pi = 2a^2 b\pi^e + 2ab(1-k)u_n$$

or,

$$\pi^* = \frac{a^2 b}{1 + a^2 b}\pi^e + \frac{ab(1-k)}{1 + a^2 b}u_n$$

If the central bank announces an inflation rate of zero and individual agents consider this to be credible ($\pi^e = 0$), the actual inflation rate will be:

$$\pi_s = \frac{ab(1-k)}{1 + a^2 b}u_n$$

This is depicted in Figure 13.14.

The optimal inflation thereby exceeds the expected value of zero as the central bank seeks to achieve a positive employment effect by means of a positive inflation rate.

Derivation of the Rational Expectations, Rules, and Discretion Outcomes

Under perfect information, the private sector knows the Phillips curve and the central bank's loss function. They will accordingly set their inflation expectations as the rational expectations equal to the central bank's optimal inflation rate, $\pi^e = \pi^*$. Then,

$$\pi_{rat} = \frac{a^2 b}{1 + a^2 b}\pi_{rat} + \frac{ab(1-k)}{1+a^2 b}u_n;$$

or,
$$\pi_{rat}(1 + a^2 b - a^2 b) = ab(1-k)u_n,$$

or,
$$\pi_{rat} = ab(1-k)u_n$$

This is depicted in Figure 13.15.

The inflation rate is higher compared to the case where the central bank deviated from its pre-announced inflation rate of zero in order to inflate the economy, $ab(1-k)u_n > [ab(1-k)/1 + a^2 b]u_n$. The social cost of discretion is then given by:

$$L_{rat} = \pi^2 + b[(1-k)u_n - a(\pi - \pi^e)]^2$$
$$= \pi^2_{rat} + b(1-k)^2 u_n^2$$

as $\pi = \pi^e$ under discretion which corresponds to $u = u_n$. Therefore,

$$L_{rat} = a^2 b^2 (1-k)^2 u_n^2 + b(1-k)^2 u_n^2$$
$$= b(1 + a^2 b)[(1-k)u_n]^2$$

This is the indifference curve as depicted in Figure 13.15. With rational expectations the social costs can be reduced by requiring the central bank to adhere to the strict rule that the inflation rate, or the growth rate in the nominal money supply, equals the target value of zero:

$$\pi_{rule} = 0$$

Then,
$$L_{rule} = \pi^2_{rule} + b[(1-k)u_n - a(\pi_{rule} - \pi^e)]^2$$
$$= b[(1-k)u_n]^2$$

as there is commitment to the rule and $\pi^e = \pi_{rule} = 0$.

It is obvious that the social costs are lower with a rule,

$$L_{rule} < L_{rat}$$

This is depicted in Figure 13.16.

Similarly, if regardless of rational expectations the central bank is able to achieve a stable price level ($\pi = 0$) the disinflation has social cost given by:

$$L_{dis} = b(1 + a^2 b)^2 [(1-k)u_n]^2$$

This is depicted in Figure 13.17.

14

Economic Growth

CRITICAL QUESTIONS

- *What is economic growth?*
- *What are the sources of economic growth?*
- *What are the determinants of long-run (steady state) growth?*
- *What is the golden rule of capital accumulation?*
- *Is there a tendency for economic growth to converge or diverge across nations?*
- *Why do economies get caught in poverty traps?*
- *How does the endogenous growth approach explain the growth process?*

14.1 Sources of Growth

The father of economics, Adam Smith, was preoccupied with the economic growth of nations and even titled his famous treatise *An inquiry into the Nature and Causes of the Wealth of Nations*. More than two hundred years since the publishing of this treatise, we are still grappling with the question of what makes some countries rich and others poor. Recall that economists use per capita income as an indicator of welfare (Chapter 1). The per capita income today varies across countries much more than it used to. Differences in per capita incomes across countries were small until the nineteenth century. They started to widen with the Industrial Revolution, and have got enlarged during the last hundred years.[1] ECONOMIC GROWTH is measured as the rate of change of real income per capita. A country with a growth rate of 1 per cent per annum doubles its living standard every seventy years. For the decade of the 1950s, the per capita income growth in India averaged 2.27 per cent. With that growth rate it takes 30.5 years for living standards to double. In the five year period from 2005–2006 to 2009–2010 per capita income in the country grew by an average of 6.93 per cent which means that if this growth can be sustained then India will double its living standard every ten years. This illustrates that differences in growth rates that persist can result in dramatic differences in the living standard.

› **Economic growth** is the rate of change of the real income (or output) per capita.

So what causes the growth rates to be different across countries? Macroeconomists emphasize the accumulation of PHYSICAL AND HUMAN CAPITAL as having the major influence on economic growth. Examples of physical capital comprise the stock of machines and equipment, whereas examples of human capital comprise the stock of education and training embodied in the labour force.

› **Physical capital** is a long-lived good that extends our ability to produce and serves as a tool at our disposal for the production of goods and services. Human capital refers to the characteristics such as education and health that enable workers to produce more output.

Robert Solow, however, demonstrated in an influential article in 1956, that accumulation of these factors in response to economic incentives would not lead to continued growth in per capita income. Instead Solow recognized that growth was due to the invention of new technologies that made labour more productive. As the source of these innovations was unexplained in the model developed by Solow, his theory come to be known as the exogenous growth theory.

Solow demonstrated that in the US economy seven-eighths of the growth in the nation's output per worker is accounted for by changes in technology and one-eighth by increases in the tangible capital per worker. Further research did depict a reduced contribution of technological change but has been unable to challenge Solow's basic result that such change accounts for more than half the growth in output per worker.[2] Moreover, Solow[3] showed that besides the fact that the real output per worker grows at a more or less constant rate on average, there are two other STYLIZED FACTS about long-run economic growth:

1. The share of labour in income is more or less constant
2. The share of consumption in aggregate income has remained approximately constant.

› The **stylized facts** about long-run growth are: (1) output per capita grows at a more or less constant rate, (2) the share of labour and capital in income is constant, and (3) the share of consumption in aggregate income is constant.

Growth theory begins with the assumption that output is related to the aggregate capital and labour through a production function:

$$Y = AF(K, N) \tag{14.1}$$

where, Y is aggregate output, K is capital, N is labour, and A is a technology parameter.[4] In applied work, a particular functional form for the production function is usually specified. A function that is frequently used is the Cobb–Douglas function:

$$Y = AK^{a}N^{1-a} \tag{14.2}$$

› The **neoclassical Solow growth** theory assumes that the economy is characterized by perfect competition with firms as price takers and output given by a constant returns to scale production function such as $Y = AK^{a}N^{1-a}$ where A is a technology parameter.

The NEOCLASSICAL THEORY assumes that output is produced by a large number of competitive firms, each of which uses the same production function. Normalizing the price of output to unity,[5] profit-maximizing firms (firms that maximize profit, Π), select the inputs capital (K) and labour (N) that solve the following problem:

$$\underset{\{K,\,N\}}{Max}\,\Pi = Y - rK - wN$$

$$= AK^{a}L^{1-a} - rK - wN$$

where, w is the wage per unit of labour and r the rental per unit of capital.[6]

The first-order profit-maximizing conditions are the usual ones, the firm should rent capital until the marginal product of capital is equal to the rental price, and hire labour till the marginal product of labour is equal to the wage. Take the profit-maximizing condition with respect to labour hiring,[7]

$$w = MP_N$$

For the case of the Cobb–Douglas production function the marginal product of labour is given by $(1 - a)A(K/N)^{a}$ allowing us to write the profit maximizing labour hiring condition as:

$$w = (1 - a)A\left(\frac{K}{N}\right)^{a} = MP_N$$

Dividing throughout by N, Eq. (14.2) gives us $Y/N = A(K/N)^{a}$, which we use to write the above labour market condition as:

$$w = (1 - a)\frac{Y}{N} = MP_N$$

where MP_N is the marginal product of labour. In this case, the share of labour in aggregate output that is the wage bill divided by the aggregate output may be written as:

$$\text{Share of Wages} = \frac{wN}{Y} = \frac{MP_N(N)}{Y} = (1 - a)$$

The Cobb–Douglas production function, accordingly, reproduces one of Solow's stylized facts that the share of labour in aggregate income is constant.

Similarly, the profit-maximizing condition for the capital stock is where the marginal cost of a unit of capital, r, equals the marginal benefit of employing that capital given by the additional output that it produces—the marginal product of capital—which in the Cobb–Douglas case is $aA(K/N)^{a-1}$.

$$r = MP_K = aA\left(\frac{K}{N}\right)^{a-1}$$

Again, dividing throughout Eq. (14.2) by K gives us $Y/K = AK^{a-1}N^{1-a} = A(K/N)^{a-1}$. The share of capital in aggregate output is then given by:

$$\text{Share of Capital} = \frac{rK}{Y} = \frac{MP_K(K)}{Y} = a$$

Solow used these results emanating from the properties of the production function to get a hold on estimating the contribution of technological progress to output growth. The contribution of technological improvements to economic growth was hard to quantify prior to Solow's pioneering work. Output can be measured by GDP, and we can measure the hours worked in a year and the stock of capital as well. But how does one measure the increased productivity in the economy due to the introduction of Fordist assembly lines and, more recently, the computer revolution?

Solow argued that the CHANGE IN OUTPUT is the sum of three components: the increased output due to technological advance, the increased output due to the growth of labour employed, and the increased output due to the availability of additional capital equipment. From Eq. (14.2) this may be written as[8]:

› Solow used the production function to argue that the **change in output** is due to the growth of the labour force, the accumulation of capital stock, and technological progress.

$$\frac{\Delta Y}{Y} = \frac{\Delta A}{A} + a\frac{\Delta K}{K} + (1-a)\frac{\Delta N}{N} \tag{14.3}$$

where, Δx represents the extent of change in a variable x. If the value of x last year is given by x_{t-1} and the value it takes currently is given by x_t, then, the change in the value of x is given by $\Delta x = x_t - x_{t-1}$. The percentage change that has taken place or the rate of growth of the variable x then is $\Delta x/x$. Hence, we may identify the variables in Eq. (14.3) as follows-

$\Delta Y/Y$: rate of growth of output
$\Delta K/K$: rate of growth of the capital stock
$\Delta L/L$: rate of growth of the labour force
$\Delta A/A$: rate of technological progress

Solow recognized that the only unobservable in Eq. (14.3) is the rate of technological progress, $\Delta A/A$. This could be calculated by taking it to the left-hand side of the equation as:

$$\frac{\Delta A}{A} = \frac{\Delta Y}{Y} - a\frac{\Delta K}{K} - (1-a)\frac{\Delta N}{N} \tag{14.4}$$

This has come to be known as the SOLOW RESIDUAL—the estimate of technological progress derived as a residual after the contributions of labour and capital growth are subtracted from the rate of growth of output.

› The **Solow residual** is the estimate of technological progress derived as a residual after accounting for the rate of growth of output due to labour force and capital stock growth.

Solow[9] applied Eq. (13.4) to the annual data on the growth rate of output ($\Delta Y/Y$), the share of capital in output ($1-a$), the growth rate of the labour force ($\Delta L/L$), and the growth rate of the capital stock ($\Delta K/K$). He reported that the rate of technological progress was about 1.2 percent per annum from 1909 to 1929 and about 1.9 per cent per annum from 1929 to 1949. As economic growth is the rate of change of the output per capita, we can write Eq. (14.3) as:

$$\left(\frac{\Delta Y}{Y} - \frac{\Delta N}{N}\right) = \frac{\Delta A}{A} + \alpha\left(\frac{\Delta K}{K} - \frac{\Delta N}{N}\right) \tag{14.5}$$

Growth Rate of Per Capita Output | Rate of Technological Progress | Growth Rate of Capital-Labour Ratio

The left-hand side is the growth rate of per capita output,[10] and the term $[(\Delta K/K) - (\Delta N/N)]$ is the growth rate of capital intensity, or the capital-labour ratio, K/N. Solow estimated that about seven-eighths of the increase in output per worker over the 40-year period 1909 to 1949 was DUE TO TECHNOLOGICAL

› Solow demonstrated that the Solow residual or the total factor productivity growth contributes the **major share** to per capita income growth.

MACROFOCUS 14.1

Growth Accounting—China and India

The Solow Residual is also called the total factor productivity (TFP) of an economy. One interpretation that is given is that it is a measure of the increased efficiency with which inputs are used, and the measure captures the technological progress that is taking place in the economy. As it is calculated as a residual by subtracting out from the output growth the contributions of the capital stock and labour, the measure is sensitive to the accuracy with which the factor inputs are measured. Labour input, for instance, is measured by the number of hours worked in a year in the aggregate. However, a person enters the labour force after accumulating years of schooling and informal education. The more the accumulated years of schooling that are present in the working age population, the more educated is the labour force, and the greater the efficiency of labour in contributing to output.

In the light of this, the measure of labour input requires to be adjusted for improvements in educational attainment (*H* representing human capital). Bosworth and Collins* accordingly write the production function as:

$$Y = AK^{a}(NH)^{1-a}$$

This leads them to decompose the economic growth ($\Delta y/y$) into the contribution of growth in capital stock per worker ($k = K/N$), increases in education per worker ($h = H/N$), and the Solow residual.

$$\underbrace{\left(\frac{\Delta y}{y}-\frac{\Delta N}{N}\right)}_{\text{Growth Rate of Per Capita Output}}=\underbrace{\frac{\Delta A}{A}}_{\text{Total Factor Productivity}}+a\underbrace{\left(\frac{\Delta K}{K}-\frac{\Delta N}{N}\right)}_{\text{Growth Rate of Capital Stock Per Worker}}+(1-a)\underbrace{\left(\frac{\Delta H}{H}-\frac{\Delta N}{N}\right)}_{\text{Growth in Educational Achievement Per Worker}}$$

or, $$\frac{\Delta y}{y}=\frac{\Delta A}{A}+a\frac{\Delta k}{k}+(1-a)\left(\frac{\Delta h}{h}\right)$$

The estimated sources of growth for the period 1978–2004 for China and India are given in Table 14.1.

› Table 1
Sources of Economic Growth

		Contribution of:		
	Growth Rate of Output per Worker	Capital Stock per Worker	Education per Worker	Total Factor Productivity
China	7.3	3.2	0.2	3.8
India	3.3	1.3	0.4	1.6

The sources of China's economic growth, as depicted in Table 1, comes from a high contribution of the large rate of capital accumulation per worker (44 per cent of per capita output growth) and from gains in total factor productivity (52 per cent). As Bosworth and Collins point out, there are historical examples of countries achieving growth rates of GDP comparable to China's such as Germany and Japan post-World War II, and Taiwan and Korea more recently. However, none of these economies were able to sustain such rapid growth for long, whereas China's high growth has continued for more than 25 years. In contrast to China, India achieved its growth with relatively more emphasis on education per worker, contributing 12 per cent to growth in contrast to China's 3 per cent, and the total factor productivity and capital accumulation contributed much less—48 per cent and 40 per cent, respectively—to the economic growth in India as compared to that in China.

*Bosworth, B. and Collins, S. M. (2007)—"Accounting for Growth: Comparing China and India", National Bureau of Economic Research, Cambridge MA, Working Paper 12943.

IMPROVEMENT and only one-eighth to an increase in the capital-labour ratio. For the period 1960–1990 for the US it is estimated that the contribution of technological progress to the increase in output per worker was 78.6 per cent, representing a drop of about 9 per cent since the time period of Solow's estimate.[11]

14.2 The Determinants of Long-Run Growth

Some readers may be wondering why there is no discussion of unemployment when issues related to the labour market variable in the production function are being addressed. Since the investigation is with reference to the determinants of long-run growth we overlook the unemployment arising from cyclical factors and concentrate instead on the aggregate output that would result if all the resources, capital, and labour are fully utilized. In growth theory we concentrate our attention on the production function with full employment of resources so as to understand the determinants of the potential output that the economy is capable of producing. In the short run there will be deviations of output from the potential because of demand conditions and rigidities in the labour market.

To facilitate a diagrammatic approach to economic growth, we proceed by drawing a graph of the production function in per capita form since economic growth is about the growth of the per capita output. In per capita terms, Eq. (14.2) may be written as:

$$y = \frac{Y}{N} = AK^{a}N^{-a} = A\left(\frac{K}{N}\right)^{a} = Ak^{a} \tag{14.6}$$

where, $y = K/N$ is per capita output, and $k = K/N$ is the capital intensity of production. For given parameters a and A, how does y respond to the changes in k? The answer to this is obtained by finding out the response of the per capita output, or the change in per capita output (Δy), to a marginal change in the capital intensity (Δk), or,

$$\frac{\Delta y}{\Delta k} = aAk^{a-1}$$

This expression is nothing but the expression for the marginal product of capital, MP_K, as can be witnessed by writing Eq. (14.6) in extensive form and finding the expression for MP_K. In extensive form, Eq. (14.6) is Eq. (14.2):

$$Y = AK^{a}N^{1-a}$$

The marginal productivity of capital from this is:

$$MP_K = \frac{\Delta Y}{\Delta K} = aAK^{a-1}N^{1-a} = aA\left(\frac{K}{N}\right)^{a-1} = aAk^{a-1}$$

The slope of Eq. (14.6) is, therefore, nothing other than the marginal product of capital. Given that the marginal product of capital is subject to diminishing returns, this translates into the slope of the graph of Eq. (14.6) diminishing as k increases. We can, therefore, depict the graph of Eq. (14.6) in Figure 14.1.

Having dealt with the labour market, which is the supply side of the economy, it is now time to turn to the demand side of the economy, which is the familiar product-market condition that in equilibrium saving equals investment

$$S_t = I_t \tag{14.7}$$

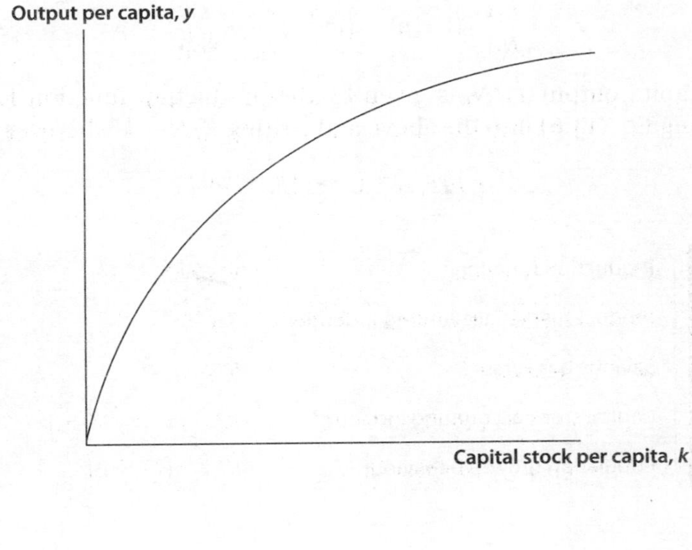

› **Figure 14.1**
Output in Intensive Form.
The output per capita increases as the capital stock per capita increases but at a diminishing rate due to the diminishing marginal productivity of the capital.

We depict savings behaviour by appealing to the other Solow-stylized fact, which is that the share of consumption and, therefore, saving in aggregate output has been more or less constant:

$$S_t = sY_t \tag{14.8}$$

where, $0 < s < 1$ is the marginal propensity to save, or the increase in saving when there is a marginal increase in income.

Finally, we incorporate an accounting identity that investment adds to the capital stock:

$$K_{t+1} = (1 - \delta) K_t + I_t \tag{14.9}$$

Equation (14.9) states that next year's capital stock is equal to the fraction of this year's capital stock that is left over after depreciation, $(1 - \delta) K_t$, plus any new gross investment in capital, I_t. Here δ represents the rate of depreciation. Finally, the population which is equivalent to the labour force by assumption[12] is assumed to grow at a constant growth rate, n,

$$L_{t+1} = (1 + n) L_t \tag{14.10}$$

Equations (14.6) to (14.10) constitute the Solow growth model, which we, for convenience, state again in Table 14.1.

Recall that growth theory attempts to explain what drives per capita output growth. Figure 14.1 depicts that changes in per capita output are due to changes in capital intensity (k) for the given parameters a, A.

The neoclassical growth equation is, therefore, an equation describing the relationship between the capital stock per capita—k—in any two successive years. We now go through the steps that enable us to derive this growth equation. First, restate the capital-stock accounting identity in per capita terms by dividing Eq. (14.9) throughout by the labour force (N),

$$\frac{K_{t+1}}{N_t} = (1 - \delta)\frac{K_t}{N_t} + \frac{I_t}{N_t}$$

or multiplying and dividing the left-hand side by N_{t+1},

$$\frac{K_{t+1}}{N_{t+1}}\frac{N_{t+1}}{N_t} = (1 - \delta)\frac{K_t}{N_t} + \frac{I_t}{N_t}$$

Substituting for the population-growth rate from Eq. (14.10) and the savings-investment identity and savings-behavioural Eqs (14.7) and (14.8),

$$\frac{K_{t+1}}{N_{t+1}}(1 + n) = (1 - \delta)\frac{K_t}{N_t} + \frac{sY_t}{N_t}$$

The per capita output Y_t/N_t is given by the production function Eq. (14.6). Substituting Eq. (14.6) into the above and writing $K/N = k$ wherever it occurs,

$$(1 + n) k_{t+1} = (1 - \delta) k_t + sAk_t^a$$

› **Table 14.1**
The Solow Model

SOLOW MODEL			
	Production function	$y = AK^a$	(14.6)
	Product market accounting indentity	$S_t = I_t$	(14.7)
	Savings behaviour	$S_t = sY_t$	(14.8)
	Capital stock accounting indentity	$K_{t+1} = (1 - \delta)K_t + I_t$	(14.9)
	Population growth behaviour	$K_{t+1} = (1 + n)N_t$	(14.10)

or,
$$k_{t+1} = \frac{1-\delta}{1+n}k_t + \frac{s}{1+n}Ak_t^a \quad (14.11)$$

Subtracting k_t from both sides of (14.11):

$$k_{t+1} - k_t = \frac{1-\delta-1-n}{1+n}k_t + \frac{s}{1+n}(Ak_t^a)$$

or,
$$k_{t+1} - k_t = \frac{s}{1+n}(Ak_t^a) - \frac{n+\delta}{1+n}k_t$$

Multiplying throughout by (1 + n),

$$(1+n)(k_{t+1} - k_t) = sAk_t^a - (n+\delta)k_t \quad (14.12)$$

This equation states that the change in capital per worker each period—the left-hand side[13]—is dependent on two terms. First, the investment per worker, sAk_t^a, increases the capital per worker, k. Second, there is a decrease in capital intensity, k, due to depreciation (δ) of the capital stock and the growth of the labour force (n). The depreciation per worker δk reduces k. In addition, in each period there are nN new workers around who were not there during the previous period. In the absence of depreciation, the capital per worker would decline because of this increase in the labour force if there were no new investments. Note that no new investments imply that the first term on the right-hand side of Eq. (14.12) is zero, and the absence of depreciation requires $\delta = 0$. Then,

$$(1+n)(k_{t+1} - k_t) = -nk_t$$

or,
$$k_{t+1} - k_t = \frac{-n}{1+n}k_t$$

or,
$$k_{t+1} = \frac{1}{1+n}k_t$$

which implies,
$$k_{t+1} < k_t$$

The capital per worker in $t + 1$, therefore, declines due to the increase in the labour force when no investment occurs to offset this decline in capital per worker.

14.3 The Solow Diagram

We now plot the graph of Eq. (14.12) in Figure 14.2. Note that the first term on the right-hand side of Eq. (14.12) is the graph of the production function $y = Ak^a$, which is depicted in Figure 14.2, but now that graph is translated down by the factor s.

The graph of the second term on the right-hand side of Eq. (14.12) is a straight line through the origin with slope, $n + \delta$, that represents the amount of the new investment per person. This new investment is required to keep the amount of capital per worker constant as both the depreciation and the growth of the workforce reduce the amount of capital per person in the economy. The difference between these two curves is the change in the amount of the capital per worker $(1 + n)(k_{t+1} - k_t)$, given by the distance PQ for an initial capital stock per capita of k_o.

Suppose an economy has a capital stock per capita given by k_o today, as in Figure 14.3. What occurs over time? At k_o, the amount of investment per

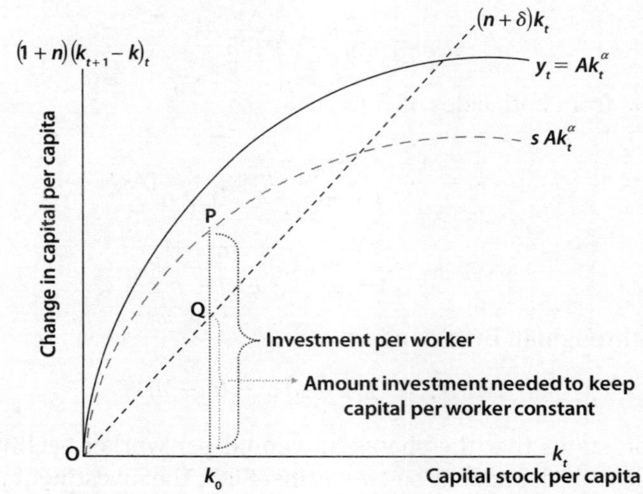

› **Figure 14.2**
Solow Diagram. The economy has a capital stock per capita given by (distance $Pk_0 = sAk_0^\alpha$) initially. Then the investment per worker[distance $Qk_0 = (n + \delta)\, k_0$] is greater than the investment required to maintain the capital stock per worker as constant due to the increase in the labour force and depreciation.

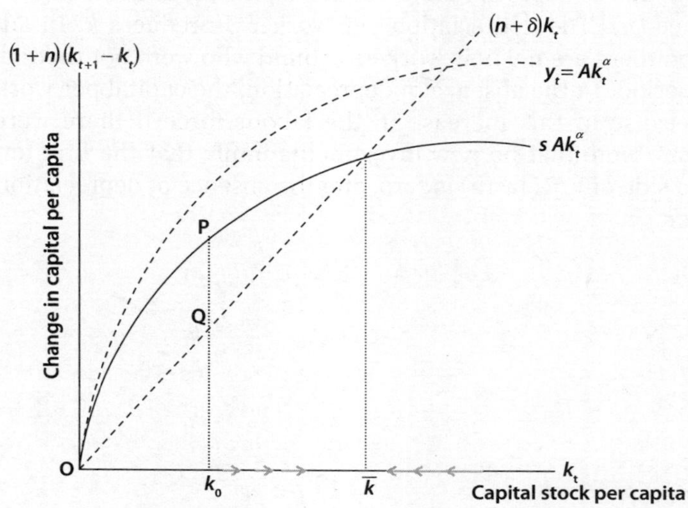

› **Figure 14.3**
Stability in the Solow Diagram. The initial capital stock per capita is k_0. As the investment per worker is greater than the investment required for the capital stock per worker to be constant, $Pk_0 > Qk_0$, the capital stock per capita increases as depicted by the arrows till $\bar{k}$. At $\bar{k}$, the investment per worker is exactly equal to that required to keep the capital stock per worker constant and the economy is in a steady state.

worker—distance Pk_0—exceeds the amount needed to keep the capital per worker constant—distance Qk_0. Accordingly, k increases over time as $(1 + n)(k_{t+1} - k_t) > 0$ or $k_{t+1} > k_t$. The capital per worker increases, as depicted by the arrows pointing rightwards from k_0 until $k = \bar{k}$, at which point, the investment per worker equals the replacement of worn-out capital per worker inclusive of the additions to the workforce. At the point $k = \bar{k}$, then, the right-hand side of Eq. (14.12) is zero so that:

$$(1 + n)(k_{t+1} - k_t) = 0$$

or,

$$k_{t+1} = k_t = \bar{k} \tag{14.13}$$

› A **steady state** is characterized by a point where the amount of capital stock per capita remains constant over time. $\bar{k} = k_{t+1} = k_t$.

A point described by Eq. (14.13) where $k_{t+1} = k_t$ is called a STEADY STATE.

Suppose that the economy began with a capital stock per worker that is greater than $k = \bar{k}$. At any point to the right of $\bar{k}$, the amount of investment per worker is less than the amount required to keep the capital-labour ratio constant, as can be verified in Figure 14.3. The right- hand side of Eq. (14.12) is negative, which implies that $(1 + n)(k_{t+1} - k_t) < 0$, or $k_{t+1} < k_t$. This means that the amount of capital per worker begins to decline in the economy. The decline will occur until the amount of capital per worker reduces to $\bar{k}$.

The steady state in the Solow model is, therefore, a STABLE STEADY STATE. If the economy has been working for a long time, we would expect it to reach the steady state as any per capita capital stock other than $\bar{k}$ pushes the economy towards $\bar{k}$. What determines the size of the capital per person in the steady-state?

› When an economy has a capital stock per capita other than $\bar{k}$ and over time the economy's capital stock per capita evolves according to the Solow equation and eventually takes the value $\bar{k}$, the economy is said to be in a **stable steady** state.

In the steady state, $k_{t+1} = k_t = \bar{k}$, and slipping this condition into Eq. (14.12) gives us:

$$0 = sA\bar{k}^{a} - (n + \delta)\bar{k}$$

or,

$$\bar{k} = \left[\frac{sA}{n + \delta}\right]^{\frac{1}{1-a}} \tag{14.14}$$

Recall that a STEADY STATE is one where the new investment per person is just sufficient to replace the worn-out capital and add to capital stock in line with population growth so that the capital stock per capita does not decline. If, after replacing the depreciated capital and providing for capital to new workers on par with the initial amount of capital per worker that existed before this new investment was undertaken, there is still some savings (equal to investment) left over, the economy will see an increment in the capital stock per person. However, as the stock of capital per capita grows, the economy will need to devote a greater amount of investment to replacing the worn-out capital thereby leaving less left over for further growth. In the steady state, savings and investment is just sufficient to keep the capital per worker constant and at this point the growth of output per person comes to a halt. Increased saving and investment then cannot cause increased growth, but it does result in high levels of capital and output per person.

› In a **steady state** investment per capita is just sufficient to replace depreciated capital stock and add to the capital stock in pace with population growth so that the capital stock per capita is constant.

14.4 Comparative Statics

Substituting the steady-state value of the capital stock per capita into the production function (14.6) gives us the steady-state quantity of the output per capita $\bar{y}$:

$$\bar{y} = A\bar{k}^{a}$$

Substituting the value of $\bar{k}$ from (14.14):

$$\bar{y} = A\left[\frac{sA}{n + \delta}\right]^{\frac{a}{1-a}}$$

or,

$$\bar{y} = A^{\frac{1}{1-a}}\left[\frac{s}{n + \delta}\right]^{\frac{a}{1-a}} \tag{14.15}$$

This equation is the Solow model's response to the question: "Why are some countries rich and some poor?" Countries that have a high savings- investment rate will tend to be richer, *ceteris paribus*. This is because such countries accumulate more capital per worker, and more capital per worker results in more output per worker. In contrast, countries with high population growth rates—high n—will tend to be poorer. This is because a higher fraction of savings in these economies go toward keeping the capital-labour ratio constant in the face of a growing population, and they find it tougher to accumulate more capital per capita.

If an economy increases the INVESTMENT RATE from s to s′ permanently, the sy curve shits up to $s'y$ (see Figure 14.4). At the current steady-state value of the

› An increase in the **investment rate** leads to a higher level of output per capita

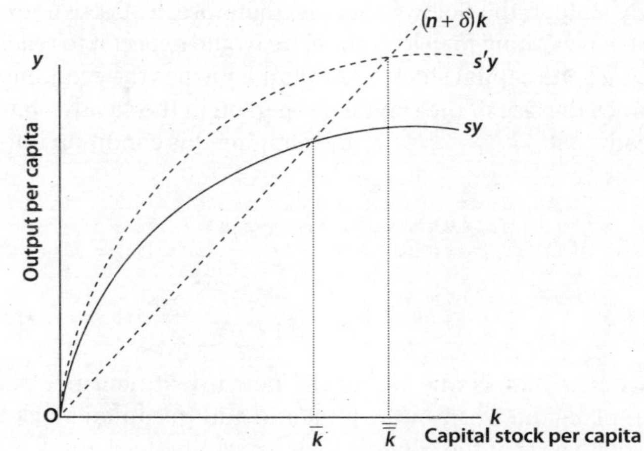

› **Figure 14.4**
Increase in Investment Rate. A higher savings/investment rate s', increases the investment per worker. The higher investment exceeds that required to keep capital per worker constant and the capital stock per capita increases till the new steady state $\bar{\bar{k}}$ is achieved.

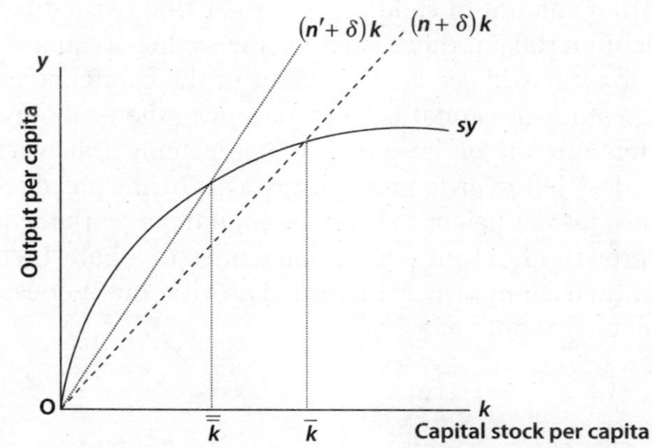

› **Figure 14.5**
Increase in Population Growth Rate. An increase in the population growth rate to n' reduces the capital stock per worker, which declines to the new steady state level of $\bar{\bar{k}}$.

capital stock $\bar{k}$ the investment per worker exceeds the amount required to keep the capital per worker constant. As a result, there is an increase in the capital per worker, which continues till the capital stock per capita reaches the new steady state $\bar{\bar{k}}$. As higher capital stock per capita is associated with higher output per capita the economy is more well off than before.

However, the higher savings rate has no effect on the long-run growth rate of output per capita. Recall that in a steady state the capital stock per worker is constant. Accordingly, the output per worker, which is dependent on the capital stock per worker, as $y = Ak^{a}$, is also constant when there is no technological progress (A is a constant). If the per capita income is constant, the growth rate of per capita income must be zero. In a long-run steady state, the savings rate has no effect on the growth rate of the output per capita, which is equal to zero. Of course, when the savings rate increases initially at capital stock per capita of $\bar{k}$ there is a TEMPORARY INCREASE in the growth rate of the output per capita as the resultant investment is higher than that required to replace the depreciated capital stock and the growth in population that enters the labour force. The capital stock per capita increases until the new steady state $\bar{\bar{k}}$ is reached where the period of growth in per capita income comes to an end.

› The **increase in savings temporarily** leads to a higher growth of output per capita but savings has no effect on the long run growth rate of output per capita which equals zero.

If an economy that has reached its steady-state witnesses an increase in the POPULATION GROWTH RATE from n to n', say, due to immigration, then, the $(n + \delta)k$ curve rotates counter-clockwise to the new $(n' + \delta)k$ curve (see Figure 14.5). The investment per worker is now no longer high enough to keep the capital-labour ratio constant in the face of the rising population and the

› An increase in the **population growth rate** reduces the level of output per capita.

capital-labour ratio begins to fall until the point at which $sy = (n' + \delta)k$ where $k = \bar{\bar{k}}$. The economy now has lesser capital per worker, and the per capita output is also lower.

What can we say about economic growth in the steady state? From Eq. (14.15), there is no growth of per capita output in the steady state as the output per worker is a constant equal to the expression of constant parameters on the right-hand side. However, an economy that begins with a stock of capital per worker below its steady state value, $k < \bar{k}$, will experience growth in k and y along the path to the steady state. Over time, however, growth slows down as the steady state is approached and in due course growth stops altogether. To see this note that the growth rate of y for the given parameters A and a is proportional to the growth rate of k,[14] as y is a function of k given by $y = Ak^a$. Now,

$$\text{Growth Rate of } k = \frac{\text{Change in Capital Stock per Capita}}{\text{Capital Stock per Capita}}$$

$$= \frac{(1+n)(k_{t+1} - k_t)}{k_t}$$

The numerator is the left-hand side of Eq. (14.12). Hence, dividing throughout Eq. (14.12) by k_t:

$$\text{Growth Rate of } k = \frac{sAk_t^a}{k_t} - \frac{(n+\delta)k_t}{k_t}$$

$$= \frac{sy_t}{k_t} - (n+\delta)$$

The first term on the right-hand side is the saving rate (s), into the average product of capital—y/k. As the production function is subject to diminishing marginal returns and since the average product declines when the marginal product declines, the graph of sy/k slopes downwards as k increases in Figure 14.6. The second term, $(n + \delta)$, is independent of k, and a horizontal line.

The difference between the graphs of the two equations, sy/k and $(n + \delta)k$, in Figure 14.6 is the growth rate of the capital stock per capita. If the economy is at a point below its steady state value of k, such as at k_0, the growth rate of the capital stock per capita is the distance AB. As the economy approaches its steady-state per capita capital stock, the diagram indicates that the growth rate of capital stock per capita, and indeed of per capita output, which is proportional to it, declines. At the steady state, given by point E, the two graphs are

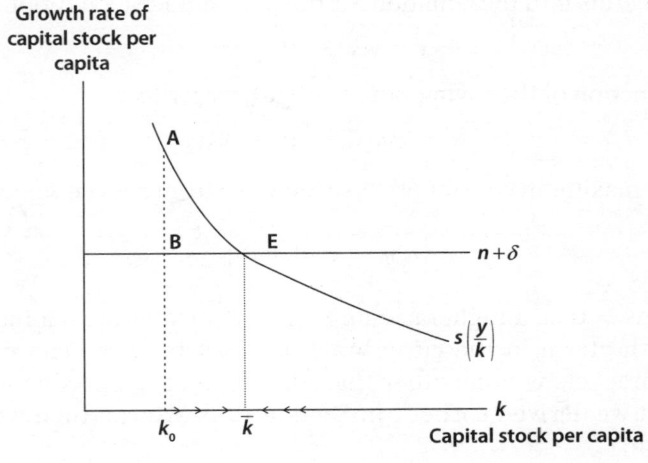

› **Figure 14.6**
Growth Rate of the Capital Stock per Capital. The savings or investment from the average product due to the capital stock, $s(y/k)$, declines with an increase in the capital stock per capita due to diminishing productivity. If this is greater than the growth in population and depreciation of the capital stock, $n + \delta$, as occurs to the left of point E, there is a positive growth in the capital stock per capita. To the right of point E, the capital stock per capita diminishes over time. The point E thus represents a steady state of capital stock per capita, $\bar{k}$.

equal and growth has ceased altogether. Of course, with $y = Y/L$, this implies that the aggregate output is growing in the steady state at the rate of population growth but per capita output growth is nil.

That economies may grow for a while and then experience stagnation, as predicted by the Solow model, does not fit an important stylized fact—that economies exhibit a sustained per capita income growth. To get around this problem, Solow assumed that technological progress occurs with the parameter A increasing over time. In the Solow set-up technological progress is exogenous—it occurs autonomously and regardless of whatever else is going on in the economy. With technological progress the parameter A increases with time, shifting the sy/k curve to the right as the capital stock per capita increases. In such a case, growth need not slow down and, eventually, stop altogether.

14.5 The Golden Rule

As a higher capital stock per capita results in a higher output per capita, should an economy keep increasing its investment rates? A rise in the saving rate increases the steady-state capital intensity (see Figure 14.5) so that we may write,

$$\bar{k} = \bar{k}(s) \text{ where } \frac{\Delta \bar{k}}{\Delta s} > 0$$

The economy achieves a steady state per capita capital stock as well as the output per capita by choosing a saving rate. However, as saving is future consumption we would be interested in that level of saving that maximizes sustainable consumption. Put another way, increasing the saving rate amounts to a reduction in consumption today. However, the increased saving results in a higher consumption in the future. Thus, sustainable consumption is that which provides the same amount of consumption to members of each present and future generation. To find this level of consumption, write the per capita consumption as the per capita output less per capita saving:

$$\begin{aligned} c &= (1 - s)y \\ &= (1 - s)Ak^{a} \\ &= Ak^{a} - sAk^{a} \end{aligned}$$

However, in the steady-state from Eq. (14.14),

$$(n + \delta)k = sAk^{a}$$

Substituting this into the equation for the per capita consumption,

$$c = Ak^{a} - (n + \delta)k$$

As k is a function of the saving rate, $k = k(s)$, we write,

$$c = [Ak(s)]^{a} - (n + \delta)k(s)$$

Hence, the maximum consumption sustainable from a given saving rate is:

$$\frac{\Delta c}{\Delta s} = \left\{aAk^{a-1} - (n + \delta)\right\}\frac{\Delta k}{\Delta s} = 0$$

Since $\Delta k/\Delta s > 0$ as a higher saving rate is associated with a higher capital intensity, the term in the curly brackets must be zero. The first term in the curly brackets is none other than the slope of the production function $\Delta y/\Delta k$ that we derived earlier[15] in Section 14.2. We can then write that for a maximum,

$$\alpha A k^{\alpha-1} - (n + \delta) = 0$$

or,

$$\frac{\Delta y}{\Delta k} - (n + \delta) = 0$$

or,

$$\frac{\Delta y}{\Delta k} = (n + \delta) \quad (14.16)$$

This CONDITION FOR MAXIMUM SUSTAINABLE CONSUMPTION requires that the slope of the production function equals the slope of the line $(n + \delta)k$, which depicts the capital needed to keep the capital per worker constant.

› The Golden Rule condition for the maximum sustainable consumption requires that the slope of the production function equals the amount of the capital stock required to keep the capital stock per capita constant. $\Delta y/\Delta k = n + \delta$.

This condition is depicted in Figure 14.7. If we do not provide less to future generations than to ourselves,[16] then the consumption per capita should be fixed at c_{gold}.

To derive the value of the golden rule savings rate, we first solve for $k = \bar{k}_{gold}$ in the equation for the maximum sustainable consumption, where, $\Delta y/\Delta k = n + \delta$,

$$\alpha A [\bar{k}_{gold}]^{\alpha-1} = n + \delta$$

This solution for $k = \bar{k}_{gold}$ is then substituted into the Eq. (14.12) where as the capital per worker is constant in the steady state at $\bar{k}_{gold}$, the left-hand side is zero which implies:

$$sA\bar{k}^{\alpha}_{gold} = (n + \delta)\bar{k}_{gold} \quad (14.17)$$

Solving this equation for s gives us the GOLDEN RULE SAVING RATE as $s = s_{gold}$. At s_{gold} saving rate the required amount of saving is generated that will sustain the golden rule steady-state capital stock per capita. This capital stock $\bar{k}_{gold}$ in turn will sustain the per capita consumption, c_{gold}, that maximizes the consumption which is equally enjoyed by members of each current and future generation.

› The savings rate that sustains the Golden Rule capital stock per capita is the golden rule savings rate. $sA\bar{k}^{\alpha}_{gold} = (n + \delta)\bar{k}_{gold}$

The golden rule is a reminder that pushing for higher saving beyond a point does not pay off because each increment to capital stock is accompanied by a diminishing marginal productivity and, thus, a diminishing incremental output. At the same time, each addition to the capital stock requires more output to be set aside to replace the depreciated capital. A diminishing incremental output and increasing requirements for the depreciated capital to

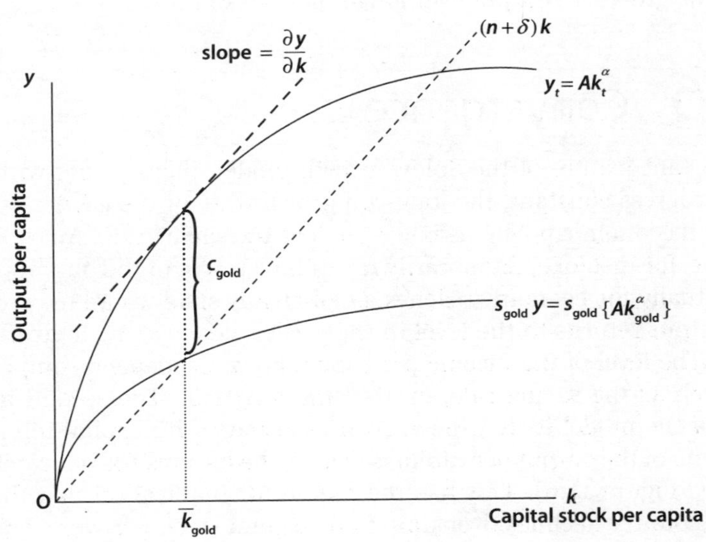

› **Figure 14.7**
The Golden Rule
The golden rule consumption is the maximum consumption that is possible across steady states. This is derived in three steps. First, is the condition that the slope of the per capita production function or the marginal productivity of capital equals the growth of population plus the depreciation rate, $\partial y/\partial k = \alpha A k^{\alpha-1} = n + \delta$. The solution to this equation gives the golden rule capital stock per capita or $\bar{k}_{gold}$. The golden rule saving rate then is the solution for $s = s_{gold}$ in the equation $sA\bar{k}^{\alpha}_{gold} = (n + \delta)\bar{k}_{gold}$. Finally, the golden rule consumption is given by $c_{gold} = y(1 - s_{gold})$ where the output per capita is that produced from $\bar{k}_{gold}$.

MACROFOCUS 14.2

Calculating the Golden Rule Saving Rate

Suppose that the economy is characterized by the following parameters for the population growth n, the depreciation rate δ, technology A, and the share of capital in output α.

$$n = 0.02 \quad \delta = 0.06 \quad A = 145 \quad \alpha = 0.4$$

To solve for the golden rule saving rate, we need to first solve for the capital stock per capita that sustains the maximum possible consumption. This requires us to solve for $k = \bar{k}_{gold}$ in the equation:

$$\alpha A[\bar{k}_{gold}]^{\alpha-1} = n + \delta$$

or, $$0.4(145)[\bar{k}_{gold}]^{0.4-1} = 0.02 + 0.06$$

or, $$[\bar{k}_{gold}]^{0.4-1} = \frac{0.02 + 0.06}{0.4(145)} = 0.001379$$

or, $$[\bar{k}_{gold}] = (0.001379)^{-\frac{1}{0.6}} = (0.001379)^{-\frac{5}{3}}$$

or, $$\bar{k}_{gold} = 58509.99$$

We then substitute this value of $\bar{k}_{gold}$ into the following equation to arrive at the golden rule saving rate $s = s_{gold}$:

$$sA\bar{k}^{\alpha}_{gold} = (n + \delta)\bar{k}_{gold}$$

or, $$s(145)(58509.99)^{0.4} = (0.02 + 0.06)\,58509.99$$

or, $$s = \frac{(0.02 + 0.06)}{145}\left(\frac{58509.99}{(58509.99)^{0.4}}\right)$$

or, $$s = \frac{0.08}{145}(58509.99)^{0.6} = \frac{0.08}{145}(725)$$

or, $$s = (0.000552)(725)$$

or, $$s = s_{gold} = 0.4$$

In other words, an economy, described by the above parameter values, which wants to maximize the consumption per capita in such a way that the consumption which the current and future generations enjoy without diminishing any generation's consumption for the benefit of another, must save 40 per cent of its aggregate income.

The previous parameter values are approximately the values that may be said to characterize the Indian economy.[17] According to the golden rule, it appears that the Indian economy is saving less than it should be. Of course, one reason that may not be true is that it is an outcome derived from the presumption that there is no technological progress.

be replaced leaves a net incremental output, which is available for the consumption that is declining. That is why additions to saving and investment beyond a point gives a diminished future consumption. An economy that saves and invests beyond s_{gold} is over saving and per capita consumption now and in the future could, in fact, be raised by lowering the economy's saving rate. Such an economy is said to be DYNAMICALLY INEFFICIENT as the path of per capita consumption is below a feasible alternative path that is attainable. Of course, this result is valid for a given technology.

› An economy that saves more than the golden rule saving rate is **dynamically inefficient** as the consumption per capita over time is lower than a feasible alternative that is available to the economy.

If there are technological improvements that enhance the productivity of capital, improvements in the saving and investment rates beyond the s_{gold} rate (that is associated with a given technology) can sustain higher present and future consumption. It is not just thrift or saving, but productivity improvements that are important for sustaining higher incomes and consumption, and higher living standards improve welfare. From a policy perspective improving saving in an economy helps up to a point: a technological change is required to sustain the growth of output over longer periods of time.

14.6 Convergence

An important feature of the Solow growth model, then, is that with technological progress constant, the long-run growth rate of the economy does not depend on economic policy variables such as the saving rate. An INCREASE IN THE SAVING RATE, for instance, temporarily raises the growth of the output per capita but eventually the economy reaches a new steady state where the growth rate of the output returns to the level in the earlier steady state, a growth rate of $(n + \delta)$. The level of the income per capita, however, depends on policy variables, such as the saving rate, even in the long run. The second important feature of the model is that the growth rates vary with capital intensity: the growth rate of the output per capita is higher, the lower is the per capita capital stock (see Figure 14.6). This has the important implication that the growth rate of a country declines over time as its capital stock per worker increases.

› Policy changes in the Solow model have **no long-run growth** effect and have only level effects on the level of the output per capita.

Also, in a comparison across economies, countries with higher capital stock per capita will grow more slowly. This implies that there is a tendency for CONVERGENCE across economies.[18]

› Economies with lower per capita incomes grow faster than richer economies and the gap in the per capita income between the two economies reduces. This catching up is called **convergence**.

The hypothesis that poor economies tend to grow faster per capita than rich ones, without conditioning on any other characteristics of economies, is referred to as ABSOLUTE CONVERGENCE. This hypothesis receives little or no support except when the test of the hypothesis is limited to a relatively homogeneous group of countries.[19] The theory gets better empirical backing if we allow for heterogeneity across economies in the sense that economies do not have the same steady states. If steady states differ, then, an economy grows faster, the further it is from its own steady-state value, a concept known as CONDITIONAL CONVERGENCE. This concept is illustrated in Figure 14.8 where two economies differ in only two respects—they have different initial stocks of capital per person, $k(0)_{poor} < k(0)_{rich}$ and second, they have different saving rates, $s_{poor} < s_{rich}$.

› **Absolute convergence** occurs when in economies with the same rates of investment, population growth, and levels of technology, the one with a smaller initial per capita income grows temporarily faster than one with an initially higher per capita income.

› Economies converge to their own steady states. **Conditional convergence** refers to the convergence of economies after we control for or condition on differences in steady states.

Then, it need not be the case that the poor economy will grow faster than the rich one. For the case illustrated in Figure 14.8, the growth rate of the per capita capital stock of the rich economy, given by distance AB, is greater than the growth rate of the poor economy given by distance CD. However, the prediction is that each economy will converge to its own steady state k and the speed of its convergence relates inversely to the distance from its steady state.

Empirically, this requires us to look at the relation between the growth in the per capita capital stock (or the growth in per capita output) and the initial capital stock per capita (or the output per capita), after holding fixed variables that account for the differences in the steady-state position. In order to compare economies, of course, they must have some thing in common. One specification is that the economies share common technological knowledge. Economies could have different values of K and N but the same value of A in the production function, $Y = AF(K, N)$.

A justification for such an assumption is that technological handbooks are easily available everywhere so that the basic commonality across economies is the knowledge of the potential production function.[20] Apart from this, the saving rates, the growth rate of employment, the rate of depreciation, and the initial per capita output would differ across economies. CONVERGENCE in the per capita output is fundamentally due TO the convergence in per capita stocks of the

› **Convergence** arises due to diminishing returns to capital. The convergence rate is an increasing function of the depreciation rate and an increasing function of the population growth rate.

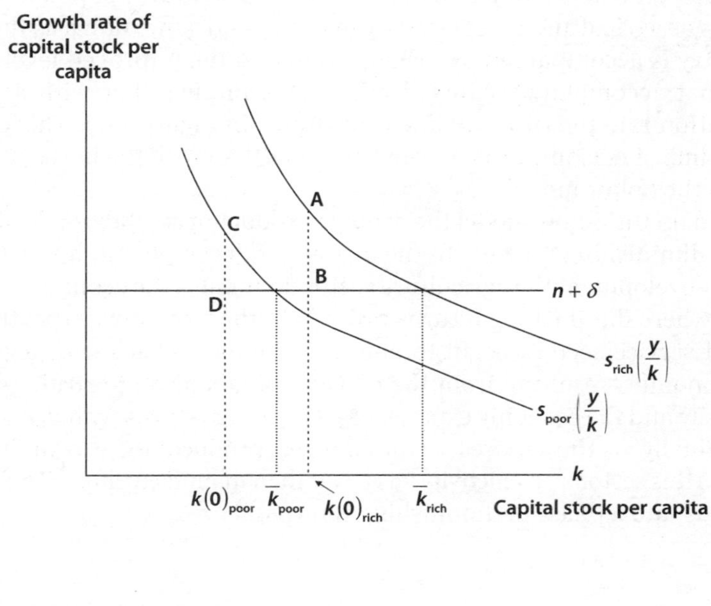

› **Figure 14.8**
Conditional Convergence.
A poor economy has less capital stock per capita than a rich one, $k(0)_{poor} < k(0)_{rich}$, and the saving rate in the poor economy is also smaller, $s_{poor} < s_{rich}$. In the case depicted, the growth rate of the capital stock per capita of the rich economy, as given by the vertical distance AB, is larger than the growth rate for the poor economy as given by the distance CD. Both economies converge to their respective steady state capital stocks per capita conditionally.

physical capital arising from the diminishing returns to capital. Depreciation offsets capital accumulation and deters the onset of diminishing returns to capital: the convergence rate is an increasing function of the depreciation rate. Population growth reduces the growth rate in the capital stock per capita and delays the onset of diminishing returns: the convergence rate is an increasing function of the population growth rate.

Cashin and Sahay[21] estimated an absolute convergence model for Indian states using 1961–1991 data and found that convergence was taking place in the Indian states. However, their findings did not go through when the share of manufacturing in each state's net domestic product (NDP), which was included as a control variable in the growth equation, was omitted from the regression model. In that case, the estimated convergence rates decreased in magnitude and became statistically insignificant. Rao and Sen[22] indicate that the share of manufacturing in NDP may be proxying for the steady-state differences in growth rates across states in which case the Cashin and Sahay findings suggest the possibility of conditional convergence and not absolute convergence. Abler and Das[23] also estimate for convergence for the period 1961–1990 using state-level annual data for the 17 largest Indian states. They find no tendency for convergence in India, a result inconsistent with the Solow model of growth.

14.7 Poverty Traps

Solow himself is circumspect about certain empirical applications of his growth model. As he states, "In my view growth theory was conceived as a model of the growth of an industrial economy.... I have never applied such a model to a developing economy, because I thought the underlying machinery would apply mainly to a planned economy or a well-developed market economy".[24]

In developing countries, the composition of output has implications for the labour and product markets which can result in outcomes that are different from the ones associated with the Solow model. Take the population growth, for instance, which is presumed to grow at a constant rate in the Solow model. In India, the current population growth rate is lower than the growth rate that applied around 1947.[25] As the income per worker rises with development, the GROWTH RATE OF THE LABOUR FORCE first rises and then diminishes. With the capital stock per worker an indicator of the level of development, the labour force growth rate n is a function of k, $n = n(k)$. The rate of population growth increases as agriculture is replaced by industry and slows down as the growth of industry is accompanied by urbanization and the improved levels of education that accompany fertility decline. This implies that with a constant depreciation rate the $(n + \delta)k$ line is as drawn in Figure 14.9. This conforms with the line of reasoning just advanced rather than with the horizontal line as stated in the Solow model.

› In a developing economy the **rate** of the population growth first increases and then declines as industrialization, urbanization, and improved education occur.

Again, in the Solow model the average product of capital y/k declines with k due to diminishing returns. In the process of development, however, at low levels of development the agriculture sector dominates the economy and this is a sector where diminishing returns prevail. As the ECONOMY DEVELOPS the industrial and service sectors begin to emerge. The industrial sector exploits the scale economies resulting from the division of labour and learning-by-doing more easily and the economy experiences increasing returns with y/k increasing with k. Finally, as the services sector emerges, productivity growth diminishes against as this sector's productivity[26] is lower than manufacturing.[27] The economy again runs into a phase of diminishing returns.

› The diminishing returns to capital is offset as an industrial sector that exploits scale **economies and learning** by doing supplants the agricultural sector.

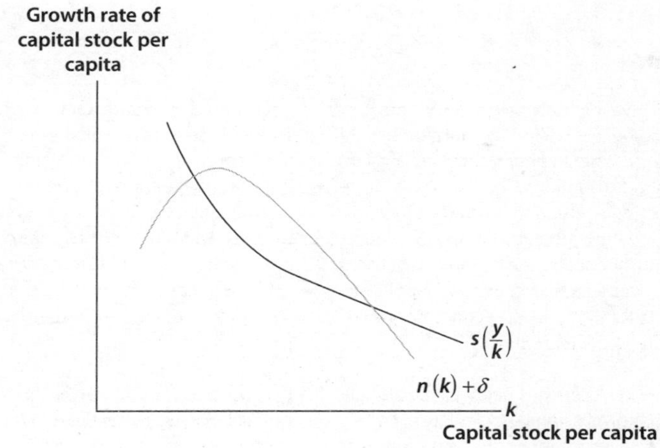

› **Figure 14.9**
Population Growth and Development. With the capital stock per capita an indicator of the development phase of the economy, the rate of population growth increases in the early stages of development when an economy is primarily agricultural, and declines as the economy becomes industrialized giving rise to the inverted U shaped $n(k) + \delta$ curve.

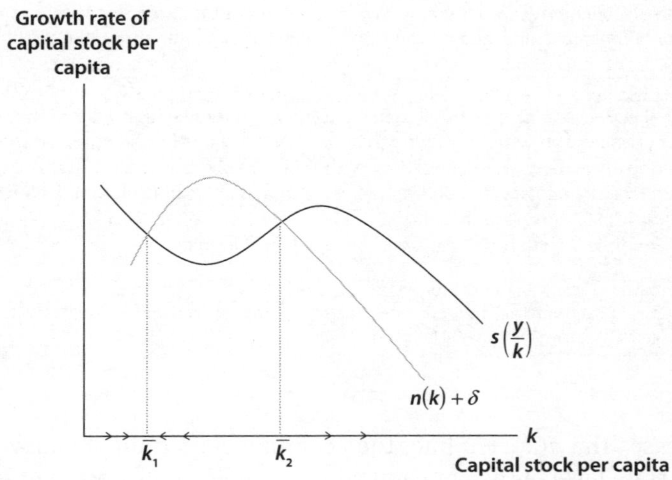

› **Figure 14.10**
Development and Productivity. In the initial stages of development with agriculture, the predominant sector, the economy is subject to diminishing returns. As industrialization occurs the economy enters an increasing returns phase and the average productivity of capital y/k rises. As the economy becomes a services economy, the productivity of the economy again declines. Multiple equilibriums then exist with the steady state $\bar{k}_1$ being a stable steady-state equilibrium and $\bar{k}_2$ an unstable steady state equilibrium. An economy with a value of $k < \bar{k}_2$ is caught in a poverty trap.

This pattern of productivity changes as the economy develops, as depicted in Figure 14.10 in the shape of the $s(y/k)$ curve, which has a negative slope at low levels of k, followed by a range with a positive slope, and a negative slope again at very high levels of k.[28]

Recall from the discussion associated with Figure 14.3 that a stable steady state involves a positive growth rate of capital stock per capita for values of $k < \bar{k}$ and a negative growth rate of the capital stock per capita for $k > \bar{k}$. As the growth rate of the capital stock per capita is given by $s(y/k) - (n + \delta)$, this implies that for any given steady state k if the $s(y/k)$ curve lies above the $n(k) + \delta$ curve to the left of $\bar{k}$ and $s(y/k)$ lies below the $n(k) + \delta$ curve to the right of $\bar{k}$, $\bar{k}$ is a stable steady state. Accordingly, $\bar{k}_1$ is a stable steady state and $\bar{k}_2$ is an unstable steady state. If the economy starts out with a value of k such that $\bar{k}_1 < k < \bar{k}_2$, it has an innate tendency for the value of k to reduce to $\bar{k}_1$.

If somehow the capital stock per capita gets to $k > \bar{k}_2$, then, the economy will have a tendency to grow further. Hence, for any $k < \bar{k}_2$, the economy is caught in a POVERTY TRAP. Any attempt to raise the per capita output and capital stock has the propensity to return the economy to the low level steady state $\bar{k}_1$.

› A **poverty trap** is the tendency for an economy to return to a low level steady state despite attempts to raise the per capita output.

There are three possible ways of overcoming the barrier to development and getting out of the poverty trap:

1. A domestic policy of raising the savings rate.[29] This results in an upward shift of the entire $s(y/k)$ curve. If the new curve with a higher savings rate

MACROFOCUS 14.3

Lawyers—Do They Reduce Economic Growth?

Solow's theory informs us that the output per worker is determined by the rate of investment and the labour force growth. It is also determined by the efficiency with which these inputs are utilized. However, why do some countries invest less than others and why are the factors of production less productive in some countries than others?

Economists have come to realize that the social infrastructure of an economy—its policies, laws and regulations, and the institutions of governance that enforce them—is a major determinant of the extent to which individuals have the incentive to make investments in the capital, the technology, and the skills that boost the long-run performance of an economy. In economies where the institutions of governance favour diversion of resources away from the production of goods and services—through theft, red tape and bureaucratic regulation that encourages corruption, the lobbying of government by special interests, defrauding investors, and frivolous litigation—individuals will be less willing to invest in new technology. They would also be less willing to augment the capital stock. When higher returns are available in wealth redistribution rather than wealth creation, individual attention is diverted towards rent seeking rather than profit seeking, with a detrimental impact on the dynamism of the economy. The search for those socio-political characteristics that support economic growth was initiated by Robert Barro.*

In this context, there has been a lively debate on whether professions such as law or the armed services promote or reduce economic growth. Murphy, Shleifer, and Vishny** argued that data on college law enrolments is an indicator of the talent allocated to diversion of resources or rent seeking. Engineering enrolments, on the other hand, reflect entrepreneurial endeavor and are argued to be good for economic growth. They found that engineering enrolments were good for growth whereas law enrolments were not. A 10 per cent increase in law enrolments reduced future economic growth by 0.3 per cent.

Revisiting this debate, Cameron and Thorpe† use data on the number of lawyers in 53 countries from the Web site of the International Centre for Commercial Law, www.Legal500.com, among others. In this data set, the USA has the highest number of lawyers among all the countries listed. China is a far second with 12 per cent of the number of lawyers in the US, and India is third. They are unable to find support for the idea that lawyers result in lower economic growth. This is because not all lawyers are involved in rent seeking through strategic litigation intended to restrict competition and impose costs on competitors. Some lawyers contribute to wealth creation through reducing the transactions and compliance costs involved in meeting regulatory authority's requirements. Finally, some lawyer, such as those involved in human rights cases, are involved in socially-useful activities that may be difficult to put a monetary value on. Not all legal cases are about junk lawsuits.

* Barro, R. J. (1991)—"Economic Growth in a Cross Section of Countries", Quarterly Journal of Economics, 106 (May), 407–43.

** Murphy, K. M., Shleifer, A. and Vishny, R.W. (1991)—"The Allocation of Talent: Implications for Growth", Quarterly Journal of Economics, 106, 503–531.

† Cameron, S. and Thorpe, A. (2004)—"Legislating for Economic Sclerosis: Are Lawyers a Baleful Influence on Growth Rates?", Kyklos, 57, 67–86.

still crosses the $n(k) + \delta$ line, the economy can attain a somewhat higher steady-state level of the per capita output and capital stock, but is unable to get away from the poverty trap. However, as the $s(y/k)$ curve gradually rises at some time, the $s(y/k)$ and $n(k) + \delta$ curves will become tangential to one another. Then suddenly the economy would find itself on an inevitable growth path towards k_2. In this case a large dose of saving and investment is required before a developing country can overcome the existing barriers to growth.

› An economy can escape a poverty trap with sufficiently large increases in the savings rate, a **decline** in the population growth rate, or, an exogenous increase in the stock of capital.

2. A REDUCTION in the population growth rate. This lowers the $n(k) + \delta$ line enough so that it no longer intersects the $s(y/k)$ curve at $\bar{k}_1$ and the economy escapes from the poverty trap.
3. An exogenous injection of additional capital, such as a foreign loan or gift or the discovery of new resources. If the World Bank, for instance, makes a contribution of some quantity of capital to a country that begins at, say $\bar{k}_1$, this bestowed capital could raise k to a level below $\bar{k}_2$. The economy will enjoy temporary higher levels of income per capita but would still return eventually to $\bar{k}_1$ and not escape the poverty trap. A sufficiently large provision of capital, which makes $k > \bar{k}_2$, is required to break out of the poverty trap.[30] In a developing economy with poverty traps, it is not hard to imagine why there may be no tendency towards convergence.

14.8 Endogenous Growth

Increasingly, it has been realized that saving and capital accumulation, population growth and exogenously driven productivity growth are not a satisfactory way to explain economic growth. At first glance, they provide an insight into the mechanics of growth but then coherence of explanation must be accompanied by completeness. Take the two emerging giants—India and China. Between 1960 and 2003, China's GDP per capita grew by 5.7 per cent per year on average compared with 2.5 per cent growth in India. India was twice as rich as China in 1969. By 2003, China had become twice as rich as India.[31] More investment has been associated with more rapid growth in China. Since 1978, investment has fluctuated between 35 per cent and 45 per cent of GDP in China whereas since the mid-1980s, investment has fluctuated between 20 per cent and 34 per cent of GDP in India. Roughly, China growing a little more than twice as fast as India has been associated with one and half times as much investment as in India.

As regards population growth there are big differences again between China and India. China adopted a one-child policy in 1980 and imposed financial penalties on families having two or more children. Subsequently, families were allowed to have two children provided the first was a girl. The reduced population enabled the expansion of human capital as fewer children meant better care at home, more and better food, clothing, and medical attention.

India's progress in population control has been much slower than China's and its population is projected to overtake China's by 2025. Also, female literacy and better health care are much better in China, where almost 90 per cent of all females know how to read and write, as compared to less than 50 per cent for India. China also sends more than 70 per cent of its youngsters to secondary school, compared to 50 per cent in India. Education improves the labour force and is necessary if individuals are to move from low-paid self-employment to better-paid jobs in manufacturing and services.

It is through education that workers acquire skills. Skill acquisition also occurs as workers learn a new technology. The acquisition of skills is considered to be the acquisition of human capital and according to the ENDOGENOUS GROWTH THEORY the accumulation of human capital is responsible for the growth in the output per capita. The determination of the long-run growth within the model itself rather than through some exogenous growth variables like technological progress is the reason behind the name endogenous growth.

› **Endogenous growth theory** does not assume that growth is the result of exogenous improvements to technology but focuses on the determinants of technological progress.

HUMAN CAPITAL is acquired by devoting resources to invest in its acquisition. However, unlike physical capital, human capital acquisition takes place through the active pursuit of learning as well as through the act of production itself. This is what is referred to as learning by doing. Romer[32] argued that knowledge creation was a side product of investment. A firm that accumulates physical capital at the same time learns how to produce more efficiently. This effect of experience on productivity is called LEARNING BY DOING.

› **Human capital** refers to the levels of education and skills embodied in the labour force.

› **Learning by doing** is the process by which individuals and firms learn better ways to produce as a by-product of some other activity undertaken such as investment.

Let S_i be the index of skills or knowledge available to the firm.[33] Then, each firm has a potential production function given by:

$$Y_i = AK_i^{a}(S_iN_i)^{1-a} \qquad (14.18)$$

Learning by doing occurs through each firm's investment—an increase in a firm's capital stock leads to a parallel increase in its stock of knowledge, S_i. This reflects the idea that knowledge and productivity gains come from investment and production. This articulation of how skills are acquired is motivated by the empirical observation of the large positive effects of experience on productivity in many production processes.[34] The Boston Consulting Group[35] has, for instance, been famous for its advocacy of learning-curve strategies. The Boston Consulting Group felt that its clients should increase production in the early stages of the product life cycle so as to secure learning economies.

Firms should use profits from cash cow products—products with a high market share in a stable or declining product market—to fund the increased production of problem-child products—products with a low-market share in a fast-growing market. As problem-child products move down their learning curves they become cash cows in the next investment cycle.

› Each firm's knowledge about the production process constitutes a public good. A **public good** is non-excludable and non-rival. A good is excludable when others cannot be excluded from its consumption as the good cannot be provided on a market for a fee. For example no citizen can be excluded from the production of the good national defense. The good is non-rival if one person's consumption does not subtract from another's. For example the ticket charge for the cinema excludes those who do not pay for a ticket but each individual admitted consumes the services of the cinema without subtracting from the benefit of others.

A key assumption of learning-by-doing models of endogenous growth is that each firm's knowledge is a PUBLIC GOOD that any other firm can access at zero cost. A public good is a good that is non-excludable and non-rival. Once produced, it is difficult to exclude somebody from the consumption of such a good and moreover one person's consumption of such a good does not subtract from another person's consumption (non-rivalness).

A classic public good is law and order or national defense, which is equally consumed by all, whereas in the case of a private good, say, food, if one person consumes more of a given supply, another has less available for consumption (rivalness). The endogenous growth theory assumes that knowledge is a public good: once discovered, a piece of knowledge escapes or spills out instantly across the whole economy. Of course, firms have incentives to maintain secrecy over their discoveries and they also file for patents to retain competitive advantage. Knowledge regarding productivity improvements thus trickle out only gradually. However, for simplicity, we assume that all discoveries are the unintended by-products of investment and these findings immediately become common knowledge. In a sense we are presuming that as a worker learns to use the new technology in a firm, he acquires skills that can be transferred to another firm. This is because a new way of production can easily be duplicated or copied by other workers in other firms,[36] or because some workers leave one firm and take up a job in another where his acquired skills are widely disseminated. As a result when firms in the economy invest more or accumulate more CAPITAL PER WORKER the skills of the workers in each firm go up proportionately as workers improve their performance of specific tasks. This happens as they gain experience and learn the appropriate tolerances for product attributes—the benefits of the learning curve. Each firm benefits from the average level of human capital in the economy as knowledge spillovers increase the higher is the average level of skills and knowledge. Thus, the increase in the level of skills at firm i (ΔS_i) with the passage of time (Δt), or $\Delta s_i/\Delta t$, increases with the increment to the capital per worker [$\Delta(K/N)$] over time:

› The accumulation of skills in a learning by doing approach to growth is a by product of another activity – an increase in the **capital stock per worker**.

$$\frac{\Delta S_i}{\Delta t} = \frac{\Delta(K/N)}{\Delta t}$$

or by choosing a coefficient of proportionality[37] equal to unity,

$$S_i = \frac{K}{N}$$

Learning by doing and knowledge spillovers thus allow us to replace S_i in Eq. (14.18) by K/N which makes the production function for firm i,

$$Y_i = AK_i^a\left(\frac{K}{N}N_i\right)^{1-a}$$

If each firm expands the capital per worker, K/N rises and imparts a spillover benefit that augments the productivity of all firms. Dividing throughout by N_i, we can write the following Eq. (14.19) in per worker terms as,

$$\frac{Y_i}{N_i} = AK_i^a\left(\frac{K}{N}\right)^{1-a} N_i^{-a}$$

or, $$\frac{Y_i}{N_i} = A\left(\frac{K_i}{N_i}\right)^{\alpha}\left(\frac{K}{N}\right)^{1-\alpha}$$

or, $$y_i = Ak_i^{\alpha}k^{1-\alpha} \tag{14.19}$$

Each firm is sufficiently small and so disregards its own contribution of increased capital intensity (K_i/N_i) to the aggregate capital intensity K/N, thereby treating K/N as given.

However, in equilibrium all firms make the same choices so that $k_i = k$ and $y_i = y$. Then,

$$y = Ak^{\alpha}k^{1-\alpha}$$

or, $$y = Ak \tag{14.20}$$

The average product of capital, then, is as follows:

$$\frac{y}{k} = A \tag{14.21}$$

The AVERAGE PRODUCT OF CAPITAL, then, is invariant with k due to the tendency for diminishing returns to capital, which permeated the Solow model, being eliminated here as a result of learning-by-doing and spillover effects. The growth rate of capital stock per capita is given by:

› In learning by doing (Ak) endogenous growth theory the **average product of capital** is not subject to diminishing returns and is a constant.

$$\text{Growth Rate of } k = \frac{sy}{k} - (n + \delta)$$

Substituting from Eq. (14.21),

$$\text{Growth Rate of } k = sA - (n + \delta) \tag{14.22}$$

The downward-sloping $s(y/k)$ curve in Figure 14.6 is replaced in Figure 14.11 by the horizontal line sA.

The vertical distance between the sA line and the line $(n + \delta)$ is the growth rate of capital stock per capita. As the two lines are parallel to one another the growth rate is constant and independent of k. Thus, the capital stock per capita always grows at the steady-state rate $[sA - (n + \delta)]$. Unlike the Solow model a higher savings rate, s, results in a higher rate of long-run per capita growth.

› In **endogenous growth theory** (1) a higher savings rate raises the long run per capita income growth rate permanently, and (2) there is no tendency for convergence.

UNLIKE IN THE SOLOW MODEL where there is a golden savings rate, here a shift to a higher savings rate at some point of time requires a reduction in consumption per capita at that time, but results in a higher level of per capita consumption in the future. An improvement in technology, A, also causes

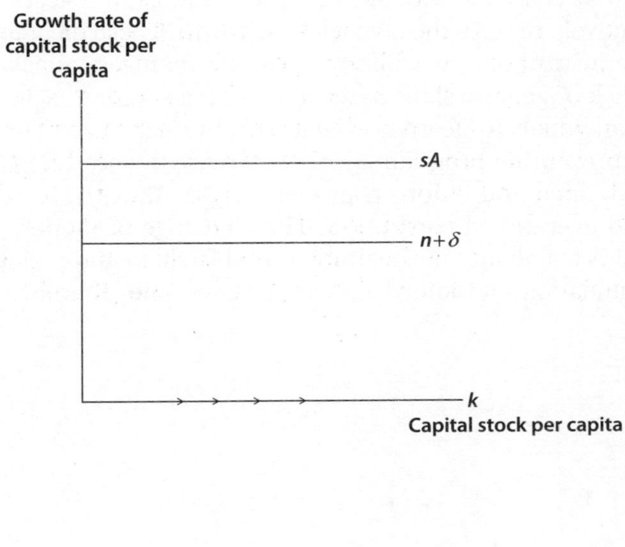

› **Figure 14.11 Endogenous Growth *Ak* Model.** Learning by doing and spillover effects result in an average productivity of the capital given by $y/k = A$ that is not subject to diminishing returns. The saving or investment from the average product due to the capital stock, $s(y/k)$ is then constant and does not decline with an increase in the capital stock per capita. The growth rate of the economy is then independent of the level of capital stock per capita and a higher saving rate increases the long-run growth rate of the economy unlike in the Solow model.

long-run growth to be higher. Finally, unlike the Solow model, the endogenous Ak model does not predict absolute or conditional convergence—the statement that smaller values of k are associated with larger values of the growth of k. In fact, if we vary the value of k, the growth rate of k as given in Eq. (14.22) does not change.

These results follow from relaxing the diminishing returns to capital condition in the Solow model. In an endogenous Romer-type model, the output depends on conventional inputs like capital and labour but it also depends on an economy's stock of knowledge and skills. The stock of knowledge rises over time as firms accumulate more capital per worker. Each firm has a production function in which the output depends on the firm's private inputs including the firm's stock of private knowledge and skills, and it also depends on the economy's aggregate public stock of skills and knowledge. Thus, the increased capital accumulation per worker in a firm results in an externality where the aggregate stock of knowledge rises and the tendency for diminishing returns is abated.

› The **engine of economic growth** is the technological progress that occurs exogenously, or the externalities (by products) of capital accumulation in the form of skills and human capital acquisition.

Growth theory then identifies the ENGINE OF GROWTH as technological change in its exogenous version and the externalities from skill and knowledge acquisition in its endogenous version. This engine of knowledge spillovers is different from most other economic goods. Knowledge is non-rivalrous—my use of a stock of knowledge, such as the use of calculus or the ideas expounded in this book, does not bar your simultaneous use of that knowledge. This property of knowledge means that we are free of the scourge of diminishing returns. Of course, producing new knowledge is costly and requires substantial investment that can result in no returns as knowledge generation is risky. But once created, knowledge and skills can be replicated at low cost. It is this externality between the private cost of creating new knowledge and the social cost of replicating it easily that provides the economic fuel for the engine of growth.

Growth theory also emphasizes that differences in growth rates across countries or regions are based on institutional differences. Knowledge spillovers will be feeble if formal credit markets are scarce, where there is a poor enforcement of property rights, in regions with a high incidence of economic and political instability, and where literacy is low and thus impedes skill acquisition. In such countries it would be difficult for growth to proceed favourably. There is a huge discrepancy between countries such as Korea and Japan where income levels are high and education is widespread, and countries like Brazil and Mexico where poverty traps prevail, literacy is low, and income inequality is high. A developing country requires to invest in the soft infrastructure of institutions that enable knowledge spillovers and capital accumulation and thereby to actively remove the obstacles to growth. These include the absence of insurance institutions that discourages risk-taking, the lack of access to credit, the lack of generic skills associated with a standard school education that teach individuals to "learn how to learn", the lack of good health services and disease prevention programmes that increase the productivity of labour, and poorly-defined and enforced property rights that reduce the incentive to invest and even breed corruption. The challenge of modern growth and development is to enhance the institutions that facilitate the engine of growth—capital accumulation and knowledge spillovers— and, thereby, make it run smoothly.

SUMMARY

- Economic growth is the rate of change of real income (or output) per capita.
- The stylized facts about long run growth are that (1) output per capita grows at a more or less constant rate, (2) the share of labour and capital in income is constant, and (3) the share of consumption in aggregate income is constant.
- The neoclassical Solow growth theory assumes: (1) the economy is characterized by perfect competition with firms as price takers, and (2) the output is given by a constant returns to scale production function such as $Y = AK^{a}L^{1-a}$ where A is a technology parameter.
- Solow used the production function to argue that the change in output is due to the growth of the labour force, the accumulation of capital stock, and technological progress.
- The Solow residual is the estimate of technological progress derived as a residual after accounting for the rate of growth of output due to labour force and capital stock growth.
- Solow demonstrated that the Solow residual or total factor productivity growth contributes the major share to the per capita income growth.
- A steady state is characterized by a point where the amount of the capital stock per capita remains constant over time. $\bar{k} = k_{t+1} = k_t$.
- In a steady-state, investment per capita is just sufficient to replace depreciated capital stock and add to the capital stock in pace with population growth so that the capital stock per capita is constant.
- An increase in the investment rate leads to a higher level of the output per capita.
- An increase in the population growth rate reduces the level of the output per capita.
- The golden rule condition for maximum sustainable consumption requires that the slope of the production function equals the amount of capital stock required to keep the capital stock per capita constant. $\Delta y/\Delta k = n + \delta$.
- The savings rate that sustains the golden rule capital stock per capita is the golden rule savings rate, $sA\bar{k}^{a}_{\text{gold}} = (n + \delta)\bar{k}_{\text{gold}}$.
- An economy that saves more than the golden rule saving rate is dynamically inefficient as the consumption per capita over time is lower than a feasible alternative that is available to the economy.
- Policy changes in the Solow model have no long-run growth effect and have only level effects on the level of output per capita.
- Economies with lower per capita incomes grow faster than richer economies, and the gap in per capita income between the two economies reduces. This catching up is called convergence.
- Absolute convergence occurs when in economies with the same rates of investment, population growth, and technology levels, the one with a smaller initial per capita income grows temporarily faster than one with an initially higher per capita income.
- Economies converge to their own steady states. Conditional convergence refers to the convergence of economies after we control for, or condition on, differences in steady states.
- Convergence arises due to diminishing returns to capital. The convergence rate is an increasing function of the depreciation rate and an increasing function of the population growth rate.
- In a developing economy, the rate of population growth first increases and then declines as industrialization, urbanization, and improved education occur.
- The diminishing returns to capital is offset as an industrial sector that exploits scale economies and learning by doing supplants the agricultural sector.
- A poverty trap is a tendency for an economy to return to a low- level steady state despite attempts to raise the per capita output.
- An economy can escape a poverty trap with sufficiently large increases in the savings rate, a decline in the population growth rate, or an exogenous increase in the stock of capital.
- The endogenous growth theory does not assume that growth is the result of exogenous improvements to technology but focuses on the determinants of technological progress.
- Human capital refers to the levels of education and skills embodied in the labour force.
- Learning by doing is the process by which individuals and firms learn better ways to produce as a by-product of some other activity undertaken such as investment.
- Skills refer to the experience and education of the labour force.
- Each firm's knowledge about the production process constitutes a public good. A public good is non-excludable and non-rivalrous. A good is excludable when others cannot be excluded from its consumption as the good cannot be provided in a market for a fee. The good is non-rivalrous if one person's consumption does not subtract from another's.
- The accumulation of skills in a learning-by-doing approach to growth is a by product of another activity—an increase in the capital stock per worker.
- In learning by doing (*Ak*) endogenous growth theory the average product of capital is not subject to diminishing returns and is a constant.
- In endogenous growth theory (1) a higher savings rate raises the long run per capita income growth rate permanently, and (2) there is no tendency for convergence.
- The engine of economic growth is technological progress that occurs exogenously, or the externalities (by products) of capital accumulation in the form of skills and human capital acquisition.

NOTES

1. Elhanan Helpman, *The Mystery of Economic Growth* (Cambridge, MA: Harvard University Press, 2004).
2. Edward C. Prescott, "Robert M. Solow's Neoclassical Growth Model: An Influential Contribution to Economics," *Scandinavian Journal of Economics* 90 no.1 (1988): 7–12.
3. Robert M. Solow, *Growth Theory: An Exposition* (The Radcliffe Lectures), (Oxford: Clarendon Press, 1970), pp. 8–9.
4. In technical parlance *A* is said to be Hicks-neutral. At a given capital-labour ratio technological progress is Hicks neutral if the marginal rate of technical substitution remains unchanged. It can be shown that Hicks neutrality implies that the output elasticity of capital and labour remains constant.
5. As $P=1$, in what follows $w/P = w$ denotes the real wage.
6. The rental on capital of course is $p^K (r + \delta)$. However, since we are considering real output and real capital the prices have all been normalized to unity. Thus, in the profit function revenue is written as $pY = Y$. Depreciation will be accounted for when we consider the evolution of the capital stock in the next section. Due to this we have taken $p^K (r + \delta) = r$ as the rental on capital.
7. The first order condition is $\Delta\Pi/\Delta N = (1 - a) AK^a N^{-a} - w = 0$ which gives $w = (1 - a) A (K/N)^a$ where the right-hand side is the marginal product of labour.
8. See the Appendix I, Part A.
9. Robert M. Solow, "Technological change and the aggregate production function," *Review of Economics and Statistics,* (1957), August, pp. 312–320.
10. See Appendix I, Part B.
11. Charles I . Jones, *Introduction to Economic Growth* (New York: W.W. Norton & Co., 1998).
12. As every member of the population is a worker, the labour force participation rate is unity.
13. See Appendix I, Part C, which interprets that $(1 + n) (k_{t+1} - k_t)$ is indeed the change in capital stock per capita.
14. From (14.6), $\Delta y/y = a\ (\Delta k/k)$. Less formally, increases in *y* are related to increases in *k* as depicted in Figure 16.2 which implies that $\Delta y/y$ is proportional to $\Delta k/k$.
15. We derived this expression while exploring the curvature of the production function depicted in Figure 14.1.
16. The Golden Rule gets its nomenclature from the maxim that "Do not do unto others what you would not like others to do unto you". Translated into the current language it requires that we do not provide less to future generations than to ourselves.
17. Bosworth and Collins (2007) report the growth in total factor productivity for the period 1978 to 2004 for India to be 1.6 percent. This implies that $A_t = A_0 + 4.95t$ where, A_0 is the technology parameter for 1978. Taking this initial value to be unity, in time $t = 29$, i.e., in 2007, $A_t = 145$. For more on this, see, Barry Bosworth and Susan M. Collins, "Accounting for Growth: Comparing China and India", National Bureau of Economic Research, Working Paper no. 12943, Cambridge, MA (2007).
18. That smaller values of *k* are associated with larger values of the growth of *k* can be seen technically by dividing both sides of equation (14.17) with respect to *k*. Then, we have the expression for the growth rate of *k*. By examining the right hand side of this expression it will be obvious that a decline in *k* increases the growth rate of *k*.
19. Robert J. Barro and Xavier Sala-i-Martin, *Economic Growth* (Singapore: McGraw-Hill, 1995).
20. Robert M. Solow, "Applying Growth Theory Across Countries," *The World Bank Economic Review*, 15 no. 2 (2001): 283–288.
21. Paul Cashin and R., Sahay, "Internal migration center-state grants, and economic growth in the sates of India," IMF Staff Papers, 43 (1996): 123–171.
22. M. Govinda Rao and Kunal Sen, "Internal migration, center-state grants, and economic growth in the states of India: a comment on Cashin and Sahay," IMF Staff Papers 44 (1997): 283–288.
23. David G. Abler and Jayanta Das, "The determinants of the speed of convergence: the case of India," *Applied economics* 30 (1998): 1595–1602.
24. Robert M. Solow, "The last 50 years in growth theory and the next 10," *Oxford Review of Economic Policy*, 23, no. 1 (2007): 3–14.
25. Tim Dyson, "India's population: The future," in T. Dyson, R.H. Cassen, and L. Visaria, 21st Century India: Population, Environment and Human Development, (New Delhi: Oxford University Press, 2005).
26. The productivity in the education sector for instance as measured by the student-teacher ratio has remained virtually unchanged for decades.
27. William J. Baumol, "Macroeconomics of unbalanced growth: The anatomy of urban crisis," *American Economic Review* 57 (1967): 415–426.
28. There are many ways in which the two curves in Figure 14.10 may intersect. Here we have depicted just one such way.
29. The sudden appearance of a Protestant work ethic in the sense of Max Weber would cause people also to save more.
30. The big push approach to development is about the requirement for large doses of savings and investment to overcome existing barriers to growth. See William Arthur Lewis, "Economic Development with Unlimited Supplies of Labour," Manchester School of Economic and Social Studies, (22 May1954), pp.139–191.

31. For an interesting comparison see Thorvaldur Gylfason (2006)—"How do India and China Grow?", Challenge, 49(1), January 2006, pp. 74–89.
32. Paul M. Romer, "Increasing Returns and Long Run Growth," *Journal of Political Economy*, 94, no. 5, (1986): 1002–1037.
33. Such indices can be constructed by multiplying the years of experience on the job by the years spent in formal education for worker and then adding across workers. Thus experience and education constitute skill.
34. For airframe manufacturing see Leonard Rapping, "Learning and World War II Production Functions," *Review of Economics and Statistics* 47, (February1965): 81–86.
35. Boston Consulting Group, *Perspectives on Experience*, 1970.
36. This could be due to reverse engineering.
37. The constant of proportionality can be set equal to 1 by an appropriate choice of the units by which we measure our variables.

TEST YOURSELF

1. What is economic growth and what are the stylized facts about economic growth?
2. Decompose the sources of economic growth and state the contribution of each source to growth.
3. What is the shape of the production function in per capita terms, and why?
4. State the elements of the Solow growth model. How does the capital stock per capita in this model grow over time?
5. What is the steady state of the Solow model? Comment on its stability properties.
6. Why does an increase in the savings rate have only a temporary and no long-run effect on the growth rate? How does it impact the level of output?
7. If there is no technological progress, how do we arrive at the savings rate associated with the maximum steady-state consumption per capita?
8. Why is the Solow model an example of an exogenous growth theory? What is endogenous growth and what are its advantages over exogenous growth as an explanation for the growth of an economy?
9. What is absolute convergence and conditional convergence? Do economies converge? What accounts for this?
10. Why do poverty traps arise and what can be done to lift an economy out of such traps?

ONLINE APPLICATION

1. To study economic growth economists have the benefit of many online data sources. A particularly popular one is the Penn World Tables (PWT). Go to the home page of the Centre for International Comparisons at the University of Pennsylvania - URL: http://pwt.econ.upenn.edu/
2. Click on the icon "Penn World Table".
3. Under the Data heading go to sub section " PWT 7.0 (189 countries, 1950–2009, 2005 as base year)" and click on "data download".
4. Select the following: Under countries, select India, Taiwan, Uganda, and the United States. Under variables, select (a) Population, (b) PPP Converted Real GDP per capita (Chain series) at 2005 constant prices (RGDPCH), (c) Investment share (RGDPL). For time period, select the years 1990 to 2009. Take the output of the data and enter it into a spreadsheet.
5. Calculate the year-on-year population growth rate for each country. Then calculate the average of the population growth rate for the period 1991 to 2009. The averages you will obtain for India, Taiwan, and Uganda are 1.7 per cent, 0.7 per cent, and 3.3 per cent. For the United States, it is 1.1 per cent.
6. Calculate the average of the investment rates for these economies for the period 1991 to 2009. The averages for India, Taiwan, and Uganda are 24.9 per cent, 24.3 per cent, and 14.8 per cent respectively. For the United States, the average investment rate is 20.6 per cent.
7. Recall that in the steady state the per capita GDP of an economy is given by the formula

$$\bar{y} = A^{1/(1-a)}\left[\frac{s}{n+\delta}\right]^{a/(1-a)}$$

This informed us that countries that have a higher investment rate will tend to be richer and those with a higher population growth rate will tend to be poorer. To test whether the model has an explanatory power in understanding why some countries are richer than others, we define the per capita GDP steady-state value of a country i in terms of the steady state per capita GDP of the US as $\hat{y}_i = \bar{y}_i/\bar{y}_{US}$. Relative income per capita in the steady state will then be given by

$$\hat{y}_i = \frac{\bar{y}_i}{\bar{y}_{US}} = \frac{A_i^{1/(1-\alpha)}[s_i/(n+\delta)_i]^{\alpha/(1-\alpha)}}{A_{US}^{1/(1-\alpha)}[s_{US}/(n+\delta)_{US}]^{\alpha/(1-\alpha)}}$$

Assume that $\alpha = 1/3$, $\delta = 0.06$, and that the relative values of the technology parameter are as follows:

Country i	India	Taiwan	Uganda
A_i / A_{US} in 1991	0.2	0.7	0.1

8. Then, relative GDP per capita in the steady state for an economy may be written as

$$\hat{y}_i = \left(\frac{A_i}{A_{US}}\right)^{1/(1-\alpha)} \left\{\frac{(s_i/s_{US})}{[(n+\delta)_i/(n+\delta)_{US}]}\right\}^{\alpha/(1-\alpha)}$$

Using the data in Step 6, calculate s_i/s_{US}, the ratio of the average investment rate of a country with respect to that in the US for the time period 1991 to 2009. Using the data in Step 5, calculate $(n + 0.06)_i/(n + 0.06)_{US}$ for the time period 1991 to 2009.

9. Substitute the calculated values of s_i/s_{US} and $(n + 0.06)_i/(n + 0.06)_{US}$ along with the values in the table above for A_i/A_{US} into the formula for $\hat{y}_i$ and compute the steady state relative GDP per capita of an economy *i*.
10. Calculate the actual relative value of the GDP per capita of the three economies in the year 2008 from the data you entered on Real GDP per capita in Step 4 above. You should obtain the relative values as follows - $y_{India}/y_{US} = .0711$, $y_{Taiwan}/y_{US} = .6842$ and $y_{Uganda}/y_{US} = .0259$.
11. Compare the computed steady state relative GDP per capita $\hat{y}_i = \bar{y}_i/\bar{y}_{US}$ from Step 9 with the actual relative value of GDP per capita y_i/y_{US} computed in Step 10. You should find that the steady state predicted value in Step 9 overestimates the actual relative value by 2.3 per cent in the case of India, and underestimates the actual relative value by 2.8 per cent and 0.3 per cent in the case of Taiwan and Uganda, respectively.
12. Given the small sample size, the result you obtained in Step 10 indicates that the Solow model is fairly good at explaining the distribution of per capita incomes across countries. Explain how the relative incomes across countries will vary as A_i/A_{US} changes—as technology in an economy *i* improves—and as the share of capital in income α increases.

Appendix 14.1 Derivations of Various Equations of the Chapter

Part A

Derivation associated with Eq. (14.3):

Take the logarithm of the production function $Y = AK^{a}N^{1-a}$:

$$\log Y = \log A + a\log K + (1 - a)\log N$$

Differentiating,
$$\frac{\Delta Y}{Y} = \frac{\Delta A}{A} + a\frac{\Delta K}{K} + (1 - a)\frac{\Delta N}{N}$$

or, alternatively,
$$\frac{\Delta Y}{Y} = \frac{\Delta A}{A} + a\frac{\Delta K}{K} + (1 - a)\frac{\Delta N}{N}$$

Part B

Derivation associated with Eq. (14.5):

Per capita output is Y/N. The growth rate of per capita output, then, is the percentage change in Y/N, or,

$$\frac{\Delta(Y/N)}{Y/N} = \frac{\Delta Y}{Y} - \frac{\Delta N}{N}$$

or the growth rate of per capita output is the growth rate of output less the growth rate of the labour force.

Similarly, $\left(\frac{\Delta K}{K} - \frac{\Delta N}{N}\right) = \frac{\Delta(K/N)}{K/N}$, or the growth rate of the capital-labour ratio.

Part C

Expression for change in capital stock per capita in Eq. (14.12):

The change in the capital stock per capita is given by the expression:

$$\begin{aligned}
\Delta k = \Delta\left(\frac{K}{N}\right) &= \frac{N\Delta K - K\Delta N}{N^2}\\
&= \frac{K}{N}\left(\frac{\Delta K}{K} - \frac{\Delta N}{N}\right)\\
&= \frac{K_t}{N_t}\left(\frac{K_{t+1} - K_t}{K_t} - \frac{N_{t+1} - N_t}{N_t}\right)\\
&= \frac{K_t}{N_t}\left(\frac{K_{t+1}}{K_t} - 1 - \frac{N_{t+1}}{N_t} + 1\right)\\
&= \frac{K_t}{N_t}\left(\frac{K_{t+1}}{K_t} - \frac{N_{t+1}}{N_t}\right)\\
&= \frac{K_{t+1}}{N_t} - \frac{K_t}{N_t}\frac{N_{t+1}}{N_t}\\
&= \frac{K_{t+1}}{N_{t+1}}\frac{N_{t+1}}{N_t} - \frac{K_t}{N_t}\frac{N_{t+1}}{N_t}\\
&= \frac{N_{t+1}}{N_t}\left(\frac{K_{t+1}}{N_{t+1}} - \frac{K_t}{N_t}\right)\\
&= (1 + n)(k_{t+1} - k_t)
\end{aligned}$$

Hence, the left-hand side of Eq. (14.12) is the change in the capital stock per capita.

15

Recent Developments in Macroeconomics

CRITICAL QUESTIONS

- *What is a rational expectation and what is its implication for macroeconomic outcomes under different schools of macroeconomic thought?*
- *With rational expectations, what is the outcome for an economy when a policy is unanticipated and when it is anticipated?*
- *How does aggregate supply differ when government spends on consumption as opposed to investment?*
- *When does public investment expenditure crowd out and crowd in private investment expenditure?*
- *Under what conditions is an increased fiscal deficit, that finances public investment expenditure, sustainable?*
- *What were the origins of the global financial crisis that began in 2007?*
- *What are the types of risk that get magnified in the goods and financial markets when a financial crisis occurs?*
- *How does a financial crisis that originated abroad affect another economy that participates in global trade?*
- *What sort of policies can a small open economy initiate to offset the impact of a financial crisis abroad?*

15.1 Rational Expectations and Macroeconomic Policy

When studying how aggregate demand and supply determine the aggregate output and income of the economy, we learned that a dominant view of the economy was that workers faced imperfections in the information they had in hand when making decisions about the supply of labour. Workers formed an expectation of the price level so as to decide on how much labour to supply at given nominal wages. If the actual and expected prices differed, workers' perceptions of their real wage earnings would be incorrect, and in the short run the output of the economy would deviate from the natural rate of output and employment. The process by which people form expectations that we considered is known as the adaptive expectations process. In the process of forming expectations adaptively, individual expectations are based on information from the past up to the present. However, recent developments in economic theory suggest that a more general theory of expectations formation than the adaptive expectations hypothesis, such as the theory of rational expectations, is more relevant to individual decisions. A rational expectation, as we shall see, takes into account not only all past information, but also includes current information such as news about the central bank's intention of changing its monetary stance. A rational expectation also takes into account the ways of the functioning of the economy.

Yet another major debate in macroeconomics concerns the effect of budget deficits. There are those who argue that a government budget deficit essentially expands the economy, which brings in tax revenues that eventually could pay for the initial deficit that is generated. We saw in Chapter XII that this will not occur if the interest rate on the government debt is larger than the growth rate of the aggregate income of the economy—in such an instance the deficit will actually keep on increasing and the government would have to increase taxes to pay off the debt. A deficit, then, implies substituting taxation today for taxation tomorrow. However, upto now we have ignored the fact that the composition of government expenditure has an important implication in all this. In Section 15.2, we segregate government expenditure into two components—government consumption expenditure and government investment expenditure. We then analyse how the composition of government expenditure has implications for the debate regarding the effect of government budget deficits on the aggregate output and income of an economy.

Finally, this chapter closes with an analysis of the recent financial crisis, that was rated as the worst setback for the world economy since the Great Depression. The financial crisis saw the advent of a blame game, whereby macroeconomists were criticized for having an inadequate understanding of such an event, as well as for not having a coherent framework with which to deal with the crisis and its spillover effects from the financial markets to the rest of the economy. In the final section of the chapter, we trace the roots of the crisis and show how it magnified the risks that financial intermediaries and individuals faced as a consequence. We then investigate how the standard macroeconomic model can help us understand a financial crisis when we incorporate the effect of risk on the decisions made in the goods and financial markets of the economy. The policy responses that enable an economy to offset the impact of a financial crisis are then considered in the context of an economy that is part of the global trade and financial system. This chapter, then, is a miscellany of recent developments in macroeconomic theory and policy.

The IS–LM model and the AD–AS model provide us with tools to enable us to understand how macroeconomic policy—fiscal and monetary—can be used to deal with cyclical fluctuations experienced by an economy. Friedman and Phelps revolutionized modern macroeconomics by clarifying the role that the expectations formation process plays in macroeconomic outcomes. It was Lucas[1] who drew the attention of economists to the importance of expectations by the public regarding policies that will be implemented and the consequence of this on the effectiveness of those policies. Lucas pointed out the importance of expectations to the outcome of a discretionary monetary or fiscal policy. In doing so, he used the theory of rational expectations.

The rational expectations approach was initially proposed by John F. Muth,[2] who argued that rational agents must use all the relevant past and current information available at the time at which they form their expectations—a property known as efficiency. Second, when forming expectations at a point in time over successive time horizons, they must utilize all the information available at that time in a logically consistent manner—the consistency property of rational expectations. This requires an individual to draw on an understanding of the factors that affect the macroeconomic variable under consideration. For example, suppose you make a forecast of inflation using information about inflation rates in the recent past. You then find out that the central bank intends to substantially increase the rate of growth of the money stock. The rational response to this finding would be to use your understanding of how an increase in the growth rate of the money supply influences the inflation rate. You would then update your forecast of inflation on the basis of this understanding of how the economy works. A rational expectation, unlike an adaptive expectation, takes into account past and current information as well as an understanding of the functioning of the economy.

Rational expectations theorists also argue, since all available information is efficiently utilized, individuals do not systematically under estimate or overestimate the actual future value of a variable—the unbiasedness property. The assertion is that individuals are correct on average, and that a rational forecast can never be completely accurate because of the occurrence of random events that influence outcomes. For instance, suppose an individual forms a forecast for inflation, but subsequently there is a drought that affects food prices and inflation. Since there was no way of ascertaining beforehand whether a drought would occur, the forecast for inflation is rational. Only if there was a report from the meteorological department about the occurrence of drought at the time of making the forecast (and the individual did not take this information into account), would the expectation no longer be rational.

When forming a rational expectation, then, individuals operate with all the available information and also a knowledge of the relevant theory that indicates how the variable being forecast evolves. Let x_t^{ratex} stand for the rationally expected value of a variable, x. A relevant theory T explains the non-random determination of the variable x_t^{T} in terms of the past and current values of the various other variables that affect the determination of this variable. For instance, suppose the relevant theory of inflation is the quantity theory approach to inflation. Inflation is then determined by the growth of the nominal money supply. The rationally expected value, x_t^{ratex}, is assumed to be determined by the value x_t^{T} predicted by the relevant theory T, which implies:

$$x_t^{\text{ratex}} = x_t^{\text{T}}$$

The actual value of the variable x can differ from the prediction by the relevant theory T by an error that is random and unrelated to the available information—the unbiasedness assumption of rational expectations. Thus,

$$x_t = x_t^{\mathrm{T}} + u_t$$

where u_t is a random variable. Variable u_t, on average, takes the value of zero[3], implying that on average the relevant theory gives a correct estimate of the variable and it is only the existence of random events that causes deviations from the predicted value. On average, then, $x_t^{\text{ratex}} = x_t^{\mathrm{T}}$ and $x_t = x_t^{\mathrm{T}} + u_t$ together imply that we can expect the value of an economic variable to be equal to that predicted by the relevant theory. The rational expectation of the variable is then the best forecast of that variable, using all the available information in a systematic manner as is worked out by a relevant theory.

What is a relevant theory for the purpose of making predictions about a variable? There are disputes among economists regarding this. So, it is wise to apply the rational expectations approach across approaches to macroeconomics in order to assess its implications. We do this for two classes of macroeconomic models—the New Classical and the New Keynesian models. The New Classical model is the Friedman–Phelps–Lucas model we saw earlier in Chapter VII. In this model wages and prices are completely flexible with regard to expected prices—an increase in the expected price, as we saw, results in this model in a rise in wages and prices as workers attempt to keep their expected real wage from declining. The short-run aggregate supply curve AS($p \neq p^e$) shifts upwards to the left with a rise in the expected price. If price expectations are realized, then the relevant aggregate supply curve results in the natural rate of output as given by the vertical aggregate supply curve AS($p = p^e$). In the new Keynesian model by contrast there is a rigidity to wages and prices, which are not completely flexible. The wage rigidity is due to the fact that wage setting across an economy is not synchronized and as workers in different sectors of the economy set wages at different points in time, wage contracts are staggered and wages adjust slowly to the natural rate of employment and output. This natural rate in the New Keynesian model is the result of a labour market outcome where firms set wages to deter shirking behaviour by workers. An increase in expected prices in the New Keynesian model may not lead quickly to a complete adjustment of wages and prices.

15.1.1 New Classical Model and Rational Expectations

Let us take the case of the New Classical approach first. In Figure 15.1 the economy is initially in equilibrium at point A. The aggregate demand curve AD_0 and aggregate supply curve $\mathrm{AS}_0(p_0^e = p_0)$ intersect at point A where the price expectations are realized ($p_0^e = p_0$) and aggregate output is at the natural rate as depicted by the vertical natural rate of output curve AS($p \neq p^e$).

Suppose the government decides unexpectedly to increase aggregate demand by increasing the money stock or government spending, or by a reduction in taxes that shifts the aggregate demand curve to the right to AD_1. This change in policy is unanticipated by workers who retain their perception of the expected price level to be p_0^e and the rise in the nominal wage they experience is attributed to the increased demand for labour due to the increase in aggregate demand. In response to the rise in the nominal wage, workers increase their supply of labour services along $\mathrm{AS}_0(p_0^e \neq p_0)$ and firms produce more output. Aggregate output increases above the natural rate of output to Y_1 and the realized price level rises to p_1. As people begin to realize that the

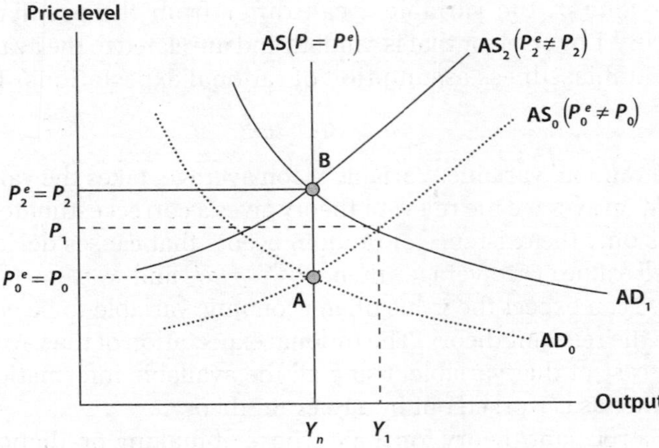

› Figure 15.1
The New Classical Outcome. The economy is at the natural rate of output at point A. An unanticipated expansionary policy shifts the AD_0 curve to AD_1, and output to Y_1 temporarily. On realizing that the expected price does not materialize, agents revise their expectations and the economic equilibrium is at point B, back at the natural rate of output. If the expansionary policy is anticipated, the economy shifts directly from point A to point B with no change in output.

government has initiated an expansionary policy and that the realized price p_1 is not the expected price, they will begin to adjust their policy anticipations and increase their expectation of the price level. The aggregate supply schedule $AS_0(p_0^e \neq p_0)$ will shift leftwards till the economy retains the natural rate of output and employment given by Y_n. This occurs when the $AS_2(p_2^e \neq p_2)$ schedule intersects the AD_1 and natural rate of output curves at a price level of p_2. However, the immediate impact of the unanticipated expansionary policy, since individuals did not predict its occurrence and thereby kept price expectations unchanged, is an increase in the real output of the economy.

In contrast to the case of an unanticipated policy change, let us take the situation where a policy change is anticipated. This may occur because the government, through the finance minister, has been announcing that it plans to increase public expenditure and introduces a bill to increase spending in Parliament. Alternatively, the central bank indicates that it plans a particular growth rate for the money stock. As expectations are rational, individuals recognize that an expansionary policy will shift the aggregate demand curve to the right and will then expect the price level to rise to p_2. The increase in the price will lead them to expect a decline in real wages, and to offset this, they revise their supply of labour services in accordance with an expected price level of $p^e = p_2$. The aggregate supply schedule will then shift leftwards to $AS_2(p_2^e \neq p_2)$. The economy then will move to point B in Figure 15.1. At point B, real output is unchanged at the natural rate, but the price level is higher at p_2.

When policy actions are anticipated or expected, there is no effect on output and they result merely in a higher price level. This is due to the way in which rational expectations are formed. The relevant theory indicates that when the aggregate demand curve is anticipated to shift rightwards to AD_1, the expected price p_0^e will not be realized. Prices are, as expected, only at $p_2 = p_2^e$, where the expected aggregate demand of the economy AD_1 intersects the vertical natural rate of output $AS(p = p^e)$ curve. The current expected price level p_0^e, then, does not equal the expected price level p_2^e that is predicted by the theory, and this amounts to a breach or failure of the rationality of expectations. It is only when the relevant supply of labour services is such that the aggregate supply of output is given by $AS_2(p = p_2{}^e)$, that expectations are rational. This is because then, the expected price equals the price predicted by the theory. In the case of an anticipated expansionary policy, then, rational expectations imply that output will always be at the natural rate of output. This proposition, that an anticipated policy has no effect on output, is called the POLICY INEFFECTIVENESS PROPOSITION. It states that when macroeconomic policy actions are foreseeable, then policy has no effect on real variables such as employment and output, and can lead only to changes in nominal variables such as the price level. It is only when policy actions are unsystematic or unpredictable, in the sense that individuals are unable to anticipate such policies, that there are impacts on output and employment.

› The **policy ineffectiveness proposition** is a conclusion of the New Classical approach to macroeconomics that anticipated or expected policy has no effect on the output of the economy.

15.1.2 New Keynesian Model and Rational Expectations

The New Keynesians do not accept complete flexibility of wages and prices. Figure 15.2 depicts the New Keynesian model. In the short run, wages are sticky because firms do not change wages often as that influences work effort by the labour force. Even though there may be rampant unemployment, firms may not reduce wages as they are set for a predetermined period of time with the aim of influencing worker performance on the job. The wages get adjusted over time as unemployment changes, and with changed current expectations regarding wage settlements by the group of workers who contract over wages in a subsequent period after their wage contract expires. As wage setting is not synchronized, deviations from the natural rate of output and employment are possible in the short run. In the long run, however, the economy settles on the vertical AS curve at the natural rate of output Y^*.

Suppose the economy is initially at point A, with the aggregate demand curve intersecting the short-run aggregate supply curve at the natural rate of output Y^*. Let the price level be p_0. An expansionary policy shifts the aggregate demand curve to AD_1. If this change in policy was not anticipated in the short run, the aggregate supply curve remains unchanged. This is because the cohort of workers who are renegotiating their wage contracts at the instant before the policy change had no information about this change in policy and did not factor it into their wage negotiations. Aggregate output increases to Y_1 and the price level increases to p_1.

What if the expansionary policy resulting in the shifting of the aggregate demand curve to AD_1 is anticipated? When the policy is anticipated and rational expectations prevail, then individuals realize that output is going to rise as well as prices. This will cause the real wage to fall and increase the demand for labour, leading to a reduction in unemployment (see Figure 10.2). As the labour market tightens, shirking increases with reduced unemployment, and firms respond to

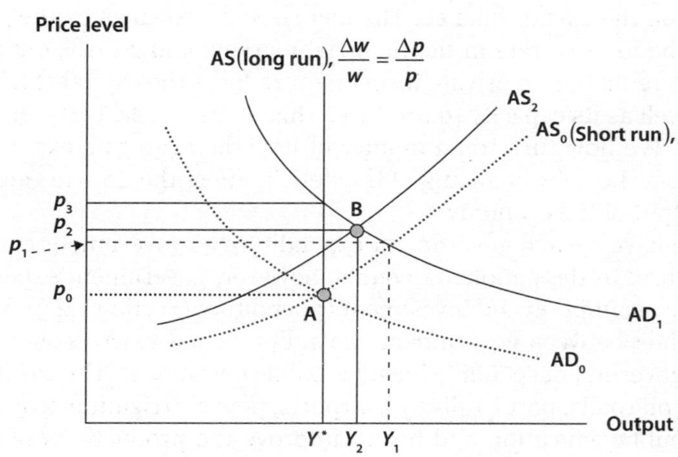

› **Figure 15.2**
The New Keynesian Outcome. An unanticipated expansionary policy increases aggregate demand to AD_1 and output and price to Y_1 and P_1. If the policy change is anticipated, staggered wage setting results in a fraction of firms changing wages and output, and prices rise to Y_2 and P_2. Unlike the New Classical outcome, here anticipated policy changes can influence the course of the economy in the short run.

this by raising wages so as to influence worker performance. However, because only a fraction of firms change wages each period, the economy does not revert to the natural rate of output as was the case in the New Classical set-up. With staggered wage setting, the short-run aggregate supply curve shifts leftwards to AS_2. The equilibrium of the economy is located at point B with output at Y_2, which is above the natural rate. The price level has risen to p_2.

› For the **New Keynesians** even when a policy is anticipated, output can deviate from the natural rate in the short run.

Unlike the New Classical case, if a policy is expected in the NEW KEYNESIAN CASE it does have an effect on aggregate real output in the short run. In the long run, as more firms adjust their wages, the economy will revert to the natural rate of output and a higher price level of p_3. In the New Keynesian set-up, policy-makers can influence the course of the economy even when it is anticipated by agents in the economy. For both approaches to macroeconomics, however, the lesson is that the effectiveness of stabilization policy that attempts to influence the course of the economy is dependent on the extent to which agents in the economy are able to assess the intentions of policymakers and predict the direction of future macroeconomic policy.

15.2 Deficits and the Composition of Government Spending

We have been considering the sustainability of deficits in the economy without considering the link between the expenditures the deficit finances, and the growth of the economy. Sustainability analysis informs us that if the rate of interest exceeds the growth rate of output, the debt will keep growing and the government will eventually face bankruptcy. Even when the rate of interest on the debt is lower than the growth rate of the economy, the debt will eventually stabilize at some constant value but never be repaid. Thus, a government must, over longer time horizons, generate primary budgetary surpluses to offset the debt issued to finance a deficit. Economists suggest that even though governments may run deficits to influence the aggregate expenditures in the economy in periods of time when there is capacity underutilization, governments must take care to generate budgetary surpluses in other periods. In times of recession, deficit financing helps to boost aggregate demand and reduce unemployment when agents respond slowly to information that enables them to update expectations. It also reduces unemployment when wages or prices are rigid. So far, however, the impact of such fiscal policy has only been considered in terms of its impact on the cost of finance. The increased borrowings by the government raises the interest rate in the financial markets and crowds out private investment. A reduction in private investment reduces the capital stock of the economy as well as its capacity to produce. This, in turn, affects the growth of the economy. We now turn to an inquiry of how the aggregate expenditures that result from the debt financing of the deficit, affect the growth rate of the aggregate output of the economy.

So far we have treated government expenditure as government consumption expenditure. In the national accounts, however, government expenditure is the sum of consumption and investment expenditure (Section 1.2.3). We now examine the link between government expenditures and macroeconomic outcomes when government spending includes public investment. The government expenditures on roads, ports, railways, airports, power, irrigation projects and canals, and public education and health improve the productivity of private factors of production. This increase in productivity occurs when, for instance, a reduction in power shortages improves the capacity of a firm to produce. Similarly, the availability of good roads reduces the time taken to transport goods. It also improves the ability to make delivery to customers in a timely manner, which again increases the productivity of business enterprises. When the productivity of business improves due to such public investments, business enterprises are able to produce more output per unit of input. This results in an upward shift of the production function. In turn, this results in a shift outwards of the aggregate supply curve.

In the New Classical set-up (the conclusions that follow in this section are also applicable to the New Keynesian approach), for instance, an improvement in productivity implies an increase in output per unit of input, and the production function shifts outwards from Y to Y_2 in Figure 15.3. At the same time, since this results in an increase in the marginal productivity of labour, the demand for labour curve shifts rightwards to $p_0MP_N^2$. Tracing out the relationship between price and output, we see that the AS $(p = p^e)$ curve has shifted rightwards to $AS_2(p = p^e)$ and the short-run aggregate supply curve has also shifted right to $AS_2(p_0^e \neq p_0)$ in Figure 15.3.

On the demand side, the increase in public expenditure is represented in the goods and financial markets by a rightward shift of the IS curve to IS_1. In Section 8.5.1, we saw how an increase in government spending induces a rise in the interest rate and crowds out the interest-sensitive components of private expenditures—investment and consumption. The extent of crowding out is given in Figure 15.4, panel A by the distance AB when the interest rate rises from i_0 to i_1 due to the increase in government expenditures.

The rightward shift of the IS curve also shifts the aggregate demand curve to the right as aggregate expenditure in the economy has increased (depicted as the shift of AD to AD_1 in Figure 15.4, panel B). This is the standard way in which the impact of the increase in government expenditures—that is financed by borrowing—is analysed. Suppose, however, as is the case, that government expenditures are of two types—government consumption

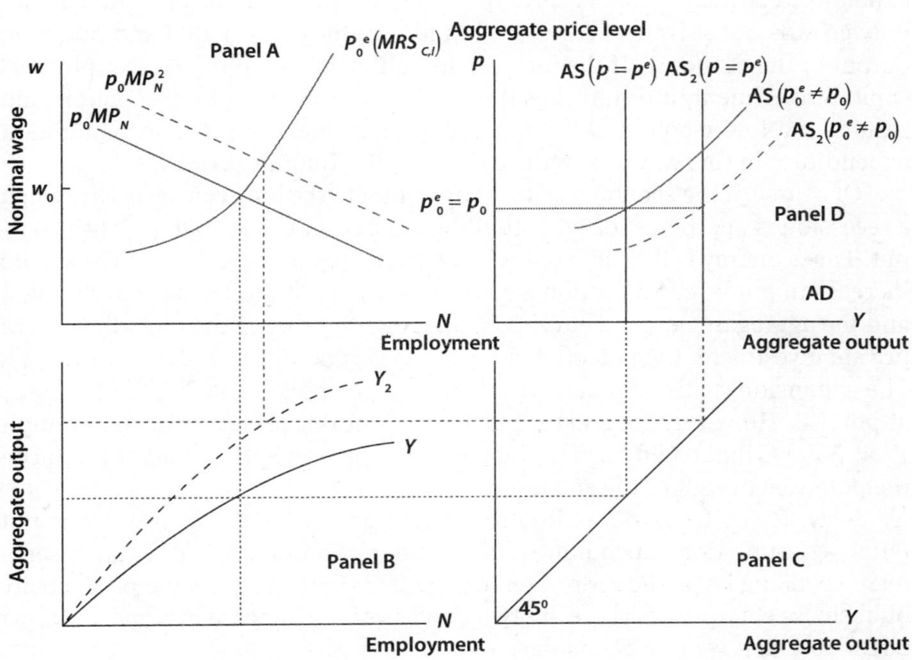

› **Figure 15.3**
Public Investment and Productivity. When public investment expenditure increases the productivity of private business, the production function shifts up from Y to Y_2 and the aggregate supply curve shifts outwards from AS to AS_2.

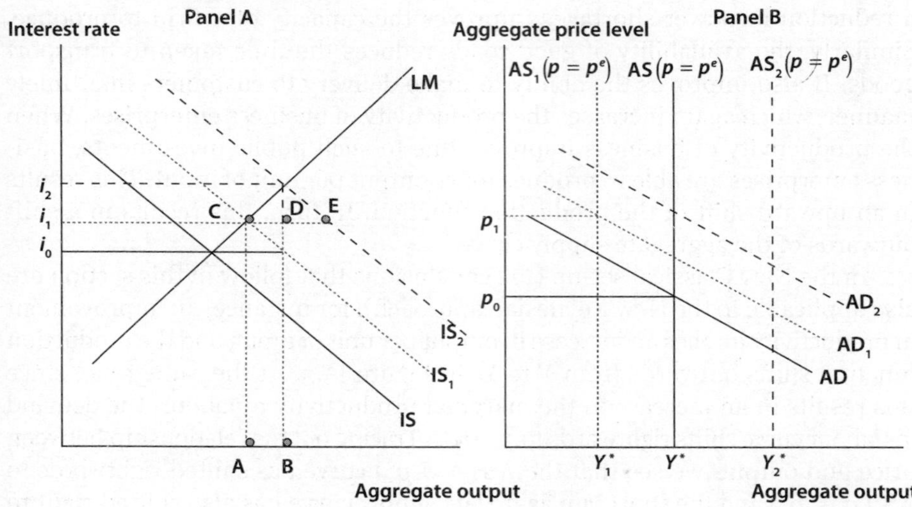

› **Figure 15.4**
Impact of Composition of Public Expenditure and Economy.
An increase in government expenditure shifts the IS curve to IS_1 and crowds out private expenditures by the amount AB. The decline in private capital stock diminishes the potential output of the economy, and the aggregate supply curve shifts leftwards to AS_1. If the government expenditure is investment expenditure, then it crowds in private investment and further shifts the IS curve to the right) (from IS_1 to IS_2) and the aggregate demand curve from AD_1 to AD_2. The potential output of the economy shifts to the right to AS_2 if the decline in private investment is less than the increase in public investment when both types of investment have equal marginal productivities, and if the productivity of public investment is sufficiently larger than that of private investment even when private investment declines by a larger amount than the increase in public investment.

expenditure (G^C) and government expenditure on capital formation (G^I). Then,

$$G = G^C + G^I$$

If all of the increased government expenditure is on consumption $G = G^C$, then there is no increase in public investment. However, there is a decline in private investment due to crowding out, and a corresponding decline in the private capital stock of the economy. A decline in the stock of capital for a given amount of labour reduces the potential output that can be produced by that labour. It also reduces the marginal productivity of labour and shifts the production function inwards. (Draw a diagram similar to Figure 15.3 to depict this outcome). The potential output of the economy then shifts leftwards to $AS_1(p = p^e)$, as depicted in Figure 15.4, panel B. The aggregate price level has increased to p_1 and output has declined from the level it was at prior to the increase in public consumption expenditure to Y_1^*. Thus, public consumption expenditure, which is financed by borrowings and a rise in the fiscal deficit, not only crowds out private investment but also reduces the actual and potential output of the economy. If the increase in public debt results in lesser physical capital investment, it diminishes the productive capacity of the economy and results in a lower potential GDP. A deficit that finances public consumption expenditure in this way may reduce the rate of economic growth.

Of course, if the economy is not equilibrium in the long run, as occurs when a recession is on, then short-run equilibrium output is less than potential output. The economy is then at a point like A in the Figure 15.5. A deficit-financed increase in public consumption expenditure will shift the IS curve to the right and the aggregate demand curve to AD_1. However, due to the crowding out of private investment, the potential output of the economy declines from Y_0^* to Y_1^*. The expansionary fiscal policy will then be successful in placing the economy at point B. However, the real output Y_1^* at point B is less than the real output Y_0^* at point C that could have been attained if the fiscal policy had not reduced the potential output of the economy.

› **Public investment expenditure** affects the economy on both the demand and the supply sides: (1) It increases the productivity of private factors of production and shifts the aggregate supply curve to the right. (2) When it is complementary to private investment, it crowds it in and shifts the IS and AD curves to the right.

Now, let us focus on a situation where government expenditure is not purely consumption expenditures. Let some portion of the additional government spending be public investment expenditure that enhances the productivity of business enterprises. There are two impacts of the increase in PUBLIC INVESTMENT EXPENDITURE that we must consider:

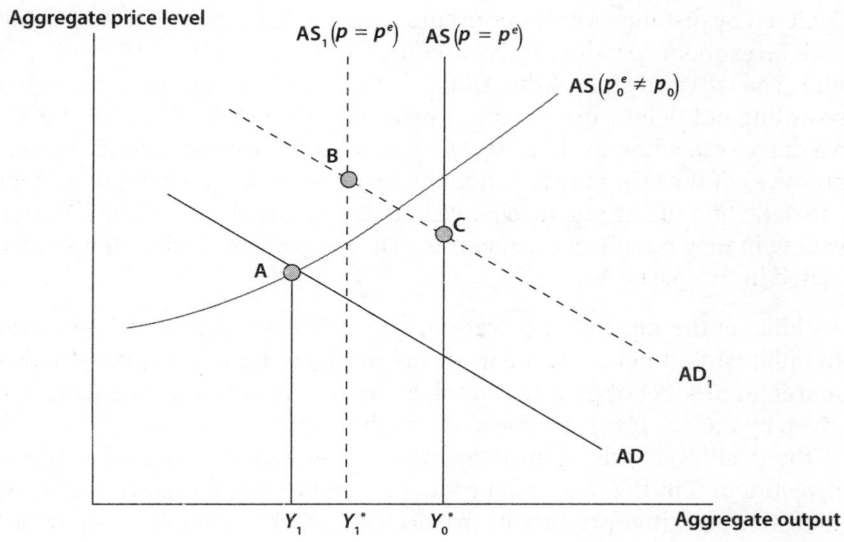

› **Figure 15.5**
Deficit Finance in a Recession. In a recession denoted by point A, short-run equilibrium output Y_1 is less than potential output Y_0*. A deficit-financed increase in government consumption expenditure shifts the AD curve to the right to AD_1. However, crowding out reduces potential output to Y_1*, placing the economy at point B rather than C.

1. On the supply side, the increase in public investment improves the productivity of business enterprises and increases the potential output of the economy with a rightward shift of the AS ($p = p^e$) curve to $AS_2(p = p^e)$ in Figure 15.4, panel B.
2. On the demand side, the deficit-financed increase in public expenditure shifts the IS curve rightward to IS_1 as in Figure 15.4, panel A. The aggregate demand curve corresponding to IS_1 is the shifted to the right AD_1 curve in Figure 15.4, panel B.

Some private investment and consumption expenditure given by distance AB has been crowded out due to the rise in the interest rate resulting from this expansionary fiscal policy, as in the case of pure government consumption expenditure. The reduction in the stock of private capital, as private investment is adversely affected, reduces the potential capacity of the output of the economy and will shift the $AS_2(p = p^e)$ curve leftwards in Figure 15.4, panel B. This is because public investment has crowded out and substituted some private investment through raising the cost of capital.

If, however, public investment is complementary to private investment, then the increase in public investment by virtue of increasing the productivity of private firms induces them to increase their investment expenditure. As reported in Chapter 4, the empirical evidence for India is that public investment is complementary to and crowds in private investment. An increase in productivity also increases the marginal product of capital, raises the value of Tobin's marginal Q, and induces greater private investment. This will cause the IS curve to shift further to the right.

Let us suppose that the increase in productivity and the increase in the wage rate and incomes from the increased public investment induces an increase in interest-sensitive private expenditures—as given by the distance CE that shifts the IS_1 curve to IS_2 in Figure 15.4, panel A. The interest rate rises further to i_2, and again DE of interest-sensitive private expenditures are crowded out. Private investment and consumption expenditure will increase by the amount CD due to the inducement effect of the increased public investment expenditures in Figure 15.4, panel A. We have shown the secondary shift of the IS_1 curve to IS_2, which results in the crowding in of interest-sensitive expenditures by CD to be exactly equal to the crowding out of these expenditures as depicted by distance AB. If this occurs then, in all, there will be no decline in private investment spending and consequently no decline in the stock of private capital. The leftward shift of the $AS_2(p = p^e)$ curve in Figure 15.4, panel B due to crowding out will be exactly offset by a rightward shift of the AS_2 $(p = p^e)$ curve due to crowding in. This $AS_2(p = p^e)$ position (of the potential capacity to produce) of the economy is due to the increase in the stock of public capital due to deficit financing and no change in the stock of private capital. Of course, crowding in may not offset CROWDING OUT. The general conclusion, however, can be stated in two parts:

› When the marginal productivity of public and private capital is equal, an increase in public investment expenditure, which is larger than the offsetting private expenditures that are **crowded out**, increases output. Second, if the marginal productivity of public capital accumulation expenditure is sufficiently larger than the productivity of the private capital stock it crowds out, aggregate output increases. In both such situations, deficit financing has beneficial impacts on the economy.

1. As long as the decline in private investment is smaller than the increase in public investment and the marginal product of public capital equals the marginal product of private capital, the potential output of the economy as given by the $AS(p = p^e)$ curve shifts to the right.
2. If the decline in private investment is larger than the increase in public investment, but the marginal product of public capital is sufficiently larger than the marginal product of private capital, the potential output of the economy, as given by the $AS(p = p^e)$ curve, still shifts to the right.

With the crowding in that shifts the IS_1 curve to IS_2 in Figure 15.4, panel A, the aggregate demand curve is shifted to AD_2 in Figure 15.4, panel B. The long-run equilibrium of the economy will then be at the level of output given by Y_2^* when public investment expenditure more than offsets the decline in private interest-sensitive expenditures or the marginal productivity of public capital is sufficiently larger than that of the private capital stock.

The composition of government expenditures is, therefore, important to the macroeconomic outcome of a deficit-financed increase in public expenditure. Debt-financed government expenditure is not necessarily a burden on the economy in the sense of crowding out private investment and reducing the potential output-producing capacity of the economy. To the extent that the financing of the deficit is for public investment expenditure, there are two avenues through which this impacts favourably on the economy. First, the increase in public investment improves the productivity of business enterprises and induces or crowds in private investment spending that offsets some of the crowing out caused by the deficit financing. Second, the increased public investment adds to the public capital stock and this, independently of the effect on private investment, enlarges the potential output of the economy. A government may then run a deficit and not harm long-run economic performance if it devotes a sufficiently large part of its expenditure to public investment and infrastructure spending.

One of the perspectives of modern macroeconomics—the Ricardian equivalence proposition—states that fiscal deficits do not matter because agents with perfect foresight would realize that tax liabilities would be higher in the future to repay the debt the government incurs currently when it runs a deficit. Agents plan for the future tax liability by increasing savings today, and this increase in private savings exactly offsets the decline in public savings stemming from the deficit, leaving total savings and investment unchanged (see Section 8.7). However, if agents have perfect foresight and are rational, then they would predict that when the deficit financing is devoted to public investment expenditures, the productivity of the economy will improve and the output and income of the economy will be greater in the future when the debt is to be retired. Then, even though more taxes will be required to repay the debt in future, the increase in productivity will result in an increase in the output of the economy. This, at an unchanged tax rate, will generate revenues to meet some of the higher tax liability. Agents with perfect foresight, then, do not need to increase private saving to the extent of the increase in public expenditure—a conclusion that reduces the sting of the Ricardian equivalence proposition. It is important, then, in a discussion of the impact of fiscal policy on the economy, to specify the composition of public expenditure. The conclusion that deficit financing is associated with crowding out is tempered to the extent that public expenditure is public investment expenditure that improves the productivity and enhances the output of the economy.

15.3 Financial Crises

› A **financial crisis** is a major disruption in financial markets, characterized by sharp declines in asset prices and the failure of financial as well as non-financial firms.

› A **hedge fund** is an aggressively managed portfolio of investments that uses advanced investment strategies (such as leveraged long, short, and derivative positions) with the goal of generating high returns. Even though hedging refers to the practice of attempting to reduce risk, hedge funds are set up to maximize the return on investment, and in fact, carry more risk than the overall market.

› A **structured credit** product is derived from the cash flows of underlying assets and is tailored to have particular risk characteristics that appeal to investors with differing preferences.

The FINANCIAL CRISIS that began in 2007 was the most serious setback experienced by the world economy since the Great Depression. The crisis started in July 2007 with the collapse of two Bear Stearns HEDGE FUNDS, the Bear Stearns High-Grade STRUCTURED CREDIT FUND and the Bear Stearns High-Grade Structured Credit Enhanced Leveraged Fund. Many factors contributed to the financial crisis. Foremost amongst them were global macroeconomic imbalances, poor risk management practices, and weak financial regulations and supervision. Since the mid-1990s, the world economy has witnessed major macroeconomic imbalances. The USA, the UK, the Mediterranean countries—including Portugal, Spain, Italy, Greece, and Turkey, and Central and East European countries run large current account deficits. On the other hand, Germany, the oil exporting countries, as well as various Asian countries such as China, Japan, South Korea, Taiwan, and Malaysia run surpluses. The current account surplus in emerging and developing economies, for instance, rose from USD 93.3 billion in 2001 to a substantial USD 741.5 billion in 2007. The surplus countries were the source of capital flows to the deficit countries, especially the USA, which financed their external deficits with the aid of these capital flows. Even though the UK, Italy, Spain, Australia, and France were net borrowers in the five years preceding the crisis, it was the USA that was primarily the recipient of the external lending by countries with external surpluses. Countries with substantial current account surpluses invested their foreign exchange in the USA government and agency securities, which raised the price of these assets and resulted in their yields declining to historical lows. The low-yield environment was an impetus to the financial industry to search for increased returns on investments by intensifying risk-taking. Low interest rates spurred mortgaged lenders to follow lax standards in approving mortgages and the subprime mortgage market saw increased volumes of business.

› A borrower who is turned away from traditional lending sources because of her low credit rating, or lack of strong credit history, or other factors that suggest she has a reasonable chance of defaulting on debt repayments is called a **subprime borrower**. Loans given to such borrowers typically do not follow standard norms for granting loans, such as underwriting, complete income documentation, etc.

SUBPRIME LOANS do not meet prime underwriting guidelines, such as full documentation and certain income and credit score thresholds. The pressure to rake in high returns increased the appetite for risk and non-prime loans, that were 10 per cent of outstanding mortgages in 2001, accounted for 34 per cent of all mortgage originations during 2006.[4] With widespread decline in underwriting standards, low interest rates, and low lending oversight by investors, the demand for housing soared in the USA and a boom in house construction followed. House prices increased dramatically with the increased demand for housing. However, by mid-2006 they began to decline as housing inventory started to exceed demand. At that point, house prices began to decline and those who had taken mortgages when the prices were high found that their properties were now worth less than what they owed on their mortgages. Foreclosures and delinquencies increased primarily in the non-prime market. Those investors who had financed these mortgages found that these mortgage securities they were holding had now declined in value and they faced the prospect of large financial losses as repayments on mortgages declined to a trickle. Before long, widespread uncertainty and loss of confidence made investors wary of the risks associated with mortgage securities, so that they were no longer traded. Investors, thus, retreated to the SAFETY OF US TREASURY SECURITIES.

› When there is uncertainty in financial markets, investors move their capital away from riskier investments towards safe investment vehicles such as government securities. This is referred to as a flight to safety or a flight to quality.

As financial losses continued to increase, investor uncertainty intensified during 2008. The crisis reached a peak in September 2008 when the US Federal Housing Finance Agency decided to put two government- sponsored enterprises, the Federal National Mortgage Association (Fannie Mae) and the Federal Home Loan Mortgage Corporation (Freddie Mac) into government conservatorship. The US Federal Reserve provided a two-year $85 billion emergency loan to an insurer of these mortgage securities, American International Group (AIG), when the investment bank Lehman Brothers filed for bankruptcy. After the collapse of Lehman Brothers, lending among banks and other financial institutions declined sharply and the risk premium on lending shot up to unprecedented levels. The difference between the three-month US Treasury bill yield and LIBOR is known as the Treasury bill–Eurodollar spread, or the TED spread. The TED spread is an indicator of perceived credit risk in the wholesale credit market as investors flee to the safety of short-term US Treasury bills. The TED spread also reflects liquidity risk as banks may prefer keeping any extra cash in treasuries rather than lending them three months unsecured. The TED spread reached a record high of 463 basis points on 10 October 2008. Historically, the spread has been around 30 to 35 basis points. It was only after a massive injection of liquidity into the financial system by central banks, that this exceedingly high spread began to decline.

15.3.1 Financial Intermediation and Risk

Banks and financial institutions face a number of risks in their day-to-day operations. Primarily, these include two types of risks—liquidity risk and default risk. LIQUIDITY RISK arises because banks engage in maturity transformation which occurs when the maturities of their assets (loans) are longer than those of their liabilities (deposits). Banks are able to support loans made out for investment in new plant and machinery that occur over long periods of time by a variety of much shorter deposits. Depositors typically want access to their funds in the event of an emergency, whereas borrowers prefer the security of funding over the life of their investment project, which involves a longer time horizon. Banks can carry out this maturity transformation as they have a large number of depositors and not all of them are likely to cash their deposits at any one particular time. The exception to this, of course, is when there is a run on the bank and large numbers of depositors attempt to withdraw their funds at the same time.

› **Liquidity risk** is the risk that the demand for repayment of deposits will exceed the liquid resources of banks.

A second risk that banks face is DEFAULT RISK—the possibility that the borrower will default and fail to repay either (or both) the interest due on the loan or the principal itself. Banks deal with this risk by pooling their loans. As they have a large number of loans, they endeavour to spread their loans across different segments of the economy—such as geographical location, type of industry, and so on. By diversifying the portfolio of loans they give, banks are able to reduce the impact of any one loan failing to be repaid. Banks also request for collateral—the requirement that borrowers deposit claims to one or more of their assets with the bank—so that in the event of default the bank can liquidate the asset and cover the default amount.[5]

› **Default risk** is the risk that a borrower will be unable to make the required payments on her debt obligations.

15.3.2 Macroeconomics with Risk Premiums

To enable an understanding of how a financial crisis affects the economy, we need to modify two assumptions that are implicit in the standard IS–LM model.[6] First, in the conventional model, there is no role for banks as financial intermediaries that link depositors in the money market with borrowers in the capital market. In the money market, banks pay households interest for keeping their funds in deposits that are liquid and subject to withdrawal without notice. In the capital market, these funds are then loaned out to support long-term financing of investment projects of borrowers. The interest charged on these loans in the capital market, i_c, is typically different from the interest paid to financial instruments, such as bonds and deposits in the financial or money market i_M. Conventionally, however, the basic macroeconomic model abstracts from this by assuming that perfect competition does not allow banks to charge a mark-up over their cost of deposits when they extend credit to firms. As a result, the interest rate in the IS–LM model is the interest rate, where $i = i_M = i_c$.

Second, the conventional model ignores the role played by risk in financial markets. When the pattern of foreclosures and defaults begin to change and banks experience and expect a higher risk that borrowers will default on their repayments, they include a RISK PREMIUM that they charge to borrowers in the capital market in order to compensate for bearing this increased risk. If we denote RP_c as the risk premium in the capital market, then borrowers in the capital market are charged a rate of interest given by:

› A **risk premium** is a compensation for the higher risk, such as default risk, that accompanies the financial intermediation.

$$i_c = i + RP_c$$

Investment demand is then affected by the risk-adjusted interest rate, $i = RP_c$. Then, when risk premiums rise, investment declines as the cost of capital has increased, and, with investment expenditure declining, the IS curve shifts to the left.[7]

In a similar fashion, if business establishments are going to slip up on their repayments, then financial instruments that individuals deploy their savings in, and which in turn finance these establishments, will be considered to be more risky. The public then expects a reduction in the returns on these financial investments, which, in the conventional macroeconomic model, is considered to be bonds. Recall that the interest rate on bonds is the opportunity cost of holding money, and a rise in this interest rate represents income forgone and causes people to rebalance their portfolio of financial assets and hold more bonds and reduce their holding of money balances. In this case, of course, individuals will demand a compensation for bearing the risk that causes the reduction in their expected returns on their financial portfolio in the form of a risk premium that we denote by RP_M. The relevant interest rate, then, for deciding on the holding of money versus bonds will be $i_M = i - RP_M$. The opportunity cost of holding money balances is i_M and the demand for money function,[8] then, is $M^d/P = f(Y, i_M)$. When the public's confidence about repayments is undermined, as occurs when a financial crisis emerges, the risk premium in the money or financial market, RP_M, increases. An increase in the risk premium in the money market reduces the expected return on financial assets, such as bonds that compete with money in financial portfolios, and result in individuals wanting to increase their liquidity or their demand for money. Accordingly, the LM curve shifts upward and to the left when risk premiums in the money market rise.[9]

Now, suppose a financial crisis emerges in which risk premiums substantially increase. If the development of the crisis permeates through the financial markets quickly—because financial markets process information and act on that at a faster speed than in other markets—then the risk premium may rise significantly in the financial market and push the economy into a situation where income and expenditures decline and interest rates increase. This is depicted in Figure 15.6 where the economy prior to the crisis is at point A and, as risk premiums increase with the emergence of the crisis, gravitates towards point B. Aggregate income during the crisis declines to Y_1 and the interest rate rises to i_1.

So far, we have proceeded as though the crisis hits an economy that has no trade or financial relations with other economies—Figure 15.6 depicts the workings of a closed economy. However, financial crises that occur in an economy have cross-border repercussions. A financial crisis is, thus, best studied in an open economy macroeconomic model such as the Mundell–Fleming model. Consider, then, an open economy which, however, is small in the sense that it does not dominate the trade and capital flows that take place in the global economy. Such would be the situation for India. Let the financial crisis emerge in the rest of the world—that is, outside the borders of the small open economy. As the financial crisis develops, the rest of the world witnesses a decline in income and a rise in interest rates due to the rise in risk premiums in that part of the world, as depicted in Figure 15.6. The small open economy that we focus on was not the location where the crisis occurred, but the decline in incomes in the rest of the world will cause a reduction in expenditures made by the residents of that region, including a reduction in expenditure on the exports of the small open economy to the region hit by the crisis.

Additionally, the increase in the interest rate due to a rise in risk premiums in the rest of the world, i^*, reduces the differential between the interest rate in the small open economy, i, and i^*. The financial crisis elsewhere reduces the value of $(i - i^*)$, and reduces the net capital inflows into the small open economy. Alternately, $NKI\ (i - i^*)$, in the balance of payments curve given by $BP = NX\ (Y, E) + NKI\ (i - i^*)$, takes on a lower value. In an open economy with imperfect capital mobility, the BP curve is upward sloping. This is because, as pointed out in the chapter on the Mundell–Fleming model, there is imperfect capital mobility and as income increases there is increased spending on imports. As net exports decline, the equilibrium in the balance of payments requires this to be offset by an improvement in net capital inflows, which is achieved when the domestic interest rate, i, rises as compared to the exogenously given interest rate abroad, i^*. As the BP curve is traced out for a given value of i^*, a change in the value of i^* shifts the BP curve. With the onset of a financial crisis abroad, i^* increases, reducing the differential $i - i^*$, and in turn reducing net capital inflows into the economy. With $BP = NX\ (Y, E) + NKI\ (i - i^*)$, the reduction

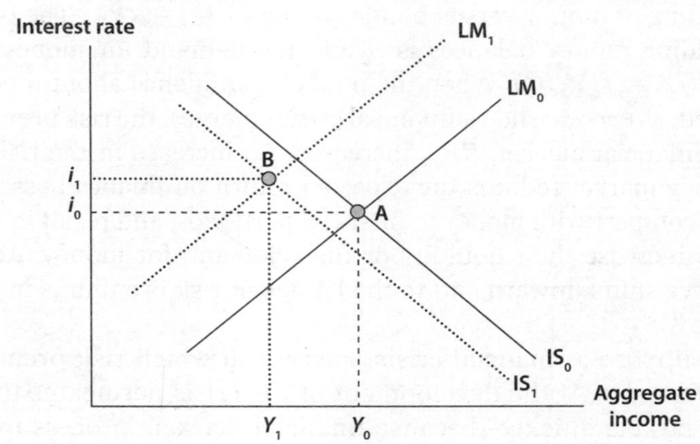

› **Figure 15.6**
Risk Premiums and Crises. The economy is at point A when a financial crisis begins. An increase in the risk premium in the financial markets raises the demand for money and shifts the LM curve to the left to LM_1. A higher default risk stemming from the crisis raises the risk premium in the capital market and shifts the IS curve to the left to IS_1. Income and expenditures decline and the interest rate rises.

in net capital inflows requires to be offset by a rise in net exports. In the space of interest rate and aggregate income, as depicted in Figure 15.7, this implies that aggregate income must decline so as to reduce the demand for imports and, thereby, cause net exports to rise. The increase in i^* will, thus, be associated with a BP curve that is allied to a lower level of aggregate income at any value of the domestic interest rate.[10] This means the BP curve shifts upwards and to the left. Prior to the financial crisis abroad, the BP curve is positioned at BP_0 in Figure 15.7. The financial crisis shifts the BP curve leftwards to $BP_1(r^* \uparrow)$, as the interest rate abroad rises due to the increased risk premiums in the financial and capital markets. If exchange rates are flexible, the reduction in net capital inflows pushes the balance of payments into a deficit and causes a depreciation of the currency. The BP curve then shifts down to the right to $BP_1(E \uparrow)$ due to the currency depreciation. The depreciation, in turn, stimulates exports and shifts the IS curve to the right to $IS_1(E \uparrow)$.

The slowdown in the global economy, stemming from the financial crisis, also reduces the incomes earned abroad and the expenditures from abroad on the exports from the domestic economy. This is an income effect that is independent of the price competitiveness effect that operates through changes in the exchange rate. Such a reduction in expenditures abroad would shift the domestic economy's IS curve to the left of IS_1, as net exports decline. Simultaneously, the reduced supply of foreign exchange in the forex market, arising from the decline in exports, will cause the exchange rate to depreciate even further and push the *BP* curve further to the right from BP_1. This depreciation of the currency improves the competitiveness of exports and shifts the IS curve back towards the right in the direction of IS_1. If the income–export expenditure effect of the economic slowdown abroad is relatively small compared to the depreciation of the currency competitiveness effect on exports, the relevant IS and *BP* curves are IS_2 and BP_2, and the economy settles to the south-west of point B at point C. If the income–export expenditure effect of the slowdown abroad is significant, then the IS and *BP* curves could even gravitate towards an equilibrium outcome at point D. The financial crisis with a genesis abroad can, then, result in a boom in a small open domestic economy, as at point C, or a downturn in economic activity, as at point D.[11]

The crisis also affected a country such as India in a somewhat different and unexpected manner. A number of large multinational firms had external bank and corporate borrowings in foreign currencies and financial markets abroad. As the financial crisis unravelled and Lehman Brothers filed for bankruptcy, the financial markets abroad began to witness a rise in risk premiums and

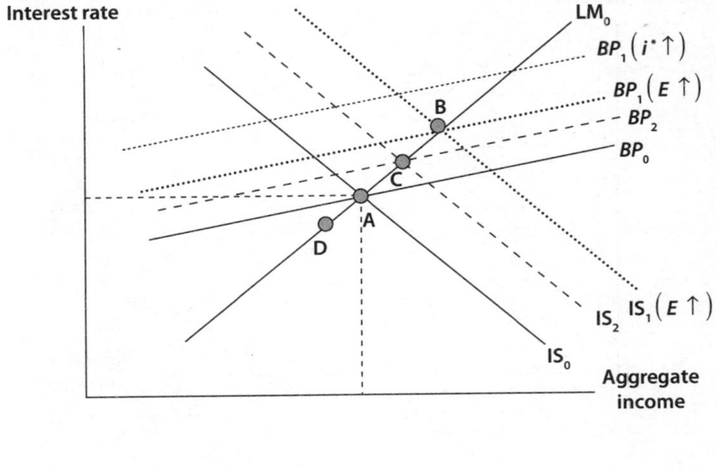

› **Figure 15.7**
Impact of a Financial Crisis that Originates Abroad. The small open economy is at point A when a crisis occurs abroad that raises the interest rate i^* abroad. The BP curve shifts upwards to $BP_1(i^* \uparrow)$. The resulting balance of payments deficit causes the currency to depreciate and the BP curve shifts to $BP_1(E \uparrow)$. Currency depreciation also stimulates exports and the IS curve shifts to $IS_1(E \uparrow)$. The small open economy experiences a boom at point B. If the income effect of the decline in incomes abroad affects expenditures from abroad on exports from the small open economy more than the stimulation to exports from depreciation, the economy will gravitate to a point like C and with a significant income effect to a point like D where a recession is experienced.

these Indian firms faced a liquidity shortage. In response, these firms began to ask for a redemption of their savings placed in Indian money-market funds.[12] In turn, these funds, facing a liquidation of their portfolio holdings, withdrew their lending to banks and financial institutions. In effect, the increase in the requirement for liquidity raised the demand for money, which raised interest rates and shifted the LM curve upwards and to the left of point C to LM_3, as depicted in Figure 15.8.

An increase in the domestic interest rate requires a currency appreciation so as to ensure that the interest parity condition is not violated and that the BP curve shifts up and to the left, to BP_3. The currency appreciation, in turn, reduces net exports from the economy and shifts the IS curve to the left, to IS_3. The economy shifts to point E where interest rates have risen and economic activity declines. In order to COUNTER THIS RECESSION that the economy begins to experience, policy makers—the Finance Ministry and the central bank or the Reserve Bank of India—began to implement expansionary fiscal and monetary policy in order to shift the IS and LM curves to the right.

› A financial crisis is **countered** by the application of an expansionary fiscal as well as monetary policy when the economy operates in a regime of flexible exchange rates.

It was the withdrawal of funds by multinational firms that caused the LM curve to shift to the left. If, in addition, the commercial banks began to have a reduced confidence in the ability of these firms to not default on their loans, then the risk premium in the capital markets would begin to rise. This would result in a shifting of the IS curve further to the left of IS_3 in Figure 15.8 and a deepening of the recession.

So far, we have analysed the crisis on the assumption that the domestic economy was operating in a regime of flexible exchange rates. What if the policy makers had fixed the exchange rate? With exchange rates unchanging, the BP and IS curves shift with changes in variables other than the exchange rate, which influences the position of these curves. For fixed exchange rates, then, the financial crisis abroad raises, and shifts the *BP* curve to BP_1 i^* as in Figure 15.7. Now, the interest differential $i - i^*$ having narrowed, there follows a reduction in net capital inflows into the economy. The reduction may also be large enough to be a capital outflow. With the exchange rate fixed, the central bank would have to provide the necessary foreign exchange that is in demand in the foreign exchange market. The central bank's stock of foreign exchange reserves declines and the money supply, which is the sum of domestic assets and foreign exchange assets, declines. The reduction in money supply shifts the LM curve to the left. The leftward shift of the LM curve continues till a new equilibrium is attained at the point where the LM curve passes through the intersection of the IS_0 and BP_1

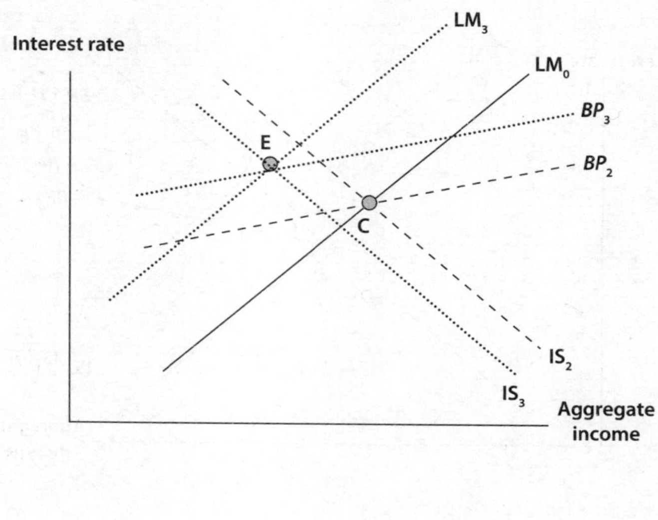

› **Figure 15.8**
Money Market Response to Financial Crisis Abroad. With firms facing a liquidity shortage abroad when the financial crisis erupted, there was a requirement for liquidity that raised the demand for money in the Indian financial markets and shifted the LM curve to the left to LM_3. This resulted in an appreciation of the currency, which shifted the BP curve upwards to BP_3. Currency appreciation, in turn, reduced net exports and shifted the IS curve to the left to IS_3. The economy went to point E and witnessed a recession as well as a rise in interest rates.

curves. The outcome is a recession, unlike the case of flexible exchange rates that results in a boom at point C, at point D in Figure 15.7. The recession in the case of fixed exchange rates occurs because, with unchanged exchange rates, the competitiveness of the economy cannot change to make the purchase of domestic goods more attractive abroad, thereby causing expenditures from abroad to contract. The reduction in net exports and the increase in the domestic interest rate, as money supply declines with the loss of foreign exchange assets arising from capital outflows, takes the economy into a recession.

Interestingly, in an economy with fixed exchange rates, EXPANSIONARY MONETARY POLICY IS NOT EFFECTIVE in dealing with the recession emerging from a financial crisis abroad. If the central bank expands the money supply and shifts the LM curve to the right, it will reduce the domestic interest rate and cause the interest differential $i - i^*$ to narrow further. This will reduce net capital inflows, as well as the stock of foreign exchange and money supply, so that eventually the expansionary policy is completely offset. With the central bank unable to stimulate expenditures in the economy, fiscal policy has the primary responsibility of taking the economy out of the recession. An expansionary fiscal policy will, in addition to stimulating spending, raise the domestic interest rate, attract capital flows, and expand the money supply. The additional liquidity in the financial market prevents the crowding out that normally occurs along with an expansionary fiscal policy.

› When a financial crisis occurs and the economy is operating in a fixed exchange rate regime, **monetary policy** is ineffective and unable to stimulate aggregate output and income in the economy.

A crisis that emerges in the money market or the capital market causes risk premiums in these markets to rise, resulting in an increase in the interest rate and a decline in income. A crisis abroad affects a small open economy differently, depending on whether it operates in a flexible exchange rate or a fixed exchange rate regime. The recession is deeper in a fixed exchange rate economy. Moreover, such an economy cannot use monetary policy to emerge from the recession and must rely on fiscal policy to offset the recession caused by a financial crisis abroad.

SUMMARY

» A rational expectation is one where agents use all available information, do not make systematic mistakes in their forecasts of economic variables, and form their expectations in a well specified way by employing a knowledge of the relevant theory that indicates how the variable being forecasted evolves.

» In the New Classical Friedman–Phelps–Lucas model, wages and prices are completely flexible. When government policy that shifts the aggregate demand curve is unanticipated, variations in the real output of the economy occur. When government policy changes are anticipated, the economy stays at the natural rate of output and price expectations change in line with the price that the theory predicts will occur as a result of the change in policy.

» The New Keynesians argue that, in the short run, wages and/or prices are sticky, as wage contracts across different sectors of the economy are not synchronized. Unlike the New Classical theory, this implies that even when a policy change is anticipated the output can deviate from the natural rate in the short run. Economic policy can influence the course of the economy.

» Government investment expenditure, unlike government consumption expenditure, has two effects on the economy. First, it increases the productivity of private factors of production and shifts the aggregate supply curve of the economy to the right. Second, to the extent that public investment expenditure and private investment expenditure are complementary, private investment is crowded in. This second effect shifts the IS and AD curves further to the right than the original rightward shift that has its origins in the increase in government investment expenditure.

» A deficit-financed increase in public expenditure does not have a long- run detrimental impact on the economy if either of two conditions is applicable. One is when public investment expenditure is larger than the decline in private investment and other expenditures that are crowded out by the rise in the interest rate for equal marginal productivities of public and private capital. The second is when the marginal productivity of public capital accumulation expenditure is sufficiently larger than the productivity of the private capital stock it crowds out.

- Countries with substantial current account surpluses, mainly emerging and developing economies, as well as oil exporting countries, invested these surpluses in US government securities from 2001 to 2007, resulting in a decline in the yields of these securities.
- Low yields pushed the financial industry to search for increased returns through an intensification of risk taking. A widespread decline in underwriting standards made available mortgages on more lax and easier financing conditions in terms of subprime loans, which caused the demand for housing and house prices to soar.
- The stock of housing inventory increased in response and, as it exceeded the demand for housing, house prices declined rapidly. Foreclosures and delinquencies on mortgages followed in the subprime market. Investor uncertainty intensified and the financial crisis erupted with risk premiums in financial markets rising to unprecedented levels.
- An increase in risk premiums raises the cost of capital, reduces investment expenditure in the goods market, and shifts the IS curve to the left. In the financial market it reduces the expected return on the holding of financial assets and raises the demand for money, thereby shifting the LM curve to the left. Interest rates rise and aggregate income declines with a financial crisis.
- A small open economy is affected by a financial crisis in the global economy by a reduction in capital inflows. In response, its exchange rate depreciates and stimulates net exports. The small open economy, then, experiences a boom. The increase in competitiveness, from an exchange rate depreciation that raises exports, however, may be offset by a reduction in spending abroad on the exports of the small open economy due to the contraction in incomes abroad. In that case, the small open economy experiences a recession.
- If there is a rise in demand for liquidity as capital markets begin to reduce financial intermediation due to a financial crisis, the small open economy will be subject to a rise in interest rates and a leftward shift of the LM curve. This causes an appreciation of the currency and a decline in net exports. The rise in interest rates and decline in net exports push the small open economy into a recession.
- If the small open economy operates in a flexible exchange rate regime, it can employ expansionary fiscal and monetary policy to emerge from a recession caused by a financial crisis abroad. If it operates in a fixed exchange rate regime, monetary policy is ineffective as any increase in money supply increases capital outflows, reduces the foreign exchange assets of the banking system, and neutralizes the money supply increase. In such a case only fiscal policy is effective.

NOTES

1. R. Lucas, 'Econometric Policy Evaluation: A Critique' (Carnegie–Rochester Conference Series on Public Policy, 1, 1976), pp. 19–46.
2. J. F. Muth, 'Rational Expectations and the Theory of Price Movements', *Econometrica*, 29, 1961), pp. 315–35.
3. Mathematically, the expected value of u_1 is zero and the correlation coefficient between x^T_t and u_t is also zero.
4. W. R. Emmons, 'The Mortgage Crisis: Let Markets Work, but Compensate the Truly Needy' (*The Regional Economist*, 16, 2008), pp. 10–16.
5. Banks also screen applications for loans so as to weed out highly risky loans and often also monitor the conduct of the borrower to ensure the security of returns on financed projects.
6. Manfred Gärtner and Jung Florian, 'The Macroeconomics of Financial Crises: How Risk Premiums, Liquidity Traps and Perfect Traps Affect Policy Options', (University of St Gallen, Discussion Paper No. 2009–15, 2009).
7. For simplicity, assume the risk premium is uniform to both firms and consumers who take out loans. The consumption function then is $C = C_0 + C_1(Y - T) + C_2(i + RP_c - \pi^e)$ and the investment function is $I = a - b(i + RP_c - \pi^e)$. The equation (8.12) for the IS curve then is rewritten as $i = [\{a + C_0 - (1 - C_1)(Y - T) - (T - G)\}/\{b + C_2\}] + \pi_e - RP_c$. An increase in then shifts this curve to the left.
8. The demand for money balances in equation (8.14) will then be $M^d/P = h + nY - ei_M = h + nY - e(i - RP_M)$.
9. The equation for the LM curve is $i = RP_M + (h - M/P)/e + (n/e)Y$ implying a rise in the risk premium increases the intercept on the interest rate axis.
10. With flexible exchange rates, the BP equation is given by $NX(Y, E) + NKI(i - i^*) = 0$. Suppose this equation is linear, as in $-\alpha Y + \beta E + \theta(i - i^*) = 0$, where α, β, θ are constants. Then, $i = i^* + (\alpha Y - \beta E)/\theta$. It is immediately apparent that a rise in i^* raises the intercept of the BP curve and shifts it to the left.
11. In India exports that grew at 25 per cent during 2005–2008 decelerated to 12.2 per cent in the crisis year (2008–2009) and declined by 2.2 per cent in 2009–2010. The exchange rate depreciated from INR 39.37 per dollar in January 2008 to INR 51.23 per dollar in March 2009. In terms of Figure 15.7, India was at point D.
12. D. Subbarao, 'India—Managing the Impact of the Global Financial Crisis' (Speech delivered at the CII's National Conference and Annual Session 2009, New Delhi, 26 March 2009) http://www.rbi.org.in/scripts/BS_SpeechesView.aspx?Id=413.

TEST YOURSELF

1. What is a rational expectation and how is it different from an adaptive expectation?
2. Consider the scenario where the fiscal deficit is reduced by the government. What is the impact on the output of the economy if this policy change is (*a*) unanticipated and (*b*) it is anticipated by agents in the economy?
3. In what way does government investment expenditure have a different effect on the economy than government consumption expenditure?
4. When government expenditure raises the interest rate in the economy, the stock of private capital declines and the production function shifts inwards. What happens to the demand for labour when this happens? Examine the impact in the labour market and the final effect on aggregate supply as a result of this change in the labour market.
5. Let the world economy be divided into two types—those with a current account surplus and those with a current account deficit. Is there a relationship between the current accounts of these types of economies and why?
6. The investment expenditure of an economy is funded from three sources—private savings, public savings, and foreign savings. If a country resorts increasingly to foreign savings, what is the impact on interest rates in that economy and on the interest rate abroad?
7. What factors were responsible for the financial crisis that began in 2007?
8. Discuss the risks that financial institutions deal with in the course of their intermediation between savers, and the uses of those savings for investment expenditures.
9. How are the IS and LM curves of the conventional IS–LM model affected by the presence of risk premiums in the financial market and in the capital market?
10. Consider a small open economy. Analyse the effect of a financial crisis that originates abroad on the aggregate income of the small open economy when the exchange rate is flexible.

ONLINE APPLICATION

1. Go to the website of the Federal Reserve System on the page where interest rate data are given. The website is http://www.federalreserve.gov/releases/h15/data.htm/. Under the instruments column scroll down to 'Treasury constant maturities—Nominal' and for the sub-category of '1-year Treasuries' download data on monthly frequencies of the yield on US Treasury securities at one-year constant maturity for the period January 2007 to the latest available month.
2. Then go to the website of the RBI where various RBI bulletins are uploaded—http://www.rbi.org.in/scripts/BS_View Bulletin.aspx/.
3. From various RBI bulletins download data on the month-end yield to maturity of SGL transactions in central government dated securities for a one-year term to maturity. This is Row 1 of Table no. 26C in the RBI bulletin. Download data again for the period January 2007 to the latest available month.
4. Compare the yield rates so obtained in India and the USA. Recall that the financial crisis began in the USA in July 2007. What does the yield rate data reveal about the way the financial crisis unfolded?

Glossary

A

Adaptive expectations: A situation where Individuals revise their price expectations in every period to incorporate a fraction of the errors in expectation ($p-p^e$) from the previous period.

Adjustment costs: The costs of integrating new capital goods into the production process. The larger the investment, the larger will be the cost of adjustment.

Aggregate demand (AD) curve: The inverse relationship between the real quantity demanded of final goods and services and the general price level.

Aggregate income: The sum of all incomes accruing to the citizens of a country within a given period of time–a year or a quarter.

Aggregate supply (AS) curve: The positive relationship between the real quantity of final goods and the services produced in an economy and the general price level.

Appreciation: Occurs when the price of the foreign currency in terms of the domestic currency decreases leading to a decrease in the exchange rate.

Arbitrage: The proposition that the expected rates of returns on two assets must be equal.

Automatic stabilizers: Expenditures that automatically increase, or taxes that automatically decrease, when the aggregate income and output decline.

Average propensity to consume (APC): The ratio of consumption to disposable income.

Average propensity to save (APS): The ratio of savings to disposable income.

B

Balance of (merchandise) trade: The value of exports less the value of imports of goods.)

Balance of payments: It summarizes a country's transactions—monetary payments for goods and services, and acquisition of financial assets—with the rest of the world during an accounting period.

Bond: A bond is a legal promise to repay a debt. The principal amount or the amount originally lent is paid at some fixed date in the future called the maturation date. A bondholder receives regular interest, or coupon payments, until the bond's maturation date.

C

Capital account: A summary of the country's financial asset transactions with the rest of the world.

Capital good: A long-lived good that is used in the production of other goods and services.

Capital theory: Informs us about the optimal stock of capital to be used as an input.

Classical supply curve: Occurs when the *AS* curve is vertical, and the quantity of output produced depends on real factors with no effect of nominal variables on output.

Consumer price index (CPI): The cost of a standard basket of goods and services consumed by a typical domestic consumer.

Consumption function: A positive function of the aggregate disposable income and is negatively related to the nominal interest rate.

Consumption smoothing theory: A preference maximization theory where individuals are forward looking.

Consumption smoothing: Occurs when the consumption in each period is set equal to the permanent income.

Consumption tilting: The case where the consumer's impatience for the present versus future consumption is not equal to the interest rate at which income is discounted.

Convergence: The catch-up phenomenon whereby poor countries would tend to grow faster than rich countries and close the gap between the two groups of countries.

Credibility: The degree to which individuals and markets believe that a policy announcement will be implemented even when there are short-term economic costs that may be imposed.

Crowding out: Occurs when the stimulative effects of fiscal policy are offset by a reduction in the interest-sensitive consumption and investment due to a rise in the interest rate.

Currency board: The requirement that the exchange rate is fixed and the monetary authority commits to buying or selling the domestic currency without any limit at this pre-announced exchange rate.

Current account balance: The statement of a country's payments to and from the rest of the world for goods and non-factor services transacted in, for factor incomes from abroad, and for transfers.

Cyclical unemployment: The unemployment associated with periods of low levels of economic activity.

D

Default risk: Risk that a borrower will be unable to make the required payments on her debt obligations.

Dependency rate: The ratio of dependents (the young and the old population) to the working population.

Depreciation: Depreciation occurs when the price of the foreign currency in terms of the domestic currency rises leading to an increase in the exchange rate.

Depth: The maximum amount or limit that a dealer stands ready to buy or sell at posted prices.

Discretionary monetary policy: Results from the deliberate and conscious choices by the central bank on money supply (or the interest rate) in order to influence output and prices in the economy.

Dollarization: Adoption of a foreign currency as its legal tender by a country.

E

Economic growth: The rate of change of the real income (or output) per capita.

Efficiency wages: The wages that maximize firm profits when workers may work or shirk.

Engine of economic growth: The technological progress that occurs exogenously of capital accumulation in the form of skills and human capital acquisition.

Exchange rate: The value of a given currency relative to another.

Exogenous variable: A variable that is taken as given and is not explained within an economic model.

F

Financial crisis: A major disruption in financial markets, characterized by sharp decline in asset prices and the failure of financial and non-financial firms.

Financial repression: The prevalence of credit controls, interest rate controls, entry barriers into banking, operational restrictions on banks, the predominance of state-owned banks, and restrictions on international financial transactions.

Fiscal deficit: The government expenditure that is not related to the repayment of the debt, G, plus repayment of the debt, rB, less government revenues, T.

Fisher effect: Describes the full adjustment of the nominal interest rate to a change in the inflation rate.

Frictional unemployment: The short-term unemployment associated with matching workers with jobs.

Full employment: A state where cyclical unemployment is zero.

G

GDP deflator: The nominal GDP divided by the real GDP.

Golden Rule: The condition for maximum sustainable consumption that does not provide less consumption to future than to current generations.

Government saving: It is equal to net government revenues less government spending.

Gross domestic product (GDP): The market value of the final goods and services produced in a country during a given time period.

Gross national product (GNP): Equals GDP plus net factor incomes from abroad.

H

Hedge: A future transaction agreeing to purchase or sell a given quantity of an asset at a future date at a price agreed today in order to offset the existing risk.

Human capital: Refers to the levels of education and skills embodied in the labour force.

I

Impossible trinity: Refers to the dilemma that a country cannot simultaneously have control over a fixed exchange rate and a monetary policy, and maintain an open-capital account.

Income effect: The change in the quantity demanded of a good or an asset that results from the effect of a change in the price on the purchasing power of the individual's budget, holding all other factors constant.

Inside lags: The delay between the time a policy change is needed and the time the policy change is implemented.

Insiders: Incumbent employees who have market power in the determination of wages.

Intermediate target: A macroeconomic variable that the central bank can influence with some predictability and is related to its ultimate objectives.

Intertemporal analysis: The analysis about the trade-offs when the present choices affect the alternatives available in the future.

Intertemporal choices: The choices that take into consideration the consequences for the current time period as well as for future periods.

Investment expenditure: The expenditure resulting in the increase in the stock of capital goods is investment expenditure.

Involuntary unemployment: Refers to a situation where the workers are willing to work at the going wage and yet firms do not employ them.

J

J-curve: The phenomenon where a depreciation of the currency causes the trade balance to initially worsen before it eventually improves.

L

Law of One Price: States that if the international arbitrage is unhindered (the market is efficient) then identical assets (with the same risk and liquidity characteristics) must earn the same rate of return. The Law applied to trade in goods is known as Purchasing Power Parity.

Learning by doing: The process by which individuals and firms learn better ways to produce as a by-product of some other activity undertaken such as investment.

Liquidity: The ease and speed with which agents can convert assets into purchasing power.

Liquidity risk: The risk that the demand for repayment of deposits will exceed the liquid resources of banks.

LM: The upward-sloping curve in nominal interest rate – aggregate income space depicting equilibrium between the demand for money or liquidity (L) and money supply (M).

M

Marginal product: The change in output that occurs in response to a unit change in the application of an input.

Marginal propensity to consume (MPC): The amount by which consumption rises when disposable income rises by INR 1.

Monetary base: The money issued by the central bank; also called high-powered money.

Monetary union: Occurs when a group of countries share a common currency and jointly manage the currency through a common central bank.

Money illusion: A situation when individuals formulate decisions on the basis of changes in nominal values rather than on nominal values adjusted for the price level (real values).

Money multiplier: The increase in the money supply as a result of an increase by one rupee in the central bank base money.

Money supply: The money multiplier times the reserve money.

N

National income: The sum of the net domestic product valued at factor cost plus the net factor incomes from abroad.

National saving: The sum of private and public savings.

Natural rate of unemployment: The sum of the seasonal, frictional, and structural unemployment. Analytically it is the unemployment rate at which price expectations are realized.

Net domestic product: GDP less depreciation.

Net investment: It is the gross investment less depreciation.

Nominal GDP: The sum of the quantities of goods produced times their current price.

Nominal incomes: Incomes measured in terms of current rupee values.

Nominal interest rate: The real rate of interest plus the rate of inflation.

O

Okun's Law: States that each percentage point increase of cyclical unemployment is associated with a three percentage point increase in the output gap.

Open market operation: The purchase or sale of government bonds by the central bank for the purpose of increasing or decreasing the money supply.

Output gap: The difference between the potential output and the actual output as a fraction of potential output.

Outside lag: The time required for a policy change to affect the economy.

Overall balance: The sum of the current account balance and the capital account balance.

P

Pareto efficiency: A condition in which no change in outcome that will make some members of society (such as the unemployed) better off without making some other members of society (such as the employed) worse off is possible.

Per capita income: The aggregate income divided by the population of the country.

Permanent income: The constant stream of income that equals the present discounted value of the fluctuating stream of current and future incomes.

Phillips curve: The mirror image of the *AS* curve that posits a negative trade-off between the price level and the unemployment in its static version and between inflation and the unemployment rate in its dynamic version.

Policy ineffectiveness, proposition: States that the government cannot systematically exploit the Phillips curve to guide the economy to a point on it.

Potential output: The maximum sustainable amount of output that an economy can produce.

Poverty trap: The tendency of an economy to return to a low-level steady state despite attempts to raise the per capita output.

Private saving: The value of the private sector's disposable income minus its consumption.

Production function: Describes how inputs like capital and labour are transformed into output.

Purchasing power parity: States that if arbitrage across national borders is unhindered, the price of a good or service in one nation should be the same as the exchange rate adjusted price of the same good in another nation.

R

Real exchange rate: The price of the average foreign good or service relative to the price of the average domestic good or service, when the prices are expressed in terms of a common currency.

Real GDP: The aggregate income measured in the prices of a base year. It measures aggregate income in constant rupees or adjusted for inflation.

Real incomes: The incomes measured in physical terms, that is, in terms of the quantities of goods and services.

Real rate of interest: The nominal interest rate minus the rate of inflation.

Rental cost of capital: Also referred to as the user cost of capital; The cost of using capital over a given period of time (a year) and is the sum of the real interest rate and depreciation rate times the unit price of the capital good.

Rental: The price of a unit of housing times the rate of interest plus depreciation.

Required reserves: The result of the central bank regulation requiring banks to hold specified fractions of their deposits—either as vault cash or as funds on deposit at the central bank.

Reserve or base money: The sum of the domestic credit advanced by the central bank and its foreign exchange assets.

Resource constraint: Depicts the locus of all possible input combinations that can be purchased for a given level of resources available to spend on purchasing these inputs.

Ricardian equivalence: The proposition that in terms of the impact on the aggregate income it is irrelevant whether increased government expenditure is financed by taxes or bonds.

Risk pooling: The process by financial intermediaries to protect themselves from excessive risk through sharing risks of independent investment projects.

Risk premium: Compensation for the higher risk, such as default risk, that accompanies the financial intermediation.

S

Seasonal unemployment: Varies predictably with the seasons.

Seigniorage: The use of money creation as a revenue device by the government.

Shock: A shock is an unexpected disturbance to the economy that affects the demand or supply side of the economy.

Solow residual: The estimate of the technological progress derived as a residual after accounting for the rate of growth of output due to labour force and capital stock growth.

Spot exchange rates: The exchange rate when two parties agree to an exchange of financial instruments and execute the deal immediately.

Stationary state: A state where the growth rate of a variable is constant, or, where there is no tendency for the variable to change with time.

Statutory liquidity ratio: Specifies the required holding of government securities as a fraction of the assets of the commercial bank.

Steady state: The state when various quantities grow at constant rates.

Sterilization: The central bank policy of altering the domestic credit in an equal and opposite direction to the variation in foreign exchange reserves so that the monetary base remains unchanged.

Structural unemployment: A long-term unemployment that does not vary with the pace of economic activity.

Substitution effect: The change in the quantity demanded of goods or assets that results from a change in the price making it more or less expensive and thereby more or less attractive relative to other goods or assets, holding constant the effect of the price change on the purchasing power of the individual's budget constraint.

Sunk cost: An investment in an asset with no alternative use, also referred to as a specific asset.

Surplus overall balance: The net increase in the country's stock of international reserves over the year.

Systemic risk: The default risk associated with general economy-wide or macroeconomic conditions that affect all borrowers and lenders.

T

Terms of trade: The relative price that is given by the price of exports (P) divided by the price of imports (EP*).

Tobin's marginal Q: The ratio of the marginal value of the capital stock (computed by adding the market value of the additional equity and the debt raised by the firm to finance the addition to capital stock) to the rental cost of capital.

Total investment expenditure: Sum of business investment, residential investment, and inventory investment.

Treasury bill: A government bond with a maturity period not exceeding one year.

Two period budget constraint: The present value of the income in the two periods less the discounted value of interest lost on account of holding money balances rather than bonds.

V

Value of waiting: The expected present value of the irreversible mistake when undertaking physical investment that would be revealed in the future should the returns fall short of the costs.

W

Walras' Law: States that the sum of the excess demand for money, bonds, and current output must equal zero.

Wealth of the private sector: Consists of its net claims on agents outside that sector—the stock of money and the stock of government bonds.

Wholesale price index (WPI): A price index of goods and services produced domestically.

Bibliography

Alan S. Blinder, *Central Banking in Theory and Practice* (Cambridge, MA: MIT Press, 1998).

Alban William Phillips, "The Relation between Unemployment and the Rate of Change of Money Wage Rates in the United Kingdom, 1861–1957," *Economica* 25(1958): 283–299.

Alberto Giovannini, "Savings and the Interest Rate in LDCs," *World Development* 11, no. 7 (July 1983): 601–607.

Albert Ando and Franco Modigliani, "The 'Life Cycle' Hypothesis of Saving: Aggregate Implications and Tests," *American Economic Review* 53, no. 1 (March 1963): 55–84.

Arthur M. Okun, *The Political Economy of Prosperity* (New York: Norton, 1970).

Assaf Razin and Efraim Sadka, "Fiscal Balance During Inflation, Disinflation and Immigration: Policy lessons," in M. Blejer and T. Ter-Minassian (eds.) *Macroeconomic Dimensions of Public Finance: Essays in Honor of Vito Tanzi* (IMF, 1996).

Assar Lindbeck and Dennis J. Snower, *The Insider-Outsider Theory of Employment and Unemployment* (Cambridge, MA: MIT Press, 1988); "Interactions Between the Efficiency Wage and Insider-Outsider Theories," *Economics Letters* 37 (1991): 193–196.

Avinash K. Dixit and Robert S. Pindyck, *Investment under Uncertainty* (Princeton, NJ: Princeton University Press, 1994); and R. S. Pindyck, "Irreversibility, Uncertainty and Investment," *Journal of Economic Literature* 3 (September 29, 1991): 110–148.

B. Bhaskara Rao and Rup Singh, "Demand for Money in India: 1953–2003," *Applied Economics* 38, no. 11 (2006): 1319–1326.

Bennett McCallum, *Monetary Economics: Theory and Policy* (New York: Macmillan, 1989).

Bruce Greenwald, Joseph E. Stiglitz, and Andrew Weiss, "Information Imperfections in the Capital Market and Macroeconomic Fluctuations," *American Economic Review Proceedings* 74 (May 1984): 194–199.

B. K. Bhoi and S. C. Dhall, "Integration of Financial Markets in India: An Empirical Evaluation," RBI Occasional Papers No. 19 (4), Mumbai 1998, pp. 345–380.

Casey B. Mulligan, "Substitution over Time: Another Look at Life Cycle Labour Supply," *NBER Macroeconomics Annual* 13, 1998.

Carl Shapiro and Joseph E. Stiglitz, "Equilibrium Unemployment as a Worker Discipline Device," *American Economic Review* 74 (1984): 433–444.

Carmen M. Reinhart, "The Mirage of Floating Exchange Rates," *American Economic Review*, May 2002.

Charles Himmelberg, Christopher Mayer, and Todd Sinai, "Assessing High House Prices: Bubbles, Fundamentals and Misperceptions," *Journal of Economic Perspectives* 19, no. 4 (Fall 2005): 67–92.

Charles I. Jones, *Introduction to Economic Growth* (New York: W.W. Norton & Co., 1998).

Charles R. Bean, "Targeting Nominal Income: An Appraisal," *Economic Journal* (December 1983): 806–819.

Charles R. Nelson and Charles I. Plosser, "Trends and Random Walks in Macroeconomic Times Series: Some Evidence and Implications," *Journal of Monetary Economics* 10 (September 1982): 139–162.

David G. Abler and Jayanta Das, "The Determinants of the Speed of Convergence: The Case of India," *Applied Economics* 30 (1998): 1595–1602.

David G. Blanchflower and Andrew J. Oswald, *The Wage Curve* (Cambridge, MA: MIT Press, 1994).

David J. Ravenscraft and F. M. Scherer, *Mergers, Sell-offs and Economic Efficiency* (Washington, DC: The Brookings Institution, 1987).

Donald A. Nichols, "Some Principles of Inflationary Finance," *Journal of Political Economy* 82 (1974): 423–430.

Douglas W. Diamond, "Financial Intermediation and Delegated Monitoring," *Review of Economic Studies* 59 (1984): 393.

Edward C. Prescott, "Theory Ahead of Business Cycle Measurement," Federal Reserve Bank of Minneapolis, *Quarterly Review* (Fall 1986): 9–22.

Edward C. Prescott, "Robert M. Solow's Neoclassical Growth Model: An Influential Contribution to Economics," *Scandinavian Journal of Economics* 90, no. 1 (1988): 7–12.

Edward S. Shaw, *Financial Deepening in Economic Development* (New York: Oxford University Press, 1973).

Elhanan Helpman, *The Mystery of Economic Growth* (Cambridge, MA: Harvard University Press, 2004).

Errol D'Souza, "Prudential Regulation in Indian Banking," in S. Arumugam (ed.) *Indian Capital Markets—Modern Perspectives and Empirical Evidence* (Mumbai: Allied Publishers Ltd., 2001).

Errol D'Souza, "Employment and Human Resource Practices in Public Sector Banks in the 1990s," in Shuji Uchikawa (ed.) *Labour Market and Institution in India–1990s and Beyond* (New Delhi: Manohar Publishers, 2003), pp. 95–120.

Fanny S. Demers, Michel Demers, and Huntley Schaller, "Irreversible Investment and Cost of Adjustment," CEPREMAP Working Paper No. 9416, 1994.

Finn E. Kydland and Edward C. Prescott, "Rules rather then Discretion: The Inconsistency of Optimal Plans," *Journal of Political Economy* 87 (June 1977): 473–492.

Fumio Hayashi, "Why is Japan's Saving Rate So Apparently High?" in Stanley Fischer (ed.) *Macroeconomics Annual* (New York: National Bureau of Economic Research, 1986).

Francesco Giavazzi and Marco Pagano, "Can Fiscal Contractions be Expansionary? Tales of Two Small European Countries," in O. Blanchard and S. Fischer (eds.) *NBER Macroeconomics Annual* (MIT Press, 1990).

Franco Modigliani, "Liquidity Preference and the Theory of Interest and Money," *Econometrica* 12 (1944): 45–88.

Franco Modigliani, "Life Cycle, Individual Thrift and the Wealth of Nations," Nobel Lecture, *American Economic Review* 76, no. 3 (June 1986): 297–313.

Franco Modigliani and Larry Cao Shi, "The Chinese Saving Puzzle and the Life-Cycle Hypothesis," *Journal of Economic Literature* 42, no. 1 (March 2004): 145–170.

Franco Modigliani and Merton H. Miller, "The Cost of Capital, Corporation Finance and the Theory of Investment," *American Economic Review* 48 (June 1958): 261–297.

Fumio Hayashi, "Tobin's Marginal q and Average q: A Neoclassical Interpretation," *Econometrica* 50 (January 1982): 213–224.

Geetha Veidyanathan, "Consumption, Liquidity Constraints, and Economic Development," *Journal of Macroeconomics* 15 (Summer 1993): 591–610.

George A. Akerlof, "The Market for 'Lemons': Quality Uncertainty and the Market Mechanism," *Quarterly Journal of Economics* 84 (August 1970): 488–500.

Gerald P. Dwyer Jr. and Thomas R. Saving, "Government Revenue from Money Creation with Government and Private Money," *Journal of Monetary Economics* 17 (1986): 239–249.

Gerard Caprio Jr., "Banking on Financial Reform? A Case of Sensitive Dependence on Initial Conditions," in Gerard Caprio Jr., Ijak Atiyas, and James A. Hanson (eds.) *Financial Reform—Theory and Experience* (Cambridge, MA: Cambridge University Press, 1996).

GOI, "Report of the Committee on the Financial System" (New Delhi: Government of India), 1991.

Gregg A. Farrell, James A. Brickley, and Jeffry M. Netter, "The market for corporate control: the empirical evidence since 1980," *Journal of Economic Perspectives* 2 (1988): 49–82.

Guillermo A. Calvo and Carmen M. Reinhart, "Fear of Floating," *Quarterly Journal of Economics* 117 (2002): 379–408.

Harvey Leibenstein, "The Theory of Underemployment in Backward Economies," *Journal of Political Economy* 65 (April 1957): 91–103.

Irving Fisher, "The Debt Deflation Theory of Great Depressions," *Econometrica* (October 1933).

J. Marcus Fleming, "Domestic Financial Policies Under Fixed and Floating Exchange Rates," IMF Staff Papers, no. 9 (1962): 369–377.

Jacob A. Frenkel, Assaf Razin, and Chi-Wa Yuen, *Fiscal Policies and Growth in the World Economy* (MIT, MA: MIT Press, 1996).

James M. Poterba and Lawrence H. Summers, "Dividend Taxes, Corporate Investment, and 'Q'," *Journal of Public Economics* 22 (1983): 135–167.

James Tobin, "The Interest Elasticity of Transactions Demand for Cash," *Review of Economics & Statistics* 38 (August 1956): 241–247.

James Tobin, "*Notes on Optimal Monetary Growth*," *Journal of Political Economy* 76, no. 4, Pt. 2 (July-August 1968): 833–859.

James Tobin, "Asset Accumulation and Economic Activity," Yrjo Jahnsson Lectures, Basil Blackwell, Oxford (1980).

Jeffrey A. Sachs, "The Debt Overhang of Developing Countries," in Guillermo A. Calvo, Ronald Findlay, Pentti Kouri, and Jorge Braga de Macedo (eds.) *Debt, Stabilization, and Development* (Oxford: Basil Blackwell, 1989).

Jeffrey Sachs and Felipe Larrain, "Why Dollarisation is More Straitjacket than Salvation," *Foreign Policy* 116 (Fall1999): 80–92.

John B. Taylor, "Staggered Wage Setting in Macro Model," *American Economic Review* 69, no. 2 (1979): 108–113.

John F. Muth, "Rational Expectations and the Theory of Price Movements," *Econometrica* (July 1961).

John Kareken and Robert Solow, "Lags in Monetary Policy," in *Stabilisation Policies*, Commission on Money and Credit (Prentice Hall, 1963).

John M. Keynes, "The General Theory of Employment, Interest and Money," *The Collected Writing of John Maynard Keynes* (London: Macmillan, 1992).

John M. Keynes, *The General Theory of Employment, Interest, and Money* (New York: Harcourt Brace Jovanovich, 1964).

John R. Hicks, "Mr. Keynes and the Classics: A Suggested Interpretation," *Econometrica* (April 1937): 147–159.

Joseph E. Stiglitz and Andrew Weiss, "Credit Rationing in Markets with Incomplete Information," American Economic Review (1981): 393–410.

Joseph G. Altonji, "Intertemporal Substitution in Labour Supply: Evidence from Micro Data," *Journal of Political Economy*, Part 2, 94 (June 1986): S176–S215.

Ken Froot and Richard Thaler, "Anomalies: Foreign Exchange," *Journal of Economic Perspectives* 4, no. *3* (1990): 179–192.

Kenneth J. Arrow and Gerard Debreu, "Existence of Equilibrium for a Competitive Economy," *Econometrica* 22 (1954): 265–290.

Kenneth Rogoff, "The Optimal Degree of Commitment to an Intermediate Monetary Target," *Quarterly Journal of Economics* 100, no. 4 (1985): 1169–1189.

Kenneth S. Rogoff, Aasim M. Husain, Ashoka Mody, Robin Brookes, and Nienke Oomes, "Evolution and Performance of Exchange Rate Regimes," IMF Working Paper No. WP/2003/243, 2003.

Lawrence Ball, "Interpersonal Substitution and Constraints on Labour Supply: Evidence from Panel Data," *Economic Inquiry* 28 (October 1990): 706–724.

Lawrence F. Katz, *Efficiency Wage Theories: A Partial Ecvaluation*, in NBER Macroeconomics Annual (Cambridge, MA: MIT Press, 1986), Vol. 1, pp. 235–276.

Lawrence H. Summers, B. P. Bosworth, J. Tobin, and P. M. White, "Taxation and Corporate Investment: A Q Theory Approach," Brooking Papers on Economic Activity, no. 1 (1981): 67–140.

Lawrence Katz and Alan Krueger, "The High-Pressure U.S. Labour Market of the 1990s," *Brookings Papers on Economic Activity* 1 (1999): 1–88.

Larry Selden, "A New Approach to the Joint Consumption-Portfolio Problem," *Journal of Money, Credit, and Banking* 12, no. 3 (August 1980): 429–447.

Leonard Rapping, "Learning and World War II Production Functions," *Review of Economics and Statistics* 47 (February 1965): 81–86.

Luis Serven, "Does Public Capital Crowd out Private Capital? Evidence from India," The World Bank, Policy Research Working Paper No. 1613, 1996.

Luis Serven, "Macroeconomic Uncertainty and Private Investment in Developing Countries—An Empirical Investigation," Policy Research Working Paper, The World Bank, Report No. 2035 (December 1998).

Luis Serven and Andres Solimano, "Private Investment and Macroeconomic Adjustment: A Survey," *World Bank Research Observer* 7, no. 1 (1992): 95–114.

Martin Eichenbaum and Charles L. Evans, "Some Empirical Evidence on the Effects of Shocks to Monetary Policy on Exchange Rates," *Quarterly Journal of Economics* 110, no. 4 (1995): 975–1009.

Martin Feldstein and Charles Horioka, "Domestic Saving and International Capital Flows," *The Economic Journal* 90, no. 358 (June 1980): 314–329.

Martin J. Bailey, "The Welfare Cost of Inflationary Finance," *Journal of Political Economy* 64 (April 1956): 93–110.

Martin Rama, "Empirical Investment Equations in Developing Countries," in L. Serven and A. Solimano (eds.) *Striving for Growth After Adjustment* (Washington, DC: The World Bank, 1993).

Matthew B. Canzoneri, "Monetary Policy Games and the Role of Private Information," *American Economic Review* 75 (December 1985): 1056–1070.

Maurice Obstfeld and Kenneth Rogoff, "Mirage of fixed Exchange Rates," *Journal of Economic Perspectives* 9 (1995): 73–95.

Maxwell J. Fry, *Emancipating the Banking System and Developing Markets for Government Debt* (London and New York: Routledge, 1997).

Michael Bruno, *Crisis, Stabilization and Economic Reform: Therapy by Consensus* (Oxford: Clarendon Press, 1993).

Michael J. Athey and Wende D. Reeser, "Asymmetric Information, Industrial Policy, and Corporate Investment in India," *Oxford Bulletin of Economics and Statistics* 62, no. 2 (2000): 267–292.

Michael Rothschild and Joseph E. Stiglitz, "Equilibrium in Competitive Insurance Markets: An Essay on the Economics of Imperfect Information," *Quarterly Journal of Economics* 90 (1976): 629–649.

M. J. Manohar Rao, "The Demand for Money in India," in K. L. Krishna (ed.) *Econometric Applications in India,* Oxford India Themes in Economics (New Delhi: Oxford University Press, 1997).

M. J. Manohar Rao and Raj Nallari, *Macroeconomic Stabilization and Adjustment* (New Delhi:Oxford University Press, 2001).

M. N. Murty and A. Soumya, "Macroeconomic Effects of Public Investment in Infrastructure in India," IGIDR, Working Paper No. 2006-2003, Mumbai, 2006.

Milton Friedman, "A Monetary and Fiscal Framework for Economic Stability," *Essays in Positive Economics* (Chicago: Chicago University Press, 1953).

Milton Friedman, *A Theory of the Consumption Function* (Princeton, NJ: Princeton University Press, 1957).

Milton Friedman, "Employment, Growth, and Price Levels," 86th Congress, First Session, (25–28 May 1958), p. 609.

Milton Friedman, "The Role of Monetary Policy," *American Economic Review* 58(1) (1968): 1–17; Edmund S. Phelps, "Phillips Curves, Expectations of Inflation and Optimal Unemployment Over Time," *Economica* 34 (1967): 254–281.

Morris Goldstein and Mohsin S. Khan, "Income and Substitute Effects in Foreign Trade," in Ronald W. Jones and Peter B. Kenen (eds.) *Handbook of International Economics* 2 (Elsevier, 1985).

M. Govinda Rao and Kunal Sen "Internal Migration, Center–State Grants, and Economic Growth in the States of India: A Comment on Cashin and Sahay," *IMF Staff Papers* 44 (1997): 283–288.

N. Gregory Mankiw, "Real Business Cycles: A New Keynesian Perspective," *Journal of Economic Perspectives* (Summer 1989): 79–90.

Nadeem U. Haque and Peter Montiel, "Consumption in Developing Countries: Test for Liquidity Constraints and Finite Horizons," *Review of Economics and Statistics* 71 (August 1989): 408–415.

Pami Dua and B. L. Pandit, "Interest rate determination in India: domestic and external factors," *Journal of Policy Modeling* 24 (2002): 853–875.

Parthasarathi Shome, "India: Tax Policy for the Ninth Five Year Plan," Report of the Working Group on Tax Policy of the Steering Group on Financial Resources, New Delhi, 1997; and the Kelkar Committee Report.

Patrick Bolton and Xavier Freixas, "A Dilution Cost Approach to Financial Intermediation and Securities Markets," Working Paper, Universitat Pompeu Fabra, 1998.

Paul A. Cashin and Ratna Sahay, "Internal migration centerstate grants, and economic growth in the sates of India," *IMF Staff Papers* 43 (1996): 123–171.

Paul Einzig, *The History of Foreign Exchange* (London and Basingtoke: Macmillan St. Martin's Press, 1990).

Paul Krugman, "Purchasing Power Parity and Exchange Rates: Another Look at the Evidence," *Journal of International Economics* 8 (August 1978): 397–407.

Paul Krugman and Lance Taylor, "Contractionary Effects of Devaluation," *Journal of International Economies* (8 August 1978): 445–456.

Paul M. Romer, "Increasing Returns and Long Run Growth," *Journal of Political Economy* 94, no. 5 (1986): 1002–1037.

Peter B. Kenen, "The International Financial Architecture: What's New? What's Missing?" *Institute for International Economics* (Washington, DC: IIE, 2001).

Prema C. Athukorala and Kunal Sen, *Saving, Investment and Growth in India* (New Delhi: Oxford University Press, 2002).

Reid W. Click, "Seigniorage in a Cross-Section of Countries," *Journal of Money, Credit and Banking* 30 (May 1998), 154–171.

Reserve Bank of India, "Report of the Committee to Review the Working of the Monetary System," Bombay, 1985.

Ricardo Hausmann, "Should There be Five Currencies or One Hundred and Five?" *Foreign Policy* 116 (Fall 1999): 65–79.

Richard A. Brealey and Stewart C. Myers, *Principles of Corporate Finance* (New York: McGraw Hill, 1991).

Robert A. Mundell, "The Appropriate Use of Monetary and Fiscal Policy Under Fixed Exchange Rates," IMF Staff Papers, no. 9 (1962): 70–77.

Robert A. Mundell, "Notes on the Development of the International Macroeconomic Model," in A. Arnon and W. Young (eds.) *The Open Economy Macromodel: Past, Present and Future* (Boston, MA: Kluwer Academic Publishers, 2002), pp. 1–16.

Robert Barro, "Democracy and Growth," *Journal of Economic Growth* 1 (January 1996).

Robert J. Barro, "Are Government Bonds Net Wealth?" *Journal of Political Economy* 82 (1974): 1095–1117.

Robert J. Barro, *Getting It Right-Markets and Choices in a Free Society* (Cambridge, MA: MIT Press, 1996), pp. 58.

Robert J. Barro and David B. Gordon, "A Positive Theory of Monetary Policy in a Natural Rate Model," *Journal of Political Economy* 91 (August 1983): 589–610.

Robert J. Barro and Xavier Sala-i-Martin, *Economic Growth* (Singapore: McGraw-Hill, 1995).

Robert E. Hall, "Stochastic Implications of the Life Cycle-Permanent Income Hypothesis: Theory and Evidence," *Journal of Political Economy* 96 (1978): 971–987.

Robert Eisner and Robert Strotz, "Determinants of Business Investment," Commission on Money and Credit, Impacts of Monetary Policy (Englewood Cliffs, NJ: Prentice-Hall, 1963), pp. 60–138.

Robert Feenstra, "Functional Equivalence Between Liquidity Costs and the Utility of Money," *Journal of Monetary Economics* 17 (1986): 271–291.

Robert Hubbard, "Capital Market Imperfections and Investment," *Journal of Economic Literature* 36 (1998): 193–225.

Robert Lane, *The Market Experience* (New York: Cambridge University Press, 1991).

Robert M. Solow, "A Contribution to the Theory of Economic Growth," *Quarterly Journal of Economics* 70 (1956): 65–94.

Robert M. Solow, "Technological Change and the Aggregate Production Function," *Review of Economics and Statistics* (August 1957): 312–320.

Robert M. Solow, *Growth Theory: An Exposition* (The Radcliffe Lectures) (Oxford: Clarendon Press, 1970), pp. 8–9.

Robert M. Solow, "Applying Growth Theory Across Countries," *The World Bank Economic Review* 15, 2 (2001): 283–288.

Robert M. Solow, "The Last 50 Years in Growth Theory and the Next 10," *Oxford Review of Economic Policy* 23, 1 (2001): 3–14.

Robert P. Flood and Peter M. Garber, "Collapsing Exchange Rate Regimes: Some Linear Examples," *Journal of International Economics* 17 (August 1984): 1–13.

Ronald I. McKinnon, *Money and Capital in Economic Development* (Washington, DC, Brookings Institution, 1973).

Ross Levine, "Financial Development and Economic Growth: Views and Agenda," *Journal of Economic Literature* 35 no. 2 (1997): 688–726.

Rudiger Dornbusch, "Fewer Monies, Better Monies," NBER Working Paper No. 8324 (Cambridge, MA: NBER, 2001).

Rudiger Dornbusch, "Expectations and Exchange Rate Dynamics," *Journal of Political Economy* 84 (1976): 1161–1176.

Rudiger Dornbush, "Policies to Move from Stabilization to Growth," Proceedings of the World Bank Annual Conference on Development Economics, 1990.

Scott Freeman, "Transactions Costs and the Optimal Quantity of Money," *Journal of Political Economy* 93 (February 1985), 146–157.

Shankar Acharya, "Macroeconomic Management in the Nineties," *Economic and Political Weekly* (20 April 2002): 1515–1538.

Sidney S. Alexander, "Devaluation Versus Import Restriction as an Instrument for Improving the Foreign Trade Balance," International Monetary Fund Staff Papers No. 1, 1951, pp. 379–392; "Effects of a Devaluation on a Trade Balance," International Monetary Fund Staff Papers No. 2, 1952, pp. 263–278.

S. S. Tarapore, "Financial Sector Reform: Retrospect and Prospect," RBI Bulletin (May 1996): 299–306.

Simon Kuznets, *National Income: A Summary of Findings* (New York: National Bureau of Economic Research, 1946).

Stanley Fischer, "Exchange Rate Regimes: Is the Bipolar View Correct?" *Journal of Economic Perspectives* 15, no. 2 (Spring 2001): 3–24.

Stanley Fischer, Ratna Sahay and Carlos A. Végh, "Modern Hyper- and High Inflations," *Journal of Economic Literature* (September 2002): 837–880.

Stephen P. Magee, "Currency Contracts, Pass Through and Devaluation," Brookings Papers on Economic Activity 1, 1973, 303–325.

Stephen S. Everhart and Mauricz A. Sumlinski, "Trends in Private Investment in Developing Countries–Statistics for 1970–2000," International Finance Corporation, Discussion Paper No. 44 (Washington, DC: IFC, 2001).

Stewart. C. Myers, "The Capital Structure Puzzle," *Journal of Finance* 39, no. 3 (July 1984): 575–592.

Stewart C. Myers and Nicholal S. Majluf, "Corporate Financing Decisions when Firms have Investment Information that Investors Do Not," *Journal of Financial Economics* (June 13, 1984): 187–220.

Svend Laursen and Llyod A. Metzler, "Flexible Exchange Rates and the Theory of Employment," *Review of Economics and Statistics* 32 (November 1950): 281–299.

Swarnjit M Arora, Mohsen Bahmani-Oskooee, and Gour Goswami, "Bilateral J-Curve between India and Her Trading partners," *Applied Economics* 35 (2003): 1037–1041.

Tarlok Singh, "Testing J-Curve Hypothesis and Analyzing the Effect of Exchange Rate Volatility on the Balance of trade in India," *Empirical Economics* 29 (2004): 227–245.

Thomas J. Sargent, "The Ends of Four Big Inflations," in Robert E. Hall (ed.) *Rational Expectations and Inflation* (New York: Harper & Row, 1986).

Thomas J. Sargent and Neil Wallace, "Rational Expectations and the Theory of Economic Policy," *Journal of Monetary Economics* 2 (1976): 169–183.

Thomas R. Saving, "Monetary Policy Targets and Indicators," *Journal of Political Economy* 75, no. 4 (1967): 446–456.

Thorvaldur Gylfason (2006), "How do India and China Grow?" *Challenge* 49, no. 1 (January 2006): 74–89.

Tim Callen and Paul Cashin, "Assessing India's External Position," in T. Callen, P. Reynolds, and C. Towe (eds.) *India at the Crossroads-Sustaining Growth and Reducing Poverty* (Washington, DC: IMF, 2001).

Tim Dyson, "India's population: The future," in Tim Dyson, Robert H. Cassen, and Leela Visaria, *21st Century India: Population, Environment and Human Development* (New Delhi: Oxford University Press, 2005).

Toni M. Whited, "Debt, Liquidity Constraints, and Corporate Investment: Evidence from Panel Data," *Journal of Finance* 47, no. 4 (September 1992), pp. 1425–1460.

Vijay Joshi and Ian Malcolm David Little, *India's Economic Reforms* (New Delhi: Oxford University Press, 1996).

Willem Buiter and Urjit Patel, "Excessive Budget Deficits, a Government-Abused Financial System, and Fiscal Rules," in Suman Bery, Barry Bosworth, and Arvind Panagariya (eds.) *India Policy Forum*, No. 2 (New Delhi: Sage Publications, 2006).

William Arthur Lewis, "Economic Development with Unlimited Supplies of Labour," Manchester School of Economic and Social Studies (Manchester: Blackwell Publishing, 22 May1954): pp. 139–191.

William J. Baumol, "The Transactions Demand for Cash: An Inventory Theoretic Approach," *Quarterly Journal of Economics* 66, no. 4 (November 1952): 545–556.

William J. Baumol, "Macroeconomics of Unbalanced Growth: The Anatomy of Urban Crisis," *American Economic Review* 57 (1967): 415–426.

William Poole, "Optimal Choice of Monetary Policy Instrument in a Simple Stochastic Macro Model," *Quarterly Journal of Economics* 84, no. 2 (May 1970): 197–216.

Index